T0399143

Aztec Latin

Aztec Latin

Renaissance Learning and Nahuatl Traditions in Early Colonial Mexico

ANDREW LAIRD

OXFORD UNIVERSITY PRESS

OXFORD
UNIVERSITY PRESS

Oxford University Press is a department of the University of Oxford. It furthers the University's objective of excellence in research, scholarship, and education by publishing worldwide. Oxford is a registered trade mark of Oxford University Press in the UK and certain other countries.

Published in the United States of America by Oxford University Press
198 Madison Avenue, New York, NY 10016, United States of America.

Library of Congress Cataloging-in-Publication Data
Names: Laird, Andrew, Dr., author.
Title: Aztec Latin : Renaissance learning and Nahuatl traditions in early colonial Mexico / Andrew Laird.
Description: New York, NY : Oxford University Press, [2024] |
Includes bibliographical references and index.
Identifiers: LCCN 2022040753 (print) | LCCN 2022040754 (ebook) |
ISBN 9780197586358 (hardback) | ISBN 9780197586372 (epub) |
ISBN 9780197586389
Subjects: LCSH: Nahuatl literature—History and criticism. | Latin literature—Influence. | Humanism—Mexico—History. | Learning and scholarship—Mexico—History. | Aztecs—Intellectual life. | Mexico—Intellectual life. | Mexico—History—To 1519. | Mexico—History—Conquest, 1519–1540. | Mexico—History—Spanish colony, 1540–1810. | LCGFT: Literary criticism.
Classification: LCC PM4068.L35 2023 (print) | LCC PM4068 (ebook) |
DDC 001.0972/09031–dc23/eng/20221202
LC record available at https://lccn.loc.gov/2022040753
LC ebook record available at https://lccn.loc.gov/2022040754

DOI: 10.1093/oso/9780197586358.001.0001

PREFACE

In 1536, only fifteen years after the fall of the Aztec empire, Franciscan missionaries began teaching advanced Latin, rhetoric, and Aristotelian philosophy to youths from the native nobility in central Mexico. The background to that initiative and the remarkable linguistic and cultural exchanges it brought about are the subject of the present study.

This book calls attention to the importance of Renaissance humanist education for indigenous history in New Spain. Such a treatment of the innovative ways in which Spaniards and native scholars alike made use of European learning is bound to challenge some common assumptions. There has been a particular tendency to romanticize the accomplishments of the first Mexican authors, but consideration of their work in relation to broader currents of early modern scholarship allows a fresh assessment of what those authors—some of whom wrote in Latin as well as Nahuatl—really did achieve.

Little prior acquaintance with specialized subjects is expected of the reader: the Introduction and Chapter 1 provide an orientation, and the grounding of this study in primary sources should also help to make it accessible. These sources are listed separately in the Bibliography, with details of available facsimiles, editions, and translations, to facilitate further enquiry.

Translations are my own unless otherwise indicated. For material in Nahuatl, I have used or consulted existing English and Spanish translations wherever possible, which are cited. The versions offered here are intended to be idiomatic, unless a precise rendering is specifically required: literal translation from Nahuatl risks 'foreignizing' writings that were actually clear and colloquial. In any case, the original language of translated passages is frequently given in accompanying footnotes. Texts and English translations of Latin sources that receive sustained discussion are assembled in Appendix 2. These historical documents have been minimally edited, in order to allow readers to make their own assessments of difficulties or ambiguities presented by the format in which they first appeared.

References to primary sources in the footnotes give the names of early modern authors in uppercase, cite each work by book and chapter (or by the original page numbers), and are often followed by a reference to a standard modern edition:

DURÁN, *Historia de las Indias de Nueva España* (1581) 1.5 [2002 i, 91].

For references to classical texts, the significance of the subsection numbers varies: '*Aeneid* 3.193' designates a single line of verse in a poetic text, while 'Livy 1.33' refers to a chapter of 260 words in a prose work. Citations of Plato consist of a book number and/or the Stephanus pagination, e.g. *Republic* 10, 616c–17c; the comparable Bekker system is used for Aristotle. Classical and patristic authors are not included in the Bibliography, apart from those found under entries for editors or commentators. Spanish double surnames are indexed by the first of those surnames: Hernando de Alvarado Tezozomoc, for example, will be listed as 'Alvarado Tezozomoc, Hernando de'.

Latin, Spanish, and Nahuatl names will normally take the form in which they appear in original documents, unless there are customary English equivalents with which non-specialists will be more familiar, such as 'Charles V' for Carlos V, 'Montezuma' for Moteuczoma, and 'Texcoco' for Tetzcoco. By the same token, titles of works like *Chronica Mexicayotl*, *Colloquios y Doctrina christiana* and *Monarchia Indiana* will be given as such, following sixteenth-century style; and the Franciscan spelling of Nahuatl words will be adopted in preference to a modern standardized system, so that *tlatoani* ('ruler') will be used instead of *tlahtoani*.

ACKNOWLEDGEMENTS

I am deeply grateful to the Leverhulme Trust in the United Kingdom for the award of a three-year Major Research Fellowship, which enabled me to plan and begin a study of humanism in sixteenth-century Mexico, and to David Brading, James N. Adams, and Sabine MacCormack, who supported the project from the outset. I have also benefited greatly from the assistance of specialist librarians at the Archivo General de Indias, Biblioteca Medicea Laurenziana, Biblioteca Nacional de España, Biblioteca Nacional de México, Bodleian Library, British Library, Warburg Institute, Benson Latin American Collection, Newberry Library, and the John Carter Brown Library in Providence.

Ed Carter, Mary L. Clayton, Alejandro Coroleu, David Cram, Cristina Monzón, and Jaspreet Singh Boparai kindly commented on drafts of individual chapters, and Sofia Guthrie took time from her important study of Antoine de Garissoles' *Adolphid* to go through all of them with extraordinary care. Three eminent historians read the whole text and each was generous enough to respond with many important suggestions: Simon Ditchfield, Ben Leeming (who also checked a number of the Nahuatl passages), and especially David Lupher. I am indebted to Roland Mayer for reviewing the entire manuscript and bringing his formidable knowledge of Latin usage to bear not only on my transcriptions and translations, but also on the argument in several places. Gordon Whittaker applied his unique expertise to almost every page of the work to follow, challenging many of my presuppositions as he gave advice on linguistic terminology, Nahuatl spelling, and Mesoamerican nomenclature.

Berenice Alcántara Rojas, Francisco Barrenechea, Amber Brian, Louise Burkhart, Rebecca Earle, Mark J. Edwards, Norman Fiering, Serge Gruzinski, Byron Hamann, Will Hansen, William Jeffett, Dylan Joy, Domingo Ledezma, Leonardo López Luján, Rosa Lucas González, Claire Lyons, Rodrigo Martínez Baracs, Barbara Mundy, Marianne Pade, Verenice Cipatli Ramírez Calva, Johann Ramminger, Michael Reeve, Alejandra Rojas Silva, Felipe Rojas Silva, Antonella Romano, John Frederick

Schwaller, Andrés Iñigo Silva, David Tavárez, Barry Taylor, Heréndira Téllez Nieto, Maude Vanhaelen, and Ken Ward have variously provided me with answers, information, images, and ideas. All the deficiencies that remain can only be my own responsibility: there would be many more, were it not for everyone thanked here.

The volume owes its final form to the vision of Stefan Vranka at Oxford University Press in New York, and to the patient work and acuity of Rachel Ruisard and Leslie Safford. The illustrations were obtained and reproduced with the support of the Brown University Humanities Research Fund. In all kinds of ways, Brown has provided an ideal environment for the completion of this endeavour, affording frequent opportunities for valuable exchanges with colleagues and students in Classics, Hispanic Studies and many other fields.

This book is dedicated to my father, John Charles Laird, and to the memory of my mother, Margaret Heather Laird, *née* Polmear.

CONTENTS

LIST OF ILLUSTRATIONS

PLATES

1. The Valley of Mexico in the sixteenth century. Map drawn by Sergio Cruz Durán and digitalized by Sylvan Cruz.
2a. *Codex Mendoza,* Mexico, c. 1542, 2r (detail). Bodleian Library, Oxford.
2b. Eagle and *atl tlachinolli* glyph, 'Teocalli of Sacred War', Tenochtitlan, c. 1507 (reverse). Museo Nacional de Antropología, Mexico. Photograph by Thomas F. Aleto.
2c. *Codex Aubin,* Mexico, c. 1576–1608, 26v (detail). British Museum.
2d. Title page of Anton Francesco Doni, *La filosofia morale,* Trent, 1588 (detail) showing the mark of the Gelmini brothers' press. British Library.
3. 'Texas fragment' of the *Lienzo de Tlaxcala,* Tlaxcala, c. 1540, depicting Cortés' meeting with Xicotencatl. Benson Latin American Collection, LLILAS Benson Latin American Studies and Collections, The University of Texas at Austin.
4a. The Mexican calendar in Motolinía, *Memoriales,* Mexico, c. 1541, *tomo* 31. Benson Latin American Collection, LLILAS Benson Latin American Studies and Collections, The University of Texas at Austin.
4b. *Trecena* period (days 6–13) with feathered serpent, *Codex Telleriano-Remensis,* Mexico, c. 1563, 18r. Bibliothèque nationale de France, Ms. Mexicain 385.
5. The convent church of Santiago, Tlatelolco. Photograph by author.
6a. *Libellus de medicinalibus Indorum herbis,* Tlatelolco, 1552, 13v. Instituto Nacional de Antropología e Historia, Mexico.
6b. *Libellus de medicinalibus Indorum herbis,* Tlatelolco, 1552, 38v (detail). Instituto Nacional de Antropología e Historia, Mexico.

FIGURES

Introduction

The coat of arms of Mexico represents an eagle perched on a *nopal*, or prickly pear cactus, clutching a rattlesnake in its beak and talons. This image derives from the legend of the foundation of Mexico Tenochtitlan. During the course of their long migration from the mythical location of Aztlan, the Aztecs were told by the god Huitzilopochtli to call themselves 'Mexica', and to establish a settlement by the lake of Texcoco (Plate 1), where an eagle had alighted on a nopal.[1]

Yet none of the initial sources for that tradition ever included a snake. The *Codex Mendoza* (c. 1542), a pictorial history dated to some twenty years after the fall of Tenochtitlan in 1521, has an eagle alone on the nopal (Plate 2a). Although it had been believed that a late pre-Hispanic stone relief showed an eagle grasping a snake, the tassel-shaped object caught in the bird's beak is really a glyph connoting sacred warfare (Plate 2b).[2] It took until at least sixty years after Spain's first incursions into Mexico for depictions of that origin myth to include a snake: one is in the *Codex Aubin*, probably painted in the late sixteenth century (Plate 2c). Another example is provided by an illustration in a manuscript history of New Spain that the Dominican Fray Diego Durán completed in the 1580s—even though the written text specified that the eagle had taken hold of a splendid bird.[3] The earliest verbal description of the eagle 'atop the prickly pear, eating and tearing apart a snake' in 1598 is attributable to a chronicle in Spanish by the native Hernando de Alvarado Tezozomoc.[4]

In Renaissance Europe the emblem of an eagle in conflict with a serpent had long been familiar. Although it did not have any Christian or biblical significance, it often appeared on medals and printers' marks that were based on Roman reliefs and coins (Plate 2d).[5] The motif was also found in a number of popular classical authors, and

[1] *Codex Aubin* (c. 1576–1608), 6v; Carrera Stampa 1960.

[2] Caso 1927; Wright Carr 2012; *Codex Mendoza* (c. 1542), 2r.

[3] DURÁN, *Historia de las indias de Nueva España* (c. 1581) 1.5 [2002 i, 91]; cf. TOVAR, *Codex Ramírez* 2 (c. 1582–1587), 91v.

[4] ALVARADO TEZOZOMOC, *Coronica mexicana* (1598) cap. 1 [2001, 54]. That detail is not in the *Chronica Mexicayotl* (1609), 18r [1997, 60–1], which the same author wrote in Nahuatl (cf. Chapter 6, p. 219, n. 113; Chapter 9 below).

[5] Wittkower 1939.

Aztec Latin. Andrew Laird, Oxford University Press. © Oxford University Press 2024.
DOI: 10.1093/oso/9780197586358.003.0001

in fact some verses in Cicero's *De divinatione* best account for the snake's first intrusion into the Mexican myth.[6] Cicero describes the general Marius witnessing a portent with a striking similarity to that supposedly beheld by the Aztecs: an eagle rose from a tree trunk by the water's edge and tore a snake apart, before flying into the sun. Jupiter confirmed the omen with a clap of thunder, as Huitzilopochtli would endorse the similar sign for the Mexica. Each of those deities could take the form of an eagle, a bird that was associated with the sun in Mesoamerica as well as in the ancient Mediterranean.[7] Most importantly, this portent for the rise of Rome also had a civic context, comparable to that of the sign for Tenochtitlan. Thus the addition of a snake to the Mexican image may have represented an attempt to dignify it with a classical association—or simply to render it readable for Europeans. Many other examples of early colonial art combined Mexican pictorial codes with Greco-Roman motifs and themes.[8]

The important part Latin played in the mediation and construction of indigenous legacies in sixteenth-century New Spain, especially in the Valley of Mexico, is the subject of this book. Within only a few years of the Spanish invasion, Franciscan missionaries had begun to provide some 'Indian' youths with an intensive humanist education. As the friars endeavoured to gain an understanding of Amerindian languages, the students under their direction translated Christian literature (and one or two classical texts) from Latin into Nahuatl, and produced accomplished writings of their own in both languages. Some native scholars assisted Fray Bernardino de Sahagún, whose extensive investigations of Mexican society and belief remain of immense value to historians and anthropologists.

The language of the dominant polities in pre-Hispanic Mexico, modern versions of which are spoken today, is now generally known as Nahuatl.[9] The various peoples who spoke it are commonly referred to as 'Nahua' (or loosely as 'Nahuas'), although that is not a word they always used themselves and it was seldom employed by Spaniards in the 1500s.[10] Each group usually took its name from the place it inhabited: the Tenochca, Tlatelolca, and Tlacopaneca respectively came from the city-states of Tenochtitlan, Tlatelolco, and Tlacopan. For the Spaniards all the aboriginal peoples of the Americas were 'Indians', while those in the Valley of Mexico and sometimes other parts of New Spain were 'Mexicans'. Both terms were also

[6] Cicero, *De divinatione* 1.47; Pliny, *Historia naturalis* 10.5.16; cf. Thompson 1895, 3. Reyes 1960 linked the Mexican symbol to Virgil, *Aeneid* 11.751–8; cf. Laird 2016a, 131, 141–3 on the *De divinatione* in New Spain.

[7] *Codex Borgia* (1400s–1500s) [1904 i, 224]. SAHAGÚN, *Historia general* (c. 1580) 7.1 [1953 viii, 1]; López Luján 2015; cf. Thompson 1895, 7 on Greco-Roman literature.

[8] Maza 1968; Gruzinski and Mermet 1994; Lyons and Pohl 2010; Hamann 2018; Rojas Silva 2018.

[9] Xelhuantzi 2018 points out the historical and linguistic misunderstandings involved in the use of the word 'Nahuatl'.

[10] The dedication of MOLINA, *Vocabulario* (1571) referred to 'Na[h]uas', but the term was not in the body of the dictionary.

adopted by natives and will be employed here. Nahuatl speakers did not generally call themselves Aztecs before or after the arrival of the Spaniards, but 'Aztec' nonetheless remains a convenient designation.[11]

Aztec Latin, the title of the present volume, connotes the use of Latin by indigenous Mexicans. Many of the texts in Latin that Indians read, translated, or composed will be discussed in the chapters to come. Some Nahuatl works will be taken into consideration as well, so that 'Aztec Latin' could double over as an explanatory metaphor for Nahuatl itself. One of the first missionaries remarked that, in New Spain, Nahuatl was like Latin because it was used to understand other tongues.[12] Once an instrument of political authority as well as a vehicular language, with its own forms of refined expression, Nahuatl had held a position in Mesoamerica that could be regarded as analogous to that of Latin in early modern Europe. On the other hand, many Nahuatl traditions were the result of European interference: the transcription of Nahuatl in the Roman alphabet, its systematization on the principles of Latin grammar, its conversion into a target language for translations from Spanish and Latin, and its new function as a medium of written literature will all be explored in the following chapters.

The conjunction of 'Aztec' with 'Latin' might, in addition, suggest parallels and points of comparison between the antiquities of Mexico and Rome. Ideas of Rome loomed large in the early history and historiography of the colonial Americas.[13] Spain's emulation of the ancient Roman empire was overt: Charles V and Philip II claimed the status of 'Caesars' and genealogies were devised to link the Hapsburg monarchy to its imagined Trojan and Roman antecedents.[14] The Spaniards also likened the Amerindian civilizations of Mexico and Peru to pagan Rome, and Indian writers in the Andes and Mesoamerica would come to embellish their narratives of the pre-Columbian past with comparisons from Roman history.[15] In New Spain, as in Europe, Aristotle, and Cicero were invoked in debates about just war and the status of the Indians, while Erasmus' opinions on Christian life and education, drawn from both Greco-Roman sources and patristic authors, appealed to missionary friars, some of whom modelled themselves on the Church Fathers of antiquity.[16]

[11] 'Aztecs' was popularized by Prescott 1843 [1915, 9] after CLAVIGERO, *Storia antica del Messico* (1780), and Humboldt 1810; see Barlow 1945a; León-Portilla 2000a, Sandstrom 2017, 707–8.

[12] MOTOLINÍA, *Memoriales* (c. 1541), 60r [1996: 330]: 'Y entre todas las lenguas de la Nueva España . . . nahu[a]tl es como latín para entender las otras'.

[13] Rowe 1965; González Rodríguez 1981; Lupher 2003; Laird 2007; MacCormack 2007; Laird and Miller 2018; Marcocci 2020.

[14] Yates 1975, 130: 'All the monarchs of Europe sought Trojan ancestors through whom to link their destinies and origins with imperial Rome.' Cf. Elliott 1989 and Tanner 1993 on the Hapsburgs.

[15] MacCormack 1998; cf. Chapter 9 below.

[16] Pagden 1982; Bataillon 1932, 1998; MacCormack 1991; Reff 2005.

The Renaissance is conventionally regarded as the period of transition from the medieval era to modernity over the course of the fifteenth and sixteenth centuries—a period that converged with, and is best identified with, the spread of humanism.[17] That immersive literary formation, which involved reading and writing in Latin, was the main vehicle for an education that would nowadays be called 'classical'. Humanism's most pervasive disciplines and practices—grammar, rhetoric, pedagogy, antiquarianism, scholarly translation—were transformed and redeployed in Mexico. They sometimes served the interests of Indian elites, as well as of the religious orders. The opening chapters trace these developments in terms of a trajectory from Europe to New Spain: Franciscan missionaries (and also some Dominicans) employed and adapted humanist educational methods as part of their effort to Christianize indigenous populations.[18] The later chapters then explore the work of native Mexican scholars, contextualizing and reassessing their achievements.

Chapter 1 begins with an introductory overview of the scope and reach of humanism and its manifestations in Spain and beyond, before showing how the first two Franciscan cohorts to arrive in Mexico in the 1520s each had quite a different intellectual character. Three bishops, the Franciscan Fray Juan de Zumárraga, the Dominican Fray Julián Garcés, and Vasco de Quiroga, who were active in the next decade, drew many of their principles from Erasmus of Rotterdam, but representations they made on behalf of the Indians were also inspired by the reading of some classical authors.

Though it tends to be overlooked by historians, the art of rhetoric had acquired new importance, and its various uses will be addressed in almost every part of this study. A short outline of the evolution of Christian rhetoric from late antiquity to the Renaissance, accounting for its vital role in colonial education and evangelical literature, will follow in Chapter 2, prior to an appraisal of Latin rhetorical treatises by missionaries who were active in Mexico in the earlier 1500s. Some of these friars argued for peaceful conversion, while others, notably Fray Diego Valadés in his *Rhetorica Christiana*, championed subjection of the Indians by force. Even as these authors relied heavily on classical *exempla* to characterize Indians, their treatises demonstrate that rhetoric soon acquired an ethnological dimension.

The radical reform of Latin teaching was at the heart of Renaissance humanism. Chapter 3 shows how the first manuals of Amerindian languages not only drew from Antonio de Nebrija's seminal Latin grammar but also relied on Erasmus' practical approach to linguistic pedagogy. Missionaries were nonetheless quick to realize that Indian tongues worked differently from the way Latin

[17] The term 'Renaissance' remains useful to scholars as a historical category: Coroleu 2004. Following Dubrow 1994, Tudeau-Clayton and Berry 2003 forcefully countered a tendency in English studies (e.g. Marcus 1992) to dissolve 'Renaissance' into 'early modern'.

[18] The Franciscans' humanist leanings were later questioned by Dominicans in New Spain, after the conservative Fray Alonso de Montúfar became archbishop of Mexico: Nesvig 2009, 119–20.

did and they sought the assistance of natives as interpreters. Some high-ranking Mexican students were actually taught in Latin at the Imperial College of Santa Cruz in Tlatelolco. Chapter 4 will give a detailed account of this institution, its curriculum, its teaching practices, and the controversies surrounding its foundation, to dispel the widely held view that the college was ever intended to be a seminary. Its purpose was to furnish youths from the indigenous nobility with the kind of schooling that humanists, including Erasmus, had recommended for Christian princes in Europe.

The central chapters focus on the native scholars' involvement in the translation of Latin texts and on their own writings in Latin and Nahuatl. Manuscripts prepared at the College of Santa Cruz, surveyed in Chapter 5, range from a trilingual dictionary and an Indian herbal in Latin to the first Nahuatl versions of the Epistles and Gospels. There were many original compositions in Nahuatl that had European models: a text still regarded as an authentic record of the Aztec priests' justification of their religion to the first Franciscan apostles actually exhibits all the hallmarks of European classical oratory. Conversely, some petitions in Latin by indigenous Mexicans are of genuine ethnohistorical interest. The little-known examples reviewed in Chapter 6 include an independent report about a claim for land made by Pedro de Montezuma, and letters to the emperor Charles V and Philip II of Spain from the rulers of Indian principalities. As well as offering unparalleled historical testimonies about the Valley of Mexico before the advent of the Spaniards, these Latin documents contain literary allusions and quotations that highlight the extent of their authors' classical learning.

Chapter 7 argues that a collection of Aesop's fables rendered into Nahuatl was directed at indigenous governors as a 'mirror for princes'. The correct identification of the Latin edition of Aesop that constituted the source text for the Mexican translations reveals their striking fidelity and ingenuity. A long-standing assumption that the Nahuatl translator conveyed a Mesoamerican worldview without always understanding the Latin original can be roundly dismissed.

The last two chapters show how, in different ways, indigenous scholars had a part in using Greco-Roman antiquity as a vehicle for presenting or explaining legacies of pre-Hispanic Mexico. Chapter 8 examines testimonies concerning Aztec belief as well as some Nahuatl speeches and sayings from the *Historia general* or *Florentine Codex,* the production of which was overseen by the Franciscan missionary Fray Bernardino de Sahagún. There are other 'moral histories' or accounts of native customs by Spaniards from the same period, but much of this particular work was originally written in Nahuatl by Indians who were trained in Latin. Their involvement may account for some distinctive evocations of episodes in Greco-Roman literature at various points in the text. The sixth book of the *Historia general* contains some formulaic Nahuatl speeches that Sahagún himself sought to present in a classical framework—his questionable characterization of these discourses as 'rhetorical orations' continues to be widely accepted.

Chapter 9 offers a brief epilogue to the developments of the 1500s by looking at parallels and analogies drawn early in the following century between Mexico's Indian past and the civilizations of the ancient Mediterranean. While both Spaniards and Indians had already made such comparisons by the 1550s, the next generation of indigenous chroniclers like Hernando de Alvarado Tezozomoc and Fernando de Alva Ixtlilxochitl used illustrations from classical literature to assert a universal significance for Mexican history. Chimalpahin, who wrote in Nahuatl, cited Greek and Roman authors in his annals to demonstrate the viability of the language as a literary medium.

Any one of the chapters just outlined can be read independently of the others as a self-standing essay. At the same time, these discussions taken together constitute a narrative of the missionaries' conveyance of humanist disciplines to New Spain, and of the resulting creation of new forms of expression in Nahuatl and Latin by a small number of their Mexican converts. Such a narrative should prompt reflection on Walter Benjamin's adage that every document of civilization is also a document of barbarism.[19] The picture of Indians engaged in scholarly 'collaborations' with the friars is often idealized and needs to be viewed in the context of the upheaval and suffering caused by the Spanish invasion and its aftermath. The effects of what Ángel María Garibay called 'the trauma of the conquest' had hardly diminished by the mid-1500s.[20]

The friars and native scholars prepared their texts and translations for a select literate elite, but these authors and their accomplishments are far from tangential to New Spain's history. Fray Pedro de Gante, Fray Julián Garcés, Fray Juan de Zumárraga and other missionary educators had a crucial role in shaping colonial society. Indian principals whose writings are discussed or quoted in the chapters to follow include the chronicler Hernando de Alvarado Tezozomoc, grandson of Montezuma II, and two Latinists who were also closely connected to the Mexica royal line by kinship or marriage: Antonio Valeriano, a hereditary lord of Azcapotzalco and governor of Tenochtitlan, and Antonio Cortés Totoquihuatzin, governor of Tlacopan, a polity that had belonged to the Aztec Triple Alliance.[21]

The varied interactions between Latin and Nahuatl also contribute important and unexpected insights to the history of western scholarship, as humanist disciplines and education came to be tested in unprecedented ways. Grammar, rhetoric, and even logic found vital new applications, while long-held precepts about language, literacy, and history—which would continue to be sustained in Europe—sometimes ended up being questioned or abandoned. In addition, knowledge of Greek and Roman literature acquired a pragmatic role, as it was instrumentalized

[19] Benjamin 1969, 256.

[20] Garibay 1954 ii, 18 [2007, 516–17]. Todorov 1984, 133–82 enumerates the atrocities perpetrated by the Spaniards. Nahuatl accounts attest to their enduring impact: Lockhart 1993.

[21] A genealogical table in Appendix 1.5 shows the noble lineages of these native scholars.

by those who sought to comprehend or to ennoble the Mesoamerican past. The inventories of college and convent libraries, along with sources by Franciscan educators and Indian Latinists alike, give a clear, if sometimes surprising, impression of which medieval and Renaissance Christian texts were being read.[22]

Many texts from sixteenth-century Mexico now deemed to be of primary importance by ethnohistorians can be better understood in the light of the Renaissance humanist practices that determined the interpretation, creation, and dissemination of many Nahuatl traditions. By drawing together themes and approaches that have been set apart in different disciplines, this book offers a more coherent perspective on the achievements of both Spanish and Indian scholars, in order to give prominence to a remarkable chapter of early modern intellectual history.

[22] Books to which native students in Tlatelolco had access are identified in Appendix 1.3.

1

Faith, Politics, and the Pursuit of Humanity

The First Scholars in New Spain

The conquest of Tenochtitlan on 13 August 1521 marked the decisive defeat of the Aztecs by the Spaniards and their indigenous allies. Hernán Cortés, who first gave the name of 'New Spain' to the areas of Mexico he claimed for the Spanish crown, was appointed Captain General of the territory by Charles V.[1] But the monarchy soon moved to curtail Cortés' power and assert its authority more directly by instituting the royal Audiencia, or high court, of Mexico.

Under its president, Nuño Beltrán de Guzmán, the first Audiencia of 1528 would turn out to be the most brutal government in New Spain's history. The chief delegates imposed heavy taxes and labour on the natives, some of whom were enslaved or murdered; and missionary friars who objected to this conduct were threatened, and risked being tortured or killed. While Cortés had made some effort to protect the interests of the indigenous population, Guzmán took advantage of his absence in Spain to defame him and persecute his supporters.[2] Guzmán's agents also censored communications from the colony, to prevent news of this conduct from reaching higher authorities in the peninsula.

In the face of those challenges, Fray Julián Garcés, the Dominican bishop of Tlaxcala, and Fray Juan de Zumárraga, the Franciscan bishop-elect of Mexico City, succeeded in sending a letter, in August of 1529, to an unnamed noble at the Spanish court. According to the chronicler Fray Gerónimo de Mendieta, Zumárraga ensured that his correspondence escaped detection by entrusting it to a sailor from Vizcaya, who concealed it in a buoy.[3] In the opening lines of the bishops' letter to the courtier, a phrase from Virgil summed up their precarious situation:

[1] CORTÉS, 'Tercera carta-relación' (1522) [1866, 272]: 'desta Nueva-España del mar Oceano'.

[2] Ricard 1933 [1966, 255–63]; García Icazbalceta 1947 i, 27–89; ZUMÁRRAGA, 'Carta a su Majestad,' (1529) [1947 ii, 182–7].

[3] MENDIETA, *Hystoria ecclesiastica yndiana* (1596) = *Historia*, 3.50, 5.27 [1870, 313, 630].

Aztec Latin. Andrew Laird, Oxford University Press. © Oxford University Press 2024.
DOI: 10.1093/oso/9780197586358.003.0002

> We see ourselves engulfed in so great an ocean of new events that wherever we turn our gaze we have lost the firmness and security of dry land; in the Poet's words: 'Coelum undique et undique pontus' ['Sky and ocean are on all sides'].[4]

Horace was quoted, too, and a verse of another Roman poet, Juvenal, was recalled to warn the reader about Gonzalo de Salazar, an ally of Guzmán, who was at that point in Spain:[5]

> He exceeds Demosthenes and Cicero in accomplishment and elegance, and says, pointing to his tongue, that if he were allowed to use it for an hour, *coram Caesare Augusto*, 'nigra et in candida vertet' [in the presence of Caesar Augustus, 'he would even argue that black is white'].

Even in such an urgent communication the two bishops were signalling their familiarity with Latin literature: a command of letters was at once an indication and instrument of power for statesmen and leading members of the church.

Latin was used in tandem with vernacular writing in Spain's new dominions, just as it was in Spain itself.[6] While there was scant opportunity for scholarly patronage and little place for humanistic study for its own sake, forms of classical learning soon found new uses in colonial Mexico. Following a brief overview of earlier intellectual developments in Europe, this chapter will indicate the importance of Renaissance humanism for New Spain's early history, showing how it served the very first missionary friars to reach Mexico in the 1520s, as well as Zumárraga, Garcés, and other influential figures who soon came after them, all within the decade that began with the destruction of the Aztec capital.

I. Humanism in Europe and the Hispanic world

Humanism evolved from the *trivium*, the curriculum of grammar, logic, and rhetoric, which along with theology, jurisprudence, medicine, and other sciences had

[4] GARCÉS and ZUMÁRRAGA, 'Carta . . . a un noble señor' (1529) [1947 iv, 99], quoting Virgil, *Aeneid* 3.193, a metaphor for disorientation or disorder: cf. Ovid, *Tristia* 1.2.23; Quintilian, *Institutio oratoria* Book 12, *praef.* 2; Jerome, *Epistles* 1.2; Hilary of Poitiers, *De Trinitate* 2.8.

[5] The quotations from Horace, *Ars poetica* 25–6, 294 and Juvenal, *Satires* 3.30 (cf. Ovid, *Metamorphoses* 11.313–15) are embedded in the writers' own Latin phrases. Salazar's persuasive powers were notorious: García Icazbalceta 1947 i, 38–41, 62–76.

[6] According to García Icazbalceta 1954, 20% (twenty-nine out of 143) of books printed in Mexico City during 1539–1600 were in Latin, as were 50% of scientific works published in Spain during the same period: cf. López Piñero 1979, 124, and Kagan 1974, 31–61 on the relation between Latin and vernacular writing in Spain.

been taught in universities since the Middle Ages. Private tutors, however, were free to teach poetry and history along with grammar and rhetoric; and they often supplemented or replaced the scholastic traditions of logic, metaphysics, and natural philosophy with moral philosophy. The totality of these disciplines came to be known as the *studia humanitatis*, 'pursuits of humanity'—an expression from Cicero, which was widely used in fifteenth-century Italy, and subsequently in Spain.[7] The term *umanista* duly gained currency in Italian from the later 1400s as a colloquial term for a teacher of classical languages and literature.[8]

Some humanists were productive scholars and authors: they restored and interpreted Greek and Latin texts to avail themselves of the insights those texts contained, thereby making their own new contributions to literature, thought, and politics.[9] While an understanding of the Greco-Roman past is usually considered an end in itself for specialists in classical studies today, Renaissance humanists were more interested in emulating and building on the achievements of the ancients.

The *studia humanitatis* had an ethical dimension. The Latin *humanitas*, like its vernacular correspondents—*humanidad, umanità*, humanity—carried connotations of philanthropy: of being humane as well as being versed in the disciplines of the humanities. The first writer to employ the term *humanista* in Spanish appears to have been the Franciscan Fray Gabriel de Toro (1500–1586). In his treatise on poverty and charity dedicated to the future Philip II of Spain, *Thesoro de misericordia divina y humana* (1536), the author noted that ancient philosophers like Seneca had advocated *humanidad* to other men without ever having had a Christian understanding of it. Toro explained why men of letters were called *humanistas*: in antiquity orators had referred to literary accomplishment as *humanitas* because, as the Roman author Aulus Gellius had remarked, only human beings could pursue it.[10] Then, echoing the Church Father Lactantius' argument that knowledge of God was the one attribute animals could not possess, Toro held that transmitting such knowledge and providing limitless charity, which transcended mere human compassion, was the true role of the humanist.[11] That proposition harmonized with the advocation of communism on Christian principles in the *Thesoro*. Eight editions of

[7] Cicero, *Pro Archia* 2.3; *Pro Murena* 61. Cf. Kristeller 1965; 1988; Kohl 1992; Black 2001; Stroh 2008. Alonso de Cartagena imported the term *studia humanitatis* to Spain: Fernández Gallardo 2016.

[8] Campana 1946. The word 'humanism' was coined in the nineteenth century: Mann 1996, 1–2.

[9] McLaughlin 1995; Hankins 2000.

[10] TORO, *Thesoro* (1536) [1548, 127v]. Aulus Gellius, *Noctes Atticae* 13.17.1: 'quod Graeci paideian vocant, nos eruditionem institutionemque in bonas artis dicimus. Quas qui sinceriter cupiunt adpetuntque, hi sunt vel maxime humanissimi. Huius enim scientiae cura et disciplina ex universis animantibus uni homini datast idcircoque humanitas appellata est.' ('What the Greeks call *paideia* we call training and instruction in the literary arts. Those who earnestly desire and seek them are by far the most human. Attention and discipline devoted to this sort of knowledge is among all living things granted to man alone, and that is why it is called *humanitas*.')

[11] Lactantius, *Institutiones divinae* 2.1.15.

this work appeared in the 1500s, and Fray Gabriel himself began despatching missionary friars to Guatemala in 1539.

What is now known as humanism was therefore not a discipline or a set of beliefs but a tendency. It sometimes intersected with the traditional scholastic disciplines that continued to develop in their own right. The resurgence of interest in texts from pagan antiquity and a pluralistic approach to philosophy did not lead to an essential opposition between the humanists' endeavours and Christian thought: *literae humaniores,* the literature of humanity, was a natural complement to the study of *sacrae literae,* religious literature. At the same time, those Renaissance authorities who attached importance to classical Latin usage derided much of the Latin used by churchmen and in the universities as 'barbarous'.[12] Their insistence on rigour in the exegesis of ancient authors led to conflict when the same exacting standards of classical philology were applied to religious texts. The linguistic authority of the Vulgate, Saint Jerome's Latin Bible, was challenged by the Italian grammarian and rhetorician Lorenzo Valla (1406–1457) and by Valla's later admirer, Desiderius Erasmus (1466–1536), the widely feted but controversial philologist, Christian thinker, and educationalist.[13] Erasmus' own Latin translation of the New Testament informed Martin Luther's version in German. Luther's *Biblia* was first published in 1522, five years after his Ninety-five Theses effectively initiated the Protestant Reformation.

It is often held that humanists in northern Europe were mainly preoccupied with religious questions, while those in Italy and France devoted their attention to classical subjects to avoid controversy with the church. Yet, prior to the Reformation, Spain had been accommodating both fields of investigation.[14] Centres for study with a strong Italian influence had long been established in Zaragoza and Valladolid, well before Antonio de Nebrija (1444–1522), a native of Andalusia who had trained in Italy, came to prominence in Spain as the greatest scholar of his age.[15] In the dedication to his *Introductiones Latinae* (c. 1487), a grammar that went through more than fifty editions in his lifetime, Nebrija railed against the poor knowledge Spaniards had of Latin.[16] Like Valla, he championed the language as the basis for all forms of learning. Ignorance of it, Nebrija warned, meant that Holy Scripture and the foundations of the Christian religion could not be correctly understood; Latin was necessary for jurists to interpret the spirit and letter of the law, and for physicians

[12] The 'barbarians' targeted in ERASMUS, *Antibarbari* (1520) were theologians opposed to the use of classical models.

[13] Bentley 1983; Hamilton 1996; Rummel 2008, and Rex 2016 survey humanist biblical scholarship; for scripture and evangelization in the early Americas, cf. Bruno and Míguez 2016 and Cervantes 2016.

[14] Gil Fernández 1967; 1981; Kagan 1974; Coroleu 1998. Bataillon 1937 saw humanism and scholasticism as contrary forces in Renaissance Spain—a view questioned in Homza 2004.

[15] Gómez Moreno 1994; Weiss 1964, 95–7 emphasized the different intellectual environments of Castile and Aragon. Cf. Codoñer and González Iglesias 1994 and Martín Baños 2019 on Nebrija.

[16] A text is in Rico 1981, 93.

to make sense of Pliny and Celsus, the two luminaries of medical science—without Latin, all the books imparting the wisdom that is every free man's due would lie buried in darkness. In another prologue, this time to his dictionary from Spanish to Latin (c. 1495), Nebrija characterized himself as an apostle and warrior ready to extirpate 'barbarism', a conceit that would acquire further resonances after Spain's incursions into the New World.[17]

While never abandoning his interest in classical Latin and antiquarianism, Antonio de Nebrija increasingly applied his philological skills to Christian literature.[18] He spent his final years in Alcalá de Henares in Castile, where Cardinal Francisco Jiménez de Cisneros was directing the production of the Complutense Polyglot, a revised text of the Bible in Hebrew, Greek, and Latin. Cisneros' university offered a progressive, academic style of instruction in theology, emphasizing the value of patristics and of historical and philological approaches to scripture. Those were priorities shared by Erasmus, whom Cisneros had invited to Alcalá by 1517—an invitation for which the Dutch humanist made clear his distaste in a letter he wrote in that year to Thomas More with the famous words 'non placet Hispania': 'I do not care for Spain.'[19] Yet Erasmus' literary, educational, and religious writing had been widely admired in Spain, even though persecution of his followers began there in the decade after the Reformation.[20] For the first evangelists in the Americas, his 'philosophia Christi', 'philosophy of Christ', which advocated simple, more practical forms of religion based on scripture and the principles of the early church, was of immense importance.[21]

It is barely ever pointed out that Erasmian ideals motivated the defender of the Indians, Fray Bartolomé de las Casas (1474–1566). Although Las Casas' arguments were presented in a scholastic style, the record he provides of his conversion in Hispaniola, from businessman and slave-owner to Dominican friar and radical reformer, is redolent of Erasmus' insistence on the realization of faith in action rather than empty ritual.[22] That conversion occurred in 1514, but years later, during the Valladolid controversy about the rights of the Indians (1550–1551), when persecution of Erasmians was at its height, Las Casas supported the objections to war on the Turks that Erasmus himself had expressed to Alberto Pio, Prince of Carpi.

[17] NEBRIJA, *Dictionarium ex Hispaniensi in Latinum sermonem* (c. 1495), aiii; cf. n. 12 above on ERASMUS, *Antibarbari* (1520a). Essays in Guzmán Betancourt and Nansen Díaz 1997 treat Nebrija's reception in New Spain.

[18] González Vega 2010.

[19] ERASMUS, *Opus epistolarum* (1529) [1906–1958, no. 597; tr. 1979 v, 12].

[20] Coroleu 2008.

[21] Bataillon 1937 [2007], 715–24.

[22] LAS CASAS, *Historia* (c. 1560), caps. 78–9 [1965 iii, 92–100], states that Ecclesiasticus 34:18–22 induced his change of heart: religious sacrifice is invalid if the offering has been wrongly obtained.

Pio was an intimate of the Medici popes and a mentor of Las Casas' own opponent, Juan Ginés de Sepúlveda. As a response to Sepúlveda's thesis—based on Aristotle's *Politics*—that the Indians were natural slaves, Las Casas' Latin *Apologia* (c. 1552) argued that Aristotle considered barbarians as such only if they were incapable of governing themselves—and the American Indians did not belong in that category.[23] In his much more extensive *Apologética historia sumaria* (c. 1558), which lambasted the continuing pagan legacies in the Old World to exonerate the peoples of the New, Las Casas displayed the wide range of his classical knowledge: he drew testimonies from ancient sources such as Herodotus, Lucian, and Pausanias, and from Renaissance antiquarians who included Lilio Gregorio Giraldi, Flavio Biondo, and the Austrian Wolfgang Lazius.[24]

II. The earliest missionaries in New Spain

The first three Franciscan missionaries to reach Mexico, who were sent from Flanders on the authority of Emperor Charles V, were highly regarded scholars. Johann Dekkers and Johann van der Auwera were priests; the third, Pieter de Muer, was a lay brother. They became better known by their Hispanicized names: Juan de Tecto, Juan de Aora, and Pedro de Gante, or 'Peter of Ghent'. Less is known of Aora, but Juan de Tecto was guardian of the friary in Ghent—a position he relinquished once he had found out about the Spaniards' discovery and conquest of 'a New World full of idolatrous people whom he desired to have ministers convert to the faith'.[25] Tecto had been Professor of Theology at the University of Paris for fourteen years: his contemporary Fray Toribio de Benavente remarked that 'no abler scholar came to this land [of New Spain] and it was to him that the Emperor went to confession'.[26] Charles V, who had been born in Ghent and educated in the Low Countries, was reluctant to lose his valued confessor; and Hernán Cortés too would hold both Tecto and Aora in high esteem.[27]

Pedro de Gante, a relative of the Holy Roman Emperor, may well have been brought up by the *Fratres vitae communis*, or 'Brethren of the Common Life'.[28] The Catholic community founded by Gerard Groote, who promoted the

[23] Aristotle, *Politics* 1, 1254b–1255a. LAS CASAS, *Apologia* (c. 1552) caps. 1–5 [tr. 1992, 25–53]; Losada 1971; Coroleu 2008.

[24] LAS CASAS, *Apologética historia* (c. 1558); Lupher 2003, 270–88.

[25] OROZ, *Relación* (1586) [tr. 1972, 279]. Acker 1992 investigates the Flemish missionaries' background.

[26] MOTOLINÍA, *Historia de los indios* (1543) = *Historia*, 2.4 [2001, 122].

[27] MENDIETA, *Historia* (1596) 5.17 [1870, 606] on Tecto; Lejarza 1948 shows that both Franciscans influenced Cortés.

[28] Gante remarked in a letter to Charles, 'Pues que VM e yo sabemos lo cercanos e propincos que somos, e tanto, que nos corre la mesma sangre': González Vera 1868, 386, cited in García Icazbalceta 1954, 91. Cortés Castellanos 1987, 79–90 lists primary sources for Gante's life.

devotio moderna, 'devotion for the present', was not a college or school, but a movement for simple piety and apostolic renewal. The Brethren, though, did attach great importance to reading and study: the anatomist Andreas Vesalius, the rhetorician Rudolph Agricola, Martin Luther, and Erasmus were all among their alumni.[29] So too was the Dutch Pope Adrian VI, who would later send twelve Franciscans from Spain to Mexico in 1524.[30] After attending the University of Leuven and working for a time in the service of the Crown (when he may have become known to Las Casas), Gante took the Franciscan habit in Ghent.[31]

Tecto, Aora, and Gante left Flanders in April 1522 and sailed from Seville on 1 May to reach Veracruz on the Mexican Gulf coast in August 1523. From there they made their way to Mexico Tenochtitlan, where they met Pedro Melgarejo and Diego Altamirano, the two Franciscan priests who had accompanied Cortés.[32] The Flemish friars then settled in the Acolhua capital of Texcoco, an important pre-Hispanic principality. When the 'Twelve Franciscan Apostles' who had been sent by Pope Adrian came from Spain nine months later, Juan de Tecto and Juan de Aora debated with them the circumstances in which the sacraments were to be administered, 'quoting excellent doctors and citing valid laws'.[33] Fray Pedro Oroz recounts a particular exchange between the two groups of missionaries:

> When the twelve apostolic men arrived . . . on seeing that the temples of the idols were still standing and that the Indians were practising their idolatries and sacrifices, they asked this Father Fray Juan de Tecto and his companions what they were actually doing and in what they were employing themselves. To this Father Fray Juan de Tecto replied: 'We are learning the theology which Saint Augustine knew absolutely nothing about'—referring to the language of the Indians as theology and giving them to understand the great advantage which was to be derived from it.[34]

The chronicler took Tecto's response to mean that the Flemish missionaries had been making advances in the language of the Indians and that conceiving Christian

[29] Hyma 1965; Van Engen 2008.

[30] The events leading to the despatching of the Twelve, their journey, and their arrival are related in MENDIETA, *Historia* 3.4–3.13 [1870, 186–215].

[31] García Icazbalceta 1941 ii, 203; LAS CASAS, *Historia* (c. 1560) [1961, 422].

[32] MOTOLINÍA, *Historia* 3.1 [2001, 164]: 'It was then [1524] that the friars arrived in Mexico and after fifteen days held a chapter at which the twelve friars and the five who had already been in Mexico received their appointments'; cf. MENDIETA, *Historia* 3.14. DÍAZ DEL CASTILLO, *Historia verdadera de la conquista* (1568) described Altamirano (caps. 188–9) and Melgarejo (caps. 143–45; 150, 158–9, 170, 172), neither of whom was named by the Franciscan chroniclers.

[33] MOTOLINÍA, *Historia* 2.4 [2001, 122].

[34] OROZ, *Relación* (1586) [tr. 1972, 280]. The episode, also in MENDIETA, *Historia* (1596) 5.17 [1870, 606], was probably based on a testimony by Fray Rodrigo de Bienvenida: Chavez 1972, 7–8.

doctrine in the Mexicans' tongue led to new formulations, of which not even the most respected Church Father could have been aware.

But the term 'theology' could still connote the science of divinity in general, including that of pagans. Saint Augustine had recognized that the ancient author Varro used the term *theologia* for accounts of the Roman gods, employing it in that sense himself in his *De civitate Dei*, 'The City of God'.[35] Fray Juan de Tecto may have meant that he was doing more than getting to grips with a new language: he was conducting researches that, like Augustine's investigations of pagan religion, were meant to defend and promote the Christian faith. The Franciscan linguist Fray Bernardino de Sahagún would later refer to the pre-Hispanic ritual discourses he transcribed and translated as 'the *theology* of the Mexican people' ('theologia de la gente mexicana').[36]

The Flemish friars succeeded in converting some members of Texcoco's native elite. According to Fernando de Alva Ixtlilxochitl, writing almost a century later, the Twelve Franciscans from Spain wept with joy on seeing how well his ancestor Ixtlilxochitl and his royal entourage knew the mysteries of the mass 'because Father Fray Pedro de Gante, to his best ability and by God's grace, had taught them Christian doctrine, the mysteries of the Passion and life of our lord Jesus Christ'.[37] The knowledge of the Nahuatl language that Gante and his companions had acquired may have enabled them or their native converts to act as interpreters for the Twelve in their first encounters with indigenous Mexicans in 1524.[38] Fray Juan de Zumárraga described in a letter to Charles V how Gante served as a translator for him when, four years later, he first addressed the native 'lords and principals' after his arrival in Mexico.[39]

Fifteen days after the Twelve arrived, a chapter for all the Franciscans in New Spain was convened in Texcoco. Fray Martín de Valencia was confirmed as *custos*, or superior, and the seventeen friars were dispersed over the principal provinces of New Spain, to preach to the native commoners, as opposed to the elites. For three and a half years, Fray Pedro de Gante remained in Texcoco, where he continued to learn Nahuatl and teach in the school he had helped to found. He outlived Tecto

[35] Augustine, *De civitate Dei* 6.5 described theology as 'the account that is given of the gods' ('rationis quae de diis explicatur'). Cf. McRae 2016, 129–41, on Augustine's interpretation of Varro and Roman paganism.

[36] SAHAGÚN, *Historia general*, Book 6 (1580) [1969 vii]. The sixth book containing the speeches was completed in 1577. Cf. Chapter 8, IV below.

[37] ALVA IXTLILXOCHITL, *Compendio histórico del reino de Texcoco* (1608), 'Décimatercia relación' [1975 i, 492]. The dating of Alva Ixtlilxochitl's works in Whittaker 2016 will be followed throughout.

[38] SAHAGÚN, *Colloquios y Doctrina christiana* (1564) related the supposed initial exchanges between the Twelve and the principals and high priests of the Mexica, excerpted in Appendix 2.5. Cf. Chapter 5 below.

[39] ZUMÁRRAGA, 'Carta a su Majestad' (1529) [1947 ii, 222].

and Aora: 'My companions died after they set off with the Captain to another territory where they suffered great toil for the love of God.'[40] On Gante's testimony, then, the two friars perished in 1524 on Cortés' expedition to Las Hibueras, now Honduras—the same expedition on which Cuauhtemoc, the last ruler of the Mexica, was summarily executed in 1525.[41]

Despite the prior presence of a handful of Franciscans in Mexico, the coming of the Twelve was of enormous symbolic value, and it came to be commemorated by friars and Indians alike as the formal beginning of evangelization in New Spain.[42] The Twelve consisted of ten priests: Martín de Valencia (the superior), Francisco de Soto, Martín de la Coruña, Juan Juárez, Antonio de Ciudad Rodrigo, Toribio de Benavente, García de Cisneros (unconnected to Cardinal Jiménez de Cisneros), Luis de Fuensalida, Juan de Ribas, Francisco Jiménez (who was ordained after his arrival in Mexico), and two lay brothers, Andrés de Córdoba and Juan de Palos. Fray Pedro Oroz' testimony quoted above hints at a difference of character between the Spanish friars and those from Ghent who had come ahead of them. While the Flemish brothers were presented as men of formidable learning, the Twelve have been portrayed as simple, practical, and ascetic. They had been selected from the humble Franciscan province of San Gabriel in the Spanish region of Extremadura by Fray Francisco de los Ángeles Quiñones, minister of the entire order, who later became Cardinal of Santa Croce in Rome.[43]

Their leader, Fray Martín de Valencia, was fifty years old when he arrived in Mexico. He had been under the tutelage of Fray Juan de Guadalupe and Fray Juan de Puebla, both of whom stringently followed the rule of Saint Francis. Their observant branch of the Franciscan order was part of a broader reform in Spain spearheaded by Cardinal Jiménez de Cisneros.[44] Fray Martín had also been inspired by the radical twelfth-century Cistercian visionary Joachim of Fiore, an influence on Saint Francis himself, whose legacy steadily endured into the 1500s.[45] Joachim had divided history into the three successive stages: those of God the Father, the Son, and the Holy Spirit. The beginning of the third stage in this scheme, marked by the

[40] GANTE, 'Epistola . . . ad Patres et Fratres Provinciae Flandriae' (1529) [1954, 102]: 'Socii autem mei cum gubernatore ad aliam terram sunt profecti, et ibidem immensos labores perpessi propter amorem Dei mortui sunt.' This Latin translation of the letter was preserved in ZIERIXEENSES, *Chronica compendiosissima* (1534), 124v–127r; the Spanish original is lost.

[41] Bernal Díaz del Castillo and Motolinía are in accord with Gante, but MENDIETA, *Historia* (1596) 5.18 [1870, 207] and TORQUEMADA, *Monarchia Indiana* (1615), = *MI*, 20.18 [1979 vi, 181] held that Juan de Aora had died soon after arriving in Texcoco.

[42] MOTOLINÍA, *Historia* (c. 1543) 3.1 [2001, 163–4].

[43] Fray Francisco de los Ángeles' Latin *Obediencia* and the Spanish *instrucción* (1523) given to his companions are translated into English in Chavez 1972, 347–60. Versions of both documents are in MENDIETA, *Historia* 3.9–10 [1870, 200–6].

[44] Holzapfel 1948, 65–117.

[45] Reeves 1999, 29–58.

foundation of the Franciscan and Dominican orders, was then harmonized with the sixth of the seven ages in traditional Christian eschatology, an epoch characterized by intensive preaching of the Gospel throughout the world. Expectation that the seventh and final age was imminent—the millennium that would lead to Christ's coming and the Last Judgement—shaped the way some 'spiritualist' Franciscans in New Spain sought to explain the conquest of Mexico and its aftermath.[46]

Such millenarianist views are evident in the chronicles written by another of the Twelve, Fray Toribio de Benavente, commonly known as Motolinía, 'Poor one', a name given to him by the Indians. The biblical books of Exodus and Revelation were the matrix for his *Historia de los indios de Nueva España*—a work beginning with a list of the ten plagues that, after the coming of the Spaniards, punished the inhabitants of the Valley of Mexico.[47] Motolinía's profound admiration for Martín de Valencia was conveyed in a hagiographic account he wrote of his superior's life: as a young priest in Extremadura, Martín fasted and was deprived of sleep to the degree that he suffered extreme temptations and delusions, before he saw the need to save the souls of infidels as the world's final era was approaching. One day, while he was reading a lesson at matins, he had a vision of multitudes of unbelievers being converted, confessing the Christian faith, and receiving baptism. What he beheld caused him to cry out so loudly that the other friars present, who assumed that he had gone mad, confined him to his cell with the door and window securely locked. There, in the darkness, Fray Martín contemplated his vision and prayed for it to be realized. According to Motolinía, it was in New Spain that God eventually answered his prayers.[48]

Reformed Franciscans like Valencia may have been wary of the abstruse theorizing of humanists and scholastics alike, but Motolinía seems to have played up the contrast between the simplicity of the Twelve and the intellectualism of the Flemish friars. That emphatic differentiation was doubtless a consequence of the chronicler's long-standing dispute with the *letrados*, 'lettered' members of the Franciscan order, who objected to the rapid baptism of large numbers of Indians.[49] It should be pointed out that Motolinía still read very widely: while scripture provided the framework for his investigation of Mexican customs and beliefs in the *Memoriales* (1527–1541), the author also drew from linguistic works by Christian humanists, including Erasmus and Nebrija.[50]

[46] Phelan 1956; Baudot 1995; Weckmann 1992, 208–16.

[47] MOTOLINÍA, *Historia* 1.1 [2001, 15–22]; Exodus 7:1–11:10.

[48] MOTOLINÍA, *Historia* 3.2 [2001, 173].

[49] Pardo 2004, 20–48, citing (at 176, n. 58) Andrés Martín 1976 i, 84 on observant Franciscans' wariness of humanist and scholastic theological speculation.

[50] The Florentine iconoclast Girolamo Savonarola, the humanist theologian Rodrigo Fernández de Santaella, Aesop's Fables, the book of Marco Polo, and Astorgan folk tales were further sources for MOTOLINÍA, *Memoriales* (c. 1541) [1996, 40–64]. Cf. Baudot 1995, 246–398 on Motolinía's work.

In his history of the Indian church, Fray Gerónimo de Mendieta, a Joachite chronicler who arrived in Mexico in 1554, remarked of the earlier missionaries that 'although they were quite used to being regarded as being simple and unlettered owing to their humility and self-depreciation, they were all educated, some in canon law, others in sacred theology'.[51] Recalling how Saint Jerome and the sixth-century encyclopedist Saint Isidore of Seville both drew attention to the importance of the Church Fathers' writings in their works, Mendieta wanted in his turn to make known the very first Franciscans who wrote in Mexican languages. He revealed that four of the original Twelve authored texts in Nahuatl: Fray Francisco Jiménez compiled the first grammar and vocabulary of the language; Motolinía wrote a Christian doctrine; Fray Juan de Ribas produced a catechism, Sunday sermons, an anthology of saints' lives, and a set of questions and answers about how to lead a Christian life; and Fray García de Cisneros composed 'preachable sermons'.[52]

As a member of the Twelve, Fray García de Cisneros left a legacy that remains underrated. Mendieta and Oroz later credited him with establishing (and indeed naming) the College of Santa Cruz, where Indians received a Latin education from the 1530s onward.[53] No less crucially, García de Cisneros was responsible for selecting and appointing the friars who taught there: Fray Arnaldo de Bassacio, Fray Andrés de Olmos, Fray Juan de Gaona, and Fray Bernardino de Sahagún. These individuals came to play a vital part in the transmission of Nahuatl texts and traditions over the course of the sixteenth century.

III. Fray Juan de Zumárraga and his associates

Erasmus' thought and writing had a profound effect on some of the most significant protagonists in New Spain's early history. Fray Juan de Zumárraga, Fray Julián Garcés, and don Vasco de Quiroga arrived in Mexico within a few years of one another. Garcés came to take up his diocese of Tlaxcala in central Mexico in 1526, although he had already held for seven years the prestigious title of *episcopus Carolensis* (the Caroline bishopric was named after the Holy Roman Emperor, Charles, or 'Carolus'). The Franciscan Zumárraga arrived in 1528 as bishop-elect of Mexico City with the title of 'Protector of the Indians'. Quiroga came to New Spain in 1531 as *oidor*, or judge, of the second reformed Audiencia to redress some of the wrongs perpetrated by the first, before he became bishop of Michoacán.

Fray Juan de Zumárraga (1468–1548) was born in Durango in the Basque province of Vizcaya, where his father, Juan López de Zumárraga, was a landowner and

[51] MENDIETA, *Historia* 3.36 [1870, 268].

[52] MENDIETA, *Historia* 4.44 [1870, 550].

[53] MENDIETA, *Historia* 5.23 [1870, 622]: 'Al colegio intituló de Santa Cruz'; cf. OROZ, *Relación* (1586) [1972, 99–100].

wealthy merchant with connections to several Italian trading centres, and his mother was from a leading family. The young Zumárraga was first educated by a local teacher, Juan Martínez de Arrazola, and later at Valladolid.[54] He joined the Franciscan order at Abrojo, eventually serving as guardian of the monastery before and after a period as Provincial of the province of Concepción during 1520–1523. Having made an impression on Charles V during the Emperor's visit to Abrojo in Holy Week of 1527, the friar was commissioned to investigate witchcraft in Pamplona before being appointed as the first bishop of Mexico in December of the same year.

Zumárraga chose a Franciscan from Burgos, Fray Andrés de Olmos, who had studied jurisprudence at the University of Valladolid and assisted as an inquisitor at Pamplona, to accompany him on his first voyage to New Spain in 1528.[55] Olmos was judged to be 'learned and discriminating' and he soon became an accomplished speaker of the Mexican language. In 1533 Fray Martín de Valencia and the president of the second Audiencia, Sebastián Ramírez de Fuenleal, entrusted Fray Andrés with the task of establishing evidence for the Indians' humanity and rationality. This task was in the context of debates in Spain and Rome about the Indians' capacity to adopt the Christian faith: missionaries were concerned that the Mexicans had governed and conducted themselves better as heathens before coming under Christian control.[56]

Fray Andrés de Olmos' resulting work focused on Mexico City, Texcoco, and Tlaxcala. His *Tratado de antigüedades mexicanas*, 'Treatise on Mexican Antiquities' (c. 1539), was a thorough investigation of pre-Hispanic religion, myth and history, the calendar, systems of social and political organization, and the Nahuatl language.[57] According to Mendieta, the stated purpose of the book was to ensure that 'there would be some record of that antiquity, that whatever was evil or nonsensical could be refuted, and anything good brought to light, just as observations are made and records are kept about other pagans'.[58] The *Tratado* was thus a scholarly enquiry, comparable to humanist study of those 'other pagans' ('otros gentiles') of the classical Greek and Roman past. The loss of the full text and of three copies of the author's own extensive *Suma*, or summary, by the end of the 1500s suggests that the work was not seen as useful to preachers. Several conjectures about the content of

[54] The few testimonies for Zumárraga's early life reveal little of his education: Larracoechea Bengoa 1987 and García de Cortázar y Ruiz de Aguirre 1999, 174–5; Greenleaf 1961, 57 n. 24.

[55] For Olmos' life and work, cf. ANTONIO, *Bibliotheca Hispana nova* (1672) [1788 i, 81–2] and EGUIARA Y EGUREN, *Bibliotheca Mexicana* (1755) [1986, 132–7] (both in Latin), as well as MENDIETA, *Historia* 5.33–5 [1870, 644–51] and TORQUEMADA, *MI* 20.38–40 [1979 vi, 240–50]. See further Baudot 1995, 163–245 and Téllez Nieto 2022, 13–40.

[56] MENDIETA, *Historia*, Book 2, 'Prólogo al Christiano Lector' [1870, 75]; cf. León-Portilla 1969; cf. Section V on Garcés below.

[57] Marcocci 2020, 20 on PANÉ, *Relación . . . acerca de las antigüedades de los indios* (1498), an important precedent for Olmos' work, usefully cites Momigliano 1950, 289–90 on what constituted *antiquitates*. Baudot 1995, 163–217 reconstructs Olmos' *Tratado* and *Suma*. Cf. Chapter 8 below.

[58] MENDIETA, *Historia*, Book 2, prologue [1870, 75].

the *Tratado* have been made on the basis of texts and pictorial codices from the 1530s and 1540s, for which it was a source.[59] Although Fray Andrés' studies of Huastec, Totonac, and Tepehuan languages were not conserved either, there are manuscripts of his foundational manual of Nahuatl, *Arte de la lengua mexicana* (1547), which incorporated a collection of idioms, and of other texts he wrote in the language, including a tract on sorcery that he translated from a Castilian original.[60]

The achievements of Fray Juan de Zumárraga himself had a far-reaching legacy. The bishop was an energetic evangelist but he would clash with the Audiencia in his first years in Mexico. He continued to prove an adept politician, protecting the interests of those Indians who were exploited by the *encomienda* system of labour, while doing his best to help Spanish colonists who were faced with severe poverty after that system was abolished. Zumárraga's Christian humanism combined his interest in scripture, patristics, and some classical authors with scholastic philosophical thought.[61] The conclusion of his *Dotrina breue* printed in Mexico City in 1544 incorporated a section of Erasmus' Christian handbook, *Paraclesis* (1516), without any acknowledgement and without reproducing its author's page-long list of pagan antecedents to his 'philosophia Christi.[62] The suppression was probably less due to any disapproval on Zumárraga's part of the use of classical sources than to a reluctance to name the scholar who had originally assembled them: Erasmus' works would soon be condemned by the Council of Trent, which first met in 1545.

The bishop had also lent Erasmus' Greek New Testament to his pupil, Cristóbal Cabrera, who in 1540 completed a Latin translation of some patristic Greek commentaries on Saint Paul's Epistles.[63] Cabrera's 'Ecstasis', a first-person fictional poem abounding in classical echoes and reminiscent of Erasmus' *Praise of Folly*, was in part inspired by the 1545 plague that killed more than eight hundred thousand people in Mexico.[64] The narrator recounted his premonitory vision of such a scourge falling upon the Spaniards and natives, a premonition that led the bishop of Mexico (a character presumably modelled on Zumárraga) to have him locked in

[59] These include *Codex Tudela* (c. 1540), *Codex Magliabechiano* (mid-1500s), and TOVAR, *Codex Ramírez* (c. 1582–1587) as well as THEVET, *Histoyre du Mechique* (1553), a translation of a lost text in Spanish: cf. Boone 1983; Gómez de Orozco 1945; Jiménez Moreno and Robertson 1980, 207–9; León-Portilla 1969; Phillips 1883.

[60] OLMOS, *Tratado sobre los siete pecados mortales* (1551); OLMOS, *Tratado de hechicerías y sortilegios* (1553) was a translation of CASTAÑEGA, *Tratado de las supersticiones* (1529); cf. Chapter 3 below on OLMOS, *Arte de la lengua mexicana* (1547).

[61] Bataillon 1937 [2007, 540–50, 810–27]: Bataillon 2007, cited here and below, is the widely available Spanish translation of the French original.

[62] Carreño 1949; Kerson 2001.

[63] CABRERA, *Argumenta in epistolas Pauli* (1540) survives in manuscript.

[64] The 'Ecstasis' first appeared in CABRERA, *Meditatiunculae ad . . . principem Philippum* (1548) 73r–77v; cf. Laird 2017a. Phelan 1956, 92–7 describes contemporaneous interpretations of the plagues.

a dark cell until he came to his senses. As the events it relates so closely recall what had befallen Fray Martín de Valencia after his vision in Extremadura, the 'Ecstasis' appears to parody millenarianist intimations of an impending apocalypse.[65] At any rate, the bookish leanings of Zumárraga and his associates distinguished them from the Apostolic Twelve, who had been directed by the zealous reformism of Cardinal Cisneros.[66]

Fray Juan de Zumárraga had a major role in creating two important educational institutions, the College of Santa Cruz and the Royal University. His awareness of some indigenous students' aptitude for Latin had led him to conceive of a school in which Indians could be trained in philosophy and theology, as well as in the humanities and Latin. On the bishop's return from Spain in 1534, those plans were developed: the Imperial College of Santa Cruz was established in Tlatelolco, to the north of Mexico City, to provide advanced instruction to youths from native elites. Zumárraga himself was present at the inauguration on 6 January 1536, and the next year he donated his own collection of books to the library of the college.[67] In February of 1537, Zumárraga next proposed the founding of a university in which all the subjects studied at 'other universities' could be taught, the arts and theology above all.[68] Five years after the bishop's death, a 1553 decree authorized the Royal University of Mexico. The institution, to which only Spaniards could be admitted, was closely modelled on Salamanca.[69] Teaching of classical poetry, rhetoric, philosophy, history, and science, conducted in Latin, would be sustained there over the next two centuries.

Zumárraga oversaw the introduction of a printing press to Mexico City, an initiative that would soon be imitated in many more of Spain's new territories. The bishop's involvement is indicated in his *memorial* to the Royal Council of the Indies, penned in Spain in 1533: 'it would be very useful and expedient to have a press and paper mill and appropriate persons to sustain the art if . . . his Majesty might supply the means for them to come.'[70] Erasmus' extraordinary success in harnessing the power of print for the dissemination of his work throughout Europe may have alerted Zumárraga to the useful potential of printing for evangelism in New Spain.

In 1539, Juan Cromberger, the German printer based in Seville, instituted a branch of his press in Mexico City under the supervision of his Italian deputy, Joannes Paulus, or Giovanni Paolo, of Brescia, who became better known as Juan Pablos.[71] The first productions were doctrines and catechisms in indigenous

[65] Cf. MOTOLINÍA, *Historia,* cited in n. 48 above.

[66] Kubler 1948 i, 9 (quoted in Greenleaf 1961, 38): 'If the Apostolic Twelve represented Cisnerian Spain, a later group of missionaries under Juan de Zumárraga represented Erasmian thought in Mexico.'

[67] Steck 1944, 35; Mathes 1982; cf. Chapter 4, III below.

[68] ZUMÁRRAGA, 'La instrucción' (1537) [1947 iv, 134].

[69] Rodríguez Cruz 1977, 53–82.

[70] ZUMÁRRAGA, 'Insigne memorial' (1533) [1947 iv, 116].

[71] Griffin 1991, 117–33.

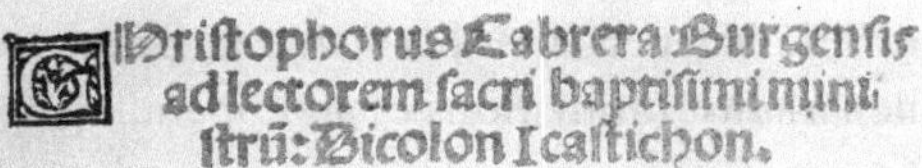

Christophorus Cabrera Burgensis
ad lectorem sacri baptisimi mini-
strū: Dicolon Icastichon.

Si paucꝫ ꝑnosse cupꝫ: uenerāde sacerdos:
Ut baptizari quilibet Indus habet:
Quᵃᵉ q; ꝑ⁹ ōbēt ceu parua elemēta doceri:
Quicqd adultus iners scire tenetur itē:
Quaeq; sient ꝑscis ꝑrib⁹ sancita: ꝑ orbem
Ut foret ad ritū tinct⁹ adultus aqua:
Utne ꝺspiciat (fors) tā sublime Charisma
Indulus ignarus terq; quaterq; miser:
Hūc māib⁹ ꝟsa: tere: ꝑlege: dilige librum:
Nil nin⁹ obscurū: nil magis est nitidum.
Siplicit docteq; ꝺdit modo Vasc⁹ acut⁹
Addo Quiroga me⁹ ꝑsul abunde pius.
Sigula ꝑpēdens nihil ide regrere possis:
Si placet) oē legas ordine dispositum.
Ne videare (caue) sacris ignauus abuti:
Sis decet ad uigilās: mittito desidiam.
Nēpe bonū nihil ūq; fecerit oscitabūdus.
Difficile est pulchrū: dictitat Antiqtas.
Sed sat ē: qd me remorarꝫ plurib⁹: ingꝫ.
Sit satis: ⁊ facias quod precor: atq; uale.

Figure 1.1 Fray Cristóbal Cabrera, 'Dicolon Icastichon', from *Manual de adultos*, printed by Juan Cromberger, Mexico City, 1540. John Carter Brown Library.

languages, and, from the late 1550s, grammars and vocabularies, which were vital for evangelization. The volumes printed in Mexico City during the sixteenth century were of a utilitarian nature: those that did not directly serve the interests of missionaries were textbooks of grammar, rhetoric, philosophy, and medicine, all in Latin, primarily for the use of university and seminary students.

Even so, such publications still contained signals of a broader culture of letters, for which surviving manuscripts and the books imported during this period supply the principal evidence.[72] Juan Pablos himself composed epigraphs in Latin prose or verse for the volumes he printed, and others showed off their talent by composing laudatory verses in Latin that frequently prefaced texts of a more practical nature. The first poem ever to be printed in the Americas (Figure 1.1), by Zumárraga's former pupil Fray Cristóbal Cabrera, was a coda to the *Manual de adultos* (1540),

[72] Leonard 1992 is the standard study of the circulation of books in early colonial Spanish America; cf. Raven 2011; Maillard Álvarez 2018 on the importing of classical texts to New Spain. 'Marcas de fuego', or brand marks, from convents and colleges show that many volumes printed in the 1500s reached Mexico in the same century: Yhmoff Cabrera 1996.

a guide for priests administering baptism in Mexico.[73] The Latin composition with a Greek title—'Dicolon Icastichon', 'An Imitative Reduplication'—mischievously echoed the opening couplet of Ovid's erotic *Ars amatoria* and quoted Erasmus.[74] The verses hint that the *Manual de adultos* itself was commissioned by Bishop Vasco de Quiroga. Cabrera assisted Quiroga with his missionary work in the 1530s, an experience he described in a memoir he wrote at the end of his life.[75]

IV. Vasco de Quiroga

Vasco de Quiroga (1470–1565), who had come to New Spain in 1531 as a judge, took office as bishop of Michoacán in 1538. He is best known for the communities he founded for native Mexicans, which were supposedly modelled on the blueprint of Thomas More's *Utopia* (1516).[76] Quiroga belonged to a noble Galician family from Madrigal de las Altas Torres, in the Spanish province of Ávila. Although little can be ascertained about his early life and education, in 1525 he served as a judge in Oran in North Africa, where he found against a corrupt governor, and later in Granada.[77] His readiness to curb the abuses of occupying Spaniards appears consistent with the judicial scrupulousness he was to show in New Spain. Quiroga prosecuted some conquistadors, including Nuño Beltrán de Guzmán, and his recognition of the Indians' grievances prompted him to set up communities for those who had been left homeless and destitute. The first *pueblo-hospital* of Santa Fé was established gradually between 1531 and 1535 on the outskirts of Mexico City.

In 1533, Vasco de Quiroga visited Michoacán, a region extending from central Mexico to the Pacific coast, where he would found further settlements for the natives near Lake Pátzcuaro. The judge's experiences in the region led to his longest work, an untitled handwritten report to the Crown, known as the 'Información en derecho' (1535).[78] Quiroga expressed amazement at the sophistication of the indigenous people and used his knowledge of jurism, Christian doctrine, and literature

[73] CABRERA, 'Dicolon Icastichon' (1540b) is extant, but the *Manual de adultos* is lost: García Icazbalceta 1954, 58–61. Lara 2006, 637 considers Quiroga to be the author of the *Manual*; Carreño 1949, 315 states that it was written on Quiroga's bidding ('por orden y nota del Obispo de Mechuacán') by a secular priest, Pedro de Logroño, and prepared for publication by Zumárraga.

[74] Laird 2019b, 84–7.

[75] CABRERA, *De solicitanda infidelium conversione* (1582), 29r–50v; cf. Chapter 2, V below.

[76] MORE, *De optimo statu reipublicae . . . Vtopia* (1518) [1995]. The association was first made by Silvio Zavala in 1937 (Zavala 1937); cf. Zavala 1955 (in English); Verástique 2000; Krippner-Martínez 2001. The *Utopia* soon circulated in vernacular translations, as well as in Latin: Cave 2008.

[77] Warren 1998 contains a transcription and study of Quiroga's litigation in Oran.

[78] The 1868 edition of the Madrid manuscript by Torres de Mendoza of QUIROGA, 'Información en derecho' (1535), used by Zavala (see n. 76 above), is the most reliable, retaining the original quotations in Latin. Quiroga's own extensive marginalia remain unedited.

to reproach the conduct of the conquistadors. The third and final chapter sought to demonstrate that the Indians should be subjected neither to 'just war' (*iustum bellum* was the routine pretext for conquest) nor to captivity and enslavement: pacification and conversion to Christianity could be achieved without abrogating the rights or legal codes of the indigenous population. Shortly after his arrival in Mexico, Vasco de Quiroga had maintained that the Indians could be brought to Christianity peacefully because they were 'naturally possessed of an innate humility, obedience, poverty and disregard for the world, and of nudity, walking barefoot with long hair and with no headwear, *amicti sindone super nudo* [a linen cloth cast over a naked body]'.[79]

Such idealization of the primitive state of the Indians must have owed at least as much to stereotypes from European literature of the period as it did to actual observation: for instance, Quiroga's 'Información en derecho' mentioned Antonio de Guevara's *Libro âureo de Marco Aurelio, emperador y eloquentissimo orador*, 'Golden Book of Marcus Aurelius, Emperor and Most Eloquent Orator', first published in Seville in 1528. In that popular work of historical fiction set in the second century AD, a 'peasant of the Danube', a barbarian subject of the Roman empire, was presented as sharing his philosophical wisdom with the emperor, providing a source for Marcus Aurelius' own *Meditations*. Quiroga, though, attached much more importance to another text that really did come from classical antiquity. In the third chapter of his 'Información en derecho', he copied a lengthy passage from the *Saturnalia*, a comical dialogue by the ancient Greek satirist Lucian (Figure 1.2).[80] The excerpt was a speech by the god Saturn, who explains that the festival of the Saturnalia was held in order to recall the 'Golden Age' of his own reign, when men did not have to sow or till the earth, when wine flowed in rivers, and there were streams of milk and honey. Saturn also declared that this age, in which all men were equal and free, without slaves or masters, would soon return.[81]

The text was quoted in Thomas More's Latin translation of Lucian's Greek.[82] Quiroga claimed that this account of the Golden Age had unexpectedly illuminated his understanding of the natives of the Americas:

> I thought I should put down Lucian's original words here because I never saw nor heard them until the very time I was writing this, and it seemed to me that God was making them available for me at this time and juncture . . . perhaps to seal, and cap, and make finally understood this (in my

[79] QUIROGA, 'Carta . . . al Consejo de Indias' (1531) [1870, 423–4] citing Mark 14:51, description of a young man, who is supposed to be Saint Mark himself.

[80] QUIROGA, 'Información en derecho' (1535), 132v–133r [1868, 483–4]. Cf. Villaseñor 1953.

[81] Lucian, *Saturnalia* 7. Cf. Chapter 4, p. 145 and Chapter 8, p. 266 below for mentions of Saturn's reign in texts from the College of Santa Cruz in Tlatelolco.

[82] MORE, with ERASMUS, *Luciani Samosatensis Saturnalia* (1521).

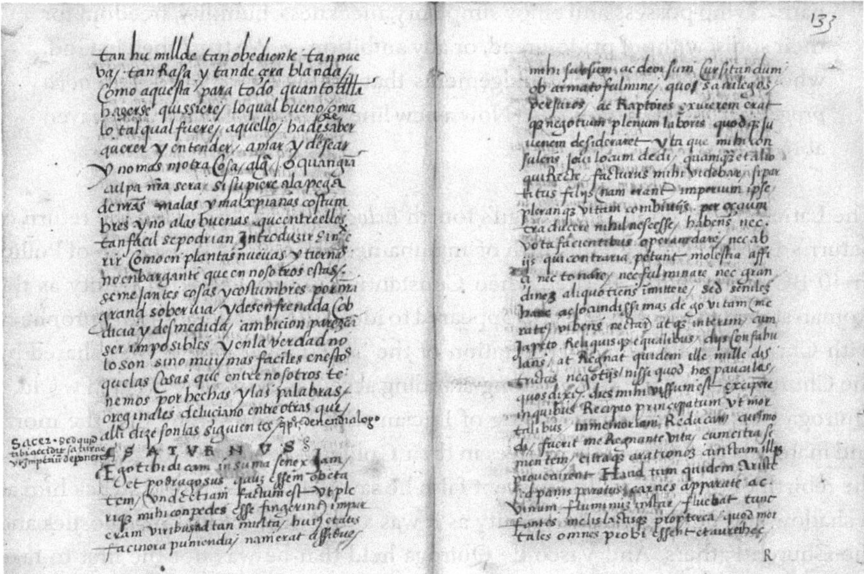

Figure 1.2 Latin translation of Lucian's *Saturnalia* quoted in Vasco de Quiroga, 'Información en derecho', Mexico City, 1535, 132v–133r. Biblioteca Nacional de España.

> opinion) so ill-understood matter of the land and the people, the properties and qualities of this New World in its Golden Age for its people, which for us, as I have said, is an Age of Iron.[83]

He elaborated at length on the innate virtues of the Indians, and on the abundant fruits of nature with which they were blessed: it was wrong for the Spaniards to impose their own legislation, designed for an Age of Iron, on the Indians, whose customs were in accordance with the Golden Age in which they lived, and whose conduct was anyway not far from the principles of the Christian religion. Lucian's distinction between the two Ages may have been what inclined Quiroga to envisage two 'republics' in the 'Información en derecho': a communitarian model was appropriate for the Indians, though not for the Spaniards.[84]

Another consideration had prompted a devout Catholic lawyer like Quiroga to bring a pagan Greco-Roman myth to bear on his understanding of indigenous Mexican society. His reasoning emerges later on when he twice recalls a greater classical authority:

> It could be said that *redeunt Saturnia regna* [the kingdoms of Saturn return], and in our own times, not among us [Spaniards], but among the

[83] QUIROGA, 'Información en derecho' (1535), 132v [1868, 483–4].

[84] Martínez Baracs 2005, 248–50 offers this important insight.

> natives who possess and enjoy simplicity, meekness, humility, freedom for their souls, without pride, greed, or any ambition . . . We trust then in God, who permits by his secret judgements that in this New World '*Jam nova progenies coelo demittitur alto* [Now a new lineage is sent down from heaven above].'[85]

The Latin phrases come from Virgil's fourth *Eclogue,* which predicted the return of Saturn's Golden Age with the birth of an unnamed child in the consulship of Pollio, in 40 BC. Four centuries later, when Constantine established Christianity as the Roman state religion, the emperor appeared to identify the child of Virgil's prophecy with Christ himself: that interpretation of the 'Messianic Eclogue' was shared by the Church Fathers and enjoyed long-standing acceptance in the Christian world.[86] Quiroga thus conjoined his reading of Lucian with Virgil to argue that the moral and material condition of the natives in their Golden Age was the ideal scenario for the rebirth of the church. The nascent faith he saw in the New World struck him as 'a shadow and outline' of Christianity as it was at the time of the holy apostles and the Church Fathers. And Vasco de Quiroga held that he was not the first to take such a view:

> This was known and understood by the author of the *best state of the republic* ['del muy buen estado de la república'] as a model from which my opinion derives, an illustrious man and one of more than human genius. As it was clear to him that the arts and customs of these uncomplicated peoples of the New World conformed to and were in every way similar to the people of gold of that first golden age, he drew, as the only remedy for the former, as one inspired by the Holy Spirit, from the customs of the latter, the ordinances and best state of government in which they would be able to keep, maintain, and work for themselves better and more easily, beyond compare, than by any other means or state that could be given them—which would not be so natural to them or in conformity with their skills, customs, and condition, nor so sufficient to provide enough that they do not waste away or perish—in order to introduce to them only the blend of faith and social conduct that they are lacking; for the rest, they have all that is proper and natural to them. For, though it is true that without grace and divine clemency no edifice of worth can be constructed, it is of great

[85] QUIROGA, 'Información en derecho' (1535), 136r–136v, 137r [1868, 489].

[86] The identification was made in a Greek text, known as the *Oratio ad sanctorum coetum,* 'Speech to the Gathering of Saints', supposedly delivered by Constantine in 323 AD and preserved by Eusebius of Caesarea. A text is in Heikel 1902; a translated excerpt is presented in Ziolkowski and Putnam 2008, 491–5; see further Courcelle 1957 and Houghton 2019, 197-8 on Juan Luis Vives' interpretation of *Eclogue* 4.

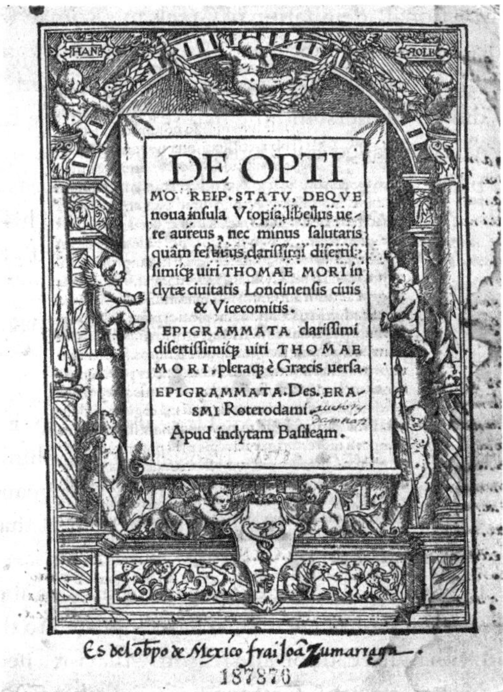

DE OPTI MO REIP. STATV, DEQVE noua insula Vtopia, libellus uere aureus, nec minus salutaris quâm festiuus, clarissimi disertissimiq; uiri THOMAE MORI inclytæ ciuitatis Londinensis ciuis & Vicecomitis.

EPIGRAMMATA clarissimi disertissimiq; uiri THOMAE MORI, pleraq; è Græcis uersa.

EPIGRAMMATA. Des. ERASMI Roterodami.

Apud inclytam Basileam.

Es del obpo de Mexico frai Joã Zumarraga.

187876

Figure 1.3 Thomas More's *Utopia*, Basel, 1518, inscribed by Fray Juan de Zumárraga. Benson Latin American Collection.

> advantage and help when this grace falls upon and gilds natural good qualities that are in line with this edifice.[87]

The words italicized above show that Quiroga was citing Thomas More's *Utopia*. The original title of that work had been *De optimo reipublicae statu, deque noua insula Vtopia, libellus uere aureus, nec minus salutaris quam festiuus*, 'On the Best State of the Republic, and on the New Island of Utopia, a truly golden book, no less salutary than enjoyable.' A Frobenius edition printed in Basel in 1518 was owned by Bishop Zumárraga in Mexico: his handwritten inscription, 'Es de obispo de Mexico frai Joan Zumarraga', is on the frontispiece (Figure 1.3). Zumárraga knew Quiroga well and consecrated him as bishop of Michoacán, and it has been speculated that Quiroga had the use of this particular copy.[88]

Quiroga's few mentions of the *Utopia* present it misleadingly as a kind of political-theological manifesto, rather like the 'Información en derecho' itself. Yet More's

[87] QUIROGA, 'Información en derecho' (1535), 139v–140r [1868, 493].

[88] MORE, *De optimo reipublicae statu* (1518); Zavala 1995, 61.

dialogue was overtly fictional, in imitation of Greek and Roman writers who passed off far-fetched stories as factual reportage.[89] The names of Utopia and of its river, Anydrus, derived from Greek, respectively mean 'No Place' and 'Without Water'.[90] Only a reader who did not understand the nature of literature could regard as veridical a story by a narrator called Hythlodaeus (whose name means 'purveyor of nonsense') about a place where gold was used for chamber pots and where newly hatched chicks followed humans instead of hens.[91] In spite of his claim 'frequently to admire' the *Utopia*, Quiroga's response to it is not in line with those of informed readers at the time.

After naming the illustrious writer of the dialogue, Quiroga revealed the real reason for his interest in him:

> This author, Thomas More, was a great Hellenist ['fue gran griego'] and a great expert of much authority. He translated some things by Lucian from Greek into Latin, where, as I have said, the laws, ordinances, and customs of the Golden Age and the most simple people of that age are set out, according to what is found and set out in what he says about these [natives] in his republic [*Utopia*] and in what Lucian says about those [in the Golden Age] in his *Saturnalia*, it must have appeared to this most prudent man—and with much caution and reason—that for a people like this, such a craft and state of government would be suitable and helpful, and that by this means, and no other, can the people be maintained, for the reasons that have been stated.[92]

More is here credited with making known Lucian's account of the mythological Saturnine Golden Age, and then for recommending that it could inform the social organization of the Indians in the New World. In other words, Thomas More is praised for doing exactly what Vasco de Quiroga was really doing himself. The 'Información en derecho' devoted several pages to Lucian's *Saturnalia*, quoting More's translation at length, with only glancing references to his *Utopia*. That at least reflected the relative dissemination of those works in the sixteenth century, when More's Lucian was far better known. By 1550 there were about 270 printings of Lucian (also rendered into Latin by Erasmus) circulating in Europe in addition to some sixty Greek editions. Even by the time the 'Información' was completed in

[89] Nelson 1973; Carver 2001.

[90] Cf. More's letter to Erasmus. London, 3 September 1516, in ERASMUS, *Opus epistolarum* (1529), no. 461 [tr. 1977 iv, 66].

[91] Wilson 1992; Williams 1981 suggests the account of the chicks was based on BREYDENBACH, *Peregrinatio in Terram Sanctam* (1486).

[92] QUIROGA, 'Información en derecho' (1535), 140r–140v [1868, 493–4].

1535, there had been fourteen editions of Thomas More's Lucian translation and only six of the *Utopia*.[93]

The 'utopianism' of Vasco de Quiroga and his manner of interpreting scripture were both primarily rooted in the thought of Desiderius Erasmus, although the Spanish judge took care not to name him. Erasmus laid constant emphasis on the importance of spreading the Christian faith by good action and setting positive examples, as opposed to merely sermonizing. Quiroga shared these positions along with the Dutch scholar's ardent pacifism, and he too, somewhat confusingly, could use the imagery of warfare to communicate his ideas.[94] Erasmus' *Praise of Folly* had reproached the church's use of violence to defend its interests:

> As if the Church really had any more deadly enemies than impious prelates who by their silence cause Christ to be obliterated, bind him with their mercenary laws, discredit him with their contrived interpretations, and murder with their noxious lives. Despite the Christian church being founded on blood [of martyrs], strengthened by blood, and increased by blood, nowadays it is just as if Christ who looks after his own in his own way, had perished, as they get things done with the sword. Even though war is so monstrous a thing that it suits animals, not men, so deranged that poets represent it as imposed by the Furies, so harmful that it involves universal ruin of morals, so wrong that it is best perpetrated by the worst criminals, and so sacrilegious that it has no relation to Christ, they still engage in it, to the exclusion of all else.[95]

Erasmus' irony was that the church, which had been established by martyrdom, was now engaged in killing. Quiroga saw the conduct of Spanish Christians in the colonies in terms of this paradox:

> I am sure on account of what I have seen and see, that the persecution of the new and early church in this part of the New World by its evil Christian

[93] Thompson 1940, 203; Branham 1985.

[94] Dealy 1975 and Dealy 1976 draw attention to the pacifism in CABRERA, *De solicitanda infidelium conversione* (1582). Lupher 2003, 155–8 shows that a manuscript treatise advocating just war, possibly dating from the 1530s (edited in Acuña 1988), has been wrongly attributed to Quiroga; the sources and style of the treatise confirm this: Laird 2009.

[95] ERASMUS, *Moriae encomium* (1511) [1979, 174]. 'Quasi vero ulli sint hostes Ecclesiæ perniciosiores, quam impii pontifices, qui et silentio Christum sinunt abolescere, et quæstuariis legibus alligant et coactis interpretationibus adulterant, et pestilente vita iugulant. Porro cum Christiana Ecclesia sanguine sit condita, sanguine confirmata, sanguine aucta, nunc perinde quasi Christus perierit, qui more suo tueatur suos, ita ferro rem gerunt. Cumque bellum res sit adeo immanis, ut feras non homines deceat, adeo insana, ut poetæ quoque fingant a Furiis immitti, adeo pestilens, ut universam morum luem simul invehat, adeo iniusta, ut a pessimis latronibus optime soleat administrari, adeo impia, ut nihil cohæreat cum Christo, tamen omnibus omissis, hoc tantum agunt.'

> sons, those of us that are in it and come to plant it, is so much greater and more brutal and fierce than that which the early church of the Old World received in the time of its enemies and unbelieving persecutors, who, thinking to destroy it with as much blood as the holy martyrs shed, rather built it up; while we are coming to build it up with our bad examples, and deeds worse than the unbelievers, and thus destroy it. For such is the contradiction and repugnance that the enemy within the house is greater than the one outside.[96]

Here Quiroga was more tactful in referring to the authorities not as 'prelates' but as 'the enemy within': unlike the sharply satirical *Moriae encomium*, his work was designed to persuade rather than to provoke.

Quiroga's 'Información en derecho' was signed in Mexico on 24 July 1535—less than three weeks after Thomas More was beheaded in London on 6 July, and the author was already referring to the English humanist in the past tense: 'Thomas More *was* a great Hellenist.'[97]

V. Fray Julián Garcés

That same summer, Fray Julián Garcés (1452–1542), the bishop of Tlaxcala, a day's journey from Mexico City, was probably drafting his own treatise about the condition of the Indians. This far more polished text, composed in elegant humanist Latin, would be presented to Pope Paul III in 1536 and printed in Rome the following year—the first work from New Spain to be published in Europe. More importantly, Garcés' short composition would elicit the celebrated papal bull of 1537, 'Sublimis Deus', which declared that Indians were 'true human beings' ('veros homines'), able and willing to adopt the Catholic faith, and that they should not be deprived of their property or enslaved.

Hailing from a noble family in Aragon, Garcés had distinguished himself as philosopher and theologian before attending the University of Paris in the late 1470s. Returning to Spain, he devoted further years to attaining the title of 'Master' from his Dominican order.[98] According to Fray Juan de Torquemada, a Franciscan writing in New Spain in the late 1500s, Garcés was 'learned in the Latin language to such a degree that the master Antonio de Nebrija said that he himself would do well to study

[96] QUIROGA, 'Información en derecho' (1535), 108v [1868, 456–7]. Dealy 1976, 14–15 identified the debt to the Erasmus in this passage.

[97] More had been imprisoned since Easter 1534: his incarceration was mentioned by Juan Luis Vives in a letter to Erasmus from Bruges, 10 May 1534: ERASMUS, *Opus epistolarum* [1906–1958, x, no. 2932, lines 30–2].

[98] LORENZANA Y BUITRÓN, *Concilios provinciales* (1769), 241–55.

in order to know more than that friar.'[99] This remark has led some to maintain that Garcés was a pupil or friend of the great Andalusian humanist. In fact, Torquemada must have relied on a comment Bartolomé de las Casas ascribed to Nebrija in his *History of the Indies* (c. 1560):

> The Bishop of Burgos, don Juan Rodriguéz de Fonseca saw to it that a Dominican named Julián Garcés should be nominated as Bishop of Cozumel, since [Garcés] was his confessor, a master in theology, a notable preacher and evidently very good at Latin, so much so that it has been said that the Master Antonio de Nebrija, on seeing his aptitude and expertise in the Latin language, said: *me oportet minui hunc aut[em] crescere* ['I must decrease and he must increase'].[100]

Las Casas seems not to have realized that Nebrija's words, which play on a verse from John's Gospel, were not so complimentary.[101] Their meaning seems to be that either Nebrija's skill in Latin would have to diminish, or that of Garcés would need to improve, for them to be on the same level. The two men may have become acquainted through Fonseca, who as minister of the Indies secured Garcés' consecration as the first bishop on the American mainland in 1519.[102] The seat of the diocese was originally on the island of Cozumel in Yucatán, but the Spaniards did not remain in the region and moved north, so that in 1526 the king, with papal approval, transferred the Caroline bishopric to the district of Tlaxcala in central Mexico.[103] Garcés finally sailed for New Spain in 1527.

Tlaxcallan had been a predominantly Nahuatl-speaking federation of four polities, or *altepetl*, at war with the Aztec empire since the 1300s. As the Tlaxcalteca had lent military support to the Spaniards, bringing about the defeat of the Aztecs, the natives of colonial Tlaxcala enjoyed special privileges at least until the mid-1500s. Spanish colonists were excluded from Indian communities, the governments of which were incorporated into Spanish principalities, and native leaders were allowed to ride horses and bear weapons.[104] Although there were some significant exceptions, the Tlaxcalteca were generally swift to embrace the

[99] TORQUEMADA, *MI* 19.31 [1979 vi, 118].

[100] LAS CASAS, *Historia* (c. 1560), cap. 118 [1965 iii, 232–3].

[101] John 3:30: 'Illum oportet crescere, me autem minui'; 'He must increase and I must decrease.' The words are spoken by John the Baptist.

[102] Nebrija dedicated his *Vafre dicta philosophorum*, 'Crafty sayings of the philosophers'; *Collationes antiquitatum*, 'Compilations of Antiquities'; and *Aenigmata iuris civilis*, 'Enigmas of civil law', to Juan Rodríguez de Fonseca in 1498, 1504–1514 and 1506 respectively: Abellán Giral 1991, 61, 72, 75, 82 n. 38, 241–5. Beuchot 1997, 145–8 explores the possible association between Nebrija and Garcés.

[103] LÓPEZ DE COGULLUDO, *Historia de Yucathan* (1688) 1.5.

[104] Gibson 1952, 143, 184, 190.

Catholic faith and some became literate in Spanish and Latin.[105] As a symbol of cultural accord, the palace of their former ruler Maxixcatzin, who died of smallpox in 1520, had been turned into a Franciscan monastery by Cortés in 1524.[106] The new bishop determined that this would be the site of his episcopal cathedral of Santa María de la Concepción.

Garcés moved to Mexico City to show solidarity with Zumárraga shortly after the latter's arrival in December 1528, and remained there until 1531. Having written to Juana of Castile to ask if Tlaxcala could be settled by Spaniards, lamenting that it was possible to construct only a makeshift cathedral 'with a straw roof', he received a firm reply from the queen, reproaching him for staying in Mexico City and urging him 'to instill holy faith and good treatment of the Indians'.[107] Zumárraga, however, was summoned to Spain in May of 1532, not to return to Mexico for at least two years: Garcés was able to take the place of his younger colleague, and it was during this second period in Mexico City that he penned his deposition to Paul III, which he entrusted to another Dominican, Fray Bernardino de Minaya, to take to Rome in person. Minaya had hoped the text would be printed along with two earlier letters—one by Fray Juan de Zumárraga, the other by Juan Bernal Díaz de Luco, a member of the Council of the Indies.[108]

Garcés' letter alone was published in Rome in 1537. A sole surviving copy of the original imprint is the only source for the text's proper title: *De habilitate et capacitate gentium sive Indorum novi mundi nuncupati ad fidem Christi capessendam, & quam libenter suscipiant,* 'On the aptitude and capacity of the peoples, or Indians, of the New World, as it is called, to adopt faith in Christ, and how willingly they embrace it' (Figure 1.4).[109] The *De habilitate* is well known for the famous bull it prompted. Garcés' purpose was to demonstrate the Indians' humanity and, like Quiroga, he sought to protect them from 'just war', slavery, or deprivation of their property. Some of his arguments anticipated those of his Dominican confrère Bartolomé de las Casas, whose defences of the Indians would gain prominence a

[105] TLAXCALA, 'Verba sociorum' (1541) is an early colonial Latin text by an indigenous author from Tlaxcala: cf. Chapter 6, I below.

[106] Maxixcatzin had ruled the *altepetl* of Ocotelolco and was a prominent ally of the Spaniards: Gibson 1952, 43–4, 54; cf. Chapter 9, I below.

[107] Cuevas 1946–1947, i: 376.

[108] LÓPEZ DE GÓMARA, *Historia general de las Indias* (1554), §217: 'fray Rodrigo [*sic*] Minaya did much to win their liberty by securing a bull from Paul III declaring that the Indians were men and not beasts, free and not slaves, and Fray Bartolomé de las Casas afterwards insisted the same.' Cf. MINAYA, 'Muy Católica Majestad' (1559), a letter to Philip II. Lillo Castañ and Camino Plaza 2021 present an edition and Spanish translation of the letters by Díaz de Luco and Zumárraga that had already been printed together, probably in 1533.

[109] Cf. GARCÉS, *De habilitate* (1537), 3–5, 7–9 in Appendix 1.1 below. Laird 2014a incorporates a complete text and translation. The edition and Spanish version of Acuña 1995 were based on the flawed, untitled copy in DÁVILA PADILLA, *Historia de la fundación* (1596).

DE HABILITATE ET CA-
PACITATE GENTIVM SIVE IN-
dorum noui mundi nũcupati ad fidem Chri-
ſti capeſſendam,& quã libenter ſuſcipiãt.

ROMAE Anno M. D. XXXVII.

Figure 1.4 Fray Julián Garcés, *De habilitate et capacitate gentium*, Rome, 1537. John Carter Brown Library.

decade or so later. The fact that the *De habilitate* was published as a self-standing work so soon after it was composed shows that its literary and moral value was swiftly recognized.

Garcés' rhetorical ingenuity is evident from the outset, as he opposed those missionaries who, in contravention of scripture, were excluding the natives from the church, simply in order to enslave them. Those same missionaries, it is maintained, were being encouraged by the Devil to argue that human beings were no more than animals or beasts of burden: 'Hence it appears that Satan, that enemy of all the human race, disguised as an angel of light, has contrived this so that, by putting off the conversion of these races, he might conserve the worship that was shown to him.'[110] The reproach turns on its head the widespread claim that the idolatrous natives of the Americas were themselves in the service of the Devil.[111] Such

[110] GARCÉS, *De habilitate*, 6–7.

[111] Cervantes 1991; Cervantes 1994, 5–39.

appropriation of an opponent's theme to a contrary end was a tactic recommended by classical rhetoricians.[112]

Even so, the charge that churchmen who deemed the Indians unfit for conversion were representing Satan was inflammatory. It is not until the closing exhortation to the pope that Garcés mentioned the Devil again—this time as a martial adversary to the Church in its fight to preserve and extend its physical borders:

> Here let us draw gold from the very insides of the faith of the Indians, gold we should send there to the support of our soldiers; let us snatch from the Devil territories which reach far further from India than those which he, with his Mohammedans, would steal away from us in Europe.[113] Let us batter the walls of the demons with a double ram: so that we pull the natives from their long-standing grasp: and there, having retrieved that gold, let us keep the demons from the borders of Europe. [114]

The conquerors' quest for gold had become an allegory for securing the souls of the Indians, who were not the Church Militant's opponents, but its prize.[115] After all, Saint Bartholomew, who taught the Indians to seek the gold mines of the faith, had proved an astonishing torment to the demons.[116] 'And you most Holy Father', Garcés implored Pope Paul, 'should imitate, emulate and accompany your God, since you see he sent, almost urged his apostles to go as soldiers to the Indies.' The position is very comparable to Quiroga's: the enemy is within, not aligned with the Indians, and the allegorical imagery here suggests a debt to Erasmus.[117]

These entreaties, culminating in an personal appeal to the pope, struck home. In his bull of 2 June 1537, Paul III wrote,

> One inimical to the human race itself, who opposes all good men in order to bring them to destruction, beholding and envying this, thought up a means not yet heard of, by which he might hinder the preaching of God's

[112] The strategy was used in *controversiae* that debated both sides of a case: Cicero, *De oratore* 1.149, 1.244; see further Clarke 1996, 17–18, 86–7, 90–5.

[113] Weighing of souls gained in the Indies against those lost in Europe to Luther or Islam would become commonplace: LÓPEZ DE GÓMARA, *Historia general de las Indias* (1554), 1.8; cf. Fuchs 2001, 144–5; Mayer 2008.

[114] GARCÉS, *De habilitate*, 13 [2014, 211].

[115] MINAYA, 'Muy Católica Majestad' (c. 1559) [1937, 83] recounted to Philip II his refusal to accept gold that had been won unjustly from Pizarro. MENDIETA, *Historia* 3.13 [1870, 214] has Cortés and the Franciscans explain to the Mexicans that they were sent by the pope to bring eternal salvation, not hunt for gold.

[116] GARCÉS, *De habilitate*, 13: the mention of Saint Bartholomew follows that of Saint Thomas, whom Christ persuaded to go to the Indies, despite his protest in *Acts of Thomas* 1:1: Elliott 1999, 439.

[117] Cf. Bataillon 1937 [2007, 818] on ERASMUS, *Ecclesiastes* (1535).

> word of Salvation to the people: he incited his agents, who, desiring to fulfil his desire, have not hesitated to publish abroad that the Indians of the West and the South, and other peoples who in these times have come to our attention, should be treated as dumb brutes created for our service, pretending that they are incapable of receiving the Catholic Faith.[118]

The opinion that the Indians could not become Christians had been propagated by agents of the Devil or Satan, 'one inimical to the human race itself' ('ipsius humani generis emulus'). The pope turned out to be in complete agreement with this, the most contentious section of Garcés' brief: his words show that he was alert to the controversial novelty of the bishop's allegation that his ecclesiastical opponents were 'instigated by devilish suggestions' and were giving voice to a 'satanic utterance'. The Dominican emissary from New Spain, Fray Bernardino de Minaya, had boldly echoed that sentiment in his short preface to the printed text of the *De habilitate,* even though such a polemical charge was something few churchmen would dare to repeat.[119] Yet Paul III was willing to underwrite it himself, by adroitly giving the impression that this was an expedient response to the Devil's latest ruse. As well as confirming that Garcés' letter precipitated the bull, such sleight of hand suggests that the Farnese pope was alert to some of the Bishop's own delicate innuendos.[120]

Garcés' eloquence was matched by his learning. He launched his refutation of objections to converting the Indians by assembling passages from the Gospels, leading to an unequivocal conclusion: 'the door is to be closed to no man who, out of his own voluntary faith, seeks baptism of the Church.'[121] Several classical sources had been quoted in the earlier letter signed by Garcés and his fellow bishop Zumárraga that opened this chapter. The *De habilitate* contained many more sustained *exempla* and quotations from Roman authors: in fact, its appeal was based more on antiquarian knowledge than on scripture and theology.

The argument was subtle. Drawing from Isidore of Seville's definition of the Greek word *anthropophagi,* Garcés began by conceding that the Indians had once been cannibals.[122] He also conceded that their former savagery and cruelty had

[118] PAUL III, 'Sublimis Deus' (1537). Acuña 1995, lii and lvi n. 2 wrongly emends 'hactenus inauditum', 'not yet heard of', to 'hactenus auditum', 'now known'.

[119] MINAYA, Letter to Tomasso Badia, in GARCÉS, *De habilitate* (1537), 2r: 'that defamatory opinion being disseminated and imposed on the Indians by the Devil's artifice'. Cf. SANDOVAL, *De instauranda Aethiopum salute* (1627) 2.3 [1956, 197–8]: 'the devil ['demonio'] has convinced masters that slaves are incapable of understanding our faith, that it is all nonsense to them.'

[120] Lupher 2003, 202–3 is cautious: '[Garcés'] eloquent and powerful document is commonly credited with helping to inspire the bull *Sublimis Deus*'. On the Pope's own humanist formation, see n. 129 below.

[121] GARCÉS, *De habilitate,* 6; cf. Revelation 4:1; Isaiah 22:22.

[122] GARCÉS, *De habilitate,* 7; Isidore, *Etymologies* 9.2.132: 'The Anthropophagi are a very savage race found hard by the region of the Seres [China]. Because they feed on human flesh they are thus

been 'beyond human measure', 'ultra humanum modum', an expression evoking a classical philosophical conception of virtue, rather than Christian morality.[123] But the Spaniards should treat the natives in the way that they would like to have been treated in the same circumstances—the native Americans were no more idolatrous or barbarous than their own people had been in antiquity—a case that would later be made by Las Casas.[124]

That point is illustrated with a couple of examples. The first is a reference to an episode recounted by Aulus Gellius to illustrate the gullibility of the ancient Iberians: the Roman general Sertorius succeeded in convincing them that he was availing himself of the clairvoyant powers of a deer, a dumb animal.[125] Secondly, the ancient Spaniards had such disregard for human life that the men would kill themselves rather than endure old age—a principle clearly contrary to the teachings of scripture.[126] According to Garcés, that proof of their savagery, 'feritas', was offered by a poet who was actually Spanish himself: 'Silius Italicus, who came from the city of Italica in Baetica pronounced a glorious eulogy of his very own ancestors!'[127]

If by his preaching 'Santiago', or Saint James the Apostle, had managed to convert the Spaniards and turn them 'from the worst to the best', the Indians could follow suit. Despite the fact that ancient Spain had once been ruled by Viriatus, a mere cattleherd, its great soldiers, glorious generals, and even some emperors eventually came to serve Rome.[128] Trajan, Hadrian, and Marcus Aurelius all came from Spain; the first Christian emperor of Spanish origin was Theodosius, who reunited the eastern and western empire under Nicene orthodoxy as the state religion. The array of such *recherché* classical authorities as Trogus, Aulus Gellius, and Silius Italicus

called *anthropophagi*'; cf. Pliny, *Natural History* 4.12.26; 6.17.20; 6.30.35; Pomponius Mela, *De chorographia* 2.14. There was no original Latin term for the Grecism *anthropophagus*. The Spanish *antropófago* is not attested before the *Historia del Monserrate* (1588) of Cristóbal de Virués; *canibal* had appeared in the *Historia de Santa Marta y Nuevo Reino de Granada* (c. 1573–1581) by Fray Pedro de Aguado: cf. Boucher 1992; Palencia-Roth 1985.

[123] Kraye 1988, 339–42.

[124] LAS CASAS, 'Carta a un personaje de la corte' (1535) followed Garcés in remarking that 'the Indians are what we were in Spain before St James' disciples converted us': Lupher 2003, 201–2.

[125] Aulus Gellius, *Noctes Atticae* 15.22.9–10: 'the credulity of this barbarian people was very helpful to Sertorius in important matters . . . none of them ever deserted him although that race is very inconstant.'

[126] Silius Italicus, *Punica* 1.225–8; GARCÉS, *De habilitate* (1537), 7.

[127] Had Silius Italicus (c. 25–103 AD) come from Italica (near Seville), he would have been named 'Italicensis', but his ancestors would have been Roman, not Iberian. The Spanish Roman poet Martial, *Epigrams* 1.61, did not include Silius in a list of Latin poets from Spain: Campbell 1936.

[128] GARCÉS, *De habilitate*, 8: Justinus' epitome of Pompeius Trogus, *Historiae Philippicae* 44.2, described Viriatus as the Spaniards' only great general, not mentioning his origins as a herdsman. Livy, *Periocha* (summary) of Book 52: 'In Spain, Viriatus first turned from shepherd to hunter, then from hunter to brigand, and soon, on becoming commander of a real army, seized all of Lusitania'; cf. Florus' epitome of Livy 1.33.3; Aurelius Victor, *De viris illustribus* 71.1.

was in part to impress Paul III. The pope, born as Alessandro Farnese, was a capable classical scholar who had read Silius with Pomponio Leto in Rome, and had studied Greek under Demetrius Chalcocondyles and other Hellenists of the Medici circle in Florence before he assumed the papacy.[129]

The observation that Spain brought forth men who became emperors in order to *serve* Rome perhaps had a contemporary resonance: Charles V, the Holy Roman Emperor, had a Castilian mother. The complex power struggles between Spain and the papacy would determine the outcome of this petition for the Indians.[130] In writing to an Italian pope, Garcés, unlike other Iberian writers of his time, did not praise Viriatus for his heroic stand against Rome any more than he idealized the ancient Spaniards.[131] There was, however, one point in their favour:

> In the age during which Sertorius was in Spain as general of the Romans among a half-wild people, the ancient Spaniards had come to know Greek and Latin letters as they were subjugated by those peoples, but it is true that if Spain had known her own strength, then, as Trogus says, she would never have bowed her neck to the Romans.[132] The Spaniards had therefore already learned the Romans' alphabet, and they were no less skilled in their language even though they were still half-barbarians.

The ancient Spaniards' acquisition of the Greek and Latin alphabets raised their status, in just a few lines, from 'once possessing great savagery' ('Feritas Hispanorum quondam tanta erat') to being 'semiferi', 'half-wild'. They could not in the end have been barbarians, but 'semibarbari', because they recognized the advantage of literacy. Ignorance of letters was what made a barbarian, and Garcés had been too careful ever to call the Mexican Indians 'barbari'.

[129] Dorez 1932 is a full study of Pope Paul III and his legacy; cf. Fragnito 2014. Farnese's Latin letters, many on classical subjects, to Chalcocondyles, Pomponio Leto, Giorgio Merula, and others are in Frugoni 1950; Paul III's correspondence with Reginald Pole was collected in QUIRINI, *Epistularum Reginaldi Poli par[te]s I–V* (1744–1757).

[130] Hanke 1937, 74–81; Dorez 1932, 249–91 examines Paul III's relation to Charles V.

[131] SEPÚLVEDA, *Democrates secundus* (c. 1545) [1951, 54] praised Viriatus; GUEVARA, *Epistolas familiares* (1539) 1.7 [1950, 56–67], echoing Livy (n. 128 above), commended don Antonio de Zúñiga as a new Viriatus; FERNÁNDEZ DE OVIEDO, *Historia general y natural de las Indias* (1557) 33.20 [1959, 97] likened Cortés to the hero, who was praised in Camões, *Lusiads* 8.6, cf. Lupher 2003, 207–9.

[132] GARCÉS, *De habilitate*, 8 was roughly quoting Justinus, *Historiae Philippicae* 44.5.8: 'Nec prius perdomitae prouinciae iugum Hispani accipere potuerunt, quam Caesar Augustus perdomito orbe uictricia ad eos arma transtulit populumque barbarum ac ferum legibus ad cultiorem uitae usum traductum in formam prouinciae redegit' ('Nor would the Spaniards submit to the yoke, even after their country was overrun, until Caesar Augustus, having subdued the rest of the world, turned his victorious arms against them, and reduced this barbarous and savage people, brought by the influence of laws to a more civilized way of life, into the form of a province').

His next move was to point out that the Indians had never been illiterate in the first place:

> Since I have pronounced that the Indians have never learned literacy ['literas'], I will now perform a recantation ['palinodiam'].[133] They used to paint instead of write. That is to say, they used not letters but images if they wished to signify anything worthy of record to those who were away ['absentibus'] in another time or in another place. Lucan [*Pharsalia* 3.220-4] also hints at it in these words:
>
> The Phoenicians first presumed, if tradition is believed,
> To seal their utterances for posterity in crude signs.
> Not yet had Egypt learned to weave together river reeds,
> And only birds, beasts, and creatures carved in rock
> Conserved the speech of wise men for their needs.

This characterization of Indian writing was really drawn from Isidore of Seville's definition of letters as signs of words that 'speak without a vocal sound to us the sayings of those absent' ('nobis dicta absentium sine voce loquantur').[134] Isidore's account of letters opened his popular *Etymologies*: Garcés' debt to this part of the work is further proven by the fact that he quoted from the same passage of the Roman poet Lucan as Isidore had.[135] But in addition the bishop included three further lines about carved Egyptian hieroglyphs that preserved 'magicas linguas', the *spoken* utterances of *magi*, or wise men, suggesting he believed Mexican pictograms had a similar capacity.

Whether or not phonographic value could be attached to them, pictures and charts did function as historical and genealogical records in Nahuatl polities.[136]

[133] GARCÉS, *De habilitate*, 9. Plato, *Letters* 319e and *Phaedrus* 243b, and Isocrates, *Helen* 64 use παλινῳδία [*palinodia*] for Stesichorus' verse retraction of his poem criticizing Helen, but the word was not transliterated by classical Latin authors. Garcés would have encountered it in Jerome, *Epistles*, 102.1 and possibly Macrobius, *Saturnalia* 7.5.4: both sources refer to Stesichorus. NIGER, *Brevis Grammatica* (1480) had included the *palinodia* as a variety of Latin lyric poetry, although there were few examples in practice: Lozano Guillén 2008, 106–7.

[134] NEBRIJA, *Comiença la gramatica . . . sobre la lengua castellana* (1492) 1.3, entitled 'De como las letras fueron halladas para representar las bozes' ('On how letters were discovered to represent utterances'), drew from Isidore, as well as Cicero, *Ad familiares* 2.4: 'Epistularum genera multa esse non ignoras sed unum illud certissimum, cuius causa inventa res ipsa est, ut certiores faceremus absentis si quid esset quod eos scire aut nostra aut ipsorum interesset' ('You are well aware that letters are of many kinds; but one kind is undeniable, for the sake of which, indeed, the thing was invented, namely, to inform those absent of anything that is to the interest of the writer or recipient that they should know').

[135] Lucan, *Pharsalia* 3.220–1 had been quoted in Isidore, *Etymologies* 1.3.

[136] Such pictures retained a documentary function after the conquest: Boone 1998; cf. Justeson 1986; Prem 1992, 53–69. Whittaker 2021 is a groundbreaking contemporary exploration of Aztec hieroglyphs.

Natives in Garcés' diocese of Tlaxcala had a motive for using such records to remind Spaniards of their support in the conquest and of the rewards and exemptions that were due to them. The earliest known visual treatments were painted on bark paper, but the more celebrated *Lienzo de Tlaxcala* (1552)—copies survive of the lost original (Plate 3)—is so called because its illustrations were on pieces of woven cloth known as *lienzos*. These 'pictorial petitions' from Tlaxcala were altered over time to be rendered more persuasive.[137] Murals relating events surrounding the conquest were to be found in the palace of the native ruler Xicotencatl and it is likely that there were similar murals in the former palace of his rival, Maxixcatzin. The episcopal cathedral was established on that site in 1527.[138]

Garcés made his case for the Indians' literacy in two ways. He dignified Mexican pictorial writing through comparison to the sign systems of the Phoenicians and Egyptians, and he explained that the Indians could now write not just in Spanish but also in Latin—which they had learned to speak and write. In fact, according to Motolinía, Fray Martín de Valencia had settled in Tlaxcala, where he taught reading and Latin grammar to native children, and the first indigenous writers were trained in Tlaxcala as well as in Mexico City.[139] Garcés further affirmed that the Latin of the Indian youths was as elegant as that of the Dominican friars themselves. The inference to be drawn from this point is obvious, although it was left unstated: if there is an inverse relation between Latinate literacy and barbarism, then the Indians could not be barbarians.

The deployment of classical learning in the *De habilitate* was strategic. The same applied to the knowledge of the Mexican language displayed in the treatise. Garcés connected two Nahuatl words in an account of the Indians' frugal nature, a description that harmonized with Vasco de Quiroga's presentation of their simple and modest customs:

> They demand nothing strenuously other than their *tla cuali,* for so they call the common meal, after the word for 'bread' or *tlaxcali.*[140]

There is no real linguistic association in Nahuatl between *tlacuali* and *tlaxcali. Tlacuali* or *tlacualli,* 'food', derives from the verb *cua,* 'eat', while *tlaxcali* or *tlaxcalli,* 'tortilla', is derived from *ixca,* 'bake'.[141] The linking of *tlacuali* to *tlaxcalli* invested

[137] Kranz 2007 analyses all these pictorial documents.

[138] MUÑOZ CAMARGO, *Historia de Tlaxcala* (c. 1592) incorporated drawings based on depictions from the *Lienzo de Tlaxcala,* which was a source for his chronicle: Kranz 2010, 53. Cf. Chapter 9, I below.

[139] MOTOLINÍA, *Historia* 3.2 [2001, 180]. Cf. Chapter 6, I below.

[140] GARCÉS, *De habilitate,* 4: 'Praeter suum tla cuali (sic enim communem escam appellant) post panem seu tlaxcali nihil obnixe flagitantes.'

[141] Karttunen 1992, 257, s.v. *tlacualli,* 'food'; 303 s.v. *tlaxcalli,* 'tortilla, baked bread'.

the Nahuatl word for 'meal' with the Christian sense of 'daily bread'. The medieval practice of etymologizing words, often in order to endow them with religious significance, was still common in Renaissance Europe, notwithstanding criticisms from humanists like Nebrija.[142] The fact that such speculative etymologies were often based on Greek bears on Garcés' second invocation of a Nahuatl term, and it reveals a more elementary misunderstanding of the Mexican language. This occurs in the bishop's description of the Indians' modesty, which he illustrated with a comparison to an ancient European custom:

> The fighters who used to train in the Campus Martius were called *campestrati* (on Augustine's testimony) because they covered their private parts with loincloths that used to be called *campestria* or, in sacred writings, *perizomata* (the Indians say *tomastli*). Amongst these Indians there is such a high regard for and observance of modesty that no one, not even a little child, would appear in public without *tomaxtli*, that is, without something around his waist.[143]

The apparent coincidence of sound and sense between *tomaxtli* and the Greek *zomata*, 'loin-cloth', is illusory, but it might have appealed to a pope with a penchant for philology.[144] It is a telling coincidence that the inhabitants of Thomas More's fictional Utopia were supposed to speak a language related to Greek.

At least Garcés considered the Mexican language worthy of attention and he criticized an 'eminent' Dominican (almost certainly Fray Domingo de Betanzos) for 'applying too little study to the Indians' language'.[145] The *De habilitate* was one of

[142] Henderson 2007 demonstrates the educational value of etymologies in Isidore; cf. the excursus (XIV) in Curtius 1953, 495–500 on their use as a category of thought in the Middle Ages. NEBRIJA, *Gramatica . . . sobre la lengua castellana* (1492) cap. 3, defined *etimología* as 'the truth of words'. Cf. Hernando Cuadrado 2008.

[143] GARCÉS, *De habilitate*, 5, recalling Augustine, *De civitate Dei* 14.17; cf. Horace, *Epistles* 1.11.8. Pausanias, *Description of Greece* 1.44.1 refers to περίζωμα; and Thucydides, *History* 1.6.5 has διαζώματα in the context of Olympic games.

[144] 'Tomastli' [sc. 'tomaxtli'] consists of the possessive prefix, *to*, 'our', and *maxtli*, the 'possessed form' of *maxtatl*. The first *a* is long, while *zōmata* or *perizōmata* in Greek has a long *o* and short *a*. For *maxtatl*, MOLINA, *Vocabulario en lengua castellana y mexicana* (1571) gives 'bragas o cosa semejante', 'breeches or similar'; Karttunen 1992, 141 (quoting Molina): 'breechclout'. Lampe 1961, 1065: s.v. περίζωμα [*perizōma*]: 'loin-cloth, girdle'.

[145] MINAYA, 'Muy Católica Majestad' (c. 1559) [1937, 100] would later tell Philip II that Betanzos, who had secured a papal audience in 1531, did not know the Indians' language or understand them: 'fray Domingo no sabía la lengua ni les entendía.' Hanke 1937, 79 shows that Betanzos' testimony to the Council of the Indies was what prompted Garcés to send Minaya to Europe. Garcés' criticism of friars 'devoted to solitude' who were neglecting their missionary duty also points to Betanzos, who had spent five years in seclusion on the Italian island of Ponza: DÁVILA PADILLA, *Historia de la fundacion* (1596) 1.22.

the earliest publications to explain Nahuatl words to Latinate readers in Europe.[146] Although Garcés' knowledge of Mexico was not extensive, he used it, along with his command of the Roman classics, to support his contention that the Indians deserved to be protected.

VI. Conclusions

The first scholars in New Spain applied their talents to defending the Indians and securing their conversion. Impelled by the exacting principles of the *devotio moderna,* the Flemish friars, notably Fray Pedro de Gante, made evident progress in mastering Nahuatl and instructing native students. The intellectual accomplishments of individual members of the Franciscan Twelve merit recognition as well: Motolinía's history and researches into Mexican society and belief remain invaluable. The endeavours of both those groups in the 1520s laid the ground for the later achievements of Olmos, Sahagún, and others who worked and taught at the College of Santa Cruz in Tlatelolco.

The religious leaders of the Franciscans and other orders who rose to prominence in the 1530s had absorbed several progressive currents of Renaissance thought—in their opposition to warfare, in their practical theology and advocation of the status and rights of the Indians, and in the value they attached to letters. They used their linguistic skills to acquire native languages and instituted systems of education for both Spanish and indigenous students. In seeking to shape colonial society more broadly, they recalled ways in which the European humanists who inspired them—Nebrija and Erasmus in particular—had applied insights derived from Latin and Greek authors to the interpretation of scripture, pedagogy, and political thought. Zumárraga's covert adherence to Erasmus' principles had a lasting impact on approaches to evangelization and the education of both natives and Spaniards. Fray Julián Garcés and Vasco de Quiroga each made distinctive use of Erasmus' writing and classical sources, and each had an enduring legacy.[147] Fray Cristóbal Cabrera, a much younger scholar educated in Mexico, imitated Erasmian invective and Roman satire in his poetry, which vehemently condemned the Spaniards' conduct and its detrimental effects on the indigenous population.[148]

[146] A few Nahuatl terms had already been glossed by the Italian humanist MARTYR D'ANGHIERA, *De orbe novo decades* (first published together in 1530): Hernández de Léon-Portilla 1986; Moreno de Alba 1996.

[147] Indians continued to inhabit the *hospitales* established by Quiroga well into the 1600s, as shown by a document affirming that they should not pay royal tribute: RIOFRÍO, 'Por el Venerable Dean . . .' (1688). The original Rome edition of GARCÉS, *De habilitate* (1537) was cited in LEÓN PINELO, *Epítome de la Biblioteca* (1629), and the copy in DÁVILA PADILLA, *Historia* (1596) was reproduced by SOLÓRZANO PEREIRA, *De Indianorum jure disputationes* (1629–1639).

[148] CABRERA, 'Ecstasis' (n. 64 above); 'Ad Emmanuelem Florez' (c. 1540), a Latin verse epistle, harshly criticized the Spaniards and likened the missionaries to Judas Iscariot.

Discourses about the Indians in New Spain had transcended the legal and scholastic controversies that would continue to hold sway in the peninsula, to involve empirical observation mediated by the full range of Renaissance learning.[149] All the domains of the *studia humanitatis*—grammar, rhetoric, poetry, history, moral philosophy—provided a framework with which to interpret and transform, for better or worse, the chaotic and alien world of Mexico after the conquest.

[149] Weckmann 1992 and others who hold that the outlook of the religious orders was 'medieval' disregard the Renaissance character of education in early colonial Mexico. It should be noted that advances in the study of classical antiquity and Erasmian sympathies (together with traditional jurism and Thomist philosophy) had been shaping the thought of humanists in Spain, such as Francisco de Vitoria: Bataillon 1937 [2007, 226–78]; Lupher 2003, 62–82.

2

Persuasion for a Pagan Audience

Rhetoric, Memory, and Action in Missionary Writing

The Roman orator Cicero attributed the origin of rhetoric to a single sage who first inclined human beings to a civilized existence by using his powers of persuasion:

> There was a time when men wandered at large over the fields like beasts and kept themselves alive with the flesh of wild animals; they managed nothing by reasoning with their minds, but relied generally on physical strength. There was not yet any principle of divine worship, nor of human responsibility . . . At this point somebody, obviously a great and wise man, realized the raw material in the minds of men and how much potential there was for maximum accomplishment, if it could be improved by instruction. He, by means of a certain reasoning, collected into one place and assembled people who were scattered over the fields and hidden in woodland dwellings, and led them on to every useful and honourable pursuit. Although the unfamiliarity of this prompted them to protest at first, they subsequently listened more readily, owing to his reason and eloquence, and he turned them from being wild and savage into people who were mild and peaceable.[1]

[1] Cicero, *De inventione* 1.2: 'Nam fuit quoddam tempus, cum in agris homines passim bestiarum more vagabantur et sibi victu ferino vitam propagabant nec ratione animi quicquam, sed pleraque viribus corporis administrabant. Nondum divinae religionis, non humani officii ratio colebatur . . . Quo tempore quidam magnus videlicet vir et sapiens cognovit, quae materia esset et quanta ad maximas res opportunitas in animis inesset hominum, si quis eam posset elicere et praecipiendo meliorem reddere; qui dispersos homines in agros et in tectis silvestribus abditos ratione quadam compulit unum in locum et congregavit et eos in unamquamque rem inducens utilem atque honestam primo propter insolentiam reclamantes, deinde propter rationem atque orationem studiosius audientes ex feris et immanibus mites reddidit et mansuetos.' Cicero incorporated versions of this account in his other works: n. 25 below.

Aztec Latin. Andrew Laird, Oxford University Press. © Oxford University Press 2024.
DOI: 10.1093/oso/9780197586358.003.0003

Evangelists in the Americas saw a parallel between their own role and that of the wise man in Cicero's story, which had long acquired an authoritative status for medieval and Renaissance readers.[2] As rhetoric and dialectic had dominated European thought and education since antiquity, missionaries were bound to reflect on how they might apply those arts of persuasion and argument to the propagation of the Christian faith.

This chapter will review Latin treatises on the subject by friars who had been in New Spain. After a preliminary account of how rhetoric had developed by the 1500s, a foundational treatise by Fray Bartolomé de las Casas will be surveyed first (Section I), in which the Dominican author affirmed the importance of rhetoric and dialectic for peaceful teaching of the Christian faith (Section II). The contrasting endorsement of just war by two Franciscans, Fray Juan Focher and Fray Diego Valadés, will be considered next (Section III), before a fuller examination of Valadés' lengthier *Rhetorica Christiana* will take into account the book's visual illustrations, its emphasis on the art of memory, and its references to the Mexican calendar (Section IV). Finally, a text by another Franciscan, Fray Cristóbal Cabrera (Section V) highlights the importance of rhetoric and classical models, even for an author who held that exemplary actions were more important than words in securing the conversion of unbelievers.

I. Rhetoric in the Christian tradition and humanist education

The rise of Christianity did not diminish the role of rhetoric but sustained and transformed it. Unlike pagan religions, the Christian faith was conveyed by preaching, as Christ himself had commanded. For all that Saint Paul had championed the simple proclamation of the Gospel over argumentative proofs and eloquence, early apostolic testimonies, epistles, and sermons showed the influence of classical rhetoric.[3] Towards the end of the fourth century Saint Augustine, who extolled Cicero, made a successful case for the accommodation of rhetorical method, and his *De doctrina Christiana*, 'On Christian teaching', gave guidance on how to induce converted audiences to act in accordance with their beliefs and lead a Christian life.[4]

[2] Cf. LAS CASAS, *De unico vocationis modo* (c. 1539), 5.33; VALADÉS, *Rhetorica Christiana* (1579), 'Praefatio'; CABRERA, *De solicitanda infidelium conversione* (1582), discussed in Section V below, and the socialization of the native Brazilians recounted in ANCHIETA, *De gestis Mendi di Saa* (1563) 2.1027–5. GARCILASO DE LA VEGA, *Comentarios reales* (1609) 1.15 [1991 i, 40–1] presents a version of Cicero's myth as a native Peruvian tradition. Copeland 2007 examines the early European reception of Cicero's myth.

[3] 1 Corinthians 1:22–31. Kennedy 1990, 195–221; 1999, 137–82.

[4] Green 1995, Green 2008.

Rhetoric accompanied grammar in medieval curricula and rose to new prominence during the Renaissance. Cicero's *De inventione* and the pseudo-Ciceronian *Ad Herennium* had been known since antiquity, but from the end of the fourteenth century Cicero's letters, speeches, and other works of rhetorical theory were being rediscovered, circulated, and eventually published.[5] Quintilian's *Institutio oratoria*, recovered in full by Poggio Bracciolini in 1416, had a seminal influence on rhetoric and, by the 1500s, knowledge of Greek authorities, notably Aristotle, was helping to reshape the subject.[6] So too did the production of new manuals by humanist scholars—more than two thousand different titles were printed during the 1400s and 1500s.[7] Their use as school texts meant that all educated members of the clergy and the laity were familiar with the principles of the discipline.[8]

Humanist theories of rhetoric were not uniform and were partly determined by whichever classical authorities took precedence. Cicero's works accentuated judicial oratory and were concerned with the preparation of subject matter, memory, delivery, and the use of certain figures of speech; Aristotle's *Rhetoric*, on the other hand, attached importance to audience psychology in terms of emotion and character.[9] Humanists were clearly developing their own distinctive methods by the 1400s: George of Trebizond set a precedent for more critical selection of ancient sources, connecting the second-century Greek rhetorician Hermogenes of Tarsus to the Latin tradition, and the work of Rudolph Agricola could compete with Greco-Roman theoretical treatises in value and originality. Together with Joannes Caesarius' *Dialectica* (1526), Agricola's *De inventione dialectica* (1515) became a standard textbook.[10] Differences in approaches to rhetoric between northern and southern Europe became more marked in the sixteenth century after the onset of the Protestant Reformation. Catholic educators generally ignored the achievements of two great synthesizers of the subject, the Lutheran Philipp Melanchthon and Peter Ramus, a convert to Protestantism, if not those of Erasmus.[11]

Despite these innovations and divergences, rhetoric in the Renaissance retained many of its features and practices from the Middle Ages. Students continued

[5] Reynolds 1983, 54–142.

[6] Reynolds 1983, 332–4; Bolgar 1954, 263, 275–6; Mack 2011, 13–32.

[7] Green and Murphy 2006.

[8] Vickers 1988, 256 notes that millions of Europeans, from princes to ordinary clergymen, had a working knowledge of rhetoric.

[9] Mack 2011, 25–6.

[10] TREBIZOND, *Rhetoricorum libri* (1522) was actually written during 1433–1434; AGRICOLA composed his *De inventione dialectica* (1515) in the 1470s. Cf. Monfasani 1976, 248–88; Patterson 1970 on Hermogenes; and Mack 1993, 130–67; 2011, 62–5 on Agricola's innovative application of Aristotelian and Ciceronian 'topics' to rhetorical argumentation. Agricola and Caesarius generally replaced medieval authors: Ashworth 1982, 790; Jardine 1982, 800–2; cf. Chapter 4, III below.

[11] Mack 2011, 310. Moisan 1997 shows that Ramus did, however, influence Sanctius, whose grammar is discussed in Chapter 3 below.

to be trained to achieve eloquence in writing as well as in speaking, and rhetoric was still the main route to knowledge of classical literature in schools and universities. Niccolò Perotti's *De conscribendis epistolis,* appended to his grammar of Latin, *Rudimenta grammatices* (1473), was the most frequently printed text on epistolography in its time, supplanting the medieval manuals known as *artes dictaminis.* Perotti's recommendations were themselves superseded by Erasmus' *Conficiendarum epistolarum formula* (1520) and *Opus de conscribendis epistolis* (1522). The latter inspired a similar work with the same title that was published by Juan Luis Vives.[12] Later, in the wake of the Counter-Reformation, humanists revived the medieval practice of composing manuals for preachers, *artes praedicandi,* and Erasmus' *Ecclesiastes,* his seminal guide to preaching, was published in 1535.[13] Erasmus' textbooks were immensely popular and went into scores of editions before his works were listed on the Index in the 1550s.[14] His *Adagia* (1500), a richly annotated dictionary of proverbs culled from classical literature to embellish a discourse, and the *De copia* (1512), a collection of formulae for amplification and variety in expression, supplemented traditional rhetorical manuals.

Cicero originally grounded the art of rhetoric in wisdom or philosophy, and drew attention to its civilizing power and importance for society. The Roman statesman's connection between *ratio,* reason, and *oratio,* speech—for the good of the republic and the service of humanity—had resonated with the civic humanism of Coluccio Salutati and Leonardo Bruni in quattrocento Florence. The social and religious value of rhetoric continued to be endorsed in the 1500s by Erasmus and his followers, including Vives, who declared that there was 'nothing more conducive to human association than well-developed and refined speech'.[15] Rhetoric thus pervaded discourse in every area of the humanities, from philosophy and law to poetry, history, and theology.[16] The humanists' desire to make the art practical and accessible was connected to methods of evangelization and to the study of Christian scripture. Antonio de Nebrija devoted the latter part of his career to reconciling his rhetorical interests with his faith.[17]

[12] Burton 2007, Henderson 2007 (in Poster and Mitchell 2007), and Mack 2011, 90–6, 228–56 highlight the success of Erasmus' treatise, often published with VIVES, *De conscribendis epistolis* (1534).

[13] ERASMUS, *Ecclesiastes* (1535) drew from Cicero, Quintilian and Aristotle, but Augustine's *De doctrina Christiana* was its primary model: Mack 2011, 98–102.

[14] Green and Murphy 2006, 181–9. On the inquisitorial Indices, cf. pp. 92–93 and pp. 170–71 below; Bataillon 1937 [2007, 715–24] and *passim.*

[15] Hankins 1995, 329; Hankins 2000; Eden 2000, 305–22 and Eden 2001 on Erasmus. VIVES, *De ratione dicendi* (1533), Preface 2 [2017, 57]: 'Ego uero nihil uideo conducibilius hominum coetibus, quam sit sermo bene institutus, atque educatus.'

[16] For Vives' theory of historiography cf. e.g. Beckjord 2007, 15–42.

[17] Cf. Chapter 1, I above; González Vega 2010.

II. Teaching religion by peaceful persuasion: Fray Bartolomé de las Casas, *De unico vocationis modo*, c. 1539

Fray Bartolomé de Las Casas was the author of the earliest known work on rhetoric to be produced in New Spain.[18] The text, entitled *De unico vocationis modo omnium gentium ad veram religionem*, 'The only way of calling all peoples to the true religion', made a broad case for the humanity of the peoples of the Indies.[19] Much of the work has been lost, but a surviving manuscript of Chapters 5–7 presents the principal thesis: the author recommended a form of persuasion that combined rhetoric, 'pleasantly coaxing or encouraging the will', with dialectic, 'persuading the reasoning of the understanding'.[20] Dialectic—the art of probable reasoning from accepted opinions—was central to the Aristotelian scholastic tradition, and Las Casas made clear that the Christian preacher or instructor had to observe its principles 'not less but all the more.'[21] Cicero's *De oratore*, on the other hand, was the source of the rhetorical techniques that would ensure listeners were well disposed, in order to 'call their feelings to whatever emotion the case demands'.[22]

The notion of 'calling', *vocatio*, in the title of the treatise was crucial: the view that souls could be won through preaching accounts for a lengthy demonstration in earlier sections that the Indians were rational, and for the insistence that a preacher bringing the true religion to unbelievers needed a greater command of rhetoric than

[18] The 220 folios of the manuscript chapters were recovered in Oaxaca: León 1886.

[19] Parish 1992, 222–6 discusses seventeenth-century summaries of the original work; cf. REMESAL, *Historia de las Indias Occidentales* (1620) 3.9. LAS CASAS, *Apologética historia* (c. 1558), cap. 263, and *Apologia* (1552), cap. 4, 22v–24v [2000, 31–5; tr. 1992, 41–5] also invoked the Indians' ingenuity in the mechanical and liberal arts and their competence in government.

[20] LAS CASAS, *De unico vocationis modo* (c. 1539), = *DUVM*, 5.1 [1942, 6]: 'Vnus et idem modus et solus docendi homines veram religionem fuit per divinam Providentiam institutus in toto orbe atque in omni tempore, scilicet, intellectus rationibus persuasivus et voluntatis suaviter allectivus vel exhortativus. Quippe qui esse debet communis universis hominibus de mundo, sine differentia discretionis ullae vel sectarum et errorum vel morum corruptorum. ('The one and the same, and the sole method of teaching men true religion has been established by divine Providence in all the world and for all time: namely the method of persuading the reasoning of the understanding and of coaxing or encouraging the will. This indeed has to be common to all the men of the world, without differentiation and distinction between sects and errors or corrupt morals.')

[21] LAS CASAS, *DUVM* 5.5 [1942, 46]: 'Non minus sed magis praedicator vel doctor, qui officium habet docendi et trahendi homines ad rectam fidem et religionem veram'.

[22] LAS CASAS, *DUVM* 5.5 [1942, 48], quoting Cicero, *De oratore* 2.19.80: 'iubent enim exordiri ita, ut eum, qui audiat, benevolum nobis faciamus et docilem et attentum' ('They bid us to begin in such a way that we render the hearer favourable to us, inclined to be taught, and attentive'); *De oratore* 2.27.115 'ut animos eorum, ad quemcumque causa postulabit motum, vocemus'.

an orator.[23] Saint Augustine had warned that the art of rhetoric can induce belief in things that are false as well as true, so that Christian believers were obliged to take advantage of its benefits to counter their opponents. Like Augustine, Las Casas endorsed the rhetorical techniques Cicero had set out in the *De oratore*.[24]

The illustration from Cicero's *De inventione* of the wise man who used eloquence to bring savage people to a more settled existence is also invoked, to prove that persuasion of the intellect and will could lead people to the Christian faith.[25] The parallels between the civilizing effect of oratory and of religious conversion were amplified by a quotation attributed to Plutarch: even though the introduction of laws succeeded in restraining people from committing offences in open view, many carried on offending in secret—until a skilful man 'ventured to bind truth with mendacious speech in order to persuade mortals that there was a God, abiding with an ageless life and powerful intelligence, who sees and hears these things'.[26] Through the example of Christ and his apostles (who practised peaceful conversion) the New World could be ordered by rhetoric—as Europe had been—with no need for 'the impetus of arms or violence'.

The detailed discussion of the power of argument and of the mechanisms for moving an audience that followed drew from scripture and from other classical authorities in addition to Cicero and Plutarch: Virgil, Valerius Maximus, Boethius, and the spurious Berosus.[27] Practical examples set by Christ and the apostles were then described, along with the traits of the ideal missionary. Before the closing summary and conclusion, Paul III's bull 'Sublimis Deus' of 1537 and the accompanying *Pastorale Officium* were quoted in full, to show that a 'multitude' of the Church's decrees shared the view that persuasion was the only way to teach the Christian faith.[28]

[23] Dealy 1976 contrasts this position with that of Erasmus, whose disdain for words alone influenced both Quiroga and Cabrera (cf. section V below).

[24] Augustine, *De doctrina Christiana* 4.2, 4.4, 4.12, 4.17, cited in *DUVM* 5.5 [50].

[25] Cicero, *'Rhetorica'* = *De inventione* 1.2, cited in *DUVM* 5.10 [1942, 98–100]. Las Casas cited the other versions of the story in Cicero, *De legibus*; *De oratore* 1.8.33; *Pro Sestio* 42 (n. 26 below. Cf. Solmsen 1932 on Horace, *Ars poetica* 391–401, which credits peace and urban existence to Orpheus and Amphion; Chapter 8, (III) below on Saturn in Virgil, *Aeneid* 8.319-25. For 'ferales antiquos homines' ('savage people of old'), cf. Garcés, *De habilitate* (1537), 8: Appendix 2.1.2 below; Chapter 1, V above.

[26] Pseudo-Plutarch, *Placita philosophorum* 1.7; cf. Cicero, *Pro Sestio* 42.

[27] LAS CASAS, *DUVM* 5.2–4 [1942, 14–154]. Parish 1992, 237 admits to purging the classical quotations and sources from her 'restoration' of the *DUVM*. Las Casas' source for the Chaldean Berosus was VITERBO, *Antiquitates* (1498), which contained forged excerpts from Berosus and other lost sources: Grafton 1991, 76–103, Ramminger 2020.

[28] The incorporation of those documents in LAS CASAS, *DUVM* 5.34 [1942, 360–70] shows the extant manuscript postdated 1537 by at least two years, although the original text may have dated back to 1534 and is thought to have influenced the papal bull: Gutiérrez 2003, 302–7. On the bull 'Sublimis Deus', cf. Chapter 1, (V) above.

Apart from an isolated mention of Montezuma in New Spain and of Atahualpa in Peru, no specific knowledge of the Americas is displayed in what survives of the *De unico vocationis modo*.[29] Its author was later criticized by the Franciscan missionary Motolinía for his lack of interest in getting to know Mexico and its inhabitants:

> He has not spent time here in New Spain, nor has he learned the Indians' language, nor has he been humble enough to apply himself to teaching them. His job has been writing up the lawsuits and wrongs that the Spaniards have perpetrated in every place . . .[30]

Las Casas would, however, describe the indigenous traditions of New Spain in some detail in his *Apologética historia*.[31] The apparent exclusion of such information from the *De unico vocationis modo* may have been a deliberate strategy: accentuation of the alien nature of the Indians' culture risked weakening claims that their capacities matched or surpassed those of Europeans. Instead, the 'sole method' was advanced through a theoretical demonstration, expressed in the elite idiom of Renaissance scholastic argument.

The theoretical approach to persuasion in the *De unico vocationis modo* served an important end. While the role of rhetoric and dialectic in evangelization was the principal subject, rhetoric and dialectic were also at work dynamically in the construction of the treatise itself. In making his case for converting the Indians by appealing to their intellect and will, Las Casas was simultaneously applying the very techniques he described, in a performative way, to win over the readers of his Latin work. His advocation of rhetoric was really aimed at Europeans in order to influence European behaviour.

III. Conversion by force: Fray Juan Focher and Fray Diego Valadés

By no means every missionary shared Las Casas' confidence that all Indians could be moved by persuasion alone. A Franciscan professor at the Imperial College of Santa Cruz de Tlatelolco, Fray Juan Focher (or Jean Foucheur), who wrote several

[29] LAS CASAS, *DUVM* 5.33 [1942, 359]: Las Casas contrasted the Spaniards' aggression toward those American rulers, each governing a vast population, with Bede's account of the peaceful evangelization of the pagan English and their lowly king. ACOSTA, *De procuranda Indorum salute* (1588), 4.5 [1987 ii, 40] saw the ancient Angles as more troublesome than the Indians: 'Legat qui volet antiquos Anglorum mores, duriores nostris indis inveniet.'

[30] MOTOLINÍA, 'Carta al Emperador' (1555) [2001, 301].

[31] LAS CASAS, *Apologética historia* (c. 1558): caps. 49–54, 62–4, 66–7, 70, 121–3, 130–2, 138–42, 169–76, 188–93, 210, 228, 233, 241.

tracts on conversion and ministry, took a different view.[32] His *Itinerarium catholicum proficiscentium ad infideles convertendos* (1574), 'Catholic itinerary for those setting out to convert unbelievers', probably written in the 1550s, assessed the merits of just war on the Indians. Focher cited the case of the 'barbarians called Chichimeca' who, he complained, 'exert tyranny on Christian worshippers . . . by tormenting some, flaying and killing others, taking goods from others again; and they obstruct the common thoroughfare by staging ambushes.[33]

The friar recognized that many did not deem it legitimate ('licitum') to make war on heathen peoples, even if those peoples killed Christians—and his opinion was contrary to the unanimous consensus of the Franciscans' Third Provincial Mexican Council, which would be convened in 1585.[34] But Focher compared the Chichimeca to the Amorrhites, whom God had ordered Moses to fight, and he cited interpretations of the biblical episode to support this comparison.[35] In Augustine's view, 'the children of Israel waged a just war against the Amorrhites, who were refusing them harmless passage, which was supposed to be open to them by the recognized law of human fellowship'; while according to the French Franciscan Nicholas of Lyra, the Amorrhites had forfeited God's grace.[36]

After Focher's death in 1570, another Spanish Franciscan, Fray Diego Valadés, who prepared the *Itinerarium catholicum* for publication in Seville, endorsed its 'very learned demonstration' of the ways in which the Chichimeca should be subjected and reduced by force of Christian arms'.[37] In his preface to the book, Valadés described his own attempt to convert the Chichimeca: he only narrowly escaped their rage ('furor')—and the ordeal resulted in the loss of all his books and of the

[32] The short biography in MENDIETA, *Hystoria ecclesiastica yndiana* (c. 1596), = *Historia*, 5.46 [1870, 677–8] lists Focher's writings and emphasizes his erudition as a 'consumatísimo letrado' ('most accomplished man of letters'), in law, theology, and canon law: cf. OROZ, *Relación* (1586) [1972, 118–20]. Focher taught at the College of Santa Cruz: '*Códice franciscano*' (c. 1570) [1889, 70]; TORQUEMADA, *Monarchia Indiana* (1615) = *MI*, 15.43 [1977 v, 175].

[33] FOCHER, *Itinerarium* (1574) 3.2 (chapter entitled 'De bello in Chichimecas') [1960, 348–9]: 'in caeteros christicolas illis in partibus commorantes exercere coeperunt tyrannidem, alios vexando, alios excoriando, alios occidendo, ab aliis sua bona rapiendo et in viis viatoribus insidiantes communem impediant viam.'

[34] Poole 1963 and Poole 1965 consider the Church's response, after that Council, to the *repartimiento* system, which forced labour on natives, and to the war against the Chichimeca.

[35] Deuteronomy 2:24 'Arise ye, and pass the torrent Arnon: Behold I have delivered into thy hand Sehon king of Hesebon the Amorrhite, and begin thou to possess his land and make war against him.'

[36] Augustine, *Quaestiones in Heptateuchum* 6.10; Nicholas of Lyra, *Biblia Latina cum Glossa ordinaria* (1502), 333r, glossing 'quia induraverat Dominus'. Cf. Reinhardt 1987 on Lyra's reception in Spain.

[37] FOCHER, *Itinerarium* (1574), fol. A 6 [1960, 18–19]: 'Quonam pacto bello et armis christianorum sint reducendi barbari, quos Chichimecas vocant . . . doctissime demonstrat.' The date of Valadés' death cannot be firmly established: according to ANTONIO, *Bibliotheca Hispana nova* (1672) [1788 i: 321], he was alive in 1580 ('Vivebat anno MDLXXX'); CHACÓN, *Bibliotheca* (1744), col. 674 suggests he was still living in 1583.

writings to which he had been devoting himself since his youth.[38] Valadés subsequently became Procurator General of the Franciscan order in Rome from 1575 to 1577 and published his own *Rhetorica Christiana* (1579) in Perugia.[39]

Assessments of Valadés and his work have been hampered by the widespread belief that he was born in New Spain, as the son of a conquistador and an indigenous woman—despite the fact that men of Indian parentage were not able to enter religious orders or the priesthood.[40] The seventeenth-century historian Augustín de Vetancurt first suggested that Diego Valadés was a native of New Spain, by stating that he was a 'natural' of Tlaxcala, the city in which he was brought up.[41] Yet Valadés' own remark that he was '*almost* a nursling of that land' ('eius terre . . . ferè alumnus') indicates that he was not born in the New World.[42] A related misunderstanding had arisen from Valadés' avowals that he had lived among the Indians for more or less thirty years and that he had been 'responsible for providing their sermons and confessions for more than twenty-two years in three of their languages, Mexican, Tarascan and Otomí'.[43] That should not be taken to mean—as it always has been—that the writer really knew any of these tongues himself: missionaries were simply able to read aloud from confessional manuals and *sermonarios* that had been prepared in Amerindian languages. Such texts were available in manuscript long before they were printed in the mid-1500s.

Two epigrams celebrating the author prove that he was a peninsular Spaniard. Fra Giulio Roscio da Orte wrote, 'He is one of our own, Diego Valadés of Iberia, a great glory to his Order and to his people'; and another Italian Franciscan, Fra Camillo Sabellio da Panicale, indulged in the conceit of 'the cultivator of warring Iberia' as a rhetorical conquistador: 'You vanquish them all, greatest

[38] VALADÉS, 'Christiano lectori salutem', in FOCHER, *Itinerarium* (1574) A 5 [1960, 14]: 'Verum dum infidelibus convertendis, quos Chichimecas vocant, insisto, illorum furore vix et cum magno vitae et sociorum dispendio ereptus, libros omnes simul ac labores, vigiliasque quibus congerendis ab ineunte aetate insuderam, amissi.'

[39] Primary sources for Valadés' life and work are surveyed in Alejos-Grau 1994, 69–88, and in Jeanne 2011, a valuable study of his career in Europe.

[40] The First Mexican Council of 1555 formalized prohibition of the ordination of Indians: Poole 1981; cf. Chapter 4, n. 67 below. Abbott 1996, 42 thus imagines that the Franciscans suppressed Valadés' supposed illegitimacy and mixed parentage, although Alejos-Grau 1994, 69–73 demonstrates he was Spanish by birth. Ramírez Vidal 2005, 14 ascribes persistent constructions of Valadés as a mestizo to modern Mexican nationalist ideology.

[41] VETANCURT, *Menologio franciscano* (1697), 142: 'El R.P.fr. Diego Valadéz natural de la Ciudad de Tlaxcalla'.

[42] VALADÉS, *Rhetorica Christiana* (1579), = *RC*, 4.19 N, 200 [1989, 456]. The Spanish translation [1989, 457] obscures this: 'porque yo sea habitante de su tierra' ('because I am an inhabitant of their land.')

[43] VALADÉS, *RC* 4.11 V, 184 [1989, 424]: 'versatus enim sum inter illos (laus Deo) plus minus triginta annos: & incubui praedicationibus, & confessionibus eorum plusquam viginti duos, in tribus illorum idiomatibus, Mexicano, Tarasco, & Otomì.'

Diego'.[44] Documents recently published confirm beyond doubt that Fray Diego came from Spain: he was born in Barcarrota, Extremadura, to a Bartolomé Valadés, and he was a nephew of the conquistador Diego Valadés, who has often been mistaken for his father.[45]

The supposition that the missionary was of dual heritage has contributed to the persistent misconception of his rhetorical work as a kind of ethnographic study, and even as a commendation of the Indians' capacities and achievements.[46] The reality was very different. While some missionaries opposed the use of physical force to convert the Indians and others justified it, Valadés had no interest in discussing the question at all. In his view, the native Americans' idolatry was proof of their 'barbarian savagery, woeful blindness and servitude'.[47] He believed that historians of New Spain and of all the New World had made 'many errors and blunders' ('multis erroribus et mendis') when they referred to abuses on the part of the Spaniards, whose conquest of the Indies was simply something to be celebrated:

> I would not wish to play down the great courage of the Romans who in open warfare and with belligerent courage brought under their control so many provinces and powerful kingdoms . . . But the extraordinary fortitude of Hernán Cortés and of those friars who came to new worlds should be proclaimed with greater praises and in language of unprecedented grandeur. It is certain that there has been no one of such lofty spirit to undertake such an arduous task and to claim its completion with the same speed . . . If the part of the Indies which has come into our hands is compared to the areas which the Romans possessed, it is ampler still in its boundless reach.[48]

[44] Both poems are among the preliminaries to VALADÉS, *RC*, at A1 [1989, 5]: (i) Roscio da Orte, 'In Rhetoricam Christianam': 'Hic est de nostris, Didacus Valadesus Iberus, / Ordinis & gentis gloria magna suae'; (ii) Sabellio da Panicale, 'Ad Auctorem': 'Sed tu, belligerae cultor Iberiae / Quem virtus stygijs ardua fluctibus / Raptum, diuitibus consecrat insulis, / Omnes exsuperas, Maxime Didace'.

[45] Ortega Sánchez 2011 presents the facsimiles.

[46] Abbott 1996, 41 likens VALADÉS, *RC* to SAHAGÚN, *Historia general* (c. 1580); cf. Moffitt Watts 1991, Nettel 1993, Cummins 1995, and Bauer 2019. The misconceptions originate in Mexican studies of Valadés: Maza 1945; Méndez Plancarte 1946; Palomera 1962; Palomera 1963; and 'Introducción' in VALADÉS, *RC* [1989], xii–xiii.

[47] *RC* 4.7 H 170 [1989, 392]: 'ferocia et infoelicissima caecitas & servitus illorum barbarorum.'

[48] *RC* 4.22 G–H 204 [1989, 464]: 'Nolim deprimere magnanimitatem Romanorum qui aperto Marte & virtute bellica tot prouincias, & potentia regna in ordinem redegerunt . . . Sed maioribus praeconijs nouaque maiestate verborum efferenda est inaudita fortitudo Ferdinandi Cortesij & religiosioru*m* qui nouos illos orbes adierunt. Certum na*m*que est, neminem fuisse animo tam excelso, qui tam arduum negotium subiret aut cui integru*m* fuisse eadem celeritate perficere . . . Deinde facta collatione eoru*m*, quae Romani possederunt, cum ea parte Indiarum, quae in nostras manus venit: haec infinitis partibus amplior est.' (Abbreviations in the original edition are expanded, here and below, with the missing letters italicized.)

IV. Fray Diego Valadés' *Rhetorica Christiana*, 1579

(i) Conception and structure

The work was not about the conversion of native peoples, but rather constituted a textbook of rhetoric in general, with some illustrations taken from accounts of the New World, as the full title makes clear:

> A Christian Rhetoric: Adapted for the practice of making speeches and preaching, with examples of both facilities inserted in their proper place, which have been very largely drawn from histories of the Indies, whence in addition to instruction, the highest pleasure will also be obtained.[49]

In his dedication to Pope Gregory XIII, Valadés presented his book about rhetoric as a digest of many others by pagan and Christian writers, since it would be impossible for preachers to study them all.[50] Contrary to 'the chatterings of heretics', Christians should not discard all the pagan authors who enabled contemporary orators to surpass their ancient precursors. The eloquence of the Church Fathers showed that argument and elegant expression could not be eschewed simply because some had abused them. Such opinions, along with the many classical sources cited throughout the work, may have appealed to a pope who was an energetic patron of the arts and sciences.[51]

Valadés explains in his preface to the reader that the work could have been entitled 'Summa Summarum Scientiarum', 'Compendium of the highest forms of knowledge', because Christian eloquence was the supreme art provided by God to direct men to goodness and fellowship, and it touched on almost every science.[52] The *Rhetorica Christiana* would enable its readers to act as 'voices of God' by 'explaining as simply as possible the art of artificial memory so long desired by

[49] 'Rhetorica Christiana: Ad concionandi et orandi usum accommodata, utriusque facultatis exemplis suo loco insertis: quae quidem ex Indorum maximè deprompta sunt historiis: vnde praeter doctrinam, sum*m*a quoque delectatio comparabitur.'

References here will be to the section (*pars*), chapter, marginal lettering, and highly erratic 1579 pagination, followed by the 1989 facsimile: e.g. *RC* 4.19 B: 200 [1989, 456].

[50] *RC* a2, [1989, 8]: 'Cum innumera fere Rhetorices artis volumina, *Beatissime Pater*, a diuersis tam paganis, quam Christianis scriptoribus edita conspexissem: qua*e* propter vitae huius mortalis breuitate ab humano nequeunt intellectu diligentius omnia perscrutari.'

[51] VALADÉS, *RC*, 'Index Auctorum' [1989, 42–4] lists 150 sources, including Greeks (Homer, Plato, Pausanias, Isocrates, Strabo; Diogenes Laertius and Xenophon will be quoted); Romans (Virgil, Horace, Propertius, Juvenal, Lucretius); Italian humanists (Petrarch, Poliziano, Pico della Mirandola), and Spaniards (Juan Luis Vives, Benito Arias Montano, Fray Alonso de la Vera Cruz, Fray Luis de Granada).

[52] The view in Plato, *Phaedrus* 260d–e that the genuine art of speaking depended on knowledge of the truth was transmitted in Cicero, *De oratore*: May and Wisse 2001, 3–48.

all'. As well as asserting the importance of the systematic art of memory for rhetoric, Valadés mentioned that he had lived in the Indies, where the precepts of rhetoric could be applied to evangelization of the natives. Like Las Casas, he invoked the story from Cicero's *De inventione* of the single orator who first united and civilized mankind. Valadés made its relevance to the Americas completely explicit: 'The admirable effects of this [art] are more clearly apparent than ever in the taming of humans of the new world of the Indies of the Ocean Sea'.[53]

Benito Arias Montano and Pedro Juan Núñez were among the many humanists in Spain who wrote rhetorical manuals in the mid-1500s.[54] But Valadés' six-part division of his work and the opening words of its title—*Rhetorica Christiana: Ad concionandi et orandi usum*, 'A Christian Rhetoric [adapted] for the Practice of Making Speeches'—pointed to its real model: the *Ecclesiastica rhetorica sive de ratione concionandi*, 'Ecclesiastical Rhetoric or the Method of Making Speeches'. That work, also in six books, had been published just three years before, in 1576, by a Spanish Dominican, Fray Luis de Granada.[55] The *Ecclesiastica rhetorica* was a response to the Council of Trent's requirement that priests should teach people 'with brevity and plainness of discourse, the vices which they must avoid and the virtues which they must cultivate'.[56] As an attempt to integrate the technical art of eloquence with sacred theology, Luis de Granada's study reflected a growing interest Catholic humanists had in adapting classical rhetoric to meet the current needs of missionaries.[57] While Fray Luis never realized his wish to go to the New World, Valadés made the most of his own experience there in his emulation of the Dominican's Latin rhetoric.

A detailed table of contents set out the six parts of the *Rhetorica Christiana* that had already been outlined in the preface.[58] The first part defined Christian rhetoric, drawing rules from scripture and church authorities; the second described its divisions, or 'canons', of invention, arrangement, memory, and elocution. Valadés

[53] *RC* b3 [1989, 28]: 'Huius, inquam, rei admirandi effectus, multo clarius, quam vnquam in noui Indiarum Maris Oceani orbis hominum mansuefactione apparent.'

[54] Verses from ARIAS MONTANO, *Rhetoricorum libri* (1569) were quoted in VALADÉS, *RC* 2.2 G 51 [1989, 148]. Antonio Ruíz de Morales, who annotated and wrote a prologue for the *editio princeps* of Arias Montano's rhetorical treatise, succeeded Vasco de Quiroga as bishop of Michoacán in 1566. Cf. Rekers 1972; Fernández López 2002; Mack 2011, 176–7 on Arias Montano and Núñez.

[55] Mack 2011, 269–72; Palomera, 'Introducción' in VALADÉS, *RC* [1989, xxxi–xl], considers the influence of GRANADA, *Ecclesiastica rhetorica* (1576) on Valadés' text. Parts of the Dominican friar's devotional works were later translated into Nahuatl: cf. Chapter 5, IV (ii) below.

[56] For the requirement of the Fifth Session of the Tridentine Council of 17 June 1546, see Waterworth 1848, 27. The twenty-five sessions of the Council of Trent during 1545–1563 were the institutional core of the Counter-Reformation: recommendations for preaching were to stem the spread of Protestantism.

[57] GRANADA, *Breve tratado* (1585); cf. Fumaroli 1994, 143–8.

[58] *RC, Praefatio* b3 [1989, 30]; *Omnium ferme capitum . . . Elenchus* [1989, 36–42]. The volume is closed with the *Magistri Sententiae*, the 'Sentences' of Peter Lombard with Valadés' commentary.

paid special attention to memory, using a tabernacle embellished with various details as an illustration, to show how an image could aid recapitulation ('anacefaleosis') of all the books in the Bible. Discussion of the interpretation of scripture and sources for sermons in the third part was followed by an account of delivery and the emotions. The fourth part of the book set out three *causae*, or subjects for rhetorical treatment, and specified the duty of an orator, with a description of the Indians' religious rites as an example of demonstrative oratory. The fifth examined the parts of a speech necessary for devising and structuring a sermon (*exordium*, narration, digression, partition, confirmation and confutation, and conclusion), with two model orations. The sixth and final part was concerned with style, listing *exornationes*, the figures and tropes used for rhetorical adornment.

That approach was conventional, but two unusual features of the *Rhetorica Christiana* made this rhetorical manual unique and led to a portrayal of native Mexicans and their traditions: twenty-seven illustrations assembled by Valadés, and an unusual emphasis on memory. Those two features will be considered in turn.[59]

(ii) Valadés' visual illustrations

The inclusion of illustrations was explained in the Preface, directly after the outline of the six parts of the work:

> Because some have not got to know letters and are not inclined to reading, we are adding a number of diagrams ['stemmata'], for the purpose of easy memorisation, and so that the rites and customs of the Indians might become better and more clearly known to our readers: having caught sight of these, their spirit may be incited to reading and they may recall to mind what they wish.[60]

The Greek word *stemma*, 'garland', often denoted a genealogical tree in Latin: Valadés uses that form to present the ecclesiastical and imperial hierarchies, the sins to which Indians may be prone, and the corresponding punishments in hell.[61] There are also pictures similar to those which can be found in many other Renaissance texts: the seven liberal arts and a phrenological diagram of the head are obvious examples. Some of the illustrations share the same model as drawings in the manuscript of Fray Gerónimo de Mendieta's *Hystoria ecclesiastica yndiana* (c. 1596).[62]

[59] Müller 2010.

[60] VALADÉS, *RC*, 'Praefatio ad Lectorem' [1989, 30–2].

[61] *RC* 4.10 181 [1989, 417]; 4.23, 216–17 [1989, 488–9].

[62] *RC* 1.3 G 17 [1989, 81]; 2.24 B 88 [1989, 222]; 4.9 172–3 [1989, 406]. The drawings are described in García Icazbalceta's introduction to MENDIETA, *Historia* [1870, xxiv–xxvi].

Figure 2.1 A missionary using *lienzos* to preach to a native audience, Fray Gerónimo de Mendieta, *Hystoria ecclesiastica yndiana*, Mexico c. 1596. Benson Latin American Collection.

These include the representation of a human sacrifice in a temple on top of a pyramid, crowned with a European arch, apparently on the shore of Lake Texcoco, and a drawing of a Franciscan friar using painted *lienzos* to preach about Christ's Passion to a large audience of native youths (Figure 2.1).

For his version of the latter picture (Figure 2.2), Valadés uses letters of the alphabet as a key to explain its content:[63]

> A: There is a trumpeter of the word of God who adapts the gifts of heaven to understanding in their own language. B: Since the [Indians] are lacking in literacy, it has been necessary to teach them by a kind of demonstration: for this reason he uses a rod to point out to them the mysteries of our redemption. This way, by afterwards running through them, they better fix them in their memory. C: Those sitting like this and holding rods in their hands are the judges among our indigenous converts, to whom the

[63] *RC* 4.23 M 111 [1989, 478]. A similar image is in the first printed edition of TORQUEMADA, *Monarchia Indiana* (1615).

Figure 2.2 Preaching with *lienzos* in Fray Diego Valadés, *Rhetorica Christiana*, Perugia, 1579. John Carter Brown Library.

> direction of the whole republic has been entrusted; the rest, sitting on the soles of their feet, are listening to the word of God.[64]

This seems to be a *mise en abyme*: the preceptive and mnemotechnical functions of the paintings shown to the audience in the picture bear on the purpose of the illustrations in the *Rhetorica Christiana* itself. The drawing in Mendieta's chronicle had a caption attributed to Isaiah 61: 'The spirit of the Lord is upon me: he hath sent me to preach the gospel to the poor'.[65] But Valadés replaced that text with an elegiac

[64] *RC* 4.23 L–Q 110, 112 [1989, 476–80]: 'Et sequenti stemmate manifestum fiet, quod per elemen*t*a etiam alphabetica explicare conabimur. A. Est verbi Dei buccinator, qui in proprio Idiomate ad sensum aptat c*ae*lestium dona. B. Quoniam vt literis carentes necesse fuit demonstratione aliqua ipsos docere: Ideo virga illis nostr*ae* redemptionis mysteria ostendit. Vt postmodum illa discurrentes melius memori*ae* h*ae*reant. C. Sic sedentes virgas in manibus tenentes sunt Iudices apud indigetes nostros, quibus commissa est totius reipublicae gubernatio. Reliqui sunt auditores verbi Dei calcibus insidentes.'

[65] 'Sp*i*r*i*tus D*o*mini sup*er* me . . . evangelizare paup*er*ibus misit me'. In fact Luke 4:18 (which takes the first four words from Isaiah) was the text in that caption. Burkhart 1996, 213–14 compares the images.

verse couplet that recalls the explanation quoted above, in order to offer a reflexive comment on his own work:

> The instructor adapts the heavenly gifts to understanding,
> And he waters parched breasts with the spring of eloquence.[66]

Another illustration corresponding to a drawing in Mendieta's manuscript has an interesting detail: Fray Pedro de Gante makes use of painted cloth *lienzos* (depicting different kinds of labour) to teach a class of Mexican students. In connection with that image, Valadés recounts that he had acted as secretary for the Flemish missionary, who was too modest to accept the archbishopric of Mexico.[67] That recollection has prompted the view that the mnemotechnical alphabets Valadés reproduced in the *Rhetorica Christiana* were inspired by Gante's celebrated use of a pictographic catechism to instruct his Indian pupils.[68]

In fact, such alphabets had long been employed in treatises on memory by European humanists: Jacobus Publicius' *Ars memorativa* (1482) was the earliest to be printed. Valadés acknowledges that his first table of alphabetic letters came from Ludovico Dolce, who had derived it from Publicius, and compares it to the images that the Indians used to record information.[69] Further on, he explains that this pictorial alphabet (Figure 2.3) was designed to instill recollection of the letters by presenting them primarily as objects they resembled: *A* was represented by a compass ('circinus') and a slanting ladder ('scala'); *B* as mandolin, 'lutina'; *C* as

[66] 'Ad sensus aptat coelestia dona magister, / Aridaque eloquij pectora fonte rigat.' The first line of this couplet recalls the prose explication of 'A' in the image (n. 64 above) as linguistic translation ('proprio Idiomate'), but the emphasis here is on eloquence. Education 'waters' ('rigat') pupils in Greco-Roman sources (Petronius, *Satyricon* 4; Plutarch, *Education of Children* 9); cf. Wittkower 1938, 82–4 on *Grammatica* watering plants in Renaissance iconography.

[67] Item P in the illustration in *RC* 4.23 S–Z 107 [1989, 471]; explanatory text at 4.23K 222 [1989, 502]: 'Representatur hoc loco Frater Petrus Gandauus vir singularis religionis & pietatis, qui omnes artes illis ostendit nullius enim nescius erat. Tantae enim erat modestiae & frugalitatis, vt oblatam sibi ab Imperatore piae memoriae Carolo V Archiepiscopatum Mexicanum renuerit, Cuius rei certissimus testis esse possum, vtpote qui multas responsiones eius nomine conscripserim, & epistolas Caesaris plenas benevolentiae & propensionis viderim.'

[68] Cortés Castellanos 1987 is a reproduction and study of Gante's catechism.

[69] *RC* 2.25 G 90 [1989, 226]: 'Vnde sequentes figuras libuit apponere, prima vsus fuisse Iacobum Publicium Ludouicus Dolce in suo de memoria dialogo attestatur.' PUBLICIUS, *Oratoriae artis epitoma* (1482) has appended the *Ars memorativa*: cf. Merino Jerez 2020. Yates 1966, 163–4 notes the debt of DOLCE, *Dialogo* (1562) to ROMBERCH, *Congestorium artificiose memorie* (1520), which also drew from Publicius, including Figure 2.4 below. Valadés' alphabetic images are on unnumbered pages in *RC* 2.28 [1989, 248–51].

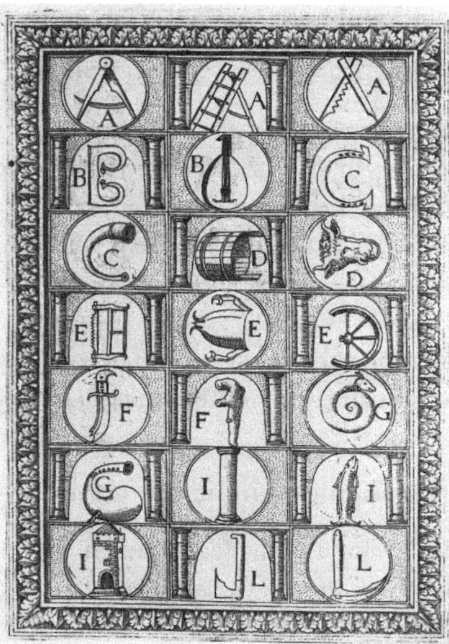

Figure 2.3 Letters A–L of an alphabet designed by Ludovico Dolce, imitated in Fray Diego Valadés, *Rhetorica Christiana,* 1579. John Carter Brown Library.

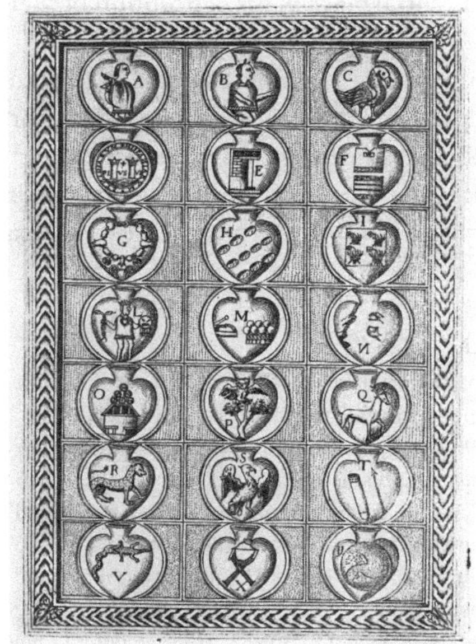

Figure 2.4 Phonic alphabet in Fray Diego Valadés, *Rhetorica Christiana,* 1579. John Carter Brown Library.

a horseshoe ('ferrum equi') and horn ('cornu').[70] The second alphabet presented (Figure 2.4), on the other hand, was entirely phonic in nature:

> With this second method, images of letters are fashioned according to the sound of the word so that from the sound of each one, the first letter may make known the name; for example, Antonius for the letter A, Bartholomeus for the letter B, Carolus for the letter C and so on for all the other letters of the alphabet.[71]

Some missionaries who employed this system may have been aware that Indians used images that were not visually symbolic but instead had a phonographic value.[72]

(iii) Art of memory in the *Rhetorica Christiana*

Renaissance rhetoricians did not usually devote much attention to *memoria*, which had been one of the traditional canons of Ciceronian rhetoric. Fray Luis de Granada omitted memory from his *Ecclesiastica rhetorica*, deeming it a natural faculty, and Vives' *De disciplinis* (1531) had amply demonstrated that all forms of knowledge, not just rhetoric, required the application of memory.[73] The proliferation of works specifically devoted to the art of memory in the 1400s and 1500s converged with a tendency to exclude the subject from rhetorical manuals. But Valadés took a different line, affirming its central place in his conception of rhetoric:

> Memory is the firm apprehension of the mind, subject matter, words and arrangement. It is pre-eminently necessary for the orator and not without reason is it called the treasure house of his ideas and the custodian of all the parts of rhetoric. It is all more greatly strengthened and increased by practice than by theory and teaching, through the use, for example, of 'places' and 'images'.[74]

[70] Oddly, Valadés did not give *bandolina* (mandolin) for *B*, or possibly *calx* for the horseshoe in *C*, even though both those names begin with the letters he depicts.

[71] *RC* 2.28 F–G 100 [1989, 246]: 'Secundo modo finguntur literarum imagines per resonantiam vocis, quatenus ex cuiusque nominis 1. litera cognoscat videlicet, pro litera A. Antonium, pro B. Bartholomeum, pro C. Carolum, & ita de omnibus alijs literis alphabeti' (*pace* Cañizares-Esguerra 2001, 93). The image for *C*, in Valadés' accompanying illustration, is not of *Carolus* but of a crow, *corvus*, probably from Dolce's alphabet of birds. Glass 1975 held that the illustrated alphabet 'contained native Mexican imagery' (cf. Palomera 1962, 105–22), but this seems unlikely.

[72] Cf. TORQUEMADA, *MI* 15.36 and ACOSTA, *Historia natural y moral de las Indias* (1590) 6.7 quoted in Chapter 4, I below, and Whittaker 2021 on Mexican writing.

[73] Cf. Merino Jérez 2007, 21–77.

[74] *RC* 2.24 Z–A 87 [1989, 220]: 'Memoria est firma animi, rerum, & verborum, & dispositionis perceptio. Est haec maxime oratori necessaria, nec sine causa thesaurus inuentorum, atque omnium

That method was then explained: artificial memory, as distinct from the innate natural capacity, could be developed by apprehending *loci,* or places, in the mind's eye. Such a *locus* was often the visualization of a palace, filled with 'images' (*imagines*) as representations of the things to be memorized which could be arranged, in order, in their appropriate locations. Valadés had relayed, a few lines previously, Cicero's story about the discovery of the system by Simonides. The poet, who had been attending a dinner, was called to the door, just before the house of his host collapsed, killing all the other guests and rendering their bodies unrecognizable; but Simonides was able to identify the corpses for burial from his recollection of where they had been positioned.[75] The principal source for the *Rhetorica Christiana,* however, was the longer, more technical exposition of the visual method of *loci* and *imagines* in the anonymous *Rhetorica ad Herennium,* which was commonly attributed to Cicero.[76]

Valadés' discussion of mnemotechnics was the cue for an account of native Mexican record-keeping in Part 2 of the *Rhetorica Christiana.* The use of shapes and images drawn on silk or papyrus remained customary for Indians, whether or not they were literate.[77] Forty years earlier, Fray Julián Garcés had likened the Mexicans' practice to the Egyptians' pictorial writing as it had been described by the Roman poet Lucan.[78] But in making the same comparison, Valadés instead cited the ancient historians Strabo, Pliny, and Tacitus; Horapollo's *De literis hieroglyphicis* (a Latin translation of an ancient Greek study of Egyptian hieroglyphs); Raphael Maffei Volaterrano's *Commentaria rerum urbanarum* (1506); and Celio Rodigino's *Antiquae lectiones* (1516).[79] The latter two encyclopaedic works contained studies of Egyptian hieroglyphs, along with elements of rhetoric and other disciplines.[80] Valadés listed some of the images Egyptians used to signal words—scarabs, bees, rivers, oxen—and maintained that American Indians produced such figures of their own, each subject to variation, and that they could spend up to an hour discussing how to interpret them.

There follows an account of how the Indians used pictures in place of writing, to transmit agreements to outsiders and to record matters of consequence. Their

partium Rhetoric*ae* custos appellatur. Confirmatur ea magis et augetur exercitatione, qua*m* arte, et pr*ae*ceptione, vte*n*do, videlicet, locis, & imaginibus.'

[75] Cicero, *De oratore* 2.351–4.

[76] *Ad Herennium* 3.28–40; Yates 1966, 1–49.

[77] *RC* 2.27 X–Z 93 [1989, 232].

[78] GARCÉS, *De habilitate* (1537), 8 (Appendix 2.1.2 below); cf. Chapter 1, V above.

[79] Strabo, *Geography* 16.4.4; Tacitus, *Annals* 11.14; Pliny, *Natural History* 7.56.192–4. Aldus Manutius' 1505 *editio princeps* popularized Horapollo in Italy and was frequently reprinted.

[80] CABRERA, 'Epigrams' (c. 1540a), written in New Spain, mentioned Rodigino and Volaterrano: Laird 2013, 199–200. Yhmoff Cabrera 1996 iii, 38–9 describes a 1542 edition of Rodigino in Mexico.

system of artificial memory is compared to the forms of encryption ('polygraphia') employed by the Greeks and Romans:

> We read that several wise philosophers, kings, and leaders in antiquity once devised various and manifold methods by which they safely committed their recondite plans to messengers to be sent to quite distant places, and whatever secret was to be entrusted could be transmitted in a suitable and secure fashion: in this way our Indians (though they may appear stupid and unlearned in other respects) used a kind of encryption to transmit their secrets in various ways, resorting not to letters but to figures and signs.[81]

Valadés explained that the Mexicans could employ a variety of objects to convey meaning: 'threads sometimes took the place of [pictorial] characters, dyed in different colours according to the nature of the message itself. Add, too, the arrows and beans of different colours and kinds, pebbles, seeds, and other things of this kind.'[82]

The dyed threads may seem reminiscent of the Andean *quipu*, but there were devices in Mexico known as *nepohualtzitzin* that used knots of various colours for calculating and recording information.[83] Valadés had observed the symbolic use of arrows, beans, and pebbles, as he describes the Indians' practice of confession a few pages later: 'the more intelligent ones show by the use of a picture the ways in which they have offended God, and they put a number of small stones, indicating their repetition of the same sin, on the symbol by which vices or virtues are represented.'[84] The Mexicans' calendars then furnish a further example of their acquaintance with the art of memory:

> But of all the amazing things I will go on to talk about, the most amazing—since the people are so stupid and born in so dense an atmosphere—are

[81] VALADÉS, *RC* 2.27 A–B, 94 [1989, 234]: 'Legimus complures ueterum sapientes, Philosophos, Reges & Principes, olim uarios atque multiplices excogitauisse modos, quibus nuncijs suis ad loca remotiora mittendis tuto committerent arcana consilij, & quid quid mysterij confidendum occurrisset secreti quo fierent in perferendis idonei, atque securi: Sic nostri (licet alioqui crassi & inculti uideantur) ueluti polygraphia quadam utentes uarijs modis arcana sua absque literis, sed signis & figuris mandabant.'

[82] *RC* 2.27, 94B [1989, 234]: 'Succedebant interdum in locum eius modi characterum, fila, diuersis coloribus pro qualitate nuncij ipsius tincta. Adde huc, sagittas, fasoles, colore diversos ac uarios, scrupulos, grana & id genus alia.'

[83] For the *nepohualtzitzin*, cf. BOTURINI BENADUCI, *Idea de una historia general* (1746), 85 [2015, 62]; GARCILASO DE LA VEGA, [Primera parte] *Commentarios reales* (1609) 6.7 described the *quipu*.

[84] *RC* 2.27 I, 95 [1989, 236]: 'ingeniosiores adhibita pictura demonstrant, in quibus Deum offenderint, & calculos ad significandum eiusdem peccati iterationem, ad signum quo vitia vel virtutes denotantur reponunt.' Cf. TORQUEMADA, *MI* 15.36 [1977 v, 157–9].

the day-books, calendars and annals they sketch out in these forms: their year consisted of eighteen months, and the month was of twenty days, as you will be able to discern from the illustration to follow. Since it may be granted from what I wrote above that the artifice of memory consists of 'places' and 'images' duly ordered, it is clear that these [calendars] are of the essence of that art.[85]

In the end the chapter of the *Rhetorica Christiana* that was supposed to 'prove the system of artificial memory from the Indians' examples' ('Indorum exemplis artificialis memoria probatur') was dominated by comparanda from classical antiquity. Valadés gave no specific examples of the feats of memorization with which the Mexicans astonished his Franciscan contemporaries.[86]

(iv) Valadés' Mexican calendar

A calendrical diagram presented in the *Rhetorica Christiana* (Figure 2.5) was possibly the first of its kind to be printed in Europe, although it should not be inferred from the inscription running alongside the lower frame ('F. Didacus Valades fecit', 'Done by Fray Diego Valadés') that this illustration was original to the author.[87] The image is a more finely executed version of a much earlier chart in Fray Toribio de Benavente Motolinía's *Memoriales* (c. 1541) (Plate 4a): Valadés' diagram can be interpreted in the light of explanations of the ancient Mexican calendar by Fray Bernardino de Sahagún, Fray Diego Durán, and others, as well as by Motolinía himself.[88]

The eighteen 'months' of twenty days mentioned by Valadés in his remarks quoted above are in the numbered segments of the smaller upper circle in the chart,

[85] *RC* 2.27 B–C, 94 [1989, 234]: 'Sed quae pergam dicere, omnium admirabilium admirabilissima sunt quod cum adeo sint stupidi, ta*mque* in crasso aëre nati: istis formis Ephemerides, calendaria & annalia delineant. Constabat autem illorum annus octodecim mensibus, & mensis viginti diebus, vt in huius rei stemmate considerare. Cum ex superioribus concedatur memoriae artificium ex locis & imaginibus debite ordinatis constare: ea esse de essentia artis perspicuum est.'

[86] According to MENDIETA, *Historia* 3.19 [1870, 226], an Indian who heard him preach in Nahuatl was immediately able to deliver the whole sermon from memory in another 'barbarian' language, possibly Otomí. TORQUEMADA, *MI* 15.18 [1977 v, 77–9] linked that example to the natives' memorization of messages, of which 'they had to render legally and precisely the contents without altering a single word', and recalled that a student understudy who had to take the lead role in a three-hour drama about Santiago 'in Castilian, Latin and Mexican' could rapidly memorize his part, and even embellish it in performance. Cf. Chapter 8, IV (i) below on native memory and speech.

[87] *RC* 2.28, 100–1 [1989, 251].

[88] Maza 1945, 39 first identified MOTOLINÍA, *Memoriales* (c. 1541) as the source. Cf. SAHAGÚN, *Historia general* (c. 1580) = *HG*, *Kalendario mexicano, latino y castellano* (c. 1585) and *Arte divinatoria de los mexicanos* (1586); DURÁN, *El calendario antiguo* (1579); TOVAR, *Historia de la benida de los yndios* (c. 1582–1587).

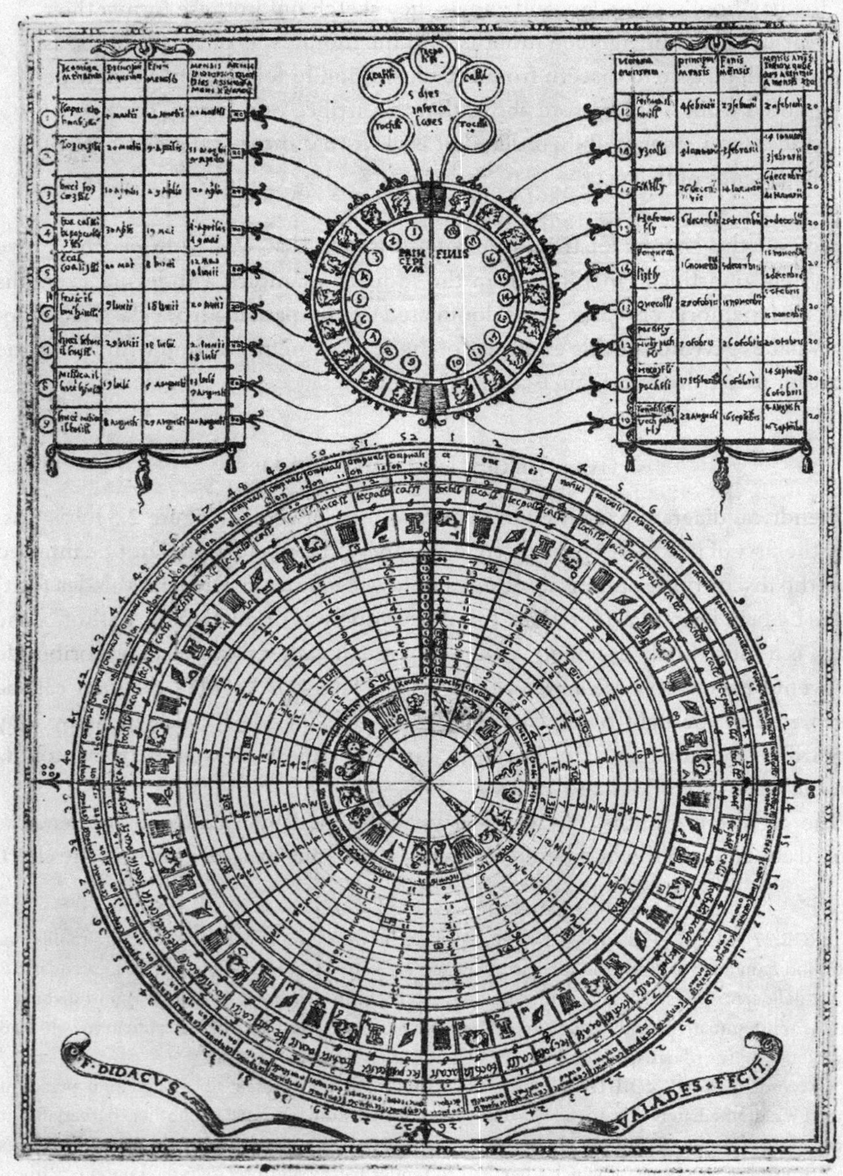

Figure 2.5 Mexican calendar, Fray Diego Valadés, *Rhetorica Christiana*, 1579. John Carter Brown Library.

running in anticlockwise sequence. Those units of twenty days, known in Spanish as *venteinas*, are also displayed on either side of the circle, in two columns of nine. Both columns are tabulated into four sections from left to right: (i) 'Nomina mexicana', identifying each *venteina* in Nahuatl; 'Principium mensis', dating the start of the *venteina* in the Julian calendar; and 'Finis mensis', stating the day it ends, and a fourth column with another set of European dates. The first line of the left-hand table opens the Mexican year in March in accord with the accounts of the calendar given by both Motolinía and Durán.[89] Above the upper circle, there are the 'dies intercalares' (*nemontemi* in Nahuatl), the five intercalary days needed to make up the total of 365 for a solar year. Although these inauspicious days were not individually named, here they are labelled in Nahuatl.[90]

In addition to that solar year of 365 days, there was another 260-day ritual cycle that Valadés did not mention: the *tonalpohualli*, or 'day count', of twenty *trecenas* of thirteen days.[91] The two systems of reckoning intersected every fifty-two years—18,980 days is the lowest common multiple of 365 and 260—instituting the 'binding of the years', *xiuhmolpilli*.[92] The larger circle in the lower part of the illustration represents, in clockwise sequence, the period of fifty-two solar years, an important unit of chronology that enabled the Mexicans to name individual years and days, and to establish when their festivals were to be held. Toward the centre of the large circle are the day signs for the twenty *trecenas* of the *tonalpohualli* and their names in Nahuatl, which again proceed clockwise from the centre: 'cipactli', Alligator; 'ehecatl', Wind (depicted with the conventional European personification); 'calli', House; 'cue[t]zpalin', Lizard, etc.[93] From each day sign radiates each of the thirteen days in concentric sections.

The Latin text of the *Rhetorica Christiana* sheds no such light on this illustration: in reference to it Valadés merely remarked, 'I want the reader to be forewarned that we have omitted elucidation of the Calendar of the Indians because it would

[89] MOTOLINÍA, *Memoriales* (c. 1541) 11r [1996, 160]; DURÁN, *El calendario antiguo*, cap. 3 [2002, 245]. Versions differed: according to SAHAGÚN, *HG* 2.1 [1981 iii, 1], the Mexican year began on the second day of February.

[90] The *nemontemi* (barren days) are here named in Valadés' diagram as 'tochtli', Rabbit; 'acatl', Reed; 'tecpatl', Flint; 'calli', House; and 'tochtli' again. Cf. SAHAGÚN, *HG* 2.19 [1981 iii, 35–41] on the associated rituals; DURÁN, *Calendario antiguo*, cap. 3 [2002, 292–3] on 'Dias demasiados'.

[91] SAHAGÚN, *HG* Book 4, Appendix [1957 v, 137–46] condemned the day count as a system of pagan divination and criticized the *Tonalamatl*, 'book of the day count', in the prologue to his *Arte divinatoria de los mexicanos* (1586) [1954, 386].

[92] I have not yet found any Spanish sources from the 1500s acknowledging that this calculation was the basis for the *xiuhmolpilli*. SAHAGÚN, *HG* 7.9 [1953, viii, 25–6] describes the ritual; cf. DURÁN, *Calendario antiguo*, cap. 1 [2002, 226] on *nexiuhilpiliztli* [*sic*], 'binding of a perfect circle of years'. In a note 'To the Reader', SAHAGÚN, *Arte divinatoria* (1586) [1954, 386, col. 2], seems unaware that the 260-day count was a factor in the calculation of the *Xiuhmolpilli* every fifty-two years: 'it has nothing to do with the Calendar nor with the number of years.' Early colonial calendar tables were inauthentic and often erroneous: Castillo Farreras 1971; Tena 1992.

[93] The sequence was conventional: cf. e.g. the anonymous *Codex Magliabechiano* (mid-1500s).

have to be put in their language.'[94] As knowledge of Nahuatl is not really necessary to make sense of the chart, it would seem that the author did not understand the meaning of the diagrams he had himself reproduced. In contrast to two of his illustrious European contemporaries, Michel de Montaigne and Joseph Justus Scaliger, who each reflected on the Aztec calendar in some depth, Valadés regarded it as a curiosity, produced by Indians whose inferior intellect, he believed, was determined by the climate in which they lived.[95]

Nonetheless, the dedication of the *Rhetorica Christiana* to Pope Gregory XIII in 1579 and its author's association with Cardinal Guglielmo Sirleto, who led the commission to correct the Julian calendar, have led to speculation that Valadés was promoting and validating the Mexican calendrical system, only three years before the introduction of the Gregorian calendar in 1582.[96] Such speculation is misguided: the pope was an appropriate, if not inevitable, choice of dedicatee because Valadés, as Procurator General of the Franciscans, would have had to preach before him in Latin, while Cardinal Sirleto entrusted Valadés with writing the *Catholicae assertiones contra praecipuos aliquot hereticorum errores*, 'Catholic declarations against several principal errors of heretics' (1581). The implicit Counter-Reformation message of the *Rhetorica Christiana* may well have prompted Sirleto to judge its Spanish author as being suitable for such an undertaking.[97] That would not have been the case if Valadés had appeared even remotely sympathetic to Motolinía's notorious justification of the Mexican day count (which Fray Bernardino de Sahagún had denounced both to Pius V and to the Holy Inquisition).[98]

For Valadés, the Indian calendar was of interest only as an illustration of artificial memory. The resemblance between the design he had copied from Motolinía

[94] *RC* 2.28 G, 100 [1989, 246]: 'Praemonitum legentem volo quod Calendarii Indorum declarationem, eo quod in illorum lingua debuisset poni omittimus.'

[95] MONTAIGNE, *Essais* (1580) 3.6 [1962, 892] and SCALIGER (the younger), *Opus novum de emendatione temporum* (1583), with the author's 1584 annotation comparing Mexican *trecenas* to the fifteen-day weeks of the Persians, are cited in Grafton 1993, 5, 361–2. Aristotle's geographical determinism had long been debated: it was espoused in SCALIGER (the elder), *Exotericarum exercitationum liber quintus decimus* (1557), a rebuttal of CARDANO, *De subtilitate* (1550): Romeo 1954; Maclean 1984; Sakamoto 2016. ACOSTA, *Historia natural y moral de las Indias* (1590) and SOLÓRZANO PEREIRA, *De indianorum jure* (1629) countered the elder Scaliger: for the controversy's impact in the Americas cf. Brading 1991, 213–27; Cañizares-Esguerra 1999; Gerbi 2010.

[96] Cf. Palomera 1963, 165–70; Cummins 1995, 152–74.

[97] Chaparro Gómez 2003 sees Valadés' *Rhetorica Christiana* as a demonstration of the utility of humanist rhetoric in the papal mission plan to oppose Protestant representations.

[98] MOTOLINÍA, *Memoriales* (c. 1541), 'Epistola prohemial' 5.5–6 and (fols.) 10v–18r [1996, 121–2, 159–84]. SAHAGÚN, *Breve compendio* (1570) reported to Pius V on the 'calendar of idolatrous feasts', and his denunciation of Motolinía's views to the Inquisition two years later is reproduced in Baudot 1991, 132. SAHAGÚN, *HG* Book 4, Appendix [1981 v, 139–42] rejected Motolinía's discussion of the calendar: Nicolau D'Olwer 1956, lv–lvi; León-Portilla 2002, 199–203, 231–3.

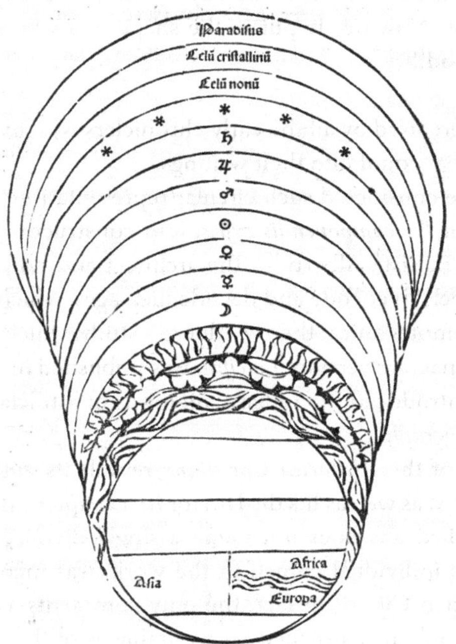

Figure 2.6 Cosmological diagram in Jacobus Publicius, *Oratoriae artis epitome,* Venice, 1485. Hay Library, Brown University.

and the circular diagrams or 'wheels' found in humanist memory treatises (including those he cited by Dolce and Publicius) is not coincidental (Figure 2.6).[99] Indigenous codices often displayed the signs for days, *trecenas,* or years in straight linear sequences (Plate 4b).[100] The device of the wheel, on the other hand, had been a method of organizing and recollecting information in Europe since late antiquity.[101] In a caption accompanying his original diagram of the Mexican calendar, Motolinía indicated that its circular design was his own innovation:

[99] Báez Rubí 2005 considers the mnemotechnical significance of Valadés' other diagrams, but not this one. Bolzoni 2001, 23–82 presents images from earlier European rhetorical texts; for Publicius and Romberch cf. Yates 1966, 101–2, 114–23.

[100] The *tonalamatl* in the *Codex Telleriano-Remensis* arranged numbered day signs in right angles around pictures of deities presiding over a *trecena*. Cf. Baird 1993, 105–17 on the illustrations of *Veintena* ceremonies in SAHAGÚN, *Primeros memoriales* (1558–1560).

[101] Laugesen 1962 (on the *rota Virgilii,* 'wheel of Virgil'); Carruthers 1993 and Carruthers 2008; Wittkower 1949, 4.

The calendar of the entire Indian race, by which means they have reckoned time until today. Now newly put in the shape of a wheel in order to be better understood'.[102]

Similar diagrams were used by all the early chroniclers who incorporated charts of the day count and year count into their writings.

Valadés may have considered such circular representations of the Mexican calendar in the light of *De componendis cyfris*, 'On constructing ciphers', written in the 1400s by Leon Battista Alberti.[103] The architect and polymath had devised a system of using wheels to encode and decode messages, which was readily applied to Renaissance mnemotechnical theory. Alberti's study, which circulated widely in Latin before the vernacular version, *La cifra*, was published in 1568, might well explain why Valadés introduced the Indians' methods of artificial memory as a form of encryption or *polygraphia*.

Overall, perusal of the *Rhetorica Christiana* reveals its author's limited knowledge of native society, as well as his disdain for it: a chapter on the number of gods venerated by the Mexicans does not name a single divinity—and Montezuma, the only indigenous individual named in the work, was incorrectly identified as the founder of Mexico City.[104] In fact, the only comments Valadés made on the pagan Indians that might be construed as favourable were about the Chichimeca in northern Mexico, whom he characterized as 'so warlike and courageous that, even with naked bodies and armed only with bows and arrows, they dare confront well-armed and equipped soldiers in formation, with the swiftness of a deer.'[105] The general presentation of the natives in the *Rhetorica Christiana* was intended, above all, to defend against detractors the success of the Franciscans' conversion of the Indians in the New World.

[102] MOTOLINÍA, *Memoriales* (c. 1541) 15r [1996, 175]: 'Calendario de toda la yndica gente, por donde han contado sus tiempos hasta hoy. Agora nuevamente puesto en forma de rueda, para mejor ser entendido.' Spitler 2005 and Aveni 2012 discuss the circular and rectangular forms of European and Mexican calendars.

[103] ALBERTI, *De componendis cyfris* (c. 1462). Yates 1966, 202–29, 248–51 discusses the 'memory wheel' in BRUNO, *De umbris idearum* (1582), which adopted the combinatory wheels invented by Ramon Llull; Báez Rubí 2005 discusses possible connections between Llull and Valadés. Cf. Bolzoni 2001.

[104] *RC* 6.7, 279 D [1989, 626]: 'Consulto quidem illam fundauit hoc loco Motectzuma, eo quod vir bellicosus esset & a multis potentissimis aduersarijs peteretur.' ('Montezuma deliberately founded the city in that place because he was a warlike man who was being attacked by many powerful foes.')

[105] *RC* 4.2, 166 M [1989, 384]: 'Item viros esse tam bellicosos & animoso pectore, vt nudis corporibus arcu, & sagittis, modo armati, se militibus bene accinctis & armaturis bene instructis, opponere audeant, celitate omnino ceruina.' Cf. Valadés on Chichimec aggression in his preface to FOCHER, *Itinerarium* (n. 38 above).

V. Conversion through action: Fray Cristóbal Cabrera, *De solicitanda infidelium conversione*, 1582

Fray Cristóbal Cabrera saw a different role for rhetoric in the evangelization of the Indians. Long after his return to Europe from New Spain, he wrote an epistolary treatise entitled 'Securing the conversion of unbelievers'. The text was a study of missionary method, containing a unique, if stylized, personal recollection of Vasco de Quiroga, whom Cabrera had assisted in his ministry fifty years earlier.[106] The work was addressed to a younger missionary appropriately named Baptista, who wanted to know in what manner unbelievers should be 'compelled' by the preaching of the Gospel to enter the Church of Christ.[107]

The wording of the enquiry was a reference to a verse from the parable of the Great Feast in the Gospel of Luke 14:23: 'Go out to the highways and hedges and compel them to come in.' Interpretation of that passage of scripture was long contested: it had been cited by Saint Augustine in response to the Donatist heretics and prompted various interpretations in the context of the conversion of the Indians.[108] Las Casas, opposing Sepúlveda's advocation of the use of force, argued that the 'compulsion' was internal, to be effected by God; but Franciscans, including Motolinía, endorsed the moderate use of coercion.[109] Fray Gerónimo de Mendieta, for instance, derived practical imperatives from the story, warning that it would be perilous to neglect the Catholic Kings' charge to call all peoples to the Lord's supper.[110]

Cabrera explained first in theory, and then with the example of Quiroga's practice, how he believed the passage from Luke was to be understood. The compulsion in question should derive from persuasive preaching and the 'power of reason'.[111]

[106] The memoir was not accessible to the Jesuit author of the earliest life of Quiroga, MORENO, *Fragmentos de la vida, virtudes del... D. Vasco de Quiroga* (1766), and it remains little known, despite the studies of Burrus 1961, Campos 1965, and Martín Ortiz 1974. For Cabrera's earlier writing, cf. Chapter 1 above.

[107] Autograph of CABRERA, *De solicitanda infidelium conversione* (1582), = *DSIC*, 1r [1974, 413]. The addressee is named in the final sentence at 50v [461]: 'And as you are called *Baptista*, endeavour to excel in what is signified by that name, that is, to convert and baptize as many people as you can to the Catholic faith from unbelief, by word and example and with the inspiration of the grace of Christ and the Holy Spirit.'

[108] Augustine, *Epistles* 93.2.5.

[109] Phelan 1956, 7–9, 15–16.

[110] MENDIETA, *Historia* (1596) 1.4–5 [1870, 24–31]. Pardo 2004, 6, 165 n. 15, contrasts Mendieta's reading of the passage to that of ERASMUS, *In Evangelium Lucae Paraphrasis* (1523), attributing Erasmus' lack of elaboration to his 'distaste for prophecies and apocalyptic fervor'.

[111] *DSIC*, 29r [1974, 414]: 'rationis vim et efficaciam'. Cabrera here cited Aquinas and others: 'A number of grave, pious and learned men who have fairly weighed up and judged the thoughts and opinions on this matter—not only diverse, but also contradictory—held by St Thomas, by Scotus, and by Thomists and Scotists, consider that the teaching of St Thomas is evidently the more commendable and closer to the truth.'

Three forms of *compulsio* were specified: miracles, which incline unbelievers to accept the truth; constant preaching of the word of God, which, without eschewing reason, promises eternal happiness or threatens eternal damnation to unbelievers; and the uprightness and sincerity of a preacher whose hearers accept the truth of his words. The second and third forms of 'compulsion' could be combined and strengthened in the figure of a good and pious apostolic preacher whose conduct was such that it would *force* those who did not yet believe to embrace the Catholic faith. Vasco de Quiroga was presented as just such a figure, because his actions were deemed to be more powerful than words, meriting both praise and imitation.[112]

After relating the writer's experience of studying, reading, and conversing with Quiroga, the letter described the bishop's strategy of purchasing land to found 'settlements' ('oppida'): the renowned *pueblos-hospitales*, residential communities that he established for the Indians' religious instruction.[113] This strategy led to the impressive sight of countless converts being baptized all over Mexico and Michoacán. The Indians would return from the *oppida* to their homes, overwhelmed with the gifts and kindnesses that had been shown to them, proclaiming to those in neighbouring territories the news of the Gospel and of the apostolic bishop, and recounting all they had seen, heard, and experienced. They had been welcomed, refreshed in body and soul, and instructed in the rudiments of the Christian faith, with men and women of any age and status comfortably accommodated. The converts displayed the images they had received of Christ, of the Blessed Virgin, and of other saints and angels, telling others about the solemn pageantry of the baptism, the processions, the music, and the chants that the Bishop had composed himself.

Cabrera then provided an exemplary narrative of an occasion on which Vasco de Quiroga received a wild-looking tribe of Indians who had come to him of their own accord to be baptized. The tenor of what he recounted concurred with a development the bishop himself reported to the Council of the Indies in 1561: 'for more than twenty years there has been and there is still being conducted here a general baptism of some fierce and savage tribes who are called Chichimeca, who come freely to it'.[114] A general image of the Chichimeca as *silvestres*, 'savage' (partly in the sense of coming from the *silva*, or forest), was corroborated by Focher, Valadés, and many other Franciscans, including Motolinía and Torquemada. Fray Bernardino de Sahagún, too, stated these natives were 'men of the woods' ('hombres silvestres').[115]

[112] *DSIC*, 41r–50v.

[113] *DSIC*, 42r (see Chapter 1, p. 23 above): cf. Cuevas 1946 i, 414–20.

[114] QUIROGA, 'El Obispo de Michoacán al Consejo de Indias' (1561) [1965, 155]: 'de más de veinte años acá siempre se ha hecho y hace baptismo general de unas gentes bravas y silvestres que se dicen chichimecas, que a él allí acuden.'

[115] SAHAGÚN, *HG* 10.29 [1961 xi, 171] identified three kinds of Chichimeca: the Otomí, the Tamime ('shooters of arrows'), and the Teochichimeca ('real Chichimeca'). FOCHER, *Itinerarium* 3.2 [1960, 348]: 'Chichimecae Indi sunt qui non laborant, sed vivunt de venatione et de his, quae ultro nascuntur. Qui neque Deum, neque idola colunt, nudi incedentes, arte sagittandi ab ineunte aetate

224 *Rhetorica Christiana*

Perfectio religiosorum in Indis.

tia viginti: Nam post orationes illico transibant ad labores, & nulla interposita quiete, à laboribus vicissim ad orationes. Erant laceri, pannosi, discalceati, quiescentes humi, Herbæ & turundæ ex Indico tritico quod Mayzium nos, ipsi verò tlahuli vocãt, illorum cibus erat: montes & valles pedestribus itineribus peragrabãt, quam cõsuetudinem Religiosi adhuc obseruant, nisi valetudo aut magna aliqua ratio diuersum postulet. Vt præsens stemma demonstrat. S

A. Religiosum armis, sed Christi crucifixi signo munitũ. Præter breuiarium nihil vult. B. Sunt pueri, quos secum tanquam coadiutores ad docendam doctrinam ducit sunt enim valde instructi ad hoc munus ita, vt ipsi maximam curam, vna cum hominibus grauibus, quos etiam tanquam coadiutores secum assumit habent. C. Est interpres religiosi Hispanicam linguam calens, ideo munitus CHRISTI IESV signo barbaros, & indomitos ad præsentiam religiosi ducit. Ideo sunt nudi, vt eorum, est mos. D. Feritatem, Arma & barbarorum incedendi modum demonstrat. X

E. Fide-

Figure 2.7 A translator escorts a band of unconverted natives to a friar. Fray Diego Valadés, *Rhetorica Christiana*, 1579. John Carter Brown Library.

The very name *Chichimeca* is the plural of *chichimecatl*, a Nahuatl term for nomad with 'both a negative "barbarous" sense and a positive "noble savage" sense'.[116]

The detailed description that follows, of the barbarian throng of both sexes, heavily armed with bows and arrows, the men completely naked, the women clad only with deerskin loincloths, was in line with Sahagún's portrayal of the Chichimeca: the men were always accompanied by the women, who had skin skirts or shifts; and they always carried bows, even when they ate or slept (Figure 2.7).[117] Cabrera next relates that a representative of the group then made a formal speech to the bishop. Praise of the man's eloquence and of its impact on those present not only rendered the savage noble; it also showed Quiroga's familiarity with classical

valde instructi' ('The Chichimeca are Indians who do not toil, but live from hunting and from what nature produces. They worship neither God nor idols, and walk forth naked, expertly trained in the art of archery from infancy'). Cf. Section III above; VALADÉS, *RC* 4.2, 165 L–M [382–4], n. 105 above; MOTOLINÍA, *Historia* (c. 1543) 3.5, 3.7 [2001, 198–9, 213]; TORQUEMADA, *MI* 1.15 [1975 i, 58–9]. See further n. 127 below.

[116] Karttunen 1992, 48: s.v. 'CHĪCHĪMĒCATL', cf. n. 123 below.

[117] SAHAGÚN, *HG* 10.29 [1961 xi, 172–3].

oratory and enabled Cabrera to display, in the telling, his own command of rhetoric and its technical terms:

> A translator and orator among them made a speech to the bishop with such great facility, full of weighty *sententiae*, and accomplished in its promptness, articulacy of thought and oral delivery, adorned with the use of oratorical figures to such a degree that, after this one man had made his address on behalf of them all, the Bishop, powerfully impressed, then turned to me and others present to say 'Have you ever seen, I ask you, barbarian Ciceros, Quintilians, and Livies like this?'[118]

The native orator's words are not quoted verbatim in Cabrera's narrative, but their presentation in indirect discourse still has a lively, declamatory quality:

> He said that it should not be considered remarkable that they presumed to approach so great a priest in this manner, naked and in such a primitive condition, in that they had lived up to now by their ancestral customs in an uncivilized and barbarous state, and had so far had no ruler or instructor like other more refined peoples, who could train them in life's skills, in moral conduct and true religion. It was for this reason that throughout the whole course of their life they had cared for nothing unless it had a bearing on their sustenance, they deemed clothing of no value, as they were constantly seeking their food and drink, from whatever place, as they wandered through the paths and passes or fields, woods and mountains, hunting wild animals—boars, bears, tigers, wolves, goats, deer, and various other living things, on the raw bloody flesh of which they used to feed—and they drank from the springs of rivers and streams, or the waters of lakes and lagoons: they always slept in the open on the ground during summer, wherever night would come upon them, or else it was in the earth's caverns, bowers, ditches, crypts, and caves, especially in the seasons of winter, that they took their nightly rest. So they knew nothing of agriculture, whether it was because they deemed themselves of too noble a condition to turn the land and demean themselves by cultivating the fields, or because they learnt nothing in any depth, except the skill of archery from the time when, as the saying goes, the fingernails are tender.[119]

[118] CABRERA, *DSIC*, 45r–v [1974, 449] 'quidam illorum interpres et orator ad Episcopum eam habuit orationem tanta facundia, sententiarumque grauitate plenam, ac dissertam, animique et linguae promptitudine ac pronunciatione, oratorioque schemate adeo ornatum, vt postquam ille suam [orationem] vnus pro omnibus fecit, ac finijt, Episcopus admirandus valde tunc ad alios praesentes meque conversus diceret, vidistisne vnquam, rogo, similes Cicerones, Fabios ac Livios barbaros?'

[119] CABRERA, *DSIC*, 45v–46r [1974, 449–50]: 'Mirandum autem non esse sic eos ad tantum Pontificem nudos, adeoque incultos ausos accedere, quippe quia patriis hucusque moribus inciuiliter

This speaker's characterization of his own people converges quite remarkably with the account of the Chichimeca in Book 10 of Sahagún's *Historia general*:

> they inhabited the plains, mountains and caves and had no fixed home but went wandering from one place to another, and wherever night came upon them, if there was a cave, they stayed there to sleep . . . The food and sustenance of the Teochichimecs were leaves . . . and the roots they knew and found in the ground, and all the meat of rabbits, hares, deer, snakes and many birds . . . When [a boy] became one year old, they placed a bow in his hand and taught him to shoot and they taught him no play, except archery alone.[120]

At the same time, the discourse of the native orator harmonized with the way in which primitive Europeans were portrayed in classical literature. Yet again, Cicero's conception of ancient society prior to the advent of rhetoric was recalled, so that the inhabitants of the new world were implicitly equated with the wild people of antiquity described in the *De inventione*. Other classical sources were in play too: the poet Ovid had imagined primeval human beings as 'living like wild animals and unconcerned with profit, the masses were still rude and without skills, for houses they knew leaves, for food greenery . . . no land was under the control of cultivation'.[121] And the attributes of the native people rehearsed to Quiroga by

barbariceque viuerint, nullumque hactenus rectoremque magistrumque, sicut aliae politiores gentes, habuerint, qui ipsos in vitae cultu, morumque conuersatione ac vera religione instruxerit. Eamque ob causam nihil aliud illi per totum vitae decursum curarint, praeter quae ad victum pertinerent, pro nihilo ducentes vestitum, quaeritantes sibi cibum et potum undecumque partium per agrorum, siluarum montiumque tractus et saltus vagantes, venantes feras, apros, vrsos, tigres, lupos, capreas, cervos, aliaque diuersa animantia, quorum crudis etiam carnibus et sanguinibus victitabant, fluuiorumque et fontium latices, lacuum aut lacunarum aquas bibebant: humi semper aestatis sub dio tempore cubitabant, vbicumque nox ipsos exciperet, vel in terrae cauernis, caueis, fossis, cryptis, et speluncis, hyemis praesertim temporibus, noctu quiescebant. Agriculturae prorsus ignari siue quod illi seipsos longe nobilioris conditionis reputarint, quam vt terram verterent, colendisque agris se deiicerent; siue quia nihil penitus praeter sagittandi artem a teneris, vt aiunt, vnguiculis didicissent.'

120 SAHAGÚN, *HG* 10.29 [1961 xi, 171–2].

121 Ovid, *Fasti* 2.291–3, 2.296: 'vita feris similis, nullos agitata per usus: / artis adhuc expers et rude volgus erat. / pro domibus frondes norant, pro frugibus herbas; . . . nulla sub imperio terra colentis erat'; cf. *Ars amatoria* 2.473–6: 'tum genus humanum solis errabat in agris, / idque merae vires et rude corpus erat; / silva domus fuerat, cibus herba, cubilia frondes: / iamque diu nulli cognitus alter erat' ('In that time the human race wandered in the lonely fields, consisting of nothing but brute strength and rude bodies. Woodland had been its home, grass its food, and leaves its bedding—and for a very long time no one had been known to anyone else'). Janka 1997, 352–3 cites ancient parallels to this passage, including Cicero, *De oratore* 1.33, and *De inventione* 1.2 quoted above (cf. LAS CASAS, *DUVM* 5.10; VALADÉS, *RC*, 'Praefatio' b3, [1989, 28]; nn. 26, 53, above) all of which would have been known to Cabrera. Cf. Seneca, *Epistulae* 17.6, 90.16, and n. 122 below.

their spokesman—sleeping on the ground, dependence on archery, and aversion to agriculture—have an uncanny resemblance to those of the Fenni from ancient Germany as they were portrayed by the Roman historian Tacitus:

> The Fenni are of remarkable savagery and appalling poverty: no arms, no horses, no homes; for food, greenery; for clothing, skins; their bed, the earth; their only hope in arrows, which, lacking iron, they sharpen with bones. The common hunt sustains men and women alike; for the women keep them company everywhere and demand their own part of the prey. Their young have no shelter from wild animals and the rains, other than coverage provided by intertwined branches; a haven for the old to which those in their prime also return. But this they deem a more blessed existence than groaning at labour in the fields, toiling on houses, and trafficking with their own or others' fortunes in hope and fear. Secure against men and secure against gods, they have reached a state very difficult to attain so that they have no need even to wish for anything.[122]

The Fenni had something else in common with the Chichimeca: their name (derived from the proto-Germanic *finne*) like *chichimeca*, designated 'nomads'.[123]

Tacitus closed the *Germania* with the example of the Fenni, prompting many modern classical commentators to interpret his text as a covert polemic, highlighting the decadence and luxury of the Romans by ennobling the values of the German barbarians—an interpretation that was also favoured by Renaissance readers of Tacitus.[124] The Fenni, at any rate, were presented as a people instinctively in accord

[122] Tacitus, *Germania* 46: 'Fennis mira feritas, foeda paupertas: non arma, non equi, non penates; victui herba, vestitui pelles, cubile humus: solae in sagittis spes, quas inopia ferri ossibus asperant. Idemque venatus viros pariter ac feminas alit; passim enim comitantur partemque praedae petunt. Nec aliud infantibus ferarum imbriumque suffugium quam ut in aliquo ramorum nexu contegantur: huc redeunt iuvenes, hoc senum receptaculum. Sed beatius arbitrantur quam ingemere agris, inlaborare domibus, suas alienasque fortunas spe metuque versare: securi adversus homines, securi adversus deos rem difficillimam adsecuti sunt, ut illis ne voto quidem opus esset.'

[123] Hellquist 1922, 137 [s.v. *finne*]: 'vandrarefolk', 'samlarefolk'; Rives 1999, 327 (ad loc.): '[*Fenni*] is usually thought to derive from Germanic **fintha-*, "to find", signifying either "gatherers" or "wanderers".' Tacitus' *Fenni* have been identified as Lapps or Finns, along with the Φίννοι in Ptolemy, *Geographica* 2.11.16 and 3.5.8, the *Finni* or *Finnaithae* in Jordanes, *Getica* 21 (sixth century AD), and the Σκριθίφινοι, 'skiing Finns', of Procopius, *De bello Gothico* 2.15.16–22 (cf. Paul the Deacon, *Historia Langobardorum* 1.5).

[124] Much 1967, 534–7; cf. *Germania* 3.3 and Rives 1999, 127 (*ad loc.*). Schellhase 1976 and Krebs 2005 consider implications for humanist historiography of Germany; Lupher 2003, 50–6, 227–8 points to intimations of the 'noble savage' in GUEVARA, *Libro áureo de Marco Aurelio* (c. 1528) (cf. Chapter 1, IV above) and in other contemporaneous Spanish sources. The circularity between Renaissance views of native Americans and ideas of ancient European 'barbarians' is explored in Burke 1995. CABRERA, 'Epigrams' (c. 1540), composed in New Spain, mentions Tacitus.

with Stoic and Epicurean ethical principles, living in freedom from hope, fear, or desire.[125] Yet the Indians whom Cabrera described differed from Tacitus' Fenni in one major respect: they were positively disposed to religion. The final part of their spokesman's appeal makes clear that his people did have gods; and that they were keen to adopt new beliefs:

> Like other peoples of this sort, they did indeed worship idols that were moulded or sculpted. Even so, they said they were humbly begging the most pious Bishop to deign to show and convey to them now the very attentive piety and charity he had practised, and was still constantly practising, for the benefit of countless other Indians, so that they could undertake, with a swift and ready spirit, as well as act, with all their heart and strength, on whatever things were to be believed, observed and performed that he might impart—with regard to the conduct of life, behaviour, faith, divine worship, and true religion—in the very way that he showed them.[126]

The ascription of idolatry to these Indians, however, does not just set them in contrast to Tacitus' Fenni, whom they had resembled up until this point. It is also incongruous with what was actually reported about the Chichimeca in several other sources. In 1540, around the time Quiroga and Cabrera were in Michoacán, Motolinía remarked that the 'Chichimeca . . . did not have idols' and Fray Juan Focher had noted that 'they worship neither God nor idols'—an observation that would be echoed in the 1600s by the chronicler Fernando de Alva Ixtlilxochitl.[127] But if Cabrera had presented the group of natives he encountered as being generally godless and antipathetic to religion, he would not have communicated so

[125] Cabrera may have known Pompeius Trogus' comparable idealization of the Scythians for putting Greek philosophy into practice in Justinus, *Historiae Philippicae* 2.2: 'Aurum et argentum non perinde ac reliqui mortales adpetunt . . . Lanae his usus ac vestium ignotus et quamquam continuis frigoribus urantur, pellibus tamen ferinis ac murinis utuntur. Haec continentia illis morum quoque iustitiam edidit, nihil alienum concupiscentibus . . . prorsus ut admirabile videatur hoc illis naturam dare, quod Graeci longa sapientium doctrina praeceptisque philosophorum consequi nequeunt. . . .' (Compare Chapter 1 above on Trogus and Garcés).

[126] CABRERA, *DSIC* (1582), 46r [1974, 450]: 'Colebant autem illi, sicut aliae huismodi gentes, ydola seu fictilia seu sculptilia. Coeterum humiliter aiebant se Episcopum pijsimum comprecari, tum eam quam erga alios innumeros indos officiosissimam pietatem charitatemque exercuerat exercebatque semper, sibi ipsis etiam praestare communicare dignaretur; vt quae credenda seruandaque et exequenda circa vitae rationem, mores, fidem, diuinum cultum veramque religionem tradidisset, ea illi omnia, sicut ostendisset, prompto alacrique animo suscipientes, toto pectore proque viribus exequerentur.'

[127] MOTOLINÍA, *Historia* (c. 1543), 'Epístola proemial' [2001, 4]; FOCHER, *Itinerarium* 3.2: 'De bello in chichimecas', quoted in Section III above; ALVA IXTLILXOCHITL, *Sumaria relación de todas las cosas . . . en la Nueva España* (c. 1603), cap. 1 ('Historia de los señores chichimecas'), [1975 i, 289]: 'no tenían ídolos; llaman al sol, padre, y a la tierra, madre'.

successfully the moral of his story: the natives, impressed by Quiroga's practice, were supposed to have come to be converted of their own accord.

The bishop assured the Indians that he would give them the teaching and introduction to the Christian way of life they required; and he offered them the shelter of his residential communities. In accord with the Indians' skills and interests, he established archery contests, as both entertainment and a form of religious instruction: the Indians should direct their attention to Christ in the manner they directed their arrows at a given target. These converts acted as apostles to other tribes whose territory they passed, encouraging them to come to the bishop. Just as Cabrera's representation of the native tribe in this narrative relied on classical sources as well as observation, so too did his portrayal of Vasco de Quiroga. In this narrative Quiroga's role resembles that of Cicero's sage, earlier recalled by Las Casas and Valadés, who first enabled men 'to turn from their previous customs to a different system of life'. And by encouraging the Indians to live in stable settlements, the bishop is shown to have re-enacted the other major accomplishment of that wise man who, in Cicero's words, had 'collected into one place and assembled people who were scattered over the fields and hidden in woodland dwellings'. The general message of the *De solicitanda infidelium conversione* may seem similar to that of Las Casas' *De unico vocationis modo*. But while Las Casas had placed emphasis on conversion through preaching, the Franciscan Cabrera echoed Erasmus' contempt for 'words alone' in regarding deeds as more important, a view shared by Vasco de Quiroga—who functions in his exemplary narrative as a model for this Erasmian position.[128]

VI. Conclusions

Consideration of subject matter, delivery, and memory are important for any preacher or public speaker. On the other hand, few of the detailed prescriptions for style or for deployment of rhetorical figures, so central to classical eloquence, could easily be applied to sermons in Amerindian languages. That much would have been obvious to any missionary who ventured to preach in them. Yet the friars were not about to discard classical rhetoric: it had constituted a major part of their education, justifying and mediating their knowledge of classical literature. Proficiency in rhetoric and dialectic had much the same symbolic value within the religious orders as it did in other spheres. Manuals of rhetorical theory by both ancient and humanist authors were available in New Spain from soon after the conquest, and many more original studies and textbooks would be produced in the Royal University and in Jesuit colleges over the course of the seventeenth and eighteenth centuries.[129]

[128] Dealy 1976.

[129] Cf. Osorio Romero 1976; Osorio Romero 1980, 95–123; Beuchot 1998.

The pervasiveness of rhetoric in the early colony is rarely acknowledged: in serving a range of practical purposes, it went well beyond other arts and disciplines such as philosophy, poetry, and history. Even though the precepts of the classical art of persuasion were, as a rule, written and read in Latin, they were tirelessly applied to spoken and written discourses in the vernacular, ranging from ceremonial speeches and sermons to official reports and chronicles.[130] The rhetorical prescriptions for epistolography, developed in the Renaissance by Erasmus and others, guided both native Latinists and Spaniards. Rhetoric provided a system of organization for Nahuatl compositions and translations, and it supplied Fray Andrés de Olmos, Fray Bernardino de Sahagún, Fray Juan Bautista, and other missionaries with a framework for interpreting and adapting autochthonous Mexican discourses.[131]

The works examined in this chapter did not just discuss rhetoric—they employed it, and they were written with quite different ends in view: Fray Bartolomé de las Casas affirmed that persuasion was the only way to call Indians to the faith in order to influence official policy; Fray Juan Focher's hardheaded advice was printed for the benefit of other missionaries; Fray Diego Valadés hoped to impress the pope and Catholic humanists in Italy by publishing his own study of Christian rhetoric; and Fray Cristóbal Cabrera was writing to inspire a young Franciscan missionary with a refined treatise and memoir that he bequeathed to the Vatican library for posterity.

In Europe, classicizing portrayals of inhabitants of the New World were very common, in Latin and vernacular chronicles alike.[132] The sixteenth-century texts from the Americas considered above, however, advocated different approaches to conversion, and thus exhibited differences, both in their respective portrayals of native groups and in their illustrative use of classical models. Las Casas drew from a range of Greco-Roman and medieval literature to promote the interests of indigenous Americans while offering barely any information about them at all. Though Valadés disparaged the original inhabitants of New Spain in his *Rhetorica Christiana*, some of the observations and images that he had taken from authentic sources were meant to give an impression of direct acquaintance with Mexican society and traditions: the author made the most of his humanist learning to belie the superficial quality of his local knowledge. In contrast, Cabrera recounted in detail a specific encounter with an indigenous group, even though the language

[130] Vernacular manuals for preachers (e.g. the *Rhetorica en lengua castellana* of 1540 by Miguel de Salinas, and Juan Bernal Díaz de Luco's *Aviso de curas muy provechoso* of 1545, both published in Alcalá) did not circulate in New Spain. The dominance of Latin in education meant that such works in Spanish were of less practical value: Mack 2011, 282–5.

[131] See Chapter 5 and Chapter 8 below.

[132] MARTYR, *De orbe novo* (1516–1532) was popular. For more examples, cf. Rowe 1965; Elliott 1970; Chiappelli 1976; González Rodríguez 1981; Todorov 1984; Grafton, Shelford, and Siraisi 1992; Greenblatt 1991, 1993; Kupperman 1995; Lupher 2003.

and tenor of this firsthand testimony were largely constituted by echoes of classical texts.

The rhetorical treatises surveyed above can be contrasted with a more practical work of missionary literature published toward the end of the sixteenth century by the Jesuit orator and historian José de Acosta, who had been rector of the College of San Pablo in Lima. This ambitious study, often known as the *De procuranda Indorum salute* (1588), combined a human geography of Peru and Mexico with recommendations for preaching and ministry in the Americas—a combination signalled by its full title: 'Two books on the nature of the New World and promulgating the Gospel among foreigners, and six books on securing the Indians' salvation.' Acosta's classical erudition was impressive, but he questioned the value of ancient authorities such as Aristotle, Pliny, and Plato for a proper understanding of the New World, and resisted the temptation to draw specious analogies between the pagans of Greco-Roman antiquity and American peoples. Rather, he urged missionaries to learn about the Indians' languages and beliefs in order to secure their conversion and, in his subsequent *Historia natural y moral de las Indias* (1590), he emphasized that the many native societies differed in their qualities and achievements.[133]

José de Acosta did not rehearse the standard parts and divisions of classical rhetoric for preaching. Instead, he recommended a simple style of speaking, encouraged missionaries to be persistent, and urged them to set an example of virtuous behaviour, simply because their preaching would not always be understood. The technical apparatus of rhetoric was, after all, of little help when it came to addressing native congregations who knew neither Spanish nor Latin. The principles of Renaissance grammar proved far more directly useful: with modifications, they could be successfully applied to learning the native tongues that the missionaries needed to master.

[133] ACOSTA, *Historia natural y moral* (1590), Book 6 [2003, 373–417].

3

Between Babel and Utopia

Renaissance Grammar and Amerindian Languages

In a letter he wrote from Mexico City in 1529 to the Franciscan community in Flanders, Fray Pedro de Gante revealed that he had lost his command of Flemish:

> I wanted to write many things to you about this country in which we are now living; but I am short of time and memory. A very great hindrance is that I have now utterly forgotten my native language; so that I do not have sufficient ability to write to you in it in accord with my wishes—and if I wrote in the Indian tongue, you would not understand me. I have got to know a little Spanish though, in which, as far as I am able, I will convey a few things to you.[1]

Another Franciscan in New Spain, Fray Cristóbal Cabrera, would apologize to Juana de Zúñiga, Hernán Cortés' wife, for forgetting his own Spanish 'after so much time in lands . . . where the language of the Indians is used more than that of Spanish'.[2] Yet those friars made no suggestion that the experience of living in the Indies had been at all detrimental to their knowledge of Latin, which they constantly employed: it was the language Cabrera generally used in his own writing and it was the language

[1] GANTE, 'Dilectissimi patres fratres et sorores' (1529) [1534, 124v]: 'multa ad vos scribere cuperem de hac regione in qua nunc viuimus, sed tempus & memoria mihi deficiunt. Plurimum etiam me impedit, quod linguam meam vernaculam iam penitus sum oblitus, vt in ea vobis pro desyderio sufficienter scribere non valeam. Et si scripsero lingua Indica, vos me non intellegetis. Hispanicae tamen linguae parum noui, in qua vobis, prout potero, pauca significabo.' This Latin translation was preserved in ZIERIXEENSES, *Chronica compendiosissima* (1534): the Spanish original is lost. Cf. Chapter 1, n. 40 above.

[2] CABRERA, *Flores de consolacion* (1549), vii: 'porque al cabo de tanto tiempo como ha que peregrino por estas tierras y naciones bárbaras, donde se tracta más la lengua de los indios que la Española', discussed in Laird 2019a, 119–22. Cf. Hernández de León-Portilla 2007, 80–1 on the missionaries' linguistic immersion.

Aztec Latin. Andrew Laird, Oxford University Press. © Oxford University Press 2024.
DOI: 10.1093/oso/9780197586358.003.0004

of the Christian texts that Gante was assiduously translating into Nahuatl.[3] It was assumed that Latin could not be forgotten, because it was identified with grammar, *grammatica*, itself.

From late antiquity onwards, Latin, or grammar, had been seen as an artificial medium that had been refined *from* 'natural' and corruptible vernaculars, and it had long been accorded a supraregional and transtemporal universality.[4] The regimen of Latin grammar was consequently applied to the study of other languages—not only European vernaculars, but also Greek, Hebrew, Arabic, and tongues spoken in Asia and the Americas. The importance Latin had for friars in New Spain who sought to learn Nahuatl and other indigenous languages will be explored in this chapter.

After an appraisal of advances in grammar that humanists had made in Europe since the late 1400s (Section I), it will be shown how their methods underpinned the achievements of missionary linguists in the Americas (Section II). Erasmus' interpretation of the Babel story also influenced Franciscans (Section III), as it became apparent that Amerindian tongues were quite unlike Latin, Greek, or Spanish, and possessed intrinsic virtues of their own (Section IV). The latter part of the chapter will highlight ways in which the earliest surviving studies of native languages in New Spain responded to this challenge: Fray Andrés de Olmos' approach to Nahuatl had to diverge from the foundational model of Nebrija's Latin grammar (Section V); and Fray Maturino Gilberti developed a different systematization for Purépecha from the one he employed in his own grammar of Latin (Section VI).

I. Latin and vernacular grammar in Renaissance Europe

Grammar had long been considered as the portal to all the other liberal arts (Figure 3.1), and it was at the heart of Renaissance humanism from its very beginnings in fourteenth-century Italy.[5] Humanists were above all concerned with increasing their pupils' proficiency at writing in a more elegant, classical style of Latin, so their reforms of linguistic study during the fifteenth and sixteenth centuries were not theoretical but pedagogical. The philosophical approaches of standard medieval grammars were rejected. Alexander de Villa Dei's verse *Doctrinale* (1199) or Martin of Dacia's *Modi significandi*, 'Modes of Signifying' (c. 1270), were among

[3] Chapter 1 II above. Gravelle 1988 shows that Italian humanists had preferred Latin to the vernacular for practical reasons. CABRERA, *Escuela de la disciplina* (1567) claimed in the prologue to use the vernacular only 'out of love for the Lord and charity for my Spanish neighbour' ('por amor de nuestro Señor y del prójimo español escribimos en lengua vulgar').

[4] DANTE ALIGHIERI, *De vulgari eloquentia* (1305) 1.9 is the *locus classicus* for this view; cf. Eco 1997, 34–9; Mazzocco 1993. Rizzo 2002 is a revisionist account of Latin's relation to the vernacular.

[5] Kristeller 1990, 113–14; Jensen 1996; Johnson 2000, 23–60.

Figure 3.1 Grammar at the door to the tower of Wisdom, Gregor Reisch, *Margarita philosophica*, Freiburg im Breisgau, 1504, 2v. John Carter Brown Library.

them: they had presented the structure of language as a reflection of logical or even theological principles.[6] The Westphalian humanist Alexander Hegius, or Von Heek, harshly criticized such works in his *Invectiva in modos significandi*, 'Invective against modes of signifying'. Hegius probably penned the *Invectiva* in the mid-1480s, when he was teaching at his school in Deventer in Holland. One of his pupils was Desiderius Erasmus, who would continue the attack on the medieval *modistae* and their disciples:

> The trails they are following show they are men born and trained in a complete state of barbarism. One orders learning the Psalter by heart, another deems that the Latin language can be acquired from the Proverbs of Solomon, another calls you to the clumsiest of authors, Michael the Modist, another to the *Mammetrectus*, another to the *Catholicon*. . .[7]

[6] Cf. Bursill Hall 1971 on medieval speculative grammar. Moss 2003 and Cummings 2009 treat the critiques of Erasmus and other humanists.

[7] ERASMUS, *Antibarbarorum liber* (orig. 1520) [1969, 57–8]: 'Vestigia quibus ipsi sint ingressi commonstrant, homines ex mera barbarie nati, simul et educati. Alius iubet edisci psalterium,

The modists, Erasmus complained, resorted to mysticism rather than proper linguistic method. Johannes Marchesinus' *Mammetrectus* (1470) and Johannes Balbus' *Catholicon* (1460) were printed versions of biblical lexicons widely employed in the Middle Ages: they were no more appropriate as sources for Latin usage than Saint Jerome's workmanlike translation from Hebrew in the Vulgate. 'Michael the Modist' was a derogatory reference to Michel of Marbais, a thirteenth-century philosophical grammarian who had come back into vogue in the 1400s.[8]

Guarino Veronese's *Regulae grammaticales* (c. 1418), on the other hand, eliminated superfluous technical vocabulary, and Lorenzo Valla recommended classical usage in his *Elegantiae linguae Latinae* (1441–1448). Niccolò Perotti's *Rudimenta grammatices* (1473) went further, making a point of citing only examples from ancient Roman authors.[9] Antonio de Nebrija's *Introductiones Latinae* (published as *Introduciones latinas,* c. 1487) which drew from Veronese and Valla, and, in the third redaction of 1495, from Perotti, represented the culmination of what had been achieved in those earlier works.[10] Even so, it was Perotti's grammar that Erasmus recommended in his *De ratione studii*, 'The principle of study' (1511), a short educational manifesto:

> Among the more recent grammarians I see barely any difference to judge, except that Niccolò Perotti seems the most conscientious of them all without verging on pedantry. While I admit that grammatical rules of this sort are necessary, I would like there to be as few as possible, as long as they are good. I have never approved of that mob of educators who hold back their pupils for several years by inculcating such rules in them. A real capacity for faultless speech [in Latin] is best provided by conversation and interaction with others who are speaking correctly, and by the continuous reading of eloquent authors.[11]

alius censet linguam Latinam petendam ex prouerbiis Solomonis, alius uocat ad insulsissimum autorem Michaelem Modistam, alius ad Mammetrectum, alius ad Catholicon.' 'Michael Modista' was lampooned in *Conflictus Thaliae et Barbariei* (c. 1489), an attack on the Latin school at Zwolle attributed to Erasmus.

[8] MARBAIS, *Summa de modis significandi* (c. 1270).

[9] PEROTTI, *Rudimenta grammatices* (1473); Percival 1981; Percival 1989. For the contents, see Appendix 1.1.1 below.

[10] Percival 1996, 108 characterizes Nebrija's *Introductiones* as 'thoroughly Italian'.

[11] ERASMUS, *De ratione studii* (1511), Aii [1971, 114–15]: 'Inter recentiores haud multum uideo discriminis, nisi quod Nicolaus Perottus videtur olim diligentissimus, citra superstitionem tamen. Verum, ut huiusmodi praecepta fateor necessaria, ita uelim esse, quoad fieri possit, quaeque paucissima, modo sint optima. Nec unquam probaui literatorum uulgus, qui pueros in his inculcandis complures annos remorantur. Nam, uera emendate loquendi facultas, optime paratur, cum ex castigate loquentium colloquio, conuictuque, tum ex eloquentium autorum assidua lectione.'

The pedagogical context of Erasmus' verdict could not better illustrate the humanist view that grammar should be a question of good practice rather than a set of theories.[12]

Appropriately enough, the most important innovation in Renaissance linguistic study was not a new concept or idea, but the emergence within Europe of grammars of languages other than Latin. The first examples were the grammars of Greek compiled in Greek by native speakers, which were translated, or composed anew, in Latin for western European scholars. For instance, Manuel Chrysoloras' *Erotemata*, 'Enquiries' (1397), was revised in a bilingual Latin and Greek edition by Guarino (1471). Further Greek grammars by Demetrius Chalcondylas, Theodore Gaza, and Aldus Manutius appeared in Italy during the 1490s and another by Francisco de Vergara, a Spanish humanist who worked on the polyglot version of the Bible at Alcalá de Henares. In Flanders, Nicolas Cleynaerts had also published studies of Greek grammar, as well as a work on Hebrew that succeeded Johannes Reuchlin's pioneering grammar and lexicon, *De rudimentis Hebraicis* (1506).[13]

While Latin had always been necessary for school or university, handbooks to vernaculars were few in number because there was little need for the formal learning of languages like Italian or Spanish. There had been guides to French and Provençal in the Middle Ages, and the Renaissance polymath Leon Battista Alberti attempted a *Regole della lingua fiorentina*, 'Rules of the Florentine tongue' (c. 1450), before Antonio de Nebrija produced the first comprehensive grammar of a vernacular, *Gramatica . . . sobre la lengua castellana* (1492).[14] Unlike the grammars of Latin, Greek, and Hebrew, guides to modern European languages did not normally employ Latin as the vehicular language. Both Alberti's *Regole* and Francesco Fortunio's *Regole grammaticali della volgar lengua* (1516) were in the same 'vulgar tongue' of Italian that they presented, and the first grammars of French were written in English in the late 1520s.[15]

Despite Nebrija's apparent championing of Castilian as the 'companion of empire' in his grammar of Spanish, the work hardly circulated at all.[16] There remained

[12] Applications of Erasmus' linguistic pedagogy in New Spain will be considered below; and cf. Chapter 4, III (i); Chapter 8, IV, (ii).

[13] The Convent of Santiago in Tlatelolco held CLEYNAERTS' *Institutiones ac meditationes in Graecam linguam* (1557), which combined his *Institutiones in linguam Graecam* (1530) and his *Meditationes Graecanicae* (1531). CLEYNAERTS' *Tabula in grammaticen Hebraeam* (1559; orig. 1529) was also in the convent, as well as VERGARA, *De Graecae linguae grammatica* (1537): Mathes 1982, 52, 68. See further n. 132 below.

[14] Percival 1975.

[15] VALENCE, *Introductions in Frensshe* (1528); PALSGRAVE, *Lesclarcissement de la langue françoyse* (1530), was in English despite the title.

[16] NEBRIJA, *Comiença la gramatica* (1492); cf. Asensio 1960; Kagan 1974, 31–61; Pym 2000, 134–64. The Spanish grammar was printed only once: Niederehe 2004, 42 characterizes it as 'una empresa malograda, un fracaso casi total' ('a doomed enterprise, an almost total failure'); cf. Fontán

a common reluctance to use the title of 'grammar' for works that were not about Latin—the application of *grammatica* to a vernacular was seen as a category mistake. Yet the accounts of European languages were grammars in all but name, and set a precedent for the *artes* of Amerindian tongues that missionaries, especially Franciscans, began to produce in abundance from the mid-1500s onward.

II. Humanist models for *artes* and vocabularies of Amerindian languages

On his visit to Spain in 1531, Bishop Juan de Zumárraga informed the royal secretary that the missionaries in Mexico were already using a rough manual of Nahuatl.[17] The chronicler Fray Gerónimo de Mendieta recalled that one of the Franciscan Twelve who came to New Spain in 1524, Fray Francisco Jiménez, 'put the Mexican language and vocabulary into a handbook [*arte*]'.[18] Fray Alonso Rengel compiled another *arte* of Nahuatl, along with a study of Otomí, a very different tongue also spoken in central Mexico.[19] The Spanish word *arte,* meaning in this context 'instruction book' or 'manual', was derived from the Latin *ars,* 'technique', 'skill', which recurred throughout Roman antiquity and the Middle Ages in titles of didactic works: *Ars rhetorica, Ars poetica,* and the like.

Artes of indigenous languages (as well as catechisms and doctrines written in them) proliferated all over the Americas throughout the colonial period. In New Spain, Nahuatl, or 'Mexican', from central Mexico, and Purépecha, 'Tarascan', from Michoacán received particular attention from Franciscan missionaries because both tongues were widely spoken and Nahuatl had been used as a means of communication between different indigenous language groups.[20] Philip II's royal cedula of July 1570 later stipulated that 'all Indians should learn the one language of Mexican which could be learned easily as it was a common tongue ['lengua general']'.[21] Spanish was the vehicular language for *artes* and vocabularies: even Fray Maturino Gilberti, a French speaker and an accomplished Latinist, produced his

Pérez 1986. Percival 1999, 23: 'we have no evidence that his Castilian grammar was ever utilized.' *Pace* Mignolo 1992 and Mignolo 1995, it had no bearing on the Americas: Laird 2018a.

[17] Morales 1993 presents a record of Zumárraga's report on the Franciscans' mastery of Nahuatl from the Archive of the Indies in Seville (AGI Justicia 1006).

[18] MENDIETA, *Historia* (1596) 3.19 [1870, 225].

[19] MENDIETA, *Historia* (1596) 4.44, 5.40 [1870, 550, 661].

[20] CERVANTES DE SALAZAR, *Chronica de la Nueva España* (c. 1566) 1.17 [1971 i, 130–1] identified both Nahuatl and Purépecha as 'lenguas generales'. CRUZ, 'Carta al Emperador' (1550) [1991, 45], had proposed that all Indians learn Nahuatl 'since they already use it and very many confess in it'.

[21] Cited in Heath 1986, 55. 'Lengua general' designated whatever indigenous language appeared to the Spaniards to be the most dominant in a given region: Cobo Betancourt 2014, 124–6.

studies of Purépecha in Spanish.[22] A treatise on the Maya language of Tzeltal by the Dominican Fray Domingo de Ara is the only known sixteenth-century *arte* to have been composed in Latin—although Tzeltal words and lemmas are glossed in Spanish throughout the work.[23]

Nebrija's *Introductiones Latinae* (c. 1487), a Latin grammar that uniquely incorporated a facing translation into Spanish, enabling readers to approach the Latin from their own language, was the model for the *artes* of Amerindian languages produced in Spanish during the 1500s. Fray Andrés de Olmos' *Arte de la lengua mexicana* (1547), Fray Alonso de Molina's *Arte de la lengua mexicana y castellana* (1571), and Fray Antonio del Rincón's *Arte mexicana* (1595)—all make reference to 'el arte de Antonio'. Nebrija's innovative inclusion of a Spanish text, proposed by Isabel of Castile, had made the *Introductiones* an immediate success, and it remained a standard textbook well into the eighteenth century.[24]

For the lexicography of Nahuatl, Nebrija's *Dictionarium* (c. 1495), a Spanish-Latin vocabulary, had an impact equivalent to that of his bilingual *Introductiones Latinae*. A handwritten copy of Nebrija's dictionary (Plate 7), to which an anonymous scribe added a column of corresponding Nahuatl terms, could be the earliest functioning Spanish-Nahuatl vocabulary, although the Nahuatl terms are based on the Latin entries rather than the Spanish ones.[25] Fray Alonso de Molina's *Aqui comiença vn vocabulario enla lengua castellana y mexicana* (1555), the first printed dictionary of Nahuatl, went from Castilian to the Mexican language. A Mexican-Castilian lexicon was later added to supplement the second edition in 1571.[26] As well as Nebrija's dictionary, two other well-known Renaissance vocabularies of Latin, both entirely *in* Latin, circulated in Mexico: Niccolò Perotti's *Cornu copiae* (1489), a glossary of every word in the poet Martial, that did double duty as a thesaurus of Latin, and Ambrogio Calepino's *Dictionarium* (1502), also based on reliable classical authorities.[27] The latter prompted Fray Bernardino de Sahagún to

[22] GILBERTI, *Arte de la lengua de Michuacan* (1558); *Vocabulario en lengua de Mechuacan* [*sic*] (1559).

[23] ARA, *Ars tzeldaica* (1560) [1983]. A fuller text of the *Ars* is in ARA, *Egregium opus* (1560).

[24] Pym 2000, 134–7. The Spanish title, *Introduciones latinas contrapuesto el romance al latin*, 'Introductions in Latin, with the Romance placed opposite the Latin', accords as much status to the Spanish translation as to the Latin. The Royal Council of Castile of 1598 ordered that no other Latin grammar be used: Esperabé de Artega 1914 i, 631; Kagan 1974, 3; and Codoñer and González Iglesias 1994.

[25] The copy was based on a later edition, *Vocabulario de romance en latín*: Hamann 2015, 47 identifies a 1520 Seville printing as the source. See further Chapter 5, I (ii) below.

[26] MOLINA, *Aqui comiença vn vocabulario* (1555) [2001]; *Vocabulario en lengua castellana y mexicana y mexicana y castellana* (1571) [2013].

[27] PEROTTI, *Cornu copiae* (1489), which went through more than thirty-six editions, also served as a Latin dictionary, even after being superseded by CALEPINO, *Dictionarium* (1502): Pade 2005. Entries on languages other than Latin were only incorporated in editions of Calepino after 1545: Labarre 1975.

lament that there had been no opportunity to compile a Nahuatl 'Calepino'—a lexicon of words with their meaning drawn from real sources.[28]

The first missionaries to preach or write in Nahuatl were Juan de Aora, Juan de Tecto and Pedro de Gante, the Franciscans who came to New Spain from Flanders in 1524.[29] Their approach to language may well have been informed by the Flemish humanist Johannes Despauter, or Jan de Spauteren, who had been teaching in Leuven for some time before his progressive grammatical works were published in the early 1500s.[30] The importance of Erasmus for Fray Alonso de Molina and Fray Maturino Gilberti will be considered in the next section, and the latter evidently knew Niccolò Perotti's *Rudimenta grammatices* as well.[31] Gilberti's successor as a grammarian and lexicographer of Purépecha, Fray Juan Baptista de Lagunas, used Nebrija and Calepino as models respectively for his *Arte y dictionario con otras obras en lengua michuacana* (1574).[32] Such debts make clear that the missionaries were imbued with humanist rather than scholastic methods in their approach to language, no less than in their approach to philosophy and rhetoric.[33]

In the decade after Erasmus' death, Julius Caesar Scaliger renewed medieval attempts to follow Aristotle by grounding grammar on the principles of philosophy in his *De causis linguae Latinae,* 'The bases of the Latin language' (1540). The later work of Franciscus Sanctius, or Francisco Sánchez de las Brozas, sometimes known as 'el Brocense', was in a similar vein. In his *Minerva seu de causis linguae Latinae,* 'Minerva, or the bases of the Latin language' (1587), Sanctius had maintained that the tripartite division of parts of speech into nouns, verbs, and particles was universal and to be found in all languages.[34] But although these studies appeared in the sixteenth century, they were not diffused in the Americas, where the less schematic thinking of Erasmus and Juan Luis Vives held sway.[35] In contrast to Sanctius and his intellectual successors (including the Cartesian Jesuits of Port-Royal), the missionary linguists in New Spain did not subscribe to a notion of 'universal grammar'.[36]

[28] SAHAGÚN, *Historia general* = *HG* (c. 1580), Book 1 'Al sincero lector' [1982 i, 50].

[29] Cf. Chapter 1, II above.

[30] Sandys 1908 ii, 212. DESPAUTER, *Commentarii grammatici* (1536) incorporated *Orthographiae isagoge* (1510), *Rudimenta* (1512), and *Syntaxis* (1515). The *Commentarii* circulated in New Spain: Osorio Romero 1980, 29–30.

[31] Laird 2012, 60; cf. Chapter 4, III (i) below.

[32] Monzón 2009; 2012.

[33] Cf. Chapter 4, Section III below.

[34] SANCTIUS, *Minerva* (1587) 1.1–1.2 [1995, 38–53]. SANCTIUS, *Verae breuesque grammatices Latinae institutiones* (1562), 'Genuine short lessons in Latin grammar', was an earlier, different book.

[35] Read 1980.

[36] ARNAULD and LANCELOT, *Grammaire générale et raisonnée* (1660) became known as the 'Port-Royal Grammar'. Padley 1985–1988 i, 298–300 examines the influence of the medieval modists (cf. Section I above) on early modern 'universal' grammarians.

III. Erasmus' interpretation of Babel and the confusion of tongues

Universal grammar, the postulation of a rational structure common to all languages, is not the same as a universal language. Conceptions of the latter emerged from debates that began in Christian antiquity about the identity of the Adamic language, which was thought to have been spoken before Babel and the ensuing 'confusion of tongues'. The Book of Genesis related that the earth had originally been 'of one tongue and of the same speech'. But after Noah's sons set about constructing, from bricks and bitumen, a city and a tower to reach heaven, God decided to 'confound their tongue, that they may not understand one another's speech . . . and scattered them abroad upon the face of all countries'.[37] In his interpretation of that episode, Saint Augustine had affirmed that there were seventy-two languages in the world, corresponding to the number of descendants of Noah, each of whom must have founded a nation with its own language.[38]

The Jesuit missionary José de Acosta, aware of the numerous languages spoken in Peru, did not agree. Without contradicting Augustine openly, he presented the great theologian's view as if it were a mistaken common opinion: 'They say that long ago the human race was thrown into confusion by seventy-two languages.' In Acosta's view the real number would have had to be much larger:

> These people, with seven hundred languages or more, sound different from one other, so that there is hardly an inhabited valley of any size which does not have its own mother tongue.[39]

Other missionaries used the Babel legend to account for, or simply to convey, the daunting number of languages spoken by the native populations in the Americas.[40]

[37] Genesis 11:1–9.

[38] Augustine, *De civitate Dei* 16.3. SCALIGER (the younger), *Diatriba de Europaeorum linguis* (1599) propagated the view that contemporary languages were descended from a few 'matrices'. The number of matrix languages was debated as well as the number of those currently spoken: Cram 2013, 44–56.

[39] ACOSTA, *De procuranda Indorum salute* (1588) 1.2 [1984 i, 92]: 'Ferunt olim septuaginta duabus linguis confusum esse genus mortalium. At hi septingentis et amplius inter se discrepant, ut vix vallis habitetur paulo latior, quae non sua materna lingua gaudeat.' Cf. ACOSTA, *Historia natural y moral* (1590) 7.28, and VIEIRA, *Sermão da Epifania* (1662) [1940, 378]: 'na Babel do rio das Amazonas já se conhecem mais de cento e cinqüenta [línguas], tão diversas entre si como a nosse e a grega' ('in the Babel of the river Amazon more than 150 languages are now known, as different from each other as our own [Portuguese] is from Greek.').

[40] Burkhart 1986 suggests that the linguistic challenges faced by the Franciscans in New Spain may account for repeated references to the tower of Babel in the Nahuatl hymns in SAHAGÚN, *Psalmodia Christiana* (1583): cf. Chapter 5 below.

Some in New Spain even found indigenous parallels to the biblical story: the Mexican creation myth, with which Fray Diego Durán began his *Historia de las Indias de Nueva España* (c. 1581), has the celestial gods routing the giants who had also used bricks and bitumen to build a tower to reach up to heaven.[41] The seventeenth-century chronicler Fernando de Alva Ixtlilxochitl would hold that the Toltecs had suffered their own confusion of tongues and were scattered abroad, after building a *zacuali*, or 'very tall tower'.[42] There is also a lighthearted elaboration on the theme of Babel and Pentecost (when the Holy Spirit enabled the Apostles to speak 'with other tongues') in an *imprimatur* commending Horacio Carochi's *Arte de la lengua mexicana* (1645): if the church father Origen had been right to hold that one angel was needed for each language conferred on an apostle at Pentecost, then Carochi must have had two angels at his disposal, because he had mastered Otomí as well as Nahuatl.[43]

Saint Augustine had further concluded that Hebrew was the original common language before Babel, and that it had been preserved by the family of Heber.[44] That conclusion was endorsed by Dante, and earlier by Isidore of Seville, who regarded Latin, Greek, and Hebrew as the three 'sacred tongues' because they were used in the inscription on Christ's cross.[45] There were comparable speculations in Renaissance Spain: Juan Luis Vives, whose edition of Augustine's works was prepared at Erasmus' behest, hinted that the contrast between the primordial language of Adam and the confusion of tongues was paralleled by Latin's relation to the vernacular; and Pedro Mexía wrote about Babel in a chapter of his popular encyclopaedia *Silva de varia lección* (1540).[46] One or two humanists elsewhere in Europe were trying to prove that all languages were descended from Hebrew.[47]

The quest for a lost originary tongue never troubled Erasmus, who was shrewd enough to realize that the search for a universal language was often connected with

[41] DURÁN, *Historia* (c. 1581) 1.1 [2002 i, 58].

[42] ALVA IXTLILXOCHITL, *Sumaria relación de todas las cosas* (c. 1603), cap. 1, 'Relación de la creación del mundo' [1975 i, 263]. Máynez 2008 draws from other sources to examine indigenous conceptions of Babel in early colonial Mexico.

[43] Don Bartolomé de Alba, 'Aprobación', in CAROCHI, *Arte* (1645), 8–9. Alba next quotes, from Cassiodorus, *Variae epistolae* 8.21, the words of Theodoric, the Ostrogothic conqueror of Rome: 'boys of Roman stock speak in our tongue, eminently showing that they want to display their future loyalty to us, whose speech they already appear to have made their own.'

[44] Augustine, *De civitate Dei* 16.5, 16.10–11; Josephus, *Antiquitates Judaicae* 1.116–19.

[45] DANTE ALIGHIERI, *De vulgari eloquentia* (c. 1305) 1.6; Isidore, *Etymologies* 9.1.1.

[46] VIVES, *De tradendis disciplinis* (1531) 3.1 [1913, 91–2]. MEXÍA, *Silva de varia lección* (1540) 1.24, 3.32. Mexía's work was in the College of Santa Cruz in Tlatelolco: Appendix 1.3, item [10] below.

[47] POSTEL, *De originibus* (1538); the Protestant orientalist BIBLIANDER, *De ratione communi omnium linguarum* (1548), held that Hebrew was the direct product of the Holy Spirit. Aramaic also enjoyed currency as the Adamic language after Giovambattista Gelli championed a fraudulent work, VITERBO, *Antiquitates* (1498), as propaganda for the Medici: Moyer 2020, 29–70. Annius of Viterbo's forged text of Berosus was cited by Las Casas: Chapter 2, n. 27.

the business of promoting one or another vernacular, often for political reasons.[48] In his *Lingua*, 'Tongue' (1525), Erasmus used Babel as a symbol of the divisions and confusions of the time, which he attributed to pride:

> But today, as we see the schools of the philosophers disputing with so many opinions, and all Christians fighting it out with so many conflicting dogmas, are we not recalling the construction of the tower of Babel? What harmony can exist among those who are so carried away when no one is giving way to anyone else? . . . Where then does such confusion of tongues and minds amongst us come from, if not from presumptuousness? Why do we not adhere to one stock, since we are tendrils of the same vine, and are one with ourselves, just as we are joined to Christ? . . . Why do we not now stop building this tower of Babel, this tower of pride and discord, and begin to rebuild Jerusalem and the fallen temple of the Lord?[49]

The new language needed to unify mankind had to be that of the Gospel itself: during Pentecost, when the apostles had begun to speak with diverse tongues, they did so 'with one accord, for they had one heart and one spirit, because one spirit had filled them all'. In his *Exhortatio ad studium euangelicae lectionis*, 'Exhortation to studious reading of the Gospel', first published in 1516 to preface his edition of the New Testament, Erasmus had expressed a desire for the Gospel and Paul's Epistles to be translated into 'the tongues of all men, so that they might not only be read and known by Scots and Irishmen but also by Turks and Saracens'.[50]

The *Lingua* more explicitly connected religion, philology, and politics, and the theological approach to language in this engaging text had an enduring role in shaping sixteenth-century thought.[51] Erasmus insisted that precision and standardization of usage and pronunciation in every language were essential for the promulgation of the faith. The *Lingua* was popular in Spain, and a vernacular translation was published in Toledo by Bernardo Pérez de Chinchón in 1533. Erasmus himself attached high value to Greek and Latin, urging that princes should encourage

[48] Eco 1997, 34–72. Cf. discussions of Nebrija's claims for Castilian cited in n. 16 above.

[49] ERASMUS, *Lingua* (1525), 343–4, 345 [1989, 174–5]: 'Hodie uero quum videmus tot opinionibus dissidere scholas philosophorum, tot dogmatibus tamque diuersis digladiari Christianos omnes, nonne referimus structuram turris Babel? Inter elatos qui potest constare concordia, ubi nemo concedit alteri? . . .Vnde igitur inter nos tanta linguarum & animorum confusio, nisi ex arrogantia? Quur non potius in una stirpe, ut sumus eiusdem uitis palmites, & unum sumus inter nos quemadmodum Christo iungimur? . . . Quin desinimus extruere turrim Babel, turrim superbiae ac dissensionis, & incipimus instaurare Hierosolymam, ac templum domini collapsum?'

[50] ERASMUS, *Paraclesis* (1516), aaa4v: 'Atque vtinam haec in omnes omnium linguas essent transfusa, vt non solum a Scotis et hybernis, sed a Turcis quoque et Saracenis legi cognoscique possint.' See further Bataillon 1937 [2007, 134–41, 192].

[51] Egido 1998; cf. Dubois 1970, 13–14; 1985.

the teaching of those languages because the vernacular gospel was a short-term solution—but Pérez de Chinchón's preface also exalted Castilian—a principle borne out by the playful title of his Spanish version: 'The tongue of Erasmus freshly put into Romance in a most elegant style'.

Some early missionary linguists in New Spain adopted Erasmus' view that the episode of Babel illustrated the confusion and conflict caused by human pride. They also shared his view that the story had contemporary implications: it was relevant to the society in which they found themselves and to the challenge of evangelization. In the opening sentence of his Spanish-Nahuatl vocabulary of 1555, Fray Alonso de Molina stated, 'It is very manifest to all who have any understanding of holy scripture and divine letters how punishable according to natural law and scripture, and how reprehensible in the law of grace is the sin of pride.'[52] Molina's Prologue then relayed a succession of accounts from Flavius Josephus' *Antiquities of the Jews* and the Old Testament to illustrate this point. After relating the downfall of the Jewish kings Saul and Rehoboam and of the Assyrian ruler Sennacherib, as well as the expulsion of Adam and Eve, the friar continued,

> Then, after the Flood, over all the earth no more than one tongue was spoken, through which all men could deal with, communicate, and understand one another. Such great pride ruled in the hearts of the men that they decided to celebrate and aggrandize their name, by contriving a way for perpetual memory of them to remain, and to that end they attempted to construct a tower that would reach to heaven. God, on seeing such folly, was minded to take them to hand, and punish a pride so great as this with a very harsh and severe punishment, namely the confusion and division of tongues.[53]

Molina had no interest in identifying the world's ancestral language: like Erasmus, he was concerned with the moral significance of the confusion of tongues in the Babel story as God's punishment for pride and (recalling Josephus) folly.[54] Molina

[52] MOLINA, *Aqui comiença vn vocabulario* (1555), aii recto: 'Muy manifiesto es a todos los q*ue* de la sagrada escriptura y diuinas letras tienen alguna inteligencia, qua*n* castigado ayasido de dios e*n* la ley de naturaleza y de scriptura y qua*n* repreh*en*dido enla ley de gracia el pecado dela sobervia.' MOLINA, *Vocabulario* (1571) had the same Prologue.

[53] MOLINA, *Aqui comiença un vocabulario* (1555), a ii verso: 'Luego despues del diluuio en toda la tierra no se hablaua mas de vna lengua, en la qual todos se tratauan, comunicauan, y entendian. Reyno entonces en los coraçones de los hombres tan gran soberuia, que determinaron de celebrar y engra*n*decer su nombre, de arte que quedasse dellos memoria perpetua: y para este fin inte*n*taron de hazer vna torre, que llegasse al cielo. Viendo dios tan gran desatino, acordo de yrles ala mano, y castigar vna soberuia tan grande como esta con muy aspero y riguroso castigo: y esta fue la confussion y diuission de las lenguas.'

[54] Josephus, *Antiquitates Judaicae* 1.116: 'οὕτως δὲ μεμηνότας αὐτοὺς ὁρῶν ὁ θεός' ('when God saw them acting so madly').

also emulated Erasmus in drawing attention to the social need for linguistic proficiency—by emphasizing the importance of language in political and judicial spheres. He outlined the difficulties faced by natives in court if they are dependent on the good or bad will of an interpreter, and he described the relief felt in Spain once the king, Charles (a native Flemish speaker), had begun to speak Castilian without needing a translator.

The theme of good government recurred in the cautionary tales of biblical kings that formed part of Alonso de Molina's Prologue. If, in the temporal realm, it was beneficial for rulers to be understood by the natives, how much more necessary it was in the spiritual realm, where nothing less than the salvation or perdition of souls was at stake? It was vital for a preacher to have a profound understanding of whatever language he used:

> To declare the mysteries of our Faith, it is not enough to know the tongue as one would wish, but to understand well the properties of terms and the ways they are used in speech, since deficiency in this could cause preachers of the truth to end up as preachers of error and falsity. For this reason (among many others) the Holy Spirit was granted to the Apostles on the Day of Pentecost in a diversity of tongues so that they could all be understood.[55]

Fray Alonso de Molina's opinions replicated those of Erasmus on language, theology, and society. In the bidirectional *Vocabulario* he published sixteen years later, the missionary's dedicatory letter to the viceroy Martín Enríquez elaborated upon the relation of language to Christian kingship and the body politic.[56]

Fray Maturino Gilberti also took up Erasmus' moral interpretation of Babel. In the lengthy dedication of his *Arte de la lengua de Michuacan* (1558) to the bishop of Michoacán, Vasco de Quiroga, Gilberti recalled 'the confused and rightly punished pride of those in former times who had *built* ['edificaron'] the necessity for erudition in various languages'.[57] The only remedy for that, Gilberti maintained, was devotion to the assiduous work of compiling *artes* and vocabularies: 'By this path of humility, the quality of once common speech ['comun eloquio'], of which arrogant

[55] MOLINA, *Aqui comiença un vocabulario* (1555), aiii: 'Y para declararles los mysterios de nuestra Fee, no basta saber la lengua, como quiera, sino entender bien las propriedad delos vocablos y maneras de hablar que tienen: pues por falta desto podria acaecer, q*ue* avie*n*do de ser predicadores de verdad, lo fuessen de error y de falsedad. Por esta causa [entre otras muchas] fue dado el Sp*iritum* s*an*cto alos Apostoles el dia de pe*n*tecostes, e*n* diuersidad de le*n*guas: paraq*ue* fuessen de todos e*n*te*n*didos.'

[56] MOLINA, *Vocabulario* (1571), 2r ('Epistola nuncupatoria').

[57] GILBERTI, *Arte* (1558), 1v [2004, 58]: 'Grave yugo y laborioso trabajo es impuesto, ilustre reverendissimo señor, sobre todos los hijos de Adam desde los dias de su nascimiento, dize el Ecclesiastico, y entre otros, este particular nos dexo la sobervia de aquellos que primero y postrero edificaron, conviene a saber, la necessidad de la erudicion de varias lenguas.'

pride deprived us, may be restored.' Not only was this objective redolent of the prescriptions for an evangelical *eloquium commune* in Erasmus' *Lingua*—so too was Gilberti's sense of a direct connection between the collective utopian ideal and obligations of an individual scholar:

> Wanting to be a participant myself in work on that new edifice (since I do not exempt myself from the common inheritance of the crime committed by our ancestors, as it is true we are descended from one first father), I have applied diligence to the composition of this *arte* and to translating this Spanish word list into the language of Michoacán, and from that language into Spanish, for the common utility of those who, to a good end and out of the zeal described above, should wish to research it, whose principal endeavour was solely the service of God.[58]

In the Latin grammar he published in 1559, Fray Maturino Gilberti openly expressed his admiration for Erasmus, drawing many examples from his *Colloquia familiaria* and other educational writings on Latin.[59] Gilberti's *Dialogo de doctrina cristiana* composed in Purépecha, or 'Tarascan', had also appeared earlier in 1559.[60]

The timing was unfortunate: in that same year Spain's General Inquisitor prohibited several works by Erasmus, including both the *Lingua* and the *Colloquia*.[61] And in December of 1559, Vasco de Quiroga petitioned the archbishop of Mexico to restrict circulation of Gilberti's Purépecha dialogue on Christian doctrine on the suspicion that 'Lutheran' views were advanced in the text. It was not until 1576 that the Holy Office of Mexico allowed the *Dialogo* to circulate.[62] The real basis for Quiroga's misgivings about the work is not clear, but it incorporated extensive translations of

[58] GILBERTI, *Arte* (1558), 2r [2004, 58]: 'y sobre dicho edificio de qual trabajo queriendo yo ser participante (pues tampoco me eximo de la comun herencia del crimen cometido por nuestros antecesores, siendo verdad que de un primer padre descendimos todos) puse diligencia en componer esta arte y traduzir esto dictionario de lengua española en lengua de Michuacan, y la de Michuacan en la española, por la comun utilidad de los que a buen fin y zelo sobredicho investigarla quisieren, cuyo principal intento solo que sea Dios servido en lo bueno todo.'

[59] On debts to Erasmus in GILBERTI, *Grammatica* (1559), see below and Chapter 4, III (i) below.

[60] García Icazbalceta 1954, 152–5 gives details. Warren 1994 is an annotated chronology of Gilberti's life and works.

[61] VALDÉS Y SALAS, *Cathalogus librorum* (1559), 44 (the pages are misnumbered). Other indexed works by Erasmus were *Moria encomium* ('Praise of Folly'), *Modi orandi Deum, Exomologesis, Encheiridion, Ecclesiastes, Explicatio Symboli sive Catechismus, Prologus in Hilarii opera, De sarcienda ecclesiae concordia, Christiani matrimonii institutio, De interdicto esu carnium, Censura super tertiam regulam Augustini, Methodus,* and *Dulcoratio.* Henderson 2007, 162–4 discusses the prohibition of Erasmus in the Indices of 1557 and 1559.

[62] QUIROGA, 'Petición' (1559); the Mexican inquisitors, *licenciados* ÁVALOS and BONILLA, 'Carta del Santo Oficio' (1576), approved the *Dialogo,* adding that there had been 'resentment' ('envidias') of Gilberti as a foreigner from Bologna.

Epistles and Gospels into Purépecha. The rendering of scripture into vernaculars was now controversial, for all that Erasmus had regarded it as a means of healing division and promoting the Christian message.[63]

However that may be, the charges against Gilberti indicate the pertinence of Erasmus' interpretation of Babel as a cautionary tale about schism and conflict. Some historians have recognized the importance of the Dutch humanist's opinions on Christian living, evangelism, and pedagogy for the religious orders and even the secular authorities in New Spain.[64] Much less attention has been paid to the ways in which Erasmus' approaches to language determined the specific methods as well as the motivations of Franciscans who engaged with Nahuatl and other Amerindian tongues.[65]

IV. Latin and the *artes* of Amerindian languages

As Latin was equated with grammar itself, missionaries naturally relied on its paradigms in their approach to the languages they encountered in the New World. A modern commentator has pointed out, with some justification, that their 'grammars' constituted a 'set of actions and strategies . . . employed to (re)organize and (re)arrange the languages of native communities'. There is, however, abundant evidence to counter the same writer's ensuing avowal that 'in grammar after grammar of Amerindian languages written during the sixteenth and seventeenth centuries, the authors took for granted that Latin was a universal linguistic system'.[66]

First, it is clear that the missionary linguists' approach resembled that of the more pragmatic Renaissance grammarians, particularly Nebrija, and not that of the medieval modists. It was noted above that the revival of universalist theories, spearheaded by Franciscus Sanctius, came too late to have any effect on the *artes* of Amerindian languages in the 1500s, and his approach had little subsequent impact in New Spain.[67] Second, numerous testimonies in the *artes* show that their

[63] Cf. García Icazbalceta 1954, 155. Translations of biblical texts into native languages remained in manuscript: Chapter 5, III below.

[64] Bataillon 1932; 1937 [2007]; Ricard 1933; Laird 2017a; Laird 2017b; Laird 2019b; Egido 1998. Roest 2004 treats early Franciscan responses to Erasmus. Cf. Chapters 1, 2, 4, and 8.

[65] The collection of Nahuatl adages and apothegms to cultivate *copia* in the language in SAHAGÚN, *HG*, Book 6 (1577) illustrates this: cf. Chapter 8, IV (ii) below. The translation of Aesop into Nahuatl (Chapter 7 below) may have been connected with the educational value Erasmus attached to the fables: Regier 2019.

[66] Mignolo 1992, 304–5. Hernández de León-Portilla 1988 i, 3–48 shows how Amerindian languages were transformed by alphabetization.

[67] *Pace* Breva Claramonte 2008, Nebrija held sway: Osorio Romero 1980, 11–12, 28. As SANCTIUS, *Minerva* (1587), 266v–271v [1995, 672–80] opposed spoken Latin, Jesuit educators in New Spain preferred ÁLVAREZ, *De institutione grammatica* (1572), which was printed twice in Mexico City.

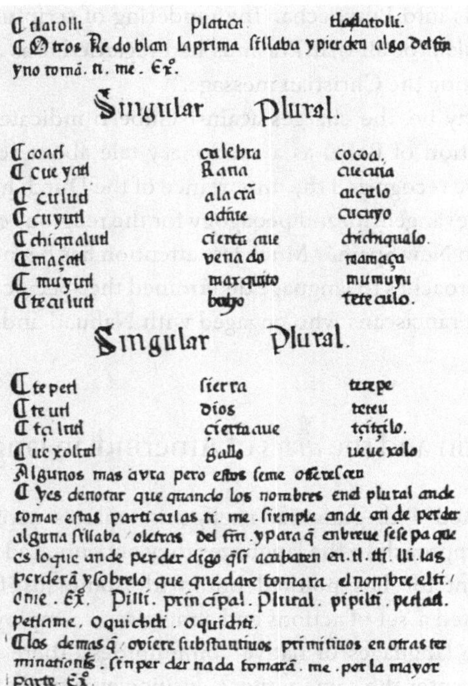

¶ tlatolli platica tlatlatolli.
¶ Otros redoblan la prima sillaba y pierden algo del fin y no tomá. ti. me. Ex.º

Singular Plural.

¶ coatl	culebra	cocoa.
¶ cueyatl	Rana	cuecueya
¶ culuctl	alacrã	cuculo
¶ cuyutl	adiue	cucuyo
¶ chiquatlutl	cierta aue	chichiqualo.
¶ maçatl	venado	mamaça
¶ muyutl	maxquito	mumuyu
¶ tecalutl	buho	tetecalo.

Singular Plural.

¶ tepetl	sierra	tetepe
¶ teutl	dios	teteu
¶ tçalutl	çierta aue	tçitçilo.
¶ uexolotl	gallo	ueuexolo

Algunos mas avra pero estos se me offrescen
¶ Yes denotar que quando los nombres end plural ande tomar estas particulas ti. me. siemple ande an de perder alguna sillaba o letras del fin. y para q̃ en breue se sepa que es lo que ande perder digo q̃ si acabaren en. tl. tli. lli. las perderã y sobrelo que quedare tomara el nombre el ti. o me. Ex. Pilli. principal. Plural. pipilti. petlatl. petlame. oquichtli. oquichti.
¶ los demas q̃ oviere substantiuos primitiuos en otras terminationes. sin perder nada tomarã. me. por la mayor parte. Ex.º

Figure 3.2 Fray Andrés de Olmos, *Arte de la lengua mexicana*, Mexico, 1547, 32r. Biblioteca Nacional de España.

authors did not believe that the system of Latin was common to all languages. In the opening chapter of his seminal *Arte de la lengua mexicana* (1547) (Figure 3.2), Fray Andrés de Olmos recognized that Nahuatl lacked many categories that were conspicuous in Latin: 'inflections, supines, and the types of words to denote the diversity of them . . . accents and other subjects do not bear on this tongue.'[68] The friar made clear that the very way he organized his exposition of Nahuatl had been determined by its distinctive nature:

> First, the conjugation [of the verb] is set out not as it is in [Latin] grammar, but as the language requires and demands, because it does not have some manners of expression we have in our own language or in Latin, and it seems to me that it will cause confusion not to depart from the principles of Latin conjugation, putting some moods in tenses that they do not fit, as

[68] OLMOS, *Arte de la lengua mexicana* (1547), = *Arte*, 1.1, 23r [2002, 15]: 'como son declinationes, supinos y las especies de los verbos para denotar la diuersidad de ellos'. The term 'declinationes' evokes general changes of form, not only 'declension'.

> will be apparent in the conjugation of verbs, so this new style will not strike anyone as being without its advantages . . . [69]

Latin did not serve Olmos as a benchmark against which phenomena of the object language could be measured. Instead, he invoked Latin and Castilian in order to highlight what was *different* about Nahuatl, which in the end had to be explained in terms of its own linguistic behaviour.

Fray Alonso de Molina was just as aware of the pitfalls of depending on Latin grammar to order Nahuatl in his *Arte de la lengua mexicana* (1571), although he kept to the general scheme of Nebrija's *Introductiones Latinae*.[70] In his *Arte mexicana* (1595), the Jesuit Antonio del Rincón used Latin terms as points of reference far more frequently than Olmos or Molina because he assumed his readers were familiar with them: 'In whatever way it is possible to make use of Latin grammar I will always be hugging it close.'[71] 'But', he continued, 'in the other respects in which the present language differentiates itself from Latin, because they involve new things, it has been necessary to reduce those to new rules, with the new style that is required.' Although claims that Rincón was himself descended from native speakers of Nahuatl are unfounded, he was well aware that the autochthonous tongues of Mexico were profoundly different from one another.[72] He opposed the application of one standardized approach to teaching them:

> It is not possible to keep wholly to the same method and technique in teaching all the languages, being, as they are, so distant and different from one another. Uniformity in this would be a great deformity that would

[69] OLMOS, *Arte*, Part 2, Prologue, 44r [2002, 59]: 'Primeramente se porna la conjugacion, no como en la gramatica, pero sino como la lengua lo pide y demanda, porque algunas maneras de dezir que nosotros tenemos en nuestra lengua, o en latina, esta no las tiene. Y pareceme que sera confusion, por no salir de la conjugacion del latin, poner algunos romances en tiempos que no les pueden cuadrar, como parecera en la conjugacion de los verbos, por tanto a ninguno le parezca nouedad sin prouecho, pues se dara en la formacion la causa dello.'

[70] MOLINA, *Arte de la lengua mexicana y castellana* (1571b).

[71] RINCÓN, *Arte mexicana* (1595), 'Prólogo al lector' [1885, 11–12]. Rincón's heavy use of Latin made for a macaronic style: e.g. at 12: 'En lugar de *hic, haec, hoc* usan, *inin,* v.g. *inincalli, haec domus;* en lugar de *iste,* usan *inon* v.g. *inoncalli ista domus. ille, illa, illud,* no le tienen propriamente. Usan de circumloqucion, diziendo *in nechcaca,* lo que esta alli. En lugar de *qui, quae, quod,* usan de este relativo, *in,* indeclinable, v.g. *intlaqua, qui comedit.*'

[72] ANTONIO, *Bibliotheca Hispana nova* (1672) [1788 i, 158] called Rincón 'Americanus' because he was born in New Spain. PÉREZ DE RIBAS, *Historia de los triunfos* (1645), stated that Rincón was 'of noble blood', from which FLORENCIA, *Historia . . . de la Compañía de Jesús de Nueva España* (1694) 3.8 inferred his descent from the native kings of Texcoco: cf. EGUIARA Y EGUREN, *Bibliotheca Mexicana* (1755), 265 col. 2: 'Hispano traxit sanguine à genitore, nobiliorem maternum junxit a Regiâ Texcucanorum stirpe ductum'. That confusion has led scholars (e.g. Guzmán Betancourt 2002) to assume that the Jesuit was indigenous or mestizo.

consequently lead to confusion and trouble for whoever might learn them.[73]

That is in line with the precept of Vives that 'no language is so copious and varied that it can respond throughout to the figures and conformations of another, even a very inarticulate one'.[74] But, needless to say, Rincón's pedagogical principle was not at all in accord with the view, being revived in Europe at the time, that all languages shared a common underlying system or *ratio*.

Those who have sought to attribute such universalism to the missionary linguists of the 1500s regularly invoke Fray Domingo de Santo Tomás' *Grammatica o Arte de la lengua general de los Indios de los reynos del Peru*, 'Grammar or *Arte* of the common language of the Indians in the realms of Peru' (1560).[75] Santo Tomás' prologue, addressed to Philip II of Spain, gave this assurance to the king about the Andean language of Quechua:

> [It is] a language so in agreement with Latin and Spanish in its design and structure that it really looks as if [it] were something preordained that the Spaniards would possess it. A language then, Your Majesty, so polished and rich, regulated and enclosed within the rules and precepts of Latin as this is, as the present *Arte* confirms, is not 'barbarous', which means (according to Quintilian and other Latin sources) full of barbarisms and defects and without moods, tenses, cases, order, rule or harmony, but rather it can be deemed very polished and refined.[76]

Yet that 'Prologue to his Sacred Majesty' was immediately followed by a second prologue that is nowadays overlooked—the 'Prologue to the Christian Reader' was more realistic: 'This language of Peru [is] so weird, so new, so unfamiliar and so

[73] RINCÓN, *Arte mexicana* (1595), 'Prólogo al Lector' [1885, 11]: 'No es posible guardarse en todo un mismo methodo y arte, en enseñar todas las lenguas, siendo ellas (como lo son) tan distantes y diferentes entresi, antes la vniformidad en esto seria gran disformidad, y por consiguiente confusion y estoruo para quien les desprendiesse.'

[74] VIVES, *De ratione dicendi* (1533) 3.57 [2017, 408]: 'Nulla est enim adeo copiosa lingua et varia, quae possit per omnia respondere figuris et conformationibus etiam infantissimae.'

[75] Mignolo 1992, 305; Breva Claramonte 2008, 16; Errington 2008, 28.

[76] SANTO TOMÁS, *Grammatica o Arte* (1560), A v verso [1995, 9]: '[Lengua], tan conforme ala latina, y española: y enel arte y artificio della, que no parece sino *que* fue vn pronostico, *que* Españoles la auia*n* de posseer. Lengua pues, S. M, tan polida y abunda*n*te, regulada en encerrada debaxo delas reglas y preceptos dela latina como es esta (como consta por este Arte) no barbara, que quiere dezir (segun Quintilian, y los demas latinos) llena de barbarismos y de defectos, sin modos, tiempos, ni casos, ni orden, ni regla, ni concierto, sino muy polida y delicada se puede llamar.' Quintilian, *Institutio Oratoria* 1.5 discusses barbarism and solecism in Latin usage.

exotic to us.'[77] In fact the alien qualities of Quechua are indicated throughout the volume. Domingo de Santo Tomás' work is the exception that proves the rule: it was the only sixteenth-century study of an Amerindian language to be printed in peninsular Spain, and it was also the only one to be billed as a 'grammar'. Hence the first words of the title—*Grammatica o Arte*—signalled the work's dual role: it was both a 'grammar', conferring upon Quechua a symbolic value comparable that of Latin or Castilian, and a functional *arte*, or handbook, for missionaries.

The author made a point of emphasizing the humanity and civilized qualities of the native speakers of Quechua: 'how clearly and manifestly . . . false', he declared, 'is the position of which many have sought to convince your Majesty, that the people of Peru are barbarians.'[78] Santo Tomás appealed to Aristotle's tenet that language was what distinguished humans from other animals, qualifying them for social and political life: 'if such is their tongue, the race that uses it does not count as barbarous, but as one we can reckon on as having a very politic nature.'[79] Fray Domingo had an ulterior motive for his specious alignment of Quechua with Latin and Castilian: he was already collaborating with his fellow Dominican Bartolomé de las Casas in defending the interests of the Indians.[80] Santo Tomás was not the first member of the Dominican order to make tendentious claims about an Amerindian language to give a favourable impression of its speakers: twenty-five years before, in Tlaxcala, Fray Julián Garcés had applied Greek etymology to Nahuatl words as a way of supporting his argument that indigenous Mexicans could not be deemed *barbari*.[81]

The Franciscans, on the other hand, did not generally pursue comparisons of Amerindian tongues with European languages because to do so was not helpful to the learner.[82] As Fray Alonso de Molina affirmed, the language ('lenguaje') and 'expression' ('frasis') used by Mexicans were very different from those of Latin, Greek, and Castilian.[83] Molina's repeated pairing of the terms *lenguaje* and *frasis* suggests that he discerned that differences between Mexican and European languages were

[77] SANTO TOMÁS, *Grammatica o Arte* (1560), A vii verso: 'Esta le*n*gua de Peru, ta*n* estraña, tan nueua, ta*n* incognita, y ta*n* peregrina a nosotros.'

[78] SANTO TOMÁS, *Grammatica o Arte* (1560), A vi recto.

[79] SANTO TOMÁS, *Grammatica o Arte* (1560), A vi recto: 'Y si la le*n*gua lo es, la gente que vsa della, no entre barbara, sino co*n* la de mucha policia la podemos contar.' Cf. Aristotle, *Politics* 1, 1253a 1–19 and Aquinas, *Summa Theologiae* I–II: *quaestio* 95 a.4.

[80] LAS CASAS and SANTO TOMÁS, *Memorial* (c. 1560).

[81] Cf. Chapter 1, IV above.

[82] A very different approach was adopted in seventeenth-century Yucatán: Hanks 2010, 204–10, notes the imposition of Nebrijan paradigms (including even the Latin conjugations) on verbs in CORONEL, *Arte en lengua maya* (1620), also adopted in later Maya *artes*.

[83] MOLINA, *Vocabulario* (1571), 2v, 'Epistola nuncupatoria': 'el lenguaje y frasis destos naturales [especialmente de los Nauas y Mexicanos] es muy diferente del lenguaje y frasis latino, griego y castellano.'

on a deeper structural level of grammar or *langue*, as well as on the level of parlance or *parole*.

Yet the profound dissimilarities of Nahuatl to Spanish, Latin, and Greek did not at all detract from its richness and aesthetic quality. Fray Andrés de Olmos had observed that 'although [the Mexican language] appears barbarous to some, it has order and concert in many things, and it is not lacking in some excellences and a fine structure'.[84] Only a few years later, Fray Alonso de Molina praised Nahuatl for being 'copious, elegant, and of great intricacy and accomplishment in its metaphors and manners of speech' and remarked on the 'variety and diversity of its vocabulary'.[85] Finally at the end of the sixteenth century the Jesuit Antonio del Rincón held that Nahuatl possessed 'exquisitos primores y elegancias' ('choice accomplishment and elegance').

Rincón described his study as a 'collection and ordering of the precepts of *Mexican grammar* ['gramatica mexicana']'.[86] That description presupposed the idea that Nahuatl had its own grammar—something that would have struck readers as novel and audacious. By seeming to take that idea for granted instead of defending it, the Jesuit was able to convey the stature and autonomy of the Mexican language. He went on to explain that Nahuatl possessed value 'not only because it is a common language ['lengua general'] in all these provinces of New Spain, but also because it is actually like the mother of all the other languages in these realms'.[87] Rincón was implying that Nahuatl was analogous to Latin without being in any way similar to it. The fact that he, along with other missionary linguists in sixteenth-century New Spain and beyond, referred to their manuals as *artes* may not have been so much due to an assumption that Nahuatl and other American tongues did not 'deserve' a grammar of their own, but more to a view that the strictures of *grammatica*, as it had been hitherto understood, should not be imposed upon them.

From the perspective of European intellectual history, the production of *artes* and *vocabularios* in the New World shows the reach of Renaissance linguistic pedagogy, and how its application facilitated the acquisition of languages completely unrelated to Latin, Greek, Hebrew, or any European vernacular. At the same time, the humanists' conceptions of language that had been sustained ever since classical antiquity were being challenged or transcended. That will be demonstrated by some observations in the next two sections, which treat in turn Fray Andrés de Olmos'

[84] OLMOS, *Arte*, part 2, Prologue, 44r [2002, 59]: 'aunque a algunos parece barbara, tiene orden y concierto en muchas cosas, ni carece de algunos primores y buen artificio'.

[85] MOLINA, *Aqui comiença un vocabulario* (1555), a iiij, 'Prólogo al Lector': 'la lengua, la qual es tan copiosa tan elegante, y de tanto artificio y primor en sus metaphoras y maneras de dezir, quanto conoceran los *que* enella se exercitare*n*. Lo segu*n*do auerseme puesto dela*n*te la variedad y diuersidad *que* ay en los vocablos. . .'

[86] RINCÓN, *Arte mexicana* (1595) [1885, 9]: dedication to Diego Romano, bishop of Tlaxcala.

[87] RINCÓN, *Arte mexicana* (1595) [1885, 9]. Cf. n. 20 above for Nahuatl as a *lengua general*.

Arte de la lengua mexicana (1547) and Fray Maturino Gilberti's *Arte de la lengua de Michuacan* (1558), the two earliest extant *artes* from New Spain.

V. Antonio de Nebrija's *Introductiones Latinae,* c. 1487, and Fray Andrés de Olmos' *Arte de la lengua mexicana,* 1547

Fray Andrés de Olmos had attended the university of Valladolid to study jurisprudence. In 1527 he was appointed as an inquisitor by Fray Juan de Zumárraga to assist in a campaign against witchcraft in the Basque province of Vizcaya, before he accompanied Zumárraga to New Spain the following year.[88] Olmos was to prove an extremely accomplished linguist: in addition to his *arte* of Nahuatl, he authored studies, now lost, of the Huastec, Totonac, and Tepehuan languages and produced Nahuatl versions of Saint Vincent Ferrer's Latin sermons and Fray Martín de Castañega's treatise on superstition and sorcery.[89] His other researches included a now lost *Tratado de antigüedades mexicanas,* 'Treatise on Mexican Antiquities'.[90]

Nebrija's *Introductiones Latinae,* which first appeared in the 1480s, the decade in which Fray Andrés de Olmos was born, would have had a central place in the friar's education. The grammar had been divided into five books: the first two were devoted to declensions of nouns and conjugations of verbs; the third and fourth covered syntax and parts of speech; and the final fifth book treated Latin syllabic quantities and accent.[91] Olmos affirmed that this was the best way of presenting Latin, but he could not use the same system for the Mexican language.[92] His own study was divided into just three 'Parts', with nouns and pronouns treated in Part 1; conjugations and formation of verbs in Part 2; and indeclinable parts of speech, orthography, and usage in Part 3. The treatise began with a discussion of 'parts of speech' because, in Nahuatl, 'the primitive substantives do not have declensions, although they do discriminate between singular and plural'.[93] As for conjugation, 'it does not come at the beginning of the present *arte* so as not to decontextualize

[88] MENDIETA, *Historia* (1596) 5.33–5 [1870, 644–51]; TORQUEMADA, *Monarchia Indiana* (1615) 20.38–40 [1979 vi, 240–50]; and the Latin bio-bibliographies in ANTONIO, *Bibliotheca Hispana nova* (1672) [1788 i, 81–2] and EGUIARA Y EGUREN, *Bibliotheca Mexicana* (1755), 132–7 are early sources for Olmos' life and work. See too Baudot 1995, 163–245.

[89] OLMOS, *Tratado sobre los siete peccados mortals* (1551–1552) was based on FERRER, *Sermones de peccatis capitalibus* (c. 1380) [1729]; OLMOS, *Tratado de hechicerías y sortilegios* (1553) translated CASTAÑEGA, *Tratado de las supersticiones y hechicerías* (1529): cf. Chapter I, III above.

[90] On the *Tratado de antigüedades mexicanas* and the collection of traditional Mexican speeches Olmos appended to his *arte,* cf. Chapter 5, IV, Chapter 8, I and IV below.

[91] Cf. Appendix 1.1.2 below.

[92] OLMOS, *Arte* 1.1, 23r [2002, 15]; cf. Appendix 1.1.3.

[93] OLMOS, *Arte* 1.7, 31r. [2002, 31].

it from the subject of verbs . . . in Part 2.'[94] Olmos also had to diverge from Nebrija's treatment of syntax ('composición') as a separate category because it could not be disentangled from the formation of words or morphology: syntax thus pervaded all three parts of his *Arte*.

That design was rooted in a division of parts of speech into nouns, verbs, and particles that originated in classical antiquity and was known to Renaissance scholars because it had been transmitted in Latin by the Roman Quintilian:

> The teacher responsible will then need to consider how many parts of speech there are, and what they are, although there is little agreement about the number. Earlier writers, including even Aristotle and Theodectes, listed only verbs, nouns, and connecting particles [*convinctiones*]; they took the forceful element in language to be in the verbs; and the material element in the nouns, because the one is what we say, and the other what we say it about, while the *convinctiones* provided the connections between them. (I know most people say conjunctions, but *convinctiones* seems the better translation of [the Greek] *syndesmos*.) The philosophers, particularly the Stoics, gradually increased the number: articles were first added to *convinctiones*, and then 'prepositions'; to nouns were added 'appellations' and 'pronouns', and the quasi-verbal 'participle'; to verbs themselves were added adverbs. Our language ['noster sermo', i.e. Latin] does not feel its lack of articles, and these are therefore divided among other parts of speech. In addition, however, there is the 'interjection.'[95]

This tripartite scheme of nouns, verbs and particles underscores many of the missionaries' *artes*.[96]

The arrangement of the *Arte de la lengua mexicana* also reflected the importance of the pronoun in Nahuatl, to which it devoted five opening chapters. After

[94] OLMOS, *Arte* 1.1, 23r [2002, 15].

[95] Quintilian, *Institutio oratoria* 1.4.18–20: 'tum videbit, ad quem hoc pertinet, quot et quae partes orationis, quamquam de numero parum convenit. Veteres enim, quorum fuerunt Aristoteles quoque atque Theodectes, verba modo et nomina et convinctiones tradiderunt, videlicet quod in verbis vim sermonis, in nominibus materiam (quia alterum est quod loquimur, alterum de quo loquimur), in convinctionibus autem complexum eorum esse iudicaverunt: quas coniunctiones a plerisque dici scio, sed haec videtur ex syndesmo magis propria tralatio. Paulatim a philosophis ac maxime Stoicis auctus est numerus, ac primum convinctionibus articuli adiecti, post praepositiones: nominibus appellatio, deinde pronomen, deinde mixtum verbo participium, ipsis verbis adverbia. Noster sermo articulos non desiderat ideoque in alias partes orationis sparguntur, sed accedit superioribus interiectio.' The translation above is a modification of Russell 2001 i, 115.

[96] At least one copy of Quintilian, *Institutio oratoria* was held in the library of the College of Santa Cruz de Tlatelolco: cf. Chapter 4, III (ii); Appendix 1.3, items [13] and [67]. Olmos taught Latin at the college: MENDIETA, *Historia* (1596) 4.15 [1870, 415].

introducing the 'pronominal' verbal prefixes, *ni* and *ti,* 'I' and 'you', in the singular; and *ti* and *an,* 'we' and 'you', in the plural, Olmos conjugated the present tense of the verb 'tetlaçotla' [*sic*], 'love oneself or another', as follows:[97]

Singular		
nitetlaçotla	yo amo	[I love]
titetlaçotla	tu amas	[you love]
Plural		
nitetlaçotla	nosotros amamos	[we love]
antetlaçotla	vosotros amais[98]	[you love]

Olmos hence explained that the pronominal forms were used in the conjugation of verbs, and that there was no third-person pronoun because its sense could simply be conveyed by what he called the 'absolute verb' ('el verbo absoluto'):

tetlaçotla	aquel ama	[he loves]
tetlaçotlah	aquellos aman[99]	[they love]

The fact that the pronominal forms *ni-*, *ti-*, *ti-*, and *an-* could be attached to nouns or adjectives, as well as to verbs, led to an important observation: 'When these pronouns are joined to nouns, the present tense of *sum, esse, fui* [the Latin verb for 'to be'] is understood.' An example is provided:

Singular		
niqualli	yo soi bueno	[I am good]
tiqualli	tu eres bueno	[you are good]
qualli	aquel es bueno	[he is good]
Plural		
tiqualhti	nosotros somos buenos	[we are good]
anqualhti	vosotros sois buenos	[you are good]
qualhti	aquellos son buenos[100]	[they are good]

[97] Verbs are nowadays identified by the root form without indefinite prefixes like *te-*, which marked only the indefinite object of the verb: Launey 2011, 28–9. The 'ç' is now always a 'z'. Hence *tlazohtla* = 'love' (as opposed to Olmos' 'tetlaçotla' = 'love someone'): cf. Karttunen 1992, 306.

[98] OLMOS, *Arte* (1547) 1.3, 24v [2002, 18–19].

[99] OLMOS, *Arte* (1547) 1.3, 24v [2002, 19]. Olmos' original spelling is retained in these quotations.

[100] OLMOS, *Arte* (1547) 1.3, 24v–25r [incorrectly transcribed in 2002, 19].

Later on in Part 1 of the *Arte,* Olmos explains that Nahuatl provides an equivalent to the present tense of Latin *esse,* 'to be'. This comes in his discussion of the way in which pronominal forms can be combined with possessive pronouns:

> A combination is made many times in this language by joining these two different kinds of pronouns and placing them before nouns, so that *ni, ti, an* will always go before *no, mo, y.* Thus joined with the noun they will make a complete articulation ['oración perfecta'] of the present of *sum, esse, fui* [the verb 'to be'] in the following manner:

nimopilhtzin	yo soy tu hijo	[I am thy son]
nipilhtzin	yo soy hijo de aquel	[I am his son]
namopilhtzin	yo soy vuestro hijo	[I am your son]
nimpilhtzin	yo soy hijo de aquellos	[I am their son]
nitepilhtzin	yo soy hijo de alguno, o de algunos	[I am someone's son or some ones']
tinopilhtzin	tu eres mi hijo	[you are my son]
tiipilhtzin	tu eres hijo de aquel	[you are his son]. . . [101]

In fact, the sense of the verb 'to be' can, on occasions, be latent in Latin or in Spanish as well: *filius meus* and *hijo mio* can in certain contexts mean 'It is/was/will be my son' or 'He is/was/will be my son': Olmos' identification of this routine feature in Nahuatl anticipated Sanctius' account of *ellipsis* in Latin.[102]

Nahuatl nouns can be inflected rather like verbs (with regard to person, though not other verbal categories): their root forms have a third-person signification and a potency as verbal propositions. For example, the simple noun *piltzintli,* 'son', 'child', standing alone, means 'he is a son' or 'it is a son'. That infringes a hitherto unquestioned distinction Quintilian had made between nouns and verbs: 'the *forceful* element in language [had] to be in the *verbs;* and the *material* element in the *nouns,* because the one is *what* we say, and the other what we say it *about.*'[103] Fray Andrés de Olmos evidently understood a characteristic Nahuatl shares with many other American languages: its fundamental structuring principle is that of the 'word-phrase', in which morphology and syntax are intertwined. A twentieth-century account of this feature of Nahuatl draws attention to its importance:

[101] OLMOS, *Arte* (1547), 1.5, 27r [2002, 23–4]: there are thirty-four singular and plural forms.

[102] SANCTIUS, *Minerva* (1587) Book 4, 164v–222r [1995, 440–581].

[103] Quintilian, *Institutio* 1.4.18: 'in verbis vim sermonis, in nominibus materiam, quia alterum est quod loquimur, alterum de quo loquimur'. These words are quoted in their context in n. 95 above.

> The word-phrase—that is, a word that contains within itself all the nuclear constituents necessary to make up a phrase—is at the base of the structure of Nahuatl. The nuclear functions of subject and predicate are inescapably present in both verbal and nominal terms. The sentence-word thus constitutes the norm for the unit of utterance in the language. This fact simply and absolutely puts English and Nahuatl on opposite ends of a linguistic spectrum.[104]

In Part 2 of the *Arte* Olmos noted that 'in the Latin language there are no particles incorporated or joined within the [active] verb' to denote the *object* ('la persona que padesce')', while Nahuatl verbs cannot be without such a particle.[105] Exceptions occur when the verb is composed out of a noun and so has the object incorporated within it: Olmos' example was 'nipetlachiua', 'I make bedrolls.' He considered instances in which a pronoun replacing the object is joined with the verb: 'ninotlaçotla', 'I love myself' (*nino-* is the first-person singular reflexive pronoun), and 'tinechtlaçotla', 'you love me' (*nech-* is the first-person singular object pronoun).

Olmos also explained pronominal prefixes, or 'particulas': he pointed out that *tla-*, for instance, is used especially for inanimate objects and roughly corresponds to the word 'something' ('lo que en nuestro romance dezimos: algo'). The example he gave was 'ni<u>tla</u>tlaçotla', 'I love something.' A second prefix, *te-*, signals that the action of the verb affects animate or rational beings: 'ni<u>te</u>tlaçotla' means 'I love someone', but without indicating whom. The first example was 'ni<u>te</u>paleuia', 'I help someone.' The second illustrated the use of *te-* in conjunction with *tla-*: 'ni<u>tetla</u>maca', 'I give something to someone.'

Nebrija, though, had held the view, inherited from antiquity, that the word (*dictio*) was an indivisible unit of meaning:

> A word is the smallest part of connected meaningful speech i.e. of speech in syntactic construction. Priscian says it is a part that is semantically complete, that is to say, it leads to understanding of the complete meaning in itself, because if a word is divided, the division does not give a sense of the whole: as, if you divide *vires* into *vi* and *res,* it signifies nothing of that part of speech where the sense of the whole is concerned.[106]

[104] Andrews 1974, xii.

[105] OLMOS, *Arte* (1547), 2.7 (2002, 108).

[106] NEBRIJA, *Introductiones Latinae* (c. 1495) Book 3 (unpaginated), cited in Monzón, 'Introducción', in GILBERTI, *Arte* (1558) [2004, 37 n. 9]: 'Dictio est pars minima orationis constructae, *id est* in ordine compositae. "Pars," inquit Priscianus, "quantum ad totum intelligendum, id est ad totius sensus intellectum: quia si dictio diuidatur: non ad totum intellegendum haec fit diuisio: ut si diuidas uires in ui. et res." nihil partes ill*ae* significant: quantum ad totius rationem pertinet.'

As Nebrija's citation of the sixth-century Roman grammarian Priscian shows, the notion of a 'word' (*dictio*) had been identified in both syntactic and semantic terms.[107] It was positioned on a hierarchical scale, with the letter, *litera*, understood as a unit of sound, as the most basic element, followed by the syllable, then the word, *dictio*; and finally *oratio*, a phrase or sentence.[108] On this basis, words are components of meaningful utterances. Unlike the syllables out of which it is composed, a word had to have an 'intelligible' or semantic function. But with a language like Nahuatl, individual nouns and verbs can be said to constitute *oratio*. They could not properly be regarded as the minimal units of speech, since they are themselves made up of particles—and the particles themselves have a semantic function.[109]

Chapters 1–5 of Part 3 of the *Arte de la lengua mexicana* deal with prepositions, adverbs, conjunctions, and interjections. Olmos' classification of numerals as adverbs is an unhelpful departure from Nebrija's practice, but his account of the Mexicans' numerical system is a fascinating explanation of their base-20 reckoning, and of the different suffixes attached to numerals in order to count different classes of things. Chapter 6 of Part 3 might raise hackles because it deals with 'orthographia'—correct transcription and spelling—for a language on which Europeans had imposed their own alphabet. But because Olmos saw the *litera*, not the phoneme, as the most basic unit of language, he employed it to produce a kind of phonology, attempting to describe how to speak and pronounce Nahuatl in terms of how to write it.

The last two chapters of Part 3 of the *Arte de la lengua mexicana* ('De unas maneras de hablar communes', 'On some common manners of speaking', and 'De las maneras de hablar que tenian los viejos en sus platicas . . .', 'On the manners of speaking the elders used in their talks . . .') contain examples of usage, apparently derived from actual Nahuatl speech.[110] Those final sections of the work might at first seem to correspond to the last part of the *Introductiones Latinae* where Nebrija had presented a set of difficult sentences and idioms. But the sustained examples of good Latinity that concluded other Renaissance grammars are the real model: Perotti's *Rudimenta grammatices*, for example, had ended with a section on how to compose

[107] Priscian, *Institutiones grammaticae* 2.14 is the passage cited: Keil 1855 ii, 53. Hyman 2005 treats *dictio* and other ancient Roman terms for 'word'. 'Dictionarium', derived from *dictio* during the Renaissance, had been used in ROSATE, *Dictionarium juris* (1481), before it was adopted by Calepino.

[108] PEROTTI, *Rudimenta grammatices* (1473) [2010, 21] relied on Priscian's itemization, seminal for Renaissance grammarians: 'Quot sunt partes grammatices? Quattuor. Quae? Littera, syllaba, dictio, et oratio' ('How many parts of grammar are there? Four. What are they? Letter, syllable, word, and sentence.'). Laird 2018a and Lucas González' introduction to GILBERTI, *Grammatica* [2003 i, 88–9] treat its use by Nebrija and Gilberti respectively.

[109] Padley 1976, 206–7 and passim; cf. Robins 1997, 110–51 on the particle in Renaissance linguistics.

[110] OLMOS, *Arte*, 3.8–3.9 [2002: 171–93].

letters; and the instructions of Erasmus and Despauter on exemplary epistolary style were imitated (or simply reproduced) by their admirers to close their own Latin grammars.

The texts incorporated at the end of the *Arte de la lengua mexicana* were for the purpose of linguistic instruction. They were therefore of a different order from the traditional Mexican discourses that would later be presented in the sixth book of *Florentine Codex* (1577).[111] Olmos' texts, however, were connected to some of the Nahuatl speeches that were later published by Fray Juan Bautista Viseo in his *Huehuetlahtolli* (1601).[112]

VI. Fray Maturino Gilberti's *Arte de la lengua de Michuacan*, 1558, and *Grammatica Maturini*, 1559

Fray Maturino Gilberti, who was probably born in France in 1508, studied arts and theology at the University of Toulouse in the mid-1530s, although some sources link him to Bologna.[113] He must have settled in Michoacán soon after he first reached New Spain in 1542, and his *Thesoro espiritual en lengua de Mechuacan* (1558) and *Dialogo de Doctrina Christiana* (1559) are among the few colonial texts written in Purépecha.[114] In 1572 Gilberti declared, before the judge of the royal Audiencia, Doctor Villanueva, that he spoke five Indian languages.[115]

Gilberti's grammar of Latin, the *Grammatica Maturini* (1559) (Figure 3.3) can serve as a control for his manual of Purépecha, *Arte de la lengua de Michuacan* (1558), highlighting the different approaches taken in the latter (Figure 3.4).[116] Both works are of roughly the same length, and both begin with grammatical rules and end with examples of usage, although they are organized in different ways. The Latin grammar is in seven clearly titled parts, the first five of which address more or less the same subjects as the five books of Nebrija's bilingual *Introductiones Latinae*. But the sixth part on *ornatus*, 'adornment', and the seventh, on exemplary formulae and

[111] Cf. Chapter 8, IV on Olmos' researches and SAHAGÚN, *HG*, Book 6.

[112] Cf. Chapter 5, IV (iv) on BAUTISTA, *Huehuetlahtolli* (c. 1601). Ruiz Bañuls 2009, 117–28 attempts to reconstruct the transmission of Olmos' texts to Bautista, even though Olmos is not mentioned in the lengthy preliminaries of the volume. Téllez Nieto and Baños Baños 2019, 93 observe that *Huehuetlahtolli*, fol. 77r implies Bautista did not have first-hand knowledge of the authorship of the texts he published.

[113] GILBERTI, *Arte* (1558) [1987, lxxii, lxxix]. Warren 1994, 277, 284–6. Some documentary sources (not always correctly interpreted) are in Fernández del Castillo 1982.

[114] Monzón 2012b.

[115] VILLANUEVA, 'Información sobre fray Maturino Gilberti' (1572).

[116] See Appendix 1.1.4 and Appendix 1.1.5 below; cf. Monzón 1999.

GRAMMA-
tica Maturini
TRACTATVS OMNIVM FE-
rè quę Grammatices ſtudioſis tradi ſolēt
à fratre Maturino Gilberto mino-
rita ex doctiſsimis collectus
autoribus.

Gloriari nos oportet in Cruce Domini
noſtri IESVCHRISTI in quo
eſt Salus Vita & Reſurrectio noſtra

MEXICI.
Excudebat Antonius Eſpinoſa.
M.D.LIX.

Figure 3.3 Fray Maturino Gilberti, *Grammatica Maturini,* Mexico City, 1559. John Carter Brown Library.

usage, drew their examples from Erasmus, a debt Gilberti explicitly signalled in his heading of the final section.[117]

The *Arte de la lengua de Michuacan,* on the other hand, is in three untitled 'partes', or sections. The first is the shortest, treating nouns and verbs in thirty folio pages, while the second and third sections each run to seventy pages. The second sets out the eight parts of speech—'as in Grammar' ('como en la Gramática')—hinting at their role as constituent elements of syntax. The third and final part deals with orthography, with composition of verbs with particles, and with the individual particles themselves, before an enumeration of *modi dicendi,* 'forms of expression', in Purépecha. Gilberti's arrangement of his *Arte* is thus looser than that of his Latin grammar. The innovative tripartite structure of Olmos' *Arte de la lengua mexicana* has been proposed as the inspiration for this format, although the methodical basis for Olmos' system of division is evidently different.[118] The Purépecha *arte* has more

[117] GILBERTI, *Grammatica* (1559), 137r [2003 ii, 597]: see further Chapter 4, III (i), n. 111 below. Gilberti's incorporation of longer passages from Erasmus is more reminiscent of the treatise on letter writing that supplemented PEROTTI, *Rudimenta grammatices* than the sentences that ended NEBRIJA, *Introductiones Latinae.*

[118] Hernández de León-Portilla and León-Portilla 2009, 82–6.

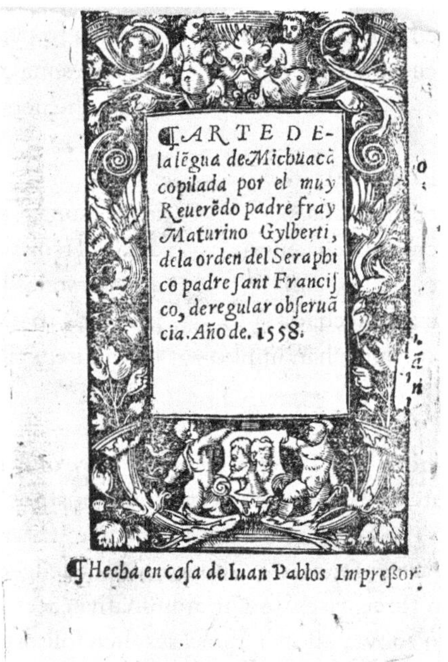

¶ARTE DE-
la lẽgua de Michuacã
copilada por el muy
Reuerẽdo padre fray
Maturino Gylberti,
dela orden del Seraphi
co padre ſant Franciſ
co, deregular obſeruã
cia. Año de. 1558.

¶Hecha en caſa de Iuan Pablos Impreſſor.

Figure 3.4 Fray Maturino Gilberti, *Arte de la lengua de Michuacan,* Mexico City, 1558. John Carter Brown Library.

affinity with Perotti's *Rudimenta grammatices,* which had rejected an overarching schematization in its presentation of Latin.[119]

Olmos had begun his *arte* by making clear that his own approach would be different from Nebrija's, but Gilberti makes no mention of the Spanish grammarian in his own opening, so that it is initially unclear whether or not Nebrija had offered a prototype for his project.[120] But Gilberti's attempt to set out paradigms for nouns and verbs in Part 1 of the *Arte,* saving explanation for the ampler second and third parts to come, resembles the style of exposition in Nebrija's *Introductiones Latinae.* What is more, at the very beginning of Part 1, Fray Maturino endeavoured to apply Latin declension to Purépecha by presenting six cases (in the singular and plural) for the noun *cuiripu,* 'person':

Nominatiuo	cuiripu	persona [person]
Genitiuo	cuiripu eueri	dela persona [of the person]
Datiuo y accusatiuo	cuiripuni	ala persona [to the person]

[119] Laird 2012, 60.

[120] Monzón 1997 shows Nebrija did have an influence on Gilberti's approach to Purépecha.

Vocatiuo	cuiripue	persona [o person]
Ablatiuo	cuiripu himbo	dela persona o enla persona [from the person or in the person]
	PLVRALI	
Nominatiuo	cuiripuecha	las personas [persons]
Genitiuo	cuiripuecha eueri	delas personas [of the persons]
Datiuo y accusatiuo	cuiripuechani	alas personas [to the persons]
Vocatiuo	cuiripuechae	personas [o persons]
Ablativo	cuiripuechan himbo	[from/in persons][121]

Yet this very example shows that Purépecha nouns have only *three* case endings, for the nominative, accusative/dative, and vocative: the postpositions *eueri* and *himbo* serve as equivalents to the Latin genitive and ablative. Later on, when discussing 'Signs of the Cases' in Part 2 of the *Arte*, Gilberti acknowledged that 'in this language there are no more than three cases, to wit, nominative, accusative and vocative'.[122] A full account of how to convey all six Latin cases then followed; and a seventh case, the 'efectivo', 'effective', was configured as an equivalent to the Latin instrumental ablative.[123]

As with the declensions, the conjugation of verbs, in Part 1 of the *Arte de la lengua de Michuacan* recalls the model of exposition in the *Introductiones Latinae*. But unlike Nebrija, Gilberti could not leave all the necessary explanation for a later part of the *Arte*. He was obliged to make clear at the outset that conjugation of the first verb introduced, *hurendahpen*, 'teach', illustrated a more general principle:

> Although this language appears to use one tense for many . . . it is not without a reason, because the adverbs or particles added or dropped give direct meaning to the tense and mood spoken, and so the subject and context of what is being said, with the aforementioned particles, make clear which tense and mood is being used. That is evident from all the examples given, in which there is no lack whatsoever of a way to express those tenses and mood, indicated in this manner. It should be a general rule, as all the

[121] GILBERTI, *Arte*, 12r [2004, 75]. The ablative plural is not given in Spanish.

[122] GILBERTI, *Arte* (1558), 57–8 [2004, 153].

[123] GILBERTI, *Arte* (1558), 60v [2004, 157]: 'The effective case is always used with *himbo* alone, as when saying "with a rock", "with a stick", "with a pitcher". In his account of the ablative at 59r–60v [2004, 156–7], Gilberti had included other postpositions as well as *himbo*, such as *hingun*, 'in', and *ynde* (= Latin *de*), 'about' or 'concerning'.

> difficulties of conjugation are present, and specific examples are given there in their places.[124]

As far as he could, Gilberti presented the forms of the Purépecha verb in terms of Latin conjugations, but only to the degree that this was practicable, for the benefit of the learner.

The importance of context in usage is raised again in Part II, with a discussion of 'conjunctiones' that signal different emotions:

> Note that in this language there are other conjunctions which by themselves do not mean anything—like the following: *Hiru quini, aru, chuhcatero, chunde, chundetero, guaru, nongua, nanhgua*—but joined to pronouns they convey an emotion. To use these conjunctions it would be necessary to look extensively at the subject concerned, because quite different states of mind can be exhibited by means of one and the same word.[125]

Such features of Purépecha, which had no equivalent in Latin, were often listed by Gilberti separately as anomalies.[126] Even so, these 'conjunctions which by themselves do not mean anything' ('que por si solas no significan nada') are described in terms drawn from the Latin grammars of antiquity. Priscian had defined the 'prepositio inseparabilis' (e.g the *con-* in the compound verb *conficio*) as 'not having the capacity to mean anything by itself' ('nihil significare possit per se'); and the ancient grammarian had explained the syllable in similar terms.[127] Gilberti's specification of these conjunctions which 'convey an emotion' ('dan a entender algun affecto') also reproduced Donatus' definition of a Latin interjection: 'a part of

[124] GILBERTI, *Arte* (1558), 29r–29v [2004, 99–100]: 'aunque parece usar de un tiempo para muchos tiempos, . . . pero no sin causa porque los adverbios o particulas añadidas o quitadas le hazen directamente significar aquel tiempo y romanze de que se habla, y assi la materia y tiempo de que se habla con las dichas particulas declaran yr por aquel tiempo y romanze de que se habla como ha parecido en todos los exemplos dados, en los quales no hay falta ninguna del hablar de aquellos tiempos y romanzes que van declarados, y esta sea regla general para que en todas las dificultades de la conjugacion acuden alli, pues ya estan dados alli en sus lugares exemplos particulares.'

[125] GILBERTI, *Arte* (1558), 103r [2004, 217]: 'Nota que en esta lengua ay otras conjunctiones, que por si solas no significan nada, como son las siguientes: *Hiru quini, aru, chuhcatero, chunde, chundetero, guaru, nongua, nanhgua* pero juntas a los pronombres dan a entender algun affecto, y para usar destas conjunctiones hase de mirar mucho a la materia de lo que se trata porque con una mesma palabra se pueden mostrar diversos afectos del anima.'

[126] Monzón 1999, 38.

[127] Priscian, *Institutiones grammaticae* 12: Keil 1855 ii, 593, on *praepositio inseparabilis*. Priscian's comparable definition of the syllable (Keil 1855 i, 53) is cited in Zwartjes 2000: 'syllaba autem *non* omni modo *aliquid significat per se*' (my emphasis), although Monzón's observation that there is no direct correspondent in Latin for the conjunctions signifying emotions can still be upheld. Zwartjes adduces the treatment of 'semipronombres', 'semi-pronouns', *te, ne,* and *tla* in RINCÓN, *Arte mexicana*

speech signifying a state of mind ("significans mentis affectum") with an unformed utterance'—a definition that Gilberti would only slightly modify for the account of interjections in his own Latin grammar.[128] Purépecha interjections are then listed on the page after the passage quoted above. Gilberti was not abandoning the traditional grammatical framework, but customizing it: a definition of one part of speech in Latin is transposed to define another part of speech in Purépecha.

Perhaps the most striking departure from the conventions of Latin grammar is to be found in the section 'On the composition of Verbs', in Part 3. This is a lengthy account of the 'particles' constituting the verb. Because of their large number and the diversity of their functions, the particles in Purépecha were a much greater challenge to the learner than those in Nahuatl. Morphemes that sound the same, at least as they are transcribed, have different meanings, depending on whether they occur as 'roots' or as suffixes, and on the different contexts in which they are found. Gilberti's prologue to his *Vocabulario en lengua de Mechuacan* (1559) confirms that he understood the 'root', *rayz*, to be the basic element of the Purépecha verb:[129]

> Certain words follow in alphabetical order, of which some could be 'roots' ['rayzes'], because it is evident that with the removal of their limbs ['miembros'], or to put it better, their subordinate parts ['las seruiles'], the root will remain without meaning anything, like a tree without branches—it is only ready to produce what is absent from simple verbs. For example, *thire* is the governing root of the verb *thireni* which means 'eat', as a command. And *ytsima* is the governing root of the verb *ytsimani* which only in itself means 'drink', as a command. I omitted these from the *Arte* so as not to confuse or daunt new students of this language, because this is a very difficult subject, even for those who are accomplished and well instructed in the language.[130]

Scholars in Europe had already used the term 'servile' of the letters that represented inflectional and derivational affixes in written Hebrew, suggesting that their system of roots and affixes provided Gilberti's model. José de Acosta's comparison of the interpositions and postpositions of 'Indian speech' (*sermo*) with Hebrew affixes

(1595) [1885, 17]: 'no tienen en si entera significación', 'they have no complete meaning in themselves' and REUCHLIN, *De rudimentis Hebraicis* (1506), book 3 [1974, 615] on the *consignificativa* in Hebrew grammar: 'Sunt enim aliquae quae per se omnino nihil significant.'

[128] Donatus, *De partibus orationis ars minor*; NEBRIJA, *Introductiones Latinae* (c. 1487) (unnumbered page): 'est pars orationis indeclinabilis affectum mentis significans voce incondita.' Cf. GILBERTI, *Grammatica* (1559), 'Prima pars', 42r [2003 i, 210]: 'Interiectio est pars orationis significans mentis affectum voce incognita, cuius significationes pene innumerę sunt.'

[129] GILBERTI, *Arte* (1558), 66v: 'se forma de la primera posicion o rayz del verbo quitada la terminación', 'the root is formed from the first position or root of the verb with ending left off'; 141v: 'All these particles or, to put it better, 'roots' of verbs'.

[130] GILBERTI, *Vocabulario* (1559), 80. Cf. Percival 1999, 21.

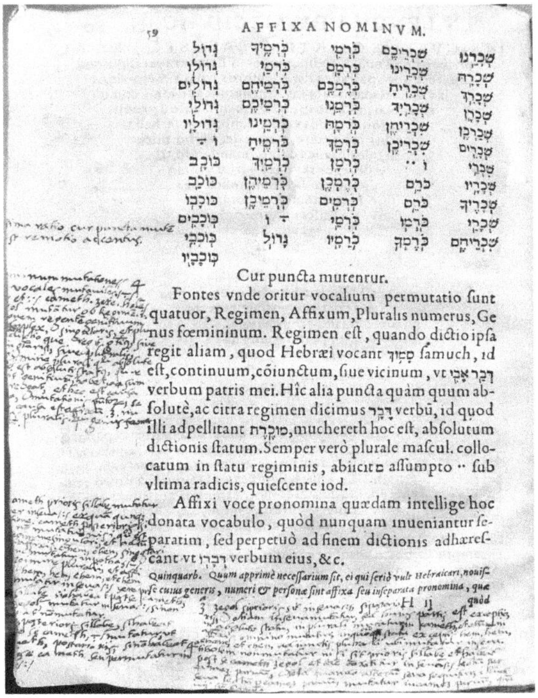
AFFIXA NOMINVM.

Cur puncta mutentur.

Fontes vnde oritur vocalium permutatio sunt quatuor, Regimen, Affixum, Pluralis numerus, Genus fœmininum. Regimen est, quando dictio ipsa regit aliam, quod Hebræi vocant סָמוּךְ samuch, id est, continuum, cōiunctum, siue vicinum, vt דְּבַר אָבִי verbum patris mei. Hîc alia puncta quàm quum absolutè, ac citra regimen dicimus דָּבָר verbũ, id quod illi adpellitant מוּכְרַת, muchereth hoc est, absolutum dictionis statum. Semper verò plurale mascul. collocatum in statu regiminis, abiicit ם assumpto ·· sub vltima radicis, quiescente iod.

Affixi voce pronomina quædam intellige hoc donata vocabulo, quòd nunquam inueniantur separatim, sed perpetuò ad finem dictionis adhærescant vt דְּבָרוֹ verbum eius, &c.

Figure 3.5 Annotation in the Tlatelolco copy of Nicolas Cleynaerts, *Tabula in grammaticen Hebraeam*, Paris, 1559, 59. Sutro Library, California State Library.

shows that categories from Hebrew grammar were being applied to Amerindian languages in the later 1500s.[131] Several handwritten annotations surround Nicolas Cleynaerts' description of pronominal affixes in the copy of his *Tabula in grammaticen Hebraeam* (1559), which belonged to the library of Santa Cruz de Tlatelolco (Figure 3.5).[132] Gilberti's analogy of a tree and its branches, which was enhanced by the typographic arrangement of this passage in the original edition of his *Vocabulario* (Figure 3.6), also reflected a conventional European visualization of

[131] ACOSTA, *De procuranda Indorum salute* (1588) 4.9 [1987 ii, 72]: 'The Indian spoken language [*sermo*] is hundreds of miles from equalling the difficulty of Hebrew and Chaldean; or the extent and daunting abundance of Latin and Greek. It is much smaller and indeed far simpler, as it has very few inflections and can be understood from just a few examples. If you have inwardly digested the interpositions and postpositions ['interpositiones postpositionesque'] that make it remote from Greek, Latin and Spanish but which are very much like Hebrew affixes ['hebraicis affixis'], it presents almost no challenge at all.'

[132] The annotated text of CLEYNAERTS, *Tabula* (1559), 59v in the Sutro Library copy reads, 'Affixi voce pronomina quaedam intellige hoc donata vocabulo, quod nunquam inueniantur separatim, sed perpetuo ad finem dictionis adhaerescant.' Percival 1999 notes that Carochi compared Nahuatl

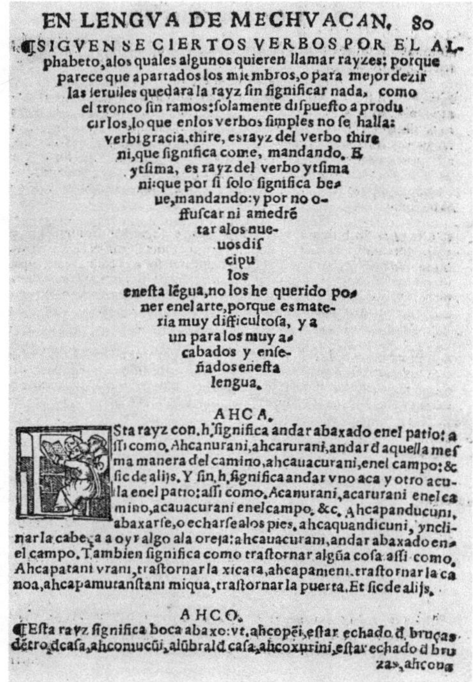

EN LENGVA DE MECHVACAN. 80

¶SIGVEN SE CIERTOS VERBOS POR EL AL-
phabeto, alos quales algunos quieren llamar rayzes: porque
parece que apartados los miembros, o para mejor dezir
las seruiles quedara la rayz ſin ſignificar nada, como
el tronco ſin ramos: ſolamente diſpueſto a produ
cirlos, lo que enlos verbos ſimples no ſe halla:
verbi gracia, thire, es rayz del verbo thire
ni, que ſignifica come, mandando. E
ytſima, es rayz del verbo ytſima
ni: que por ſi ſolo ſignifica be-
ue, mandando: y por no o-
ffuſcar ni amedrẽ
tar alos nue-
uos diſ
cipu
los
eneſta lẽgua, no los he querido poner enel arte, porque es materia muy difficultoſa, y a
un para los muy a-
cabados y enſe-
ñados eneſta
lengua.

AHCA.

Eſta rayz con. h. ſignifica andar abaxado enel patio: a
ſſi como. Ahcanurani, ahcarurani, andar d aquella meſ
ma manera del camino, ahcauacurani, enel campo: &
ſic de alijs. Y ſin. h. ſignifica andar vno aca y otro acu-
la enel patio: aſſi como. Acanurani, acarurani enel ca
mino, acauacurani enelcampo. &c. Ahcapanducuni,
abaxarſe, o echarſe alos pies. ahcaquandicuni, yncli-
nar la cabeça a oyr algo ala oreja: ahcauacurani, andar abaxado enel campo. Tambien ſignifica como traſtornar algũa coſa aſſi como.
Ahcapatani vrani, traſtornar la xicara, ahcapameni. traſtornar la ca
noa, ahcapamuranſtani miqua, traſtornar la puerta. Et ſic de alijs.

AHCO.

¶Eſta rayz ſignifica boca abaxo: vt. ahcopẽi, eſtar echado d. bruças
dẽtro d caſa, ahcomucũi, alũbral d caſa, ahcoxurini, eſtar echado d bru
ças, ahcoua

Figure 3.6 Fray Maturino Gilberti, *Vocabulario en lengua de Mechuacan*, Mexico City, 1559, 80r. John Carter Brown Library.

grammar as a tree (Figure 3.7).[133] Some years before in New Spain, Fray Cristóbal Cabrera had likened the *doctrina*, 'taught science', of language to a tree-trunk, and the various everyday vernaculars to its branches.[134]

As had been the case with Nahuatl in Olmos' *arte*, the interdependence of morphology and syntax determined the manner in which Gilberti presented Purépecha.

particulate pronouns to Hebrew affixes and that Molina, who, like Olmos, would naturally have derived the verb in Nahuatl from the third person, had also observed this in *artes* of Hebrew.

[133] PASTRANA, *Grammatica Pastranae* (1497) used illustrations of trees to represent functions of Latin grammar and syntax; cf. Báez Rubí 2005, 88–91 on Ramon Llull's use of the tree to symbolize encyclopaedic knowledge.

[134] CABRERA, *Flores de consolación* (1549), vii: 'no soy muy curioso del romance . . . Tomemos el tronco, que es la doctrina. Dexemos las ramas que son las palabras, las quales al fin no pueden ser mas que palabras.' ('I am not very interested in the vernacular . . . Let us keep the trunk which is our education. Let us leave behind the branches, which are spoken words, and that in the end cannot be more than spoken words.')

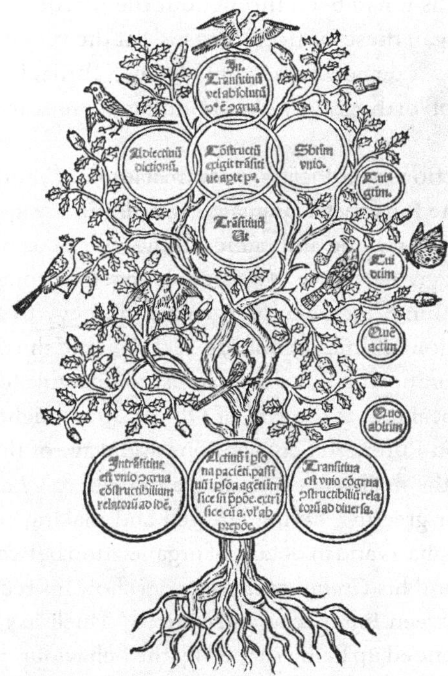

Figure 3.7 Illustration of Grammar, Juan Pastrana, *Grammatica Pastranae,* Lisbon, 1497. Biblioteca Nacional de Portugal.

But the demands of phonology ('vocablos y orthographia') also accounted for the layout of the *Arte de la lengua de Michuacan*:

> I have tried to produce and order in what seemed to me the best way possible, and to correct and emend, the *spoken words and their transcription,* which have until now been badly set down in the writings of my predecessors, and *so that what is put here in the present Arte and vocabulary and the order in which it comes may be better understood,* it will be helpful to bear in mind the following preliminary notices.[135]

Gilberti had no corresponding discussion of phonology in his Latin grammar—both the pronunciation and spelling of Latin continued to be determined by local,

[135] GILBERTI, *Arte,* Prologue, 6v–7r [2004, 63]: 'He acordado de hazer y ordenar lo mejor que me ha sido possible esta artezica en la qual va reformado y emendado en los vocablos y en la orthographia lo que hasta ahora ha sido mal puesto en las escripturas de mis antecessores, para que mejor se entienda lo que en este arte y vocabulario se pone y la orden que lleva sera menester notar los avisos siguientes . . .'

regional convention, as it had been throughout the Middle Ages.[136] More significantly, the positioning of these 'notices' ('avisos') at the very beginning of the *Arte* of Purépecha was also a departure not only from Nebrija, but also from Olmos, whose examination of 'orthography' or phonology comes toward the end of his *Arte*.[137]

The last two subsections of Gilberti's study treat idioms ('modos dicendi') and the 'division of time' in the Purépecha language. The idioms are appropriate to various social situations: 'for quarrelling and name-calling', 'for praising someone for such and such a thing', 'for giving advice', 'two people together going or coming', 'when a place is full of something' 'for when two go on a journey', 'to give orders at home'. Examples of the division of time set out the 'reckoning of the days' and of 'parts of the night'. The incorporation of such expressions, comparable to the inclusion of the 'elders' manners of speaking' at the end of Olmos' *Arte*, might prompt reflections of a broader nature on Purépecha conventions and ways of thinking. But another parallel is offered by the final section on usage in Gilberti's *Latin* grammar, which contains 'formulae for greeting, saying farewell and making enquiries'.[138] Overall, the divergences in emphasis and in details of organization between Gilberti's *Arte de lengua de Michuacan* and his *Grammatica Maturini* show his recognition of the profound differences between Purépecha and Latin.[139] Much in the way that Olmos' approach to Nahuatl ended up being shaped by the behaviour of the language itself, Gilberti adapted classical linguistic paradigms, ingeniously transforming them to facilitate his exposition of Purépecha. The flexible and pragmatic practices of both missionaries show that they were not constrained by long-standing assumptions about linguistic pedagogy.

VII. Conclusions

The rapid progress made by the missionary linguists was rooted in Renaissance approaches to grammar, which were largely practical. Guides to romance vernaculars and humanist grammars of Greek and Hebrew, for example, offered precedents for the missionaries' endeavours, and categories from Hebrew were sometimes used to explain features of Nahuatl and Purépecha.

[136] Quintilian, *Institutio oratoria* 1.7.30 had advocated writing according to pronunciation: 'Ego, nisi quod consuetudo optinuerit, sic scribendum quidque iudico, quomodo sonat', 'For my own part, unless usage makes a claim, I think that something should be written in the way that it sounds'. ERASMUS, *De recta Latini Graecique sermonis pronunciatione* (1528) attempted to systematize the multiple ways of pronouncing Latin across Europe. Waquet 2001, 151–73 describes the controversies.

[137] Cf. Suárez 1992, 82–95 and Smith-Stark 2004.

[138] See n. 117 above.

[139] Monzón 1999, 151 suggests that Gilberti may have first envisaged a common approach to Latin and Tarascan that proved impossible to realize.

But Latin grammar supplied the principal framework used to describe and systematize Amerindian languages. Nebrija's bilingual *Introductiones Latinae* and his Spanish-Latin dictionary were respectively the principal templates for the missionaries' *artes* and vocabularies, although the works of Despauter, Perotti, and Erasmus were all known and used in New Spain by the mid-1500s. At the same time, it was recognized that Latin rules and taxonomies could not always be applied to languages like Nahuatl and Purépecha—a realization that had little impact outside Spanish America because it conflicted with the universalism of Sanctius and his successors.

The study of languages had been accorded an important ideological status by Erasmus' utopian conception of a 'lingua', a tongue that would unite all of mankind in shared understanding of the Gospel. This philosophy explains why the missionaries' interest in the Babel story lay in its moral significance for the future, not in enquiries about the Adamic language of the prehistoric past. Erasmus' theological linguistics were again bound up with the practical importance that humanist grammarians attached to *usus*—achieving refinement of expression through the close imitation of classical models. This scrupulous attention to quality of eloquence, which left no time for the speculations of the medieval *modistae*, also went well beyond rote learning of grammatical rules. The high level of proficiency in Latin attained by European humanists would have motivated Fray Alonso de Molina and other missionaries to gain the fullest possible understanding of Nahuatl idioms and the ways they were used.[140]

An emphasis, after Valla, on the benefits of models for improving expression in Latin had especially important consequences in New Spain. From the 1400s humanist grammars had been supplemented with texts illustrating good Latin usage, from classical authors or exemplary Renaissance digests of ancient sources. It seems that Fray Andrés de Olmos, at least, had been attempting something similar by including the 'elders' manners of speaking' at the end of his *Arte de la lengua mexicana*. Following Olmos, other Franciscans, including Fray Juan Bautista and Fray Bernardino de Sahagún, collected texts that exemplified good Nahuatl usage and that could also ennoble broader aspects of Mexican thought and tradition. In this way the acquisition of an alien language and investigations of the *mores* (hence 'historia moral') of an alien society could be closely related. The missionaries' ethnographic enquiries were pursued in tandem with their linguistic work, much as European humanists acquired their broader knowledge of ancient Greece and Rome as a by-product of their study of classical grammar and rhetoric.[141]

[140] Cf. MOLINA, *Aqui comiença* (1555), aiii r–v: n. 55, above; CHIMALPAHIN, *Relaciones* 7 (c. 1630), 219v–220r [1998 ii, 252].

[141] Mack 2011, 307.

4

Education of the Indigenous Nobility

The Imperial College of Santa Cruz at Santiago Tlatelolco

As they struggled to learn Nahuatl and other Amerindian tongues, the missionaries in New Spain must have been daunted by the overwhelming task that faced them. Throughout the sixteenth century, there were never more than a few hundred friars to convert a population of millions, amongst which more than a hundred different languages were spoken.[1] Sacred images and relics, the spectacles of rituals and processions, pictorial catechisms, and many other forms of visual display would have played a vital role in conveying the Christian message to large numbers of people who could not understand Spanish or Latin, let alone read and write.[2] But the successful communication of that message still depended on linguistic translation: indigenous recruits were required as interpreters and preachers.[3] The Franciscans taught Latin to some Mexicans who acted as intermediaries and from whom in turn they eventually 'received great help and much light in the implanting of the faith.'[4]

In 1536 the Imperial College of Santa Cruz was established in order to provide a higher education to youths drawn from the region's indigenous elites. This institution in Tlatelolco, two miles from the centre of Mexico City, became the principal site for the translation and composition of Christian texts in Nahuatl, and some of the Latinists trained there assisted Fray Bernardino de Sahagún with his researches

[1] Cook and Borah 1979 iii, 97 estimate the native population of central Mexico at 2.65 million by 1568, while there were barely more than 800 missionary friars in all of New Spain: cf. Chapter 6, n. 1 below. A letter to Philip II from the provincials of the mendicant orders reported that there were only 380 Franciscans, 210 Dominicans, and 212 Augustinians in the entire viceroyalty: SANTA MARÍA, TORAL, and VERA CRUZ, 'Sacra Catholica y Real Magestad' (1559) [1877, 141–2].

[2] Lara 2008; Ditchfield 2017; Boone, Burkhart, and Tavárez 2017.

[3] Cf. Karttunen 2000 on the linguistic challenges faced by the missionaries.

[4] SAHAGÚN, *Historia general* (c. 1580) = *HG*, Book 10, 'Relación del autor' [1982 i, 82]: 'hemos recibido y aun recibimos, en la plantacion de la fe en estas partes grande ayuda y mucha lumbre de aquellos a quien hemos enseñado la lengua latina.'

Aztec Latin. Andrew Laird, Oxford University Press. © Oxford University Press 2024.
DOI: 10.1093/oso/9780197586358.003.0005

on Mexican traditions and beliefs. But the real purpose of the advanced instruction of youths from the native nobility was to prepare them for service as Christian governors and judges in their own communities.

This chapter will begin with a description of earlier educational initiatives in Hispaniola and New Spain, for which there had also been political as well as religious motives (Section I). An account of the foundation of the College of Santa Cruz (Section II) will then show conclusively that the institution was never meant to train a Mexican clergy, as has often been assumed, although the teaching of the Indians still provoked controversy. The latter part of this discussion (Section III) will throw some light on what was actually taught at the college, and on how the teaching was conducted, before some concluding remarks (Section IV).

I. Initial contexts and motives for the Indians' Latin education

All catechized converts had to know by heart the *Pater Noster, Credo, Ave Maria,* and the confession, *Ego peccator confiteor Deo.* Fray Juan de Torquemada recalled two methods used by Indians to memorize and sound out the Latin words. The first, which relied on counting, had long been used by Mexicans and Europeans alike:[5]

> Some proceeded by counting the words of the prayer ['Oración'] they were learning with pebbles or grains of maize, putting down a stone or grain, one after the other, for each word or each group of words they were pronouncing, so for the expression or word *Pater Noster* (as we say it) there was one stone, for *qui es in coelis,* another, for *santifiquetur,* another; and, afterwards, signalling with a finger, they began, by means of the first stone, to say *Pater noster* and then *qui es in coelis* on the prompting of the second, and they went through all of them until the end; and they used to go through this several times until the whole prayer stayed in their memory . . .

The second method is likely to have derived from non-alphabetic Mesoamerican writing, in which depictions could have a phonic value:[6]

> Another way (in my view very difficult, though remarkable) was to apply the words in their language that conformed and approximated to some

[5] Cf. VALADÉS, *Rhetorica Christiana* (1579), = *RC,* 2.27 B–C, 94 [1989, 234] quoted in Chapter 2 nn. 81, 82 above. Cf. Small 1993, 14, 34, 89–93, 188 on the role of number in memorization from European antiquity.

[6] Cf. Whittaker 2021, a study of Aztec hieroglyphics.

extent with the pronunciation of the Latin words. They put them, in order, on a sheet of paper, not as written words formed in letters, but what those words conveyed; *because they did not have letters of their own but paintings, and these were interpreted as characters.* This will be more easily understood by an example. The word they have that comes closest to the pronunciation of *Pater* is *pantli,* which signifies a kind of little flag and that prompts them to say *Pater.* For the second word *Noster* the term they have closest to it in pronunciation is *nuchtli,* the name for what our people call *tuna* [prickly pear] or 'fig of the Indies' in Spain. In order to align it with the word *Noster* they paint it next in sequence to the little flag, a *tuna,* which they call *nuchtli*; and in that fashion they go on until the end of their prayer; and by a similar means they find other corresponding characters that could be understood, to memorize what they had to recite in chorus.[7]

Torquemada's specification above that the paintings were 'interpreted as characters' ('así se entendían por caracteres') implies that they were phonographic.[8] If so, they operated differently from the way that ideographic or pictographic catechisms did with which Indians depicted the content of words and phrases in prayers and responses.[9] All these means of instilling either the sound or the meaning of prayers in Latin were a long way from conventional instruction in the language.

On the other hand, several sources indicate that some Mexicans were taught Latin before any institutions were formally established for this purpose.[10] In a royal cedula of 1536, which retroactively authorized the foundation of the College of Santa Cruz, the Emperor Charles himself recognized that Indian children had a talent for Latin.[11] At around the same time Fray Julián Garcés reported that although

[7] TORQUEMADA, *MI* 15.36 [1977 v, 158–9].

[8] ACOSTA, *Historia natural y moral de las Indias* (1590) 6.7 [2003, 382–5] also referred to 'characters' that may have been indigenous phonographic signs: 'donde faltan imágines, ponen caracteres, como en qué pequé, etc. de donde se podrá colegir la viveza de los ingenios de estos indios, pues este modo de escrebir nuestras oraciones y cosas de la fe ni se los enseñaron los españoles, ni ellos pudieran salir con él, si no hicieron muy particular concepto de lo que les enseñaban' ('where images are lacking, they insert characters, as with 'wherein I have sinned', etc., from which one is able to gather the liveliness of these Indians' intellects, for the Spaniards never taught them this way of writing').

[9] Cf. Cortés Castellanos 1987 on Fray Pedro de Gante's catechism in pictograms; Gaillemin 2014 on Testarian catechisms; VALADÉS, *RC* 2.27 I, 95 [1989, 236]: Chapter 2, n. 84 above. These systems may have derived rather more loosely from pre-existing indigenous practices than the phonographic method earlier described by Torquemada. Boone, Burkhart, and Tavárez 2017, 21–31 is an important revisionist account. Cf. Ødemark 2017, 331–67.

[10] Cf. nn. 26, 27, 29, 37 below.

[11] The cedula conferred in Valladolid on 3rd September, addressed to Bishop Zumárraga and communicated to the viceroy, is quoted in García Icazbalceta 1947 i, 287: 'mucho he holgado de lo que decís, que yendo a examinar la inteligencia de los niños hijos de los naturales de esa tierra, a quienes enseñan gramática en los monasterios, hallasteis muchos de gran habilidad y viveza de ingenio y

the Indians 'used to paint instead of write', their children now wrote in Latin and Spanish: 'they know and speak Latin more elegantly than our [Spanish children], and no less than our own [friars] who have devoted themselves to the study of this subject'.[12]

The first educators in New Spain left no testimony about how systematic knowledge of Latin was first transmitted, doubtless because they assumed that the process was less worthy of comment. The practice, customary in the 1500s, of teaching Latin in Latin must have been adopted, and the enormous popularity of Erasmus' textbook of elementary dialogues, *Colloquia familiaria*, 'Dialogues among friends', first published in 1518, and Juan Luis Vives' *Exercitatio linguae Latinae* (1538) point to the pervasiveness and success of that technique.[13] In Europe it had long been common for humanists to teach children to read first in Latin rather than in the spoken vernacular, and the friars would have done the same.[14] Fray Gerónimo de Mendieta hinted at this when he remarked that the Indians soon learned to read in Spanish *as well as* in Latin.[15]

The schooling of aboriginal American children began in the Caribbean. In 1503, the crown issued an instruction to Nicolás de Ovando, the governor of Hispaniola, to build houses next to parish churches, in which the local children could assemble twice a day to learn how to 'read, write, make the sign of the cross and recite the *Pater noster*, *Ave Maria*, *Credo* and *Salve Regina*'. On 23 January 1513, the Laws of Burgos specified the obligations of *encomenderos* and Franciscans to inculcate literacy and elements of the Christian religion. The next month a royal order charged that twenty Latin textbooks, desks and reams of paper, and ten books of the Gospels

memoria aventajada . . . para aprender gramática y para otras facultades' ('I have dwelled much on what you say, that in proceeding to examine the intelligence of the little children of the natives of that land, and those who teach grammar in monasteries, you found many with great aptitude, lively intellect and remarkable memory . . . to learn Latin and other subjects').

[12] GARCÉS, *De habilitate* (1537), 5v (see Appendix 2.1.2 below): 'nostris pueris elegantius Latine sciant atque loquantur: non minus quam nostri qui se eius rei studio dedidere.' SAHAGÚN, *HG*, Book 10, 'Relación' [1982 i, 82] and TORQUEMADA (n. 8 above) also imply that the Indians' pictorial writing had once served as a kind of counterpart to Latin letters. The fundamental role of *literae* in Latin grammar and recognition of their pictorial significance in Isidore, *Etymologies* 1.1.3 might account for this.

[13] See Section III below for the use of the *Colloquia* and *Exercitatio* in teaching. 'Venatio', a dialogue on hunting in the *Colloquia*, was echoed in CABRERA, 'Dicolon Icastichon' (1540), the first poem printed in New Spain: cf. Laird 2019b, 86. Salmon 1960 examines a debate about Latin pedagogy among Erasmus, Vives, Despauter, and George Halewyn, Charles V's Belgian courtier.

[14] Black 2015, 99: 'The first stage of the Italian medieval, Renaissance and early modern curriculum consisted of learning to read: this skill was always acquired through the Latin language'. The missionary educators themselves would have been taught in a similar manner. See further Black 2001.

[15] MENDIETA, *Hystoria ecclesiastica yndiana* (c. 1596), = *Historia*, 4.14 [1870, 410]: 'con mucha brevedad aprendieron á leer, así nuestro romance como el latín.' Mendieta then states in 4.14 [411] that the Indians subsequently appropriated the Roman alphabet for their own language.

and homilies be supplied to a *bachiller,* or high school graduate, named Hernándo Xuárez.[16]

Ferdinand of Aragón entrusted a sum of money to Xuárez 'to teach Latin ('gramática') to the sons of the native rulers ('caciques') of Hispaniola'.[17] Fray Bartolomé de las Casas later objected to such discrimination, complaining that the Franciscans who had accompanied Ovando to the Antilles took in only a few such pupils.[18] Xuárez, however, recruited others to instruct Indians and Africans in Santo Domingo in Latin, the arts, and theology, and his efforts continued to succeed in securing approval and material resources from the crown and church authorities.[19] The diocesan bishop of Hispaniola, Sebastián Ramírez de Fuenleal, asked the Empress Isabella in 1530 to seek a papal bull supporting a college that would produce 'masters of all the sciences'.[20] Ramírez de Fuenleal later had a major part to play in establishing the College of Santa Cruz.

The Flemish missionaries Pedro de Gante, Juan de Aora, and Juan de Tecto were the first European educators in New Spain. Soon after their arrival in 1523, they were accommodated in the residence of Ixtililxochitl, the ruler of Texcoco, so that they could teach his sons and other children in the household.[21] Fray Pedro de Gante was singled out by the king's great-grandson, Fernando de Alva Ixtlilxochitl, for his extraordinary success in teaching Christian doctrine and the Gospel to Mexican children.[22] For more than three years Gante continued to work in the school he had helped to found in Texcoco. He then moved to Mexico City in 1527, where he oversaw the education of Indians in the chapel of San José de Belén de los Naturales, 'Saint Joseph of Bethlehem of the Natives', adjacent to the convent of San Francisco.

Boys at San José were able to learn 'the most common kinds of job in the workshops . . . those of tailors, shoemakers, carpenters, and others'.[23] Music, precious-metal work, painting, sculpture, and embroidery were taught, too, but Gante saw the benefits of an education that could equip Mexican students for civic life. More than thirty years later he would ask Philip II to consider the advantages of training Indian judges, mayors, and governors.[24] Latin was probably added to

[16] Konetske 1953 i, 257, cited in Kobayashi 1985, 157.

[17] Olaechea Labayen 1958, 182; Kobayashi 1985, 160.

[18] LAS CASAS, *Historia* (c. 1560) 2.13 [1961, 37]. Las Casas had sailed on Ovando's 1502 expedition to Hispaniola as a youth.

[19] Kobayashi 1985, 160–1.

[20] Utrera 1932, 14–18, cited in Méndez Arceo 1952, 41.

[21] MENDIETA, *Historia* 5.17 [1870, 606].

[22] ALVA IXTLILXOCHITL, *Compendio histórico* (1608), 'Décimatercia relación' [1975 i, 492]: cf. Chapter 1, II above.

[23] MENDIETA, *Historia* 4.13 [1870, 407–9].

[24] GANTE, 'Carta . . . al Rey' (1558) [1941, 225]: 'es necesario ayudar esta obra y sustentarla, de donde salen jueces de los pueblos, alcaldes, regidores y los que ayudan á los frailes' ('it is necessary to help and sustain this endeavour, to produce judges for the towns, mayors, rulers and those to help the friars').

the curriculum at San José de los Naturales some time after 1530, by a Franciscan scholar from Aquitaine, Arnaud de Bassac, or Fray Arnaldo de Bassacio, who was the first teacher of Latin to the Indians in Mexico City.[25]

Sebastián Ramírez de Fuenleal wrote again to the Empress Isabella in 1533, having arrived from Hispaniola two years earlier to assume the presidency of the second reformed Audiencia of New Spain. The main aim of his letter was to request support for the residential community that Vasco de Quiroga had founded for the 'poor Indians' two leagues from Mexico City, but it also reported that the Franciscans at San José de los Naturales were successfully teaching Spanish to native children in the Mexican language. Bassacio's command of Nahuatl was proving so useful that Ramírez de Fuenleal estimated that, within two years, there would be fifty Indians themselves capable of teaching Spanish. He pleaded for additional funding to sustain the students, to pay their instructors, and to achieve a further objective:

> once they know and understand some grammar, there will be a need for people to read them books of good Latinity and oratory, and it will be enough that they should be instructed in the Latin language, even though the teachers may not be Nahuatl-speaking friars ['frailes naguatatos'], nor any who know their language, as they will have to read to them and teach them doctrine in Latin . . . the expense is small and the benefit will be great.[26]

Something that occurred toward the end of Ramírez Fuenleal's presidency suggests that his idea was not just prompted by religious considerations. According to Vasco de Quiroga, the two young sons of the last *cazonci*, or king of Michoacán, had been taken to Mexico City in 1535 and offered as hostages by the leaders of the Purépecha to guarantee their loyalty to the Spaniards.[27] This was five years after the boys' father, Tangaxuan, had been summarily executed on false charges by the rogue conquistador Nuño Beltrán de Guzmán.[28] Francisco Cervantes de Salazar reported that both children were given tuition in Latin and Spanish—probably at the court of the first viceroy, Antonio de Mendoza, who had succeeded the auditor, Ramírez Fuenleal. Following their return to Michoacán in 1538, the elder son, Francisco

[25] MENDIETA, *Historia* 4.15 [1870, 414].

[26] RAMÍREZ, 'Carta a la emperatriz' (1533) [1939 iii, 118]: *naguatato* was a corruption of the Spanish loan word from Nahuatl, *nahuatlato*, 'clear speaker', i.e. 'Nahuatl speaker'.

[27] QUIROGA, 'Información en derecho' (1535) cap. 2 [1868 x, 343–5]: 'en días pasadas vi que vinieron al acuerdo de esta audiencia los principales de Mechuacan y traían consigo á dos hijos pequeños del Caçonçi'. On the 'Información en derechocf. Chapter 1, IV above.

[28] ALCALÁ, *Relación de Michoacán* (1540), cap. 29, fols. 56v–59r [2016, 274–9], cf. Afanandor-Pujol 2015, 17–108; CERVANTES DE SALAZAR, *Chronica* (c. 1566) 6.28 [1971 ii, 282, col. 1].

Tariacuri, became governor of the region, to be replaced on his death by his brother, Antonio Huitzimengari, who produced a revealing account of the services he and his father had rendered to the Spanish crown.[29]

Cervantes de Salazar, a professor of rhetoric appointed at the inauguration of the Royal University of Mexico, knew Huitzimengari personally, recalling that 'he prided himself on owning many books in Latin that he very well understood'.[30] In fact, Huitzimengari bequeathed ninety-one volumes to his son Pablo, and although no details of those volumes are recorded, fourteen titles are given in a bookseller's hastily scrawled *poder* for payment from Huitzimengari.[31] The bill, reproduced in Appendix 1.2, includes three dictionaries: editions of Nebrija's Spanish-Latin *Dictionarium,* or 'Vocabulario'; Niccolò Perotti's *Cornu copiae* (the commentary on Martial that functioned as a Latin lexicon); and Fray Maturino Gilberti's *Vocabulario en lengua de Mechuacan.*[32] Such items, along with the commentaries on Aquinas and the Gospels that were included in this purchase, would have been helpful for Huitzimengari's attested translation of a catechism and a lectionary of Gospels and Epistles into his native Purépecha.[33] The other works listed were on a range of topical subjects: they included Ptolemy's *Geography*, Ginés de Sepúlveda's *Democrates* (his dialogue on the value of military experience for a Christian), and Bernardo Pérez de Chinchón's Spanish translation of Erasmus' *Lingua*—a text that, in contrast, was pacifistic in tenor.[34] The acquisition of the *Lingua* points to another connection with Gilberti: the friar's dedication of his *arte* of Purépecha contained several conspicuous echoes of that text by Erasmus.[35]

Another renowned professor at the Royal University of Mexico, Bartolomé Frías de Albornoz, who held the chair of Civil Law, elaborated upon Antonio Huitzimengari's capacities:

[29] HUITZIMENGARI, 'Información' (1553–1554).

[30] CERVANTES DE SALAZAR, *Chronica* (1566), 6.28 [1971 ii, 282, col. 1]: 'presciábase de tener muchos libros latinos, las cuales entendía muy bien. Era muy gentil Escribano y especialmente en Castellano escrebía con mucho aviso una carta, y no menos en latín.'

[31] A document (Pátzcuaro 114) on the guardianship of Huitzimengari's son, 'Sobre la tutela de don Pablo, hijo de Don Antonio Huitziméngari y sus bienes' (1571), is noted in López Sarrelangue 1965, 180. The existence of the bookseller's charge, MENDOZA, 'Poder' (1559), examined in Jiménez 2002, was initially signalled by Martínez Baracs and Espinosa Morales 1999, 63–4: cf. Appendix 1.2 below.

[32] Cf. Chapter 3, nn. 25, 27 and Chapter 3, VI above.

[33] León 1888, 173 attested Huitzimengari's autograph manuscript of a *Devocionario,* a catechism and prayer book containing Gospels and Epistles. A Purépecha manuscript by Huitzimengari may have been among the documents León retrieved from convent archives and sold to an unidentified library in the United States: Corona Núñez 1982, 59.

[34] SEPÚLVEDA, *Democrates* (1535) was translated into Spanish in 1541; his *Democrates secundus* (c. 1545) was a defence of just war in the Indies: cf. Chapter 1, n. 131 above. For PÉREZ DE CHINCHÓN, *La lengua de Erasmo* (1533), cf. Chapter 3, III above.

[35] GILBERTI, *Arte* (1558), 1v–2r [2004, 58–9]: Chapter 3, III, VI above. See below III (i) for Gilberti's use of Erasmus in his Latin grammar.

> The present witness has sufficient foundation in the Latin, Greek, and Hebrew languages to recognize who excels in them, and though he is well above average ability in them all, where Latin is concerned, you should know that the same Don Antonio is very proficient and can easily understand and read quite well any Latin poet or orator. As for the Greek he knows, there are not two better Hellenists in all of New Spain—though there are many who are regarded, or who regard themselves, as gifted in Greek—because this witness saw him, on one of many occasions, reading an Olynthiac speech of Demosthenes and pronouncing the tricolons very competently ['dezir los ternos muy diestramente']. He knows the elements of Hebrew, but is not as advanced in that as he is in Greek or Latin: in those languages and in literature he is more thoroughly rehearsed than many who earn their keep from it . . . He is busy writing about questions of the Christian faith in which he is also well trained. His learning is a great example to the natives—who tend to imitate the virtues as well as the faults of their superiors.[36]

The final remark in the quotation above clarifies the real benefits to the Spaniards of the Purépecha leader's erudition. The object of educating both sons of the *cazonci* was to ensure that they sustained Spanish influence and secured social stability in the administration of their ancestral realm. The Franciscan missionaries were already employing much the same strategy in central Mexico: boys and youths from the local elites were taken or abducted as 'hostages' and schooled, before they were eventually returned to their communities as governors.[37]

The crown and the religious authorities alike saw the creation of an Indian ruling class imbued with Christian humanist principles as a means of consolidating the faith and loyalty of native communities. By 1537 the Augustinians had secured funds for their College of the Name of Jesus, where Indians and Spaniards were taught by a salaried professor.[38] Two colleges in Michoacán admitted Spanish, mestizo, and indigenous students: in 1540 Bishop Vasco de Quiroga founded the celebrated College of San Nicolás Obispo, which would later incorporate the College of San Miguel, endowed by the viceroy Mendoza in 1541.[39] But in central Mexico there was already another institution to which the most outstanding students from San José and other 'Indian' schools could proceed.

[36] Frías de Albornoz's testimony of March 1554 is quoted in HUITZIMENGARI, 'Información' (1554), 59r–v [2019, 185–6]: at 15v [135] Gonzalo Gómez and at 20r [140] the Augustinian professor Fray Alonso de Castañeda also attest to Huitzimengari's learning.

[37] TORQUEMADA, *MI* 15.19 [1977 v, 83]; cf. Trexler 1987, 552.

[38] Méndez Arceo 1952, 34–6; Osorio Romero 1990, l–li.

[39] Miranda Godínez 1972; Herrejón Peredo 1989.

II. Foundation of Santa Cruz: Objectives and controversies

The Imperial College of Santa Cruz was established with Mendoza's patronage and support from Ramírez de Fuenleal, Bishop Zumárraga, and Fray García de Cisneros, who was one of the Franciscan Twelve. Located in Santiago Tlatelolco, an Indian enclave to the north of Mexico City, the college had already begun operating some months before its official inauguration in 1536 on January 6, the Feast of the Epiphany.[40] That celebration of the visit of the Magi to the infant Jesus, which had long been interpreted as a call to gentiles to recognize Christ, was deemed an appropriate occasion for the sons of indigenous Mexican rulers to be invited to join the Christian society of the Spaniards.[41] There was a solemn procession from the Convent of San Francisco in Mexico City, in which Mendoza, Ramírez de Fuenleal, and Zumárraga took part. Three sermons were preached to mark the occasion: the first in the Convent of San Francisco by the church's treasurer Rafael de Cervantes, the second en route to coincide with mass at the Convent of Santiago Tlatelolco by Fray Alonso de Herrera, and the third, by Fray Pedro de Rivera, in the refectory of the new college, where all present were invited to dine at Bishop Zumárraga's expense.[42]

Before the arrival of the Spaniards, Tlatelolco had been a powerful Mexica *altepetl*, or polity, closely allied to Mexico Tenochtitlan. Its dedication to 'Santiago', or Saint James, the bellicose patron saint of Spain often known as *Matamoros*, 'Killer of Moors', and later as *Mataindios*, was grimly appropriate. Thousands of Mexica warriors had perished on that site, as their commander, the young emperor Cuauhtemoc, had made his last stand against the Spaniards before his capture by Cortés brought the Aztec resistance to an end on 13 August 1521.[43] But Santiago Tlatelolco would retain a high degree of political and cultural independence as an Indian republic for some time after the Spanish invasion: the status of the district made it an appropriate location for a college to educate native students.[44] The

[40] Previous studies of the College of Santa Cruz include Ricard 1933 [1966, 217–38]; Steck 1944; Kobayashi 1985; Gil 1990; Gonzalbo Aizpuru 1990, 111–34; Osorio Romero 1990; SilverMoon 2007; Hernández and Máynez 2016; Téllez Nieto 2019a. Not all the opinions in those works are shared here.

[41] Matthew 2:1–12; MOTOLINÍA, *Historia de los indios* (c. 1543) 1.13 [2001, 76; tr. 1951, 142]: 'The feast of the three kings also makes them very happy because they regard it as properly theirs.' 'Cédula real', 3 September 1536, in García Icazbalceta 1947 i, 288 (n. 12 above).

[42] MENDIETA, *Historia* 4.15 [1870, 414–15]; TORQUEMADA, *MI*, 15.43 [1977 v, 175].

[43] CORTÉS, 'Tercera carta-relacion' (1522) [tr. 1986, 263–5].

[44] According to the 1536 cedula (n. 12 above), Zumárraga had stated that the Indians should have a college in Santiago because it was 'better disposed than any other area' ('porque había mejor disposición que en otra parte'). For Tlatelolco's post-conquest identity, cf. Estrada Torres 2000; Guilliem Arroyo 2013 gives archaeological evidence.

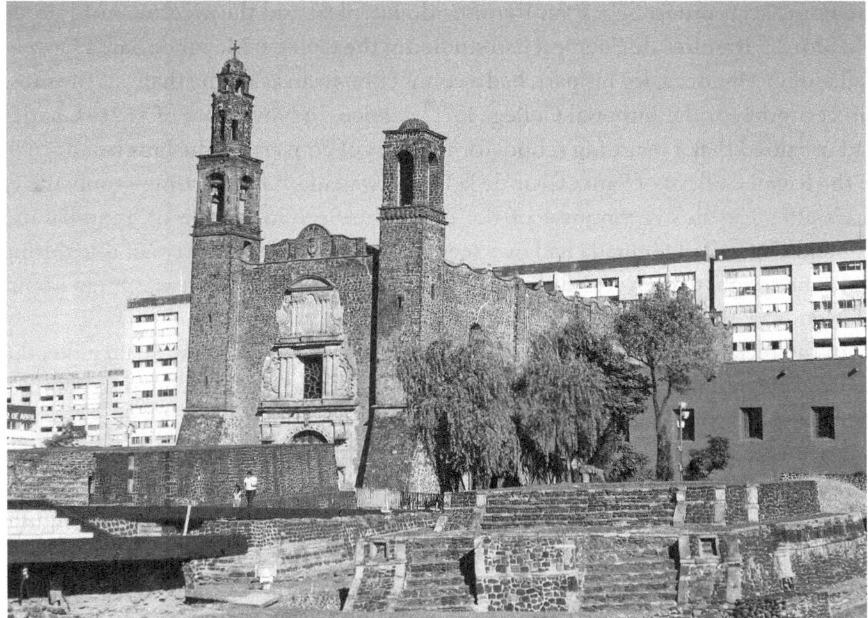

Figure 4.1 The church and convent of Santiago, site of the College of Santa Cruz, with remains of pre-Hispanic Tlatelolco in the foreground.

convent and church (Plate 5) were constructed only a few steps away from where an Aztec temple had stood, so that the College of Santa Cruz may well have been near or on the site of a pre-Hispanic *calmecac*, a residential part of the sacred precinct in which Aztec priests, officiants, and nobility had been trained (Figure 4.1).[45] Such a coincidence may not have appealed to the Franciscans, even though the friars adopted the practice of raising indigenous children in religious institutions 'because we discovered that in their ancient republic the [Mexicans] reared the boys and girls in the temples and there disciplined them and taught them the worship of their gods and submission to their state.'[46]

The college, designated 'Imperial' in honour of the Emperor Charles V, was under the financial control of a *mayordomo*, or treasurer, appointed by the viceroy. The dedication to the Holy Cross, Santa Cruz, though chosen by Fray García de Cisneros, had important associations for the two most powerful supporters outside

[45] SAHAGÚN, *HG* 8.20 [1979 ix, 71]; anon., *Codex Mendoza* (c. 1542) [1992 iii, fols. 61v–63r]; Calnek 1988.

[46] SAHAGÚN, *HG* 10, 'Relación' [1982 i, 77]. Comparisons between pre-Hispanic and Franciscan education (cf. Kobayashi 1985, 178–80, 183) have led to the questionable view that the friars were engineering a symbolic continuity between them: e.g. Nesvig 2006, 77: 'the Franciscans had adopted the Mexica concept of a *calmecac*.'

the Franciscan order: Sebastián Ramírez de Fuenleal and the viceroy, Antonio de Mendoza.[47] Ramírez de Fuenleal had studied at the Colegio Mayor de Santa Cruz in Valladolid. Mendoza, for his part, had a connection to an academy that was the most direct model for the Imperial College in Tlatelolco. In November of 1526, Charles had ordained that a boarding school for the sons of converted Muslims be attached to the Royal College of Santa Cruz de la Fe, in Granada.[48] By this time—only thirty years after Castile's reconquest of the city—the Second Conde of Tendilla and Captain General of Granada had overseen almost a decade of Christian rule during which he sought to convert Muslims by education and example. He was Íñigo López de Mendoza, the viceroy Antonio de Mendoza's father.[49]

In the reclaimed emirate of Granada, in Hispaniola and in New Spain alike, the practice of training an elite from a subjugated population was intended to complement and reinforce that population's conversion to Christianity. Such a practice was not exceptional or enlightened: it was naturally adopted as a consequence of the presupposition, widely shared even before the Renaissance, that the objective of an advanced education was to prepare students to be leaders. Since the Middle Ages, *specula principum*, 'mirrors for princes', had presented various forms of knowledge under the guise of instructing rulers on the art of kingship. The most successful of these, a scholastic application of Aristotelian political theory, was studied in universities all over Europe: *De regimine principum*, 'Guidance for Princes' (1279), long attributed to Saint Thomas Aquinas, but in fact the work of his disciple, Aegidius Romanus, or Giles of Rome.[50]

Well before Niccolò Machiavelli wrote *Il principe*, 'The Prince' (1513), there had been a succession of Renaissance treatises in Latin on princely education containing precepts and admonitions for a ruler.[51] These texts did not engage with political theory or strategy, and were in effect rhetorical works that followed classical models, not least Cicero—who had held that a trained orator was bound to serve the public interest and that he 'must be accomplished in every kind of discourse and in every realm of the humanities'.[52] The *De regno et regis institutione*, 'Kingship and instructing a king', composed in the 1480s by Francesco Patrizi of Siena, and the

[47] OROZ, *Relación* (1586) [tr. 1972, 99] reports that Fray García de Cisneros founded the College as it was conceived by Mendoza and Zumárraga and that Cisneros 'gave [it] the title of Santa Cruz' ('intituló Santa Cruz').

[48] López Rodríguez 1979; Coleman 2003, 1–9, 113–43.

[49] Nader 1972, 156.

[50] Briggs 1999, 20 notes that the popularity of Giles' *De regimine principum* (there are 350 known manuscripts) eclipsed that of Saint Thomas Aquinas' *De regimine principum*, completed by Ptolemy of Lucca (27 mss.), of Vincent of Beauvais' *De morali principis instructione* (3 mss.) and of the anonymous *Liber de informatione principum* (6 mss.).

[51] Skinner 1988, 423–34, 441–52.

[52] Cicero, *De oratore* 1.16.71: 'quod in omni genere sermonis, in omni parte humanitatis dixerim oratorem perfectum esse debere.'

De principe (1494) by the Neapolitan humanist Giovanni Pontano were influential examples of the genre. Both secured a wide readership and were reprinted several times. Patrizi's work, dedicated to Alfonso of Aragón, was repeatedly printed in the sixteenth century and it was translated into English as well as Spanish.[53]

Although Erasmus' *Institutio principis Christiani,* 'Instruction of a Christian Prince' (1516), was rooted in the same rhetorical tradition, it represented a significant departure in several ways.[54] This work, especially the long opening chapter, was concerned with very specific aspects of pedagogy. The recommendation that a prince should be selected for his skill rather than on the basis of noble ancestry anticipated the more overt challenge to hereditary privilege in More's *Utopia* (1518). Erasmus' instructions for a *princeps* dealt with such matters as taxation, enactment of laws, magistrates, and marriage alliances, along with the stock themes of generosity and avoidance of flattery. Three separate chapters advocated pacifism—as the optimal method of ruling, as a means of improving the realm, and as a general principle—and thus went beyond humanist commonplaces to address contemporary political concerns. Erasmus' *De querela pacis,* 'The Complaint of Peace' (1517), which overtly countered scholastic doctrines of a just war, had also appeared in 1516, before being published as a volume in its own right.[55]

The *Institutio principis Christiani* contained a panegyric to the Archduke Philip of Austria, and it was dedicated to the future Emperor Charles, who ascended to the Spanish throne in 1516. Despite its polemical tone with regard to the church and the religious orders, Erasmus' tract was evidently known to the friars and students of Santa Cruz, even though, like the *Lingua* and the *Moriae encomium,* it was never actually named by the authors from sixteenth-century New Spain who echoed it. Sahagún, for example, remarked that the Indians would be subject to a 'most Christian prince' ('principe christianjssimo') as a result of the education the friars were providing.[56] The *Institutio principis Christiani* at once offered inspiration, a rationale, and an agenda for the schooling of youths from the indigenous nobility.

[53] PATRIZI, *De regno et regis institutione* (1531). The work continued to circulate in New Spain: Yhmoff Cabrera 1996 ii, 522–25 gives details of two later imprints (Paris, 1582 and Strasbourg, 1594) found in Mexico, and the Spanish translation: GARCÉS, *Francisco Patricio, De Reyno* (1591).

[54] Skinner 1978, 213–48.

[55] Fernández-Santamaria 1977, 130–44.

[56] SAHAGÚN, *HG* 10, 'Relación' [1982 i, 83], quoted below. A 1519 edition of ERASMUS, *Institutio principis Christiani* (1516) was listed in a Victorian sale catalogue of imported Mexican books: Simpson 1890, 142. The Old Testament books of wisdom literature recommended in *Institutio principis Christiani* (1516) 2.15 [1974, 180] to show 'what pertains to the duty of a good prince' ('quid ad boni principis officium pertinet'), were translated into Nahuatl at Tlatelolco (Chapter 5 below). In his Latin letters to Philip II, Pablo Nazareo, an Indian rector of the College, seems to have drawn wording and conceits from Erasmus' *Institutio principis Christiani*: NAZAREO DE XALTOCAN, 'Invictissimo Hispaniarum' (1556), 'Sacrae Catholicae Magestati' (1566); cf. Carrera de la Red 1998 on Nazareo's use of ERASMUS, *Opus de conscribendis epistolis* (1522); and Chapter 7, III below.

The possibility of another motive for the establishment of the Imperial College of Santa Cruz, over and above that of preparing Indians to serve as governors and magistrates, has long been entertained: the formation of an indigenous clergy. As early as 1525, Rodrigo de Albornoz, a prominent member of the Audiencia of New Spain, wrote to ask Charles V to ordain 'a college where [the sons of lords and chieftains] may be taught reading, Latin, philosophy and other arts to become priests'.[57] In the same letter Albornoz proposed establishing a convent to teach the Christian faith and handiwork to the daughters of principal lords 'which would render them orderly and suitable until they marry, as the Beguines do in Flanders'. Motolinía may have considered the possibility of natives entering the church in the 1530s, but the ramifications were controversial.[58] To concede such a position to Indians in the sphere of religion would have accorded them equal status in civil life.[59] In practice, Indians, mestizos, and Africans were not admitted to the priesthood—a prohibition that was formalized by the First Mexican Church Council of 1555.[60]

The opinion of the French historian Robert Ricard that the purpose of the Imperial College of Santa Cruz was to train an indigenous clergy has been generally accepted for nearly a century, and a great deal of emphasis has been placed on that unlikely objective.[61] Given that Latin was the customary vehicle of formal education, the long-standing association of the language with the church and the priesthood might account for the wide acceptance of Ricard's view, along with the realization that Santa Cruz would have been modelled on the schools and colleges at which the friars themselves had been educated.

Yet the original idea, expressed by Sebastián Ramírez Fuenleal, had been only for an unspecified 'great fruit' to be born from training Indian students in 'good Latinity

[57] ALBORNOZ, 'Carta al emperador Carlos V' (1525) [2008, 38]: 'ay neçesidad nos mande vuestra majestad se haga un colegio donde les muestren a leer y gramatica y philosophia y otras artes para que vengan a ser sacerdotes'.

[58] MOTOLINÍA, *Memoriales* (c. 1541), 60r [1996, 330]; *Historia* 2.9 (c. 1543) [2001, 151–6] discussed in Pardo 2004, 49–50.

[59] Osorio Romero 1990, v (my translation): 'The polemic about the teaching of Latin to the Indians, and especially about their access to the priesthood, was the reflection, on the superstructural level, of another more grievous reality, the reality of the conquest.'

[60] LORENZANA Y BUITRÓN, *Concilios provinciales primero y segundo* (1769) lib. 1, tit. 4, §3, 31: 'Inde etiam nec Mixti, tam ab Indis, quam Mauris, nec non ab illis, qui ex altero parente Aetiope nascuntur, descendentes in primo gradu, ad Ordines sine magno delectu admittantur.' ('Wherefore not even those of mixed race, bred from Indian or Moors, or indeed from those born with an African parent, in the first stage of descent, are to be admitted to Holy Orders without great discernment.') Pardo 2004, 183 n. 5, notes the crafted ambiguity of the phrasing. See further Poole 1981.

[61] Ricard 1933 [1966, 217–24]. Ricard's work was known to Francis Borgia Steck before it was translated into Spanish in 1947. Kobayashi, Osorio Romero, Mathes, and other Mexican scholars followed Steck in regarding the College in Tlatelolco as a 'failure', because it did not function as a seminary. That consensus was adopted by historians writing in English and is still entertained: Dumont 2016, 103; Zwartjes 2016, 190. Contrast the neglected study of Estarellas 1962.

and oratory' and in theology ('doctrina').[62] Bishop Zumárraga's proposal had been made in similarly general terms.[63] In his *Historia ecclesiástica indiana*, Fray Gerónimo de Mendieta recounted how Fray Francisco de Bustamante visited a former student from the Imperial College of Santa Cruz, a native from Cuauhtitlan named Miguel, who was dying of the plague that devastated Mexico City and Tlatelolco in 1545. The piety and learning displayed by don Miguel as he conversed in Latin with his teacher prompted Mendieta to rehearse the arguments that someone might raise for Indians taking the habit or entering the priesthood: their conduct showed they have a natural inclination to become good Christians; newly converted Jews and Gentiles had after all been admitted to the early church; and Indian priests would be advantageous for the conversion of other Mexicans who would be more likely to listen to those who spoke their own languages.[64]

Mendieta's rebuttal was that the situation in the time of the early church was different. Then God had worked with miracles through the agency of recent converts, who were saints and well prepared to martyr themselves for their faith. In contrast, the church in Mexico was facing setbacks and problems with its new converts, so that it had ordained in its statutes, on papal authority, that natives should not enter the religious profession. Mendieta further argued that the Indians shared a disposition to be ruled rather than to rule: 'they are not to be masters but disciples, not prelates but subjects, and the best in the world.' The chronicler ended his discussion on a conciliatory note—though without changing his mind—after another short narrative:

> An eminent foreign man of letters from Spain's dominions [Fray Jacob the Dacian, a Dane] who came to these parts, relying on his learning, presumed to declare that this new Church of the Indies was mistaken not to receive native ministers amongst its converts, as in the Early Church: he held the opinion that Holy Orders should be conferred on the Indians and that they should be made ministers of the Church. The most learned and devout father Fray Juan de Gaona convinced him of his error in a public disputation, so that he was obliged to do penance. And his apology which he expressed in writing still circulates amongst us to this day. I have thought about this at greater length but 'it is not in man's power to stop the spirit' [Ecclesiastes 8:8]. I conclude with this: what we find in Indians we find in all other nations of the world, that among them there are good and bad ones.[65]

[62] RAMÍREZ DE FUENLEAL, 'Carta a la emperatriz' (1533): cf. n. 26 above.

[63] The 1536 royal cedula (n. 12 above) reveals the gist of Zumárraga's proposal.

[64] MENDIETA, *Historia* 4.23 [1870, 447–8].

[65] MENDIETA, *Historia* 4.23 [1870, 450].

There were indeed debates about Indians entering the priesthood, although such debates had never impinged upon the foundation or the function of the Imperial College of Santa Cruz—at which both Juan de Gaona and Jacob the Dacian were instructors. Fray Bernardino de Sahagún, who had been involved with the institution for more than forty years, made clear that Indians had been unfit to be admitted to the Franciscan Order, let alone to become priests.[66] There had never been any expectation that the college would produce an indigenous clergy. He recalled the response the friars offered to those who warned that a Latin education might incline Mexicans to heresy:

> To these objections it was responded that, admitting they were not to be priests, we wished to know how far their capabilities might be expanded. Knowing this from experience, we could bear witness to what was in them, and in accordance with their capabilities, there would be done with them what would seem to be just as nearly as possible. To their saying that we gave them the opportunity to become heretics, it was replied that there was no expectation of that, but rather the opposite would happen, that is, that they would better understand matters of the Faith, and being subject to a Most Christian Prince, it was very easy to remedy it, should something of this sort appear.[67]

Sahagún explained that lay Spaniards and members of other religious orders were at first amused by the Franciscan initiative, because they assumed Latin could not be taught to a people apparently so incapable. The idea of the pedagogical experiment he described must have been to determine the kind of intellectual training most suitable for preparing an Indian ruling class to help manage the viceroyalty.[68]

After only two or three years the friars' students came to understand every area of grammar ('todas las materias del arte de la gramática'), knowing how 'to speak Latin, and understand it, and to write Latin, and even to compose hexameter verses.'[69] Motolinía, writing soon after the foundation of the college, praised the students' speeches and disquisitions ('oraçiones y rrazonamientos') in Latin as well as their compositions in hexameters and pentameter verse, and he noted that they

[66] SAHAGÚN, *HG* 10, 'Relación' [1982 i, 76]: two native youths who were early on given the Franciscan habit proved inadequate: 'nunca mas se a recibido indio a la religion: nj aun se tienen por abiles para el sacerdocio' ('never since has an Indian been received into the religious order, nor are they even deemed suitable for the priesthood').

[67] SAHAGÚN, *HG* 10, 'Relación' [1982 i, 83].

[68] Estarellas 1962, 234.

[69] SAHAGÚN, *HG* 10, 'Relación' [1982 i, 82]. In his preliminary catalogue of sources on the Indies, ZORITA, *Relación de la Nueva España* (1585) [1999 i, 104] remarked that the former student Pablo Nazareo was a good Latinist, rhetorician, logician, and philosopher 'and not a bad poet in any genre of [Latin] verse' ('buen latino, y retórico, lógico, y filósofo y no mal poeta en todo género de versos').

astonished their teachers with their capacity to elaborate on their arguments for half an hour or more. The friar illustrated his observations with a memorable anecdote:

> I think a funny thing that occurred in Mexico City should be revealed. A clergyman could not believe that the Indians knew Christian teaching or even the *Pater noster* and the Creed. Despite the fact that other Spaniards told him this was so, he was still incredulous. At the time two students had gone out of the College, and the clergyman, thinking they were typical Indians, asked one if he knew the *Pater noster*. He said he did, and the clergyman made him say it, which he did correctly. Not content with that, he made him say the Creed and he did that too. But the clergyman challenged the Indian about a word he had used quite correctly. As the Indian insisted the word was right and the clergyman that it was not, the student had to prove it was correct by asking him, in Latin, *Reverende Pater, cuius casus est?* [Reverend Father, what grammatical case is it?]. Then the clergyman who had thought of confounding his neighbour ended up being confounded himself, because he did not know his grammar.[70]

Some who recognized the Indians' abilities were still opposed to their receiving such an education. A notary and an *encomendero*, Jerónimo López, for instance, was appalled that 'each day there were more collegians who could speak Latin as elegantly as Cicero', as he sought to warn the Emperor Charles that their knowledge of Latin and the sciences would lead to heresy and perversion of the Bible and all the Holy Scriptures.[71]

In another letter written to the crown in 1545, López complained that the students had now discovered that the Spaniards had once been pagans themselves—and that, after being subjugated by the Romans, they had revolted and rebelled before being converted. 'There are many Indians who have studied and are studying this sort of thing', the notary continued, 'and they speak and preach what they like about these and other things that take their fancy.'[72] It could be held that there was an element of prescience in those remarks: Fray Julián Garcés had after all compared the Mexicans to the ancient Spaniards, and indigenous and mestizo chroniclers would come to draw explicit analogies between pagan antiquity in Europe and New Spain's pre-Christian past.[73]

[70] MOTOLINÍA, *Memoriales* (c. 1541), 63v [1996, 343]; cf. MENDIETA, *Historia* 4.15 [1870, 417]; TORQUEMADA, *MI* 15.43 [1977 v, 177].

[71] LÓPEZ, 'Carta . . . al emperador' (1541).

[72] LÓPEZ, 'Carta . . . al emperador' (1545) [1939 iv, 168–9]. The copy of Appian's Roman history attested in the inventory of books at the college for 31 July 1572 (cf. Appendix 1.3, item [5] below) is unlikely to have prompted López's remarks: Lupher 2003, 232–3.

[73] For Garcés' comparison see Chapter 1 above and Appendix 2.1; cf. Chapter 9 below for native chroniclers.

But given that ancient history was not on the curriculum at Santa Cruz (even if some classical texts were available to the students), there would have been little basis in fact for Jerónimo López's alarmist comments, which must have represented a singular and rather contrived line of attack. Fray Gerónimo de Mendieta and Fray Juan de Torquemada embellished Motolinía's story about the clergyman who was outdone by an Indian to make the point that those who knew little Latin themselves feared that their errors would be detected by the native collegians. Objections to the advanced education of the Indians were really rooted in simple prejudice—and such prejudice endured throughout the 1500s.

That point is well illustrated by an episode that occurred more than thirty years later. After the Feast of Saint Francis on 4 October 1584, the incoming Franciscan Commissary General for New Spain, Fray Alonso de Ponce, was formally welcomed to the College of Santa Cruz in Latin and Castilian with a performance by a chorus of indigenous students. Their teacher then asked the Commissary to pardon them, because, just like parrots or magpies, these Indians were reciting what they had learned without understanding it—a reproach that was probably designed to recall Saint Augustine's distinction between senseless singing, like the noises of those types of bird, and intelligent singing, born of understanding God.[74] One of the students then made a short Latin speech in reply:

> It is entirely true, very Reverend Father, as many may compare us to magpies and parrots that are taught with much effort but forget swiftly. This is not without good reason, as we certainly possess very weak aptitude and so we are in constant need of a great deal of help.[75]

The student then translated that Latin response into Spanish, adding that he and his fellows needed such help to become 'whole human beings' ('hombres cabales'). The irony of this request became more evident when a tall Indian dressed as a Spaniard came onstage and derisively remarked that '[the students] indeed deserved to be

[74] Augustine, *Enarrationes in Psalmos*, Commentary on Psalm 18 (Dekkers and Fraipont 1956, 105): 'Nam et meruli et psittaci et corui et picae et huiusmodi uolucres, saepe ab hominibus docentur sonare quod nesciunt. Scienter autem cantare, naturae hominis diuina uoluntate concessum est.' ('In fact blackbirds, parrots, ravens, magpies, and birds of this kind are often taught by men to make sounds they do not understand. Singing with understanding, on the other hand, is granted to human nature by divine will.') The Dominican MINAYA, *Memorial* (1559), complained to Philip II that Cardinal Loaysa, president of the Council of the Indies, likened the Indians to 'parrots' ('papaguayos'): the comparison may have been conventional.

[75] CIUDAD REAL, *Relación* (c. 1586) [1872 i, 22–3]: 'Ita res habet ad omnem veritatem, Reverende admodum Pater, quia a non paucis estimemur tanquam picae et psittaci qui laboriose docentur et cito obliviscuntur, et hoc non gratis, quia certe tenuissima habilitate dotati sumus, sed ob id egemus magno et continuo auxilio.'

helped so that they could be raised to be as drunken and disreputable as the rest'. Finally, a speech from the teacher brought the short piece of theatre to an end:

> That scoundrel is lying because in fact they are good sons, attentive of their virtue and of their study, but you only know how to open your mouths to speak badly of them and whatever good fortune they have upsets you, as you only want them to go about carrying loads on their backs, busy in your service. So then, see that God is just, who says *Beatus qui intelligit super egenum et pauperem* [Psalm 41:1 'Blessed is he that understandeth concerning the needy and the poor'].

This rebuttal of the *habillé* Spaniard's taunt advertised the students' true capacities and reproached the audience for disparaging them. The short performance was engineered so that the Indians themselves did not need to say anything in their defence: their own words endorsed the opinions of those who held them in low esteem, but at the same time their good use of Latin showed that those opinions were unfounded. Fray Antonio de Ciudad Real, who described the event, says nothing of Ponce's reaction, mentioning only that he stayed in the convent of Tlatelolco until the following Sunday. But the very inclusion of this episode in the friar's account could imply that the distinguished visitor was impressed by what he witnessed.

There were, in addition, graver material difficulties the college was facing: many teachers and pupils perished in the severe epidemic of 1545.[76] That may have been a factor in the Franciscans' withdrawal from the institution, which was run by its alumni for more than twenty years. In 1554 Cervantes de Salazar identified the native Antonio Valeriano as a *lector,* or lecturer, at Santa Cruz, and by the 1560s, a second indigenous scholar, Pablo Nazareo of Xaltocan, had succeeded Fray Arnaldo de Bassacio as rector, and he in turn was replaced by another Indian, Martín Jacobita.[77] The 'Codex of Tlatelolco' (c. 1587) named eleven more former students who were involved in teaching at the college.[78]

While Viceroy Mendoza and his successor, Luis de Velasco, had ensured that Santa Cruz received adequate financial support, it was left virtually destitute after Velasco's death in 1564, and had to depend on donations and a small annuity for its

[76] MENDIETA, *Historia* 4.36 [1870: 513–19]; TORQUEMADA, *MI* 5.13 [1975 ii, .371]; cf. León-Portilla 2002, 114; Reff 2005, 122–9.

[77] CERVANTES DE SALAZAR, *Dialogi* (1554), 267r (quoted in Section III, (i) below); for Nazareo, cf. nn. 56, 69 above, Chapter 5, II, and Chapter 6 nn. 6, 31; Chapter 5, II n. 50 for Valeriano; Valeriano and Jacobita collaborated with Sahagún on the *Florentine Codex*: cf. Chapter 8, V, and Appendix 1.4 below.

[78] Appendix 1.4 below lists alumni of the college named in the 'Codex of Tlatelolco' (c. 1587), a manuscript record of proceedings at the College of Santa Cruz, a work that should not be confused with the pictorial *Codex Tlatelolco* (c. 1562).

survival.[79] The Franciscans reassumed control in the early 1570s, but another plague struck in 1576: in that year Fray Bernardino de Sahagún gave a gloomy account of how the college had diminished as a consequence of both epidemics.[80] Teaching did continue into the early years of the seventeenth century, although Fray Gerónimo de Mendieta remarked that (by the 1590s) the college was operating only to impart 'reading, writing and good manners' to the local children of Tlatelolco.[81]

III. Education and the *trivium* at Santa Cruz

In design, the college in Tlatelolco was not unlike those in Oxford and Cambridge, which were being established at the time of its foundation. The classrooms, dining hall, and dormitories were arranged around a cloister next to the Franciscan convent and church of Santiago. The original adobe constructions were eventually rebuilt in the grey volcanic stone purloined from the adjacent ruins of the Great Temple of Tlatelolco (Figure 4.1). Sahagún described how the students in Santa Cruz 'slept and ate in the College itself, not going out except on a few occasions'.[82] Fray Juan de Torquemada, who was the guardian, emphasizes that 'the collegial children were raised and instructed with great care', and offers a fuller picture of the immersive nature of the education they received: the youths would share meals with the friars in the refectory, but they slept in different quarters on platforms of timber, each with a blanket and mat, and a lockable trunk for books and clothing. There was a light in the dormitory all night, and wardens were on duty to ensure peace and quiet as well as propriety. In the morning the students sang matins, and heard mass before attending their lessons.[83]

The college had a sizeable library, to which Bishop Zumárraga donated some of his own books in 1537 and bequeathed many more after his death in 1548.[84] Seventy volumes from Santa Cruz and the convent of Santiago can still be consulted, many containing glosses and marginal notes in a number of hands.[85] The 'Codex of Tlatelolco' (1587) contains inventories of the books at the college itself that were made in 1572, 1574, and 1582: the *mayordomo* was periodically required to present a judge with a sworn statement of all the goods held there.[86] As

[79] MENDIETA, *Historia* 4.15 [1870, 415–16].

[80] SAHAGÚN, *HG* 10, 'Relación' [1982 i, 84–5].

[81] MENDIETA, *Historia* 4.15 [1870, 418]; cf. TORQUEMADA, *MI* 15.43 [1977 v, 178], quoted in Chapter 9 below.

[82] SAHAGÚN, *HG* 10, 'Relación' [1982, 82].

[83] TORQUEMADA, *MI* 15.43 [1977 v, 174–8].

[84] Titles from Zumárraga's library are in Mathes 1982, 93–6.

[85] The Tlatelolco Collection of the Sutro Library, now held in San Francisco State University, is catalogued in Mathes 1982.

[86] 'Codex of Tlatelolco' (1587): cf. n. 78 above. The inventories are largely deciphered in Appendix 1.3.

the registers were not compiled by scholars, the titles and authors of many books are often garbled: 'Contentus mundi de Jason', for instance, refers to Jean Gerson's *De contemptu mundi*. But these early inventories give a far more accurate picture of the volumes that officially belonged to the college in the later 1500s than catalogues compiled in later centuries.[87] Allowing for multiple copies and the reduplication of some items from one year to another, during 1572–1582 between eighty and ninety different titles were in Santa Cruz, although collegians would have had access to books from other sources.[88]

Seven Latin grammars, six dictionaries, and six copies of a textbook by Vives, along with a very large number of individual titles on logic and rhetoric, indicate that the library was geared to the teaching of the *trivium*, discussed below. There were a few single texts of popular devotional manuals and of Augustine, Jerome, and Ambrose, who were widely read in the 1500s, but only a couple of strictly theological works. Although Latin scripture was obviously to be found in any scholarly library, in Santa Cruz there were four Latin Bibles, two copies of the New Testament (probably Erasmus' edition), three commentaries on Saint Paul's Epistles, and some further books of Jerome's Old Testament. The importance of biblical translation into Nahuatl in the college is likely to account for the prominence given to scripture. In that regard, it is significant that all three inventories record two copies of Fray Alonso de Molina's active dictionary from Spanish to the Mexican language, *Aqui comiença un vocabulario* (1555).

The greater part of the library was devoted to a wide range of classical literature: Cicero's *Orationes* and *De officiis*, editions of Livy, Virgil, Juvenal, Martial, Pliny, Seneca, and Quintilian and four copies of Sallust; along with Latin translations of Greek texts by Plato, Aristotle, Plutarch, Appian, Josephus, and Diogenes Laertius.[89] The works of late antique authors, namely Prudentius, Sedulius, Boethius, and

[87] More books from the college were catalogued by Fray Francisco Antonio de la Rosa Figueroa, but he did not specify the collections in which those titles had originated: ROSA FIGUEROA, *Diccionario bibliográphico* (c. 1758); cf. Téllez Nieto 2019b, 47–8 nn. 85–6. Mathes 1982, a catalogue of many of the volumes surviving from Santa Cruz and the Convent of Santiago in Tlatelolco, includes items acquired in the 1590s, after the college had declined as a teaching institution.

[88] The 'Codex of Tlatelolco' (1587) states that, in 1582, further books were in the care of Sahagún. Mathes 1982, 44 notes that its inventories (Appendix 1.3 below) were not complete and perhaps overgenerously estimates that there were more than 370 volumes in the college and convent: cf. Tibesar 1988, 509. There was also a library at the nearby Convent of San Francisco in Mexico City, to which the college of San José de los Naturales was adjoined: cf. Chapter 9, n. 28. Relaxation of restrictions on the sale and import of books in New Spain by the mid-1500s made more titles available (Fernández del Castillo 1982, Leonard 1992, Maillard Álvarez 2018), as did printing (Zulaica Gárate 1939; Griffin 1991, 105–33).

[89] The standard school authors Horace, Ovid and Terence were not in the sixteenth-century inventories. George 2009, 280 attributes their absence to the 'more austere Christian humanism' of the friars, but there are indications that these authors were read (cf. nn. 90, 91 below).

Martianus Capella, and some Renaissance humanists—Battista Mantovano, Pietro Crinito, and Pico della Mirandola—are listed, too. It is important, however, to bear in mind that in the 1500s there was no study of classics as it is conceived today: ancient authors were mainly read in order to extend knowledge of 'grammar', or Latin, and as models for composition in the language. On that basis, Cato's *Distichs* and some fables of Aesop (also in the college library) were studied in Latin at elementary level, before students advanced to Cicero, Sallust, Virgil, and Horace, along with Ovid's *Tristia,* which was a favoured model for verse composition.[90] After they arrived in New Spain, the Jesuits would recommend a similar set of readings for their own colleges.[91]

It was therefore no coincidence that the Mexican youths were using the same classical texts as those prescribed for boys at St Paul's School in London—where Erasmus himself had been invited by John Colet to devise the programme of study. The proposals in Erasmus' *De ratione studii* (1511) were recalled in Juan Luis Vives' *De tradendis disciplinis* (1531), a seminal encyclopaedic treatise on education that the Spanish humanist wrote in Oxford during the 1520s. As Erasmus' and Vives' strategies for developing spoken and written fluency in Latin were being implemented all over Europe, they were similarly applied in New Spain.[92] An account of the routine in a sixteenth-century English grammar school gives an idea of how intensive the teaching at the Imperial College of Santa Cruz would have been:

> Grammar was studied first . . . Gradually pupils ascended to the writing of themes on a set subject and impromptu disputations in Latin, while working through Latin literature in stages of increasing linguistic difficulty . . . The curriculum was not large, but the teaching was incredibly thorough . . . after the master's explanation the pupil would repeat it, memorize it, be asked to recite it; be tested again, repeat it, and be made to use it over and over again until there was no chance of forgetting it . . . School

[90] The Latin writings by Indian rulers considered in Chapter 6 allude to these authors. Osorio Romero 1980, 32 mentions two different copies of an edition of Cato by ERASMUS, *Catonis Disticha moralia* (1539), printed in 1559 and 1567, in the Biblioteca Nacional de Mexico. According to TORQUEMADA, *MI* 15.43 (quoted in Chapter 7, IV below), Antonio Valeriano translated Cato into Nahuatl. The anonymous *Tam de Tristibus quam de Ponticis* (1577), the first poetic anthology published in Mexico, contained verse by Ovid and later Latin authors: Osorio Romero 1984, 192–200; Laird 2020, 139–41.

[91] In his license for the printing of TOLEDO, *Introductio in dialecticam Aristotelis* (1578), Viceroy Martín Enríquez reproduced a list of classics, including Aesop, Cato, Vives, Cicero, Virgil, Valla, and Ovid's *Tristia,* which the Jesuits sought to publish in Mexico: García Icazbalceta 1954, 297. From the copy of *Tam de Tristibus* (cf. n. 90 above), A4r in New York Public Library, it seems that the lost preceding folio contained the same list.

[92] Baldwin 1944 i, 75–93 discusses ERASMUS, *De ratione studii* (1511) and the curriculum at St Paul's.

> hours were from 6 a.m. till 9, then breakfast; 9.15 till 11, then lunch; 1 till 5, then supper; 6 till 7, for pure repetition, for thirty-six weeks a year for six years. First thing in the morning pupils were tested on the facts they had been given to learn the previous day.[93]

The lack of a detailed description of the teaching at Santa Cruz from any of the Franciscan chroniclers suggests that they considered their methods of education to be so familiar to their readers that they did not need to be explained. On the other hand, there are many more testimonies about the operation of the Royal University of Mexico, which was inaugurated in 1554.[94] That institution, to which Spaniards alone could be admitted, was modelled on the University of Salamanca in Castile, but it would have had many practices in common with the college founded in Tlatelolco nearly twenty years before. The establishment of both of those centres of learning in Mexico City had been largely due to the efforts of the same individual, Bishop Juan de Zumárraga.[95] More importantly, the *trivium* of grammar, rhetoric, and dialectic dominated the curricula of Santa Cruz and the Royal University, as the writings of Mendieta and Cervantes de Salazar make clear.[96] Fray Juan de Torquemada, echoing Mendieta, identified the teachers of each of the three subjects at Tlatelolco:

> The [students] had notable and weighty masters in Latinity, after Fray Arnaldo de Bassacio, such as Fray Bernardino de Sahagún who was in this College for forty years and Fray Andrés de Olmos. And for rhetoric, logic, and philosophy, they had the very learned Fray Juan de Gaona, Fray Francisco de Bustamante, and Fray Juan Focher.[97]

Advanced Latin was taught first, before students proceeded to rhetoric, the art of elegant and persuasive speech or writing. The final component was dialectic, which consisted of both logic—defining terms and making accurate statements—and

[93] Vickers 1988, 257, epitomizing parts of Baldwin 1944.

[94] See e.g. Carreño 1961 and the bibliography in Martínez López-Cano 2006, 103–51. The dialogue 'Academia mexicana' in CERVANTES DE SALAZAR, *Dialogi* (1554), 247v–57r [Eng. tr. 1953, 23–36] gives a contemporary description of the university.

[95] ZUMMARÁGA, 'La instrucción que yo' (1537); cf. Chapter 1, III above.

[96] CERVANTES DE SALAZAR, n. 94 above; MENDIETA, *Historia* 4.15 [1870, 415].

[97] TORQUEMADA, *MI* 15.43 [1977 v, 175]: 'Tuvieron notables y gravisimos maestros en la latinidad, después de fray Arnaldo de Bastacio, como fue fray Bernardino de Sahagún que estuvo en este colegio cuarenta años; y a fray Andrés de Olmos. Y en la retórica, lógica y filosofía, a los doctísimos fray Juan de Gaona, fray Francisco de Bustamante y fray Juan Fucher.' MENDIETA, *Historia* (n. 97 above) does not mention Focher.

disputatio, the business of constructing arguments and detecting fallacies in the arguments of others.[98]

The system of the *trivium*, inherited from the Middle Ages, was of far more practical benefit than is generally recognized today: its three components were not so much subjects as practices, or 'ways of dealing with subjects', and they conferred versatile, transferable skills.[99] Even medicine could be conceived in terms of the *trivium*, with 'grammar [enabling the physician] to understand or explain what he reads . . . rhetoric, to delineate what he treats in true arguments . . . and dialectic to apply reason to examining and curing the causes of infirmities'.[100] Medicine was in fact taught at the College of Santa Cruz: the evidence for this—not least Sahagún's reference to purging and bloodletting—strongly suggests that European rather than indigenous methods of healing were being taught.[101] The 'Indian' herbal authored at Santa Cruz by the native Latinist Juan Badiano (discussed in the next chapter) offers little to change that impression, despite suppositions to the contrary.

But rather more light can be shed on the teaching of the constituent elements of the *trivium*, not only from the titles of European books attested at the college in the 1570s, but also from some important works that were printed in Mexico City in the mid-sixteenth century.

(i) Grammar and Latin expression

The teaching of Latin was informed by the Renaissance humanists' practical approach, rather than the speculative grammatical theory of medieval scholasticism.[102] Although friars with the linguistic skills of Sahagún or Olmos would hardly have needed textbooks, the college had acquired at least five copies of Nebrija's *Introductiones Latinae* (or '*arte*'), three of Despauter's *Commentarii grammatici* (1536)—the standard Latin textbook in France and the Low Countries—and Martianus Capella's more colourful *De grammatica*, which had hardly diminished in popularity more than a millenium after it was composed in the 400s AD.[103] Fray

[98] Jensen 1996 and Mack 1996 are overviews of education; Percival 2004, Vickers 1988, and Ashworth 2008, respectively, explore Renaissance grammar, rhetoric and logic.

[99] Sayers 1948, 8.

[100] Isidore, *Etymologies* 4.13.1–2: 'Nam et Grammaticam medicus scire debet, ut intellegere vel exponere possit quae legit. Similiter et Rhetoricam, ut veracibus argumentis valeat definire quae tractat. Necnon et Dialecticam propter infirmitatum causas ratione adhibita perscrutandas atque curandas.' Isidore then makes a similar argument for geometry, music, and astronomy—disciplines that may have been taught informally at Santa Cruz: compare e.g. Steck 1944, 25. Lawn 1993 and Ashworth 2008, 615 treat the relation of medicine to the Renaissance *trivium*.

[101] SAHAGÚN, *HG* 10, *Relación* [1982 i, 85]; MENDIETA, *Historia* 5.41 [1870, 664]; TORQUEMADA, *MI* 15.43 [1977 v, 178].

[102] Chapter 3, I above.

[103] Cf. Appendix 1.3 below. Martianus' *De grammatica*, which formed part of his *De nuptiis Philologiae et Mercurii* (early 400s AD), was published as a self-standing volume.

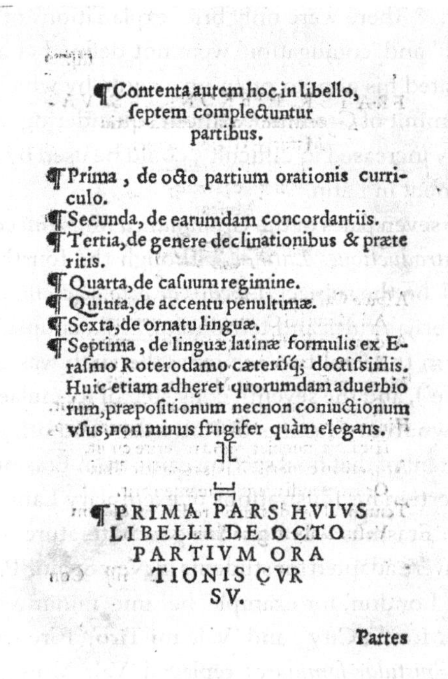

¶Contenta autem hoc in libello,
ſeptem complectuntur
partibus.

¶Prima, de octo partium orationis curriculo.
¶Secunda, de earumdam concordantiis.
¶Tertia, de genere declinationibus & præteritis.
¶Quarta, de caſuum regimine.
¶Quinta, de accentu penultimæ.
¶Sexta, de ornatu linguæ.
¶Septima, de linguæ latinæ formulis ex Eraſmo Roterodamo cæteriſq; doctiſsimis. Huic etiam adhęret quorumdam aduerbiorum, præpoſitionum necnon coniunctionum vſus, non minus frugifer quàm elegans.

¶PRIMA PARS HVIVS
LIBELLI DE OCTO
PARTIVM ORA
TIONIS ÇVR
SV.

Partes

Figure 4.2 Contents of Fray Maturino Gilberti, *Grammatica Maturini*, Mexico City, 1559. John Carter Brown Library.

Maturino Gilberti's *Grammatica Maturini* (1559), the first Latin grammar to be composed and printed in New Spain, was almost certainly used as well, and the approach it adopts gives an impression of how Latin is likely to have been taught at the College of Santa Cruz (Figure 4.2).[104]

Gilberti drew from the Renaissance grammars of Niccolò Perotti and Antonio de Nebrija, and from Erasmus: his *confrère* Francisco Beteta praised him for 'plucking his flowers from all sides, like bees' ('flores undique seligens apes ceu').[105] The *Grammatica Maturini* resembled its antecedents in many respects, but it was a trimmer, clearer work, without digressions, annotations, or lengthy examples of usage from classical sources. Theory was eschewed altogether: not even *grammatica* was defined—its constituent parts were simply listed with examples as the opening

[104] VETANCURT, *Menologio franciscano* (1697), 139 states that Gilberti wrote his grammar specifically for the instructors at the College of Santa Cruz ['escribio para los grammaticos de Tlatiluco vn Arte latino'], although that claim cannot be verified and the grammar would have been useful to Spanish and Mexican students alike.

[105] Laird 2012; Beteta in GILBERTI, *Grammatica* (1559), Iv [2003 i, 72].

sentence of the work.[106] There were only brief explanations of the parts of speech; terms like 'declension' and 'conjugation' were not defined at all. In his dedication Maturino Gilberti stated his aim 'to open up a route by which students might ascend almost to the summit of Grammar without squandering too much time'.[107] His work, which gradually increased in difficulty, could be used by readers with various levels of accomplishment in Latin.[108]

The first five of the seven parts of the *Grammatica Maturini* correspond to the five books of Nebrija's *Introductiones Latinae,* although the fourth section, on syntax, copied Erasmus' work on the subject, *Libellus de octo orationis partium constructione* (1513), retaining Nebrija's rules and terminology in a couple of places.[109] Matters of style were treated in the final two sections: the sixth was on 'adornment' ('De ornatu linguae Latinae'), and the seventh consisted of formulae for greeting and social interactions, 'drawn from Erasmus of Rotterdam and other learned authors'.[110] In fact, the entire content of that final section came from Erasmus—who was boldly commended by Gilberti in his illustrations of exemplary Latin usage, e.g. 'Erasmus excels in Latinity' or 'Erasmus was born for good literature to be restored.' Some expressions, though, were adapted for students in New Spain. 'Paulo vivitur Londini', 'One lives on little in London', for example, became 'minimo vivitur Mexici', 'One lives on very little in Mexico City'; and 'Vale mi Tiro', 'Fare well dear Tiro', a salutation from Cicero's *Epistulae familiares,* replaced 'Vale More', an adieu to Thomas More.[111] Gilberti removed coarse references or passages in which Erasmus had disparaged the monastic orders or ridiculed religious fasting or abstinence.[112] These

[106] 'There are four parts of grammar, namely the letter, such as *a, b, c;* the syllable, such as *ba, be;* the word, such as *Pater,* and sentence [*oratio*], such as *Pater noster qui es in caelis.*' PEROTTI, *Rudimenta grammatices* (1473) began with the *Pater Noster*: Laird 2012.

[107] GILBERTI, *Grammatica* (1559), 2r [2003 i, 74]: 'aperire viam, qua citra tanti temporis iacturam Grammatices pene fastigium tenerent.'

[108] Cf. the tabulation of contents in Appendix 1.1.5 below.

[109] Cf. Appendix 1.1.2 below. In her edition of GILBERTI, *Grammatica* (1559) [2003, 62–3], Rosa Lucas González notes instances at 72v and 82v.

[110] GILBERTI, *Grammatica* (1559), 137r [2003 ii 597]: 'Quaedam pro pueris linguae Latiné salutandi, valedicendi, percontandi exercitamenta ac formulae ex Erasmo Roterodamo aliisve doctissimis' ('Some exercises and formulae, for students of the Latin language, for greeting, saying farewell, and making enquiries from Erasmus of Rotterdam or others who are very learned'). The Erasmian sources are *Colloquia familiaria* (1518), *Opus de conscribendis epistolis* (1522), *De copia* (1512), and *Paraphrasis* (1529), a concordance summary of Valla's foundational study on Latin expression. The commendations of Erasmus are in GILBERTI, *Grammatica* (1559), Part 6, 123r–123v [2003 ii, 526–8]; 133v [2003 ii, 576] and in Part 7, 152v–152r [2003 ii, 650].

[111] These were from ERASMUS, *Epistolae* (1516), *Epistolae familiares* (1538), and *Colloquia familiaria* (1518) and referred to by Gilberti as 'Erasmicae formulae'. Another letter, to Thomas More, prefaced ERASMUS, *Moriae encomium* (1511).

[112] See e.g. the selective rendering in GILBERTI, *Grammatica* (1559), 141v–142r [2003 ii: 616] of 'Percontandi forma in valetudine', a dialogue in ERASMUS, *Colloquia familiaria* (1518), a work prohibited in 1559 by Spain's General Inquisitor in both Latin and vernacular versions, along with

expurgations actually made it easier for students to apply in their own writing oratorical and epistolary formulae transmitted in this final part of Gilberti's grammar—and those formulae were evidently employed in Latin texts written by alumni of the College of Santa Cruz.[113]

The six books of 'Juan Luis bibas' [*sic*] counted in the college's holdings in 1574 were almost certainly copies of Juan Luis Vives' most popular Latin textbook, the *Linguae Latinae exercitatio*, or 'Practical application of the Latin language', sometimes entitled the *Colloquia*. This collection of dialogues that first appeared in 1538 continued to be published well into the seventeenth century.[114] The dialogues were designed to enable students to discuss everyday subjects in Latin in the vein of Erasmus' *Colloquia familiaria*, although they were lengthier and rather more elaborate. An edition of the *Linguae Latinae exercitatio* was printed in Mexico City by Juan Pablos in 1554 to coincide with Francisco Cervantes de Salazar's appointment to the Royal University's chair of rhetoric, which was inaugurated in that year. That edition, *Ad Ludovici Vivis Valentini exercitationem, aliquot Dialogi*, 'Appended to Luis Vives of Valencia's *Exercitatio*, several Dialogues', contained a commentary and a prefatory biography of Vives along with the seven new Latin dialogues Cervantes de Salazar had written himself, indicated by a separate title page (Figure 4.3).

The Royal University, the centre of Mexico City, and the city's environs were the setting for three of those additional dialogues: 'Academia mexicana', 'Mexicus interior', and 'Mexicus exterior'. Texts like these went much further than Gilberti's grammar in supplying students with the idioms and vocabulary they needed to talk about the commodities, practices, and localities of the world they actually experienced. In 'Mexicus interior', one of the interlocutors refers to the College of Santa Cruz in passing, as he describes the marketplace in Tlatelolco:

> In the Franciscan monastery a college has been founded for the Indians who are taught to speak and write Latin. They have a teacher from their own people, Antonio Valeriano, in no way inferior to our own Latin instructors, learned in the observance of the Christian faith, and very devoted to cultivating eloquence.[115]

the *Lingua, Moriae encomium,* and other Erasmian works on religious questions: VALDÉS Y SALAS, *Cathalogus librorum* (1559), 44 (pages misnumbered). Mahlmann-Bauer 2008, 348–50 treats censorship of the *Colloquia familiaria* in Europe; cf. Henderson 2007, 162–4.

[113] Erasmian formulae mediated by Gilberti's grammar were deployed in surviving Latin writings by native Mexicans: Chapter 6 below.

[114] Noreña 1970, 303–4 lists forty-nine editions of VIVES, *Linguae Latinae exercitatio* in the 1500s.

[115] CERVANTES DE SALAZAR, *Dialogi* (1554), 267r: 'Franciscanorum positum est monasterium, et in ipso Indorum collegium qui latine loqui et scribere docentur. Magistrum habent ejusdem nationis Antonium Valerianum nostris grammaticis nequaquam inferiorem, in legis christianae observatione satis doctum et ad eloquentiam avidissimum.'

Figure 4.3 Francisco Cervantes de Salazar, *Dialogi,* Mexico City, 1554. Benson Latin American Collection.

The speaker of these words in the dialogue has a clear interest in education: his name, Camora, was probably Cervantes de Salazar's sobriquet for Bishop Zumárraga.

(ii) Logic and rhetoric

Fray Juan Focher, Fray Francisco de Bustamante, and Fray Juan de Gaona taught logic, rhetoric, and philosophy at the College of Santa Cruz in the middle decades of the 1500s. Focher's expertise in theology and canon law—evident in his attested and extant works—would certainly have qualified him to teach philosophy.[116] There are no known writings by the logician Francisco de Bustamante, but a speaker in Cervantes de Salazar's 'Academia mexicana' described a master of philosophy who is named 'Bustamantius':

> He interprets authors carefully, solves problems, and notes the more important points in a most learned fashion. He is very well versed in Philosophy

[116] Cf. Chapter 2, III above.

> and Dialectic in which he is a master, and, because he has tirelessly taught native Mexican youths for twenty-six years, there is hardly anyone who speaks in public or teaches who would not have been one of his pupils.[117]

Bustamante may indeed have taught indigenous students, presumably at Tlatelolco, although this claim (made in 1554) that he had done so for twenty-six years cannot be correct, as he first came to New Spain in 1542[118] Gaona, whose attested writings include two dialogues in Nahuatl, was, according to Fray Gerónimo de Mendieta, an excellent Latinist and rhetorician.[119] Gaona's defence of the Franciscans' opposition to an indigenous clergy in a formal disputation (recounted above in Mendieta's words) indicates that the use of dialectical *disputatio* to resolve differences of opinion and uncover scientific or theological truth had a role in the life of the college beyond the classroom:

> Here begins the counter to the opponent's first Proposition. The opponent's first Proposition is: *To establish faith in Jesus Christ without sufficient ministers and without practice of the sacraments necessary for salvation, is to establish faith without the Holy Spirit. This Church in the Western Indies has been instituted in this way, so it has not been established in the Holy Spirit.* But this new Church, a little plant in the World of the Indies, has been planted *by* the Holy Spirit, and day by day, with the same Spirit sustaining it, grows in the Lord, receiving increase in strength in Christ Jesus.[120]

It is possible to identify the books on logic that were in Santa Cruz by the 1570s, despite the rough transcriptions of their titles in the 'Codex of Tlatelolco'

[117] *Dialogi* (1554), 250v: 'explicat auctores sedulo, labyrinthos solvit, et quae sunt potiora docte satis observat. In Dialectica et Philosophia, quarum est magister, non leviter versatus; et quia per annos viginti sex indefessus juventutem mexicanam instituit, vix est ullus qui aut concionetur aut doceat, qui non ejus fuerit discipulus.'

[118] García Icazbalceta 1875, 56 n. 6; O'Gorman 1963, 81–2 n. 19.

[119] For GAONA, *Colloquios de la Paz* (c. 1540) cf. Chapter 5 below.

[120] GAONA, *Antidota quarundam Propositionum cuiusdam famigeratissimi Theologi . . . Dat. Mexici Kal Maii 1553*, 'Responses to some propositions by one renowned Theologian . . . given in Mexico City on the Kalends of May 1553', is lost apart from this opening quoted in Beristáin de Souza, *Biblioteca* 1883 i, 340: 'Incipit antidotum primum ad primam adversarii propositionem. Prima adversarii propositio: "Fundare fidem Jesu Christi sine sufficientibus ministris et sine usu sacramentorum ad salutem necessariorum, est fundare fidem sine Spiritu Sancto . . . Haec Ecclesia in Occidentali India sic instituta est: ergo non est in Spiritu Santo fundata." Nova haec Ecclesia plantula in orbe Indiarum a Spiritu Sancto plantata est, et in dies, eodem fovente Spiritu, crescit in Domino, virium augmentum in Christo Jesu recipiens.' The account of the disputation, in MENDIETA, *Historia* 4.23 [1870, 450], is quoted in Section II above. Angelelli 1970 describes the 'argument method' in Renaissance doctrinal disputation, which focused on the truthfulness and substance of an initial thesis, not simply on argumentation.

DIALECTICA
resolutio cum textu
ARISTOTELIS EDITA PER
REVERENDVM PATREM
ALPHONSVM A VERA CRVCE
Augustinianum. Artium atq; sacrę Theo
logię magistrum in achademia Me
xicana in noua Hispa-
nia cathedræ pri
mæ in Theo
logia
moderatorem. ab eo dē autore
nunc [illegible] 2° edita et in aliquibus
locis addita.
MEXICI
Excudebat Ioannes paulus Brissensis.
Anno. 1554.

Figure 4.4 Title page of Fray Alonso de la Vera Cruz, *Dialectica resolutio*, Mexico City, 1554, showing indigenous figures as atlantes. John Carter Brown Library.

(c. 1587).[121] They comprised canonical works of Aristotle, Saint Thomas Aquinas' *Logica,* and Renaissance textbooks that had come to be widely used all over Europe: Pierre Tartaret's *Expositio* (1483), Siliceus' *Logica brevis* (1518), Johann Caesarius' *Dialectica* (1526), Franz Titelmans' *Dialectica consideratio* (1543), Augustine Hunnäus' *Progymnasmata* (1553) and Fray Alonso de la Vera Cruz's *Dialectica resolutio* (1554) (Figure 4.4).[122] Those more modern works exemplified a humanist conception of logic as an instrument of argument and communication, rather than as something to which eloquent language had to be subordinated.[123]

In his *Recognitio summularum* (1554), one of the first philosophical works to be published in Mexico, Fray Alonso de la Vera Cruz made a case for the practical benefits of dialectic. The Augustinian scholar commended Franz Titelmans, giving him pride of place among those who followed Rudolph Agricola in rejecting

[121] The titles are reconstructed in Appendix 1.3.

[122] The dates given here are of years of first publication for these books, not those of the volumes in the college. The 1572–1582 inventories in the 'Codex of Tlatelolco' do not include Duns Scotus' *Quaestiones,* although two surviving copies from the college are noted in Mathes 1982, 54. Tartaret's *Expositio* could indicate the Franciscans' broad allegiance to Scotism: cf. Murillo Gallegos 2016.

[123] This is a distillation of varying accounts: Giard 1984, 35–55; Jardine 1988; Ashworth 2008.

sophistries and restoring 'the reign of Saturn and a golden age' of sound reasoning.[124] Agricola's insistence on contextualizing the use of argument in real-life situations had led to rhetoric and dialectic becoming more intertwined in sixteenth-century Europe, an evident trend at the college in Tlatelolco.[125] The Franciscans' adoption of a more modern 'natural logic' in their teaching paralleled their preference for practical linguistic pedagogy and rejection of the speculative grammar of the medieval modists.

A copy of Quintilian's *Institutio oratoria,* which was in the convent library, provides evidence of the thoroughness with which rhetoric was studied in Tlatelolco (Figure 4.5). The edition, printed by Nicolaus Savetier in 1527, has Latin annotations written in several hands (Figure 4.5). Edward George has observed that the comments of one scribe go beyond glossing individual words to offer further instructions about eloquence for students.[126] Moreover, the same scribe proposes variant readings of Quintilian's text, and even adduces parallels from other classical authors including Plutarch and Euripides. But these observations were not original, as has been supposed: they reproduce, more or less verbatim, commentary from two earlier authorities. The first was the German humanist Petrus Mosellanus, who produced *Annotationes* on Books 1–7 of the *Institutio oratoria* in the 1520s; the second was Antonius Pinus' commentary on Book 3.[127] Both works had been incorporated, along with Joachim Camerarius' commentary on Books 1–2 of the *Institutio* and Pierre Gallande's text of the *Institutio,* in a single book first published by Michael Vasconsanus in 1538. Gallande in fact appears to be the unnamed source ('al[iu]s') for the variant readings that were added in handwriting to the Savetier edition.[128] As there was a 1543 copy of the Vasconsanus text in the library of the Convent of San Francisco in Mexico City, the date of 1543 might

124 VERA CRUZ, *Recognitio* (1554), 4r, 'Proemium: De vtil. dialect.': 'Venerunt vero Saturnia regna, iam aureum seculum, reuertuntur ad sanam mentem. . . Titelmanus (iudicio meo) palmam obtinet.' AGRICOLA, *De inventione dialectica* (1515) was originally written c. 1476–1479.

125 Mack 1993, 130–67; and n. 123 above. CABRERA, 'Epigrams' (c. 1540), number 13 praised Agricola for applying Aristotelian and Ciceronian 'topics' (*loci*) to rhetorical argumentation; number 15 commended CAESARIUS, *Dialectica* (1526) for dispelling 'barbaries', echoing Erasmus' words in a 1524 letter to Caesarius: Laird 2013, 200–1; ERASMUS, *Opus epistolarum* (1529) [1908–1958 iii, 262]. Editions of Erasmus' *Epistolae* and Caesarius' *Dialectica* were inventoried in Santa Cruz in 1572: Appendix 1.3 below.

126 George 2009 discerns that one example—the scribe's warning (52v) to a speaker to avoid the disgrace of forgetting his text, especially in the opening (*exordium*) of a speech—is based on Quintilian's advice (*Institutio* 4.1.54–5) that a scripted speech can appear sponteaneous if it begins with an improvised *exordium.*

127 These are the sources of particular annotations described by George 2009, 283–7: a reference to the Greek Aristoxenus' perplexity about God reproduces Pinus' comment on *Institutio* 3.7.2; and the quotations of Euripides and Plutarch inscribed at 68r come from Mosellanus' comment on *Institutio* 5.10.24.

128 The readings proposed by the scribe at 66v, noted by George 2009, 284 indicate this.

LIBER QVINTVS. Fo.LXVIII.

quid accidit exequendum mihi est:vt pleriq; fecerunt:sed vnde argumenta sumi possunt. Ea porro sunt,genus. Nam similes parentibus : ac maioribus suis filii plerunq; creduntur:& nonunq̃ ad honeste : turpiterq; viuendum in de causę fluũt. Natio:nã & gẽtibus proprii mores sunt:nec idẽ in Barbaro, Romano, Græco, ꝓbabile est. Patria:quia similiter etiã ciuitatũ leges insti tuta, opiniones habẽt differentiã. Sexus:vt latrociniũ facilius in viro:vene ficiũ in fœmina credas. Aetas: qa aliud aliis ãnis magis cõuenit. Educatio & disciplina: quoniã refert a qbus, & quo quisq; mõ sit institutus. Habitus corporis. Ducit eñ frequẽter in argumẽtũ species libidinis:robur petulãtiæ. His cõtraria in diuersũ. Fortuna. nec eñ tã idẽ credibile est in diuite ac pau pere: ꝓpinquis, amicis:clientibus:abundãte, & his oĩbus destituto. Cõditio nis etiã distantia est:nã clarus an obscur⁹:magistrat⁹ an priuatus:pr̃ an fili⁹: ciuis an pegrin⁹:liber an seru⁹:marit⁹ an cęlebs:parẽs liberoꝝ:an orbus sit, plimũ distat. Animi natura:etẽñ auaritia, ira, iracũdia, misericordia, cru delitas, seueritas, aliaquę iis si\'ia, afferunt freqnter fidẽ:aut detrahunt:sicut victus:luxuriosus:an frugi:an sordidus, quæritur. Studia quoq;: nãq; rustic⁹, forensis:negociator, miles, nauigator, medicus:aliud atq; aliud efficiũt. In tuendũ etiã quid affectet quisq;:locuples videri an disertus:iustus an potẽs. Spectantur ante acta dictaq;. Ex præteritis enim æstimari solent pręsentia. His adiiciũt quidã cõmotionẽ:hanc accipi volunt ⁂ tẽporariũ animi motũ sicut iram, pauorẽ. Consilia autẽ, & præsentis & præteriti & futuri tẽporis: quæ mihi etiam si personis accidunt:referenda tamen ad illam partem ar gumentorum videntur:quam ex causis ducimus: sicut habitus quidam ani mi:quo tractatur amicus an inimicus. Ponunt in persona & nomen : quod quidem ei accidere necesse est: sed in argumẽtum raro cadit: nisi cum aut ex causa datum est: vt sapiens, magnus, plenus: aut ipsum alicuius cogitatiõis attulit causam:vt Lentulo coniurationis:ꝙ libris Sibyllinis haruspicumque responsis dominatio dari tribus Corneliis dicebatur : seq; eum tertium esse credebat post Syllam, Cinnamque: quia & ipse Cornelius erat. Nam & il lud ♂ extat apud Euripidem:frigidum sane:ꝙ nomen Polynicis vt argu mentum frater morum incessit. Locorum enim ex eo frequens materia : qua Cicero in Verrem non semel vsus est. Hęc fere circa personas sunt: aut his si milia. Nec enim complecti omnia:vel in hac parte:vel in cæteris possumus, contenti rationem plura quæsituris ostendere. Nunc ad res transeo : in qui bus maxime sunt personis iuncta quę agim⁹:ideoq; prima tractãda. In om nibus porro quę fiunt:quęritur aut quare:aut vbi:aut quãdo: aut quomodo: aut per quæ facta sunt. Ducuntur igitur argumenta ex causis factorum: vel futurorum:quorum materiam quam, ὕλην alij : δύναμιν alij nominauerunt: in duo genera:sed quaternas vtriusq; diuidunt species. Nam fere versatur ra tio faciendi circa bonorum adeptionem : incrementum : conseruationem: vsum:aut malorum euitationem:liberationem:imminutionem, conuersio nem:nanque hæc in deliberando plurimum valent. Sed has causas habent

A genere
A natiõe.
A patria.
A sexu.
Ab ętate.
Ab educa tione.
Ab habi tu.
A fortũa.
Cõditiõe
Natura animi.
Victu.
Studiis.
Affectib⁹
Ab ante actis di ctisq;
⁂ tẽpora rio animi motu
♂ 'est.
Arg. a re bus actis.
A causis factorum vel futuro rum.

i iiij

Figure 4.5 Annotations in a Tlatelolco copy of Quintilian, *Institutiones oratoriae*, Paris, 1527, 68r. Sutro Library, California State Library.

be a reasonable *terminus post quem* for those scribal annotations in the Tlatelolco volume of Quintilian.[129]

[129] GALLANDE, *M. Fabii Quintiliani . . . Libri XII* (1543). Yhmoff Cabrera 1996 iii, 6–7 gives a detailed description of the book and itemization of its content, noting it has the brand marks of the Convent of San Francisco, and the convent's *Ex libris* inside the second cover. There were other copies

While the Indian students' own writings in Latin and even in Nahuatl offer ample proof of their accomplishment in rhetoric, there is less direct evidence for their formation in logic.[130] Unlike Spanish students in the Royal University of Mexico or Lima, they were not required to produce Latin treatises or commentaries on Aristotle.[131] On the other hand, the ability to define terms, make accurate statements, and draw correct inferences that was conferred by a training in logic would have helped them to prepare accurate translations of Christian texts 'free of heresy' or any other unwelcome implications.[132] And that training might have had a further symbolic and ideological value, given that the status and capacities of native Americans were the subject of vigorous debate in Europe as well as in New Spain. If literacy in Latin and the pursuit of the *studia humanitatis* showed that the Indians were civilized—and human—in the fullest sense, then their capacity for logic would have been incontrovertible proof that they were rational as well.

IV. Conclusions

Fray Juan de Torquemada summarized the beneficial outcomes of the education at Santa Cruz de Tlatelolco in response to objections that the Indians' study of Latin 'would be of no actual use to the republic'.[133] First, the friars acquired knowledge of the Mexican language from the Latinists whom they had taught, and drew from their expertise in order to translate works on doctrine and religious treatises into Nahuatl, and to determine that they were redacted and printed correctly. Second, the Indians' competence in Latin enabled them to assist the missionaries in scrutinizing the legitimacy of marriages and in the administration of the sacraments. Third, the Indians were appointed as judges and governors: 'They did this better than others, as they were men who could read, know and understand.' Elaborating on this point, Torquemada cited the example of Antonio Valeriano, a native of Azcapotzalco, whose training equipped him to be governor of the Indians of Mexico City for more than thirty-five years, securing 'the acclaim of the viceroys and the edification of the Spaniards'.

in Mexico City, printed by Hieronymus Scotus (Venice, 1546) and Sebastianus Gryphius (Lyon, 1549): Yhmoff Cabrera 1996 iii, 8–9.

[130] Dialectic was employed in the Nahuatl text of SAHAGÚN, *Colloquios y Doctrina christiana* (1564): cf. Appendix 2.6 and Chapter 5, IV (i) below. CHIMALPOPOCA, *Lógica en el idioma mexicano* (1876), a manuscript Nahuatl translation of the *Elementa logicae* from HEINECKE, *Elementa philosophiae* (1740), 76–190 (cf. Schwaller 2001, 72), might attest to an enduring tradition of teaching logic to Mexicans.

[131] Beuchot 1998; Redmond 1972; Hampe Martínez 1999.

[132] SAHAGÚN, *HG* 10, 'Relacion del autor' [1982 i, 83–4], quoted in Chapter 5 below.

[133] TORQUEMADA, *MI* 15.43 [1977: 5:176–17].

Torquemada's arguments confirm that the vocational purpose of their training had always been to enable them to become governors of their own communities, not priests. Theology was not taught at Santa Cruz, because the college was not a seminary. Nor was the formal education 'liberal' or 'classical', although literary and historical works of Greco-Roman authors were clearly available. The curriculum was the standard Latin *trivium*, a practical training in clear, critical thinking and composition that would enable the Indian students to become judicious and eloquent leaders. A command of grammar, logic, and rhetoric was, of course, no less useful to ensure they could help prepare precise translations of Latin religious texts into Nahuatl and other Mesoamerican languages.

Opposition to the college never abated, even at the end of the sixteenth century. The students at Tlatelolco were conscious of the controversies about their education, as the content of the brief dramatization put on for Fray Alonso de Ponce shows. But they were also aware of their high standing in indigenous communities, conferred by their ancestry. In assuming positions of leadership, it is unlikely that they would have seen themselves as mere agents or deputies of the Spanish administration. Trained to think, argue, and hold their own among both Spaniards and Indians, they were uniquely empowered to manoeuvre and operate between the two worlds.[134]

Nonetheless, those students, some of whom had been separated from their parents, were brought up as Christians from their infancy and had no direct experience of pre-Hispanic society—which they were too young to remember and many features of which would have been difficult for them to understand or explain.[135] For all that their knowledge as speakers of Nahuatl was of great value to the missionaries, the collegians were in an unusual diglossic situation: as a result of linguistic immersion some of them ended up speaking, reading, and writing Latin (as well as Spanish) with impressive proficiency, but the command they had of their Mexican language would not have been developed in an equivalent way. At the same time, the active translations those indigenous scholars helped to produce *from* Latin are by far the most important legacy of their training, and led to the creation of a written literature in Nahuatl.

[134] Burkhart 1996, 59: 'Interpreters between European and Nahua worlds, the young men became cultural brokers negotiating the exchange of symbols and meanings between conquerors and conquered.' See the Latin petitions in Appendix 2, examined in Chapter 6 below.

[135] SAHAGÚN, *HG* 2, Prologue [1982 i, 54] makes clear that information about pre-Hispanic Mexico was supplied by elders or principals from outside the college, in Tepepulco, Tlatelolco, and Mexico City: the Indian Latinists served as interpreters and scribes. Trexler 1987 describes how the friars' indoctrination of their charges required them to be sequestered and alienated from their parents.

5

From the *Epistolae et Evangelia* to the *Huehuetlahtolli*

Indian Latinists and the Creation of Nahuatl Literature

The Franciscan order stood to lose much ground in New Spain, if the costly and controversial schooling of indigenous youths had not proved effective. The work done by those educated at the College of Santa Cruz in Tlatelolco provides the best evidence that the enterprise did in fact succeed: an abundant and varied corpus of literature survives, ranging from Latin compositions to Nahuatl translations of Christian texts and original dialogues in the Mexican language. These different kinds of writing, however, are seldom examined in conjunction with one another. The following survey of a variety of texts produced in Tlatelolco seeks to demonstrate that they all share a reliance on Latin learning—which was also the matrix for a new literature in Nahuatl.

The opening examination of an 'Indian' herbal and an early vocabulary of Latin, Spanish, and Nahuatl reveals that native authors and scribes presupposed the centrality of Latin—even when they were conveying forms of knowledge particular to Mexico (Section I below). Testimonies from both friars and indigenous collegians at Santa Cruz confirm that the difficulties encountered in putting Christian texts into Nahuatl lay not in understanding the meaning of the Latin, but in finding appropriate ways to express that meaning in a very different language (Section II). Despite the value the friars attached to the collegians' translations of scripture and their importance for religious and linguistic history, the lectionaries of Epistles and Gospels in Nahuatl that survive from the 1500s have long been overlooked. Comparison of surviving examples, with inspection of some specific passages, offers fresh insights on the way in which the translations were made and transmitted (Section III). As later restrictions on scripture in native languages led to the generation of a new Christian literature in Nahuatl, the focus in the latter part of the chapter (Section IV) will be on the production of original works in the language, including the *Colloquios y Doctrina christiana* (1564) and the *Huehuetlahtolli* (1601).

Aztec Latin. Andrew Laird, Oxford University Press. © Oxford University Press 2024.
DOI: 10.1093/oso/9780197586358.003.0006

The crucial role Latin humanism had in shaping that literature will be considered in the concluding discussion (Section V).

I. Latin manuscripts by Mexican scholars

(i) Juan Badiano, *Libellus de medicinalibus Indorum herbis*, 1552

An illustrated 'Booklet on the medicinal herbs of the Indians' is the best-known Latin text by a native Mexican. The work was commissioned by the rector of Santa Cruz, Fray Jacobo de Grado, to be presented to the Emperor Charles V in the hope of eliciting royal support for the college after its main patron, the viceroy Antonio de Mendoza, departed to Lima in 1550.[1] The full title of the *Libellus* affirms that it was compiled by an 'Indian physician, one taught not by any systems, but thoroughly instructed by experimental results alone' ('Indus medicus composuit, nullis rationibus doctus, sed solis experimentis edoctus'). That form of words precisely recalls Isidore of Seville's definition of the Greco-Roman 'Empirical School' of medicine.[2] A dedication follows, in which the native physician identifies himself as 'Martinus de la Cruz'—a name possibly connected to the College of Santa Cruz—although the same individual was also known as Martín Momauhti.[3] Along with another Mexican from Tlatelolco, Antón Hernandez, Martín had received a license from the viceroy, Luis de Velasco, 'to heal and have the right to heal the native Indians of the diseases they have in this city of Mexico, in Santiago and other quarters'.[4]

Although Martín de la Cruz appears to have been the author of the dedication, he did not write the text of the *Libellus* itself. In a note to the reader at the end of the manuscript, 'Joannes Badianus', or Juan Badiano, 'an Indian by race, a native of Xochimilco, and professor in the same College', refers to himself as the

[1] This information can be gleaned from the dedication on the title page and the coda: Appendix 2.2 below. Somolinos D'Ardois 1991, 167–75 describes the transmission of the *Libellus*.

[2] BADIANO, *Libellus* (1552), 1r [1991 ii, 12]. Cf. Isidore, *Etymologies* 4.4: 'Secunda Enpirica, id est experientissima, inventa est ab Aesculapio, quae non indiciorum signis, sed solis constat experimentis'. Isidore here described three schools ('haereses') of medicine and their inventors: Apollo's methodical school, Aesculapius' empirical school, and Hippocrates' logical school. Cf. Chapter 4, III, nn. 100 and 101 above on Isidore and medicine at Santa Cruz.

[3] The anonymous Nahuatl *Annals of Juan Bautista* (c. 1569), 51v [2001, 299], named don Martín Momauhti as one of a group of officials appointed in San Sebastián. A similar list in the *Codex Osuna* (1565) includes him as 'Martín de la Cruz' (and also mentions another Tlatelolco collegian, Pedro Atecpanecatl de Coatlayhuacan, referring to him as 'Pedro de Gante').

[4] VELASCO, 'Mandato' (1551) stated that the two healers 'make and have made very good remedies, especially among the collegians at the college of Santiago in this city': cf. Viesca Treviño 1995a, 489. Martín acknowledged Antonio de Mendoza, the previous viceroy, as his patron ('meo maecenati') in BADIANO, *Libellus*, 1v.

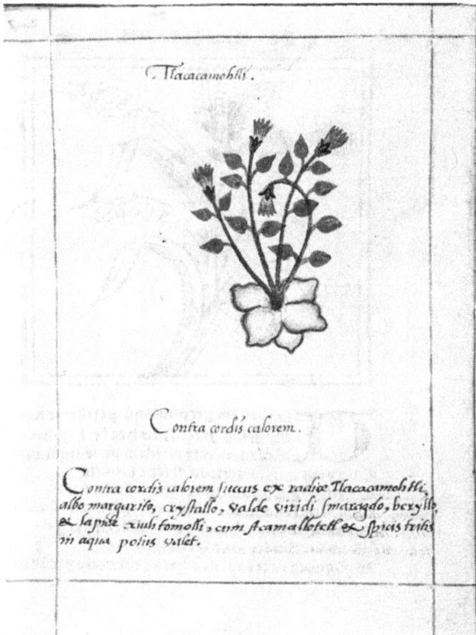

Figure 5.1 Libellus de medicinalibus Indorum herbis, Tlatelolco, 1552, 28v. Instituto Nacional de Antropología e Historia, Mexico.

'translator' ('interpres') of the work.[5] This description has led to a general supposition that Badiano produced a Latin version of a prior text by Martín in Nahuatl. There is, however, no record of such a document and there may never have been one. The indication in the extended title of the *Libellus* quoted above that Martín had 'compiled' ('composuit') the work does not at all imply that he committed anything to paper: his words are more likely to have been dictated or recited from memory.[6] While some of the content may have been informed by an oral testimony from the physician, it is evident that the overall conception of the herbal was rooted in Badiano's Latin learning. Juan Badiano can be regarded as the author in all but name, even if he did conceive of his work as a translation.

The *Libellus,* with its paintings of the medicinal plants described in the text (Figure 5.1, cf. Plate 6a), is often compared to manuscripts of Dioscorides' *Materia medica.*[7] But the *De virtutibus herbarum,* 'The virtues of herbs', a medieval verse

[5] BADIANO, *Libellus,* 63r [1991 ii, 88]: Appendix 2.2.2 below. The primary sense of *interpres* is 'go-between' or 'mediator'—the Spanish *intérprete* often had the same sense. Badiano may be hinting at something broader than linguistic translation: 'Quicquid operae in huius libelli herbarii qualicunque uersione a me collocatum est'. ('Whatever labour has been expended by me in the rendering, such as it is, of this booklet on herbal medicine').

[6] Garibay 1954 ii [2007, 716] recognized this possibility; cf. Biondelli 1858, xvii quoted in n. 70 below, and Chapter 7, p. 227 below on dictation.

[7] Cf. Riddle 1984 on the transmission of Dioscorides.

De verbena herba. lviii.

Verbenam gerobotanũ peristereonq
Appellãt greci. spẽs hec fert habere
Binas. effect⁹ est idem pene duabus
Cum vino iuuat ictericos si sepe bibatur
Pestiferos morsus curat superaddita trita
Cum vino renouanda quidã per quattuor ista
Est medicina dies horis bene vulnera purgat.
Illius succus tepidus si voluitur ore
Hoc quoq3 facta recens herbe decoctio prestat.

Figure 5.2 Macer Floridus, *Carmen de virtutibus herbarum*, Paris, 1511, 58v. Wellcome Collections, London.

treatise long attributed to a 'Macer Floridus', was far more popular as a school text in the 1500s: it was published in Basel, Paris, and Venice, and translated into German, French, Spanish, and English.[8] Printed editions of that work, which contained numerous woodcut illustrations (Figure 5.2), should be considered as the most likely model for the Mexican herbal.

At the same time, the images in the *Libellus de medicinalibus Indorum herbis,* though generally European in style, accommodate indigenous conventions of representation as well. The standard glyphs for *atl,* 'water', and *tetl,* 'rock', which are employed several times, can have a phonetic or a pictographic value, depending on the context.[9] Alejandra Rojas Silva has identified an illustration that appears to combine Mexican and European significations: an image of the *couaxocotl* plant with two snakes positioned vertically on either side of it (Plate 6b).[10] As well as representing *couaxocotl,* 'serpent fruit' (the Nahuatl *coatl* means both 'twin' and 'serpent'; *xocotl* is 'fruit'), that depiction evokes the classical *caduceus,* a staff garlanded with two

[8] The *De virtutibus herbarum* is now attributed to Odo of Meung-sur-Loire: Crossgrove 2010. The last sixteenth-century printing was in 1590 by Henricus Ranzovius in Leipzig; GIL, *Libro de medicina llamado Macer* (1527) was a Spanish translation.

[9] Fernández 1991; Hassig 1989; Stols 1992; Reyes Equiguas 2016, 29–35.

[10] Rojas Silva 2018, 50; cf. Retief and Cilliers 2006, 194.

serpents.[11] The tableau of snakes around a fruit tree might also recall medieval iconography of the temptation of Adam and Eve that portrayed both Lilith, Adam's earlier wife, and Eve as serpents (Figure 8.3 below).[12]

Along with the painted illustrations, the frequent incorporation of Mexican names for plants in the written text has led many to view the *Libellus* as a vehicle for Mesoamerican knowledge. An excerpt from Badiano's description of a remedy for sleeplessness (Plate 6a) exemplifies the macaronic quality of his Latin:

> Somnum intermissum alliciunt et conciliant herba tlahçolpahtli, quae iuxta formicarum foveam nascitur, et cochizxihuitl cum hirundinis felle trita frontique illita. Tritae uero herbulae huihuitzyocochizxihuitl ex frondibus liquore expresso corpus ungi debet.[13]

> When sleep is interrupted it can be brought on and induced by the *tlahzolpahtli* herb, which grows around anthills, and by *cochizxihuitl* when ground with the gall of a swallow and rubbed on the forehead. Then, after the little herb *huihuitzyocochizxihuitl* has been ground, the body ought to be anointed with juice squeezed from its leaves.

The Nahuatl compound words in this quotation appear to be unique to the *Libellus*, but that does not necessarily mean that these and other such terms in the work were neologisms coined specifically for this text.

The pathology and ailments that determine the structure of the herbal are European, for all that it has been argued that they had independent analogues in Mexico.[14] A hundred or so short entries, each prescribing botanical remedies for a given infirmity, are grouped into thirteen chapters. The first eight chapters address diseases and injuries to the body, keeping to the convention of *a capite ad calcem*, or 'head to toe', common in post-Galenic medical texts; chapters 9–12 are concerned with fevers and various systemic conditions, informed by classical humoral theory.[15] The sequence roughly corresponds to that of the *Medicina Plinii*,

[11] For *coatl* and *xocotl*, see Karttunen 1992, at 36 and 329 respectively. The *caduceus*, owing to its connection with Mercury in antiquity, was associated with eloquence and commerce in the early modern period and was distinct from the rod of Asclepius, a symbol for medicine: Bayard 1978.

[12] Rojas Silva 2018, 51. The Aztec goddess Cihuacoatl ('Woman-Serpent') was identified with the biblical Eve in the Spanish version of SAHAGÚN, *Historia general* (1580) = *HG*, 1.6 [2016, 31]: Chapter 8, III below.

[13] BADIANO, *Libellus*, 13v [1991 ii, 24]. Humanists followed the classical practice of not inflecting names in Hebrew and other exotic languages: Adams 2013, 205–7. Viesca Treviño 1996, 147–61 discusses this passage.

[14] Viesca Treviño 1995b; Ortiz de Montellano 1993, 37 on *abderetica mens* and *siriasis* in BADIANO, *Libellus*, 53v, 61r.

[15] The *a capite ad calcem* principle, which originated in the first century AD with Apollonius Mys, was adopted by Dioscorides and pseudo-Galen. Cf. Hinojo Andrés 2015, 709–37 on classical sources for the *Libellus*.

a collection of remedies compiled in the fourth century AD from Books 20–32 of Pliny's *Natural History*.[16] Badiano took Greek pathological terms from Pliny, whom he actually named and quoted in a reference to the *alectoria*, the crystalline stone found in the gizzards of cocks.[17]

A section appended to the eighth chapter, accompanied by an outstanding set of richly coloured illustrations of flowers and plants, constitutes the formal centre of the *Libellus*.[18] There remedies are proposed for a very specific kind of fatigue—of 'one administering the Republic and holding a public office' ('contra rempublicam administrantis, et munus publicum gerentis fatigationem'). This special inclusion may bear on the eminence of the intended recipients of the manuscript: the dedicatee Francisco de Mendoza, son of the former viceroy, and ultimately the Emperor Charles himself. The herbal was implicitly fashioned for such readers as an example of European princely *speculum* literature.[19]

There were, however, characteristically Mexican manners of expression in the personal dedication to Mendoza by Martín de la Cruz, although it was given in Latin:

> Vtinam librum *regis conspectu dignum* Indi faceremus, hic enim prorsus *indignissimus* est, qui veniat *ante conspectum tantae maiestatis*. Sed memineris nos *misellos pauperculos* Indos omnibus mortalibus inferiores esse, et ideo veniam nostra a natura nobis insita *parvitas et tenuitas* meretur.[20]
>
> If only we Indians could make a book *worthy of the king's glance*: this book is obviously *very unworthy* of coming before the *glance of such great majesty*. But bear in mind that we *poor little wretched little* Indians are inferior to all other mortals, and the *smallness and insignificance* ingrained in us by nature therefore merits pardon.

[16] The *Medicina Plinii*, popular in the Middle Ages, was consulted in monastic infirmaries: Matthews Sanford 1949, 463.

[17] BADIANO, *Libellus*, 19v [1991 ii, 32]: 'alectoria quae quidem gemma invenitur, teste etiam Plinio, in ventriculis gallinaceorum, crystallina specie, magnitudine fabae indianae vel hispanae'; cf. Pliny, *Natural History* 37.54.144: 'alectorias vocant in ventriculis gallinaceorum inventas crystallina specie, magnitudine fabae' and Isidore, *Etymologies* 16.13.8: 'electria quasi alectoria'. The stone's medical application in the *Libellus*—to prompt flow of saliva and check excessive thirst—is from a later tradition, probably derived from the *De lapidibus* (c. 1070) by Bishop Marbode of Rennes and attested in RUEUS, *De gemmis* (1547): Duffin 2007, 333; Forbes 1973, 49. Despite these references in the *Libellus*, Mackenzie Cooley has pointed out to me that 'bezoar stones' are not among the Mexican remedies in SAHAGÚN, *HG* Book 11.

[18] Rojas Silva 2018, 43 compares the format of the central folios in the *Libellus* to pre-Columbian screenfolds 'in which the centre marked the most significant point of meaning'.

[19] The collegians of Santa Cruz were themselves trained for positions of leadership: cf. Chapter 4 above. On mirrors for princes: cf. pp. 126–7 above, and pp. 248–9, 316 below.

[20] BADIANO, *Libellus*, 1v [1991 ii, 12]: Appendix 2.2.1 below. Emphases here are mine.

While rhetorical repetition is common in Latin, the wording of Badiano italicized above seems to be reproducing the pleonastic quality of 'synonymic diffusion' in Nahuatl.[21] But the most striking feature of this address is its abject tone, exemplified here by Martín de la Cruz's apology for the inferiority of his Indian race. In the next sentence he beseeched Mendoza 'to receive the *Libellus* in the spirit in which it is offered from the hand of [his] little servant or else . . . to cast it away to whatever place it deserves'. The document had involved two years of intellectual and artistic labour, and the very suggestion that it might be discarded by its dedicatee seems preposterous. In Nahuatl, however, self-depreciatory devices were a component of formal speech and did not necessarily indicate genuine submissiveness on the part of speakers who employed them.[22]

Thus the dedication could be the one part of the manuscript in which Juan Badiano rendered Martín de la Cruz' words directly. The physician's technical knowledge, on the other hand, must have been radically overhauled in a treatise with a classical structure that relied heavily on European models and frames of reference. Badiano's showcasing of indigenous medicine was packaged as a Renaissance mirror for princes, in the hope of better impressing the eminent readers to whom the *Libellus* was directed.

(ii) A trilingual vocabulary of Spanish, Latin, and Nahuatl, c. 1545

This manuscript is actually a copy, penned in black ink, of a 1520 printing of Antonio de Nebrija's *Dictionarium ex Hispaniensi in Latinum sermonem* (c. 1495), with Nahuatl translations added in red lettering to most of the original entries (Plate 7).[23] The copy, which can be dated to the 1540s, thus transforms Nebrija's Spanish-Latin dictionary into a trilingual vocabulary of Spanish, Latin and Nahuatl.[24] The scribe probably did not compile the Nahuatl text himself, because the entire content

[21] Garibay 1940, 115 used the term 'difusión sinonímica'. The 'maneras de hablar' in OLMOS, *Arte de la lengua mexicana* (1547) 3.8 [2002, 177–93] include examples of such repetition, and Serafino 2015 notes instances in modern Nahuatl prayers. TLAXCALA, 'Verba sociorum' (1541) also reproduced this effect in Latin: Chapter 6, p. 190 below.

[22] Cf. Karttunen and Lockhart 1987, 22. Maxwell and Hanson 1992, 20–1 note that 'constant potential for antonymic interpretation gives the Nahuatl author the power to say one thing but to mean another'. Compare the avowal of the student at Tlatelolco that he and his cohort are of 'very weak aptitude' ('tenuissima habilitate') in Chapter 4, II above.

[23] The words 'Vocabulario trilingüe' are on the nineteenth-century binding of the anonymous 155-folio document, which is in the Newberry Library. NEBRIJA, *Dictionarium* (c. 1495) was the first full edition of the Spanish-Latin dictionary: Hamann 2015, 47 identifies an unauthorized 1520 Seville printing of a shorter 1513 version (with a given date of 1516) as the one copied in the Newberry manuscript. On editions of Nebrija's 1513 dictionary, cf. Vidal Díez 2007.

[24] This estimate of the date is based on the view that this trilingual vocabulary was produced well before MOLINA, *Aqui comiença vn vocabulario* (1555) superseded it. Molina would probably have started work on the dictionary before his Nahuatl *Doctrina Christiana* (1546) was published. It is

of the manuscript seems to have been copied from a lost earlier version, which itself incorporated all three languages.[25]

Both the extant trilingual vocabulary and its lost source are likely to have been produced at the College of Santa Cruz. Physical characteristics of the existing copy—the quarto size, European paper, ink colour, and style of lettering—are shared by other manuscripts copied under the direction of the Franciscans.[26] In the mid-1500s Fray Juan de Torquemada states that Sahagún himself wrote 'a trilingual vocabulary of great accomplishment in the practice of the Mexican language.'[27] The scribe of the present copy, however, was a native speaker of Nahuatl as the distinctive spelling of some Spanish and Latin words reveals—but that does not preclude a connection to the college in Tlatelolco.[28]

As the trilingual vocabulary retains the format of Nebrija's *Dictionarium*, it presents Spanish headwords with their Latin correspondents (nominative and genitive case for nouns, and conjugations for verbs), with Nahuatl equivalents supplementing 70% of the entries.[29] Those equivalents are of the *Latin* words in Nebrija's dictionary rather than the Spanish ones. Even Latin loan words that Nebrija had included in his Spanish entries were put into Nahuatl:

> [Spanish] Consul romano.[Latin] consul consulis.
> [Nahuatl] teuctláto[30]

unlikely that the labour of either compiling or copying out the trilingual manuscript would have been undertaken if Molina's vocabulary had been known to be in progress. See further nn. 34 and 36 below.

[25] Clayton 1989, 398–9 discerned this from scribal errors deriving from misread handwriting, incorrect ordering of some entries, and the occasional absence of Spanish and Latin terms for which Nahuatl words are supplied.

[26] Schwaller 2001, 11. Early manuscripts of Epistles and Gospels considered below, including one at the Newberry (cf. Plate 8 and Section III of this chapter), are similar in format and appearance. Téllez Nieto 2010, 177–84 makes the case for the trilingual vocabulary's Franciscan provenance.

[27] TORQUEMADA, *MI* (1615), 20.46 [1979 vi, 266]: 'Escribió también otro vocabulario, que llamó *Trilingüe*, en lengua mexicana, castellana, y latina, de grandísima erudición en este ejercicio de la lengua mexicana.' Ramírez 1898 i, 121, the first attestation of the extant trilingual vocabulary, asserted its connection with Sahagún but (as Torquemada noted) it was different from the projected 'Calepino' based on Nahuatl usage: SAHAGÚN, *HG* Book 1, 'Prólogo al sincero lector' [1982 i, 53].

[28] Indicative misspellings are pervasive: in the incipit (Plate 7), 'Neprissensi' has replaced *Nebrissensi*, the standard form in the Latin ablative. That variant is characteristic of Mexican writers because the voiced *b* did not exist in Nahuatl and was confused with the unvoiced *p*: Launey 2011, 3–8. Karttunen 1988 first proposed that the scribe was a Nahuatl speaker—a thesis developed in Clayton 2003. Cf. SAHAGÚN, *HG*, Book 10, 'Relación del autor' [1982 i, 83–4] (quoted below, p. 166).

[29] Clayton 2003, 100 notes that 11,058 of 15,479 of Nebrija's entries are given Nahuatl equivalents, with 9,230 different Nahuatl words and phrases used in the text.

[30] Anon., *Dictionarium* (c. 1545), 44r.

Teuctlato[*ani*] was specifically used for the governor of a locality, and it was related to the verb *teuctlatoa*, 'to hold court, public hearing, council', as distinct from *teuctli*, a common word for 'lord'.

In other cases, the translation involved the coining of a suitable paraphrase. The entry for the month of August is one example:

> [Spanish] Agosto mes. [Latin] sextilis. augustus, i.
> [Nahuatl] tlachicuacencayutia méztli.[31]

The Nahuatl text for this entry can be translated as 'the month is in sixth position'.[32] That is clearly not an explanation of the Spanish 'Agosto mes' but of 'sextilis': in the ancient Roman system of reckoning, August was the sixth month of the year counted from March.[33] Such examples show the translator was more concerned, if not more conversant, with Latin than with Spanish.

Not only are the Latin terms in Nebrija's dictionary translated instead of the Spanish headwords: there are often explanations in Nahuatl of the Spanish words rather than simple functional equivalents, and the translator occasionally misunderstood some of Nebrija's terms.[34] These considerations have led scholars to regard the trilingual lexicon as a *passive* dictionary—with Spanish as the source language, foreign to the anticipated user, and Nahuatl as the target language, tantamount to the user's first language.[35] On that hypothesis, Nebrija's *Dictionarium* would have provided a ready list of Spanish words, with the Latin offering a further resource for the elucidation of those words in Nahuatl. Hence the Nahuatl words added to the Spanish-Latin entries have often been referred to as 'glosses': glosses are annotations serving to explain alien or unknown words, and, crucially, they are normally in the language or idiom of their intended reader.

But the annotations would not have been glosses in that conventional sense for someone who was not a speaker of the Mexican language, and it cannot be assumed that anyone consulting the work would have a knowledge of Nahuatl as extensive as that of the writer who translated the entries in Nebrija's vocabulary. Those

[31] *Dictionarium*, 15r.

[32] This is Gordon Whittaker's translation from a personal communication comparing SAHAGÚN *HG* 7.7 [1953 vii, 21]: 'tlanauhcaiotia' ('is fourth in order'). Whittaker also observes that 'meztli' here, in place of *metzli*, the correct term for 'moon' or 'month' (cf. Chapter 6, p. 192, n. 27 below) suggests interference from *mes*, the Spanish for month.

[33] Clayton 2003, 113 first pointed out that the Nahuatl translation follows the Latin terms for July and August, *Quintilis* and *Sextilis*. Macrobius, *Saturnalia* 1.12.35 recorded the Roman senatorial decree that renamed *Sextilis* as *Augustus* in 8 BC: see further Brind'Amour 1983.

[34] Karttunen 1988 observes that the trilingual vocabulary uses paraphrases, or analogous terms, in Nahuatl rather than Spanish loan words—a practice that suggests it preceded MOLINA, *Aqui comiença un vocabulario* (1555), the first printed Spanish-Nahuatl dictionary.

[35] Clayton 2003, 101–8 makes a forceful case for this point.

translations could still have been made to create an *active* dictionary to identify Nahuatl expressions for the Spanish or Latin words that were already known to the *user* (despite the Spanish words causing confusion for the native copyist). This possibility would mean that the resulting trilingual vocabulary followed the directionality of Nebrija's dictionary—from Spanish to Latin—extending it to Nahuatl; and it better accounts for the Latin being retained in the surviving copy of the lost document.

It is important to consider the kind of user this trilingual dictionary would have served. Although some Mexicans soon learned to read and write wills, letters, and other documents in their own language, they would have gained little from a passive dictionary, since literacy was rarely if ever acquired without knowledge of Spanish or Latin in the first place. On the other hand, the ability to translate both Spanish and Latin into Nahuatl was of paramount importance to the missionaries and indeed some of their educated Indian collaborators, whose unusual diglossic situation meant that in certain respects they too were learners of the Mexican language.

Fray Alonso de Molina, for example, remarked that his first dictionary from Spanish to Nahuatl, *Aqui comiença un vocabulario enla lengua castellana y mexicana* (1555), had been 'necessary to help ministers in this new church with the obligatory performance of their duties, in administering the word of God and the holy Sacraments to these natives'. Its purpose, he added, had been 'to begin opening a path, so that, over time and with the diligence of others with a livelier understanding, there would be the gradual discovery of an inexhaustible mine (so to say) of words and manners of speaking possessed by this very copious and well structured Mexican tongue'.[36] Similar objectives could account for the manuscript trilingual vocabulary, even though it was really a rudimentary prototype for an active dictionary of Nahuatl. While Molina's *Vocabulario* was an accomplished work of lexicography in its own right, the word list in the trilingual manuscript was constituted from Nebrija's *Dictionarium*.

There was at least one precursor for this kind of conformity in peninsular Spain: Pedro de Alcalá's *Vocabulista arauigo en letra castellana* ('Arabic word-finder in Castilian lettering'). That Spanish-Arabic dictionary had been published in 1505 at the behest of Hernando Talavera, first archbishop of Granada, who sought to ensure that 'all priests and sacristans who live in . . . towns recently converted would be able

[36] MOLINA, *Vocabulario* (1571), 'Prologo al lector', unnumbered page, corresponding to 124v: 'Quando imprimi la primera vez el Vocabulario dela lengua Mexicana (obra a mi parecer harto buena y necessaria, para ayudar a los ministros desta nueva yglesia, ala deuida execucion de sus oficios en la administracion dela palabra de Dios y delos sanctos Sacramentos a estos naturales) no fue otro mi intencion, sino començar a abrir camino, para que en el discurso del tiempo y con la diligencia de otros mas biuos, se fuesse poco apoco descubriendo la mina [amanera de dezir] inacauable de vocablos y maneras de hablar que esta copiossima y artificial lengua Mexicana tiene.' These comments of Molina on his 1555 vocabulary precede the Nahuatl-Spanish section of his later bidirectional dictionary.

to learn Arabic'.[37] Pedro de Alcalá's *Vocabulista* kept very closely to the precedent of Nebrija's Spanish-Latin dictionary, although the Latin terms were not retained, and some new Spanish headwords were added.[38]

Missionaries in New Spain would have been inclined to elicit *ad verbum* translations and explanatory equivalents in Nahuatl for the terms in Nebrija's *Dictionarium* in a similar fashion. The desire to assemble an abundance (or 'copia,' as Erasmus called it) of vocabulary, etymology, and paraphrase—a standard practice of humanist language learning—might well account for the contrivance of Nahuatl terms to harmonize with a lexicographical scheme and linguistic categories designed for Latin. Such a process parallels the *reducción* involved in the composition of missionary *artes,* which relied to some degree on the conventions of Latin grammar to systematize Amerindian languages.[39] The apparently eccentric Nahuatl explications of Nebrija's terms in the trilingual vocabulary involved a principle that would continue to underpin many endeavours undertaken in the College of Santa Cruz in Tlatelolco.[40] The central position instinctively accorded to Latin, no less than the directionality *from* Latin *to* Nahuatl, characterized the linguistic works, translations, and new compositions in the Mexican language whether they were authored by native scholars or the Franciscan friars.

II. Status and achievements of the native translators

For the Indian students who had acquired a thorough working knowledge of Latin grammar and idiom, the challenge of making translations from Latin to Nahuatl lay not in comprehending the source texts—they would have come to understand these no less well than their Franciscan instructors—but in finding the appropriate expressions to put the content of those sources into the Mexican language. That process often required a capacity for innovation and circumlocution in situations when, as will be shown in examples to come (cf. Section III below), no direct correspondents existed.

Versions of Christian texts had to be free from error or potentially perilous misunderstandings. Writing in the 1570s, Fray Bernardino de Sahagún, who had

[37] *Breve suma de la santa vida del reverendissimo y bienaventurado don fray Fernando de Talavera,* manuscript, quoted in Amador de los Rios 1861–1865 vii, 358, translated in Dannenfeldt 1955, 105–6.

[38] Zwartjes 2014, Gilbert 2020, 155–7.

[39] Cf. Chapter 3 above.

[40] The changing role of Latin in early missionary linguistics can be compared to that of English in 'machine translation', which had involved putting source texts first into English and then into the target language—until a neural machine-translation engine could produce 'whole sentences at a time, rather than just piece by piece': Turovsky 2016. The missionaries' *ad literam* translation soon yielded to an *ad sensum* approach (cf. nn. 43–45 below).

been involved with the College of Santa Cruz from its foundation, described the vital assistance of the indigenous scholars in the preparation of evangelical material:

> They have helped and still help in many things in the implanting and maintaining of our Holy Catholic Faith, for if sermons, *postillas* and catechisms ['doctrinas'] have been produced in the Indian language, which can appear and may be free of all heresy, they are those which were written [in collaboration] with them. And they, being knowledgeable in the Latin language, inform us as to the properties of words, the properties of their manner of speech. And they correct for us the incongruities we express in the sermons or write in the catechisms.[41]

Some thirty years later, Fray Juan Bautista Viseo, who oversaw the publication of numerous religious works in Nahuatl at the College, also emphasized the importance of the help he received from native Latinists in the Prologue to his *Sermonario en lengua mexicana* (1606). There he gave detailed information about several individuals:

> I have been helped in this task by some accomplished natives very well trained in Latin, especially by one Hernando de Ribas (one of the first sons of the Royal College of Santa Cruz founded in the Convent of Santiago Tlatilulco in Mexico) local to the city of Tetzcuco, a very good Latinist, who with great dexterity could translate anything from Latin and from the Spanish vernacular ['romance'] into the Mexican language, paying more attention to the sense than the literal meaning. What he wrote and translated for me on various things amounted to thirty hands of paper . . . With his help, Fray Alonso de Molina put together his Mexican *Arte* and his *Vocabulario,* Fray Juan de Gaona his *Dialogos de la paz y tranquilidad del alma,* and I have compiled a *Vocabulario ecclesiastico* (which I think is very necessary for preachers), and most of the *Vanidades* by Estel[l]a.[42]

The capacity for 'paying more attention to the sense than to the literal meaning' ('atendiendo más al sentido que a la letra') is a quality Bautista praised in similar terms elsewhere.[43] The classical and humanist predilection for *ad sensum* rather than

[41] SAHAGÚN, *HG* Book 10, 'Relación' [1982 i, 83–4].

[42] BAUTISTA, *Sermonario* (1606), vii verso [1954, 474–5].

[43] BAUTISTA, *Huehuetlahtolli* (1601), 77 (cf. Section IV below) remarked on Fray Andrés de Olmos' translation of the Mexican discourses: 'Las quales romanço de la lengua Mexicana sin añadir, ni quitar cosa que fuesse de substancia: *sacando sentido de sentido, y no palabra de palabra*' ('He put these into the vernacular from the Mexican language without adding or removing anything of substance: *taking it sense for sense, not word for word.*') The italics are mine.

ad verbum translation for the sake of elegance went back to Cicero.[44] But the importance of the application of that principle to sacred texts in late antiquity tends to be overlooked by early modern intellectual historians. *Ad sensum* translation had appealed to Jerome and other Church Fathers because they were actually aiming at fidelity to the thematic essence of their sources. Franciscan missionaries in the 1500s had the same inclination: they eschewed literal renditions, not for stylistic reasons, but to capture the actual meaning of a given passage.[45]

As well as offering unique portrayals of individual Mexican scholars, Bautista's Prologue is of value because it specifies the skills that were required of the native translators. The friar's description of how he was assisted by Antonio Valeriano, Sahagún's best-known collaborator, gives way to some illuminating reflections:

> He helped me a great deal, both with specific things I consulted him about and with the etymology and meaning of many [Nahuatl] terms, explanations of which have gone into the text of my *Sermonario*, so as better to advise ministers who would not be able to discover them without effort. That is because in today's world the Indians whom one can ask things about their language are so few that they can be counted, and many of them employ corrupt forms of speech, just as Spaniards do. This is something that anyone whose knowledge of this language has an accurate and systematic grounding is bound to notice; and so it is necessary to proceed cautiously in asking things and getting advice, especially about words and expressions involving mysteries of the faith and moral matters. I have come across an Indian with Latin and a good degree who, in conversing with me, said 'Dios itlaneltoquilitzin', which means 'the faith which God believes', when he should have said, 'Dios ineltococatzin', 'the faith in which God is believed in', and I could find many examples of this sort of thing.[46]

These considerations led the writer to single out and describe at length the ability of another assistant of Sahagún, as a scribe, editor and typesetter: Agustín de la Fuente, a native of Tlatelolco and teacher at Santa Cruz, was praised for his 'excellent comprehension, reasoning and precise knowledge of his language and its peculiarities'.[47] The other Mexicans whom Bautista acknowledged were trained in

[44] Cicero, *De optimo genere oratorum* 5.14 is the *locus classicus*; cf. Pliny, *Epistles* 7.9.2–3. Botley 2004, 164–77 shows how humanist translation *ad sensum* could convey the meaning of the source text in a less precise manner, sometimes omitting or altering passages in favour of greater elegance and fluency; cf. Den Haan 2016.

[45] Jerome, *Chronicle of Eusebius*, 'Praefatio'. This important difference is discussed in Adler 1994, 321–48; cf. Canellis 2016 on Jerome's biblical exegesis.

[46] BAUTISTA, *Sermonario* (1606) [1954, 475].

[47] BAUTISTA, *Sermonario* [1954, 476]: 'Es de muy buen entendimiento y razón, y sabe su lengua e idiotismos de ella con gran propiedad.'

the College of Santa Cruz as well: don Juan Berardo of Huexotzinco, a good writer of Latin prose and a singer; Diego Adriano from Tlatelolco, the typesetter who could translate from Latin to Nahuatl with great precision; don Francisco Bautista de Contreras from Cuernavaca, a good writer of Spanish prose; Esteban Bravo of Texcoco, who helped Bautista to translate and edit the *Sermonario* in Nahuatl; and 'Pedro de Gante', or Pedro Atecpanecatl from Texcoco, who took his name from Peter of Ghent.[48]

Unfortunately, the indigenous scholars could never be credited as authors or co-authors of the texts on which they worked. Their translations and writings were either anonymous or attributed to individual Franciscans directing the given enterprise: in the latter case, though, the friars often named their Indian collaborators in their prefaces, sometimes providing extensive acknowledgements. But there are a couple of interesting testimonies from native translators. Don Pablo Nazareo of Xaltocan drew attention to his own efforts, in the first of his petitionary letters in Latin to Philip II:

> So I toiled to the utmost night and day, to translate the Gospels and Epistles into my mother tongue to be read in church over the course of the whole year. Not only these: I also took the trouble to translate a very large number of other texts, all of which have been emended in accordance with the discretion and judgement of experts, especially those qualified in theology and acquainted with our language. These translations are now widely circulated amongst almost all the holy preachers, friars and clergy who are helping many inhabitants of the Indies by using my works and sampling the fruit of my labour.[49]

In a letter to Fray Juan Bautista, again written in Latin, Antonio Valeriano described the difficulties he had with a particular text:

[48] Cf. Appendix 1.4. SilverMoon 2007 names some fifty native collegians, but wrongly assumes that Fray Diego Valadés (cf. Chapter 2 above) was connected to the college, a claim also made in Kobayashi 1985, 268. A 'Pedro Juan Antonio', for whom the first attestation seems to be García Cubas 1896, an unreliable source, should be discounted as well.

[49] NAZAREO, 'Invictissimo Hispaniarum . . . Domino Philippo' (1556), 2 [1970, 18]: 'sic noctes, diesque summopere laboraui vt que per anni totius discursum in ecclesia leguntur euangelia et epistolas in linguam maternam traducerem, nec hec solum sed et complurima alia e latino in nostrum ydioma transferre procuraui, que omnia correcta judicio ac censura peritorum, precipue theologie candidatorum, nostraeque lingue peritorum passim habentur apud fere omnes sacros concionatores, religiosos et clericos qui nostra opera fruentes, sudorisque nostri fructum degustantes multis prosunt indiarum incolis.'

> I know not for sure whether I am successful in my translation of it. Indeed there are many things in [the source] weighty with implication, so that I do not know what is the better sense into which they should be rendered. I beg you to pardon anything done in error; and to apply to it your authoritative censorship.[50]

That ready submission to the senior friar's formal *censura* makes clear the directionality of the translation: the writer was referring to a Latin religious text he had put into Nahuatl.

The efforts made by Nazareo, Valeriano, and other native translators still receive scant recognition. Historians concerned with Nahuatl texts authored at the College of Santa Cruz have focused largely on material of putative pre-Hispanic origin: Fray Bernardino de Sahagún's *Historia general de las cosas de Nueva España* (or *Florentine Codex*) and other texts of ethnographic interest have diverted attention from dozens of diligently composed works on Christian themes—including those overseen by Sahagún himself. The persistent misconception that the College of Santa Cruz was founded to train an indigenous clergy (and that it failed in such an unlikely objective) has diminished understanding of what the students really achieved.[51] They were not theologians but linguists, with a valuable range of broader learning. Their activities in this respect can be seen as analogous to those of countless Christian humanists in Europe—of whom Valla, Nebrija, and Erasmus are now the best known. Such individuals belonged to the laity, yet they dedicated much of their philological and textual scholarship to the translation and transmission of scripture and Christian literature, sometimes authoring works of their own on religious subjects.

III. Biblical translation

A large number of lectionaries or books of Epistles and Gospel readings in Mesoamerican languages were copied by hand. There are at least twenty extant examples from the 1500s, mostly in Nahuatl, which have been barely studied, individually or collectively. Three early Nahuatl manuscripts, however, each unsigned and undated, have received some scholarly attention:

[50] VALERIANO, 'Hic gerulus litterarum' (c. 1600): 'Nescio profecto an in traductione eius sim felix. Multa quippe in eo sunt praegnantia; vt nesciam in quem sensum meliorem verti debeant. Si quid est erratum parcas obsecro. Et tuam gravem censuram adhibeas.' See Appendix 2.5 below for the entire letter, which is discussed again in Chapter 6, III.

[51] See Chapter 4, II above.

1. Milan: *Sequuntur communes epistolae de apostolis*, Manoscritti, AH_X.9, Biblioteca nazionale Braidense

An annotation on the second folio of the manuscript states that it was held by Fray Diego de Cañizares from 1552, a firm *terminus ante quem*.[52] The selection and order of lessons predated recommendations by the Council of Trent in 1545, and the palaeographical evidence is consistent with this finding.[53] This is the only Nahuatl lectionary to have been printed. It was edited in the nineteenth century by the Italian philologist Bernardino Biondelli, who wrote an important and informative Latin introduction to the text.[54]

2. Chicago: *Incipiunt Epistolae et Evangelia*, Newberry Library, Ayer Ms. 1467

The Newberry manuscript (Plate 8) is generally thought to have been a prior draft of the Milan lectionary, and the writing of both documents has been attributed to Fray Bernardino de Sahagún.[55]

3. Toledo: *Incipiunt epistolae et evangelia*, Biblioteca Capitular, Ms. 35-22

This recently discovered manuscript was definitely copied by 1561, the year in which it was brought to Spain by Fray Francisco de Bustamante—and it could have been completed some years before.[56]

In accordance with the Roman Rite, lectionaries customarily begin with the Sunday Epistle and Gospel readings at the start of the church liturgical year on the First Sunday of Advent, opening with the Epistle from Romans 13:11–14. The initial verse (13:11) of that reading is as follows:

> Fratres: Scientes, quia hora est jam nos de somno surgere.
> Nunc enim propior est nostra salus, quam cum credidimus.
>
> Brothers, knowing that it is now the hour for us to arise from sleep,
> For now our salvation is nearer than when we became believers.

[52] Cañizares was appointed as a censor to correct Latin bibles in Yucatán: AGN Inquisición, vol. 76, exp. 31, cited in Nesvig 2009, 142.

[53] Biondelli 1858, xiv.

[54] Biondelli 1858.

[55] Chavero 1948, 30; Nicolau d'Olwer and Cline 1973, 204. Schwaller 2001, 8–9, in accord with these studies, discerns marginal notes in Sahagún's hand 'in the period up to about 1563'. Bustamante García 1990, 91–157 gives the lectionaries extensive consideration.

[56] Téllez Nieto 2015a, 171; Téllez Nieto and Baños Baños 2018.

Here, as on some other occasions, the Latin text of the Roman Rite diverges a little from the Vulgate.[57] The three manuscripts detailed above give slightly different Nahuatl versions of the verse. These are as follows (with the orthography and spacings between the words as they appear in the manuscripts):

> Milan:
>
> Noteiccauene [*sic*], yeanquimomachitia, cayeymman yequalcan intiçazque, intitoquetzazque.
> Auh inaxcan cacenca yeyzca yntomaquixtiloca, ynamoyuh yehuecauh iniquac çanoc titlaneltocaya.[58]
>
> Chicago:
>
> Noteyccauane, yeanquimomachitia, cayeimman ye qualcan intiçazque, intitoquetçazq[ue].
> Auh ynaxcan cacenca yeizuitz intomaquixtilloca, yn amo yuh titomatia, yeoquiz in youalli: otlatuic.
>
> Toledo:
>
> Noteicauane, yeanquimomachitia, ca yeimman yequalcan intiçazque intitoquetzazque.
> Ahuinaxcancacencayeizhuitz intomaquixtiloca ynamoyhu [*sic*] titomatia, yeoquiz inyoalli: otlatuic.

There are discrepancies between these renditions. The most notable is in the Milan manuscript where the last part of the second sentence is different from the others: 'ynamoyuh yehuecauh iniquac çanoc titlaneltocaya'. Yet in general, despite the different orthographic conventions in play, these versions exhibit remarkable uniformity, given the real potential for radical variation between translations from Latin into a very different language. Such uniformity suggests that the translations had a common provenance. They must have originated in the College of Santa Cruz in Tlatelolco, as Sahagún indicated in his account quoted above (Section II) of the role indigenous collegians had in the preparation of evangelical material:

[57] The Vulgate has 'hoc scientes tempus quia hora est iam nos de somno surgere nunc enim propior est nostra salus quam cum credidimus'. The entire running Latin text of Biondelli 1858 is different again: it is a careful, close translation *from* the Nahuatl of the Milan lectionary for benefit of the modern Latinate reader. Thus the Latin version of Romans 13:11 in Biondelli 1858, 251 reads, 'Mei fratres, jam scitis, quia venit hora venit tempus expergiscamur, surgamus. Nunc enim magis proxima est nostra salus, quam longinquam usquedum credebamus.'

[58] Biondelli 1858, 251 has 'Noteiccahuane, yeanquimomachitya, cayeimman yequalcan intiçazque, intitoquetzazque. Auh inaxcan cacenca yeizca intomaquixtiloca, inamoyuh yehuecauh iniquac çanoc titlaneltocaya.'

> And whatever is to be rendered in their language, if it is not examined by them, if it is not written congruently in the Latin language, in Spanish, and in their language, cannot be free of defect. *With regard to orthography, and good writing, there are none who write it other than those reared here.*[59]

The difficulties faced in Christian antiquity by the first translators of the Bible from Hebrew and Greek into Latin doubtless acquired a new salience in Mexico.[60] Some of the most familiar and foundational phrases in liturgy would have presented problems. 'Ecce agnus Dei', 'Behold the Lamb of God', from John's Gospel 1:36 is one example. In all the lectionaries of Epistles and Gospels in Nahuatl it was conveyed as follows:

> Izcatqui in yichcatzin *Dios.*[61]
>
> Behold God's sheep.

The Franciscans used the Spanish *Dios* as the word for God in Nahuatl, to avoid any confusion or association with pre-Hispanic conceptions of the divine.[62] 'Yichcatzin' is a third-person possessed form of the noun *ichcatl,* incorporating the honorific suffix '-tzin'. *Ichcatl,* 'cotton', had come to designate wool and sheep, items introduced to Mexico by Europeans. A formulation like this and others would soon have become absorbed by converts who came to be familiar with many new expressions.[63] Some must have been obvious choices, like *cuaatequia,* 'to sprinkle on the head', for 'baptize'; while others were less so, such as *nezcaliliztli,* 'a reviving' or 'resuscitation', for resurrection.[64] As Nahuatl speakers

[59] SAHAGÚN, *HG* Book 10, 'Relación' [1982 i, 83–4]: 'y qualqujera cosa que se sa de conuertir en su lengua, y si no va con ellos examjnadano puede yr sin defecto, [sin] escrivjr congruamente en la lengua latina, nj en romãnce, nj en su lengua, *para lo que toca a la orthographia, y buena letra: no ay qujen lo escriua, sino los que aquj se crian'* (my italics).

[60] Cf. n. 45 above; n. 66 below on the sixteenth-century reprise of the ancient debate about John 1:1. CABRERA, *Meditatiunculae* (1548), 75v, composed in New Spain, alluded to Jerome's controversial Vulgate translation of the Hebrew *qiqqayon,* 'gourd', as *hedera,* 'ivy': Laird 2017a, 88–9.

[61] Biondelli 1858, 241 (my translation). The text of the Toledo lectionary, 168v, differs only in orthography: 'Jzcatqui ynichcatzin Dios'.

[62] Murillo Gallegos 2010; Baudot 1993; Tavárez 2000. On other occasions *teotl,* 'god', could be used, unmodified by *Dios.*

[63] Cf. Karttunen 1992, 92 on *ichcatl;* Launey 2011, 106–7 on the suffix *-tzin.* ACOSTA, *De procuranda Indorum salute* 4.9.2 (1588) [1987 ii, 74–8] stated that missionaries should not be concerned if correspondents for some terms could not be found in native languages. As Ditchfield 2017 has shown, the physical 'translatability' of material devotional objects and representations, rather than of texts and languages, brought about the successful diffusion of Catholicism.

[64] Tavárez 2000 addresses Nahuatl translation of Christian terms.

accommodated these usages in the context of their conversion, it is likely that the language they employed in other situations may have undergone change as a result.

The Nahuatl lectionaries sometimes show more notable departures from the text of the Roman Rite. The traditional opening verses of John's Gospel 1:1–2 for the Christmas mass, for example, were in precise accord with the wording of the Vulgate:

> [1] In principio erat Verbum et Verbum erat apud Deum et Deus erat Verbum:
> [2] Hoc erat in principio apud Deum.

> [1] In the beginning was the Word and the Word was with God, and the Word was God.
> [2] The same was in the beginning with God.

But those verses were given in Nahuatl as follows:

> [1] In ipan peuhcayotl moyetzticatca in *tepiltzin* Dios, auh inyehuatzin itlantzinco catca inDios, auh inyehuatzin *inipiltzin* Dios cateotl.
> [2] Inin moyetzticatca inipan peuhcayotl itlantzinco inDios.[65]

> [1] In the beginning was God the *Child*, and he was with God, and the *Child* of God was divine.
> [2] In the beginning this one was with God.

Verbum, 'the Word', which had long replaced *sermo*, 'discourse', as the standard equivalent to *logos* in the Greek text of John's Gospel, is here translated as 'tepiltzin Dios', 'God the Child', to be understood as 'God the Son'.[66] The Nahuatl *tlatolli* was the obvious term for *verbum* or *sermo*, but it must have had a value that was deemed inappropriate or insufficient for the sense of the Incarnate Word.[67]

Yet forms and cognates of *tlatolli* commonly recur elsewhere in the lectionaries, and they denote 'tongue', or language, as well as speech in the reading from Acts 2 for the Feast of Pentecost:

[65] Biondelli 1858, 376 (my emphases); Toledo Ms. 7r: '[1] INipanpehucayotl moyetzticatca in tepiltzin itlantzinco catca indios, auhindios ca yehuatl intepiltzin. [2] ininmoyetzticatca inipanpeuhcayotl itlantzinco indios.' (Initial capitalization is as in the manuscript; verse numbers are added.)

[66] See Karttunen 1992, 230 on 'tēpiltzin'. The Latin translation of John 1:1 was debated in the 1500s, as it had been in Christian antiquity. ERASMUS, *Apologia de In principio erat sermo* (1520) defended the change of 'verbum' to 'sermo' in his own own translation of the New Testament: O'Rourke Boyle 2004.

[67] Christensen 2013 explores the significance of many comparable examples.

[7] Stupebant autem omnes, et mirabantur, dicentes: Nonne ecce omnes isti qui *loquuntur*, Galilæi sunt?
[8] et quomodo nos audivimus unusquisque *linguam nostram*, in qua nati sumus?
[9] Parthi, et Medi, et Aelamitae, et qui habitant Mesopotamiam, Judaeam, et Cappadociam, Pontum, et Asiam,
[10] Phrygiam, et Pamphyliam, Aegyptum, et partes Libyae, quae est circa Cyrenen, et advenae Romani,
[11] Judaei quoque, et Proselyti, Cretes, et Arabes: audivimus eos loquentes *nostris linguis* magnalia Dei.

[7] And they were all amazed, and wondered, saying: Behold, are not all these that speak Galilean?
[8] And how have we heard, every man our own tongue wherein we were born?
[9] Parthians and Medes and Elamites and inhabitants of Mesopotamia, Judea, and Cappadocia, Pontus and Asia,
[10] Phrygia and Pamphylia, Egypt and the parts of Libya about Cyrene, and strangers of Rome,
[11] Jews also, and proselytes, Cretes, and Arabians: we have heard them speak in our own tongues the wonderful works of God.

[7] Icmochintin cenca miçahuiyaya, tlamahuiçohuaya, quitohuaya: Tlaxiquimittacan: inixquichtin *tlatohua*, cuix amo Galileatlaca?
[8] Quenin mochihua axcan, iniquac *tlatohua* cecenyaca, ticcaqui *intotlatol* in ipan otitlaque?
[9] Inyehuantin parthos, yuan medos, yuan Elemitas, auh inyemochintin ompa inchan Mesopotamia, Judea, yuan Cappadocia, Ponto, yuan Asia
[10] Phrigia yuan Pamphilia, Egipto, yuan inixquichtin ompa hualehua Lybia, inachi itlanca Cyrene yuan inRomatlaca inhueca hualehuaque,
[11] NoyehuantininJudiome, yuan proselites inCretes yuan Arabiatlaca, inizquican inaltepetlipan tihualehua, timochintin oticcacque *totlatol* inicquitenehua, inicquitenquixtya incenca mahuiçauhqui inoquimochihuili totecuyo dios.[68]

The gift of tongues was obviously connected to the missionary enterprise. Erasmus' moral interpretation of the Babel story pervaded prefaces of *artes* and vocabularies of Amerindian languages, but importance was also attached to Pentecost for its association with baptism in Christian antiquity.[69] A short clarificatory phrase in verse 11 of the Nahuatl reading above may be relevant, as it makes the biblical text inclusive of native Mexicans: 'in izquican in altepetl ipan tihualehua', 'we come forth from all *altepetl*

[68] Acts 2:7–11; Biondelli 1858, 319–20 (my emphases). For verse 8, Biondelli had *mipan* for *inipan*.

[69] Tertullian, *De baptismo* 19: 'paschae celebrandae locum de signo aquae ostendit. exinde pentecoste ordinandis lavacris laetissimum spatium est' ('By the sign of water, [our Lord] showed the

(towns)'. The fact that this additional phrase—which was never in the Latin—is to be found in other manuscript translations of the same passage from Acts is important: it suggests that all the lectionaries now known shared a common model, despite the apparent variations between them. Different manners of transcription are more likely to be the cause of those variations than a succession of recensions. In the absence of much needed further investigation, the Nahuatl '*Epistolae et Evangelia*' (c. 1540) can be provisionally conceived of as a single work rather than as a plurality of separate translations.

Dictation would have been the quickest way of obtaining multiple copies and that might well account for differences of orthography between manuscripts as well as errors within them.[70] Sahagún recounted preparing in exactly this manner a *postilla*, a commentary in Nahuatl on the Epistles and Gospels, along with a set of *Cantares*, religious canticles:

> Also at this time I dictated ['dicte'] the *Postilla* and the *Cantares*. The Latinists wrote them down, in the same village of Tepepulco.[71]

The *Postillas sobre las Epístolas y Evangelios de los Domingos de todo el año* were written in collaboration with 'four Latinists [who] taught grammar in the College of Santa Cruz in Tlatilulco'. They were supplemented with an 'appendix' of admonitions in a similar style to the traditional Nahuatl discourses Sahagún would later assemble and translate in his *Rethorica, y philosophia moral, y theologia* (1577).[72] The religious canticles in Nahuatl that Sahagún published more than twenty years later as the *Psalmodia Christiana* (1583) were designed to supplant older Nahuatl songs 'which praised false gods'.[73] These new *cantares*, composed to be sung on feast days through the year, transmitted biblical stories and the exemplary lives of saints. Further digests and retellings of biblical episodes and saints' lives and exegeses of specific passages of scripture, for which the same or other

place for the Passover to be celebrated. After that, Pentecost is the most felicitous period for arranging baptisms'). Cf. Chapter 3, III above for Erasmus' interpretation of Babel and Pentecost.

[70] Biondelli 1858, xvii–xviii deemed that dictation accounted for the nature of the scribal errors he corrected in the Milan manuscript: 'Sed ipsa errorum indoles clarius ostendit codicem ex dictantis voce fuisse exaratum. Sic exempli gratia, *chipahuac* (purus) pro *chicahuac* (fortis) is solus scriberet qui male vocabulum aure perciperet, non vero qui tanto magisterio veste mexicana Biblia sacra adornavit. Sic *tletl* (ignis) pro *tetl* (lapis), *leltiloca*, nullius significationis pro *neltiloca* (in fide) . . . caeteraque de genere hoc.' Transmission involving dictation can explain variations in other Nahuatl manuscripts: cf. Chapter 7, I below on the texts of Aesop's Fables.

[71] SAHAGÚN, *HG* Book 2, Prologue [1982 i, 54].

[72] SAHAGÚN, *Postillas* (1540s) [1993]. The *Rethorica, y philosophia moral y theologia* (1577) became Book 6 of SAHAGÚN, *Historia general* [1969 vi]. Cf. Section IV below.

[73] SAHAGÚN, *Psalmodia Christiana* (1583) [1993]. Cf. Burkhart 2003 and Alcántara Rojas 2008 for a full exploration of the work's bicultural significance.

Indian collaborators must have given their assistance, were written in Spanish and Nahuatl.[74]

The use of scripture in such texts, like the incorporation of readings from Gospel and Epistles in Nahuatl lectionaries, had been permitted, although translation of the Bible became increasingly controversial over the course of the sixteenth century. The issue loomed large in debates about biblical reform at the Council of Trent in the spring of 1546. Cardinal Pacheco had vehemently opposed the translation of scripture into any other tongue, deeming that in itself to be an 'abuse', but his views met with much opposition, and the Council made no pronouncement on the matter. Vernacular 'Epístolas y Evangelios' remained popular in Spain at any rate, and the steady run of new printed editions continued unabated through the 1550s.[75] The dissemination of vernacular translations of the Bible was neither condoned nor condemned, so that different jurisdictions could be directed to act in accordance with their specific needs.[76]

It would have been in the wake of this compromise that Fray Luis Rodríguez, some time before he left New Spain in 1562, undertook the translation of the Proverbs of Solomon into the Mexican language.[77] A variorum manuscript presenting lemmata of the Vulgate text of Proverbs 2:1–15:23 with a Nahuatl translation and commentary was discovered and identified in 2013 as a copy of Rodríguez' work, dating to the mid-1500s.[78] This unusual example of a version of a sustained passage of scripture shows how European conventions of scholarly biblical exegesis could be applied in Nahuatl—at least before legislation moved toward the explicit suppression of such endeavours.

In 1564 Pope Pius IV had published the bull *Dominici gregis custodias* stating that the reading of vernacular bibles required written permission from a local bishop or inquisitor.[79] Rodríguez's Nahuatl text of the Proverbs of Solomon was banned in 1577—the same year in which the *Suprema*, or General Council of the Spanish Inquisition, extended the prohibitions of the 1559 Index to ban a manuscript translation of Ecclesiastes 'into an Indian language', along with all translations of the Bible into Amerindian tongues.[80] In 1577 the Mexican inquisitors circulated a questionnaire to friars who knew Nahuatl, including Bernardino de Sahagún and Alonso de Molina, in order to establish which books

[74] Nahuatl manuscripts (BNM Ms. 1628 bis and Bancroft M-M 464) include accounts of the healing of Jairus' daughter, a narrative of the Passion and exposition of Leviticus 1:9: Chapter 7, I below. Christensen 2014, 15–26 includes a Nahuatl narrative of Paul's conversion that was loosely based on Acts 9.

[75] The most popular, MONTESINO, *Epistolas y euangelios*, went through more than twenty editions between 1506 and 1558: Griffin 1991, 188; Bataillon 1937 [2007, 44–8].

[76] McNally 1966; cf. O'Malley 2013, 19, 183, 190, 269.

[77] MENDIETA, *Hystoria ecclesiastica yndiana* (c. 1596) = *Historia*, 4.44 [1870, 551]: 'Fr. Luis Rodriguez tradujo los proverbios de Salomon de muy elegante lengua, y los cuatro libros del *Contemptus mundi*.'

[78] Tavárez 2013a.

[79] McNally 1966, 226–7.

[80] The banning of the Nahuatl Proverbs of Solomon by the inquisitors Alfonso Granero Davalos and Alfonso Fernandez de Bonilla is recorded in AGN, Inq., vol. 450, exp. s.n., fols. 575–6; the interdict on Ecclesiastes is in AGN, Inq., vol. 1A, exp. 41. Both documents are cited in Nesvig 2009, 153. According

of Holy Scripture had been translated, and whether their suppression would have any detrimental consequences for the religious instruction of the Indians.[81] The consensus of the friars was that the suppression of scripture in native languages would hinder their attempts to Christianize the native population. But it is notable that while Pablo Nazareo had proudly called attention to his translations of the Gospels and Epistles in his letter to Philip II in 1556, Sahagún's testimonies in the 1570s were much more circumspect, giving emphasis to sermons and catechisms instead.

Irrespective of the controversy they provoked, the various biblical translations were scrupulously executed, offering viable equivalents for challenging expressions in the Vulgate or the Roman Rite. Despite some superficial variations arising from dictation, the different manuscripts of lectionaries of Epistles and Gospels can be provisionally regarded as versions of a single authoritative work.

IV. Religious literature in Nahuatl: Translations and new compositions

Increased restrictions on the dissemination of scripture in vernaculars did not diminish the need for native Latinists: a wide range of Christian material still needed to be translated, and knowledge of Latin would in fact remain essential for rendering *Spanish* texts into Nahuatl, as it would for producing original compositions in the Mexican language.

(i) *Colloquios y Doctrina christiana*, 1564

Latin was integral to a work of missionary literature which was written in Spanish and translated into Nahuatl under the direction of Fray Bernardino de Sahagún in 1564: 'Colloquies and Christian Learning, with which the Twelve Friars of Saint Francis, sent by Pope Adrian the Sixth and Emperor Charles the Fifth, converted the Indians of New Spain, in the Mexican language and in Spanish'. This text presented a narrative that was not a veridical history but an idealized exemplary account of the initial exchanges between the first Franciscan missionaries and the Mexica principals and priests in 1524.[82] The first words of the Spanish title, 'Colloquios y Doctrina christiana', recalled two educational texts, both well known and widely studied in the 1500s: Erasmus' *Colloquia familiaria*, which was intended to develop

to Beristáin de Souza 1883 ii, 248, Fray Luis Rodríguez was the translator of Ecclesiastes: Tavárez 2013b, 215, n. 46.

[81] AGN, Inq., vol. 43, exp. 4, fols. 133–36. Nesvig 2009, 306–7, nn. 69–70 dates and quotes the document.

[82] Cf. Garibay 1953–1954 [2007, 738–44]. The unreliable account of the same events in MENDIETA, *Historia* 3.51 [1870, 314–17] may be based on Sahagún's text: cf. Chapter 1, II above on the Twelve.

students' Latin in practical situations, and Saint Augustine's *De doctrina Christiana*, which championed the benefits of classical rhetoric for preaching.[83] Although the two works were different in style and tone, both promoted eloquence as a crucial part of Christian education, and both were models for Sahagún's endeavour.[84]

As the *Colloquios y Doctrina christiana* was intended to supply preachers with the kind of language and arguments they needed to communicate Christian doctrine in their ministry, the manuscript presented the prior Spanish text along with an 'active' Nahuatl translation to show how the content could be expressed in Mexican idiom. In the Prologue, Sahagún described the way in which the text was prepared:

> There had been no opportunity before for the present work to be placed in order, or converted into a form of Mexican that would be suitably congruent and polished. It was thus translated and polished in this College of Santa Cruz at Tlatelolco, in the above stated year, with the help of the collegians most adept and accomplished in the Mexican language and in the Latin language.[85]

The collegians involved were named as Antonio Valeriano of Azcapotzalco and Alonso Vegerano of Cuauhtitlan, along with Martín Jacobita and Andrés Leonardo, both from Tlatelolco.

Scrutiny of the surviving part of the *Colloquios y Doctrina christiana* soon reveals why Latinists were required to turn the Spanish text into Nahuatl.[86] Book 1, chapter 7 will be reviewed here (the Spanish original is reproduced below in Appendix 2.7). The chapter consists of a speech given by one of the Aztec 'priests of the idols' in response to the Franciscan missionaries. After some preliminary courtesies, the substance of the response begins thus:

[83] Cf. p. 92 and p. 119 above on ERASMUS, *Colloquia* (1518); Chapter 2, p. 44 on Augustine's *De doctrina Christiana*, which was not an exposition of doctrine, but a treatise on how to study and teach the Christian faith. Augustine's work was emulated in ERASMUS, *Encheiridion militis Christi* (1503), which was popular in Spain. Translated excerpts of the *Encheiridion* were incorporated in ZUMÁRRAGA, *Dotrina breue* (1544): cf. Bataillon 1937 [2007, 166–255, 821–5]; Chapter 1, p. 20 above, on the use of ERASMUS, *Paraclesis* (1516) in Zumárraga's *Dotrina*.

[84] Augustine, *De doctrina Christiana* is in four books—the number Sahagún had first projected for his *Colloquios*: n. 86 below.

[85] SAHAGÚN, *Colloquios* (1564), 27v, 'Al Prudente Lector' [1986, 75]: 'antes no vuo oportunidad de ponerse en orden ni conuertirse en lengua mexicana bien congrua y limada: la qual se boluió y limó en este Colegio de Santa Cruz del Tlatilulco este sobredicho año con los colegiales más habiles y entendidos en lengua mexicana y en la lengua latina.'

[86] SAHAGÚN, *Colloquios*, 27v–28r, 'Al Prudente Lector' [1986, 75] describes the four projected books; chapter summaries of Books 1–2 [1986, 76–7] come next. The extant text consists of Book 1, chapters 1–14 alone.

> You say those whom we worship are not gods. This way of speaking is very new and very shocking to us: we are horrified at such speech, because our forefathers, who engendered and ruled us, did not tell us such a thing.[87]

The speaker then explains how the Aztecs' ceremonies and sacrifices were ordained long ago; that the gods, to whom they pray for rain, brought their people into being, and provide everything that sustains them. The gods inhabit the divine realm of Tlalocan, and their worship was instituted before recorded time, in a number of sacred places including Tula, Tamoanchan, and Teotihuacan: to destroy these traditions would risk unsettling the people and incurring the wrath of the gods themselves. He ends by saying that it is enough for the Mexica leaders to have lost their power: they would prefer to perish rather than forsake worship of their gods.

That oration has wrongly been interpreted as a unique and authentic testimony of pre-Hispanic 'Aztec thought' by ethnohistorians who insist on regarding the Nahuatl rather than the Spanish text as the source—despite Sahagún's clear statement to the contrary quoted above.[88] While there are devices characteristic of traditional Mexican address, notably the self-depreciatory locutions at the opening ('We are not worthy ourselves, so low and dirty'), such devices are found in the words ascribed to the Franciscan spokesmen in the previous chapters.[89] As a whole, the speech just summarized displays evidence of artifice that is markedly European. The content, as a point-by-point retort to the friars' preceding arguments in Book 1, chapters 1–5 of *Colloquios*, follows the convention of dialectical disputation. The structure of this reply from the Aztecs also conforms to the *dispositio*, or arrangement, for a speech recommended by Cicero and Quintilian as it incorporates, in the correct sequence, an introduction (*exordium*), preliminary division of the speech into parts (*partitio*), statement of facts (*narratio*), proof (*confirmatio*), rejection of opponent's argument (*refutatio*), and conclusion.[90]

The courteous *exordium* leads into the *partitio*, labelled 'A' in the manuscript, in which the speaker explains that the Mexica will 'reply to and counter with two or three arguments' what they have heard ('con dos o tres razones responderemos y contra diremos las palabras'). That is in defiance of the assertion the friars had

[87] SAHAGÚN, *Colloquios* 1.7 (36r, paragraph B in the manuscript).

[88] León-Portilla 1956 [1963, 62–70]; Klor de Alva 1982, 142–84; Baudot 1987; Mignolo 1995, 96–103 (refers to the 'original Nahuatl' at 97); Dehouve 2000; Johansson 2002, 211–34; Bayardi 2016.

[89] For comparable effects in the Latin of native Mexicans, cf. n. 22 above. Valeriano, who collaborated on SAHAGÚN, *Colloquios* (1564), had used remarkably similar expressions in a Latin letter from the rulers of Azcapotzalco to Philip II: VALERIANO, 'Invictissimo Hispaniarum Regi' (1561), quoted in Chapter 6, III below.

[90] The standard sources for *dispositio* in the Renaissance were [ps.-Cicero] *Rhetorica ad Herennium* 1.3.4–1.10; Cicero, *De inventione* 1.9–109; and Aristotle, *Rhetoric* 3, 1414a–1419b.

made earlier that no one can contradict scripture.[91] The ensuing *narratio* (labelled B) recapitulates the Franciscans' claim that the Aztecs' divinities are not gods, and explains the Mexicans' opposition to it, invoking the authority of their ancestors and the beliefs they ordained. A *confirmatio* (C) then sets out the gods' attributes, explains where they reside, and lists (D) the places in which their worship was initiated long ago. That 'proof' incidentally parallels and counters the Franciscans' emphasis on the importance of the city of Rome for the Christian faith.[92]

The *refutatio* (E–F) consists of admonitions, employing the rhetorical commonplaces of what is practical (*utile*), safe (*tutum*), and prudent (*prudens*): it would be unwise to change laws of ancient standing; the gods might be provoked and the people rise up if their traditional beliefs are rejected; it is advisable to proceed slowly and calmly. The formal conclusion (G) appeals to honour (*honestum*): it is enough that their power and royal jurisdiction have been taken away; where the gods are concerned, the Mexica have determined they would die before leaving their service and worship.

That distinction made at the end of the speech between political power ('la potencia y juridición real') and divine authority ('lo que toca a nuestros dioses') was in essence European—as was the convention of *controversiae*, pairs of opposed speeches arguing both sides of a case, in dialectic and rhetoric. Clinching proof that conscious rhetorical artistry is at work in the Mexican leader's speech can be found in the sentence that led into it:

> one of the satraps got up and, *seeking the goodwill* ['captando la benevolencia'] of the Twelve, began to speak and he gave a long speech as follows.

The Nahuatl version could offer no more than a circumlocution for '*captatio benevolentiae*', the strategy of winning an audience's favour at the beginning of an oration:

> qujmmotlapalhuj in teupixque, tlatlatlauhti, achi veyx yn jtlatol. . .
>
> he greeted the priests, he entreated, his speech was a little long.[93]

The indigenous scholars responsible for the Nahuatl version of Sahagún's text needed to be 'adept and accomplished in the Latin language' because knowledge of dialectic and rhetoric could be acquired only from sources in Latin. The sustained application of classical rhetoric to writing in Nahuatl has important implications: on the level of discursive organization at least, such texts must have represented something

[91] SAHAGÚN, *Colloquios* 1.3: 32r B [1986, 82].

[92] SAHAGÚN, *Colloquios* 1.1: 30r E; 1.2 31r A [1986, 79, 81].

[93] SAHAGÚN, *Colloquios* 1.6: 35r D (Appendix 2.6 below).

strikingly new, as Latin learning had a part in transforming the Nahuatl *tlatolli* into a Latinate oration. The *Colloquios y Doctrina christiana* was by no means the only work that involved this process, akin to what the missionaries called 'reducción'.

(ii) Translations of the *Contemptus mundi* and Spanish devotional literature

The prohibitions of scriptural translation probably contributed to the generation of an original and varied Christian literature in Nahuatl from the 1560s to the 1600s. The very fact that doctrines, confessional manuals, and lectionaries had been among the first texts to have been written in Nahuatl may have had the effect of dignifying subsequent works in the language by association, endowing them with an aura of canonicity and authority. In contrast to far more numerous writings in Spanish that were often of a functional or ephemeral nature, works in Nahuatl—like those in Latin which they replicated—would be perceived as hallowed vehicles of wisdom, painstakingly crafted and composed.

Two incomplete but distinct Nahuatl translations of Thomas à Kempis' *Contemptus mundi*, 'Contempt of the world' (1418), now more often known as *Imitatio Christi*, 'The Imitation of Christ', are a case in point. These translations, which were produced in the 1560s, 'elevated the humble *Imitatio* to the place of Scripture or of a received commentary on it, following the model of the catena in medieval and early modern scholarly texts'.[94] At least parts of two popular books in Spanish that had been closely modelled on Kempis' work seem to have been put into Nahuatl: Fray Luis de Granada's *Libro de la oración y meditación*, which appeared in Salamanca in 1554, and Fray Diego de Estella's *Libro de la vanidad del mundo*, first published in Toledo in 1562. Nahuatl renderings of the 'nocturnal meditations' from Luis de Granada's text are in Fray Juan Bautista's *Libro de la miseria y brevedad de la vida del hombre y de sus postrimerías* (1604). Granada's authorship of those sections was not acknowledged in that volume, but Bautista did report in the prologue to his *Sermonario en lengua mexicana* (quoted in Section I above) that the native Hernando de Ribas helped him to translate 'gran parte de las *Vanidades* de Estela' [*sic*]—although the translation was never printed and is not extant.[95]

[94] Tavárez 2013b, 215–18 describes the manuscript versions of Books 1–2 of Kempis' *Imitatio* in the John Carter Brown Library and the version of Books 1–3 of the four books in the El Escorial monastery library, noting at 234 that the latter was produced before 1570. MENDIETA, *Historia* 4.14 [1870, 41] recounted that he himself took to Spain this text 'in lettering by an Indian, well formed, even and gracious' in that year and later mentioned the earlier translation initiated by Fray Luis Rodríguez, before 1562 when Rodríguez left Mexico for Spain, which was left unfinished and 'recently' (i.e. shortly before 1595) completed by Fray Juan Bautista.

[95] BAUTISTA, *Sermonario* (1606), viii r, quoted in Section I above. Bautista goes on to state that don Francisco Bautista de Conteras, native governor of Xochimilco, also assisted with the translation of the *Libro de la vanidad del mundo*.

This cluster of texts has been convincingly identified by David Tavárez as evidence of a concerted attempt to propagate tenets of the *devotio moderna*, developed by the Brethren of the Common Life in Windesheim in the Netherlands.[96] Thomas à Kempis himself, as well as Martin Luther and Erasmus, was among their associates. The founder of the quasi-monastic community, Gerard Groote, stressed the importance of learning as well as private contemplation. That movement for simple piety and apostolic renewal had found an enthusiastic reception in Spain, where the popularization of mysticism followed that of scripture and patristic writing, owing much to the wide appeal of Kempis' *Contemptus mundi*.[97]

The spread of the *devotio moderna* to Mexico may have begun still earlier, with the arrival in 1523 of the first Franciscan missionaries from Flanders: Pedro de Gante may possibly have received his own education from the Brethren.[98] In the years that followed, however, the status of the movement in New Spain and the implementation of its practices in the College of Santa Cruz would have been a matter of concern for the viceroyalty and for a counter-Reformation Inquisition. The indigenous students were expected to put their talents to the service of the colonial hierarchy rather than to develop a contemplative, intellectual faith.

(iii) The *Colloquios de la paz*, c. 1540, and *Espejo divino*, 1607

Yet it is evident that many of the disciplines of the *devotio moderna*—penance, prayer, meditative reading, scholarly work, and, notably, the copying of manuscripts—were being fostered in the College at Tlatelolco. David Tavárez has linked two Nahuatl dialogues that originated there to the movement, suggesting that both of them were modelled on Book 3 of Kempis' *Imitatio*, in which Jesus was in conversation with a disciple.[99] The first, Fray Juan de Gaona's *Colloquios de la paz*, has a collegian being instructed by a friar or 'Padre'; while Fray Juan de Mijangos' *Espejo divino* consists of a set of exchanges between a natural father and his son. Students of the Franciscans and other native converts were expected to treat and address friars as 'fathers' (*patres*, or *padreme* in Nahuatl).[100]

Hernando de Ribas, the indigenous Mexican scholar who assisted Fray Juan Bautista, had helped Gaona to prepare the manuscript of a new work in the early 1540s. This was later published in 1582 as *Colloquios de la paz, y tranquilidad*

[96] Tavárez 2013b; Hyma 1965; Van Engen 2008; cf. Chapter 1, pp. 13–14, 41 above.
[97] Bataillon 1937 [2007], 44–51.
[98] Cf. Chapter 1, p. 13 above.
[99] Tavárez 2013b, 211.
[100] Trexler 1987, 551. This discussion of Gaona and Mijangos draws from Laird 2019c, 13–21.

Ad laudem Auctoris.

FRATER ANTONIVS A
Cruce, Minoritanus, ad suũ Theo-
logiæ magistrum, Fratrem
Michaelem à çarate.

Iã tua lata nouæ patefacta p̱ æquora fama
Spargitur hesperiæ, Michael: iã nubila cœli
Cõcutit, & validis totũ quatit æthera pẽnis
Suppeditãtq́; locũ: sicq́; mirantur àb alto
Astra, nouæq́; isti nimiũ iubilantia voce
Grata ferũt patriæ: siquidẽ produxit alũnû
Hic, sibi quã pepit, mulcẽtẽ cũcta minerua
Corda virũ, miroq́; dei præcepta potẽtis
Ordine pãdẽtẽ, sophiæq́; ænigmata sacræ
Floret & ingenio, ꝙ iam videatur acutos
Exupare aĩos: rabidus velut æquoris æstus
Grãdisono placidi fremitu trãsuerberat o-
Littoris, & siccæ fũdos obducit arenæ. (rã
Eia age mellifluis çarate d̄corata magister
Arce tuæ fluuijs animæ labẽtibus ãpla (ctus
Facta rigẽt aridos: sapida labor arbore fru
Prodat odoriferos, ꝗbus ĩflãmata freq̃nti
Flamine diuino gentes alimẽta resumant.

Figure 5.3 Latin verses by Fray Antonio de la Cruz in Fray Juan de Gaona, *Colloquios de la paz y tranquilidad christiana en lengua mexicana*, Mexico City, 1582. John Carter Brown Library.

christiana, with revisions by Fray Miguel de Zárate (Figure 5.3).[101] Despite external evidence for Gaona's skill as a dialectician, the twenty exchanges that make up the work are didactic expositions rather than philosophical disputations.[102] The Nahuatl text has never been translated and no direct Latin or vernacular source for this work has yet been identified.[103] But the *Tractatus de pace* by the thirteenth-century Franciscan Guibert de Tournai has many themes in common with the *Colloquios de*

[101] Zárate's prologue of the printed edition reveals that the text had been drafted forty years before: the manuscript has now come to light as a section of the Toledo Ms. 35–22: Téllez Nieto and Baños Baños 2018, 678–9.

[102] MENDIETA, *Historia* 4.15 [1870, 415] credited Gaona with teaching rhetoric, logic, and philosophy, and in 4.23 [1870, 450] recounted his victory in a dialectical *disputatio*, in which he countered Fray Jacobo Daciano's proposition that natives should enter the priesthood. Part of Gaona's rebuttal (preserved in Beristáin de Souza 1883 i, 340) is quoted in Chapter 4, III, (ii) above.

[103] Garibay 1954 ii, 191 [2007, 689–90]. Zulaica Gárate 1939, 189 discerned 'affinities' with Fray Juan de los Ángeles—although Ángeles' writings began to circulate widely only in the 1590s.

la paz and could be considered as a possible template: Gaona, who had studied in Paris, would have known Guibert's treatise, which continued to circulate.[104]

The lack of an obvious model for the *Colloquios de la paz* is all the more remarkable, given that it refers to several classical figures, as well as Church Fathers. The 'great wise man' ('vuetlamatini') Plato, Pythagoras, Archytas, and Apollonius of Tyana are all invoked in chapter 5, 'On the varied forms of knowledge in the soul . . . and the desirability of knowledge'.[105] In the original manuscript their names were rubricated (Plate 9), making them conspicuous to viewers of the page, whether they knew Nahuatl or not. Those ancient Greek sages were mentioned in various works by Erasmus, but Traversari's Latin translation of Diogenes Laertius' *Lives of the Philosophers*, inventoried at the College of Santa Cruz, was a possible source for information about them too.[106] A fragmentary epigram on Diogenes Laertius by Fray Cristóbal Cabrera suggests that the text of his *Lives* was available to Franciscans in Mexico by the 1540s, although Cabrera, unlike the 'Padre' in Gaona's *Colloquios*, is dismissive of the pagan philosophers.[107] The *Colloquios de la paz* also elaborated on Hannibal and Alexander as cautionary *exempla*: Alexander is censured in chapter 13, 'On the definition of patience', for the impetuous killing of his friend Clytus. Conversely, the unworldliness and poverty of Stilpo, Diogenes the Cynic, Zeno, and Socrates are extolled in chapter 17, 'On the loss of temporal things'. But a declaration attributed to Stilpo here—that he needed only eloquence and wisdom rather than material possessions—did not come from Diogenes Laertius:

> Omnia mea bona, mecum porto. quitoznequi. Inixquich naxca, çan nitic in nicpie.[108]

'Omnia mea bona, mecum porto.' This means, 'All that is mine, I keep within me.'

[104] TOURNAI, *Tractatus de pace* (1200s) [1925]. Baudot 1968 identifies other texts read by Gaona; see also Téllez Nieto 2019b.

[105] GAONA, *Colloquios* ms. (c. 1540), 271r; and (1582), 22v–22r: 'Macamo nimitzteneutli icenca veitlamatini Platon, amono nimitzteneuiliznequi in Pythagoras, noyehuatl in Architas, noyehuatl Apolonio' ('Let me not refrain from praising then the great sage Plato, nor should I omit to mention Pythagoras, nor another, Archytas, nor another, Apollonius').

[106] TRAVERSARI, *Diogenes Laertius: Vitae et sententiae philosophorum* (1472): cf. the books listed for 1574 in Appendix 1.3 below. The Nahuatl author Chimalpahin knew of Diogenes Laertius: Chapter 9, II below.

[107] CABRERA, 'Epigrams' (c. 1540), no. 43, 'In Laertium', can hence be reconstructed: 'Philosophorum [*vitas et dicta*] Laertius offert. / Sunt quae forte probes, sunt mage quae reprobes' ('Laertius provides the Philosophers' [*lives and sayings*]. / There are things you may approve, there are more to reproach').

[108] GAONA, *Colloquios* (1582), 106.

Seneca the Younger had ascribed such a comment to Stilpo, but the precise Latin wording used here may well have originated in a Renaissance digest or commonplace book, possibly Erasmus' *Adages* or Alciati's *Emblemata*.[109]

Even though it was primarily an instructive guide to spiritual discipline, the later printed edition of the *Colloquios de la paz, y tranquilidad christiana* advertised the work's literary or rhetorical qualities—perhaps to detract from any potentially controversial asceticism in its content.[110] This was a new departure: marginal notes printed in Latin called attention to *exempla, comparationes*, or *figurae* in the Nahuatl text. In addition, a series of Latin poems was specially composed by Fray Antonio de la Cruz to open the 1582 publication: elegiacs and sapphic stanzas were addressed respectively to the *opus* and to the reader, while the introductory hexameters 'in praise of the author' actually commended the editor, Fray Miguel de Zárate, without any mention of Juan de Gaona, let alone his native translator (Figure 5.3). A manuscript translation of the *Colloquios de la paz* into Otomí (c. 1600) is further evidence of the importance that was attached to the work.[111]

The *Espejo divino*, first published in Mexico City in 1607 by an Augustinian friar, Fray Juan de Mijangos, was written in collaboration with a Mexican who was emphatically thanked by Mijangos on the last page of the volume:

> The Corrector of the Language was Agustín de la Fuente, native of Santiago Tlatelolco, very skilled (who, in this work and in all the others done by Father Fray Juan Bautista of the Order of the seraphic father Saint Francis, has helped a great deal and served our Lord), may the Lord reward him and keep him many years.

A still more profound acknowledgement to Agustín de la Fuente is implicit: the *father* whose dramatized discourse constituted the greater part of the book is named 'Augustin'. The son, to whom he offered guidance, was called Joan, a variant of Mijangos' own Christian name, Juan. The apparent homage could reflect Agustín

[109] The earliest version of the statement as 'nam omnia mea, mecum porto' attributed to Bias of Priene in Cicero, *Paradoxa Stoicorum* 1.8, was recalled in Alciati's *Emblemata* as 'Omnia mea mecum porto', and quoted and linked to Bias in ERASMUS, *Adagia* (1508) 4.4.9. The words attributed to Stilpo by Seneca the Younger excluded 'porto' ('omnia bona mea mecum sunt' in *Epistulae morales* 1.9.19 and 'omnia mea mecum sunt' in *De constantia sapientis* 5.6).

[110] In contrast, the printed marginalia in Sahagún's *Psalmodia Christiana* (n. 74 above) printed in 1583, the following year, contain only explanatory glosses, mostly liturgical excerpts in Latin, and there is no attempt to signal any poetic or rhetorical virtues in the preliminaries. The evangelical function of the work may have made such 'aesthetic' justification unnecessary, for all that the Nahuatl text has some radical departures from the declared liturgical model.

[111] The manuscript also contains essential prayers and devotional texts in Otomí.

de la Fuente's seniority in age—he had assisted Fray Bernardino de Sahagún more than twenty years before—and it could be a tribute to the Indian's erudition.[112]

It has never been remarked that the title *Espejo divino*, 'Divine Mirror', was purloined from that of a Spanish book of themes for sermons for the church year, published in Madrid by Pedro Suárez de Escobar, another Augustinian missionary in Mexico and a former student of Fray Alonso de la Vera Cruz.[113] That work by Suárez de Escobar may have been a model for a Nahuatl sermonary that Mijangos would publish, much later, in 1624.[114] The text on the first page of Mijangos' *Espejo divino* contains a Nahuatl approximation, here in italics, of that Spanish title:

> Nican vmpehua (tlaçomahuiztlacaè) ontzinti, centlamantli tenonotzaliztlahtolli, intlacahuapahualoni tlacazcaltiloni *teoyotica tezcatl* tocayotilo, nepanotl mononotzihui ce tlacatl tettatzin itoca Augustin yhuan ce tlacatl ipiltzin, itoca Joan.[115]

> Here begins (o dear revered one), originates, a set of words of admonition, for the bringing up of people and the raising of people, called a *Mirror through Holiness*, [in which] one person, a father named Augustin and [another] person, his son named Joan, go on counselling each other.

David Tavárez has observed that a metonymy for wisdom, 'in coyauac tezcatl necoc xapo', 'the wide mirror polished on both sides', had designated the teacher's words in the Nahuatl version of the *Contemptus mundi*.[116] That translation, dating from the 1560s, was a crucial precedent for Mijangos' text. The locution *teoyotica tezcatl* on the Nahuatl title page therefore had its own genealogy, deriving from the long-standing Mexican association of the mirror with divinity (and divination), exemplified by the name of the all-knowing pre-Hispanic deity Tezcatlipoca, 'Smoking Mirror'.[117]

The *Espejo divino* is a textual cornucopia, interspersing prayers and sermons with the preceptive dialogues between father and son.[118] Printed marginal notes in

[112] Cf. BAUTISTA, *Sermonario* (1606), quoted in Section I above. Whittaker 2016, 64–5 proposes that Agustín de la Fuente may have been an informant for Alva Ixtlilxochitl.

[113] SUÁREZ DE ESCOBAR, *Primera parte del libro intitulado Espejo divino* . . . (1591): Yhmoff Cabrera 1996 iii, 210–11. Such a title evokes the popular convention of *speculum*, or 'mirror', literature (cf. Chapter 4 above): according to ANTONIO, *Bibliotheca Hispana nova* (1672) [1788, 241], Suárez, who took the name Fray Pedro de Medellín from his native Badajoz, was bishop-elect of Guadalajara in Mexico at the time of his death in Tlayacapan in 1591.

[114] MIJANGOS, *Primera parte del Sermonario* (1624).

[115] MIJANGOS, *Espejo divino* (1607), 1.

[116] Tavárez 2013b, 224–5 further notes that SAHAGÚN, *HG* Book 6 (1577) employed the metonymy for wisdom (associated with Tezcatlipoca's attributes of knowledge and prescience), also used as an epithet for Christ in SAHAGÚN, *Psalmodia Christiana* (1583).

[117] Cf. Saunders 2001, 220–36 on mirrors in pre-Hispanic Mesoamerica.

[118] Garibay 1954 ii [2007: 693–6] gives a useful conspectus of the work's content.

Latin and Spanish do not just highlight similes: they contain citations of scriptural passages and authorities ranging from Saint Augustine to Seneca and Aesop.[119] More remarkably, large portions of some biblical books can be reconstructed from the Nahuatl translations in the text. The conversation in the *Espejo divino* was designed to be engaging as well as enlightening. The reprinting of the book in 1626, nearly twenty years after its first publication, indicates that its appeal endured.

(iv) The *Huehuetlahtolli*, c. 1601

The contrived elegance of the *Colloquios de la paz* and the *Espejo divino*, quite absent from the austere Latin texts likely to have inspired them, invites comparison with another Nahuatl work printed in 1600 or 1601 at the Convent of Tlatelolco: the *Huehuetlahtolli*, 'Speeches of old', published by Fray Juan Bautista Viseo (Figure 5.4).[120] The texts in the volume were presented as the talks native fathers and mothers gave to their children, and rulers to their subjects. Such discourses had long attracted the attention of missionaries and chroniclers, and Fray Andrés de Olmos' collection of texts was in part the basis for Bautista's book—and its title, *Huehuetlahtolli*, could well be a calque for Olmos' original designation in Spanish: 'maneras de hablar que tenian los viejos'('the elders' manners of speaking').[121] But Fray Juan Bautista had 'added and inserted new, important and necessary contents' so that the twenty-nine speeches in Nahuatl and six translations in Spanish conveyed a Christian message, and most of them addressed Christian themes.[122] Although they are in monologue form, the discourses—of fathers to sons, of sons to fathers, and (implicitly) of missionaries to converts—show an obvious community with the dialogues of the *Espejo divino* and the *Colloquios de la paz* in terms of the pious instruction they contained.

As was the case with those dialogues, the *Huehuetlahtolli* are commended by their editor as much for their style as for their moral quality: Bautista remarked upon the 'cultivation, urbanity, respect, courtliness, good diction, and elegance in the speech of Indians of old', and later commented that 'the Mexicans had seemingly

[119] *Pace* Sell 2010, 193 which states that there are no glosses or marginalia in MIJANGOS, *Espejo divino* (1607). There are also Spanish glosses for Nahuatl words in the body of Mijangos' text, e.g. at 42: 'muchihuanih (durables)'.

[120] BAUTISTA, *Huehuetlahtolli* (c. 1601) [2011]. The 2011 facsimile includes a transcription (and translation) of the Nahuatl text, but not of the Spanish preliminaries, and the added subtitle, *Testimonios de la antigua palabra*, is not authentic: although 'HVEHVETLAHTOLLI' is a running head of the 1601 edition, the title page is lost.

[121] See Chapter 3, V, n. 112 above on the texts in Olmos' *arte* and Chapter 8, IV nn. 102–103 on the Nahuatl term *huehuetlatolli* in Sahagún, and its subsequent uses.

[122] BAUTISTA, *Huehuetlahtolli*, 'Aprobación del Doctor Francisco de Loya' (unnumbered folio): 'El Padre Fray Joan Bautista . . . con mucha erudición a añadido y puesto cosas nuevas, importantes y necesarias . . . sin tener cosa que contradiga a nuestra Religion'.

HVEHVETLAHTOLLI.
PLATICA QVE HAZE EL PADRE
al hijo auiſandole, o amoneſtandole
que ſea bueno,

¶ Tenonotzaliztli intetta yc quinono-
tza ycquizcalia inipiltzin, inic qualli
yectli ycmonemitiz.

NOpiltzè, nocozquè, noquetzalè, otiyol otitlacat, otimotlalticpacquixtico
initlalticpactzíco in Totecuiyo omitzmo
yocolili, omitzmopiquili, omitzmotlaca
tilili inipalnemohuani Dios. Auh mixco
mocpac otitlachixque intimonanhuã in-
timottahuan, yhuan immahuihuan, immo
tlahuan, immohuayolque, omixco mocpac tlachixque, ochocaque, otlaocoxque
mopampatzinco: ynic otiyol, inic otitla
cat in tlalticpac. Auh in axcan achitzin-
ca otihuallachix, otihualmozcali, otihua-
lizcallohuac, otihualchamahuac, yuhqui-
ma titototzintli quinyetimotlachopinilia
yuhquin otimã otizcallohuac, otimozcal
B ti, oti-

Figure 5.4 Fray Juan Bautista, *Huehuetlahtolli*, Tlatelolco, c. 1601, 1r. John Carter Brown Library.

learned and imbibed all the colours of Rhetoric'.[123] These commendations recalled the way Sahagún had framed a larger manuscript collection of apparently more authentic Nahuatl speeches that he affirmed he himself translated into Spanish in 1577.[124] That collection had been calculatedly entitled *Rethorica, y philosophia moral, y theologia de la gente mexicana* and later appeared as the sixth book of the *Historia general* (c. 1580)—the only book in the twelve-book history to be dignified with an elegant dedication in Latin.[125] The effect of the Latin verse panegyrics

[123] BAUTISTA, *Huehuetlahtolli*, third unnumbered folio of Prologue, verso and 92r. The case made in Pollnitz 2017, 146 for an Erasmian contextualization for this work prompts some caveats: despite Erasmus' importance for earlier missionaries including Molina, Gilberti, and Sahagún, his popularity sharply declined after 1559 (Chapter 3, III above) and Bautista was born in 1555; and the Nahuatl *qualli tlatolli*, good speech, does not correspond to *bonae litterae*, good literature, which connotes written discourse. For 'qualli tlatolli', cf. Chapter 8, p. 276 below.

[124] SAHAGÚN, *HG* Book 6, colophon [1969 vii, 260] specified this translation was his own: 'Fue traduzido en lengua española por el dicho padre bernardino de Sahagun: despues de treynta años, que se escriujo en la lengua mexicana: este año de mjll y qujnjentos y setenta y siete.' Spanish versions of the Nahuatl sources in the *Historia general* were usually produced in collaboration with native Latinists.

[125] This work is discussed in Chapter 8, IV below.

heralding the printed version of Gaona's *Colloquios de la paz* only five years later was rather similar. A general trend is clear: Nahuatl texts were becoming aestheticized and endowed with the hallmarks of Christian humanist literature.

Many more works were authored in manuscript and some were printed in the College after Pedro Ocharte's press was transferred there by his widow, Maria de Sansoric, in 1597.[126] The trilingual students Hernando de Ribas, Agustín de la Fuente, and Diego Adriano were employed as typesetters, initially under the direction of the Dutch printer Cornelius Adrian Caesar. But after Caesar was imprisoned by the Inquisition for being a Lutheran (usefully serving part of his sentence in the convent of Tlatelolco), Pedro Ocharte's son Melchor took charge.[127] In all, more than forty books and pamphlets were printed in Santiago Tlatelolco over the next twenty years—although from 1601 onward the place of publication was given as 'Mexico'.[128] The first volume to go to press was Fray Juan Bautista's *Confessionario en lengua mexicana y castellana* (1599), which appeared the year after the author became guardian of the College, followed by the two volumes of his 'Advice for Confessors' in Spanish, Latin and Nahuatl, *Advertencias para los Confessores* (1600), and the *Huehuetlahtolli.*

V. Conclusions: Latin humanism and Nahuatl literature

The use of *gramática,* the term for 'Latin' in the sixteenth-century Hispanic world, reflected a general identification of Latin with grammar itself. This had long been mirrored in practice: in Europe Latin had generally been the only language to be systematically taught.[129] Hence Latin was not seen as the historical source of the romance vernaculars, but as an artificial medium that was refined from every language: though it had to be learned and acquired, it was a universal *langue.*[130] Everyday spoken tongues, whether they were European or Amerindian, could be systematized only by *artes,* which were based on the categories of grammar or Latin.[131] The very existence of written literature was subject to grammar,

[126] Compare the contents of the anonymous *Miscelánea sagrada* (1550s–1570s) enumerated in Alcántara Rojas 2022, and the Bancroft and BNM manuscripts listed in Chapter 7; Téllez Nieto and Baños Baños 2018 list further Nahuatl compositions copied in the Toledo Ms. 35–22. Schwaller 2001, Sandoval Aguilar and Rojas Rabiela 1991, and Hernández de León-Portilla 1988 are catalogues of Nahuatl manuscripts and imprints.

[127] Pascoe 2017.

[128] Mathes 1995.

[129] Bloch 1961 i, 77.

[130] Mazzocco 1993; Kagan 1974, 31–61.

[131] See Chapter 3 above.

because the most fundamental, atomic unit of grammar was the alphabetic letter, *littera*.[132]

Native Mexican scholars who recognized Latin as the language of the church and of knowledge, and who had seen how its alphabet (which the Spaniards called 'Latin' or 'Roman') could be used for other languages, including their own, attached importance to 'litterae', letters:

> Our ancestors, in the time they were pagan, were very simple, lowly, and bare of ornaments for body and soul alike, including the most important ones: moral virtues and letters, which they certainly did not come to know even in their dreams.[133]

From letters and words (*dictiones*) to discourse (*oratio*), Latin laid the ground for writing in Nahuatl because the traffic of written translation was almost always in one direction—from Latin, or from Spanish via Latin, to Nahuatl. The collegians of Tlatelolco, who were trained to play an instrumental role in the government of Mexico as indigenous rulers and judges, were just as instrumental in facilitating the government of Nahuatl by Latin.

Yet the texts surveyed above show that Latin's capacity to govern Nahuatl was not comprehensive or complete—and could sometimes be threatened. Just as the missionary linguists soon found that the distinctive 'excellences and design' ('primores y buen artificio') of Nahuatl challenged the universality of Latin, the Mexican tongue could not always compliantly convey the language of scripture: there is some irony in the lack of an equivalent for the *Verbum*, or the Incarnate Word, in John 1:1.[134] Conversely, 'teoyotica tezcatl', the formulation that was used in place of the Spanish 'Espejo divino', had potent associations of its own.

One consequence of all the first printed books in Nahuatl being *Doctrinas* and *Confesionarios* was touched upon in Section IV of this chapter: the canonization of their content through translation 'elevated' the language of Nahuatl itself. In Europe the effect of translating from modern vernacular languages into Latin had been similar: a translation not only raised the profile of a given text, but also affirmed and contributed to the status of the target language as a medium. The authority and

[132] GILBERTI, *Grammatica* (1559), Vr, following PEROTTI, *Rudimenta grammatices* (1473): 'There are four parts of grammar, namely the letter, such as *a, b, c;* the syllable, such as *ba, be;* the word, such as *Pater,* and the sentence [*oratio*] such as *Pater noster qui es in caelis*.' The partition derived from the early 500s AD: Priscian, *Institutiones grammaticae* 1.3–2.21.

[133] VALERIANO, 'Invictissimo Hispaniarum Regi . . .' (1561), 1: 'praedecessores suae tempore gentilitatis fuere admodum rustici, abiecti, nudi et corporis et animae dotibus, inter quas primas habent virtutes ac litterae, quas profecto ne per somnium quidem novere.' Cf. Appendix 2.4 below.

[134] 'Primores y buen artificio': OLMOS, *Arte de la lengua mexicana*, Part 2, Prologue, 44r [2002, 59].

importance of the Nahuatl lectionaries was signalled by their fine lettering and occasional decorative illumination: a copy of the *Epistolae et Evangelia* recently identified in the Chapter Library of Toledo Cathedral is especially striking. The careful design and execution of the manuscripts containing translations of the Proverbs of Solomon and the *Contemptus mundi* give a further indication of the high value accorded to their content.

The original Nahuatl dialogues described above—the *Colloquios y Doctrina christiana, Colloquios de la paz,* and the *Espejo divino*—were adorned in quite a different way, with rhetorical flourishes and explicit evocations of both classical and Christian sources. An obvious mechanism for this accommodation was provided by the versatility of dialogue:

> In the sixteenth century in particular, everything from rhetorical handbooks to medical treatises to travel narratives to manuals on duelling to erotic fiction to utopias can be found in dialogue form. Dialogue became a convention, even an institution for representing the margins of what could be represented in the Renaissance literary system of generic codes and forms. That dialogue would also gain greatly in prestige in the eyes of the Renaissance from its origins in ancient Greek and Roman philosophy is not hard to understand.[135]

The application of humanist learning to dialogues in Nahuatl, and also to Bautista's *Huehuetlahtolli,* could be seen as a kind of reverse appropriation, rather than as a demonstration of Latin's capacity to govern Nahuatl. The vernacular literatures that had emerged in Europe in the previous centuries had depended on Latinate conventions of genre, rhetorical structuring, poetical devices, and classical references. As there had been no alphabetically written texts in Mexico before the Spanish incursion, such conventions were automatically commandeered for the rapid institution of a Nahuatl literary canon within only fifty years—a process that would continue in the 1600s.[136]

Latin and Nahuatl alike were integral to the culture of the College of Santa Cruz, where the two languages had a sustained and intensive connection. Ethnohistorical research on colonial Mexico has naturally accommodated study of Catholicism and the missionary enterprise in New Spain.[137] But the traditions and practices of Christian humanism—grammar, rhetoric, dialectic, poetics, antiquarianism,

[135] Snyder 1989, 7–8; cf. Burke 1989.

[136] Cf. Chapter 9, I, II below on Alvarado Tezozomoc and Chimalpahin.

[137] Cf. e.g. Christensen 2013; 2014 (nn. 67, 74 above); Baudot 1995; Burkhart 1989; Pardo 2004; Lara 2008; Tavárez 2011.

translation, and textual scholarship—are no less crucial. Recognition of their relevance and of the importance of Latin culture to Nahuatl literary history will afford new insight into the works produced by Franciscans and native Mexican scholars in Tlatelolco. The 'wide mirror polished on both sides' could be a perfect symbol for the knowledge of both Nahuatl and Latin that is required for this clearer understanding.

6

Humanism and Ethnohistory

Petitions in Latin from Tlacopan and Azcapotzalco

The Valley of Mexico, an area greater than six thousand square miles, was inhabited by several different peoples and language groups when the Spaniards first arrived in 1519 (Plate 1).[1] In the dominant city states the language spoken was Nahuatl: Mexico Tenochtitlan and the adjacent city of Tlatelolco, whose inhabitants were together called the Mexica, or 'Aztecs', had become the most powerful. With the states of Texcoco and Tlacopan, the Mexica are believed to have forged the Triple Alliance (Plate 10) in 1428, through which they sought to control the area covered by Mexico City today.[2] In whatever way that alliance operated, the Aztec empire might best be seen as a mutable, symbolic confederation led by the Mexica, who had as much control over regions beyond the Valley of Mexico as they did within it.[3]

After the Spaniards' defeat of the Aztecs, tensions remained between the Nahuatl-speaking principalities, some of which were ruled by Christianized descendants of their original pre-Hispanic *tlatoque,* or lords.[4] By the mid-1500s, many native governors were lodging appeals to the Spanish crown for the restoration of territory, reduction of tribute, coats of arms, and other privileges for their polities.[5] Their petitions were usually in Castilian or Nahuatl, but on occasions Latin was used: the

[1] The native population, estimated at 2.65 million in 1568 (Cook and Borah 1979 iii, 97), would have been greater on the Spaniards' arrival. There may have been 27 million inhabitants of Mesomerica as a whole: Prem 1997, 124–5; cf. Knight 2002, 132–92 and Kline 2008.

[2] Carrasco 1999. Herrera Meza, López Austin, and Martínez Baracs 2013 relate the Nahuatl term 'excan tlatoloyan', 'parliament in three places', to the Triple Alliance. CLAVIGERO, *Storia antica del Messico* (1780), 'Dissertazione' 6.7 [2003, 778] had referred to the confederation between Mexico, Acolhuacan, and Tlacopan as a 'triplice alleanza'.

[3] The only equivalent for *imperium* or empire in Nahuatl sources is *tlatocayotl*, 'authority', 'rulership', a term derived from *tlatoani*: cf. Van Zantwijk 1990 and *Nican ompehua y çaçanillatolli* (1550s), fable 36, quoted in Chapter 7, III below. On the word 'Aztec', cf. Introduction n. 11, above.

[4] Gibson 1964a, Lockhart 1992.

[5] Indigenous principals from New Spain petitioned in other Mesoamerican languages, as well as in Spanish: Zimmermann 1970, Pérez-Rocha and Tena 2000; Restall, Sousa and Terraciano 2005.

Aztec Latin. Andrew Laird, Oxford University Press. © Oxford University Press 2024.
DOI: 10.1093/oso/9780197586358.003.0007

letters written to Philip II and Isabel of Valois by Pablo Nazareo of Xaltocan, the Indian rector of the College of Santa Cruz, are the best known examples.[6]

Although the Latin documents that are the focus of the present chapter have received less attention than Nazareo's letters, these earlier texts are of greater interest because they involve prominent indigenous nobles and they offer unparalleled testimonies about the histories of their principalities. A short official report about a contested claim for lands made by Pedro de Montezuma will be described briefly (Section I), before two Latin letters—both presented in Appendix 2 below—are discussed in full: an appeal to the Emperor Charles V by the governor of Tlacopan (Section II); and a petition to Philip II of Spain by the rulers of Azcapotzalco (Section III). The rhetorical strategies and literary allusions employed in these letters show how some indigenous nobles taught by the friars were able to make practical use of the humanist education they had received for their own ends. A short concluding discussion (Section IV) considers why the documents examined in this chapter were composed in Latin.

I. Juan de Tlaxcala, 'Verba sociorum domini petri tlacauepantzi', 1541

Don Pedro de Moctezuma Tlacahuepantzin (1510–1570) was the younger son of Montezuma II by María Miahuaxochtzin, daughter of the pre-Hispanic ruler of Tula, Ixtlilcuechahuacatzin.[7] During 1528–1531 don Pedro had accompanied Hernán Cortés to Spain, and in 1539 he made a second journey there to obtain a royal cedula confirming his ancestral rights to lands and income in Tula. On his return to Mexico in 1540, however, those holdings had been taken over by local principals, leading to a legal dispute that would continue almost until his death in 1570.[8] Abundant records of the proceedings survive in Nahuatl and Spanish, but a single document is in Latin, headed 'Verba sociorum domini petri tlacauepantzi', 'Words of the partners of don Pedro de Tlacahuepantzi' (Figure 6.1).[9] This was the work of a judge whom the Viceroy Mendoza had commissioned to visit Tula

[6] NAZAREO, 'Invictissimo Hispaniarum…Domino Philippo' (1556), 'Serenissimae Hispaniarum Reginae' (1556) and 'Sacrae Catholicae Magestati' (1566) [1970, 18–31]: cf. Gil 1990; Osorio Romero 1990; Carrera de la Red 1998; Laird 2014b, 160–1; Chapter 4, II; Chapter 5, II above.

[7] ALVARADO TEZOZOMOC, *Chronica Mexicayotl* (1609) [1998, 151]; cf. Chapter 9, II below; Ramírez Calva 2010, 133–45.

[8] CHIMALPAHIN, *Relaciones* 7 (c. 1630), 199v [1998 ii, 183] records Pedro de Montezuma's return from his first journey to Spain in 1531; cf. Chipman 2005, 75–95. Jiménez Abollado and Ramírez Calva 2011 is a study of the legal documents.

[9] TLAXCALA, 'Verba sociorum' (1541) and the other records ('Vínculos y Mayorazgos', vols. 255–257) are in the Archivo General de la Nación, Mexico. Laird 2024 provides a transcription, English translation, and analysis of the Latin text.

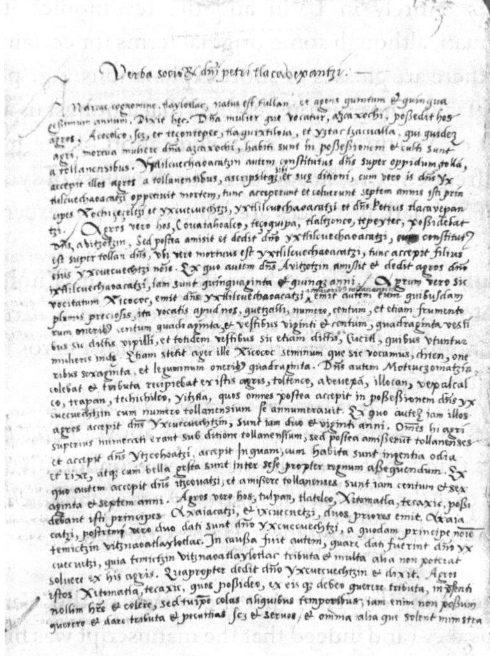

Verba socio[rum] d[omi]ni petri tlacauepantzi.

Figure 6.1 'Verba sociorum domini petri tlacauepantzi', Tula, 1541. Archivo General de la Nación, Mexico.

and assemble an impartial record of statements from local elders about Pedro de Montezuma's claim.[10]

The 'Verba sociorum' begins with five testimonies from don Pedro's supporters, who explain how the lands had passed to his possession from various parties (9r–10r). Two lengthy counter-testimonies and endorsements from witnesses who hold that the Mexica had appropriated territory belonging to Tula come under a second heading (10r–12r): 'Tollanorum verba quibus respondent Petro ac sociis ejus' ('Words of those from Tula in reply to Pedro and his partners'). The name, age, and place of origin of each witness are supplied without any further explanation or comment, and it is not made clear how many of their accounts were delivered in person or how they were collected. The report is dated at the end: 'All these enquiries were made in the town of Tula on the 6th September in the 1,541st year from the Virgin Birth.'[11]

[10] Ramírez Calva 2010, 103; Xelhuantzi 2017.

[11] 'Verba sociorum' (1541), 12r: 'Hec omnia inquisita in oppido tulla*n* fuere, die 6.ª mensis Septembris, A virgineo partu Milissimo. D. 4i.'

The document is entirely in Latin and the testimonies it comprises were translated from Nahuatl, although some original terms for certain commodities are retained, for which there are glosses or short explanations: e.g. 'plumis preciosis ita vocatis apud nos quetzalli', 'the precious feathers that amongst us are called *quetzalli*'. Like the translation of Martín de la Cruz's dedication of the herbal discussed in Chapter 5, this text frequently replicates in Latin the effect of synonymic diffusion, a standard feature of Nahuatl. Instances are italicized in this excerpt:

> Eadem que *sentit & attestatur* Andreas tlaylotlac supra nominatus *sentio & dico*, verum non satis ita et firma fronte *affirmarim & dixerim mulierem illam, dominam* nomine azcaxochi *possedisse et coluisse* agros hos, acocolco, teçontepec, tlaquixtiloja . . .
>
> The same things as Andrés Tlailotlac named above *thinks and attests* are what I say and I think, but in truth not so very confidently *would I affirm and would I say* that *the woman, the mistress* Azcaxochitl *owned and tended* those lands of Acocolco, Tezontepec, Tlaquixtiloyan . . .[12]

But there is also interesting evidence that the author of the 'Verba sociorum' was himself a Nahuatl speaker (and indeed that the manuscript was his autograph) from an error that he corrected in his own hand on folio 9v:

> Joannes cognominatus Nexpanecatl, natione Mexicanus de moiotla qui vivit quind~~ecim~~ et ~~quadra~~ quinquaginta annis.
>
> Juan, with the surname Nexpanecatl, a Mexican by birth, from Moyotlan, who is fif~~teen~~ and ~~for~~ fifty years old.

As the use of 'fifteen and forty', instead of 'five and fifty' or 'fifty-five', is as irregular in Latin as it would be in Spanish or English, 'quindecim et quadraginta annis', 'fifteen and forty years old', is altered to 'quin[que] et quinquaginta annis', 'fifty-five years old'. Mesoamerican peoples multiplied in twenties: the writer had first literally translated the number *ompohualli oncaxtolli* (forty and fifteen) into Latin, before remembering that he should give it as a decimal figure.[13]

The writer in question was identified by Pedro de Montezuma himself as a native judge, 'don ioan, natural de Tlaxcala', who was sent to Tula by the viceroy to establish

[12] TLAXCALA, 'Verba sociorum' (1541), 9v. On 'synonymic diffusion', see Chapter 5, I, (i) n. 21 above. A 1563 will in Nahuatl, quoted in Pérez Rocha and Tena 2000, 262, offers a pertinent parallel to the excerpt quoted above: 'yn *notlalnamiquiliz y notlahiyaliz* oc noyolococopan, y *niquitohua y nictenehua* notlatol', 'In complete possession of *my thoughts and my judgement* even in my state of sickness; thus *I say and I affirm* my words' (my translation).

[13] Cf. OLMOS, *Arte de la lengua mexicana* (1547) 3.4 [2002, 161–5]; Lockhart 2001, 50; Launey 2011, 59. Latin does not use this vigesimal system: Hofmann–Szantyr 1965, 210–14.

who owned the disputed lands.[14] A judge from Tlaxcala might have been deemed especially suitable, because the region probably had few connections of interest or kinship with Mexico or Tula, owing to its historic enmity with the Mexica. To be qualified for the role, don Juan would have been seconded from an Indian *cabildo* (council), or *alcaldía* (mayoralty) and was therefore of high social standing. On that basis it has been asserted—without any evidence—that Juan was an alumnus of the College of Santa Cruz in Tlatelolco.[15]

Even allowing for the narrow scope of its remit, the limited vocabulary and repeated formulae of the 'Verba sociorum' make its Latin style look pedestrian compared to that of writings by former students of Santa Cruz. The college, which was for pupils of grammar school age, opened only in 1536: if Juan had been one of them, he could hardly have become a senior judge by 1541, when he compiled this document. It is far more likely that he was educated in Tlaxcala, where friars had begun teaching native students from the mid-1520s.[16] The 'Verba sociorum' may well be the sole extant Latin text written by an indigenous author who was not trained at the College of Santa Cruz.

II. Antonio Cortés Totoquihuatzin, 'S.C.C. Majestati' to Charles V, 1552

Don Antonio Cortés was the son of Totoquihuatzin, who had been *tlatoani*, or ruler, of Tlacopan when the Spaniards first reached Mexico.[17] Tlacopan (now Tacuba in Mexico City), an *altepetl* on the western shore of Lake Texcoco, was once part of the Tepanec empire of Azcapotzalco, before it joined Tenochtitlan and Texcoco in the Aztec Triple Alliance.[18] The town initially retained its importance after the Spanish conquest, but only for the early part of the colonial period.[19] Totoquihuatzin had been descended from the royal line instituted there by the Mexica in the 1430s, after their overthrow of the Tepanec empire.[20] The chronicler Motolinía remarked that the pre-Hispanic rulers of both Texcoco and Tlacopan 'might well be called kings

[14] Xelhuantzi 2017, 12 quotes don Pedro's letter to the Audiencia, a work that follows the Latin document in AGN, Vínculos y Mayorazgos, 256 at fol. 13r.

[15] Cf. e.g. Ramírez Calva 2010, 26–7; Kalyuta 2011, 490.

[16] On early education in Tlaxcala cf. GANTE, 'Carta al emperador' (1532) [1877, 52], MOTOLINÍA, *Historia* (1543) 3.2 [2001, 180], GARCÉS, *De habilitate* (1537), 9 (Appendix 2.1.2) below.

[17] Cf. Castañeda de la Paz 2013, 301–20; Villella 2016, 73–122; and part (ii) of this Section, p. 200 below. The *Codex Huixquilucan* (c. 1660–1750s), 3v (Plate 12a) depicts Totoquihuatzin the elder, not Antonio Cortés, *pace* Pérez Rocha and Tena 2000, 49.

[18] Wagner 1944, 117 (citing Zorita and Alva Ixtlilxochitl); Carrasco 1999, 176–204.

[19] Gibson 1964a, 309, 477; Gibson 1964b.

[20] ALVA IXTLILXOCHITL, *Sumaria relación de la Historia general* (c. 1625) [1975 i, 543]; Carrasco 1984, 89–90.

because they lack nothing to be such.'[21] Totoquihuatzin died in 1520, and his immediate successor, don Antonio's brother Tetlepanquetzatzin, was summarily executed with Cuauhtemoc on Hernán Cortés' expedition to Honduras in 1525.[22]

Various individuals were placed in charge of Tlacopan until Antonio Cortés, who had been brought up by Franciscans, was appointed governor by viceroy Antonio de Mendoza on 21 April 1550, re-establishing the authority of Tlacopan's royal lineage.[23] Don Antonio was charged with 'securing the good governance of the town, seeing to everything with a bearing on the service of God, ensuring that the Indians learned Christian teaching and attended church services, taking care that they would not indulge in drunkenness, sacrifice, or idolatry, and seeing that tribute would be collected.'[24] The coat of arms [Plate 11a] conceded to Antonio Cortés Totoquihuatzin in 1564 symbolized his standing as a hereditary *tlatoani* and his role in promoting the Christian religion.[25] He supplied labour and resources to help build the first Jesuit church in Mexico in 1572—the year that the Society of Jesus reached New Spain.[26] Cortés Totoquihuatzin died in 1574, having named his son Pedro Alvarado Tetlepanquetza as his heir and successor.[27]

(i) Context and argument of the Latin letter to Charles V

In January of 1552 Antonio Cortés had written twice in Spanish to Charles V, requesting the return of estates that had been handed over to Spanish settlers.[28] Both his letters were dated on the Feast of Epiphany, often called 'el Día de los Reyes', 'the Day of the Kings'—an appropriate occasion for one ruler to write to another. At the end of the same year don Antonio wrote again to the Emperor on 1 December, this time in Latin (Figure 6.2), to seek relief from the servitude and excessive tribute

[21] MOTOLINÍA, *Historia* (c. 1543), 3.7 [2001, 209]: 'se podían bien llamar reyes, porque no les faltaba nada para lo ser'.

[22] CORTÉS, 'Quinta carta' (1526) [tr. 1986, 366–7]; cf. (iii) below.

[23] Gibson 1964a, 171; Castañeda de la Paz 2013, 206–8.

[24] AGN, ramo Mercedes, vol. 3, exp., 48, folio 22, cited in Pérez-Rocha and Tena 2000, 50 (my translation); Pérez-Rocha 1982, 82–3.

[25] The shield incorporated two *tlacotl* flowers standing for 'Tlacopan', three *xiuhuitzolli* (turquoise regal diadems), and a motto ('águila blanca pequeño' [*sic*], 'small white eagle', apparently connecting Totoquihuatzin's name with *tototl*, 'bird'—see, however, Whittaker 2021, 164–5), as well as images of a crowned *tlatoani* before a Christian cross and of a cross being affixed to an orb of the world.

[26] SÁNCHEZ BAQUERO, 'Patri Everardo Mercuriano' (1573) [1956, 65, 67]; SÁNCHEZ BAQUERO, *Fundación de la Compañia* (c. 1580) [1945, 54]. ALEGRE, *Historia de la Compañia* (c. 1767) [1841 i, 65].

[27] CORTÉS TOTOQUIHUATZIN, 'Jueves ic XXIX ilhuitl metztli' (1574); cf. Ruiz Medrano 2010, 43. Alvarado Tetlepanquetza was succeeded in 1585 by his brother Juan Cortés Chimalpopoca Moteuczoma Totoquihuatzin: Gibson 1964a, 171.

[28] CORTÉS TOTOQUIHUATZIN, 'Don Antonio Cortés y otros yndios' (1552), 'Sacra Cathólica, Cesarea Magestad' (1552).

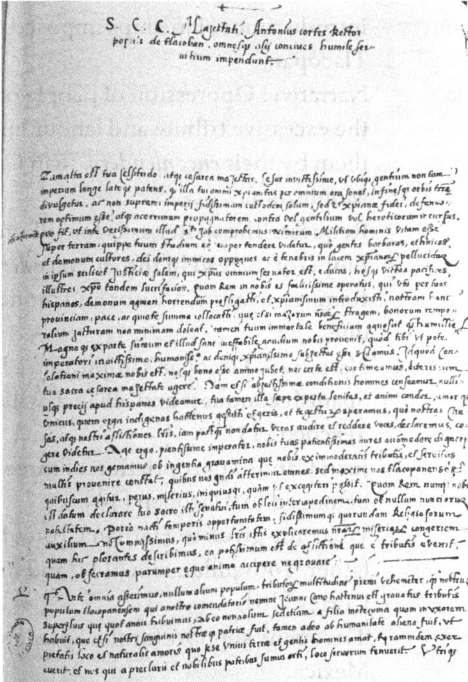

S. C. C. Majestati. Antonius cortes rector populi de tlacoban. omnesque alii cives humile servitium impendunt.

Figure 6.2 Latin letter of Antonio Cortés Totoquihuatzin to Charles V, Tlacopan, 1552. Archivo General de Indias, Seville.

imposed on Tlacopan by the *encomenderos* Juan Cano and his late wife Isabel, daughter of Montezuma II. The governor also called attention to Tlacopan's former greatness in pre-Hispanic Mexico and explained that the town had supported the Spaniards at the time of the conquest.[29]

The letter conforms to the guidelines for *dispositio,* or 'arrangement,' in humanist manuals on epistolography:[30]

[1]–[2]	*Salutatio*	Greeting: Praise (*laudatio*) of the Emperor [1], and an appeal to his good will (*captatio benevolentiae*) [2].

[29] He expressed similar concerns in a Spanish letter to Philip II in February 1561, and in 1566, with other leading citizens, appealed to the Audiencia of Mexico for Tlacopan to be placed under direct control of the Spanish crown, commuting payment of tributes to any other party.

[30] ERASMUS, *Conficiendarum epistolarum formula* (1520) [tr. 1985, 261–2] opposed the conventional five-part format proposed in the *artes dictaminis*; cf. VIVES, *De conscribendis epistolis* (1534) [1989, 82]; Chapter 2, I above.

[3]–[10]	*Exordium*	Introduction: Hardships imposed on the people of Tlacopan.
[11]	*Narratio*	Narrative: Oppression of people of Tlacopan and the excessive tribute and labour imposed upon them by their *encomendero,* Juan Cano, and Isabel de Montezuma.
[12]	*Petitio*	Request: The writer asks for tribute to be paid to the Emperor instead of the *encomendero* and for Jacobo Ramírez to act as Visitor and moderate the amount due.
[13]–[17]	*Narratio*	Narrative: Tlacopan's importance before the Spanish conquest and alliance with Mexico and Texcoco [13]. Juan Cano's appropriation of three more towns that belonged to Tlacopan [14]. Welcome given to Hernán Cortés by the writer's father, Totoquihuatzin [15], and his speech to Cortés [16]. Tlacopan's support for the Spaniards against the Mexica. The writer's brothers killed by the Mexica [17].
[18]–[20]	*Conclusio*	Profession of loyalty to the Emperor [18]. Summary of the preceding petition [19]. Signatures [20].

The lengthy greeting to Charles V begins with a flourish:

> So lofty is your eminence and Caesarean majesty, most invincible Caesar, that among peoples everywhere the Christian quality of your soul, as well as your empire stretching far and wide, sounds on the lips of all and is proclaimed to the ends of the earth . . . [1]

It was conventional to address the Holy Roman Emperor as Caesar, but further classical usages in this sentence—'longe lateque' ('far and wide'), and 'omnium ora' ('on the lips of all')—may have been a response to the Hapsburg monarchs' avowal of their ancient Trojan and Roman ancestry.[31] An echo of Psalm 18, 'in fines . . . orbis

[31] Cf. Yates 1975, 130–4 and Tanner 1993 on the Hapsburg identification with Rome. Philip II claimed the title of 'Caesar': Elliott 1989. Wölfflin 1933, 265 notes 'longe late[que]', 'far and wide', in Caesar and Cicero. For 'omnium ora', 'on the lips of all', cf. Virgil, *Georgics* 3.9: 'victorque virum volitare per ora'; *Aeneid* 12.235: 'succedet fama vivusque per ora feretur' (recalling Ennius, *Epigram* 18: 'Volito

terrae', 'to the ends of the earth', is followed by an explicit quotation from scripture, as the Emperor is praised for using his power to spread the Christian faith:

> This has led us to commend in your case those words of the holy prophet Job [7: 1] as very true, namely, that 'the life of man upon earth is warfare', since your exertions seem always to be directed towards fighting against barbarous peoples, pagans, and worshippers of devils, in short, against God's enemies, then leading them from darkness to the clear light possessed of Christians, indeed to that Sun of Justice which is Christ, saviour of all, and towards pacifying them once conquered, enlightening them, and at last winning them for Christ . . . [1]

Thomas Aquinas had interpreted Job's verse to mean that human life, with its threats and dangers, was like a military campaign, but here the text is taken literally.[32] The title *Sol Justitiae*, 'Sun of Justice', which originated in the Old Testament as well, was given to Christ and used in the Votive Mass of the Blessed Virgin, said between Epiphany and the Feast of the Purification—the period in which this letter is likely to have reached Spain.[33] In Christian antiquity Saint John Chrysostom had connected *Sol Justitiae* to the pagan *Sol Invictus*, 'Invincible Sun', because the date of Christmas had once been the celebration of the birthday of the solar deity.[34] Though *invictus* or *invictissimus* was a customary epithet for the Holy Roman Emperor, its

vivus per ora virum', 'Alive I fly about on the lips of men'); Apuleius, *Metamorphoses* 6.8.1: 'per omnium ora populorum discurrens', 'coursing through the lips of all peoples'. Cf. Psalms 18:5: 'In omnem terram exivit sonus eorum: et in fines orbis terrae verba eorum' ('Their sound hath gone forth into all the earth: and their words unto the ends of the world'). The *exordia* of two letters to Philip II by NAZAREO, 'Invictissimo Hispaniarum . . . regi' (1556) and 'Sacrae Catholicae Magestati' (1566), also employ classical devices: Carrera de la Red 1998, 142–4; Laird 2014b, 160–1.

[32] Aquinas, *Expositio super Job* (1200s) on Job 7: 1: 'hoc est quod dicit "militia est vita hominis super terram", ac si dicat: vita praesens qua super terram vivimus non est sicut status victoriae sed sicut status militiae' (He says, "Man's life on earth is combat", as if to say: The present life which we live on earth is not like a state of victory, but like the state of a military campaign.')

[33] Malachi 4: 2: 'et orietur vobis timentibus nomen meum sol iustitiae' ('But unto you that fear my name, the sun of justice shall arise'); cf. the 'Propers' or Offertory of the Votive Mass: 'Felix namque es sacra Virgo Maria et omni laude dignissima, quia ex te ortus est sol justitiae, Christus Deus noster' ('For thou art happy, O sacred Virgin Mary, and most worthy of all praise, since out of thee hath arisen the sun of justice, Christ our Lord.')

[34] Chrysostom, 'Sermo XXVII', in *Opera* (1530) ii, 342: 'Sed et dominus noster nascitur mense decembri, hyemis tempore VIII Cal. Ianuarias . . . Sed & invicti natalem appellant. Quis utique tam invictus nisi dominus noster? . . . uel quod dicant solis esse natalem, ipse est sol iustitiae' ('But Our Lord, too, is born in the month of December in the season of winter, the eighth day before the calends of January [25 December] . . . But they also call it the "Birthday of the Invincible One." Who indeed is as invincible as Our Lord? . . . Or, if they say that it is the birthday of the Sun, He is the Sun of Justice'). Editions of Chrysostom would have been in New Spain by the mid-1500s: Yhmoff Cabrera 1996 ii, 200–17.

use to hail Charles V is especially pertinent to this context: the Caesars of antiquity had long been associated with the *Sol Invictus*.[35] While Augustine and Tertullian had both rejected any identification of Christ with the pagan sun god, that repudiation would only have ended up making such a connection better known in the 1500s, when Chrysostom's works were widely read in Latin.[36]

The sun was also crucial to the calendrical epistemology of pre-Hispanic Mexico and it was prominent in some interpretations of the catastrophe of the Spanish conquest that were attributed to the Indians.[37] According to sixteenth-century sources, the Mexicans initially connected the Spaniards with the sun and even venerated them as 'sons of the sun'.[38] Such reports, which reflect post-conquest ideology, could underlie the connection between the Emperor Charles' capacities both to 'enlighten' ('illustres') and to 'pacify the conquered' ('victos pacifices')—a principle inherited from the pagan Roman empire by early Christian authors.[39]

Motolinía, the Franciscan guardian of Tlacopan, had already associated the Christian *Sol Justitiae* with Tonatiuh, the Aztec solar deity.[40] His *Memoriales*, an ethnological work drafted more than a decade before Cortés Totoquihuatzin's letter and finalized in 1549, contained a chapter entitled, 'The many and varied festivals the natives held in this land in which many idolatries are revealed, and how in order to destroy them, the Sun and the Moon were on our side, that is Christ, Sun of Justice, and his most precious Mother and Our Lady'.[41] Motolinía's use of this

[35] Berrens 2004.

[36] Tertullian, *Apologeticum* 16 (cf. *Ad nationes* 1.13; Origen, *Contra Celsum* 8.67); Augustine, *In Evangelium Iohannis* 34.

[37] Cf. Lockhart 1993, 5, 18; and Chapter 8, III on the omens in the *Florentine Codex* and references in Chapter 8, n. 59 below.

[38] TOVAR, *Codex Ramírez* (c. 1582–1587). León-Portilla 1962, 59 translates, 'The Indians knelt . . . and adored the Spaniards as sons of the Sun, their god'; in the *Annals of Tlatelolco* (c. 1550) [tr. 1993, 256, 264], Pedro de Alvarado is called 'Tonatiuh', 'Sun.' In the *Codex Telleriano-Remensis* (c. 1563), 46r, an image of the sun with a human face depicts Alvarado, captioned 'al cual llamavan los yndios tonatihu que quiere dezer el sol' ('the Indians called him Tonatiuh, which means Sun'). Hamann 2013, 529–30 discusses the sun's central position on the *Lienzo de Tlaxcala* (1552) at a turning point in this pictorial history of the conquest. Compare the visual personification of the sun in the map of Mexico City in CORTÉS, *Praeclara . . . de Noua maris Oceani Hyspania narratio* (1524), discussed in the General Conclusions, II below.

[39] Cf. Orosius, *Historiae adversum paganos* (c. 416 AD), 6.1.7–8, 6.22.5.

[40] CERVANTES DE SALAZAR, *Chronica* (c. 1566) 4.125, cited below in II (iii), states that Motolinía had once been guardian of the people of Tlacopan after their conversion. While 'Thoribius' is one of the signatories of this letter (Appendix 2.4, A2P102 / p. 380 below), this is *not* Fray Toribio de Benavente, who signed himself 'Motolinía' (cf. MENDIETA, *Historia* 3.12 [1870, 211]) but the native Toribio Feliciano, who put his full name to don Antonio's later 1561 letter. Toribio may have taken Motolinía's Christian name at baptism.

[41] MOTOLINÍA, *Memoriales* (c. 1541), 9r [1996, 151]: 'De muchas y diuersas fiestas que en esta tierra tenían en las quales se declara muchas ydolatrías, y como para las destruir estuuo en nuestro fauor el sol y la luna, esto es Cristo, sol de justiçia y su muy preçiosa madre y señora nuestra.'

association as a strategy for conversion is paralleled in a number of other texts by missionaries in Mexico.[42]

The topos of pacification through conquest in Cortés Totoquihuatzin's greeting effected a transition to a *captatio benevolentiae*:

> To this end you have laboured very happily among us: by the agency of your own Spaniards you have overthrown the dreadful army of devils, introduced Christianity and, with the utmost peace and tranquility, given order to our province, which has the humblest recognition of your immortal kindness, even though it may grieve at the slaughter of our elders and at the very great loss of our worldly wealth. [2]

The courteous tone could be double edged, as the writer highlights the human cost of Charles V's victory, just as the earlier remark that the people of Tlacopan regarded Job's dictum 'the life of man upon earth is warfare' as being especially true of the Emperor. The request to the Emperor Charles to look sympathetically on petitioners who 'may be judged to be humans of the lowest condition and may be seen to be of no worth in the eyes of the Spaniards' ('abjectissimae conditionis homines censeamur, nulliusque precii apud hispanos videamur') [2] may be ambiguous as well. Erasmus had disparaged the use of such obsequious formulae in formal letters, but Cortés Totoquihuatzin appears to be providing another example of the importation into Latin of the self-depreciatory tone that was a conventional feature of courtly Nahuatl expression.[43] A revered pre-Hispanic *tlatoani*, for example, in a traditional speech supposedly pronounced to the nobles who elected him, would describe himself in these terms:

> I am an imbecile, and I cannot bring forth a word or two of discourse. And the truth is now that I have spent my life in excrement, in refuse. And perhaps in truth my lifetime is not for [the position] to which our lord inclineth his heart.[44]

[42] Burkhart 1988 notes uses of a similar association: SAHAGÚN, *Historia general* (c. 1580) = *HG*, Book 1, Appendix [1970 ii, 65]; *Sermonario* (1563); and especially the *Psalmodia Christiana* (1583, orig. 1560) at e.g. fols. 55v, 130r–130v, 172r; ANUNCIACIÓN, *Sermonario* (1577); and BAUTISTA, *Sermonario* (1606). The presentation of Christ as a solar entity in the El Escorial Nahuatl translation of Kempis alludes to 'Lux Mundi', 'Light of the World', in John 8:12: Tavárez 2013b, 223, 225; Chapter 5, IV (ii) n. 94 above.

[43] ERASMUS, *Opus de conscribendis epistolis* (1522) [1971, 276–85]. The collegian's speech made before Fray Alonso de Ponce (Chapter 4, II above), Cruz's dedication of BADIANO, *Libellus* (1552) (Appendix 2.2.1 below) and the opening of VALERIANO, 'Invictissimo' (1561) (Appendix 2.4 below), discussed below, contain similar expressions.

[44] SAHAGÚN, *HG* 6.12 [1969 vii, 61]: 'Ca anommati in njxco, in nocpac, auh ca avel cententli, cencamatl njcqujxtia, in jhijotl, in tlatolli: auc ca nelli axcan ca cujtlatitlan, ca tlaçultitlan nonemja. Auh at amo nelli nonemja, invncan tlacoa yiollotzin totecuyo.' Cf. *HG* 6.9 [1969 vii, 41–5].

On the basis of this and many other parallels, the native governor's wording, despite appearances, may be a coded signal of his prestige.

As noted above, the main subject of this letter was the servitude and excessive tribute imposed on Tlacopan by Juan Cano and his late wife, Isabel de Montezuma, whom Cano had married in 1532 after he became an associate of Hernán Cortés.[45] The aggravation Isabel caused the principals of Tlacopan is expressed in forthright terms at the beginning of the first *narratio*:

> Even though she was of our own blood and from our own native land ['sanguinis nostraeque patriae'], she was herself so remote from humanity that instead of the duty and natural love which men of the same country and race ['vnius terrae et gentis'] usually show to each other, she exercised tyranny and kept us in the position of slaves, when we were born of renowned and noble parents. [4]

There is clear rhetorical emphasis on the fact that Montezuma's daughter had the same ethnic and national origins as the inhabitants of Tlacopan.[46] At the same time, the 'tlacopanenses' were a distinct group, as the previous sentence had indicated: 'no other people is so fiercely oppressed by such a multitude of tributes as our Tlacopaneca people' ('nostrum populum tlacopanensem') [4], reiterating the complaint made a few lines above [3]: 'all we Indians are worn down by tribute and much servitude, but especially we Tlacopaneca' ('maxime nos tlacopanenses').

The substantial dues to both Juan Cano and Isabel are then described in detail [5–8]: as well as money, they received fruit, wood, wild fowl and poultry, and many other goods. For certain commodities, loanwords from Nahuatl—'huipiles', 'mastiles', 'ocote'—are used and glossed much as they were in the 'Verba sociorum'.[47] Other terms are examples of Spanish usage that had acquired currency in the

[45] Juan Cano de Saavedra (1502–1572) had arrived in Mexico in 1520 on Pánfilo de Narváez's expedition against Cortés, but changed loyalties to the Captain, for which he was later rewarded. Kalyuta 2008 examines Cano's appeal for full restitution of Isabel's patrimony in 1548, before her death. Another appeal was made in 1553: Pérez-Rocha 1998, 16, 23; Sagaón Infante 1998; Megged 2010, 201. Juan Cano instructed some unnamed Franciscans (possibly Motolinía was involved) to compile an account of pre-Hispanic genealogies and inheritances for Charles V, of which some pages survive: MOTOLINÍA, undated manuscripts [1941 iii, 240–80]. FERNÁNDEZ DE OVIEDO, *Historia general y natural* (1535–1557) 33.54 staged a dialogue between the author and Juan Cano on the conquest of Mexico: Martínez 1986; Myers 2008, 166–73. Cano's lost *Relación* is considered below.

[46] Chipman 2005, 27–74, examines the Spaniards' accommodation of Isabel de Montezuma and her subsequent status. For the complex assignation of the *encomienda* of Tlacopan to Isabel, cf. Gibson 1964a, 423–6.

[47] The *huipil* was the traditional upper garment worn by women; for 'tomastli', literally 'our breeches', with the possessive *to-* preceding *maxtli*, cf. Chapter 1, p. 40 above. Here the words have a Latin plural form. 'Ocote' is a Hispanization of *ocotl*, a pine-torch: Karttunen 1992, 90, 141, 176.

Americas, although they had less currency in Spain: 'nagua' and 'axi' were loanwords from Taíno, the Arawakan Caribbean language; *tortilla* in Castilian Spanish has always designated an omelette, not the unleavened flat bread of Mesoamerica; and 'hanega' was a variant (more widely used in the New World at this time) of the usual Castilian *fanega*, a Spanish bushel.[48] In showing awareness that such words might not be familiar to a reader in peninsular Spain, don Antonio reveals the extent of his acculturation—and he conveys the authoritative status of Latin as a stable and effective vehicle of meaning. By writing in Latin he can make a conclusive statement of what the items given various names in Nahuatl, Spanish, or Taíno actually are.

The letter lists land, towns, or estates belonging to Tlacopan that had been ceded to Juan Cano [9–11, 14] or had been appropriated by him, or to which he was laying claim after his wife's death the previous year. These allocations are confirmed in sources attesting the dowry Hernán Cortés had given to Isabel de Montezuma in 1527, including the pictorial *Codex Osuna* (1565) and the anonymous *Memorial* of towns subject to Tlacopan from the mid-1500s.[49] The latter document, produced in Tlacopan, enumerated the polity's towns and estates, and mentioned Capolhuac, Ocoyacac, and Tepehuexoyocan among the five *pueblos* under Juan Cano's control: 'they serve him and they do not know of Tlacopan as an authority.'[50] Cortés Totoquihuatzin's Latin letter, however, contradicts this, stating that Juan Cano had taken the same three *oppida* that properly belonged to Tlacopan [14]. The *Memorial* was probably compiled at the same time as the letter, or afterwards, since it makes no mention of doña Isabel.

In the context of this discussion of the appropriations of land from Tlacopan, Antonio Cortés Totoquihuatzin makes clear that his town had once been a major power, with dominions of its own:

> In the first place, then, we inform your most excellent majesty that in former times these Indies were divided into three parts, namely Mexico, Tlacopan, and Texcoco, and as a consequence had three masters or rulers who ruled the other surrounding peoples. [13]

The three polities of the Triple Alliance were normally listed as Mexico, Texcoco, and Tlacopan, in descending order of importance. But in this passage Tlacopan, which was the smallest and had the fewest dominions, comes second, after Mexico City.[51]

[48] Cf. Helmer 2009 on the semantics and diffusion of the word *ají* (*axi*) in colonial Spanish America.

[49] *Memorial de los pueblos* (1550s); Carrasco 1999, 177 n. 8.

[50] Anon., *Memorial de los pueblos* (1550s), item 3 [1970, 5]: 'Estos cinco que agora se siguen traxo Juan Cano, y le siruen y a Tlacupan no la conoçen por señorio ninguno.'

[51] The *Memorial de los pueblos* from Tlacopan uses the sequence 'Mexico, y Tezcuco, y Tlacupan' on all six occasions the three *altepetl* are named.

The sentence echoes the beginning of Julius Caesar's *Gallic Wars*: the Indies of New Spain had been divided into three parts like Gaul.[52] Although the opening of Sallust's *Bellum Catilinae* had been recalled in this text as well, this particular evocation may have been designed to appeal to the Holy Roman emperor as a latter-day Caesar.[53] While recognizing that the conquistadors and missionary friars in New Spain had been aware of Tlacopan's importance, don Antonio emphasizes that his own people were never in servitude, in order to lend weight to his plea for Tlacopan to be relieved from tribute, as far as might be possible. He also asks for one of its former subject peoples to be returned to serve the polity, [13], and for the *oppida* that had been appropriated by Juan Cano to be restored [14].

(ii) Further narratives in the 1552 letter

Opportunely calling attention to his own Christian name, 'Antonius Cortés', the writer explains how his father, Totoquihuatzin (Plate 12a), had rejoiced at the first arrival of the Spaniards: he sent gifts to them and received them in Tlacopan 'with open arms' ('obuiis manibus') [15].[54] The *tlatoani* had even invited Hernán Cortés to destroy the town's temple, and to take from it anything he liked; he offered him his daughters as wives for the Spaniards; and he proposed an alliance with them, in order to defeat the nations in Mexico that were hostile to them both [16]. The tone of this welcome recalls the overture made to Hernán Cortés by Xicotencatl, ruler of the Tlaxcalteca, if not the more confused reception proffered by Montezuma.[55] While none of the genealogies for Totoquihuatzin and his descendants make reference to any daughters, those of Montezuma II—the most prominent of whom was

[52] Caesar, *Bellum Gallicum* 1.1: 'Gallia est omnis divisa in partes tres . . .' ('All of Gaul was divided into three parts . . .'). A Vascosanus edition of Caesar (Paris, 1543) was in the convent library of Santiago Tlatelolco: Mathes 1982, 51.

[53] See n. 31 above on Caesars. The remark in Sallust, *Bellum Catilinae* 1.1 that men 'should not go through life in silence like cattle' ('ne vitam silentio transeant veluti pecora') is recalled earlier at [7]: the men of Tlacopan worked so hard for Juan Cano that they had become 'unmindful of the salvation of their souls, like cattle' ('immemores suae anime salutis veluti pecora').

[54] ERASMUS, *Adagia* 2.9.54 [1992, 111] noted the proverbial quality of 'obuiis manibus' in Jerome, *Epistles* 53.11. The sentence 'et accedentes ad hoc nostrum oppidum obuiis manibus, vt dicitur, recepit' means 'as they approached this town of ours, he welcomed them, as the saying goes, "with open arms".' Pérez-Rocha and Tena 2000, 175 fatally confuse *manus*, 'hands' (sc. 'arms'), with *Manes*, the ancient Roman spirits of the dead: 'y cuando se acercaban a nuestro pueblo *amenazados por los Manes, como a veces se dice*, los acogió.' Hence Domínguez Torres 2011, 77 and Domínguez Torres 2013, 144 translate, 'every time they approached our town, threatened by the Manes [Mexicas] as sometimes they are called [!], he welcomed them.'

[55] Cf. Xicotencatl's speech in CORTÉS, 'Segunda carta-relación' (1520) [1866, 66–7; tr. 1986, 66] and ALVA IXTLILXOCHITL, *Historia de la nación chichimeca* (c. 1648), cap. 90 [1977 ii, 236]. Restall 2003, 77–99 reviews sources for the encounter between Cortés and Montezuma.

Isabel—did end up being married to conquistadors.[56] The claim that the *tlatoani* of Tlacopan was prepared to give up his own daughters to the Spaniards is obviously a strategic fabrication, but one that is understandable in the context of a letter about the abuses inflicted upon the town by the daughter of another *tlatoani* and her husband.

Don Antonio avers that he is quoting 'the very words' ('haec sunt quidem verba') that his father spoke to Cortés, although he was an infant when Totoquihuatzin first encountered the Spaniards and his account of that meeting cannot be based on personal recollection. The formulae used at the beginning and end of Totoquihuatzin's welcoming speech to the Captain strongly suggest that the whole episode was instead crafted as a fiction to win over the Emperor Charles:

> May your arrival with your army be most auspicious, and may you know that we are prepared to serve you, and the one in whose name you come. Along with my people I will worship the same god you praise . . . In any case, you should know that I have no wish to wage war against you and your army, lest my people come to a bad end. [16]

This passage is far more than a promise of cooperation with the invaders: the elder Totoquihuatzin's language is oddly consonant with the demands of the *Requerimiento*, a legal text asserting Spain's sovereignty over the territories of the New World and formally recited to their inhabitants when the Spaniards first encountered them.[57] Natives were addressed 'in the name of' the Pope and the Catholic monarchs, informed that they were 'subjects or vassals of their Highnesses', and enjoined to accept the Christian faith. Furthermore, they were told that failure to comply would result in their being killed or enslaved and deprived of their property—and that they would be to blame for these losses. Missionaries introduced themselves as representatives of the Pope and Holy Roman Emperor in a similar style, albeit without the threats of violence or coercion.[58] The script of Totoquihuatzin's oration, in which the ruler pledged to serve the Captain and 'the one in whose name [he] came' and promised not to wage war against the Spaniards, suggests that its author was familiar with those protocols.

Don Antonio explains how Totoquihuatzin and his people subsequently lent their support to the Spaniards:

> To that I add that my aforementioned father often tried to prevent Montezuma, the ruler of Mexico, from campaigning against the Spaniards,

[56] Cf. Chipman 2005, 53–95 on the strategic marriages of Montezuma's daughters Isabel and Mariana, and of other descendants.

[57] Hanke 1949; Williams 1992, 88–93; Restall 2003, 87–99; Laird 2018b.

[58] Cf. the friars' speech in SAHAGÚN, *Colloquios* (1564), caps. 1–5, 29v–33v [1986: 79–85].

> but in defiance of my father's warning he nonetheless prepared for war. What is more, the Spaniards fleeing Mexico passed through this community of mine, which, as it had already entered into an alliance with them, again supplied them with all the things they needed to survive, and freed them from the severe hunger that was devastating them . . . [17]

There are several narratives of the occasion in the summer of 1520 that came to be called the 'Noche Triste'.[59] The Spaniards suffered heavy losses as they escaped Tenochtitlan by night after the death of Montezuma, crossing the lake of Mexico on rope bridges while under heavy attack from the Aztecs. In his letter of April 1522 Hernán Cortés related that he found his men in Tlacopan after they reached dry land and was keen to lead them out to the countryside before they were attacked by the enemy pursuing them. The chronicles of Francisco López de Gómara and Bernal Díaz del Castillo told the same story, adding that the Mexica were inciting the men of the town to fight the Spaniards. According to Díaz, they were being attacked by soldiers from Tlacopan as well as Azcapotzalco and Tenayocan from under the cover of high maize plants in fields nearby so that they wanted 'to leave that town as soon as possible'.[60]

Francisco Cervantes de Salazar knew the accounts of Hernán Cortés and López de Gómara, but as he compiled his *Chronica de la Nueva España* in Mexico City later, probably around 1560, he was able to collect further reports and testimonies. Cervantes' narrative of the Spaniards' arrival in Tlacopan on the *Noche Triste* shows that there had been some debate about what happened there:[61]

> They reached Tacuba: the Spaniards in the rearguard, believing that Cortés (who was in the vanguard) would rest in the lodgings and the house of the lord [Totoquihuatzin] of that city, entered the guest accommodation of that house. About that there are two opinions:
>
> (i) One is that once our men arrived there the Mexica who were in pursuit of them turned around, either because they were tired of fighting by then or because they dared not enter foreign boundaries, fearing the Tacubans would come out to confront them because they gave a good

[59] Records of the date and fatalities vary: CORTÉS, 'Segunda carta-relación' (1520) [1866, 139] gives 30 June 1520, stating that 150 Spaniards and more than 2,000 indigenous allies were killed. DÍAZ DEL CASTILLO, *Historia verdadera* (1568–1575), cap. 128, in line with LÓPEZ DE GÓMARA, *La historia general de las Indias* (1554), cap. 110, who dated the *Noche Triste* to 10 July 1520, affirming that 450 Spaniards and 4,000 native allies perished. Cf. FERNÁNDEZ DE OVIEDO, *Historia general y natural* (1535–1557), 33.14 on Cortés' flight from Tenochtitlan, and the dialogue staged with Juan Cano in 33.54; SAHAGÚN, *HG* (c. 1580) 12.24 [1975 xiii, 67–9]. Wagner 1944, 300 tabulates the differing estimates of the losses.

[60] DÍAZ DEL CASTILLO, *Historia verdadera* (1568–1575), cap. 128.

[61] CERVANTES DE SALAZAR, *Chronica* (c. 1566), 4.125 [1971 ii, 60].

> welcome to Christians—something the Mexica among them afterwards complained about greatly and they reproached [the Tacubans] for not finishing off the slaughter of the Spaniards in their town. This is what Motolinía and the people of Tacuba say: their guardian, after they were converted, was that same Motolinía, a Franciscan friar and conqueror of souls.
>
> (ii) The truth is, on the testimony of many conquistadors, that the Mexica followed the Spaniards as far as Tacuba, and more than a league beyond, and as it was night the Tacubans gave neither help nor hindrance. The Spaniards in the rearguard, once they realized Cortés was not resting in the accommodation but going on ahead, left in a frenzy not to lose him . . .

The first opinion Cervantes de Salazar reported is consistent with what Antonio Cortés Totoquihuatzin had maintained in all three of his letters in Spanish. Cervantes, though, believed the second opinion he reported to be the truth: the people of Tacuba (Tlacopan) did nothing for the Spaniards on this occasion.

Alonso de Zorita, whose manuscript *Relación de la Nueva España* was completed in 1585, contained yet another description of the Spaniards' reception in Tlacopan after their flight from Tenochtitlan:[62]

> And [Cortés] gave the order to stop in Tlacopan, the dry land at the end of all the causeways, in the lodgings in the town, and he said this to everyone . . . Many went on until they reached Tlacopan and some went into the lodging Cortés has spoken of, and there they killed them all. But Cortés went a long way ahead without stopping in the place. The place was full of high maize plantations full of men, who leapt out and killed the Spaniards as they were fleeing and in confusion.

This testimony, in which the Tlacopaneca were aggressive opponents of the Spaniards, apparently without any incitement, runs counter to Antonio Cortés Totoquihuatzin's characterization of his people as firm allies who prevented Cortés' men from dying of starvation.[63]

Among the many sources Zorita catalogues at the opening of his work was a manuscript of which he would make frequent use: a *Relación* about New Spain and its conquest by Juan Cano, the *encomendero* of Tlacopan, with whose family the

[62] ZORITA, *Relación* (1585), 3.29 [1999 ii, 582–3].

[63] An indigenous view of events contemporary with Cortés Totoquihuatzin's letter is in line with Zorita's opposing account: the *Lienzo de Tlaxcala* (n. 38 above) shows, at cell 19, the Spaniards being attacked at Tlacopan. See Kranz 2007 and Kranz 2010 on the versions of the *Lienzo*.

author was acquainted.[64] Cano's lost memoir was not available to other chroniclers, although its gist can be reconstructed from content in Zorita that is not found elsewhere.[65] Zorita's characterization of the hostility the Tlacopaneca showed to the Spaniards on the occasion of the *Noche Triste* is likely to have been based on Cano's version of events. Accordingly, those governing Tlacopan in the mid-1500s may well have had cause to be concerned about how Cano and others were presenting the town's role in the conflict. Antonio Cortés Totoquihuatzin's claims about his father's friendliness to the Spaniards, fanciful as they may be, were an expedient to counteract detrimental testimonies.[66]

On the other hand, don Antonio's report of Totoquihuatzin's death the following year—'my father had died, by no means in battle but of an illness' [17]—would be endorsed: Fernando de Alva Ixtlilxochitl recorded that the ruler perished in a smallpox epidemic.[67] But the next event related, toward the very end of the letter, is not corroborated anywhere:

> One year went by and the Spaniards returned to Mexico, and the Mexicans were strenuously warned not to enter into a war against them, by my father's other sons who were my brothers. Receiving an evil return for their good deed, my brothers were killed by the Mexicans: one was called Tepanecatzintli and the other Tlacatecatzintli.

The names given for Totoquihuatzin's sons here are actually titles in Nahuatl. The heir of Totoquihuatzin as king of Tlacopan was widely identified as Tetlepanquetzatzin (or, inaccurately, as Tetlepanquetzal): Alva Ixtlilxochitl would describe how Tetlepanquetzatzin had formed an alliance against the Spaniards with Cuauhtemoc, Montezuma's successor as leader of the Mexica, and with Cohuanacoch, *tlatoani* of Texcoco.[68] After the fall of Tenochtitlan, the three *tlatoque* were captured by Hernán Cortés. In a letter of 3 September 1526 to Charles V, the Captain explained that he had taken these leaders 'who appeared prone to cause instability or revolt in those regions' with him on his 1524 expedition to Honduras. After receiving intelligence from a native informer that Cuauhtemoc, Cohuanacoch, Tetlepanquetzatzin, and 'a certain Tacatelz' were plotting to kill him and the other Spaniards on the journey,

[64] ZORITA, *Relación* (1585), 'Catálogo de los autores' [1999 i, 112], Part III, 'Proemio' [1999 ii, 413].

[65] Martínez Baracs 2006.

[66] Megged 2010, 184–248 considers indigenous accounts that competed with the 'canonic narratives', although Cortés Totoquihuatzin's fabrication of parallel realities had a strategic purpose.

[67] ALVA IXTLILXOCHITL, *Historia de la nación chichimeca* (1625–1640), cap. 90 [1977 ii, 236]. Gibson 1964a, 171, implies that the *tlatoani* met a violent end ('Totoquihuatzin was killed in the conquest') but gives no source.

[68] *Historia de la nación chichimeca* (1648), cap. 91 [1977 ii, 242–3].

Cortés had Cuauhtemoc and Tetlepanquetzatzin hanged as the instigators.[69] Cortés' letter of 1526 was not printed until the nineteenth century but several early sources tell a similar story, and confirm that Tetlepanquetzatzin was executed with Cuauhtemoc and Cohuanacoch.[70]

The names don Antonio gives for his brothers, Tepanecatzintli and Tlacatecatzintli, have some resemblance to those of the conspirators respectively identified by Hernán Cortés as 'Tetepanqueçal', lord of Tacuba, and 'Tacatelz'.[71] Don Antonio's use of similar-sounding names in the Latin letter enables his revisionist narrative to compete with different accounts without flatly contradicting them. His intention may even have been to bamboozle his reader—the very emperor to whom the conquistador had recounted his version of events twenty-five years before. Alternatively, if Tepanecatzintli and Tlacatecatzintli did exist, the phrase 'alij filij patris mei qui mihi erant fratres', 'my father's *other* sons who were my brothers', would suggest that the elder Totoquihuatzin had had two further sons in addition to Tetlepanquetzatzin. Whatever the truth of the matter may be, it remains the case that Antonio Cortés Totoquihuatzin had a brother who was put to death by the very conquistador from whom he took his own Spanish name.

In seeking an end to the abuses of Juan Cano, Totoquihuatzin's Latin letter was not simply promoting the interests of Indians vis-à-vis the Spaniards, but asserting the distinctive prestige and patrimony of the town of Tlacopan. The closing narrative laid emphasis on the stature of the *altepetl* before the conquest and, more questionably, on its support of the Spaniards against the Mexica, offering a contrast to details presented in other primary sources.

III. Rulers of Azcapotzalco, 'Invictissimo Hispaniarum Regi' to Philip II, 1561

(i) Context and argument of the Latin letter to Philip II

In February 1561 the native principals of Azcapotzalco wrote to Philip II of Spain to secure a number of privileges and exemptions for their town. Although the

[69] CORTÉS, 'Quinta carta' (1526) [1866, 420; tr. 1986, 366]: 'aquel Guateumucin, é Guanacaxín, señor que fué de Tezcuco, y Tetepanqueçal, señor que fué de Tacuba, y un Tacatelz, que á la sazon era en esta ciudad de Méjico en la parte de Tatelulco, habían hablado muchas veces y dado cuenta dello á este Mexicalcingo, que . . . les habia parescido que era buen remedio tener manera como me matasen á mí y á los que conmigo iban . . .' ('This Cuauhtemoc, and Cohuanacoch, who was ruler of Texcoco, and Tetlepanquetzatzin, ruler of Tlacopan, and a certain Tacatelz, who was at the time in the city of Mexico in the Tlatelolco area, had spoken many times recounting to Mexicalcingo that . . . it had seemed to them that the best solution was to arrange to kill me and those travelling with me . . .').

[70] Restall 2003, 147–53 reviews different accounts.

[71] 'Tacatelz' looks like an approximation of *tlacateccatl*, a Nahuatl title for high official: Piho 1972. Hernán Cortés use of Nahuatl names was imprecise, as shown by the quotation in n. 69 above.

illustrations originally sent with the letter have not survived, the document remains a unique source for the history of Azcapotzalco, the seat of the Tepanec empire, which had fallen to the Mexica, nearly a century before the Spaniards arrived in Anahuac (Figure 6.3).[72]

After the formal opening greeting, or *salutatio*, the text was divided into eight parts labelled 'Primum', 'Secundum', 'Tertium', etc. (here and in Appendix 2.4, indicated by [1], [2], [3], etc.):

Salutatio (a) Deliberation: Should Indians dare to address a king?
(b) *Captatio benevolentiae*: The king is kind and ready to hear requests from his subjects.

[1] Account of the constriction of Azcapotzalco's boundaries, as Spanish settlers and the people of Tlacopan have intruded into the town's traditional territory.

[2] The king is asked to issue a seal for the protection and preservation of the town's original boundaries.

[3] Plea for exemption from public building work in Mexico City and from farm labour for the Spaniards.

[4] The issue of the town's frontiers is raised again: in former times the Azcapotzalca used to cut wood and quarry stone anywhere within three days' journey from their town, but are now prohibited from doing so.

[5] History of Azcapotzalco as a great *provincia* under the rule of Tezozomoc, culminating in a plea for the town to have the right to be a *civitas*, 'city state'.

[6] More about Azcapotzalco's heritage, with a request for insignia for the town.

[7] The writers ask for an academy to be established in Azcapotzalco for the teaching of Latin and Spanish.

[8] The final plea is for the town market, *tianquizco*, to be allowed on a second day in the week.

Valedictio beseeching a long life for the king.

The writers point out that their *encomendero*, Francisco de Montejo, was away in Yucatán and no longer able to defend their interests [1]. As Montejo's earlier campaigns in Yucatán had taken the lives of many conscripts from Azcapotzalco, a royal cedula of 28 January 1550 reduced the tribute imposed on the town.[73] The mention of Montejo's name forged an implicit connection to the request for another

[72] The text is in Appendix 2.4. The writers refer in [2] to the pictures, 'picturas', they sent that showed the estates taken by the Spaniards: cf. Mundy 1996 on native paintings and maps in early colonial Mexico.

[73] LANDA, *Relación* (1568) described how Francisco de Montejo the younger (1508–1565) conquered Yucatán. Chuchiak 2007, 221 n. 58 mentions Azcapotzalco's involvement.

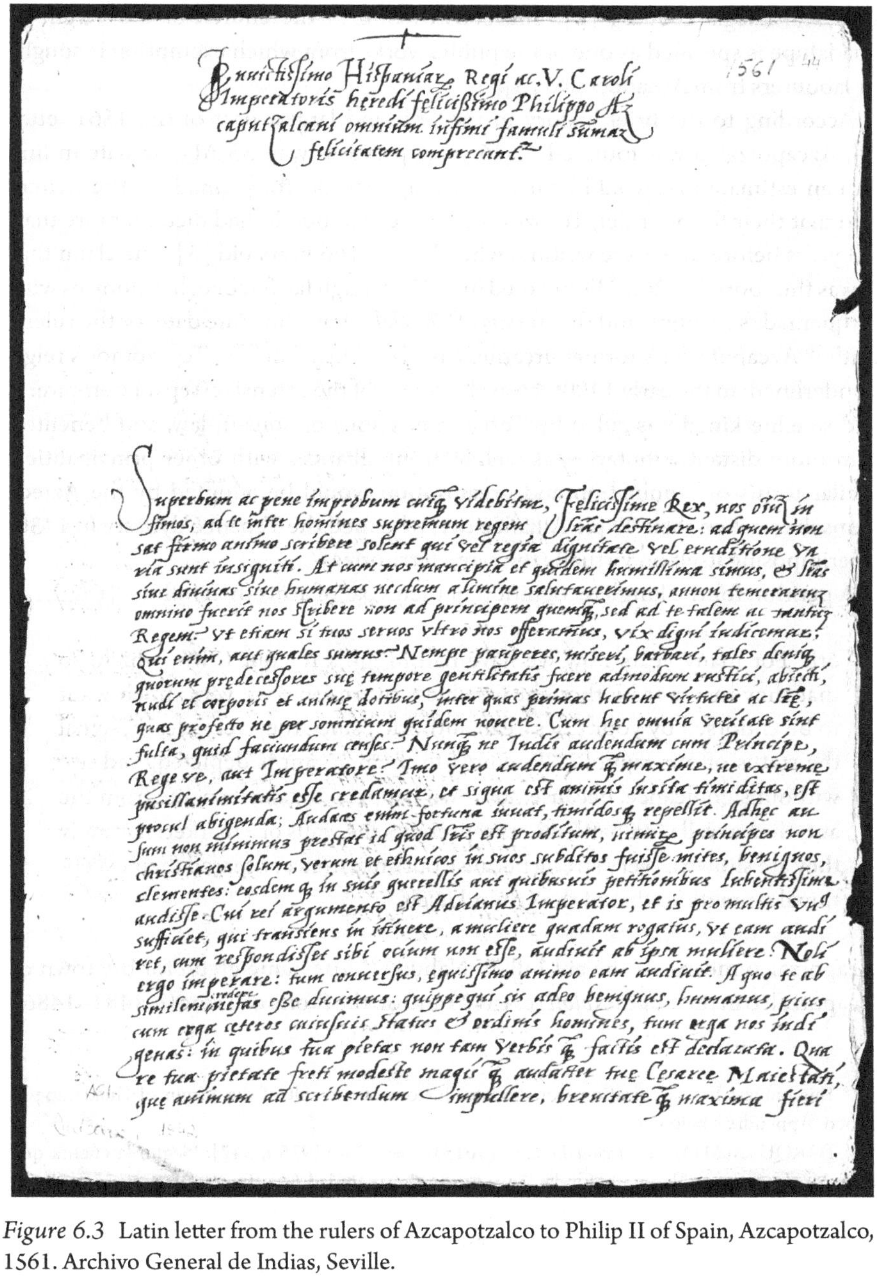
1561 44

Invictissimo Hispaniarum Regi ac V. Caroli
Imperatoris heredi felicissimo Philippo Azcaputzalcani omnium infimi famuli summam
felicitatem comprecantur.

Superbum ac pene improbum cuique videbitur, Felicissime Rex, nos omnium infimos, ad te inter homines supremum regem literas destinare: ad quem non
sat firmo animo scribere solent qui vel regia dignitate vel eruditione varia sunt insigniti. At cum nos mancipia et quidem humillima simus, et literas
sive divinas sive humanas necdum a limine salutaverimus, annon temerarium
omnino fuerit nos scribere non ad principem quemque, sed ad te talem ac tantum
Regem? Ut etiam si tuos servos ultro nos offeramus, vix digni iudicemur?
Qui enim, aut quales sumus? Nempe pauperes, miseri, barbari, tales denique
quorum predecessores sue tempore gentilitatis fuere admodum rustici, abiecti,
nudi et corporis et anime dotibus, inter quas primas habent virtutes ac leges,
quas profecto ne per somnium quidem novere. Cum hec omnia veritate sint
fulta, quid faciundum censes? Nunquamne Indis audendum cum Principe,
Rege ve, aut Imperatore? Imo vero audendum quam maxime, ne extreme
pusillanimitatis esse credamur, et si qua est animis insita timiditas, est
procul abigenda; Audaces enim fortuna iuvat, timidosque repellit. Adhec animum non minimum prestat id quod literis est proditum, nimirum principes non
christianos solum, verum et ethnicos in suos subditos fuisse mites, benignos,
clementes: eosdemque in suis querellis aut quibusuis petitionibus lubentissime
audisse. Cui rei argumento est Adrianus Imperator, et is pro multis unus
sufficiet, qui transiens in itinere, a muliere quadam rogatus, ut eam audiret, cum respondisset sibi ocium non esse, audivit ab ipsa muliere: Noli
ergo imperare: tum conversus, equissimo animo eam audivit. A quo te absimilem credere nefas esse ducimus: quippe qui sis adeo benignus, humanus, pius
cum erga ceteros cuiuscuis status et ordinis homines, tum erga nos Indigenas: in quibus tua pietas non tam verbis quam factis est declarata. Quare tua pietate freti modeste magis quam audacter tue Cesaree Maiestati,
que animum ad scribendum impellere, brevitate quam maxima fieri

Figure 6.3 Latin letter from the rulers of Azcapotzalco to Philip II of Spain, Azcapotzalco, 1561. Archivo General de Indias, Seville.

royal seal ('regia cedula') [2]. The construction of the church of the Virgin of Guadalupe is specified as one of the public works from which exemption is sought for labourers from Azcapotzalco [3].[74]

According to the brief history in the fifth and largest part of the 1561 letter [5], Azcapotzalco was founded 1,526 years previously, in 35 AD—a date in line with an estimate that would be made by Fray Juan de Torquemada.[75] The writers hold that their former ruler, Tezozomoc, or 'Teçoçomoctli', had died no more than 133 years before they were writing, when he was 166 years old [5]. The claim that he was thus born in 1262 AD and died in 1427, though far-fetched, harmonizes with Torquemada's account, and the *Annals of Tlatelolco* give the same date for the ruler's death.[76] Azcapotzalco's former greatness as a 'provincia' during Tezozomoc's reign is underlined: in the early 1400s it was the centre of the extensive Tepanec empire: it held satellite kingdoms ruled by Tezozomoc's sons or sons-in-law, and benefited from more distant tributaries, as well as from alliances with other principalities. Similar forms of domination and organization would be adopted by the Aztecs themselves, when their Triple Alliance overwhelmed the Tepanec dynasty in 1430, superimposing itself on virtually the same territories.[77]

A petition for the king's recognition of their coat of arms then follows [6]:

> 6th. For many years now we have had insignia for our town, which, so that they may not be thought worthless by anyone, we very much want to be endorsed by your Caesarean authority, since they very clearly signal the status of our republic. Foremost in them an ant is depicted, and not without significance, because our town happens to take its name from the ant; then a wall with battlements represents the walls of a market: naturally they are shown as very strong because our ancestors compared their exceptional strength to that of the ground itself.

Azcapotzalco means 'At the ant hill' in Nahuatl.[78] The name glyph for the town of Azcapotzalco in the *Codex Xolotl* (c. 1542) and on the Stone of Tizoc (c. 1481–1486)

[74] This request has ramifications for the later history of the cult of the Virgin of Guadalupe in Mexico: Appendix 3 below.

[75] TORQUEMADA, *Monarchia Indiana* (1615) = *MI*, 3.6 [1975 i, 347]: 'Según la cuenta que tienen los de Azcapotzalco de la fundación y origen de su ciudad (que fue en otros tiempos de las mayores poblazones que hubo en estos reinos) ha mil y quinientos y sesenta y uno años que se fundó.' Torquemada was actually writing c. 1596: Carrasco 1984, 74.

[76] TORQUEMADA, *MI* 3.6 [1975 i, 348]; *Annals of Tlatelolco* (c. 1550) [1980, 55, para. 258]. The convergence with Torquemada may be explained by Valeriano acting as the friar's informant: *MI* 15.43 [1977 v, 176–7], quoted in Chapter 7 below.

[77] Carrasco 1984, 88–9.

[78] MOLINA, *Vocabulario* (1571), 10r: 'Azcaputzalli. Hormiguero' ('ant hill'); 'Azcatl. hormiga' ('ant'). For *-co* as a locative suffix in Nahuatl, cf. n. 105 below.

was an ant, *azcatl*, with four legs.[79] Other components of the desired coat of arms—the market walls, the heart, and the indigenous head-dress 'similar to the mitre worn by bishops'—would later appear in a heraldic emblem for Azcapotzalco in the *Codex Techialoyan García Granados* (Plate 11b).[80] Philip II ceded a coat of arms in 1565, probably in response to this very request: a song in Nahuatl to honour this event was composed by one of the signatories of the 1561 letter, the drummer-poet don Francisco Plácido, who was governor of Xiquipilco.[81]

Philip II's authority is also sought for the foundation of an educational institution in Azcapotzalco [7]:

> We consider it very advantageous for our town to be endowed with a home for the Muses, and we seek from your Caesarean Majesty the resources to enable us to found it in our own town. Although there may be no need for all the sciences to be taught there, instruction in Latin and the Spanish language can certainly be provided by some of us who have frequently taught it as well as the Spaniards have.

This idea for such an academy could well have been inspired by the inauguration of Santa Cruz de Tlatelolco as an 'Imperial College' in 1536, six years after Charles' coronation in Bologna as the Holy Roman Emperor Germanicus Caesar by Pope Clement VII in 1530. The rulers of Azcapotzalco were writing in 1561, six years after Philip II had succeeded Charles to the Spanish throne in 1555. Given the timing of their request for a college, the evocation of Philip's imperial '*Caesarean* Majesty' in this very context may not be coincidental.

After seeking permission for the town's market to be open on a second day in the week [8], the letter ends with a reprise of the *captatio benevolentiae* at its opening, trusting in Philip's clemency, liberality, and Christian faith.

[79] *Codex Xolotl* (c. 1542) [1980, plate 6 E3]; cf. Lockhart 1992, 578, n. 15. Umberger 1998, 251 n. 9 notes a glyph on the Stone of Tizoc depicting an ant hill, with a four-legged ant resembling the Azcapotzalco glyph in the *Codex Xolotl*: see further Whittaker 2021, 168–71.

[80] Glass 1964, 94–5, plate 50. The *Codex Techialoyan García Granados* (1600s) has the glyph for rock (*tetl*), which denoted the Tepaneca in the Azcatitlan, Boturini, and Xolotl codices, either as a logogram, 'people of the rock', or as a phonogram for the first syllable of 'Tepanec': Santamarina Novillo 2007, 74.

[81] *Cantares mexicanos* (1560s–1580s), 41r [1985, 268–73]. The song moves through the Creation, Flood, Incarnation, and Resurrection to end with Azcapotzalco: praise of the poet's patron or locality as the culmination of a broader narrative was common in European panegyrical poetry. A preface naming Valeriano as the town's governor in 1565 could suggest he transcribed Plácido's song: *Cantares mexicanos* [1985, 12]. Plácido's Christmas song in the *Cantares*, 37v–38v [1985, 254–9] was performed in the house of Azcapotzalco's previous governor and confirms Plácido's association with the town.

(ii) Competing accounts of the Tepaneca and Mexica

The writers of the 1561 letter explain that Tenochtitlan had once been one of Azcapotzalco's tributaries [5]:

> So that we might reveal the matter in a few words: when the Mexica had been fought by the Azcapotzalca near the mountain called Chapultepec, on which the former had earlier settled after a long period of wandering, and were now again driven to wander about from one place to another, having no idea where they should choose to live, the said Tezozomoc, taking pity on them, decreed that they could be settled in a part of the region where Tenochtitlan is now. And so the Mexica served our town for eighty years, by making a payment in the place of tribute, of what they were able to gather from the lake: fish, frogs, ducks, and other kinds of aquatic creatures.

Tezozomoc's relaxation of the tribute imposed on the Mexica, with the exception of fauna from the lake, would be recounted, in very similar terms, in two chronicles written later in the sixteenth century. The first was Fray Diego Durán's *Historia de las Indias de Nueva España* (1581):

> Tezozomoc sent his messengers to Mexico to say to the king and the other lords that . . . he was relieving them from the standard tribute they were paying . . . and that from then on they should provide each year two ducks reared in the lake and some fishes and frogs, with other creatures ['con los demas sauandijas'] reared in the lake.[82]

The second was the *Coronica mexicana* (1598), authored by Montezuma's grandson, Hernando de Alvarado Tezozomoc.[83] There the messengers' speech is quoted directly, and Nahuatl words are used to identify the 'other kinds of aquatic creatures' ('aliaque id genus aquatilia') referred to in the Latin letter:

> Tezozomoc sent ambassadors to the Mexica saying to them 'Lords and Mexicans . . . now there will no longer be the burden of tributes and personal services that there was before, except that fish, frogs, and every kind of small fish that is born and reared in the lake, with the *yzcahuitle, tecuitlatl,*

[82] DURÁN, *Historia* (c. 1581) 1.7 [2002 i, 110].

[83] On Alvarado Tezozomoc, see Chapter 9, I below.

> *axaxayacatl, acoçil, anenez, cocolli, michpilli,* only this should the Mexica provide and render to Azcapotzalco . . .'[84]

Durán and Alvarado Tezozomoc are both thought to have derived their knowledge of this episode from the same lost source in Nahuatl, '*Crónica X*', on which their works were based.[85] The appearance of such similar details in the earlier Latin letter indicates that at least one of the traditions attributed to *Crónica X* was circulating by 1561, more than twenty years before Durán was writing.

The account in the letter, however, elides the more complex series of events presented from the Mexica perspective by Durán and Alvarado Tezozomoc. According to both those sources, the Mexica had already established themselves in Tenochtitlan, and Tezozomoc had increased their tribute, before later relaxing it, because the Tepaneca had been concerned about the growing independence of the Mexica. Durán's providential narrative even has Tezozomoc himself declare that the Mexica were the chosen people of Huitzilopochtli and that some day they would 'rule over all the nations'.[86] Unsurprisingly, the Azcapotzalca do not record anything like this: instead they refer to the Mexica settlers who turned on their people as *proditores*, 'traitors' [5].[87]

(iii) Humanist style and Nahuatl idiom

It is not only the historical data yielded by the rulers of Azcapotzalco in their petition that distinguishes it from other such appeals. The text is in remarkably fluent Latin and an accomplished example of Renaissance epistolography. The writers appear to have been familiar with Erasmus' *Opus de conscribendis epistolis* (1522), perhaps because some of its content was reproduced verbatim in Fray Maturino Gilberti's *Grammatica Maturini* (1559), which had been written and published in Mexico.[88] Erasmus favoured succinct expression in letters, along with an arrangement (*dispositio*) suited to the contents, refined Latin diction, and the adroit use of commonplaces and *exempla* to win over the reader. The writers of the 1561 letter draw attention to their recognition of the importance of clarity and brevity:

> So then, relying on that piety of yours, more modestly than boldly, we shall set out for your Caesarean Majesty, in the greatest brevity possible, what incited our desire to write, all of which will be assembled in order so that

[84] ALVARADO TEZOZOMOC, *Coronica mexicana* (1598), cap. 7 [2001, 67–8].

[85] Barlow 1945b first postulated *Crónica X* as the common source for Durán and Alvarado Tezozomoc; Peperstraete 2007 is a reconstruction.

[86] DURÁN, *Historia* (1581) 1.6 [2002 i, 102].

[87] Cf. Megged 2010 cited in n. 66 above.

[88] Cf. Chapter 2, I above on the popularity of Erasmus' recommendations.

> the things we are trying to obtain from your clemency can be clearly and distinctly discerned. [1]

Again, in the final *Valedictio* it is remarked that the epistle should not 'exceed the appropriate limit or "go beyond the pale", as the expression goes' ('Ne vero modum seu septa ut dicitur epistola transiliat'). At just over two thousand words, the length is in line with Erasmus' precept that the greatest amount of material be conveyed in the fewest words possible. While older humanist manuals on letter writing had recommended a classical structure (*salutatio, captatio benevolentiae, narratio, petitio, conclusio*), Erasmus and his associate Juan Luis Vives proposed that, after the opening *salutatio* or greeting, the main argument could be devised as the subject required.[89] In their *salutatio* to Philip II, the Azcapotzalca adopted the latter strategy: the greeting moves on to a deliberation about whether the writers should even be addressing the king and culminates in a persuasive anticipation of his kindness and mercy, making an effective transition to the eight concerns that shape the rest of the letter.

As well as displaying a remarkable richness of expression, the Latin is precise and idiomatic.[90] Classical terms are used to designate categories and institutions in New Spain: 'senatus' [4] and 'senatores' [1] respectively denote the Audiencia and its *oidores*; and 'vectigales' [5] are *terrazgueros*, or payers of tribute. The Azcapotzalca ask for their 'oppidum', i.e. *pueblo*, to be elevated to the status of a 'civitas', city state [5], and Tezozomoc's domain at its apogee is tactfully referred to not as an *imperium*, but as a 'provincia', the Roman term for a part of an empire. On the other hand, 'com[m]endatarius' [1], which thrice serves as a translation for the Spanish *encomendero*, is barely attested in classical Latin. As a word in Christian canon law for someone who held an ecclesiastical benefice *in commendam* ('in trust'), 'commendatarius' is a reasonable approximation for *encomendero*—the same term had been used in Cortés Totoquihuatzin's Latin petition. The word 'chirographum' in the request to the king for a royal seal 'fortified in handwriting' ('chyrographo munita') [3] is a classical expression for a written pledge or authentication.[91]

There is recurrent emphasis throughout this petition on the value of 'litterae', or letters. At the very opening of their appeal, the rulers of Azcapotzalco introduce themselves as 'vassals . . . who have not even touched upon letters, whether divine

89 For Erasmus and Vives on structure cf. n. 30 above.

90 Roland Mayer has pointed out to me the *variatio* employed in the various requests: 'digneris', 'may you think it right to' [1]; 'summopere contendimus', 'we earnestly entreat' [2]; 'suppliciter petimus', 'we humbly beseech'; 'suplicamus [*sic*] terq*ue* quaterq*ue*', 'we beg once and again' [3]; 'submisse postulamus', 'we humbly ask' [4]; 'maxime volumus', 'we very much want' [6]; 'expetimus', 'we seek' [7]; 'testamur atque obsecramur', 'we call upon and entreat' [8].

91 *Chirographum*, the Latin equivalent of the Greek χειρόγραφον, had that sense in Cicero (*Ad Atticum* 2.20.5; *Philippics* 2.4.8) but later acquired the same meaning of 'bond' or 'record of a debt' in Roman law (*Digest* 20.7.57) as it had in patristic Greek: Lampe 1961, 1522.

or human', and they maintain that illiteracy was to blame for the primitive condition of their ancestors.[92] Fray Julián Garcés had already noted that predicament of the Indians in New Spain before the arrival of the Spaniards, echoing Antonio de Nebrija's affirmation that letters were necessary to adorn human life.[93] The request of the Azcapotzalca for an academy where Latin could be taught in their town also presents knowledge of *litterae* as a means by which 'the hearts of Christians are greatly strengthened in the faith' [7].

Commonplaces from ancient Roman authors are used strategically in the 1561 letter. The opening deliberation about whether it is appropriate for the Indian subjects to address their king is the first example:

> Should Indians never dare to speak with a prince, king or emperor? On the contrary, we must so dare to the utmost, in order not to be believed cowardly in the extreme—and if there is any timidity ingrained in our mind we should drive it far away, since 'Fortune helps the bold and drives back the fearful.'

'Audentes fortuna iuvat' ('fortune helps the bold') was a popular adage, from an incomplete verse of Virgil's *Aeneid*. The phrase 'timidosque repellit' ('and drives back the fearful'), which is found here, was often added by later authors to make up the hexameter.[94] Hernán Cortés had echoed the Virgilian formula in Spanish in the letter he originally wrote to the Emperor in October 1520.[95] In the sentence following this quotation, the Azcapotzalca invoke *litterae* again, this time in the sense of 'literature'. It is classical literature that supplies them with a sustained *exemplum* to illustrate their own boldness, and to guide the king's response to their suit:

> Daring things like this is very well supported by what is shown in literature: there is no doubt that not only Christian princes but pagan ones, too, have been lenient, kind, and merciful to their own subjects, and they have been very willing to hear their complaints or suits of every kind. The emperor Hadrian is proof of this principle and this one figure will serve

[92] This passage is quoted in Chapter 5, V above.

[93] NEBRIJA, *Comiença la gramatica* (1492) 1.2: 'para polir e adornar la vida umana: ninguna otra fue tan necessaria . . . que la invencion delas letras' ('nothing was so necessary as the discovery of letters to adorn human existence'); GARCÉS, *De habilitate* (1537), 5r (Appendix 2.1 below): '[nullis] aliisque humanae vitae ornamentis praediti, nullo literarum commertio' ('They have had no other adornments of human existence, no dealings with letters').

[94] Virgil, *Aeneid* 10.284; The apocryphal Latin verse was supposedly quoted by Pedro Alonso Casco, the mutineer on Lope de Aguirre's ill-fated Amazon expedition of 1560: Simón 1942, 68.

[95] CORTÉS, 'Segunda carta-relación' (1520) [1866, 142; tr. 1986, 145]. 'La fortuna ayuda a los osados' became proverbial in Spanish, as it had been used in the first act of Fernando de Rojas' *La Celestina* (1499).

> for many. On a journey he was making, he was asked by a certain woman to hear her: when he replied that he did not have time, he heard that very woman say 'In that case, do not be an emperor'. At that he was moved to hear her very readily.

The inclusion of this episode is remarkable because it was not in the standard Roman life of Hadrian that had circulated in the *Scriptores historiae Augustae* since the late Middle Ages.[96] The story is told, however, by the Greek historian Cassius Dio, whose biographies of the emperors supplemented a popular edition of Suetonius' *Lives of the Caesars* annotated by Erasmus of Rotterdam and Giovanni Battista Egnazio.[97] The anecdote found in the 1561 letter was probably gleaned from that volume which was first printed in 1546.[98]

Whatever led the rulers of Azcapotzalco to this *exemplum*, they deploy it to good effect. It could be a cautionary tale for the king: the woman's reprimand to the Emperor could potentially be levied at any monarch who does not respond to his petitioners. The invocation of Hadrian as a model for Philip II is appropriate, as he was one of the Roman emperors who was born in Spain.[99] A preoccupation with Iberia's classical past might even explain why the Azcapotzalca refer to the academy of Latin that they want to establish as a *Musarum domus*, 'home for the Muses' [7]—a distinctive expression coined by the classical poet Silius Italicus, who was widely believed to have been of Spanish origin.[100] The request for the establishment of an academy was introduced with an adage [7]:

> The following divine oracle is not at all obscure to us: 'Wisdom steadies the heart, giving it weight against the winds' ['Sapientia cor stabilit ventis

[96] Marshall 1983. In medieval and Renaissance Europe this story was far more often told about the emperor Trajan: cf. Paris 1878; Boni 1906. Singleton 1973, 210 identifies Vincent of Beauvais' *Speculum historiale* as the ultimate source for Dante's inclusion of the episode in *Purgatorio* 10.73–93.

[97] ERASMUS and EGNATIUS, *Vitae Caesarum quarum scriptores hi C. Svetonius Tranquillus, Dion Cassius* (1546). Many copies were printed and a second edition appeared in 1551.

[98] A Latin translation of Dio's lives of Nerva, Trajan, and Hadrian had appeared in an edition of Censorinus: MERULA, *Censorini de die natali* (1503). Giorgio Merula also published Joannes Xiphilinus' eleventh-century epitome of Dio in *Scriptores historiae Augustae* (MERULA 1519, MERULA 1521) from an edition of 1516, with Erasmus' annotations from a similar title printed in Basel in 1518. STEPHANUS, *Dionis Nicaei . . . epitome* (1551) was an *editio princeps* of Xiphilinus (1551). These texts were unlikely to have reached New Spain, but GUEVARA, *Una década de Cesares* (1539) included a life of Hadrian.

[99] Cf. n. 31 above and Introduction above, nn. 13–15 on Spain's emulation of Rome.

[100] 'Musarum aedes', 'temple of the Muses', is much more common in classical Latin, but *aedes*, 'temple', had pagan connotations. LIPSIUS, *De constantia* (1584) 2.3 used 'musarum mihi domus', 'my Muses' home', of his study; Silius Italicus, *Punica* 8.595 is the only instance of 'musarum domus' in Roman literature. GARCÉS, *De habilitate* (1537), 5r (Appendix 2.1 below) believed Silius was a Spaniard: cf. Chapter 1, p. 36 above.

> pondus ponit']. From this it is rendered very clear to all, that the hearts of Christians are greatly strengthened in the faith through knowledge of letters, and that those who were at one time buffeted by the winds of paganism now have anchorage in their Christianity.

The phrase '[God] who made a weight for the winds' ('qui fecit ventis pondus') is found in the Book of Job (28: 25), although the 'divine oracle' quoted here may conceivably have originated in a Nahuatl expression.[101]

Finally, in their closing *valedictio*, the rulers of Azcapotzalco use a couple of classical commonplaces to emphasize their lowly standing:

> The poverty and worthlessness of us all does not at all dissuade us [from our petition]; though we are poorer than Irus and more worthless than seaweed ['licet Iro pauperiores atque alga viliores'], we are nonetheless loyal servants of your holy Catholic Caesarean Majesty.

The poverty of Irus, an itinerant beggar in Homer's *Odyssey*, was proverbial.[102] A shepherd in Virgil's *Eclogues* claims he would be 'more worthless than seaweed' ('vilior alga') if he were not telling the truth, and a satire by Horace has the hero Ulysses remark that breeding or virtue without wealth is, again, 'vilior alga'.[103] Both the comparison with seaweed and the *exemplum* of Irus were adopted by early modern authors, who normally used them to disparage others.

The extravagant humility shown at the end of the letter is in keeping with the abject manner of the writers' opening *salutatio* to Philip II, which is comparable to that in Antonio Cortés Totoquihuatzin's letter to the Emperor Charles discussed above. The self-abasement of the Azcapotzalca here, though, is more protracted:

> It will seem to anyone proud, if not ill judged, that we, the most lowly of all, are sending a letter to you, the supreme king among men, to whom even those endowed with royal rank or a range of erudition do not write in too confident a spirit. But as we are vassals and indeed of the most insignificant sort . . . is it not altogether rash for us to write to any prince, let alone to a

[101] SAHAGÚN, *HG* 6.17 [1969 vii, 89, 91–2], recording an admonitory speech in Nahuatl from a ruler to his sons, has the expressions 'wherever my heart goeth, it sinketh, it riseth' ('in canin nemi noiollo, in temo in tleco') and 'do not rise up, do not blow as a violent wind against one' ('ma tevic teoa, ma titehecavitivetz'); cf. *HG* 6.2, 6.9 [1969 vii, 7–10, 41–5], prayers to Tezcatlipoca for a calm temperament in adverse conditions.

[102] Homer, *Odyssey* 18.1–116; Ovid, *Tristia* 3.7.42: 'Irus et est subito, qui modo Croesus erat', 'And one who was as rich as Croesus is suddenly Irus'; ERASMUS, *Adagia* (1508) 1.6.76: 'Iro pauperior', 'poorer than Irus'. GILBERTI, *Grammatica* (1559), 157v [2003 ii, 666] copied Erasmus: 'Opes? At vel Iro ipso pauperiores', 'Wealth? You are even poorer than Irus!'

[103] Virgil, *Eclogues* 7.42; Horace, *Satires* 2.5.8.

> king such as yourself, so great, that even if we offer ourselves as your slaves of our own accord we may scarcely be judged worthy?

It has already been noted that such a servile tone could be explained by the courtly style of speech that Mexican nobles used to express themselves in formal contexts in their own language. That tone is sustained in the ensuing sentence—'Who, then, or what are we? Nothing but paupers, wretches, barbarians . . .' ('qui enim aut quales sumus? Nempe pauperes, miseri, barbari')—which looks strikingly similar to the opening of the speech of the Aztec 'priest of the idols' in Sahagún's *Colloquios y Doctrina christiana* (cf. Chapter 5 above, Appendix 2.6) and they resemble the Nahuatl version of the *Colloquios* even more closely than the original Spanish (presented in Appendix 2.6):

> mach titlatin? ca çan timacevaltonti, titlalloque, tiçoquiyoque, tivaço[n]que titoxonque, ticocoque, titeuhpouhque, ca çan otech tlaneuj, in tlacatl totecujo inic ipetlanacazco, ycpalnacazco otech motlalili?[104]
>
> Are we perchance something? Since we are only the poor class of the people, we are full of earth, we are of mud, we are ragged, we are wretched, we are afflicted, we are sorrowful; indeed the man, our lord, only lent us the corner of his reed mat and the corner of his seat [where] he placed us.

The position and sense of the words 'mach titlatin?', 'Are we perchance something?,' parallel those of the rhetorical question 'qui enim aut quales sumus?' with which the authors of the letter introduce themselves. The sequence of idioms in Nahuatl—'we are only the poor class of the people, we are of earth, we are of mud'—matched the Latin writers' claim to be 'pauperes, miseri, barbari'. Again, like the principals of Azcapotzalco who signed themselves with their Spanish titles of 'governor,' 'mayor,' or 'ruler,' the Aztec priests' characterization of themselves as 'the poor class of the people' and as 'ragged' stood in contrast to their actually exalted social position and fine attire: Sahagún called them 'sátrapes', 'satraps', which was rendered as 'quequetzalcoa', 'feathered serpents', in the Nahuatl version.

Throughout the 1561 letter, places are called by their indigenous names and not the Spanish approximations: 'Quauhnauac' [5] is used instead of Cuernavaca; 'tianquizco' is introduced as a term for market, 'mercatum' [8]; and the etymologies for both Azcapotzalco [6] and Tlatelolco [5] are given too.[105] There are, in addition, a couple of occasions on which Nahuatl idioms or categories could be behind some Latin expressions used in the text. The phrase 'atque ut rem paucis aperiamus', 'and so

[104] SAHAGÚN, *Colloquios* (1564), 35v (Appendix 2.6, Section A below).

[105] *Quauhnahuac,* 'place near the trees', cf. Lockhart 2001, 23; *tianquizco* 'at the market place', cf. Karttunen 1992, 240; *Tlatelolco,* 'at the earth mound', cf. MOLINA, *Vocabulario* (1571), 134v: 'Tlatelli, altoçano, o montón de tierra grande' ('hillock, or big mountain of earth'). Compare Karttunen 1992, 35 and n. 78 above on 'Azcapotzalco'.

that we might reveal the matter in a few words', [5] comes at a crucial juncture, prior to an account of how the Azcapotzalca brought about the settlement of Tenochtitlan by the Mexica. Comparable usages can be found in classical and Renaissance texts, but a similar formula—again to signal the importance of the argument to follow—is found in the Nahuatl passage of Sahagún's *Colloquios y Doctrina christiana* referred to above.[106] Secondly, the image of the heart as the 'vitae fons et origo', 'the fount and origin of life', on the coat of arms proposed for Azcapotzalco could derive from pre-Hispanic tradition or from classical Galenic medicine.[107] The organ symbolizes the town's role as 'the origin of all the nobility that has been scattered among the peoples of New Spain' [6].

In addition, the style of dating employed at the end of the letter may have had a special significance:

> Written in Azcapotzalco on the fourth day before the Ides of February in the true year, the one thousand five hundred and sixty-first from Christ's birth.

The Roman style for the day of the month, common in humanist correspondence, is conjoined with the standard manner of indicating the Christian year. But the addition of the word 'true' ('vero') to this conventional formula to characterize the year could allude to systems of annual reckoning that are *not* true.[108] That implicit disavowal of pre-Hispanic chronology is still a subtle reminder that such chronology existed.

Finally, the first-person plural used throughout is common in Nahuatl petitions, chronicles, and other kinds of discourse, but it is less regular in classical or Renaissance Latin epistolography: the choral 'we' form here might therefore be functioning as a marker of hybridity.[109] The *valedictio* at the end, though, contains

[106] SAHAGÚN, *Colloquios* (1564), 35v: 'in axcan achitzin ic tictlapoa in itop iniipetlacal' ('now we will open the coffer [the chest and the basket] a little'); cf. Appendix 2.6, Section A below. Karttunen 1992, 293 gives 'recitation' for *tlapohuiliztli*, but MOLINA, *Vocabulario* (1571), 132v glosses *Tlapouiliztli* as 'desatadura o abertura de puerta o de carta' ('unfastening or opening a door or letter'). Cf. 'rem aperio' in Petrarch, *Epistolae familiares* 4.1. *Aperio*, 'open', has the sense of 'to make known or clear by words': *Oxford Latin Dictionary* 1996, 146.

[107] The heart was seen as the source of vitality in medicine after Plato: cf. Singer 1997, xi–xii and Wear 1995 on Galenic theories of the circulation of blood. SAHAGÚN, *HG* 10.27 [1961 xi, 130–1]: 'Toiollo . . . teiolotia, tenemjtia' ('Our heart . . . makes one live, sustains one'). *Yollotl*, 'heart', is related to *yoli*, 'live', 'come to life': the diphrasis *in ixtli in yollotl*, 'face and heart', signifies both the distinguishing characteristics and living essence of an individual: Karttunen and Lockhart 1987, 54–5; León-Portilla 1956, 190–1.

[108] Forms of dating in ERASMUS, *Opus de conscribendis epistolis* (1522) [1971: 298–300] were reproduced in GILBERTI, *Grammatica* (1559) [2003 ii, 608].

[109] Other examples include: letters to Philip II in Nahuatl from Esteban de Guzmán and from Pedro de Montezuma (1554) [Zimmermann 1970, 15–16], and in Spanish from nobles of Xochimilco (1563)

an exceptional use of the first-person singular before a prompt reversion to the first-person plural:

> And so that this letter may not go beyond the appropriate measure or 'go beyond the pale', as the expression goes, may it come to an end here, *once I have added* ['subiecero'] that there had been a resolve to send *two of us* ['duos ex nobis'] to Spain so that they might represent these concerns, but this was not permitted by the Viceroy nor did *we want* ['voluimus'] to cause any further trouble with this matter, because *we knew* ['sciremus'] you were equally unwilling too.

As well as being the only first-person singular form in the entire text, the future perfect 'subiecero', 'once I have added', has a performative role because the proposition to be added is made in the very same sentence.[110] By making a remark in the letter about the letter, the writer momentarily highlights his existence as an individual and his control over what has been written ('may it come to an end here')—before he rejoins the plurality of 'azcaputzalcani' whose collective sentiments have been generally expressed throughout. The single author's subtle signalling of his presence could hint that he alone is responsible for the composition.

(iv) Antonio Valeriano as author of the Azcapotzalco letter

It remains to establish the identity of that individual author. The names of the signatories with their titles (in Spanish) are on the final folio. After the two governors, don Hernando de Molina and don Baltasar Hernandez, and the *alcaldes*, Pedro Zacharias and Pedro Dionisio, Antonio Valeriano's name is next to that of the poet Francisco Plácido (Figure 6.4), in the third of five lines of signatures. Valeriano's signature therefore appears above several other native rulers of rank, including four *regidores*, although at the time this letter was written he held no formal title.[111] His proficiency in Latin, though, which was already renowned, makes it more than likely that he was the writer, and a couple of the sources reviewed below strengthen the case for this suggestion.

In 1554 Francisco Cervantes de Salazar was the first to commend in print Valeriano's skill in Latin and eloquence, stating that he taught at the College of Santa

[Restall, Sousa and Terraciano 2005, 64–71]; *Cantares mexicanos* (1560s–1580s); and the *Annals of Tlatelolco* (c. 1550). Erasmus (cf. n. 108 above) opposed using the first-person plural in normal letters, but this was not recalled in GILBERTI, *Grammatica* (1559) [2003 ii, 652].

[110] Austin 1971 distinguishes 'constative utterances', which describe things, from 'performative utterances', which bring things about: cf. Quintilian, *Institutio oratoria* 12.10.43.

[111] Later in 1576, as governor of Tenochtitlan, Valeriano signed himself 'Don Ant[oni]o Valeriano, g[obernad]or' in a Spanish letter to Philip II: León-Portilla 2015.

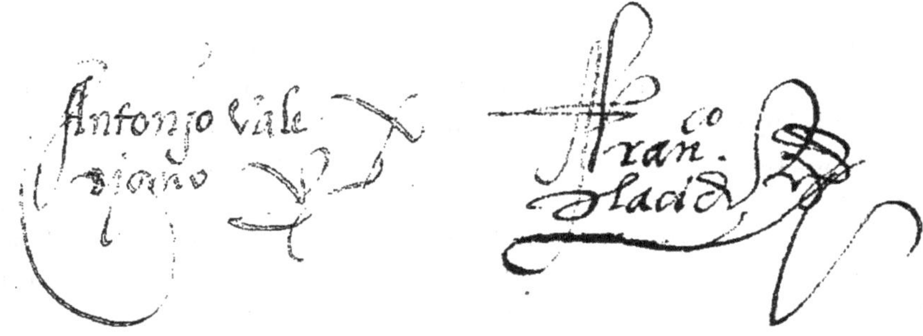

Figure 6.4 Letter from the rulers of Azcapotzalco, 1561: signatures of Antonio Valeriano and Francisco Plácido. Archivo General de Indias, Seville.

Cruz.[112] The Nahuatl *Chronica Mexicayotl* even implied that Valeriano's capacity for Latin, rather than his ancestry, accounted for his marriage to doña Isabel, daughter of don Diego de Alvarado Huanitzin, king of Tenochtitlan, and Montezuma II's daughter doña Francisca. The writer states that Valeriano was 'not noble' ('amopilli') and 'only a collegial student of Latin speech' ('zan hueymomachtiani Colegial Latin tlatolli').[113] In fact, Valeriano was descended from an eminent line of pre-Hispanic 'huei tlatoque' or 'great rulers': his father was don Francisco Alvarado de Matlaccohuatl of Azcapotzalco, son of Tezozomoc Acolnahuacatl and brother of Montezuma II.[114]

Fray Bernardino de Sahagún credited Valeriano with being the 'principal and most learned' of his Latinate collaborators on the production of his *Historia general*, which was compiled in Nahuatl through the mid-1500s and translated into Spanish in the 1570s.[115] Sahagún had already acknowledged Valeriano's help in rendering the *Colloquios y Doctrina christiana* (1564) from Spanish 'into a very suitable and polished Mexican idiom' ('en lengua mexicana bien congrua y limada'). 'Antonio Valeriano, resident of Azcapotzalco' was the first of four students named in the same

[112] CERVANTES DE SALAZAR, *Dialogi* (1554), 267r, quoted in Chapter 4, III (i) above.

[113] ALVARADO TEZOZOMOC, *Chronica Mexicayotl* (1609) [1998, 171, cf. 176]: these comments lend weight to the case that Alvarado Tezozomoc, not Chimalpahin, wrote at least this part of the *Chronica Mexicayotl* (cf. Chapter 9, II below). As Alvarado Tezozomoc's father was don Diego de Alvarado Huanitzin and his maternal grandfather was Montezuma II, each a *tlatoani* of Tenochtitlan, he was better placed than Chimalpahin to disparage Valeriano's illustrious ancestry as 'not noble', even if this characterization was unjustified: cf. Appendix 1.5 and n. 114 below.

[114] Castañeda de la Paz 2013, 275–9 notes an affirmation (AGN-V 110, exp. 2, 338v–339r) by Antonio Valeriano's grandson (of the same name) that his great-grandfather was Francisco Alvarado de Matlaccohuatl, brother of Montezuma II: CHIMALPAHIN, *Relaciones* 7 (c. 1630), 199v [1998 ii, 183]. For the genealogy see Appendix 1.5.

[115] SAHAGÚN, *HG*, Book 2, Prologue [1982 i, 55]: 'y en todos estos escrutinjos, vuo gramaticos colegiales. El principal y mas sabio, fue antonjo valeriano, vezino de azcaputzalco'; cf. Chapter 8, p. 293 and Appendix 1.4(c) below.

preface who were 'the most capable and knowledgeable in the Mexican language and in the Latin language who up to now have been raised in this College'.[116]

The fullest testimony of the native scholar's capacity for composition in Latin was provided by Fray Juan Bautista, who described Valeriano as 'one of the greatest Latinists and rhetoricians to come out of [the College of Santa Cruz] . . . he spoke [Latin] *ex tempore* with such precision and elegance that he seemed like a Cicero or Quintilian'.[117] To prove his point, Bautista reproduced in full the last of many letters he had received from him. That text was long believed to be the only existing example of Latin writing by Valeriano.[118] The following excerpt contains several features of interest:

> & his litteris tam male formatis simul & ignoscas: illiturae enim videntur potius quam litterae. Nec mirum vestrae paternitati videatur: manus n[amque] iam vacillant: oculi caligant, & aures occlusae. Iterum atque iterum parcas. Deus optimus maximus longaeuam tuae paternitati vitam concedat.
>
> And [may you] overlook these badly formed letters: indeed they look more like litterings than letters. And that should seem no wonder to Your Paternity: as my hands now quiver, my eyes grow dim and my ears are blocked. Again and again pardon. May God the Best and Greatest grant a long life to Your Paternity.

Valeriano had probably written, or had meant to write, *liturae*, 'blots'—but *illiturae*, a word that cannot be construed (and is here translated loosely as 'litterings') was transmitted by Bautista.[119] The likely play on *liturae* and *litterae* originated in Ovid's image of an epistle blotted with tears: '*littera* suffusas quod habet maculosa *lituras*' (*Tristia* 3.1.15). *Tristia* 3.1 was among the examples of Ovid's exile poetry that were recommended as models for students composing Latin verse—in New Spain as

[116] SAHAGÚN, *Colloquios* (1564), 27v [1986, 75]: 'mas habiles y entendidos en lengua mexicana y en la lengua latina que hasta agora se an en el dicho colegio criado'. Valeriano's involvement in the *Colloquios* may account for the resemblance noted above between the excerpt from the Nahuatl text and the *salutatio* of the Latin letter. The other Latinists are listed in Appendix 1.4(c).

[117] BAUTISTA, *Sermonario* (1606), Prologue [1954, 475]: 'uno delos mejores latinos, y rethoricos que del salieron . . . y fue tan gran latino, que hablaua ex tempore con tanta propriedad, y elegancia, que parecia vn Ciceron, o Quintiliano.' Comparison to the Roman orators was conventional: cf. GARCÉS and ZUMÁRRAGA, 'Carta . . . a un noble señor' (1529) and LÓPEZ, 'Carta . . . al emperador' (1541), respectively quoted in Chapters 1 and 4 above.

[118] Valeriano, 'Hic gerulus litterarum' (c. 1600): Appendix 2.7; see Chapter 5, II above for the earlier section of this letter and on Bautista's Prologue.

[119] *Illiturae* 'about to soil' (translated above as 'litterings' to parallel the assonance with *litterae*) is a future participle from *illino*, 'besmirch with mud'. EGUIARA Y EGUREN, *Bibliotheca Mexicana* (1755), 290; Beristaín y Souza 1883 ii, 84; and Osorio Romero 1990, xxv retained Bautista's reading.

well as in Europe—during the 1500s.[120] The verse had inspired similar puns in Latin by Erasmus, and in English, by his associate John Colet, the founder of St Paul's School in London, who disparaged writing that 'ratheyr may be called *blotterature* thenne *litterature*'.[121] Thus reconstructed, Valeriano's sentence would end thus:

> his litteris tam malè formatis simul & ignoscas: liturae enim videntur potius quam litterae.
>
> May you overlook these badly formed letters: indeed they look more like blots than letters.

The ink blots would be a consequence of the trembling and diminishing vision that are described in the next sentence.

The symptoms of old age listed—shaking hands, dimming eyes, and blocked ears—echo specific phrases from a medieval treatise by Pope Innocent III, *De miseria conditionis humanae* (c. 1196):

> If anyone has proceeded to old age, . . . his eyes grow dim and joints quiver . . . , and his ears go deaf.[122]

Manuscripts of that text abounded in European monasteries, and Bishop Zumárraga's own copy of the 1540 edition of Innocent's works may have passed to the Imperial College library at Tlatelolco.[123]

The idea of longevity leads to Valeriano's closing farewell to Bautista:

> Deus Optimus Maximus longaevam tuae Paternitati vitam concedat.
>
> May God the Best and Greatest grant a long life to Your Paternity.

The writer here applies the traditional epithet of Jupiter to the Christian God in his farewell—exactly as it was applied some years before, in the 1561 letter from the rulers of Azcapotzalco to Philip II:

[120] *Tristia* 3.1 was in the first anthology of classical verse printed in New Spain, the anonymous *Tam de Tristibus quam de Ponticis* (1577), 23v–25r. Cf. Chapter 4, III n. 90 above.

[121] Valeriano could be recalling 'illiterata literatorum turba', 'an illiterate horde of literates', from ERASMUS, *Opus de conscribendis epistolis* (1522) [1971, 211]. Lupton 1909, 280 quotes Colet's 1509 statutes for St Paul's.

[122] INNOCENT III, *De miseria* (c. 1196) [1855, col. 706]: 'Si quis autem ad senectutem processerit, . . . caligant oculi et vacillant articuli . . . , et aures surdescunt.' This is the text recalled by Valeriano above, not the erotic motif of Catullus 51 or Lucretius 3.152–9: *pace* Gil 1990, 122 n. 75.

[123] Cf. Moore 1981 on the diffusion of the *De miseria*: the text was included in the printed edition of INNOCENT III, *De sacro altaris mysterio* (1540) which circulated in Mexico: Mathes 1982: 25, 94; Yhmoff Cabrera 1996 ii, 154.

a Deo Optimo Maximo tuae Caesareae Maiestati precamur vitam longaevam,

we beseech from God, the Best and Greatest, a long life for your Caesarean Majesty

That similarity, along with the recurrent preoccupation with *litterae*, strongly suggests that the short letter to Bautista and the petition from Azcapotzalco were by the same author.

Fray Juan de Torquemada included a detailed account of Valeriano's life and achievements in his *Monarchia Indiana*, remarking that 'since he was a man of very great talent, the king took notice of him and wrote him a very favourable letter, offering many kindnesses'.[124] Torquemada also mentioned the coat of arms Philip II conferred on Azcapotzalco, in response to the 1561 letter discussed in this chapter. Valeriano served as a judge, and then as a governor in Mexico City for more than thirty years before his death in August 1605. The *Codex Aubin* recorded the appointment of 'Vareliano' [*sic*] as judge of Tenochtitlan, from 18 January 1573.[125] The illustration (Plate 12b) accompanying that information shows him sitting on a throne in the manner of a *tlatoani* wearing a turquoise *xiuhuitzolli*, the headdress compared to a mitre in his 1561 letter [6], but he is holding a Spanish staff of office. A glyph above the throne has the three-pronged symbol for water, *atl*, below the image of a bird, *tototl*: these terms contain the phonetic values, *a-* and *to-*, that combine to convey the name 'Anton'.[126]

Antonio Valeriano is more renowned as the alleged author of the 'Nican mopohua', a Nahuatl narrative about the apparitions and miracles of the Virgin of Guadalupe, than he is for his actual role in the production of Sahagún's *Florentine Codex* and *Colloquios y Doctrina christiana*.[127] But as well as assisting with the translation of Christian texts into Nahuatl under the direction of Fray Juan Bautista and other Franciscans, the native noble from Azcapotzalco made a substantial contribution to civic life in sixteenth-century New Spain as a judge and as governor in Mexico City.[128] The two surviving letters Valeriano penned in Latin are

[124] TORQUEMADA, *MI* 15.43 [1977 v, 176–7], quoted in Chapter 7 below; an earlier notice of Valeriano was in *MI* 5.10 [1975 ii, 361].

[125] *Codex Aubin* (c. 1576–1608), 58v. Nahuatl has no 'r', but some Spanish writers sometimes also confused 'r' with 'l': Lockhart 2001, 119.

[126] Lacadena and Wichman 2008, 14; Whittaker 2009, 69; 2021, 201. The same glyph appears in another portrait of Valeriano in the *Codex Aubin* (c. 1576–1608), 78v.

[127] Appendix 3 below offers evidence against Valeriano's involvement in the 'Nican mopohua' published in LASO DE LA VEGA, *Huei tlamahuiçoltica* (1649). Karttunen 1995, SilverMoon 2007, and Tavárez 2013b consider Valeriano's role as a scholar and translator.

[128] Valeriano's importance as a political leader is attested by his 1575 letter in Spanish to Philip II (n. 111 above) and other documents: cf. Connell 2011, and Mundy 2015, 190–2, 202–8 who highlights

modest achievements in comparison but they exhibit a sensibility and tact appropriate for a statesman who was successful in mediating between Spanish and native communities, as well as a depth of Latin culture that matches the writer's abilities as a translator of Nahuatl.[129]

IV. Conclusions

The sources examined in this chapter offer valuable insights on the origins and governance of Tula, Tlacopan, and Azcapotzalco, showing how disputes between competing native groups for control and territory during the early colonial period were often rooted in historical pre-Cortesian rivalries. These Latin documents also offer a fresh perspective on many better-known histories and chronicles that demonstrate the enduring importance of both lineage and the *altepetl* for the indigenous nobility under Spanish rule. The native rulers who wrote to the crown naturally sought to affirm the historic renown of their polities in the hope of sustaining, or increasing, the economic security of the communities they ruled. At the same time, requests for coats of arms indicate that a desire for recognition of their symbolic standing was in play as well.

Given that Castilian had long been the prevalent language for official documents and communications to the Spanish crown, it remains to consider why the texts surveyed in this chapter, each of which addressed questions of critical importance, were composed in Latin. The most likely explanation is that Latinity had an ideological value, as forceful proof of an author's humanity in the fullest sense. The command of Latin, like literacy, had been invoked as evidence of the Indians' civilized qualities and their readiness to profess the Christian faith.[130] Latin's perceived identity with grammar and its capacity to systematize and explain other languages may have been another related factor: Juan de Tlaxcala, Antonio Cortés Totoquihuatzin, and Antonio Valeriano alike used Latin as a vehicle to explain some Nahuatl words.

In addition, the writers of the two longer letters reviewed in this chapter were able to exploit the knowledge of rhetorical techniques that could be acquired only through a humanist education and the reading of manuals of rhetoric or epistolography—all of which were themselves in Latin. The principles of rhetorical arrangement, the elegant opening *salutatio,* and the explanatory narratives that characterize both letters could, in principle, all have been deployed in the romance

his achievements as governor, notably the proposal of an aqueduct to supply water to Mexico City from Chapultepec.

129 BAUTISTA, *Sermonario* (1606) [1954, 475] states that he consulted Valeriano about Nahuatl on 'particular things, like etymologies and the meanings of words'.

130 Cf. GARCÉS, *De habilitate* (1537), 7–9 (Appendix 2.1.2, below).

vernacular. But such elaborate features are not found in the Spanish letters written by either of these authors—and the same divergence in practice between Latin and Castilian letters is found in the correspondence of Franciscans in the same period.[131]

There is a further consideration. Allusions to Latin works are more naturally made and recognized if they are in the same language—an effect not so easily achieved in a Spanish composition. Besides, a native Mexican with a Christian humanist education would have had little knowledge of sources or models in vernacular Spanish. The use of Latin facilitated the seamless accommodation of classical or biblical references, some of which hinted at parallels between European and Mesoamerican traditions. The writers of these petitions were, after all, seeking to reassure, impress, and win over the Spanish monarchs to whom their appeals were directed.

[131] Cf. Zumárraga's letters written during 1528–1548 [García Icazbalceta 1947, ii–iv].

7

A Mirror for Mexican Princes

The Nahuatl Translation of Aesop's Fables

In common with the vernacular literatures that had emerged in early modern Europe, the nascent Nahuatl literature in New Spain consisted of translations as well as original compositions—a clear signal of the importance and functionality of the Mexican language. The material translated into Nahuatl, under the direction of the Franciscans at Tlatelolco, usually consisted of religious texts and preceptive works of Christian literature: in comparison with such content, the version of Aesop's Fables, a source in a much lighter vein, may seem incongruous. But Aesop was a staple of grammar school curricula and it is likely that the immersive teaching of Latin to Mexican students was what engendered this translation of the Fables. In addition, the set of fables in Nahuatl is unique among other Renaissance collections for its emphasis on the art of government. The Nahuatl Aesop thus reflects two defining features of the College of Santa Cruz: its culture of humanist translation and its official function of training native principals for positions of leadership.

After a short account of the manuscript transmission of the texts of the Nahuatl fables (Section I), this chapter will identify the particular Latin edition that constituted their source. The precise identification at last makes a proper assessment of the Mexican translation possible, dispelling the persistent misunderstandings and fanciful assumptions that have impaired previous discussions (Section II). The purpose of the Nahuatl fables will be considered too, in the light of their unusual focus on statecraft (Section III). That will be the basis for a conjecture about who the translator or translators might have been (Section IV), before some general concluding remarks (Section V).

I. Manuscripts of Aesop's Fables in Nahuatl

A collection of forty-seven of Aesop's fables survives in two manuscripts dating from the late sixteenth or early seventeenth century, one in the Biblioteca Nacional

Aztec Latin. Andrew Laird, Oxford University Press. © Oxford University Press 2024.
DOI: 10.1093/oso/9780197586358.003.0008

de México (BNM) in Mexico City and the other in the Bancroft Epistles Library in Berkeley.[1] A later copy (c. 1800) of just thirty-five fables, now in the Bibliothèque nationale de France, was made by the Mexican linguist and historian Padre José Antonio Pichardo from another document, which is now lost.[2] The two earlier manuscripts may have been copied by Jesuits, but the contents of each (itemized below) are characteristic of Franciscan miscellanies of Nahuatl text produced at the Imperial College of Santa Cruz at Tlatelolco in the later 1500s.[3] The fact that Fray Bernardino de Sahagún is thought to have authored the *Kalendario* and *Arte adivinatoria* in the BNM manuscript, along with his own affirmation that only those trained at the college could write Nahuatl well, gives grounds for supposing that the material presented in both manuscripts originated there.[4] The contents of each of the manuscripts are given below, with the translations of Aesop's Fables highlighted in bold.

Biblioteca Nacional de México Ms. 1628 bis

1–85	*Cantares mexicanos*
86–100	*Kalendario Mexicano Latino y Castellano*
101–125	*Tonalamatl / Arte adivinatoria*
126–139	*Iz pehua in Neixcuitl machiotl* ['Aquí comienza el ejemplo', in reference to Eucharist]
140–146	*Plática indiferente para donde quiera* [Sermon on Paul's Epistles]
147–151	*Breve sermón sobre Hic est panis*
152–156	*Curación de la hija de Jairo*
157r	'Teoyautlatohoa huitzilopotchtli Cuetzpali huan/ Coyotl Miquiztli Ocelotl Cohuatl' [a text of two lines]
158–162	*Exposición de Leviticus 1:9*
163–169	*Recuerdo de la Muerte*

[1] BNM Ms. 1628 bis, fols. 179r–191v: *Nican ompehua y çaçanillatolli* (ed. Tena 2019 in León-Portilla, Curiel Defossé and Reyes Equigas 2019 iii, 569–630), hereafter 'BNM manuscript' or '*Nican ompehua*'. Bancroft M-M 464, fols. 421–426: *Nican vmpeua y çaçanillatolli* (1550s), ed. Kutscher, Brotherston, and Vollmer 1987, hereafter 'Bancroft manuscript'. Vollmer 1987, 219 and Tena 2019, 572 discuss the dating of the manuscripts.

[2] PICHARDO, *Traduccion* [*sic*] *de Algunas Fabulas* (c. 1800). Pichardo was chair of Latin and philosophy at the College of San Juan de Letrán: Castañeda 1952. The 'severe orthographic deviations' in Pichardo's copy noted by Vollmer 1987, 209 suggest it was made from a manuscript distinct from those in n. 1 above.

[3] Cf. Ms. 35-22 from the Biblioteca Capitular in Toledo (Chapter 5 above) and the *Miscelánea sagrada*, BNM ms. 1477 (n. 68 below), a manuscript that contains biblical commentary, treatises, and preceptive texts in Nahuatl. Tena 2019 makes a case for the Jesuit provenance of the manuscripts in which the fables are presented.

[4] SAHAGÚN, *Historia general* (c. 1580) =*HG*, Book 10, Prologue [1982 i, 84]. For attribution of the *Kalendario* and *Arte adivinatoria* to Sahagún, cf. Nicolau D'Olwer and Cline 1973, 201.

170–178	*Vida de S. Bartolomé*
179–191	***Fábulas de Esopo***
New pagination:	
1–68	*Historia de la pasión.*[5]

Bancroft Library Ms. MM-464

197–244	*Santoral*
245–251	*Oraciones diversas*
253–260	*Publicación de la bula*
261–266	*Pláticas diversas*
270–289	*Pláticas y oraciones diversas*
290–295	*Explicación de la misa y ornamentos que se usan*
296–303	*Oraciones*
307–345	*Ejemplos diversos sobre los santos*
347–412	*Más ejemplos tomados de vidas de santos*
413–417	*Algunos refranes de la lengua mexicana con traducción al español*
418–420	*Metáforas muy elegantes de esta lengua mexicana, con traducción al español*
421–426	***Algunas fábulas de Esopo***
427–446	*Cuentos diversos en mexicano.*[6]

The role of dictation in the copying of documents best accounts for the hitherto unexplained differences of orthography among all three texts of the Fables.[7] There are other divergences: the Bancroft manuscript is the only one of the three to place the seventeenth fable ('Telpopochtotonti yhuan molchichiuhqui', 'The youths and the cook') at the end of the collection. The Bancroft text also departs from that of the BNM by inserting an explanatory phrase into one of the fables and by adding a second moral to another.[8] The distinguishing features suggest that the full set of forty-seven fables in the BNM is the more reliable, and that (Figure 7.1) will generally be cited here.

The title common to all three copies of the Nahuatl fables, 'Nican ompehua y çaçanillatolli yn quitlali ce tlamatini ytoca Esopo', 'Here begin the fables set down

[5] Garibay 1953 i, 152. León-Portilla, Curiel Defossé and Reyes Equigas 2019 iii comprises editions and translations of all the items in the BNM manuscript.

[6] Schwaller 2001, 131–2. The extant Bancroft manuscript begins at folio 197.

[7] SAHAGÚN, *HG* Book 2, Prologue [1982 i, 54]; cf. Chapter 5, III above.

[8] In the BNM text fable 42, 'Quauhtlamaçatl', reads coherently without the interpolated phrase: Torres López 2019, 51. The interpolation has no analogue in the Latin, and the second moral added to BNM fable 47, 'Ce cahcatzactli' in the Bancroft manuscript, discussed in Section III below, is not in the Latin either.

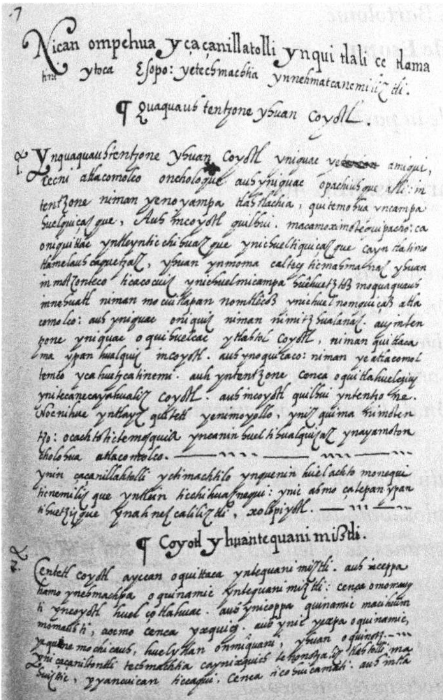

Figure 7.1 'Nican ompehua y çaçanillatolli', Mexico, 1550s. Biblioteca Nacional de México.

by the sage called Aesop', gives no indication that the ensuing content is a translation; and neither the Bancroft nor the BNM manuscript makes any reference to a Latin original. In the Paris manuscript, on the other hand, there are corresponding Latin texts for all but two of the thirty-five Nahuatl fables. Those texts, though, were inserted by José Antonio Pichardo at the beginning of the nineteenth century: they were certainly not the ones from which the translations were first made, and they followed Aldus Manutius' widely used edition of Aesop. Pichardo's incorporation of Aldus' text into his copy of the Nahuatl fables has long impeded identification of the Latin collection on which they were based.

II. The source of the Nahuatl fables: Joachim Camerarius, *Fabellae Aesopicae*, 1538

The Nahuatl translation in all three manuscripts was actually made from Joachim Camerarius' distinctive text of Aesop. This first appeared with a life of Aesop when it was published in 1538 as *Fabellae Aesopicae plvres quadringentis*, 'More than four

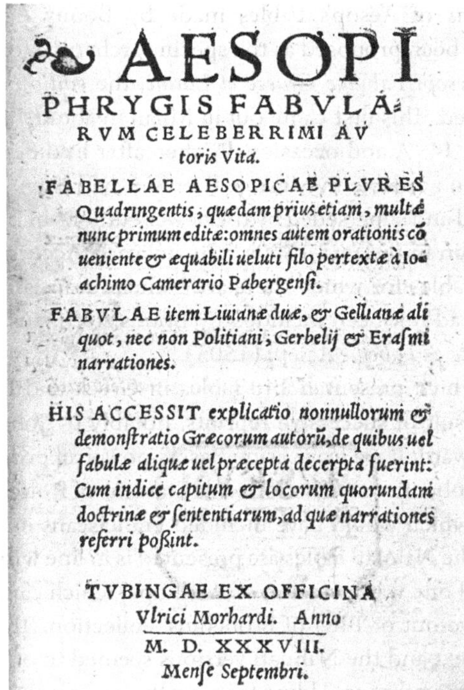

AESOPI PHRYGIS FABVLARVM CELEBERRIMI AVtoris Vita.

FABELLAE AESOPICAE PLVRES Quadringentis, quædam prius etiam, multæ nunc primum editæ: omnes autem orationis cõueniente & æquabili ueluti filo pertextæ à Ioachimo Camerario Pabergensi.

FABVLAE item Liuianæ duæ, & Gellianæ aliquot, nec non Politiani, Gerbelij & Erasmi narrationes.

HIS ACCESSIT explicatio nonnullorum & demonstratio Græcorum autorũ, de quibus uel fabulæ aliquæ uel præcepta decerpta fuerint: Cum indice capitum & locorum quorundam doctrinæ & sententiarum, ad quæ narrationes referri poßint.

TVBINGAE EX OFFICINA Vlrici Morhardi. Anno M. D. XXXVIII. Mense Septembri.

Figure 7.2 Joachim Camerarius, *Aesopi Phrygis . . . vita. Fabellae Aesopicae,* Tübingen, 1538. British Library.

hundred Aesopic Fables'.[9] (Figure 7.2) Camerarius' collection went through some forty editions in the second half of the sixteenth century and was a popular school textbook.[10] It is important to provide a full and conclusive demonstration that Camerarius' edition was used for the translation into Nahuatl: the singular degree of variation between the many printed texts of Aesop available in the 1500s and the complexity of that print tradition has led to considerable confusion.[11]

[9] CAMERARIUS, *Aesopi Phrygis fabularum celeberrimi auctoris vita: Fabellae Aesopicae plvres quadringentis* (1538), hereafter *Fabellae Aesopicae.* The identification of Camerarius as the source, confirmed here, was tentatively proposed by 'Ayac' 2014.

[10] Philipp Melanchthon prefaced a later edition: *Fabellae Aesopicae qvaedam notiores, et in scolis vsitatae,* 'Some more notable Aesopic fables used in schools' (1545): Elschenbroiche 1990 ii, 258–69; Springer 2011, 50.

[11] Brotherston 1987, 13 relied on Hausrath 1957–1959, a survey of Aesop manuscripts, without considering print circulation; Ríos Castaño 2015, 248–9 misidentifies a Basel 1616 reprint of Frobenius' Aldine edition as 'Maximus Planudes' edition, *Aesopi Phrygis fabulae Graece et Latine,* a compilation which Accursius imbibed': Aldus' text of 1505 had been printed long after Bonus Accursius' death in c. 1485. Latin versions of Aesop differed widely, as they derived from a complex Greek tradition, on which Perry 1952 is the standard guide.

Earlier collections of Aesop's Fables made by Bonus Accursius and Aldus Manutius have both been proposed as the specific archetype for the Nahuatl translation. Accursius' *Aesopi Fabulae Graece et Latine*, the *editio princeps* of Aesop, is most easily eliminated. This first came out in Milan in about 1478, to be reprinted in Italy in 1480 and 1497, and occasionally thereafter in different forms, but it is unlikely to have been available in Mexico. Even if it had been, it would have been greatly outnumbered and superseded by the newer editions in Latin that were being shipped to New Spain in the mid-1500s.[12] In any case, Accursius' collection does not contain all the fables for which there are Nahuatl translations. The 'Aethiops' fable, for example, had not been included by Bonus Accursius, although it was in Aldus Manutius' *Vita, & Fabellæ Aesopi* (1505).[13]

Aldus' edition, which presented 148 fables in Greek and Latin, circulated far more widely as a result of successive reprints, notably by Johannes Frobenius in Basel from 1517 onward. If we leave aside Basel's powerful position in the international book trade, Frobenius' association with Erasmus of Rotterdam helped attract an avid readership, which would have included Franciscans in the earlier 1500s.[14] The order in which the Nahuatl fables are presented is in line with that of the Aldine edition, and the final one was a version of 'Aethiops', which came at the end of the first half (seventy-five out of 148) of Frobenius' collection. That clear correlation between this Latin text and the Nahuatl versions seemed to offer further grounds, prima facie, for believing that an Aldine text was their source.[15]

Joachim Camerarius, however, worked from Aldus Manutius' edition and presented the same fables, without a Greek text, in almost exactly the same sequence in his *Fabellae Aesopicae*. The correspondence can be seen in the first seventy-four titles (cf. the conspectus in Appendix 1.6.1 of this volume): the ordering of the Nahuatl fables is just as much in line with Camerarius' edition as it is with that of Aldus. But the contents of Joachim Camerarius' text are different when it comes to the style and wording of his Latin fables, which are often longer and more rhetorical. Wherever there are divergences from Aldus Manutius, the Nahuatl translator's dependence on Camerarius is revealed. This influence is obvious even from the titles of a couple of Nahuatl fables: 'Nehtolle yn ahmo huel moneltilia', 'The promise that

[12] Francisco Valverde, 'Obligación de pago', 16 November 1545, recorded the book dealer Alonso Losa's purchase of six texts of Aesop in Mexico, probably new copies: 'seis Fábulas de Esopo latín, en 714 maravedíes': Mijáres 2014.

[13] MANUTIUS, *Vita et Fabellae* (1505), 39 (Greek text); sig. c3v (Latin). Barker and Kaplan 2001, 94–5 gives a conspectus of Aldus' edition. Massing 1995, 183 notes that 'the first Latin translations of the fable appeared in the fifteenth century', citing Omnibonus Leonicenus' *Aesopus e Graeco in Latinum*, printed in Venice around 1570. Massing, observing that the Frobenius version of the fable 'published for the first time in Basel in 1524' became the standard one, does not recognize that Frobenius was reproducing Aldus Manutius' 1505 text, in fact from 1517 onward.

[14] Bataillon 1932; Bataillon 1937, 540–50, 810–27.

[15] Téllez Nieto 2015b made a case for Aldus Manutius as the source for the Nahuatl fables.

Plate 1 The Valley of Mexico in the sixteenth century. Map by Sergio Cruz Durán.

Plate 2a *Codex Mendoza*, Mexico, c. 1542, 2r (detail). Bodleian Library, Oxford.

Plate 2b Eagle and *atl tlachinolli* glyph, 'Teocalli of Sacred War', Tenochtitlan, c. 1507 (reverse). Museo Nacional de Antropología, Mexico. Photograph by Thomas F. Aleto.

Plate 2c *Codex Aubin*, Mexico, c. 1576–1608, 26v (detail). British Museum.

¶ Con Licentia, & Priuilegio.

IN TRENTO,
Per Gio. Battista, & Giacomo fratelli, de Gelmini,
di Sabbio. M. D. LXXXVIII.

Plate 2d Title page of Anton Francesco Doni, *La filosofia morale*, Trent, 1588 (detail), showing the mark of the Gelmini brothers' press. British Library.

Plate 3 'Texas fragment' of the *Lienzo de Tlaxcala*, Tlaxcala, c. 1540, depicting Cortés' meeting with Xicotencatl. Benson Latin American Collection, University of Texas at Austin.

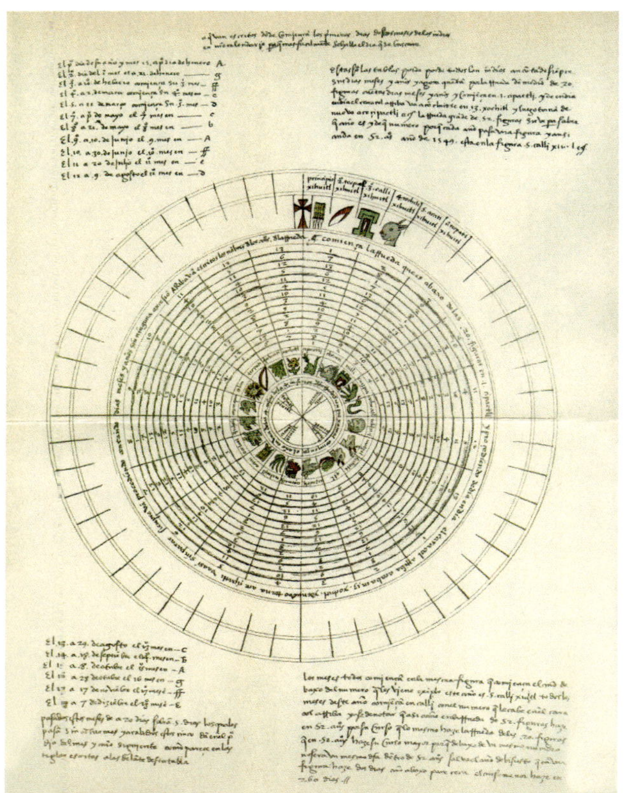

Plate 4a The Mexican calendar in Motolinía, *Memoriales,* Mexico, c. 1541, *tomo* 31. Benson Latin American Collection, University of Texas at Austin.

Plate 4b *Trecena* period (days 6–13) with feathered serpent, *Codex Telleriano-Remensis,* Mexico, c. 1563, 18r. Bibliothèque nationale de France.

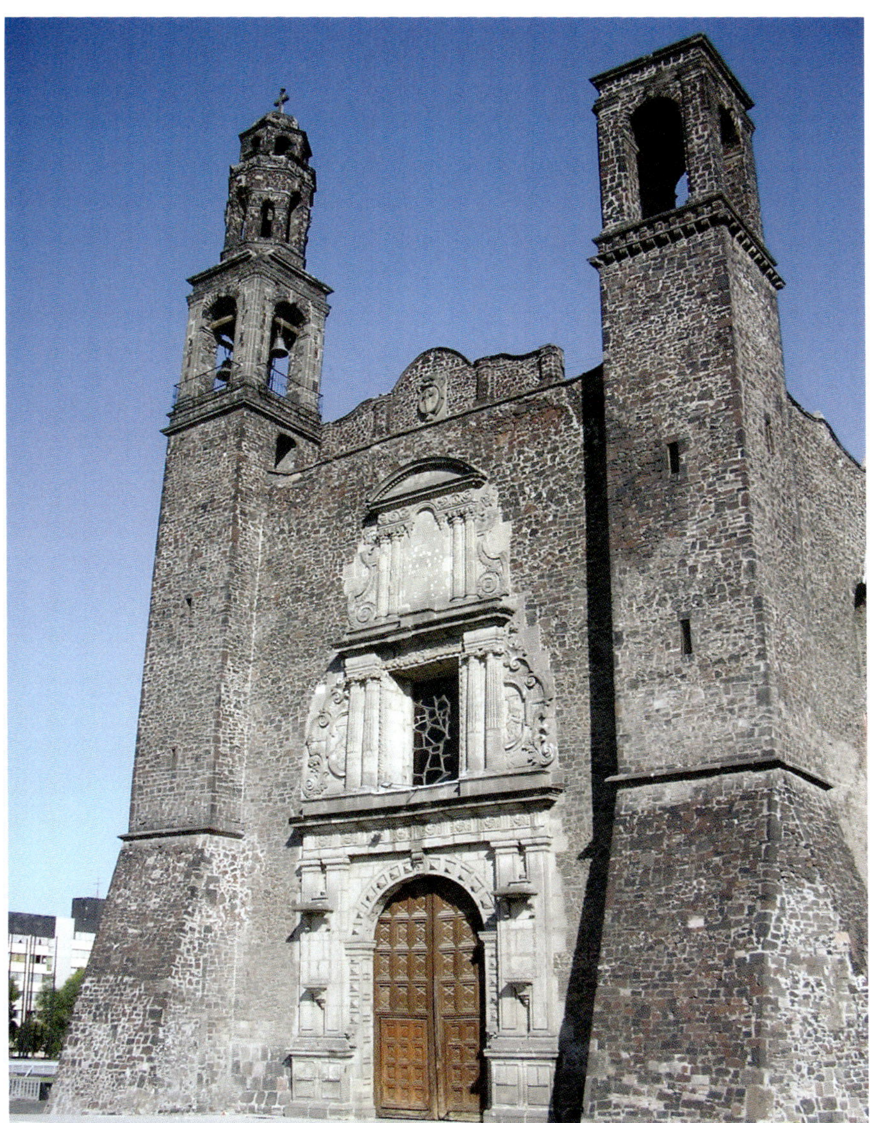

Plate 5 The convent church of Santiago, Tlatelolco. Photograph by author.

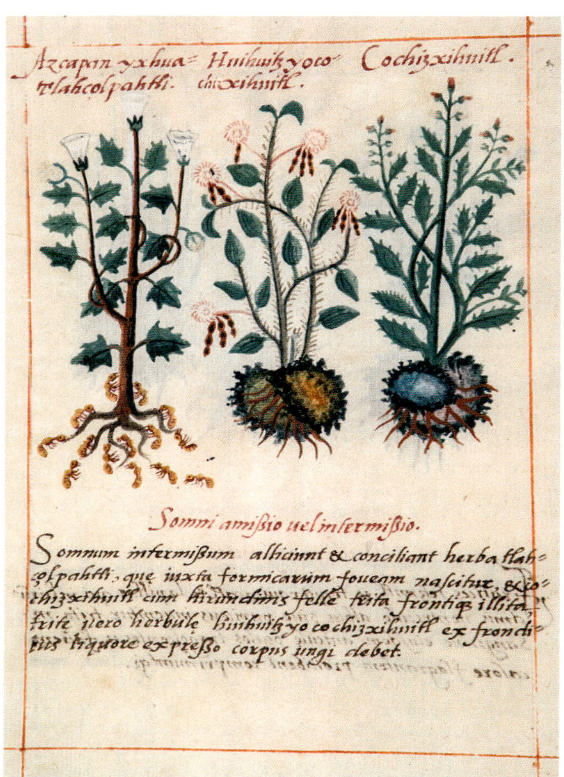

Plate 6a Libellus de medicinalibus Indorum herbis, Tlatelolco, 1552, 13v. Instituto Nacional de Antropología e Historia, Mexico.

Plate 6b Libellus de medicinalibus Indorum herbis, 38v (detail). Instituto Nacional de Antropología e Historia, Mexico.

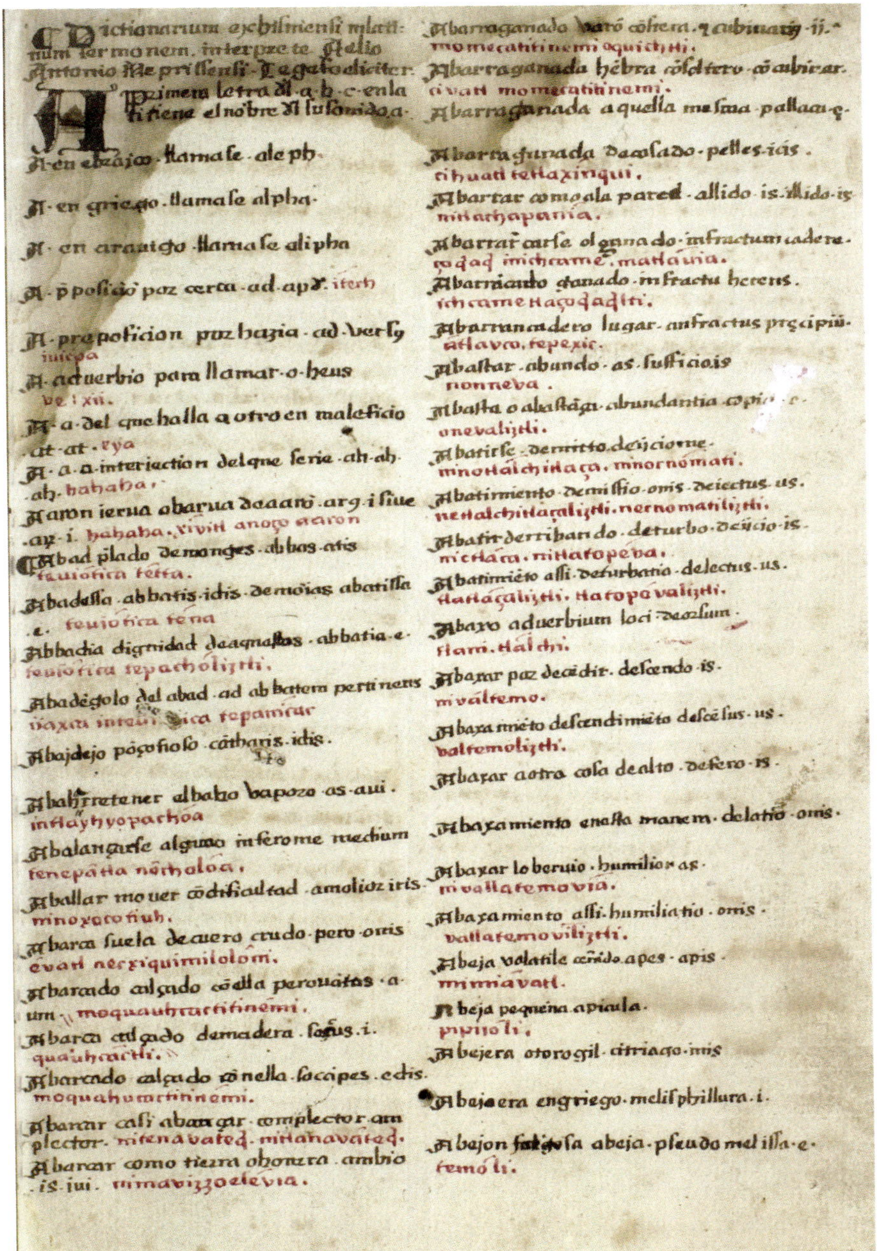

Plate 7 Manuscript copy of Antonio de Nebrija, *Dictionarium ex Hispaniensi in Latinum sermonem* (1516), with Nahuatl terms added in red, Mexico, c. 1545, 3r. Newberry Library, Chicago.

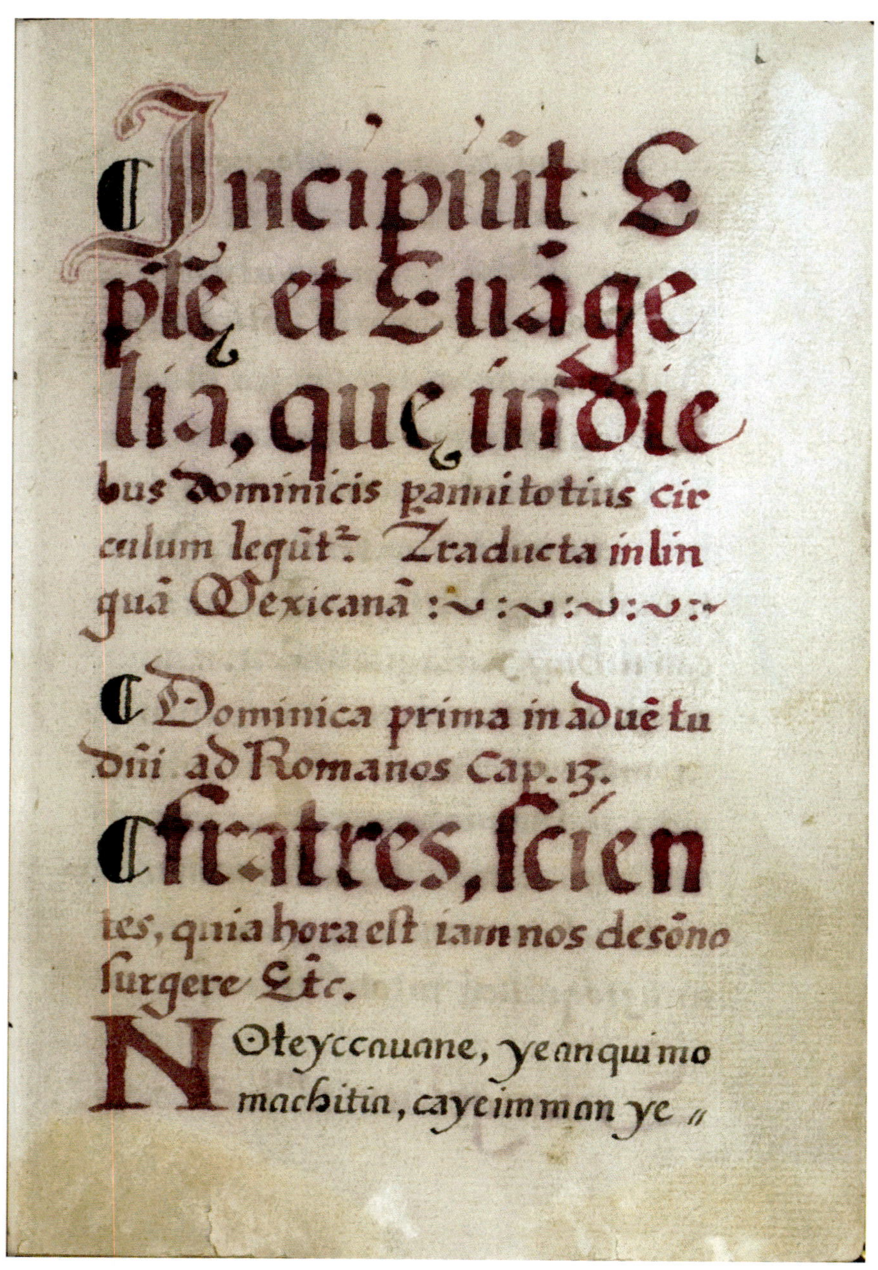
Incipiũt E
plẽ et Euãge
lia, que in die
bus dominicis p anni totius cir
culum legũt. Traducta in lin
guã Mexicanã
Dominica prima in aduẽtu
dñi ad Romanos Cap. 13.
Fratres, scien
tes, quia hora est iam nos de sõno
surgere &c.
Noteyccauane, yeanquimo
machitia, cayeimman ye

Plate 8 Title page and opening Epistle in Nahuatl, *Incipiunt Epistolae et Evangelia . . . Traducta in linguam Mexicanam,* Mexico, c. 1550. Newberry Library, Chicago.

271

nymo, yn quenin cenca q̃nmauiçotia. q̃nteyotia. quiyectenevar: yntlamatinime.
caq̃ cuilotia ynquenin yevecahu cenca mauiz temoloya. yntlamatinime, yn ce
q̃nti cencaveca iuallehuaya yn q̃ntemo tinenca, macamo nimitzontenevilli yn cẽ
cauey tlamatini. Platõ: Amo no nictenevaz neq̃ in Pythagoras. noyehuatl
yn architas. noyehuatl yn apollonio yuan inoccencamiequinti ynachto=
oc nouian q̃ntemotinenca yntlamatinime ynicmomachtiz que. Ahuiniq̃c
yetlamatinime, cencanotemoloya cencanomauiztililoya. Cuixamotiquitta in
quenin axcan nouian cacauantihu ynintehyo yninmaviço iyehuanti cenca
tlamatinime yn Origenes. Hylario. Hieronymo. ambrosio. Augu
stino. Gregorio: Cuixmochinti niquintenevaz: ma ciuintopan youaz cen
ca çanihuq̃ntepiton noconitoz. Coll. Notatcine amomo neq̃ yncencamiec
tic mitalhuiz. Caihu quin cencayetlatla noyollo ymic yeniquelehuia tlama
tiliztli. Ye el nicmati caynnicantlaca yntlanel centzonxiuitl tiq̃mmonono=
chiliz, Caamo moyollevaz que ynic quitemoz q̃ tlamatiliztli: ahu maciuin cẽ
ca teyollehu inihuqui teyolquima tlatolli tiq̃mmolhuiliz amo ymel quicaq̃
que atlevel ynnacazco onchipiniz Pa. Ynincayevelnicmati yccenca nite q̃.
pachiui. yc ninentlamati. Cahuelyehuantin ynmonomanextia. caihuq̃n co
conetotonti momati. uelquinextia ynincoconeyo yninpipilo Cainihuq̃ co
netontli, yntlacentlapal ymactictlaliliz yncoztic teocuitlatl yuan epyollotli, q̃
tçaliztl ahuinoc centlapal ymac yntlatictlaliliz tçaputl. ahuin tlayeyatihu.
cuixamoçãço quititlan yca onmayauiz ynteocuitlatl ynepyolotli ynquetçaliz
tli. ahuĩ tçaputl amoyequitetehutçiz quiz. Yntlaaca q̃cuiliz teocuitlatl. atle
ypan quittaz ahuin tla qui cuiliz tçaputl yc chocaz. cauelihuque ynnicantlaca
caynttleinitech momati atleipan motta, çanihuq̃npillutl coneyotl. Ahuincen
ca tlaçotli tlamatiliztli atleypan quitta: Ypampahi yyehuatçin SSto. q̃ntoca=
yoti coconetotonti yollo tlaueliloque, yniquac quimitalhui. Yncoconetotonti
yvan yollo tlavelilo que çanquitelchiua atleypan quitta yntlamatiliztli. Ahu
ynoccenca techocti ynoccen ca tetlaoculti, caamo çah yeiyo yntlamatiliztli qui
telchiua, çan noivan ynitlatollo nemaquixtiliztli. Nelli yncatichoca yncatinen
tlamati yn topilhuã ynixquichtin nicantlaca. Caynnemachtiliztlatolli ỹ nel
toconi yn teonauatilli çanquipoloua çanquilcaua. Ahuiniquac tiq̃ncuitlavil
tia yhuq̃ntequitl ypanq̃mati Maçanoc yxquich nopiltzine. quiceppa tiq̃toz q̃.
Ynitechpa ynçan cencamatl ynnimitzilhuiz. cencatemamahuti techocti. Yna q̃n

Plate 9 Rubricated names of Greek sages and Church Fathers, Fray Juan de Gaona, *Colloquios de la paz y tranquilidad christiana en lengua mexicana*, Mexico, c. 1540, 271r. Biblioteca Capitular, Toledo Cathedral.

Plate 10 *Altepetl* emblems of Texcoco, Mexico, and Tlacopan, *Codex Osuna*, Mexico, 1565, 34r. Biblioteca Nacional de España, Madrid.

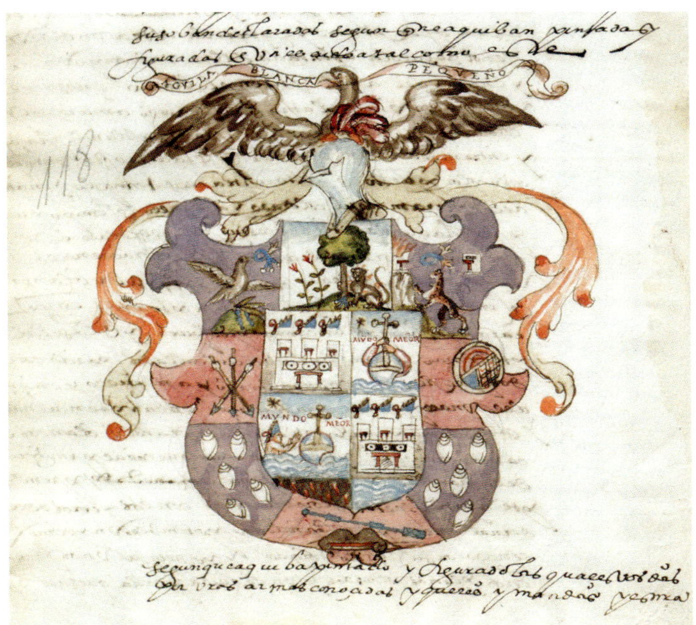

Plate 11a Coat of arms ceded to Antonio Cortés Totoquihuatzin in 1564. Archivo Ducal de Alba, Madrid.

Plate 11b Glyph for Azcapotzalco, *Codex Techialoyan García Granados*, Mexico, 1600s (detail). Instituto Nacional de Antropología e Historia, Mexico.

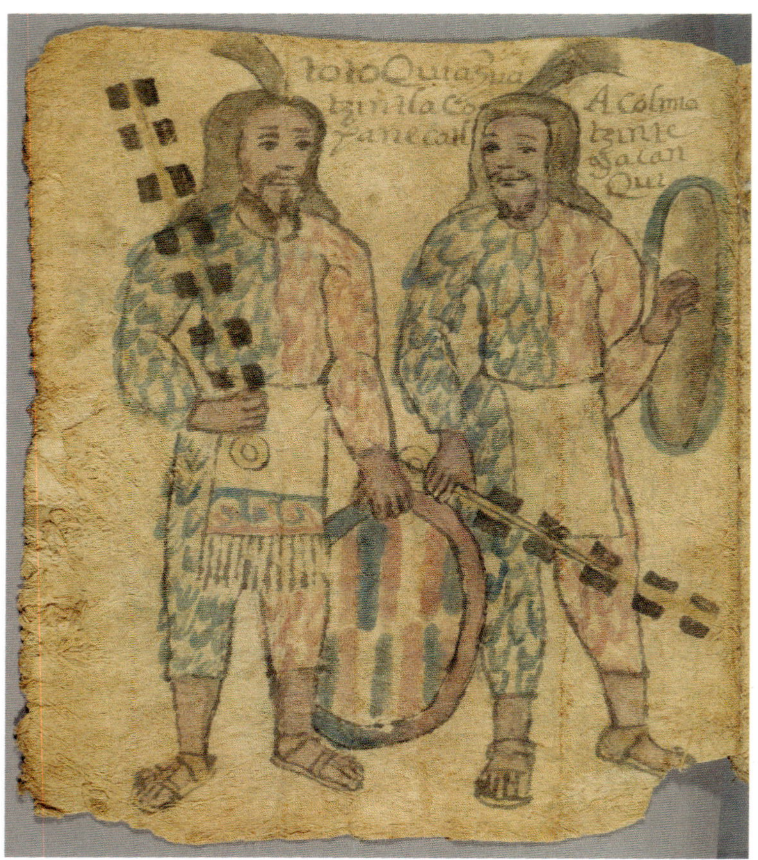

Plate 12a Totoquihuatzin (the elder), ruler of Tlacopan, shown with Acolmiztli, a noble, *Codex Huixquilucan*, Mexico, c. 1660–1750, 3v. Tozzer Library, Harvard University.

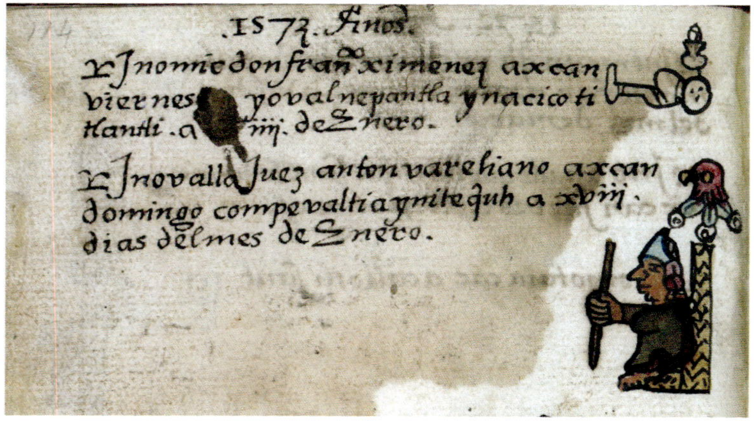

Plate 12b Depiction of Antonio Valeriano, *Codex Aubin*, Mexico, c. 1576–1608, 58v (detail). British Museum.

Plate 13 Portrayals of the first four Mexican divinities, *Florentine Codex*, Mexico, c. 1580. Ms. Med. Palat. 218, f. 10r., Biblioteca Medicea Laurenziana, Florence.

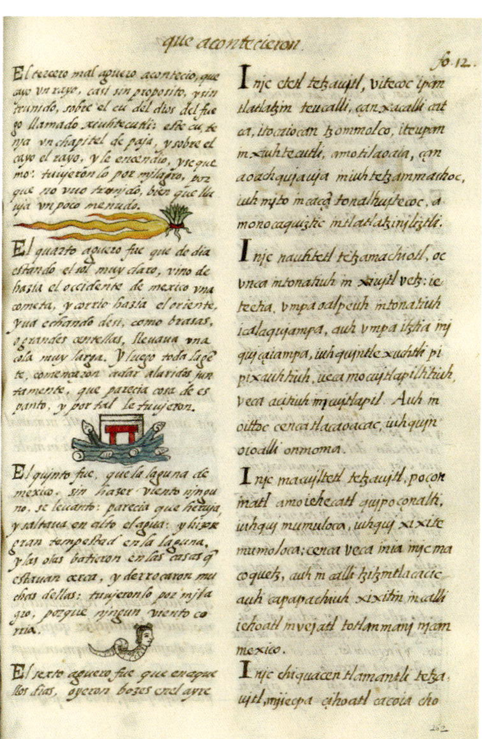

Plate 14a Omens of the Spaniards' arrival in Mexico, *Florentine Codex*, Mexico, c. 1580, Ms. Med. Palat. 219, f. 262r. Biblioteca Medicea Laurenziana, Florence.

Plate 14b Cihuacoatl, *Florentine Codex*, Ms. Med. Palat. 218, f. 10v (detail). Biblioteca Medicea Laurenziana, Florence.

Plate 15 Painting of Nezahualcoyotl, *Codex Ixtlilxochitl,* Mexico c. 1552, 106r. Bibliothèque nationale de France.

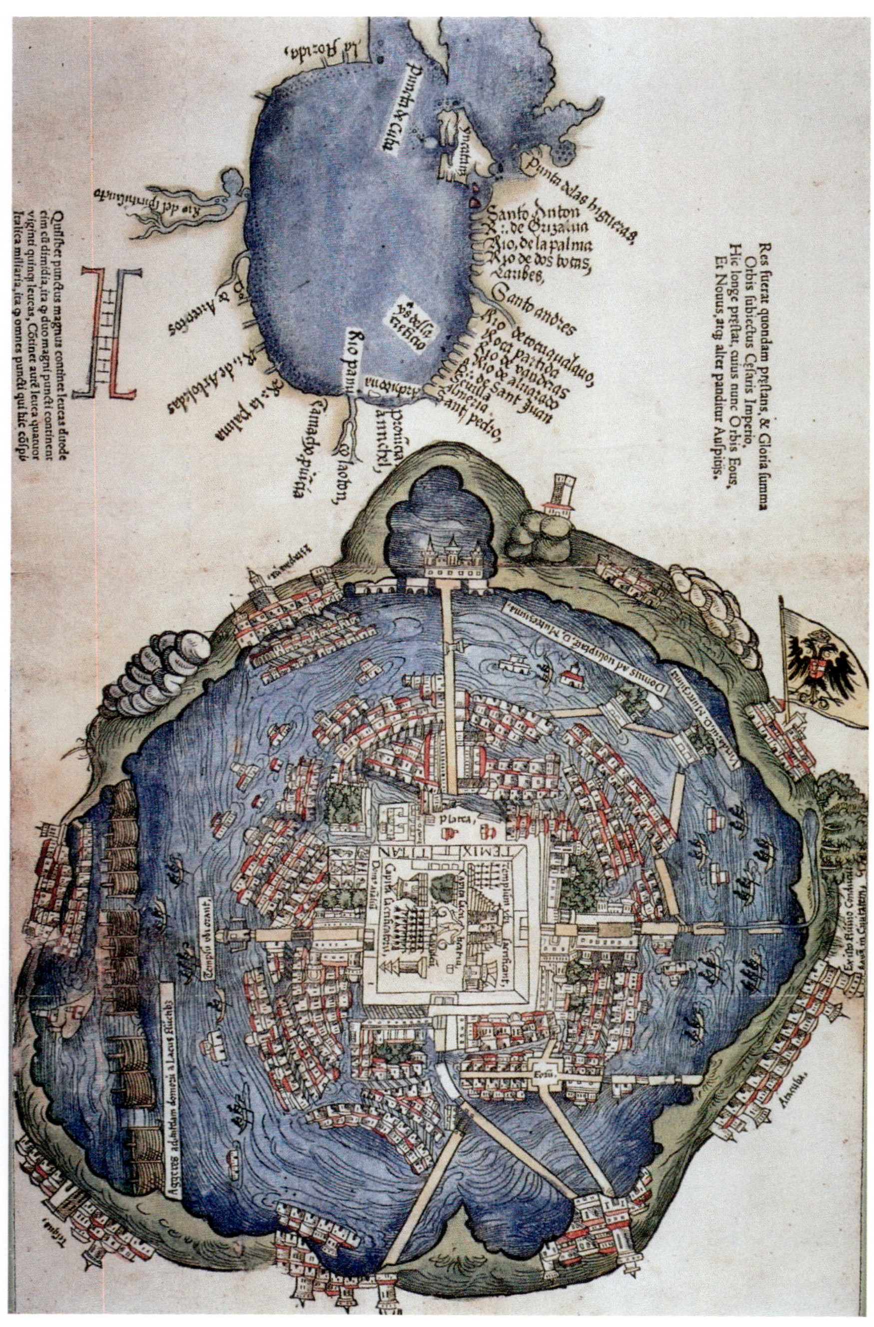

Plate 16 Map of the Gulf of Mexico and Tenochtitlan, *Praeclara Ferdinandi Cortesii de Noua maris Oceani Hyspania narratio*, Nuremberg, 1524. Newberry Library, Chicago.

could not be kept' (8), is nearer to Camerarius' 'Votum quod solvi non posset' than to Aldus' 'Impossibilia promittens'; and 'Ylamaton yxcocoxqui', 'Old Woman with Bad Eyes' (12), comes from 'De Anu Laborante ex oculis' in Camerarius, not 'Anus et medicus', 'Old woman and Doctor', which is in the Aldine text.

A careful reading of the very first fable of the Nahuatl collection, 'Quaquauhtentzone yhuan coyotl', 'Goat and Coyote', points to the correct Latin model. It is based on 'Vulpes et hircus', 'Fox and Goat': the two animals in the story are stuck in a well, and the fox tells the goat how to position himself in such a way that he can climb over him to escape. In Aldus Manutius' text, the fox's words were as follows:

> Si enim rectus steteris, & anteriores pedes parieti firmaueris, & cornua pariter in anteriorem partem inclinaueris, cum percurrerim ipsa per tuos humeros, & cornua, & extra puteum illinc exiliuerim, & te postea extraham hinc.[16]
>
> If you stand up straight, and place your forefeet firmly on the wall, and similarly direct your horns in front of you, once I have myself run up over your shoulders, and horns, and from there leapt out of the well, I will then get you out too.

The Nahuatl content is very similar:

> Ca yntla timotlamelauhcaquetzaz, yhuan yn moma caltech ticmahmanaz, yhuan in motzonteco ticacocuiz ynic huel micampa huéhuetztoz moquaquauh, in nehuatl niman mocuitlapan nomtlêcoz ynic huel nomquiçaz atlacomolco: auh yniquac oniquiz niman nimitzhualanaz.
>
> If you stand up straight and spread your forefeet against the wall and raise your head so that your horns hang back behind you, I shall then climb up on your back to get out of the well, and when I have come out, I will bring you out.[17]

The mention of the goat's head ('motzonteco'), which was absent from Bonus Accursius and Aldus Manutius, has been put down to the Mexican translator being perplexed by 'anteriores pedes'.[18] But the Latin for 'head', *caput*, along with the detail

[16] MANUTIUS, *Aesopi Phrygis uita et Fabellae* (1534), 107–9. This Frobenius edition of Aldus Manutius' Latin text is the one cited here and in Appendix 1.6.

[17] *Nican ompehua,* 179r. Quotations of the Nahuatl fables are from the Biblioteca Nacional de México Ms. 1628 bis with one exception (n. 63 below). The translation of the Nahuatl text in this chapter has drawn from the Spanish versions of Tena 2019 and Torres López 2019, and it has been reworked in the light of the Latin source: I am grateful to Ben Leeming for many valuable suggestions.

[18] Cf. ACCURSIUS, *Aesopi Fabulae* (1480), fol. a ii: 'si enim rectus stans & anteriores pedum parieti firmabis: & cornu similiter in anteriorem partem inclinabis'.

of the reclining horns, was already in Joachim Camerarius' more explicit narrative, which must have been the translator's model. The relevant words are here italicized:

> Si enim te in posteriores pedes erigens, priores parieti isti applicueris, *& caput alte, cornua vt oblique reclinentur, extuleris,* tum ego de tergo tuo in haec ascendere, atque deinde exiliere de puteo, & te mox etiam attrahere facile potero.[19]
>
> If you stand on your back feet and put your forefeet on this wall *and you hold your head high, so that your horns rest back,* then I can climb onto them from your back, and from there jump out of the well, and I can soon bring you out easily too.

Examination of a couple of fables short enough to present in their entirety will suffice to give clear confirmation that Camerarius, not Accursius or Aldus, was the source for the Nahuatl translation, and to dispose of some more general misconceptions about it.

This is Bonus Accursius' text of 'De Leone & Rana', 'The Lion and the Frog':

> Leo audiens olim ranam ualde clamantem conuersus est ad uocem putans magnum quoddam animal esse. expectans autem paullulum postquam uidit ipsam exeuntem a stagno accedens ipsam conculcauit.
>
> Fabula declarat. quod non oportet ante aspectum ab auditu solo perturbari.[20]
>
> A lion once heard a frog croaking loudly and went towards the noise, thinking that it was some kind of large animal. Then the lion waited a little and after he saw the frog coming out of a pond, he went up and trod on her.
>
> The fable makes clear that it is better not to be worked up by hearing something before having sight of it.

Aldus' *Leo et rana* is similar:

> Leo audita aliquando rana ualde clamante, uertit se ad uocem, ratus magnum aliquod animal esse, parumper autem expectando, ut uidit stagno egressam, accedens propius proculcauit.
>
> Affabulatio
>
> Fabula significat, non oportere, ante quam uideas uoce sola perturbari.[21]

[19] CAMERARIUS, *Fabellae Aesopicae* (1538), 40r–40v.

[20] ACCURSIUS, *Aesopi Fabulae* (1480), b iiii.

[21] MANUTIUS, *Aesopi Phrygis uita et fabellae* (1534), 137.

A lion once heard a frog croaking loudly and went towards the noise, thinking that it was some kind of large animal. But after a short wait, it saw the frog coming out of a pond, went up to it, and trod on it.

Moral:

The fable means that it is better not to get worked up by the mere sound of something before you see it.

The Nahuatl fable, 'Tequani miztli yhuan cuiyatl', 'Fierce Lion and Frog' (25), is more extensive than either of those versions:[22]

> Yn tequani miztli ceppa oquicac cuiyatl cenca tzahtzi in cotalohua, cenca yc *omomauhti*, momatia ca huey manehnemi yn iuh tzahtzia; *çan in omotlali yyollo, nohuiampa tlahtlachiaya, mochihchihuaya ynic quinamiquiz y çaço quenami cotalohuaya*. Auh yn oquittac atlampa cholotihuitz cuiyatl y ye hualquiçaya atenco; in tequani *cenca oquala[n] yhuan opinahuac, yehica ca atle ypan motta yn oquimauhttiaya*, oquicxixaxaqualo, oquimicti.
>
> Yni çaçanilli techmachtia ynic amo çan ilihuiz titomauhtizque ytechpa in tlein ticcaqui tetecuica, hanoço yhcoyoca, auh amo no çan tlapic titomauhtizque yn ayamo huel tiquitta in tlein techmauhtia.

> A fierce lion once heard a frog calling out and croaking a lot, at which he was very *afraid*: thinking that it was a large beast that was calling out like that. *But he settled his heart, he looked around him in all directions, preparing himself to meet whatever it was that croaking.* But upon seeing the frog quickly leap out of the water and come on the shore, the lion *got very angry and felt ashamed because the one that frightened him was considered of no importance* [and so] he crushed it with his paws, and killed it.
>
> This fable teaches us that we should not be afraid without reason when we hear any noise or roar, and that we should not be afraid before we know what it is that frightens us.

The addition of the phrases (here italicized) that give a far more detailed account of the lion's thoughts and emotions has always been regarded as an innovation on the part of the Mexican translator or translators. Gordon Brotherston went so far as to attribute the apparent elaboration in the Nahuatl text to the 'power of Mesoamerican philosophy draw[ing] out what is there in Aesop's original', and further commented:

> The Aztecs however take time to explain that the jaguar [sc. 'lion'] trod on the frog because he was angry and ashamed at having been in the least

[22] *Nican ompehua*, 185r. 'Tequani', equivalent to English 'man-eater', could refer to the jaguar (*ocelotl*) or to the mountain lion (*miztli*). On *miztli*, cf. n. 31 below.

> put out by such a tiny creature. There is here an interest in the jaguar's motives and sensitivity, a feeling one's way into the animal's skin practised literally by those Aztec knights who dressed for battle as jaguars, eagles, or coyotes . . .[23]

In fact all those details in the Nahuatl text come from the 1538 Latin version prepared by Joachim Camerarius. The relevant phrases are again italicized:

> Leo auditis ranae clamoribus, quos illa toto rictu edebat quam maximos, primum *percelli animo valde* coepit, quod crederet ingentem animantem esse autorem tanti clamoris. *Animo tamen confirmato, circumspicere, & contra illum clamatorem, quiquis esset, sese parare, & ad pugnam accingere.* Cum videt prorepentem ranam de propinquo lacu, ibi leo, *simul indignatione, simul etiam pudore affectus,* pede illam conculcatam attriuit.
>
> Docet fabula, non esse ad quemlibet strepitum expauescendum, neq[ue] nos inexplorata re terreri oportere.[24]

> A lion heard the cries of a frog, which the frog made as loud as she could with her mouth wide open, and at first *his heart was very startled,* because he thought a huge animal was the source of such a cry. *After quieting his heart, the lion looked around, and he prepared himself and girded himself for battle against the source of the cry, whoever it might be.* When he saw the frog crawling forth from a nearby pool, the lion at that point *was moved by indignation and shame* and trod on her with his foot and squashed her.
>
> The fable teaches that we should not needlessly be frightened by what we hear howling or roaring, nor should we be frightened without reason before we are able to see what frightens us.

So it was not the Aztecs, but a professor of Classics and Theology, far away in the university town of Tübingen, who endowed the lion with emotions of fright, anger, and shame, and who envisaged the animal dressing for battle.

The firm knowledge that Camerarius' *Fabellae Aesopicae* was the source for the Mexican translation should help to address a prevalent misunderstanding about the fourth Nahuatl fable, 'Acuetzpali yhuan coyotl', 'Alligator and Coyote', a translation of 'Vulpes et crocodilus', 'Fox and Crocodile':

[23] Brotherston 1987, 23. Cf. Brotherston 1993, 316. The suggestion in Torres López 2019, 164–5 that the translation dramatized the fable's narrative to align it with aspects of Mexican culture is a more restrained expression of this view.

[24] CAMERARIUS, *Fabellae Aesopicae* (1538), 49v.

> Centlamantli acuetzpali mochihua yn ompa Egipto, atlan nemi, cenca temahmauhti yn itlachieliz, huel yuhqui tzitzimitl, ytoca cocodrillo; yuhquin cuetzpali yc mahmaye, auh cenca huey temahmauhti yn ixincayo. Quilmach ceppa canin monamique coyotl yhuan ynin acuetzpali, motlatzohuilique ytechpa yn intlacamecayo.
>
> A kind of alligator exists over there in Egypt that lives in the water; its appearance is very frightening, very much like a monstrous figure, it is called a 'crocodile'; it is just like a lizard because it has legs and and its scales are very large [and] terrifying. It is said that once a coyote and this alligator met somewhere, and got involved in an argument about their lineages.[25]

The fable in the Aldine text was shorter and began directly with the story:

> Vulpes & crocodilus contendebant de nobilitate: cum multa autem crocodilus superba de progenitorum narrasset splendore . . .[26]
>
> A fox and a crocodile were arguing about their nobility: when the crocodile had recounted many proud things about his ancestors . . .

That has led commentators on 'Acuetzpali yhuan coyotl' to affirm that whoever translated the text into Nahuatl was responsible for supplying this preliminary explanation about the crocodile, perhaps drawing from Isidore or Pliny. It is supposed that this would have been for the benefit of the Mexican reader, because there were no crocodiles in Mesoamerica.[27] In fact the information came straight from Camerarius:

> Crocodilus Aegyptiacum est animal, tetrum aspectu, atque monstrosum, specie lacertae, cute rugis & squamis horrida, vastum atque informe. Inter hunc & vulpem quodam tempore certamen de generis nobilitate extitisse narrant.[28]
>
> The crocodile is an animal from Egypt, frightful in appearance, and monstrous, like a lizard, its skin is rough with wrinkles and scales, it is huge and

[25] *Nican ompehua*, 179v–180r.

[26] MANUTIUS, *Aesopi Phrygis uita et fabellae* (1534), 113.

[27] E.g. Brotherston 1987; Ríos Castaño 2015, 251: 'The translator(s) . . . were cognizant of their audience's unfamiliarity [with the crocodile] . . . and resorted to explanatory translations.' The focus on the crocodile's skin, noted by Brotherston 1993, 23 and Ríos Castaño 2015, 252, is not original to the Nahuatl text: the skin was mentioned by the fox at the end of the Latin fable ('nam de pelle apparere omnia', 'everything is evident from your skin') and this description is given in Nahuatl as 'ca niman ytech neci ym mopanehuayo yn ac tehuatl', 'your skin makes clear who you are'.

[28] CAMERARIUS, *Fabellae Aesopicae* (1538), 41v.

> misshapen. They say that on one occasion there was a contest between this creature and a fox about the nobility of their ancestral line . . .

That is a salutary reminder that crocodiles were not at all common in Europe either. If the Latin text had not begun by pointedly introducing 'Crocodilus' as a new term for an unfamiliar animal, the translator could have referred to an alligator, *acuetzpalin*, throughout.[29] Instead the Nahuatl retains the sense of the Latin by maintaining the status of the crocodile as something exotic and monstrous, but accentuates its threatening nature by the word 'tzitzimitl'.[30]

Further evidence of sensitivity to some nuances in the Latin might be provided by the penultimate fable in the Nahuatl collection: 'Leon tequani yhuan cuitlachtli', 'Fierce *León* [lion] and Wolf'.[31] This is based on Camerarius' 'Leo et lupus', in which the lion, who has fallen ill, is visited by all animals in his kingdom, except the fox. The wolf seeks to take advantage of this state of affairs to turn the lion against the fox, before the fox appears and finds a way to reverse the situation:

> Hac occasione capta, lupus uulpem grauissime accusare, quæ tam superbe despiceret regem suum, neque ad illum ægrotantem uiseret. Haec illo declamitante aduenit uulpes, et de clausula orationis, quam uehementer accusata esset, intelligens, & cernens leonem fremere ira, consilium coepit callidum & sui defendendi, & ulciscendi inimici, ac dicendi copia impetrata: Quænam igitur de cunctis animantibus inquit, tantam curam gerit salutis Regie, aut de tua uita ita, leo, solicita est, ut ego? Que omnia loca peragro, uestigans medicinam qua sanari posse uidearis . . . [32]

> Seizing the opportunity, the wolf made a very serious charge against the fox for haughtily disrespecting her king and not coming to see him when he was ill. But the fox arrived when the wolf was declaiming like this, and as she understood from the conclusion to his oration how forcefully she had been accused, and as she saw that the lion was seething with rage, she initiated a crafty plan both to defend herself and to take revenge upon her

[29] The literal translation of 'acuetzpali' as 'water lizard' in Kutscher, Brotherston, and Vollmer 1987 reflects the word's formation from *atl*, water, and *cuetzpalin*, but implies that such a creature was unfamiliar to the translators. *Acuetzpalin* normally designates the alligator or caiman.

[30] For 'tzitzimitl', here given in English as 'monstrous figure', Tena 2019, 606 has 'monstruo'. Torres López 2019, 186–7 retains 'tzitzimitl'—the word appears in sources on pre-Hispanic belief, including SAHAGÚN, *HG* 7, Appendix 1 [1953 viii, 37], 8.1 [1979 ix, 2], listed in Bierhorst 1992, 212–13—and cites its associations with the demonic in Christian Nahuatl literature: SAHAGÚN, *Colloquios* (1564) 1.10, 38v [1986, 173]; BAUTISTA, *Huehuetlahtolli* (c. 1601), 55r, 71r, 73v [2011, 438, 482, 489].

[31] The Spanish *león* is used here for *leo* in the Latin title, but *miztli*, the word for an American mountain lion or puma, is used in the fable itself.

[32] CAMERARIUS, *Fabellae Aesopicae* (1538), 59r.

> enemy, after securing the chance to speak: 'But who out of all the animals', she said, 'shows as much anxiety for your Royal health, or is so concerned about your life, Lion, as I am? I am the one who trailed through every place, tracking down a medicine with which you can clearly be cured . . .'

In Camerarius' narrative the debate in the lion's court has a mock grandeur: the wolf is described as 'declaiming' ('declamitante') and he closes his speech formally 'clausula orationis'). There are no equivalents to terms like these in Nahuatl and the effect of the Ciceronian clausula ('posse videaris') in the fox's speech cannot be captured either.

To achieve a comparable dramatic effect, the Nahuatl translation—which substitutes a coyote for the fox—has to use different techniques, indicated here by italics and double quotation marks:

> Auh in cuitlachtli yniquac ayac quitta coyotl yn oncan tetlahpaloloyan, (ca cenca mococoliaya) opeuh ye quiyollococoltia miztli, quilhui: "Tlahtohuanie, *tla ye xicmotili* yn inepohualiz coyotl, yn ahmo tehuan ohualla yn *mitzmotlapalhuiz*: ca nelli hamotle ipan *mitzmotilia*." Auh in coyotl quin tepan ohuacico, ça achi in quicac yn ixqui teixpanhuiaya cuitlachtli. Auh in miztli yn iquac oquittac coyotl, cenca otlancuitzo, quilhui: "Can oticatca, nocne. Cuix amo titlachia y nican omocenquixtique noteycahuan manehnemi nechtlapaloco. Auh ça tio yn ahmo nimitzitta." Auh in coyotl oquinanquili yn miztli, quilhui: '*Tla oc yhuian xinechmocaquiti*, totecuiyoe. *Cuix timomatzinohua* haca yuhqui tequipachohua yn mococolitzin, yn iuh nehuatl nechtequipachohua. Ca oc nohuian oninemia yn nictemohua yn tlein yc pahtiz monacayotzin. . . .'[33]

> When the wolf noticed that the coyote was not where the visitors were being greeted (as they greatly hated each other), he began to upset the lion by saying: "O king! *Be so kind as to look at* the arrogance of the coyote who has not come with the others *to greet you*, for truly *he does not value you* at all". Then the coyote arrived in time to hear a little bit of the wolf's complaint. The lion, upon discovering the coyote, bared his teeth and asked him: "Where were you, scoundrel? Can't you see that my younger animal brothers are gathered here to greet me? You were the only one I had not seen." The coyote replied to the lion, saying: '*Be so kind as to listen to me calmly*, my lord. *Do you know* of anyone who cares about your illness as much as I do? For that reason I was looking everywhere for a remedy to cure you. . . .'

[33] *Nican ompehua* 1500s, 191r–191v: quotation marks and italics indicating reverential forms have been added. Quotations of the Nahuatl fables are from the Biblioteca Nacional de México Ms. 1628 bis with one exception (n. 63 below).

Here the wolf's motivation is made completely explicit by the narrator, who explains that the wolf and coyote hated each other. The propositions of the wolf's speech, which had been in indirect discourse in the Latin, are expressed in a speech that is directly quoted, and a spoken reproach from the lion is also inserted to convey the gravity of the accusation against the coyote. In addition, reverential forms of address in Nahuatl (indicated above in italics) are used by both the wolf and the coyote in their spoken words. That device operates as a substitute for the oratorical proficiency implicitly ascribed to the animals in the Latin narrative.[34]

There is a presupposition in many assessments of the Nahuatl fables that whoever produced them struggled to understand the Latin or did not have the necessary contextual knowledge to comprehend it fully. For instance, the opening words of 'Chichime yhuan intecuio', 'Dogs and their master' (14), have prompted a repeated claim that the translators could not grasp the notion of being snowbound:[35]

> Ce tlacatl ymilco mocaltzauc hamo nicmati tle ypampa yn aocmo huel oncalaquia altepetl yttic, ca amo huehca quitzticatca.
>
> A man was confined to his farm; I don't know the reason he didn't go into the city anymore, since it was not far.

Yet none of the Latin sources makes mention of snow—the Nahuatl sentence really is an attempt to unpack and clarify the compact wording of Camerarius' text:

> In praedio sub urbe quidam tempestate inclusus
>
> A man was confined by the season to his farm near the city.[36]

Mistaken and sometimes condescending assumptions about the Nahuatl translation have been largely if not entirely due to a failure to identify the correct Latin original.[37] The Mexican versions are bound to look like misprisions or creative elaborations of their source texts if they are set against the Aesops of Bonus Accursius and Aldus Manutius, when they were never in fact based on those editions.

[34] The first exchanges in Nahuatl between Mexicans and Spaniards presented in SAHAGÚN, *HG* Book 12 and *Colloquios* (1564) contain locutions similar to those in this fable. A comparable effect in another council scene in 'Quetzaltototl yhuan toznene' (36) will be discussed below.

[35] *Pace* Brotherston 1987, 19 and 1993, 315, a snowfall, *cepayauitl*, was familiar enough to Mexicans for them to believe it augured a good harvest: SAHAGÚN, *HG* 7.6 [1953 viii, 19] (Nahuatl text); 7.7 [2016, 418], 'De la helada, nieve, y granizo' (Spanish text). Snow was also depicted in the *Codex Telleriano-Remenis* (c. 1563).

[36] CAMERARIUS, *Fabellae Aesopicae* (1538), 46r. Cf. MANUTIUS, 'Vir quidam a tempestate in suo suburbio deprehensus'.

[37] Compare the Nahuatl text of SAHAGÚN, *Colloquios* (1564), which scholars have endowed with primary significance even though it was translated from Spanish: Chapter 5 above.

Such misunderstanding is often connected with an equally mistaken view that the translations have been unduly inflected by indigenous categories or assumptions. It is true that certain words used in the Nahuatl fables do carry connotations specific to Mexico: *tlatoani*, 'ruler', is one example. At the same time it is hard to see what other term could be used as an equivalent for *rex* or *princeps*. Or what word apart from *cuauhtli*, eagle, could convey *aquila*?[38] One gets the impression that some would prefer the Mexican translation not to be as accurate and successful as it actually is.

The recognition of Joachim Camerarius' text as the Latin source provides some extra insights on the provenance and transmission of the Nahuatl translations:

1. The *terminus post quem* for their production has to be 1538, the date of the first printing of Camerarius' *Fabellae Aesopicae*.
2. The *Fabellae Aesopicae* was in Latin alone, putting an end to speculation that the Nahuatl translator was working from an edition that contained a Greek text.[39]
3. There is a stronger case for connecting the Nahuatl translations to the College of Santa Cruz in Tlatelolco because Camerarius' edition may have been available there.[40]
4. With Camerarius identified as the Latin source, minor differences between the BNM and Bancroft manuscripts indicate that the translation in the BNM manuscript is slightly closer to the original.[41]

There are, though, one or two significant departures from Camerarius that will be considered in the next section: these have to be understood within the general picture that emerges from the decisive identification of the source text. The fact that the Nahuatl translations are accurate and convey delicate nuances of the Latin original should not be surprising. Whichever scholars were responsible are likely to have faced the far more daunting challenge of putting Latin sermons, doctrines, and even Gospels into an alien language with alien categories, in which they nonetheless perceived canons of correct expression and *elegantia*.[42]

[38] *Pace* Brotherston 1987, 25; Ríos Castaño 2015, 259.

[39] Such speculation in Díaz Cíntora 1996, 9 is rightly dismissed by Téllez Nieto 2015b, 718–19. Greek was not well known or taught, so it is unsurprising that there are no Greek loan words or glosses in the manuscripts of the Nahuatl fables.

[40] The inventories of books at the college from the 1570s, reproduced in Appendix 1.3), do not specify which texts of Aesop were held, but ROSA FIGUEROA, *Diccionario bibliográphico* (c. 1758), 994, 1023 lists Camerarius' edition, which may have been at Santa Cruz (cf. Chapter 4, n. 87). I am grateful to Andrés Iñigo Silva for locating these references.

[41] See p. 227 above. The sequencing of fables in the BNM manuscript also follows Camerarius more exactly than the Bancroft manuscript, which transposed BNM fable 17.

[42] Cf. OLMOS, *Arte de la lengua mexicana* (1547), 44r and MOLINA, *Aqui comiença* (1555), unpaginated 'Prólogo al Lector' on the 'elegancias' of Nahuatl.

III. The purpose of the Nahuatl translation

Seventy years ago, Ángel María Garibay concluded his foundational survey of Aesop's Fables in Nahuatl by remarking that they were very useful for study of the language.[43] He was referring to the benefits they could offer to modern-day learners of classical Nahuatl, but some have taken him to mean that the fables originally served as a kind of textbook. Salvador Díaz Cíntora, for example, envisaged Fray Arnaldo de Bassacio employing the Nahuatl fables to teach his native students to read and write.[44] That notion is unlikely, because the friar is reported to have relied on his command of the Mexican language to teach *Spanish* grammar and literacy ('gramática romanzada') at the College of San José de los Naturales.[45] For such an end, a Castilian version of Aesop would have been more practical.

More recently it has been suggested that the Nahuatl translation facilitated the learning of *Latin* at the Imperial College of Santa Cruz de Tlatelolco.[46] This suggestion runs against the abundant evidence available for how Latin was actually taught there: multiple copies of Nebrija's grammar, the *Grammatica Maturini* that Fray Maturino Gilberti published in Mexico City, and the text books of Despauter and Erasmus—all of which seem to have been used in the college—presupposed what would now be called the 'direct method' of immersion in the target language.[47] Bilingual or grammar-translation approaches were not favoured for Spanish learners of Latin, and would have had even less appeal if they involved a polysynthetic language like Nahuatl. Aesop's Fables were essential for elementary Latin instruction, because they were read in Latin. For Franciscans who were concerned with education and conversion, texts turned into Nahuatl were conceived as an end product, rather than as instruments of linguistic instruction.

The miscellanies in which the translation of the fables has been transmitted might offer a clue about its purpose. The inclusion of Aesop in those collections is not as anomalous as it might seem: for early modern educators the classical provenance of Aesop's Fables was of far less interest than their perceived utility.[48] As well as constituting a standard elementary text for students of Latin, the content of the fables was considered to be morally edifying.[49]

[43] Garibay 1954 ii, 184: '. . . utilísimas para el estudio de la lengua, nada de particular ofrecen en el campo puramente literario, si no es la cuidadosa forma en que están traducidas'.

[44] Díaz Cíntora 1996, 9 offered no evidence to support his suggestion that Basaz was the translator.

[45] RAMÍREZ DE FUENLEAL, 'Carta a la emperatriz' (1533) [1939, iii, 118].

[46] Ríos Castaño 2015, 258.

[47] Cf. Chapter 4, III above.

[48] Contrast Vollmer 1987, 207: 'no relationship of content or form' can be discerned between the different parts of the manuscripts containing the Nahuatl fables.

[49] Vollmer 1989.

It is unlikely that the Nahuatl translations were made simply as an exercise or display of linguistic competence—the preceptive nature of the collection is conveyed by its full title:

> Nican ompehua y çaçanillatolli yn quitlali ce tlamatini
> ytoca Esopo, yc techmachtia yn nehmatcanemiliztli.
>
> Here begin the fables set down by a sage
> called Aesop, in which he teaches us prudent living.

'Nican ompehua', 'Here begin(s)', which might once have signalled the start of an oral presentation or performance, was a conventional opening formula for written texts, but there are no apostrophes to give any hint as to the identity of the readers or their situation.[50]

On the other hand, the structure and character of the collection as a whole are distinctive, and unusual enough to yield some new insights into its overall conception. The forty-seven fables put into Nahuatl were selected from the first seventy-four items in Camerarius' volume. Despite twenty-seven of the tales being omitted from the Nahuatl translation, those that were retained were presented in precisely the same order as they had appeared in the Latin text. The Conspectus (Appendix 1.6.1) makes it easier to identify the items from that grouping that were *not* translated. Most of the exclusions can be easily explained: the stories that were left out had condoned acts of revenge, trickery, and other undesirable forms of conduct, or the stories had contained unseemly elements. The case of 'Fiber' (32 in Camerarius' unnumbered edition), in which the beaver removed his genitals to avoid being killed, is a telling example. Fables with morals that are elusive, obscure (49, 'Malus et pirus'; 50, 'Talpa'; 51, 'Vespae et perdices'), or simply inconsequential (17, 'Piscatores'; 53, 'Aper et Vulpes'; 55, 'Hinnuleus'; 63, 'Cerva et Leo') were also suppressed.

Other omissions include 18, 'Fraudulentus', which repeatedly referred to the Greco-Roman gods ('dii'), and some fables that had named individual deities such as Apollo (16, 'De Apollonis tentatore'), Hercules (61, 'Pulex'), Mercury (42, Lignator et Mercurius'; 46, 'Viator'), and Venus (67, 'Sus et canis'). The version of 44, 'Asinus et Olitor', on the other hand, replaces Jupiter's name with 'dios', the Spanish loan word that customarily designated God in Nahuatl Christian texts. The eschewal of pagan divinities is to be expected because even in the 1500s the gods of classical antiquity could still be considered a threat.[51]

[50] Compare: (i) the opening of the Nahuatl translation of SAHAGÚN, *Colloquios* (1564), 29v [1986, 100]: 'Nican vmpeva yn temachtiliz tlatolli'; and (ii) the *Cantares mexicanos* (1560s–1580s) e.g. fols. 7, 15, 16v, 37v. The words 'Nican mopohua' began the Nahuatl narrative of the apparition of the Virgin of Guadalupe in LASO DE LA VEGA, *Huei Tlamahuiçoltica* (1649): cf. Appendix 3.

[51] Cf. Chapter 8, II below.

Thus, in the Nahuatl translation 'dios' is substituted for any references in the original Latin to *dii*, Greco-Roman gods, or to *numen*, a divine agency that had a pagan association.[52] A resurgence of interest in Christian texts was propelling humanist endeavours on both sides of the Atlantic, but the fables are not doctrinal in any religious sense, even if the author of the Latin source text was a Lutheran theologian.

The Mexican fables, however, do seem to have a more specific kind of didactic purpose, which is made evident by the selection of stories that closes the collection (33–47). A clear preponderance of these, seven out of the last eleven fables (36–47), have stories or morals of a political import, concerned either with the social order or with the art of government.[53] What is more, although most of the Nahuatl translations show remarkable fidelity to the Latin, three fables in the final group exhibit some notable departures from their Latin sources, apparently in order to magnify political themes.

Questions of statecraft are introduced in the narrative of 'Totoanqui yhuan acatzanatl', 'Birdcatcher and Thrush' (33).

> A birdcatcher was setting his snares in place and scattering food for the birds. From the top of a tree a reed-thrush was watching him, very intrigued by what the birdcatcher was doing; so it approached him to ask him, and said 'What are you doing?' The birdcatcher replied: 'I am setting up a city.' The birdcatcher left his snares and went to hide somewhere. Then the reed-thrush said: 'Let me see how the city is laid out here for living.' The reed-thrush flew over the snare and, when it was caught, the birdcatcher ran to seize it. Already caught, the thrush said to the birdcatcher: 'If this is how you set up your city, you will not be seeing many citizens at all soon.'

The Nahuatl text translated here follows that of Camerarius' 'Auceps et cassita' closely, but both protagonists' spoken words are externalized in direct discourse, whereas in the Latin only the final pronouncement was quoted directly. In addition the bird's desire to see the city, which had been a simple expression of purpose in the original ('Cassita ad nouam urbem aspiciendam celeriter advolat', 'The lark swiftly flew over to see the new city'), is reformulated so that the bird's intention is expressed in direct speech:

[52] *Numen* connoted pagan divinity: Augustine, *Enarrationes in Psalmos* 96.11, *Sermones* 62.6.10. In 'Quauhtlacihuamaçatl yhuan xocomecatl', 'Forest Doe and Vine' (43), 'itetlatzacuiltiliz Dios', 'God's punishment', is thus used for 'vltionem numinis', 'vengeance of a divine power', in 'Cerva et Vitis'. Ríos Castaño 2015, 245–6 has argued that the Nahuatl translation of this and other fables functioned as stories or *exempla* for conversion purposes. But even if that were so, Aesop was never, as Ríos suggests, a 'liturgical source' (245) or used in 'liturgical contexts' (246, 255), at least not in the usual sense of liturgical.

[53] Cf. Appendix 1.6.2.

> auh yn acatzanatl quimolhui, Tla niquitta quenami yn altepetl quimana nican onemiya.
>
> Then the reed-thrush said: 'Let me see how the city here is laid out for living.'

Those words anticipate the political value of the moral in the original Latin fable:

> Fabula monet, male coli atque habitari cum oppida tum domus, in crudelitate & rapinis principum.
>
> The fable advises that it is bad to live and dwell in towns and households amidst the cruelty and depredations of those in charge.

That value is accentuated in the Nahuatl moral by the use of the term 'altepetl', 'city-state(s)', to convey 'towns and households'. The potential abuses of those in government are stated more explicitly:

> Yni çaçanilli techmachtia ca niman ahmo huel oncan nemohua yn altepetl yttic yn canin tepachohua çan no yehuantin teca mocacayahua tetlacuihcuilia yhuan tetolinia.
>
> The fable teaches us that one cannot live well in a city-state where those who govern people are the ones who deceive them, steal from them, and harm them.

This Nahuatl version of the moral is deployed on a second occasion in the Bancroft manuscript alone: there it is appended to the closing fable, 'Ce cahcatzactli', 'Black man' (47), which will be discussed below.

A second tale involving birds, 'Quetzaltototl yhuan toznene', 'Quetzal Bird and Parrot' (36), is in the final group of fables that addresses questions of society and governance. It is a version of Camerarius' 'Pavo et monedula', 'Peacock and Jackdaw':

> Cum haberent comitia volucres regi creando, petijt regnum pauo, quod se ob formam eximiam illo dignum prae cunctis esse diceret. Qui cum omnium suffragia laturus videretur: Hic tamen rex, inquit monedula, si forte sit factus, & aquilam hostem habuerimus, quidnam opis auxilijque poterit afferre?
>
> Monet fabula, in principibus legendis non speciem modo, sed etiam virtutem & sapientiam spectari oportere.[54]

[54] CAMERARIUS, *Fabellae Aesopicae* (1538), 54r.

> When the birds were holding an election to appoint a king, the peacock asked for the kingdom, because, he said, he was deserving above all of them on account of his exceptional beauty. But when it seemed as if he were about to win the votes of them all, the jackdaw said, 'If this one happens to be made our king and we end up having the eagle as enemy, what help or support could he provide?'
>
> The fable advises that in electing leaders, it is important not just to look for a fine appearance, but also for strength and wisdom.

While the story and the moral of the Latin text are retained in the Nahuatl presentation, some notable stylistic embellishments have been added to the speech by the parrot (who takes the place of the jackdaw):

> Ceppa omocentlalique yn ixquich nepapan totome ynic quipehpenazque yn aquin yntlatocauh yez. Auh yn ocenquizque yhuan in ye quinemilia yn ac yehuatl quixquetzazque intlahtoca yez, niman ymixpan moquetz in quetzaltototl, oquimihtlani yn tlatocayotl. Auh yn iquac ye achi mochintin quitlahuelcaquilia ynic yehuatl ye quixquetzaznequi yn intlatocauh yez, niman tetlan hualquiz. yn toznene ye quinnonotza, quimilhui, Tla xicmocaquiltican totecuiyohuane, yn amiquecholhuan ypalnemohuani, Yntla yehuatl anquimotenehuilia totlatocauh yez in nican yhcac quetzaltototl: auh intla quenmanian techyaochihuaz quauhtli, quexquich yn itlapalihuiz oncatqui? Cuix huel quinamiquiz? Auh yehica in nehuatl yuh niquitta yehuatl technequi tiquixquetzazque in totlatocauh yez quauhtli.
>
> Yni çaçanilli techmachtia. Ca yn iquac pehpenalo tlahtoque in quimocuitlahuizque altepetl hamo yehuatl mottaz yn inchipahualiz yn inqualnexiliz, ça yehuatl mottaz yn inchicahualiz yhuan yn imixtlamatiliz yn innezcaliliz.

> Once upon a time all the different birds met to decide who should be their ruler. When they had come together and were thus thinking about whom they should choose to be their ruler, the quetzal bird got up in front of them and asked for the power to rule. Nearly all the birds were already agreeing that they wanted to choose him to be their ruler, but then the parrot went before them and admonished them, saying: 'Please listen, our lordships, o you flamingos of the One through whom there is life. If you nominate the quetzal who stands here before you to be your king, and if the eagle declares war on us one day, what are his strengths? Will he be able to stand up to him? So then I am of the view that we should nominate the eagle—our ruler should be the eagle.'
>
> This fable teaches us: when the rulers are chosen to look after the town, beauty and looks should not be considered, but only strength, prudence and aptitude.

A kind of grandeur is conferred on this avian debate by the use of a Nahuatl reverential form in the parrot's address to the other birds ('Tla xicmocaquiltican'), whom he hails as 'totecuiyohane' ('our lordships').[55] The effect is very much like that of the courtly exchange of speeches in 'Leon tequani yhuan cuitlachtli', 'Fierce *León* and Wolf' (46), described above—but on this occasion there is no corresponding effect in Camerarius' Latin. A second courteous epithet employed by the parrot, 'amiquecholhuan ypalnemohuani', 'you birds of the One through whom there is life', is tantamount to 'you birds of Our Lord God'.[56] There is no corresponding theistic reference in the Latin source.

A version of 'Aethiops', 'An African', is the final fable in the Nahuatl corpus. The narrative in Camerarius' text was as follows:[57]

> Emptum aethiopem quidam putabat ita in negligentia prioris domini decoloratum fuisse. Itaque ad se deductum, summa cum cura lauare, & destringere, & omni ratione anniti, vt sordes illas, quemadmodum rebatur, abstergere posset. Verum mutare illum colorem non valuit, aethiops autem afflictus cura, in morbum incidit.[58]

> Someone who bought an African thought he had been discoloured by the negligence of his previous master. So after bringing him back, he took great pains to wash, scrape, and work on him by every means, to be able to cleanse away, as he thought, the grime. In fact he had no success in changing his colour, but the African was harmed by these efforts and fell ill.

'Ce cahcatzactli', 'Black man' (47), translates this closely:

> Ce tlacatl quimocohui ce cahcatzactli; momatia ça can[59] tlaxiccahualli ynic opochehuac, cayc omalti yn ompa achto otetlayecolti. Yehica quipehualti in cahaltia quipahpaca momuztlaye, cenca quimamatelohua quitequixaqualohua yn inacayo. Auh in cahcatzactli ayc huel oquicauh yn icatzahuaca yn ipochehuaca, ça ye ilhuice yc peuh ye mococohua, omic.[60]

[55] The formula 'tla xicmocaquitican', 'Please listen', is common in Christian literature: cf. ESCALONA, 'Dominica in albis' (1500s), 237r; Sell and Burkhart 2009, 136, 188, 196, 200.

[56] *Ipalnemohuani* was used of the Christian God: SAHAGÚN, *Colloquios* (1564) [1986, 120–1] translated 'el verdadero Dios, Señor universal, que da ser y vivir a todas las cosas' as 'Uel Nelli Teotl, Tlatoani, in Ipalnemoani'; cf. OLMOS, *Tratado de hechicerías* (1553) [1990, 13]. 'Ayac' 2014 notes that *Ipalnemohuani* was far more rarely used of the Aztec god Tezcatlipoca, finding only one instance in SAHAGÚN, *HG* 3.2 [1978 iv, 11]. Psalms for the third day of Nativity in SAHAGÚN, *Psalmodia Christiana*, 'Pro tertia die' [1993, 373] associate angels singing in heaven with various tropical birds.

[57] The Latin *Aethiopia* generally designated sub-Saharan Africa, rather than Ethiopia.

[58] CAMERARIUS, *Fabellae Aesopicae* (1538), 60r.

[59] BNM ms: 'ca çan', misplacing the cedilla.

[60] BNM and Bancroft: 'mic'.

> A man bought himself a black man. He thought it was only neglect that made him so smoke-grey, that he had never bathed where he had served before. Therefore he began to bathe him. Day after day he washed him, he rubbed him hard with his hands, he scraped his body firmly. But the black man never lost his blackness, his smokiness. He became more ill through this treatment; he died.

There is, however, one significant alteration: the addition of 'omic', 'he died', as the very last word. That changes the tenor of the story, endowing it with far more gravity as the master who abused his bought man is made responsible for his death.

A second alteration is an abbreviation and subtle adjustment to the Latin moral, which Camerarius had amplified with a maxim from Aristophanes:[61]

> Significat fabula nullo pacto mutari ingenia & naturas, sed retinere insitas semper proprietates, & quasi personas attributas sibi. Recte igitur dicitur & hoc apud Aristophanem:
>
> Non poteris rectum cancris inducere gressum,
> Nec leves horrentis echini reddere sentes.
>
> The fable means that characters and natures can by no means be changed, but always keep their ingrained properties, and the characters, so to say, assigned to them. So in Aristophanes it is correctly said:
>
> 'You will not be able to get crabs to walk in a straight line,
> Nor to make smooth the spines of the spiky hedgehog.'

In contrast, the lesson of the Nahuatl fable highlights the agency of the one who seeks to transform another, rather than the subject's incapacity to undergo change:

> Yni çaçanilli techmachtia, ca yn quenami ceceyaca yyeliz yn ipan tlacat ayac huel occentlamantli ypan quicuepiliz.
>
> This fable teaches us that in whatever way each one is born is his nature; nobody can change it into another.

The alterations to the story and moral both put the master-servant relation into sharper relief. This new slant also represents a departure from Erasmus' interpretation of the saying 'Aethiops non albescit', 'An African does not whiten', in his popular collection of adages, *Adagiorum chiliades* (1508):

> De iis dici solitum, qui nunquam mutaturi sunt ingenium. Quicquid enim nativum id haud facile mutatur. Fertur Aesopicus apologus de quodam,

[61] The Latin hexameters are versions of Aristophanes, *Peace*, verses 1083 and 1088.

> qui empto Aethiopi, cum eum colorem arbitraretur non nativum esse, sed domini superioris accidisse neglectu, assidua lotura faciem divexavit, ita ut morbum etiam adiungeret, colore nihilo, quam antea fuerat meliore.[62]

> This is usually said about those who will never change their nature, as whatever is inborn is not easily changed at all. An Aesopic tale is told about someone who, as he had bought an African and did not think his colour was natural but had come about from the previous owner's neglect, damaged his appearance with constant scrubbing, to the point that he actually made him ill, with his colour no better than it had been before.

This elucidation of 'Aethiops non albescit' converged with the moral of 'Aethiops' in the Aldine edition, and the ensuing summary of the Aesopic story here looks like a paraphrase of Aldus' text. It would seem that Erasmus had given no more attention than Camerarius would to the relation between master and servant that furnished the background for the fable.

The changes the Nahuatl translator made to the story and moral of *Aethiops* are perhaps too subtle to attract attention. Nonetheless, it is still surprising that there has been no discussion of the relevance of the theme and interpretation of 'Ce cahcatzactli' to the society of early colonial New Spain. In that environment, in which social hierarchy was determined by ethnic discrimination, the affirmation made in Nahuatl that 'whatever nature a person is born with, nobody can change into another' could have more than one sense. It might convey resigned compliance: the natives, *naturales* in Spanish, cannot change their 'inborn human nature' ('yyeliz yn ipan tlacat')—'quicquid nativum' in Erasmus' commentary above. Or it could be taken to suggest a kind of resistance: masters cannot change the nature of those who are supposed to serve them. That second implication is more salient in the Nahuatl translation of the moral than it had been in the Latin.

In the Bancroft manuscript the fable is endowed with a further ideological charge, because it is followed by a second moral, repeated from 'Totoanqui yhuan acatzanatl', 'Birdcatcher and Thrush':[63]

> Yni çaçanilli techmachtia ca niman ahmo huel oncan nemoa in altepetl itic in cani tepachoa çan no yehuanti teca mocaiahua tetlacuicuilia ihuan tetolinia.

> The fable teaches us that one cannot live well in a city-state where those who govern people are the ones who deceive them, steal from them, and harm them.

[62] ERASMUS, *Adagia* (1508), 237v [1981, 580–1].

[63] The repetition is noted, but without comment, by Vollmer 1987, 213.

As well as making the political significance of the story more evident, this additional moral achieves a kind of ring-composition for the whole collection: here, at its very end, the counsel on 'living well' ('nemoa') recalls the claim that the fables taught 'prudent living' ('nematcanemiliztli'), which was made in the opening title.

It would be a mistake to assume that either of the Nahuatl morals appended to this fable was a comment on the inequity of Spanish rule. The art of government had long been a dominant theme in European humanism and pedagogy. The objective of training leaders was what had led to the advanced education of indigenous students in New Spain, and Erasmus' *Institutio principis Christiani*, 'Instruction of a Christian prince' (1516), circulated in the viceroyalty, along with comparable Latin treatises by Francesco Patrizi, and Juan Ginés de Sepúlveda.[64] The enthusiasm for *specula principum*, or 'mirrors for princes', was shared by Franciscan and Dominican missionaries, extending even to their grammars and vocabularies of indigenous languages.[65]

At least one Latin study of the art of government was put into Nahuatl in the 1560s: a version of *De regimine politiae*, 'The regulation of a polity', originally authored by Denis the Carthusian in the 1400s, has been convincingly attributed to Fray Alonso de Molina.[66] That translation would have been made in Tlatelolco—Fray Juan Gaona and Hernando de Ribas were possibly involved—and its title, *Izcatqui yn innemiliz yn tepachoa*, 'Behold the manner of living for governors', has some resonance with the full title of the Nahuatl Aesop given above.[67] Just as importantly, another text produced in the 1500s, *Izcatqui yn intezcaamauh, in tlahtoque*, 'Here is a mirror-book for rulers', was an original work of *speculum* literature in Nahuatl.[68]

Fray Antonio de Guevara's *El reloj de príncipes* (1529) exemplifies an abundance of vernacular writing from Spain on the same theme, and production of works in this mode would continue unabated into the seventeenth century, on both sides of the Atlantic.[69] Other authors packaged their work to make it a part of this trend: in

[64] See Chapter 4, II above. Many other such works were in circulation: cf. SEPÚLVEDA, *Democrates* (1535) acquired by Huitzimengari: cf. Chapter 4, I, p. 122 above; Appendix 1.3; and Lupher 2003, 111.

[65] Cf. LAS CASAS, *De regia potestate* (1571). For the trend in missionary literature, cf. TORO, *Thesoro* (c. 1536) (cf. Chapter 1), the preliminaries of MOLINA, *Vocabulario* (1571) and SANTO TOMÁS, *Grammatica o arte* (1560) discussed in Chapter 3 above.

[66] Tavárez 2019. The *De regimine politiae* (1400s) was in CARTHUSIANUS, *Opera minora* (1532) ii, 319–34. Sánchez Aguilera 2022, 36–54 discerns connections between the Nahuatl translation and SAHAGÚN, *Sermonario* (1563).

[67] The frontispiece of the Tlatelolco copy of CARTHUSIANUS, *Opera minora* (1532), which was signed by Gaona, is reproduced in Mathes 1982, 30.

[68] The anonymous *Izcatqui yníntezcaamauh, in tlahtoque* (c. 1550) is included with a copy of MOLINA, *Innemiliz yn tepachoa* (c. 1550), in the *Miscelánea sagrada* manuscript (1550s–1570s): Alcántara Rojas 2022, 257–8.

[69] MARIANA, *De rege et regis institutione* (1599), SIGÜENZA Y GÓNGORA, *Theatro de virtudes políticas* (1680). Cf. Chapter 9, IV for Fernando de Alva Ixtlilxochitl's portrayal of Nezahualyotl.

his dedication of *La Vlyxea de Homero* (1556) to Philip II, for example, Gonzalo Pérez claimed that his verse rendering of Homer's *Odyssey* was useful reading for a king. The Nahuatl Aesop seems to share this tendency: the content has been delicately arranged in such a way as to accentuate questions with a bearing on statecraft.

The few Mexicans who were in a position to read the Nahuatl fables (or to hear them read aloud) would have been high-ranking nobles. The moralistic tenor of the collection as a whole and the emphasis, in the final fables it contains, on the conduct of rulers of an *altepetl,* lend weight to the possibility that it was fashioned as a kind of mirror for princes. A preoccupation with good governance as central to 'prudent living', however, had not been a conventional feature of early modern collections of Aesop in Europe—that seems to be unique to this Mexican corpus.

IV. The identity of the translator or translators

These considerations bear on the status and identity of whoever authored the Nahuatl fables. The content of the other texts in the manuscripts in which the fables were copied suggests that they could have been translated by Franciscan missionaries, by their students from the indigenous nobility who were themselves in a position to rule their own principalities, or by both friars and Indians who worked together.[70] It is likely that a group of translators was involved, not just a single individual, as Nahuatl versions of European texts were nearly always collaborative endeavours. The use of different Nahuatl locutions to convey particular Latin terms that recur from one fable to another strongly suggests that various translators were involved, each making their own interpretative choices.[71]

The possibility of Fray Bernardino de Sahagún's participation must be taken seriously, given that he directed the production of many works in Nahuatl.[72] Gerdt Kutscher, the German editor of the Nahuatl fables in the Bancroft manuscript, took the view that 'the Aesop translations owe their existence to the Franciscan spirit, and behind them stands no less a figure than Bernardino de Sahagún himself'.[73] That carefully expressed opinion does not amount to a declaration of Sahagún's exclusive authorship.[74] Sahagún himself made clear that he worked with native collaborators, and his introductory note to the *Colloquios y Doctrina christiana* (1564) credited by

[70] Chapter 4, I; cf. Villella 2016, 29–72.

[71] Torres López 2019, 169–71, 182, 201 makes this important point, citing a number of convincing examples.

[72] Chapter 5, Chapter 8 below.

[73] Kutscher quoted in Vollmer 1987, 222–3.

[74] Garibay 1954 ii, 184 identified Sahagún as the translator because the Fables in the BNM manuscript are in the same hand as the *Cantares* and *Kalendario,* but this is no proof that those different works were by the same author.

name Antonio Valeriano of Azcapotzalco, Alonso Vegerano, Martín Jacobita, and Andrés Leonardo.[75] Several years later, in the preface to his *Historia general*, Sahagún again paid tribute to three of those Latinists—Vegerano, Jacobita, and Valeriano—describing Valeriano as 'the principal and wisest'.[76]

All the instructors and students at the College of Santa Cruz would have known Aesop's Fables, which were a standard component of a Latin education. But putting them into Nahuatl would require a resourceful and extensive command of the language, with knowledge of diction to address themes that were different from those of Gospel lectionaries and sermons. As the friars who possessed such capability might have been less inclined to translate Aesop than texts of religious import, the work may have been done by one or more of the indigenous scholars.

The Franciscan chronicler, Fray Juan de Torquemada, offers some information that could point to the collegian whom Sahagún considered to be the most accomplished Latinist as the translator of the fables:

> Don Antonio Valeriano, an Indian, a native of the town of Azcaputzalco, one league from this city, governor of the district of San Juan, which they call Tenuchtitlan. Having proved a good Latinist, logician, and philosopher, he succeeded the masters named above [Arnaldo de Bassacio, Bernardino de Sahagún, Andrés de Olmos] as Lecturer in Grammar at the College for some years, and after that he was elected Governor of Mexico, and he governed the Indians of this city for more than thirty-five years . . . I myself know very many of the particular aspects of his talent, because for some years he had been my master in teaching me the Mexican language. I was present when he died and, among other things, he gave me his works, worthy of his knowledge, translations into the Latin language and also into Mexican: there was one of Cato, something very worthy of esteem, which (if God pleases) will be printed in his name.[77]

[75] SAHAGÚN, *Colloquios* (1564), 'Al Prudente Lector' [1987, 59], quoted in Chapter 5, IV (i) above.

[76] SAHAGÚN, *HG* Book 2, Prologue [1982 i, 55].

[77] TORQUEMADA, *Monarchia Indiana* (1615) 15.43 [1977 v, 176–7]: 'don Antonio Valeriano, indio, natural del pueblo de Azcaputzalco, una legua desta ciudad, gobernador de la parte de San Juan, que llaman Tenuchtitlan, que habiendo salido buen latino, lógico y filósofo, sucedió a sus maestros, arriba nombrados, en leer la gramática en el colegio algunos años; y después desto fue elegido por gobernador de Mexico, y gobernó más de treinta y cinco años a los indios desta ciudad . . . y de su talento sé yo muchas particularidades por haber sido algunos años mi maestro en la enseñanza de la lengua mexicana. Y cuando murió estuve presente, y entre otras cosas que me dio de sus trabajos, dignos de su saber, así de lengua latina como de traducción de mexicana, fue una, a Catón traducido, cosa cierto muy para estimar, el cual (si a Dios place) se imprimirá en su nombre.' Torquemada gave an earlier notice of Valeriano at 5.10 [1975 ii, 361].

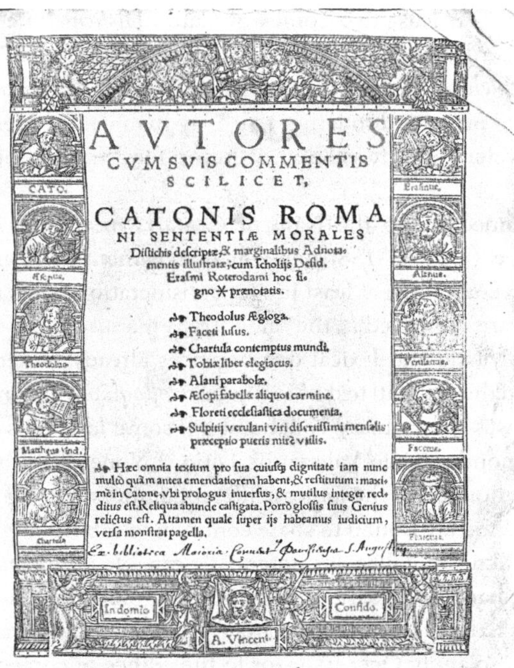
AVTORES
CVM SVIS COMMENTIS
SCILICET,

CATONIS ROMANI SENTENTIÆ MORALES
Diſtichis deſcriptæ, & marginalibus Adnotamentis illuſtratæ; cum ſcholijs Deſid. Eraſmi Roterodami hoc ſigno ✳ prænotatis.

Theodolus Ægloga.
Faceti luſus.
Chartula contemptus mundi.
Tobiæ liber elegiacus.
Alani parabolæ.
Æſopi fabellæ aliquot carmine.
Floreti eccleſiaſtica documenta.
Sulpitij verulani viri diſertiſſimi menſalis præceptio pueris mirè vtilis.

Hæc omnia textum pro ſua cuiuſq; dignitate iam nunc multò quàm antea emendatiorem habent, & reſtitutum: maximè in Catone, vbi prologus inuerſus, & mutilus integer redditus eſt. Reliqua abunde caſtigata. Porrò gloſſis ſuus Genius relictus eſt. Attamen quale ſuper ijs habeamus iudicium, verſa monſtrat pagella.

Figure 7.3 Erasmus' edition of the *Autores*, Lyon, 1539. Beinecke Library.

Several of Valeriano's contemporaries bear witness to his excellent command of Latin and Nahuatl, but this is the only one to mention that he had translated Cato. 'Cato' was generally taken to refer to the widely read *Disticha moralia*, 'Moral couplets', which had long been attributed to Cato the Elder, the Roman soldier and statesman born in the third century BC.[78]

The proverbial sayings ascribed to Cato, together with medieval Latin versifications of Aesop's Fables, formed part of the *Auctores octo morales*, a canon of preceptive texts that dominated school curricula from the early fourteenth century.[79] The collection continued to be used and remained in print well into the sixteenth century—a version edited by Erasmus, with a couple of further inclusions, was published in 1539 (Figure 7.3). Aesop and Cato also headed the list of classical authors whom the Jesuits sought to publish in the 1570s, soon after their

[78] The *Disticha moralia* actually date from the third or fourth century AD. The suggestion made by León-Portilla 2000b, 34 that Valeriano translated Cato the Elder's *De agri cultura* can be discounted: that text which was far less common than the *Distichs* would have had little educational or practical value in New Spain, and there is no evidence that it circulated there.

[79] *Auctores octo* (1400s); Ziolkowski 2006, 114.

arrival in Mexico.[80] At least two copies of Cato's *Distichs*, one probably copied by hand, were recorded in the College of Santa Cruz in the 1570s.[81] If Valeriano translated the *Distichs*, it is conceivable that he translated Aesop's Fables too. The texts were so often presented together that Fray Juan de Torquemada might have been mistaking Valeriano's translation of Aesop for a translation of 'Cato' in the first place.

Valeriano's connection to the Nahuatl *Cantares mexicanos*, or 'Songs in the Mexican Language' (c. 1560–1580), in which he is mentioned and which he may have had a part in compiling, at least invites consideration of his role in producing the fables, which are preserved in the same BNM manuscript as the *Cantares*.[82] In addition to the stylistic and lexical convergences already hinted at between the Nahuatl fables and the Nahuatl text of Sahagún's *Colloquios y Doctrina christiana* (for which Valeriano was the primary collaborator), some locutions in the *Colloquios* have clear correspondences in Valeriano's Latin.[83] None of this though, amounts to proof of his authorship of the fables: different authors writing in Nahuatl in the same place and period are bound to share common vocabulary.

The number of known collegians potentially capable of the task is certainly not confined to those name-checked by Sahagún.[84] But only a few have testimonies to their capacities as Latinists and as translators, and none has as many as Valeriano.[85] If it is appropriate to apply Occam's razor to the edifice of conjectures involved in postulating just one Mexican author, and thus to choose the hypothesis that involves the fewest (of many) assumptions, then don Antonio Valeriano seems to be the best bet. This hypothesis also harmonizes with the interpretation of the Mexican fables offered here, given Valeriano's political experience and his pre-eminent position in the Mexican nobility. A thirty-five-year term as Indian governor of the San Juan Tenochtitlan in Mexico City—the jurisdiction once ruled by his uncle, Montezuma II—would certainly have qualified him to conceive of the Aesop translation as a guide for rulers of an *altepetl*.

[80] The *Distichs* came second after Aesop's Fables in a list of school texts the Jesuits sought to publish in Mexico. Cf. Chapter 4, n. 91 above.

[81] Cf. Appendix 1.3, items [24] and [98]. Both texts in Santa Cruz would have predated the editions by Nebrija and Erasmus that were later available in Mexico. Osorio Romero 1980, 32 notes two different printings of ERASMUS, *Catonis Disticha moralia* (1559, 1567) in the BNM.

[82] *Cantares mexicanos* (1560s–1580s), 41r [1985, 268–73] presents a song that was composed by Francisco Plácido, one of the co-signatories of the 1561 Latin letter to Philip II from the rulers of Azcapotzalco: Chapter 6, n. 81 above.

[83] Chapter 6, pp. 215–16 above.

[84] Cf. Appendix 1.4 below.

[85] Chapter 6, III, (iv) above.

V. Conclusions

Crucial to any assessment of a translation in its historical context is the question of its directionality—whether it was made into or out of a language better known to the translator. The challenge for the translator of Aesop into Nahuatl never lay in making sense of the Latin source, but in finding the appropriate idioms to convey it in the target language. It cannot be assumed that even native Mexican Latinists, who were subjected from childhood to the Franciscans' immersive teaching of *grammatica,* would necessarily possess the capacity for innovation, circumlocution, and correctness of speech in a language that was rapidly becoming corrupted.

By the same token it should not be imagined (as it generally has been) that the translator or translators had any particular regard for pre-Hispanic beliefs and systems of thought. Identification of Joachim Camerarius' *Fabellae Aesopicae* as the Latin source used helps to dispel such notions. Many of the details and stylistic elements—notably speeches in direct discourse—in the Nahuatl fables that had been deemed to bespeak the intrusion of an 'indigenous' sensibility were already evident in the original Latin. The rendering is far more proficient and precise than scholars have realized.

The rare modifications that have been made to Camerarius' text intensify or occasionally introduce references to statecraft, reflecting the apparent character of the Nahuatl collection as a 'mirror for princes'. As noted above, such concerns were a conspicuous feature of Spanish vernacular literature and the influential Christian humanist works of Erasmus, Patrizi, and others—and they percolated into missionary literature and even into *artes* and *vocabularios* of Nahuatl and other Amerindian languages. The *Cantares mexicanos* also exhibit a preoccupation with rulers and with kingship, in keeping with the high status of their indigenous composers. But whatever the context and purpose of the Nahuatl translations of Aesop may have been, the definitive identification of their Latin source means that systematic linguistic analysis and more informed interpretation of the contents can now begin.

8

Aztec Gods and Orators

Classical Learning and Indigenous Agency in the Florentine Codex

Christian missionaries in New Spain had to be vigilant for evidence of lingering pagan beliefs:

> The sins of idolatry, idolatrous rituals, idolatrous superstitions, auguries, abuses, and idolatrous ceremonies are not yet completely lost. To preach against these matters, and even to know if they exist, it is needful to know how they practiced them in the times of their idolatry, for, through our lack of knowledge of this, they perform many idolatrous things in our presence without our understanding it.[1]

Fray Bernardino de Sahagún thus described the motive for his thorough study of Mexico as it had been before the coming of the Spaniards. The resulting history, which was concluded in the late 1570s after three decades of research, went beyond an examination of the Aztecs' religion to provide a record of their forms of knowledge and aspects of their everyday life. Presented in both Spanish and Nahuatl and illustrated with ink drawings and coloured paintings, the work was originally entitled *Historia universal de las cosas de la Nueva España*, 'Universal enquiry into the matters of New Spain'. It is now better known as the *Historia general de las cosas de Nueva España* or as the *Florentine Codex*, after the final and most complete manuscript of twelve books, which is held in the Biblioteca Medicea Laurenziana in Florence (cf. Bibliography below).[2]

[1] SAHAGÚN, *Historia general* (c. 1580) Book 1, Prologue [1982 i, 45–6].

[2] '*Historia general*' or '*HG*' will be adopted here, and *Florentine Codex* will designate the Laurentian manuscript. Citations of the twelve books will usually give references in brackets to Dibble and Anderson 1950–1982, an edition of the Nahuatl text in thirteen parts with an English translation. The introductory volume [1982 i], the last to be published, contains Sahagún's Spanish prologues and appendices to the twelve books. Garibay's edition of the *HG* [2016] will sometimes be cited for the

Aztec Latin. Andrew Laird, Oxford University Press. © Oxford University Press 2024.
DOI: 10.1093/oso/9780197586358.003.0009

The greater part of the history is based on testimonies from indigenous elders, painstakingly transcribed and interpreted by a group of Nahuatl-speaking Latinists trained at the College of Santa Cruz. Sahagún's own contribution was that of editor, redactor, and Spanish co-translator. The essential distinction between the Nahuatl text effectively produced by the Mexican scholars and Sahagún's Spanish translations and shorter editorial commentaries will bear on the following discussion of the use of classical and Christian sources in the *Historia general*. The role of Sahagún as the architect of the work will be accentuated first—in a review of its relation to some medieval and Renaissance precursors (Section I), and in its treatment of paganism and idolatry (Section II). On the other hand, some latent echoes of Greco-Roman literature in the Nahuatl text can firmly be attributed to the native Latinists who transcribed it (Section III). The last part of this chapter (Section IV) examines the Nahuatl ceremonial speeches, adages, riddles, and metaphors that are presented in Book 6. It will be argued that the common perception that all these discourses are 'rhetorical' actually has its origins in Sahagún's strategic attempts—evident from his Spanish translations and prefaces to individual chapters—to confer upon them a kind of classical stature.

I. Conception of the *Historia general*; models and precedents

Writing in the earlier 1600s, the Nahuatl chronicler Chimalpahin gives a good impression of the content of the *Historia general* and the way in which it was acquired:

> [Sahagún] wrote in accordance with his enquiries of those who were elders, who were preserving the inscriptions in books of paintings, with what they were accustomed to paint in them, and with what they said about everything that happened in ancient times.[3]

Those methods, which have led to the contested claim that the friar was an anthropologist *avant la lettre*, were really inquisitorial in origin.[4] Many assessments of the

Spanish text. Unless otherwise indicated, the translations of Dibble and Anderson, sometimes lightly updated, are used in this chapter.

[3] CHIMALPAHIN, *Memorial breve* (1631), 40v [1998 i, 136]: 'quimicuilhui yn iuh quinmotlatlanili ye huecauh huehuetque catca yn quipixticatca tlapallamatlacuilolli yn iuh quicuillotihui yn ocno nepa ye huecauh huehuetque catca; yn itechcopa tlahtoa yn ixquich tlamantli ye huecauh omochiuh. . . .' Cf. León-Portilla 1980, 118–19.

[4] Cf. Vicente Castro and Rodríguez Molinero 1986; Nicolau D'Olwer 1987; León-Portilla 2002. Browne 2000 attributes Sahagún's 'ethnography' to conventions of medieval scholasticism. Ríos Castaño 2014a, 151–98 explores the inquisitorial origins of Sahagún's practice.

Historia general have thus emphasized the extent to which its findings were shaped by the agenda of the missionary's questionnaires.[5] More recent surveys, however, have stressed the importance of the part played by his Mexican collaborators.[6]

The detailed account Sahagún himself gave of the way in which the work was compiled indicates that both perspectives are pertinent.[7] Four native Latinists who had been taught at the College of Santa Cruz spent two years writing down in Nahuatl the testimonies of ten or twelve elders from Texcoco and the explanations they gave of their books of paintings. Latinists from the college were also involved in checking and discussing the resulting transcriptions with two further groups of indigenous subjects, first in Tlatelolco for a further year, and then—after Sahagún had edited and arranged the material into twelve books—in Mexico City. It is therefore evident that the native Latinists were responsible for the Nahuatl text of the *Historia general*. That text, with a concomitant Spanish translation in a parallel column, runs to between one and two hundred folio pages per book (Figure 8.1).

As well as designing and structuring the work as a whole, Sahagún was involved in its translation into Spanish after a manuscript had been finalized at the request of Fray Rodrigo de Sequera, the Franciscan Commissary General, in August 1575.[8] Sahagún also wrote Spanish prologues to each of the twelve books, occasionally adding appendices or supplementary *relaciones*. The prologues explain the procedures and challenges involved in compiling the books, calling attention to features of interest and censuring sacrilegious content.

The twelve books of the *Florentine Codex* were grouped by their subjects under the three areas of enquiry set out in the preface: 'divine, or rather idolatrous, human, and natural things'. Divine matters were the subject of Books 1–5:

1. *De los dioses que adorauan* [The gods they worshipped]
2. *Del Calendario, fiestas y ceremonias* [The calendar, festivals and ceremonies]
3. *Del principio que tuuieron los Dioses* [The origin of the gods]
4. *De la astrologia judicario o arte de divinar* [Judicial astrology or divination]
5. *De los agueros y pronosticos* [Auguries and predictions]

Books 6–10 treated human and technical concerns:

6. *De la Rethorica, y philosophia moral, y theologia* [Rhetoric, moral philosophy, and theology]

[5] Cf. Todorov 1984, 219–42 and Grafton, Shelford and Siraisi 1992, 116–17, 146–7. Cline and Glass 1973, 186–239 is a bibliographical guide to earlier studies of Sahagún.

[6] Cf. e.g. León-Portilla 2002; Peterson and Terraciano 2019, 14.

[7] *HG* 2 Prologue [1982 i, 54–5], summarized in this paragraph. For the evolution of the *HG*, see further Dibble and Anderson 1982 i, 9–23; León-Portilla 2002, 132–224; Baird 1993, 13–20.

[8] *HG* 2 Prologue [1982 i, 56]: León-Portilla 2002, 204–24.

Libro. 1. delos dioses. fo. 1.

Libro primero, enque se trata, de los dioses que adorauan, los naturales, desta tierra: que es la nueua españa.

Capitulo primero, que habla, del principal dios: que adorauã, y aquien sacrificauan los mexicanos. llamado vitzilubuchtli.

Inic ce amuxtli. vncan motenehoa. in teteuh: in quinmoteutiaia in nican tlaca.

Inic ce capitulo. ynitechpa tlatoa, ynoc cenca tlapanauja teteuh: yn quinmoteutiaia. yoan yn quijntlamanjliaia, yn ievecauh.

Figure 8.1 *Florentine Codex*, Mexico, c. 1580, beginning of Book 1, 'On the Gods'. Biblioteca Medicea Laurenziana, Florence, Ms. Med. Palat. 218, f. 13r.

7. *De la astrologia natural* [Natural astrology]
8. *De los reyes y señores* [The kings and lords]
9. *De los mercaderes y oficiales* [The merchants and artisans]
10. *De los vicios y virtudes de esta gente Indiana* [The vices and virtues of this Indian people].

Aspects of nature were addressed in Book 11, 'on the properties of animals, birds, fish, trees, herbs, flowers, metals, rocks and on colours', while the final Book 12 was a narrative: 'The conquest of Mexico'. This organization of the subject matter has led to several models being identified for the *Historia general*, including the Latin Aristotelian corpus, Pliny's *Natural History*, Isidore of Seville's *Etymologies*, the Franciscan Bartholomaeus Anglicus' *De proprietatibus rerum* ('The properties of things'), and even Olaus Magnus' Latin history of Scandinavia.[9]

[9] Cf. Garibay 1953–1954 [2007], 566–71 on the role of Aristotle, *Historia animalium* and *Partes animalium*, and for tabulations of parallels between Sahagún and Pliny; Robertson 1966; León-Portilla 1999. León-Portilla 2002, 34–5 considers the analytical index of Aristotle's works

Yet the influence on Sahagún of the best-known encyclopaedia of the Middle Ages, parts of which were printed in the 1400s, has never been considered. The *Speculum maius* of Vincent of Beauvais or Vincentius Burgundus (c. 1190–1264) was well known in Renaissance Spain: though it would later be disparaged by Juan Luis Vives, it was cited several times by Las Casas and other authors.[10] Vincent's huge compilation was divided into three sections: divinity and the cosmos (*Speculum naturale*); humanities and technical arts (*Speculum doctrinale*); and history (*Speculum historiale*). That is the sequence adopted in the *Historia general*. Medieval *speculum* literature had a moral purpose, showing the ideal image of conduct not just for princes, but also for other classes of people, such as teachers, students, and children.[11] The *Florentine Codex* followed suit: the first six books contained 'much material urging upon [people] the theological virtues', and the exposition of Nahuatl ethical terms in Book 10 recalled the scholastic tradition of moral instruction established in Aristotle's *De virtutibus et vitiis*, 'On virtues and vices'.[12] The Council of Trent had stipulated that priests and missionaries should explain to their congregations, in concise and plain terms, the vices that were to be avoided and the virtues that were to be pursued.[13]

In New Spain, Fray Andrés de Olmos' *Tratado de antigüedades mexicanas*, 'Study of Mexican Antiquities' (c. 1539), prepared some forty years before the final completion of the *Historia general*, was a crucial precedent.[14] Although Olmos had been charged to 'collect in a book the antiquities of these native Indians, especially those of Mexico, Texcoco and Tlaxcalla', the *Tratado* was lost by the end of the sixteenth century—perhaps because it was not regarded as useful to

and sources published by the Abbot of Sahagún in León at a press established there: RUIZ, *Index locupletissimus . . . in Aristotelis Stagiritae opera* (1540). BURGOS, *Propriedad de las cosas* (1494) was the Spanish translation of ANGLICUS, *De proprietatibus rerum* (c. 1240). Mathes 1982, 60 notes that a copy of MAGNUS, *Historia de gentibus septentrionalibus* (1555) had been in the Convent of Tlatelolco, and Yhmoff Cabrera 1996 ii, 337 lists a 1565 edition that was at the Convent of San Francisco. This has prompted Escalante Gonzalbo 2019 to argue that one or two illustrations in the *HG* imitate features of those in Olaus Magnus.

[10] LAS CASAS, *De unico vocationis modo* (1539) 5.11, 5.31, and 6.6, [1942, 116, 332–8, 348–60]; LAS CASAS, *Apologia* (c. 1552), caps. 47 and 51 [2000, 295–6, 313, 319]. Vergara Ciordia and Comella Gutiérrez 2014 note references to Vincent in Gonzalo Fernández de Oviedo, Pedro Mexía and other Spanish authors in the 1500s.

[11] Cf. Chapter 4, pp. 126–7 on *specula principum*; Chapter 5, I, IV; Chapter 7, III above.

[12] See the Spanish text of *HG* 10.1 [2016, 528]: 'se pretende en este tratado aplicar el lenguaje castellano al lenguaje indiano, para que [se]pan hablar los vocablos propios de esta manera de vitiis de virtutibus', 'The aim of this treatment is to apply the Castilian language to the Indian language so that the right words can be spoken on the subject *de viciis et virtutibus*': Ríos Castaño 2014a, 111–50; Anderson 1983.

[13] Waterworth 1848, 27. Cf. Chapter 2, p. 54 above.

[14] Hanson 1994, 29; Marcocci 2021, 27–40. PANÉ, *Relación* (1498), a study of the 'antiquities' of Hispaniola, was an important precursor to Olmos' undertaking: cf. Chapter 1, n. 57 above.

preachers.[15] But Olmos may have written the preface to the *Historia de los mexicanos por sus pinturas*, 'History of the Mexicans through their paintings' (1532), which shows that the practices of interviewing native informants and of using pictorial illustrations, both of which were essential to the *Historia general*, had been previously adopted.[16]

As noted above, the reworked transcriptions of the informants' testimonies in Nahuatl that constituted the main text of the *Historia general* were only subsequently translated into Spanish. That directionality, from Nahuatl to Spanish, was unusual and contrasted with the other texts prepared under Sahagún's supervision. All of them, including the *Colloquios y Doctrina christiana*, had been translated *from* Spanish or Latin source texts into the Mexican language for evangelical purposes. The main body of the *Historia general*, which had been in Nahuatl from the outset, was intended to assist missionaries in a different way—by providing complete illumination of the Mexicans' language and forms of speech.

It is important to emphasize that the Nahuatl text of *Historia general* (including the preceptive content of Book 6) was not aimed at an unconverted native audience, but to serve as a resource for those who needed to develop the language for their preaching. Readers would also acquire knowledge of the pre-Hispanic past as a by-product of the primary linguistic endeavour:

> The work is like a dragnet to bring to light all the words of this language ['lenguaje'] with their exact and metaphorical meanings, and all their ways of speaking ['maneras de hablar'] and most of their ancient practices, the good and the evil. It will be a source of great satisfaction, because, with much less effort than it costs me here, those who may so desire will be able to know many of their ancient practices ['antiguallas'] and all the language of this Mexican people in a brief time.[17]

In an ensuing note to the reader, Sahagún laments that the absence of written sources made it impossible to compile a full lexicon of Nahuatl on the model of Calepino's Latin dictionary, although his endeavour could be the basis for one in future by supplying 'all the expressions and all the terms as authorised and as reliable as those written by Virgil, Cicero and other Latin authors'.[18] He also affirmed that in the year

[15] MENDIETA, *Historia* Book 2, Prologue [1870, 75] states that the *Tratado* was commissioned by Sebastián Ramírez de Fuenleal and Fray Martín de Valencia in 1533. See Ruiz Bañuls 2009, 46–59 for bibliography. There are several conjectures about the lost content based on THEVET, *Histoyre du Mechique* (1553) and on pictorial codices (Phillips 1883; Jiménez Moreno and Robertson 1980; Boone 1983); Gómez de Orozco 1945; León-Portilla 1969. Baudot 1995, 163–217 attempts a reconstruction of Olmos' *Tratado* and *Suma*.

[16] Wilkerson 1974, 72–3; Robertson 1959.

[17] *HG* 1, Prologue [1982 i, 47].

[18] *HG* 1, 'Al sincero lector' [1982 i, 50]. Cf. Chapter 5, I (ii) n. 27.

he was writing, 1569, 'a clean copy of these twelve books' had been prepared with 'a grammar and vocabulary as an appendix'. That may have been in line with Fray Andrés de Olmos' likely inclusion of the *Arte de la lengua mexicana* at the end of his own encyclopaedic study of Mexican society and belief in 1547.[19] But by the time work had begun on the *Historia general* in the 1550s, the lingering paganism of the native peoples was perceived to be a pressing concern, not the object of curiosity for more disinterested enquiries.[20]

II. Greco-Roman paganism and the extirpation of idolatry

The missionary friars called the Mexican deities 'demons', 'devils', or 'false gods', reflecting the stark polarity that was presupposed between Christianity and all other religions.[21] That outlook had been endorsed in medieval jurism, which set the *populus Romanus,* those who belonged to the Holy Mother Church, against the *populi extranei*—the Greeks, Tartars, Saracens, and Jews—who did not.[22] Theology is often political theory in disguise, but the thinking behind that uncompromising opposition rested on a deliberate step that had been taken more than a thousand years before by the first fathers of the Christian Church, who identified the Greek and Roman gods with the demons driven out by Christ in the Gospels.

Such an identification would not have been obvious in the second century AD: new gods and cults had previously been absorbed into the official Roman religion (as in the case of the Greco-Egyptian Serapis), or they supplemented it (as in the case of the Persian Mithras) or blended with it (as the Greek Dionysus had merged with Liber, the Italian wine god). But the early Christians in Rome wanted nothing to do with the 'gods' of the gentiles, abiding by Saint Paul's declaration that 'the heathens sacrifice to devils and not to God' (1 Corinthians 10:20). In a seminal letter written in Greek to the pagan emperor Antoninus Pius in the 150s, Justin Martyr argued that evil demons who appeared long ago had been mistaken for gods and were even known *by name* as gods—such as Jupiter, Apollo, and Venus—until their true nature had been revealed, first by Socrates, and then by Reason incarnate in Jesus Christ.[23] The later Church Fathers, including Tertullian, Augustine, and Jerome, inherited this view, which was still generally held by Christians in the 1500s.[24]

[19] *HG* 1, Prologue [1982 i, 46]. Maxwell and Hanson 1992, 10.

[20] Boruchoff 2003.

[21] Cervantes 1991; 1994. Burkhart 1989, 35–45.

[22] Laird 2009.

[23] Justin, *Apologies* 1.5; Minns and Parvis 2009, 88–91.

[24] Kristeller 1974, 127, 245; Marrou 1976.

Understanding of that position resolves an apparent contradiction in the thinking of the missionary friars, who could maintain that Aztec gods were invented and not real, and yet still regard them as potent, pernicious demons. The missionaries' point was that the Mexicans were venerating divinities that, like those of ancient Greece and Rome, were masquerading as gods and celestial beings.[25] At the same time there was a broader Renaissance fascination with classical polytheism to which educated churchmen would not have been immune, and Cicero's dialogues on Roman religion, *De divinatione*, 'Divination', and *De natura deorum*, 'The nature of the gods', were popular in sixteenth-century Spain.[26]

Consciousness of pagan Roman tradition is evident in the very structure of the first book of the *Historia general*, on the Mexican gods. Each of the twenty-two chapters treated an individual divinity, but the introduction to Chapter 13 began the description of 'gods that are lesser in rank': the six male and six female deities surveyed in the first twelve chapters were therefore the *greater* Aztec gods.[27] It cannot be coincidence that the Romans had twelve great gods of their own; again, six female and six male:[28]

Juno Vesta Minerva Diana Ceres Venus Mars
Mercurius Jovis Neptunus Vulcanus Apollo.

That enumeration in verse by the archaic poet Ennius was often quoted or recalled in later Latin literature.[29] Alternatively, Virgil's different group of twelve, which included Pan and Bacchus, and the list of *di selecti*, 'select gods', mentioned by Augustine in his *De civitate Dei*, or *City of God*, may have determined the distinction between greater and lesser Mexican deities.[30]

The chronicler Gonzalo Fernández de Oviedo had already compared specific Mexican gods to those of ancient Rome.[31] Such associations were also made in the

[25] SAHAGÚN, *HG* 1 includes an untitled confutation [1970 ii, 70]: 'In many other ways the devils tricked your ancestors and made fun of them, making them believe some women were goddesses so that they worshipped and venerated them.'

[26] Escobar Chico 1997.

[27] That sense of the Nahuatl, 'tepitoton teteuh', is reflected in the Spanish: 'dioses que son menores en dignidad': *HG* 1.13 [1970 ii, 29; 2016, 37].

[28] Schilling 1992, 73–5. In the 1500s there was scant knowledge of the twelve Greek Olympian gods, transmitted from Herodotus and Pindar to the Platonic tradition.

[29] Ennius, *Annales* fragment 240, ed. Skutsch 1985, 91, 424–6; quoted in Apuleius, *De deo Socratis* 2, and Martianus Capella, *De nuptiis Philologiae et Mercurii* 1.42: Skutsch 1968, 103–18. Livy, *Ab urbe condita* 22.10.9 described the same gods being honoured in the Roman ritual of the *lectisternium* in 217 BC: Nouilhon 1989: cf. Suetonius, *Vita Divi Augusti* 70. Manilius' *Astronomica*, recovered in the 1460s, aligned each god listed by Ennius with a sign of the zodiac: Bull 2005, 28–9.

[30] Virgil, *Georgics* 1.5–25; Augustine, *De civitate Dei* 7.2 (drawn from Varro).

[31] FERNÁNDEZ DE OVIEDO, *Historia general* (1557) 33.46 [1959 iv, 221]; see Fabregat Barrios 2003. Cf. LAS CASAS, *Apologética historia* (c. 1558), caps. 121–30.

TABLE 8.1 **Equivalences between Mexican and Roman gods in drafts of *Historia general*, Book 1**

	Memoriales en tres columnas	*Memoriales complementarios*	*Florentine Codex*	
	(Nahuatl)	(Spanish)	(in Spanish and Nahuatl)	
	1564	1565	1577	
Huitzilopochtli	Mars	Hercules	Hercules	cap. 1
Paynal	Mercury	–	–	cap. 2
Tezcatlipoca	Jupiter	Jupiter	Jupiter	cap. 3
Tlaloc	–	–	–	cap. 5
Quetzalcoatl	Hercules	Hercules	–	cap. 5
Cihuacoatl	Venus	–	–	cap. 6
Chicomecoatl	Ceres	Ceres	Ceres	cap. 7
Temazcalteci	–	–	–	cap. 8
Tzaputlatena	–	–	–	cap. 9
Ciuapipiltin [Diseases]	–	–	–	cap. 10
Chalchiuhtlicue	Neptune	Juno	Juno	cap. 11
Tlazolteotl	–	Venus	Venus	cap. 12
Xiuhtecutli	Vulcan	Vulcan	Vulcan	cap. 13
Tezcatzoncatl	Bacchus	wine god	wine god	cap. 22
Teteoinnan	Artemis	–	–	*Appendix*

first book of the *Historia general*: 'Huitzilopochtli is another Hercules', 'Tezcatlipoca is another Jupiter', and so on (Plate 13).[32] The pairings are to be found in the opening sentences of the Spanish versions of some chapters and in captions accompanying illustrations in the *Florentine Codex*, but they are not in the Nahuatl text. Some of those pairings were changed or abandoned through successive draftings of the work, as indicated in Table 8.1.[33]

[32] Todorov 1984, 231; Gruzinski 2002, 103; Lyons and Pohl 2010, 17. As Gordon Whittaker has pointed out to me, the association of both Huitzilopochtli and Quetzalcoatl with Hercules could reflect recognition of traditions that they were once human.

[33] Table 8.1 has been adapted from Nicolau D'Olwer 1987, 112. The progressions it summarizes are also discussed in Olivier 2016, 192–201.

The characterization of the Mexican goddess of water, Chalchiuhtlicue, as 'another Juno' may throw some light on the function of these comparisons for Sahagún. Chalchiutlicue's principal attribute was to have 'power over the water of the sea and rivers, to drown those who go on the waters, and to make storms and whirlwinds, and to sink ships and boats'.[34] Yet control over water had not been a prominent attribute of Juno in Roman or Renaissance traditions. An aquatic deity who could whip up storms was best compared to Neptune—and that was exactly the comparison that had been made in the version first produced in 1563.[35] The substitution of Juno in the 1565 revision of the *Memoriales*, which was retained in the final *Historia general*, makes sense only in terms of Juno's unique role in Virgil's *Aeneid*, in which she instigated the minor god Aeolus to stir up a storm at sea, with the aim of preventing Aeneas and the Trojans from reaching the coast of Italy: 'Whip up the might of your winds, flood their ships and sink them, or drive them in all directions and scatter their bodies over the deep.'[36] In fact it was the part of Neptune in the epic to pacify the tempest that Juno had caused.[37]

That connection to Virgil suggests that the equivalences between Mexican and Roman gods were only superficial illustrations, revealing less about the essential nature of the Aztec divinities than they do about how a Franciscan missionary sought to present them. The association of Chalchiuhtlicue with a markedly poetic portrayal of Juno further suggests that the Mexican deities are as fictitious as the classical personages to whom they are compared. Many passages in the *Historia general* make clear that the Aztec gods are spurious, and Sahagún's Spanish prologue to Book 3 affirms that they have no more credibility than those of the ancient Romans:

> The divine Augustine did not consider it superfluous or vain to deal with the fictitious theology of the gentiles, in the sixth Book of the *City of God*, because, as he says, the empty fictions and falsehoods which the gentiles held of their feigned gods could easily make them understand that those were not gods, nor could they provide anything that would be beneficial to a rational creature. For this reason, the fictions and falsehoods that these natives held regarding their gods are placed in this third Book because the vanities they believed regarding their lying gods being understood, they may come more easily, through Gospel doctrine, to know the true God, and to know that *those they held as gods were not gods, but lying devils and deceivers* ['aquellos que ellos tenjan por dioses non erã dioses sino diablos mentirosos y enganadores'].[38]

[34] *HG* 1.11 [2016, 33]; cf. Nahuatl text [1970 ii, 21].
[35] Cf. Isidore of Seville, *Etymologies* 8.11.38.
[36] Virgil, *Aeneid* 1.69–70.
[37] Virgil, *Aeneid* 1.124–7. Isidore, *Etymologies* 8.11.69 states that *poets* associated Juno with water.
[38] *HG* 3, Prologue [1982 i, 59].

The Greco-Roman pantheon was not viewed with detachment in the sixteenth century. Even Renaissance authors who were sympathetic to the classics emphasized, first and foremost, the falsity of the ancient gods, who were still seen by the Church as a source of potential confusion or danger.[39] In his popular Spanish work of *speculum* literature, *Libro áureo de Marco Aurelio*, Fray Antonio de Guevara felt impelled to describe the deities of antiquity as 'mere human inventions . . . doomed toadstools rooted in shifting sand'.[40]

The confutation of Mexican idolatry in the Spanish text of the *Historia general*, Book 1 was in the same spirit. It elaborates on a biblical verse quoted in Latin from the Book of Wisdom 12:13: 'For there is no other God but thou, who hast care of all.' For his part, Sahagún writes, 'This is thus revealed: Huitzilopochtli is no god; Tezcatlipoca is no god; Tlaloc, or Tlaloca[n]tecutli is no god; Quetzalcoatl is no god, nor is Cihuacoatl.'[41] After the negation of some twenty deities in this manner, there is another scriptural quotation from Psalms 5:5: 'All the gods of the gentiles are demons.' The intercultural alignment Sahagún cared about is the one that has been stressed already: the Church's long-standing connection of all pagan gods with the demons cast out by Christ. This is the real respect in which he believed that the Aztec gods resembled the Roman ones. And this alignment explains why Sahagún could associate the omnipresent, invisible prime mover Tezcatlipoca with Jupiter, yet at the same time see no affinity between Tezcatlipoca and the Christian God.[42]

In outlining the rationale for his entire project, Sahagún compared the missionaries' understanding of heathen practices to a physician's recognition of an illness:

> The physician cannot advisedly administer medicine to one infirm without first knowing of which humour or from which source the ailment derives. Wherefore it is desirable that the good physician be expert in the knowledge of medicines and ailments, in order to administer adequately the cure for each ailment. The preachers and confessors are healers of the souls for the curing of spiritual ailments. . . .[43]

[39] Seznec 1972, 263–4.

[40] GUEVARA, *Libro áureo de Marco Aurelio* (1528) [1994, 82].

[41] *HG* 1, unheaded section of manuscript (after chapter 16 of the Appendix), confuting Mexican idolatry.

[42] Todorov 1984, 233: 'Sahagún expects the Aztec gods to resemble the Roman gods, not the God of the Christians!' An untitled confutation in *HG* 1 [1970 ii, 68] compared Tezcatlipoca to Lucifer, who was cast out from heaven. Olivier 2016, 198–9 considers parallels between Tezcatlipoca and Jupiter.

[43] *HG* 1, Prologue [1982 i, 45]: 'El medico no puede Acatadamente aplicar Llas medicinas al enfermo sin que primero conozca: de que humor o de que causa proçede la enfermedad. De manera que el buen medico conuiene sea docto en el conocimiento de las medeçinas y en el de las enfermidades para aplicar conueniblemente a cada enfermedad la medeçina contraria. Los predicadores, y confesores, medicos son de las animas para curar las enfermedades espirituales. . .'

That passage recalls a celebrated early Christian exploration of classical paganism. In the *City of God*, Augustine had used a similar analogy to criticize the ancient Roman religion for its lack of moral teaching and for the obscenity of its rites:

> If only the infirm understanding of human custom did not presume to resist the reason of evident truth, but yielded its weakness to healthy doctrine as if to medicine, until it were healed with divine assistance procured by devout faith . . . But now, since the ailment of the souls of those foolish people is greater and more virulent. . . .[44]

Purloining Augustine's medical conceit at the outset, Sahagún shared his agenda and demonized—quite literally—the gods of the Mexicans. The precedent of Augustine's work was a powerful justification for the researches of the *Historia general*: the pious disclaimers of Sahagún's Spanish prologues stood in contrast to the often controversial ethnographic material in the books they introduced. Renaissance humanists in Italy, including Francesco da Fiano, Coluccio Salutati, and Battista Mantovano, had employed similar tactics in their studies of Greco-Roman myth and poetry in order to avoid repercussions from the Church.[45] The renowned poet and scholar Giovanni Boccaccio frequently invoked Christ in the prefaces to the fourteen books of his *Genealogiae deorum gentilium*, 'Genealogies of the Pagan Gods' (c. 1360), and ended the entire work with a profession of faith.[46] Boccaccio's classical mythography in Latin appeared in illustrated editions and remained the principal source for the classical gods until the later 1500s. Versions circulated in Spain and the *Genealogiae* were cited in Guevara's *Libro áureo de Marco Aurelio* (1528)—a 1529 edition of which was acquired by the Convent of Santiago in Tlatelolco.[47]

[44] Augustine, *De civitate Dei* 2.1: 'Si rationi perspicuae ueritatis infirmus humanae consuetudinis sensus non auderet obsistere, sed doctrinae salubri languorem suum tamquam medicinae subderet, donec diuino adiutorio fide pietatis inpetrante sanaretur . . . Nunc uero quoniam ille est maior et taetrior insipientium morbus animorum . . .'

[45] Baron 1966, 291–313; Bull 2005, 7–36; Marrone 2000, 28–37.

[46] BOCCACCIO, *Genealogiae* (1472) was the *editio princeps*: the author had continued to revise the manuscript until his death in 1374. Solomon 2011, viii–xi. Laird 2016b and Boone 2019, 102–3 indicate the relevance of Boccaccio's work to the *Historia general*.

[47] Cf. Álvarez Morán and Iglesias Montiel 2001 on the reception of BOCCACCIO, *Genealogiae* in Spain. Mathes 1982, 57, lists the 1529 copy of Guevara's work in the convent library: *Marco Aurelio cõ el relox de principes*, printed in Valladolid.

III. Classical allusions in the *Historia general*

In contrast to Sahagún's occasional practice in his prologues and in the Spanish translation of the *Florentine Codex,* the writers of the Nahuatl text do not draw explicit analogies between Mexican and Greco-Roman traditions.[48] The interference of classical literature, when it is discernible, is implicit and enigmatic. A description, in Book 3, of the legendary reign in Tula of Quetzalcoatl 'who was esteemed and regarded as a god' is a salient example. The peoples of Anahuac were scattered all over the region until Quetzalcoatl used a herald to call them from a mountain range to bring them together so that they would heed his commands. The ruler's role recalls the sage who in ancient times, according to Cicero, first assembled people in civilized communities.[49] Quetzalcoatl's Toltec subjects, who were endowed with the skills of working with jewelry, precious metals, shells, and feathers, wanted for nothing:

> And the ears of maize were each indeed like hand-held grinding stones, very long. They could only be embraced in one's arms. And palm-tree-like amaranth plants: they could climb them, they could be climbed. And also the varicolored cotton grew: chili-red, yellow, pink, brown, green, blue, verdigris color, dark brown, ripening brown, dark blue, fine yellow, purple, coyote colored cotton, this. All of these came forth exactly so; they did not dye them.[50]

Here the story has some more marked resemblances to classical narratives of the myth of Saturn. In the *Aeneid,* Virgil had described how the god came down from Olympus to earth and 'gathered together the untaught race, dispersed among the high mountains, and gave them laws', in an age of plenty that was called 'golden'.[51] The 'varicolored cotton' ('tlapapal ichcatl') growing in Quetzalcoatl's reign recalls the naturally dyed wool imagined in Virgil's fourth *Eclogue,* a poem that envisaged the return of the Golden Age of Saturn's rule:[52]

[48] *HG* 10.29 [1981 xi, 165], however, compares the Toltecs to 'the inhabitants of Babylon, wise, learned, experienced' ('babylonja tlaca, in mjmatinj in tlamatjnime, in jxtlamatque'); the Spanish translation [2016, 578] states that they were like the Trojans ('troyanos'). See further Rojas Silva 2022.

[49] *HG* 3.3 [2016, 189]. The sense of being called together is clearer in the Spanish: 'pregonaua, un pregonero, para llamar a los pueblos apartados: los quales distan, mas de cien leguas, que se nombra Anaoac, y desde alla oían y entendían el pregón, y luego con brevedad venían y a saber y oir lo que mandaba el dicho Quetzalcoatl.' Cf. Cicero, *De inventione* 1.2, quoted in Chapter 2, p. 43.

[50] *HG* 3.3 [1978 iv, 14].

[51] Virgil, *Aeneid* 8.319–25: 'primus ab aetherio venit Saturnus Olympo . . . is genus indocile ac dispersum montibus altis / composuit legesque dedit . . . / aurea quae perhibent illo sub rege fuere / saecula'. Cf. Ovid, *Metamorphoses* 1.89–113.

[52] *Ichcatl* is also the word for 'wool' in Nahuatl: cf. Chapter 5, III n. 63 above.

Every land will bring forth everything . . .
Wool will stop learning to fake varied colours.
Instead the ram in the meadow will himself change his fleece,
now to a sweet blushing purple, now to a saffron yellow:
of its own accord scarlet will clothe the grazing lambs.[53]

Celebrated as a pagan Roman prophecy of Christ's birth, Virgil's fourth 'Messianic' *Eclogue* also came to be regarded as a prophecy of his second coming by churchmen and friars who agreed with Lactantius' interpretation of the text.[54] The poem also predicted that this new order would be established with heroes sailing in another Argo, captained by another Tiphys, leading to different wars and Achilles being sent once again to Troy.[55] Columbus had identified himself with the Argonaut Tiphys and apparently believed that the discovery of the Garden of Eden or the earthly paradise was a sign of Christ's imminent advent.[56]

Independent confirmation that the Toltecs had been looking forward to the return of their own Golden Age suggests that the evocation in Book 3 of Virgil's *Eclogue* was not coincidental. Sahagún's Spanish Prologue to Book 8 states that the Toltecs had established Tula in the course of their own search for an earthly paradise that they called 'Tamoanchan' and that they were still awaiting the restoration of Quetzalcoatl's kingdom: 'they say he is still alive and that he is to reign again and rebuild that city which was destroyed and to this day they wait for him.'[57] In this same passage, Sahagún likened Quetzalcoatl to 'King Arthur among the English.'[58] That analogy would have been more obvious to a Spaniard familiar with vernacular *libros de caballerías* than to the Indian collegians, as they were trained only in Latin literature. But the import of Sahagún's remarks is clearly in keeping with the delicate parallels between the time of Quetzalcoatl and the Golden Age of Saturn in the main text of Book 3: Quetzalcoatl's reign, like that of Saturn, was destined to return.

On other occasions, however, classical learning was employed covertly in the *Historia general* to manipulate, or even generate, testimonies that could be

[53] Virgil, *Eclogue* 4.39, 42–5: 'omnis feret omnia tellus . . . nec varios discet mentiri lana colores, / ipse sed in pratis aries iam suave rubenti / murice, iam croceo mutabit vellera luto, / sponte sua sandyx pascentis vestiet agnos.'

[54] Houghton 2019, 205–10. Cf. Chapter 1, III above on Quiroga and *Eclogue* 4.

[55] Virgil, *Eclogue* 4.34–6: 'alter erit tum Tiphys et altera quae vehat Argo / delectos heroas; erunt etiam altera bella / atque iterum ad Troiam magnus mittetur Achilles.'

[56] COLUMBUS, *Libro de las profecías* (c. 1504), 59v [1997, 290–1]. Columbus' identification with Tiphys was primarily prompted by his reading of Seneca, *Medea* 374–9: cf. Clay 1992, Romm 1993, Delany 2006, Bartosik-Vélez 2014, 38–43.

[57] *HG* 8, Prologue [1982 i, 69]; cf. *HG* 1, Prologue [1982 i, 49].

[58] *HG* 8, Prologue [1982 i, 69–70]. Earlier in *HG* 1, Prologue [1982 i, 48] Sahagún noted that the citizens who fled the destruction of Tula went on to found Cholula, and remarked that 'the affairs of these two cities went the way of Troy and Rome': cf. n. 48 above.

compatible with a Christian perspective. The omens recounted in Books 8 and 12—by which the Aztecs had supposedly foretold the destruction of their empire—are a striking example (Plate 14a). These were based on portents from classical and early Christian literature, although there is no explicit indication of this.[59] The sword-shaped light in the sky listed as the first omen of the Spanish conquest had an antecedent in Josephus' first-century history of the Jewish War. Comets, lightning flashes, and other signs described recall the portents that marked Caesar's death in Virgil's *Georgics* and augured civil war in Lucan's *Pharsalia*.[60] Several sets of connections could be explored, but the sixth omen listed in the *Historia general* deserves special attention because it has a bearing on the gods, and is related on three separate occasions. The first is in Book 8, chapter 1:

> In the days of this same [ruler, Montezuma], it happened that [the demon] Cihuacoatl went about weeping, at night. Everyone heard it wailing and saying: 'My beloved sons, now I am about to leave you.'[61]

The next tellings, later in Book 8 and in Book 12, are similar, without naming the goddess Cihuacoatl, or 'Snake Woman', although in the *Florentine Codex* there is a small ink painting of a snake with a woman's head that accompanies the text in Book 8 (Figure 8.2).[62] On both those occasions the nocturnal weeping was attributed in the Nahuatl text to 'a woman' and, in the Spanish version, to 'cries in the air, as of a woman':[63]

> A sixth evil omen: often was heard a woman going weeping, going crying out. Loudly did she cry out at night. She walked about saying: 'O my beloved sons, now we are about to go!' Other times she said: 'O my beloved sons, whither shall I take you?'[64]

The topos of gods abandoning a doomed city was common in classical literature and associated with Thebes and Troy, as well as Jerusalem.[65] But it has long been

[59] Fernández-Armesto 1992 and Rozat Dupeyron 1993 are foundational studies of these omens. Cf. Lockhart 1993; Loera de la Llave 1994; Townsend 2003, 659–87.

[60] Josephus, *Jewish War* 6.289; Virgil, *Georgics* 1.466–88; Lucan, *Pharsalia* 1.524–695.

[61] *HG* 8.1 [1979 ix, 3].

[62] For pre-Hispanic representations of Cihuacoatl, see Figure 8.3 and Plate 14b, and cf. n. 81 below.

[63] The story is one possible source for the popular Hispanic American tradition of 'La Llorona', the weeping woman, who calls out at night for her lost children: Fuller 2015.

[64] *HG* 12.1 [1955 xiii, 2–3].

[65] Tacitus, *Histories* 5.13 and Josephus, *Jewish War* 6.300 (cf. n. 60 above) describe nocturnal voices announcing their departure before the fall of Jerusalem—to which the fall of Tenochtitlan was often compared: cf. Brading 1991, 25, 104–14, and Chapter 9, II below. Pelling 1988, 303 (on Plutarch, *Life of Antony* 74.4–5) lists further examples including Aeschylus, *Seven against Thebes*, verses 217–18 and Virgil, *Aeneid* 2.351–2 on Troy.

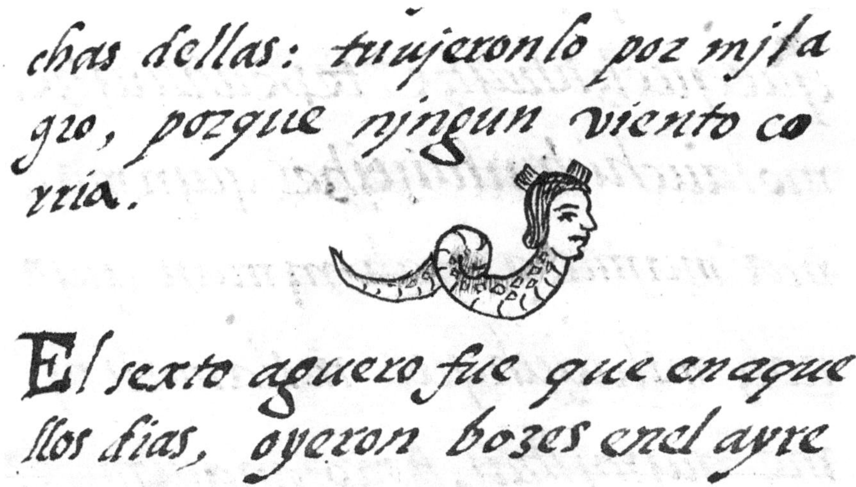

chas dellas: tuujeronlo por mjla
gro, porque njngun viento co
rria.

El sexto aguero fue que enaque
llos dias, oyeron bozes enel ayre

Figure 8.2 Ink drawing of a snake woman, *Florentine Codex*, c. 1580, Book 8, detail. Biblioteca Medicea Laurenziana, Florence, Ms. Med. Palat. 219, f. 262r.

noted that this episode in the *Historia general* has a particular resemblance to a story told by Plutarch in the first century AD.[66] In a treatise on oracles the Greek author reported that the helmsman of a ship named Thamus heard a voice coming from an island announcing, 'Great Pan is dead', an utterance accompanied by 'loud lamentation, not of one, but of many, mingled with amazement'.[67]

Several texts by Plutarch were available in the College of Santa Cruz, where Sahagún and the native Latinists who assisted him were at work.[68] The tradition of Pan's death was also well known because it was discussed by the third-century Christian author, Eusebius of Caesarea.[69] After quoting Plutarch's account to explain why the Greeks had come to abandon their polytheistic religion, Eusebius commented,

[66] Without realizing that the omen in the *HG* was probably based on Plutarch's story, Nicolau d'Olwer 1987, 111 remarked that Sahagún should have spotted the resemblance, since he and his collaborators had access to Plutarch's *Moralia*.

[67] Plutarch, *Moralia* 419c–e.

[68] Editions of Plutarch's works are in the 1572 and 1574 inventories of books in the College of Santa Cruz: Appendix 1.3 below. Mathes 1982, 64 lists a 1552 Isingrin edition of Plutarch's *Moralia* in the library of the Convent of Tlatelolco.

[69] Eusebius, *Praeparatio evangelica* 206c–207d. TREBIZOND, *De euangelica praeparatione* (1470) was an early Latin translation, of which there were many later editions cf. Monfasani 1976, 78, 127. Yhmoff Cabrera 1996 i, 597–8 lists a 1539 edition in Mexico.

Figure 8.3 Statue of Cihuacoatl emerging from a serpent's mouth, holding an ear of maize and a snake, Cuernavaca, c. 1325–1521 AD. Museo Nacional de Antropología, Mexico.

> It is important to observe the time at which [Plutarch] said the death of the demon [Pan] took place. For it was the time of [the emperor] Tiberius, in which our Saviour, making His sojourn among men, is recorded to have been ridding human life from demons of every kind: so that there were some of them now kneeling before Him and beseeching Him not to deliver them over to the Tartarus that awaited them.[70]

Pan's death was hence seen as a consequence of Christ's triumph. For the friars and their converts in New Spain, Eusebius' next sentence had an even more acute resonance:

> You have, therefore, the date of the overthrow of the demons, of which there was no record at any other time; just as you had the abolition of human sacrifice among the gentiles as not having occurred until after the preaching of the Gospel had reached all mankind.

[70] *Praeparatio evangelica* 5.17: 208a.

Human sacrifice had been far more common in Mexico than it had ever been in the pagan Mediterranean. That further comment from Eusebius reveals why the elements of the Aztec omen may have been fashioned to recall this episode in Greek literature, as it had acquired so much significance in the Christian world.

The Jesuit José de Acosta was an early reader of the *Historia general* who discerned a connection between Cihuacoatl's departure and the death of Pan. Acosta's history of the Indies included a chapter on the prodigies in Mexico before the passing of Montezuma's empire, which he prefaced as follows:

> You should read Eusebius, who treats this matter at length in his *Praeparatio Evangelica* . . . I have mentioned all this on purpose, so that no one may look down on what the histories and annals of the Indians recount about the strange prodigies and prognostications that had marked the end of [Montezuma's] reign and that of the devil.[71]

The 'histories and annals of the Indians' mentioned here could only be the accounts in the *Historia general*: it is very significant that the construction of these omens is ascribed to *native* authors—and it has been shown that there were no other creditable Nahuatl sources for them.[72] In this way Acosta's recommendation of Eusebius drew attention to the classical and biblical precursors of the Aztec omens—'some of which', the Jesuit conceded, 'may not have happened exactly as described' ('algo de estas cosas no hubiese acaecido tan puntualmente').[73]

Christian interpretations of the attributes of both Pan and Cihuacoatl in their respective traditions explain why Sahagún's assistants forged a parallel between them. Pan represented much more than the Arcadian shepherd god portrayed in classical poetry and Renaissance art.[74] The Greek meaning of 'Pan', 'All', led to a conception of 'Great Pan' as the supreme divinity of nature that the Stoics recognized as Zeus-Cosmos.[75] For Christians, Pan thus came to represent *all* the unwelcome pagan divine powers.[76] François Rabelais, a former Franciscan, knew this legacy and that of Eusebius' interpretation of Pan's death: earlier in the 1500s, in his felicitously entitled *Pantagruel*, he had playfully associated the god with Christ himself.[77]

[71] ACOSTA, *Historia natural y moral de las Indias* (1590) 7.23 [2003, 465].

[72] Lockhart 1993, 5, 18.

[73] ACOSTA, *Historia*, 7.23 [2003, 468].

[74] Wernicke 1903 is a full survey of Pan in antiquity; see also Borgeaud 1988.

[75] Cornutus, *Theologiae Graecae compendium* 27 (c. 60 AD); cf. the wordplay in Plato, *Cratylus* 408b.

[76] Eusebius, *Praeparatio* 124a–b: see Sirinelli 1961; 200; Lane Fox 1986, 130–2.

[77] RABELAIS, *Pantagruel* (1532) 4.28, analysed in Krailsheimer 1948. Rodríguez Garrido 2005 examines a Spanish eclogue, 'El Dios Pan', in MEXÍA FERNANGIL, *La segunda parte del Parnaso antartico* (c. 1617), which alluded to the grim portents provoked by the conquistadors' atrocities in Peru.

The reason Cihuacoatl was selected, out of all the Mexican gods, to correspond to Pan might be gleaned from the chapter about her in Book 1 of the *Historia general.* In that chapter there is an unusual discrepancy between the Nahuatl and Spanish versions. The Nahuatl text gave a description of her attributes and appearance (Plate 14b):

> Ciuacoatl [was called] a savage beast and an evil omen. She was an evil omen to men; she brought men misery. For, it was said, she gave men the digging-stick, the tumpline; she visited men therewith. And as she appeared before men, she was covered with chalk, like a court lady. She wore ear-plugs, obsidian ear-plugs. She appeared in white, garbed in white, standing white, pure white. Her womanly hairdress rose up. By night she walked weeping, wailing; also was she an omen of war. And in this wise was her image arrayed: her face was painted one-half red, one-half black. She had a head-dress of [eagle] feathers; she had golden ear-plugs. She wore a triangular shoulder-shawl. She carried a turquoise [mosaic] weaving stick.[78]

But the corresponding Spanish text added a crucial detail:

> This god was called Cihuacoatl which means 'Woman of the Serpent' and they also called her Tonantzin which means 'our mother'.

That in turn prompted an interpretation that was absent from the Nahuatl text as well:

> In these two respects it seems that this goddess is our mother Eve, who was tricked by a serpent, and that they had some notice of what occurred between our mother Eve and the serpent.

The tradition of Eve herself as a Serpent Woman had originated in the 190s AD, when Clement of Alexandria claimed that the aspirated Hebrew name of Eve, *Hevva*, translated into Greek as 'female serpent'. Clement also linked this interpretation to the use of serpents and the ritual invocation of Eve, 'Euhoe', in Greek Bacchic orgies, and Eusebius took the same view.[79] The association was sustained in the Middle Ages:

[78] SAHAGÚN, *HG* 1.6 [1970 ii, 11].

[79] Clement of Alexandria, *Protrepticus* ('Hortatory discourse') 2.12.2. Eusebius, *Praeparatio* 62c: 'The Bacchanals celebrate with their orgies the frenzy of Dionysus, and organise a holiday feasting on raw flesh each month . . . they are crowned with garlands of serpents and they invoke *Eve,* that Eve through whom deception came into the world and who was closely followed by death. Therefore,

Figure 8.4 Eve as reflection of a serpent, Porte de la Vierge, Cathedral of Notre Dame, Paris.

> We should not pass over what Bede says about the serpent which seduced Eve: that the devil chose a particular kind of serpent with a woman's face, because like approves of like, and he prompted its tongue to speak.[80]

These remarks made by Gervase of Tilbury in the early 1200s help account for the common medieval depictions of Eve as the reflection of a serpent (Figure 8.4). The miniature illustration of a snake with a woman's head in Book 8 of the *Historia general* accordingly evoked European imagery as well as indigenous representations of Cihuacoatl (Figure 8.3).[81]

according to the precise pronunciation of the Hebrews, the name *Heva,* with an aspirate, is at once interpreted as the female serpent.'

[80] GERVASE OF TILBURY, *Otia imperialia* (c. 1211) [2002, 87] attributed his explanation of odd images like this to the Venerable Bede; his mention of a belief that women who turned into serpents wore white fillets on their head uncannily converges with the description of Cihuacoatl's white attire in *HG* 1.6.

[81] Cf. a similar glyph denoting the official title of 'cihuacoatl' in the *Codex Mendoza* (c. 1542), fol. 2v. Sculptures of Cihuacoatl include a stone statue from Cuernavaca (c. 1325–1521 AD) (Figure. 8.3)

The connection of the white-clad Mexican goddess to Eve in the *Historia general* was therefore disingenuous.[82] Its purpose was to suppress a far more threatening identification prompted by Cihuacoatl's epithet in Nahuatl, 'Tonantzin', 'Our mother': secular missionaries—in contrast to those in the religious orders—had been using this expression to refer to the Virgin Mary. In a note, written only in Spanish, to accompany Book 11 of the *Historia general,* Sahagún complained that practices of Marian worship at the site of Tepeyac, where people had once made human sacrifices, were conducive to idolatry:

> At this place they had a temple dedicated to the mother of the gods whom they called Tonantzin, which means Our Mother . . . And now that a church of Our Lady of Guadalupe is built there, they also call her Tonantzin, taking their cue from the preachers who call Our Lady, the Mother of God, Tonantzin. It is not known for certain where the beginning of this Tonantzin originated, but this we know for certain, that, from its first usage, the word means that ancient Tonantzin. And it is something that should be remedied, for the correct [native] name of the Mother of God, Holy Mary, is not Tonantzin but rather 'Dios inantzin' [The Mother of God].[83]

The use of the word 'remedy' at this significant juncture recalled the medical analogy taken from Augustine at the outset of the *Historia general.* Sahagún would again express his concern about the Mexicans' confusion in a note on the manuscript of his *Kalendario mexicano, latino y castellano,* compiled toward the end of his life in the 1580s:

> When they say they are going to Tonantzin or that they are arranging a fiesta for Tonantzin, they understand the old [Aztec] one, not the modern [Christian] one.[84]

The persistent and perilous association of Cihuacoatl-Tonantzin with the Virgin Mary explains why this goddess was so troublesome and why Sahagún's collaborators

representing the goddess as emerging from the mouth of a serpent, with an ear of maize in one hand and a snake in the other; she is depicted in costume in *HG* 1; compare Baird 1993, fig. 34(a).

[82] TORQUEMADA, *Monarchia Indiana* (1615) = *MI,* 6.31 [1976 iii, 98]: 'according to the etymology of this name given by Fray Bernardino de Sahagún, this woman or goddess that they called Cihuacoatl was the first woman in the world, mother of all the human race, the one indeed that was tricked by the snake.' Torquemada thus gave Sahagún full credit for the identification, possibly hinting that he did not accept it himself.

[83] *HG* 11, 'Nota' [1982 i, 90].

[84] SAHAGÚN, *Kalendario* (c. 1585): cf. García Icazbalceta 1954, 368–9.

may have sought to stage a definitive departure for her, modelled on that of Pan. The repetition of the catalogue of omens in the *Historia general* enabled Cihuacoatl to give voice to her own valediction at three different points in the work.

IV. Book 6: *De la Rethorica, y philosophia moral, y theologia,* 1577

Taken in its entirety, the *Florentine Codex* shows that the Mexican people were not solely to be characterized by their idolatrous beliefs and practices. In the prologue to Book 1 of the *Historia general,* Sahagún affirmed that the work's comprehensive exposition of the Mexicans' language would reveal their true 'carat value' ('quilate'). Comparing their defeat by the Spaniards to God's curse on Judah and Jerusalem in the book of Jeremiah, he insisted that the Mexicans should not be held as barbarians: 'in matters of social conduct ('policia') they are a step ahead of many other nations which take great pride in being politic, if one casts aside some tyrannies their manner of ruling contained'.[85] The point was later elaborated in the prologue to Book 6, after Sahagún remarks that the Spaniards, French, and Italians, like the Greeks and Romans, have looked to the wise, to the powerful and to experienced warriors for accomplishment in the art of persuasion:

> The same was practiced in this Indian nation, and especially among the Mexicans, among whom the wise, superior, and effective Rhetoricians ['los sabios, Rethoricos virtuosos y esforçados'] were held in high regard. And they elected these as priests, lords, leaders, and captains, no matter how humble their estate. These ruled the states, led the armies, and presided in the temples.[86]

That practice was in accord with the opinion that a wise man 'armed with eloquence' is best able to serve the interest of his country—an opinion expressed by Cicero in the first paragraph of his famous textbook on rhetoric, *De inventione,* which was very familiar to educated Europeans.[87]

[85] *HG* 1, Prologue [1982 i, 47], quoting Jeremiah 5:15.

[86] *HG* 6, Prologue [1982 i, 65].

[87] Cicero, *De inventione* 1.1: 'Qui vero ita sese armat eloquentia, ut non oppugnare commoda patriae, sed pro his propugnare possit, is mihi vir et suis et publicis rationibus utilissimus atque amicissimus civis fore videtur' ('The man who arms himself with eloquence, not to attack the interests of his country but to fight for them, this man, I think, will be a citizen most supportive and well-disposed to the purposes of the community as well as his own').

Sahagún's account of the response he received from the native principals in Texcoco to his request for information for his researches shows he had seen for himself how seriously Mexicans took public speaking:

> [The leaders] replied that they would consult one another . . . and that they would answer me the next day. And thus they took their leave of me. The next day the lord came with the leaders. And, having made a very solemn speech ['muy solemne parlamento'], as they were wont to do at that time, they assigned me as many as ten or twelve leading elders.[88]

The importance the Mexicans had attached to good speech is affirmed at other points in the body of the *Historia general*. In Book 3, an account of customs in the *calmecac*, the residential school in which youths were trained for the Aztec priesthood, shows that this skill was paramount: '*Most especially* ['cenca vel'] there was teaching of *good speaking* ['qualli tlatolli']. If there was one who did not speak well, who did not greet others well, they then drew blood from him [with maguey spines]'.[89] Again, it is reported in Book 8 that noble children were brought up to speak in a cultivated way with good diction and in a respectful manner.[90] There are speeches in various parts of the *Historia general*—including Montezuma's welcoming words to Cortés—but the greatest number are to be found in the sixth book.[91]

That book, entitled *De la Rethorica, y philosophia moral, y theologia de la gente mexicana*, 'Rhetoric, moral philosophy, and theology of the Mexican people', amounted to a self-contained work. As the Latin dedication to Fray Rodrigo de Sequera affirmed, this single book was 'greater than all of the others in both size and clout': its forty-three lengthy chapters filled one of the four volumes in which the twelve books of the *Florentine Codex* were bound.[92] According to the Prologue of Book 6, its contents alone sufficed to demonstrate the truth of the *Historia general* as a whole:

> In this Book it will be very clearly seen (as to what some rivals have asserted, that all written in these books, preceding this one and following this one, is

[88] *HG* 2, Prologue [1982 i, 54]. The procedure recalls the sequence of communication that was supposedly required to secure a reply from the Aztec priests to the Franciscan Twelve, related in SAHAGÚN, *Colloquios* (1564) 1.6 [1986, 86–7].

[89] *HG* 3, Appendix 8 [1981 iv, 67]. Cf. *Codex Mendoza* (c. 1542) [1992 iii, 61v–63r.]; Calnek 1988.

[90] *HG* 8.20 [1979 ix, 71].

[91] Montezuma's speech at *HG* 12.16 [1955 xiii, 44] is exceptional because it was delivered just once. It has formulae similar to those in the Nahuatl text of SAHAGÚN, *Colloquios* 1.7: cf. Chapter 5, IV (i) above. *HG* 9.1–12 [1959 x, 1–57] presents statements made to merchants embarking upon or returning from trading expeditions.

[92] 'Hic sextus omnium maior, cum corpore tum vi'. The dedication comes after the *Sumario* of *HG* Book 6 [1969 vii, page unnumbered]. Cf. n. 8 above on Sequera's role in the production of the *HG*.

> invention and lies)—that they speak as intolerant and as liars, because the inventing ['el fingirlo'] of that which is written in this Book is not within the understanding of human beings, nor is there a living man who could invent the language which is in it, and, if they are asked, all the informed Indians will assert that this work is characteristic of their ancestors and the works they produced.[93]

Chapters 1–40 generally consist of the text of a single Nahuatl speech, while the last three chapters take the form of collections of Nahuatl idioms—adages (41), riddles (42), and metaphors (43). All of this material was presented with a facing Spanish text, in keeping with the practice throughout the *Historia general*. While Sahagún and his assistants worked on the Spanish translation, he emphasizes that he himself translated Book 6 into Spanish in 1577, after it had been written in the Mexican language thirty years previously.[94]

The indication that this Nahuatl text of Book 6 dated back to 1547 has led some to identify the speeches it contains with those Fray Andrés de Olmos had appended to his *Arte de la lengua mexicana* (1547).[95] Olmos' collection of the 'talks the Lords of Mexico gave to their sons and vassals' is generally considered to be the source for Mexican 'pláticas', which were quoted and enthusiastically commended for their moral value by Alonso de Zorita, Fray Juan de Torquemada, and Fray Bartolomé de las Casas. Las Casas went so far as to declare that the advice they contained surpassed anything composed by 'Plato, Socrates, Pythagoras and . . . Aristotle', and that they were compatible with Christian law'.[96]

Part of the appeal of the discourses lay in the fact that Olmos had substantially Christianized them in the first place, to exemplify good linguistic usage for preachers and missionaries.[97] The monologues published in Fray Juan Bautista Viseo's *Huehuetlahtolli* (c. 1601) have long been thought to derive, at least in part, from Olmos' collection, after undergoing some alterations and the addition of new content. But Bautista's texts, though they are not conventional sermons, have

[93] *HG* 6, Prologue [1982 i, 65–6].

[94] *HG* 6, colophon [1969 vii, 260], quoted in Chapter 5, n. 124 above.

[95] Cf. Chapter 3, V above. OLMOS, *Arte* (1547) 3.8, entitled 'De las maneras de hablar que tenian los viejos en sus platicas' [2002, 177–93: the edition of that chapter is based on the BNF and NLC manuscripts]. León-Portilla 2002, 115–17 hints at Sahagún's debt to Olmos; Hanson 1994 makes a more explicit case.

[96] LAS CASAS, *Apologética historia sumaria* (c. 1558), cap. 223 [1967 ii, 448]; cf. ZORITA, *Breve y sumaria relación* (1576), cap. 9, addressed to Philip II (cf. n. 112 below); TORQUEMADA, *MI* 13.36–7 [1977 iv, 260–72].

[97] Dehouve 2014 is a salutary discussion of the Christian content and conception of Olmos' and Bautista's texts. Téllez Nieto 2022, 29–30 remarks that 'Olmos' *De sacramento communionis* shows that his *Ueuetlatolli* are fully Christianized and contain fragments of those [Christian] texts he wrote in 1533' (my translation).

a great deal in common with other religious writings in Nahuatl produced under Franciscan supervision.[98]

Some speeches in Book 6 of the *Historia general* resemble the preceptive discourses described above in certain respects: there are instructions offered to youths or children by parents or elders (chapters 17–22), and words to be said by nobles and public figures on the election of a new *tlatoani,* or ruler (chapters 10–16). Overall their subject and style signal that these texts originated in a pre-Hispanic Mexican setting. Each of the opening chapters consists of a prayer to a god (Tezcatlipoca in chapters 1–7, Tlaloc in chapter 8) which was pronounced by an Aztec priest, and the greatest number of speeches (chapters 24–38) are for the occasion of pregnancy and childbirth, in which the midwife is the most frequent speaker.[99] The content was probably based on the testimonies of the primary informants, although the native Latinists who transcribed and revised the text may well have made excisions, and they certainly seem to have made some interpolations. A passage in the noble father's advice to his son, for example, recalls Christ's dictum in the Sermon on the Mount that 'whosoever shall look on a woman to lust after her, hath already committed adultery with her in his heart'.[100]

Overall, however, the historical or documentary nature of the speeches in Book 6 distinguishes this collection from the one made by Olmos that was used for evangelical purposes.[101] Confusion between the two has been magnified by the now standard practice of referring to both groups of speeches as 'huehuetlatolli', 'talks of the elders', a generic label extended to some other Nahuatl texts.[102] Yet that term, employed in the title of Fray Juan Bautista's volume, *Huehuetlahtolli* [*sic*], was never originally used to label the corpus of speeches in *Historia general* Book 6, although the word 'huehuetlatolli' itself is to be found in certain passages of Sahagún's Nahuatl

[98] Cf. Chapter 5, IV above. Locutions common to both *HG* 6 and SAHAGÚN, *Sermonario* (1563) [2022] noted by Bustamante García 1989, 7 and Ríos Castaño 2014b, 58–60 also recur in BAUTISTA, *Huehuetlahtolli* (c. 1601), 1r and *passim*. (Texts of Nahuatl sermons which appeared in the *Sermonario* were first drafted in the 1540s.)

[99] The speeches are listed (with details of speakers, addressees, and themes) in Appendix 1.7.

[100] Dibble 1982, 10 has useful conjectures on the preparation of Book 6. The scripture quotation is from Matthew 5:28. In English, *HG* 6.22 [1969, 122] reads, 'ca mjtoa, teixtlaxima in aqujn quijcecemjtta ixco tlatlachia in tecioauh' ('for it is said he who stareth at, who peereth into the face of another's wife, with his eyes committeth adultery').

[101] Olmos and Sahagún may still have collaborated: Dibble 1982, 10; Ríos Castaño 2014b, 58–9.

[102] Cf. Ríos Castaño 2014; Peterson and Terraciano 2019. Karttunen and Lockhart 1987 reify the 'huehuetlatolli' as a genre in their edition of the 'Bancroft Dialogues', an early-seventeenth-century manuscript of exchanges exemplifying polite speech in Nahuatl. Gingerich 1988, 518, however, understands *huehuetlatolli* 'as a rough catch-all term for any discourse in the vast body of traditional learning'. Ruiz Bañuls 2009, 66–7 justifies her use of the term on pragmatic rather than historical grounds. Sánchez Aguilera 2019, 134–40 (on Sahagún's sermons) is relevant: cf. n. 107 below.

text.[103] The most evident convergences with Olmos' material are in chapters 41–43, which enumerate adages, riddles, and metaphors.

(i) The Nahuatl speeches in Book 6, chapters 1–40

Fray Bernardino de Sahagún's application of the title '*De la Rethorica*' to Book 6 of the *Historia general* has had a long reach.[104] The Nahuatl speeches contained in the book are often called 'rhetorical orations' and they continue to be likened to classical or Renaissance epideictic oratory, despite the fact that Ángel María Garibay, himself a scholar of ancient Greek as well as Nahuatl, long ago warned against such misleading comparisons.[105] In pre-Hispanic Mexico there was certainly nothing to correspond to the systematized art of rhetoric as it would have been recognized in sixteenth-century Europe.[106] To regard these Nahuatl speeches as examples of 'rhetoric', even in a looser, less technical sense, risks obscuring the very qualities that make them distinctive.

As noted above, the speeches in Book 6 consisted of standard prayers that priests made to the gods, precisely formulated pronouncements for the institution of a new *tlatoani*, set words of advice to youths or children, and conventional pronouncements occasioned by childbirth, that last of which included exhortations to a new mother and the naming of a newborn child. Their counterparts in early modern Europe might be the legal, religious, or magical formulae that constituted hymns, prayers, and addresses for coronations and investitures, initiations, confirmations, baptisms, and other rituals related to birth, such as the churching of women. Such events were (and in some cases still are) contexts for utterances that could be meaningfully redeployed, again and again.[107] On this basis, the Nahuatl discourses presented in

[103] *HG* 6.21 [1969 vii, 113]: 'Here is that which they gave us, entrusted to us as they left, the words of the old men ['vevetlatolli'], that which is bound, the well-guarded [words]'; 6.43 [1969 vii, 250] in an explanation of the 'metaphor' *Tecujc, Tetlatol*: 'It means the one who spoke words not his own—perhaps *the words of the old men* ['vevetlatolli'], *the words of the noblemen* ['pillatolli'].'

[104] Sullivan 1974, 83 remarks that Sahagún was referring to Renaissance rather than Greco-Roman rhetoric, but the distinction is vulnerable, as humanists followed classical models: Chapter 2, p. 45 above; cf. Mack 2011; Patterson 1970.

[105] Garibay 1969 ii, 293. Classical epideictic was the source of European panegyric and *speculum* literature: Curtius 1953, 180, 388 and Vickers 1988, 391, 408–9. For reliance on the questionable comparison, see e.g. Peterson 2019, 171 who (also calling the speeches in Book 6 'huehuetlatolli'; cf. n. 102 above) holds that 'in Aristotelian terms, the majority... fall into the category of civic speeches that are epideictic', in line with Abbott 1996, 36: 'an art so persistently important in European politics and religion occupied a comparable position in Mexica society'.

[106] Cf. Chapter 2, I above for an overview of Renaissance rhetoric.

[107] On 'reusability' of language, cf. Conte 1986, 40–52; Laird 1999, 81–2. Sánchez Aguilera 2019, 134 hypothesizes that in Mexico there had been 'a genre, the pragmatic aspects of which point to solemn discourses, pronounced by figures of authority in ritual contexts, that invoked an oral tradition of old with very specific ways of saying things' (my translation).

Book 6 can be conceived as more akin to orders of service that were required on certain occasions.

In many chapters of the book, the speeches are followed by a passage commenting on the manner and context in which the words were to be delivered, or by descriptions of the gestures, conduct, or attire appropriate for the situation.[108] This excerpt, from an account of how a noble was expected to address a newly installed *tlatoani,* comes straight after the text of the speech itself:

> This one who spoke, who thus brought forth the words, was perhaps a great priest . . . Or perhaps it was some great lord, or some wise person or a counselor, one having wisdom, who did not hesitate as he spoke, who struck nothing out, and who spoke in the manner his heart required. And truly such was necessary, for it was said, when we replaced one, when we selected someone, when he died, he was already our lord, our executioner, and our enemy. Therefore the discourse with which he was greeted, with which he was supplicated, was most complete. And he spoke carefully when he made the greeting, when he said it. And he spoke with weeping.[109]

By speaking 'in the manner his heart required' the officiator—perhaps prompted by a pictorial text—could choose how he said the words, but the essence of what he was required to say was preordained.[110] As the Aztec speaker was the performer of an oral text, he had no need for the primary classical rhetorical canon of *inventio,* the 'finding' or devising of content.[111] On the same basis, the canon of *dispositio,* deliberate arrangement, which was also fundamental to the production of all forms of classical or Renaissance oratory, was similarly irrelevant.[112] Instead, the speeches

[108] *HG* 6.9 [1969, vii 45], 6.10 [54–5], 6.11 [58], 6.12 [62], 6.26 [150], 6.28 [160], 6.30 [169], 6.31 [173], 6.32 [177], 6.35 [196], 6.37 [204], 6.38 [206–7], 6.39 [210–11].

[109] *HG* 6.10 [1969 vii, 54–5]: 'Injn tlatoa, in juhquj qujqujxtia, in tlatolli: iehoatl in aço vei tlamacazquj . . . anoço aca vei tecutli, anoço aca tlamatinj in aço nonotzale matile: amo moquequetza in tlatoa, atle qujtzotzona: auh tlatoa in juh qujnequj ijollo: auh ca nel iuh monequj, ca mjtoa: quac ticcoa, in jquac aca tiqujana, iquac mjquj, ca ie totecujo, ca totequacauh: auh ie toiauh, ipampa in nelli mach ontlatlatlamj tlatolli, injc tlapalolo, injc tlatlautilo. Auh in çan mocxiieiecotiuh tlatoa, in tlatlapaloa qujtoa: auch choqujztica in tlatoa.'

[110] In practice there may have been additions or alterations to the oral text: Foley 2002, 11–21 describes south Slavic oral poets' insistence that they were reciting the same song (or section of a song) in the same way each time, when their text was in fact customized for a specific occasion. See e.g. Boone 1998, Bleichmar 2017, and Boone, Burkhart, and Tavárez 2017 on codices eliciting oral recitation.

[111] The Aristotelian canons of rhetoric (*inventio, dispositio, elocutio, actio, memoria*) had been transmitted through Cicero, *De inventione* 1.7 and *Rhetorica ad Herennium.* See Lausberg 1998, 119–208 on *inventio.*

[112] Cf. Lausberg 1998, 209–14 on *dispositio.* Sahagún makes no comment on the speeches' arrangement, but ZORITA, *Breve y sumaria relacion* (1576), cap. 9 [1942, 21] describes a *plática* as 'not very systematic' ('no bien ordenado'), before quoting it. Contrast SAHAGÚN, *Colloquios* (1564) 1.7

in Book 6 of the *Historia general* are structured associatively, with rhythmic and repetitive formulations characteristic of oral discourse.[113] Nor was there any place for the third canon of classical rhetoric, *elocutio*, the conscious selection of figures and metaphors, although figurative language and metaphors—prominent in oral texts—abounded in the speeches, as this excerpt from the noble's words to the new *tlatoani* makes evident:[114]

> And now, O lord, O our lord: our lord of the near, of the nigh, causeth the sun to shine, bringeth the dawn. It is thou: he pointeth the finger at thee; he indicateth thee. Our lord hath recorded thee, indicated thee, marked thee in the books. Now verily it was declared, it was determined above us, in the heavens, in the land of the dead, that our lord place thee on the reed mat, on the reed seat, on his place of honour. The spine, the maguey of thy progenitors, of thy great-grandfathers—which they planted deep as they departed, which they planted, which they placed in the earth as they departed—sprouteth, flowereth.[115]

Two canons of classical rhetoric, however, always have a general bearing on oral texts: *actio*, delivery, and *memoria*, memory. *Actio* was defined by Cicero as 'regulating of the voice and body in a manner suitable to the dignity of the subjects spoken of and of the language employed'. A noble father's instruction to his son shows that spoken delivery in Nahuatl also required similar discipline:[116]

> Thou art to speak very slowly, very deliberately; thou art not to speak hurriedly, not to pant, nor to squeak, lest it be said of thee that thou art a groaner, a growler, a squeaker. Also thou art not to cry out, lest thou be known as an imbecile, a shameless one, a rustic, very much a rustic ['timjllacatl, titequjmjllacatl']. Moderately, middlingly, art thou to carry, to

(discussed in Chapter 5, IV above) where the fictional speech attributed to the Aztec priests exhibited classical *dispositio*.

[113] Foley 1991; 2002. According to Ong 2002, 34, 'rhythmic, balanced patterns, in repetitions or antithesis, in alliterations or assonances, in epithetic and other formulary expressions' facilitated performers' retention and retrieval of material. Cf. Lockhart 1992, 394–8 on the structure of Nahuatl song.

[114] The capacity of metaphors to evoke or convey a larger context in a brief phrase accounts for their prominence in oral traditions: cf. Foley 1991, 7; Foley 1995, 5.

[115] *HG* 6.10 [1969 vii, 48]. Cf. OLMOS, *Arte de la lengua mexicana* (1547) 3.8, [tr. Maxwell and Hanson 1992, 171: 'For the family tree, for the line of descent, the lineage head sustains the vital essence, the progenitor establishes the line.'

[116] Cicero, *De inventione* 1.7: 'pronuntiatio est ex rerum et verborum dignitate vocis et corporis moderatio.' Cf. Cicero, *De oratore* 3.40–6; Aristotle, *Rhetoric* 3.1, 1404a.

> emit thy spirit, thy words. And thou art to improve, to soften thy words, thy voice.[117]

Quintilian, too, had recommended expression that was free of 'rusticity': 'the voice should be healthy . . . not dull, coarse, exaggerated, hard, stiff, feeble, soft, or effeminate, and the breath is neither too short nor difficult to sustain or recover.'[118]

Memory was necessary for good delivery, as is evident from the description of how the noble was supposed to address the newly enthroned *tlatoani*. It was also memory, not rhetorical method, that provided the mechanism for generating new speeches, in order to meet needs as they arose. In a society without alphabetic writing, memorized sequences of phrasing (sometimes in conjunction with pictorial codices) had been the building blocks for the construction of new discourses. Fray Gerónimo de Mendieta and Fray Juan de Torquemada give separate accounts of how Indian converts who acted as interpreters could relay perfectly the content of the friars' sermons in their own language, occasionally making appropriate additions after hearing them in Spanish only once or twice.[119]

Whether or not the native Mexican scholars who transcribed the text of the *Historia general* were able to accomplish similar feats of memorization, their thorough grounding in the *trivium* meant they would have been well aware—perhaps far more aware than Sahagún—of the categorical difference between the Nahuatl Christian texts they themselves composed on European rhetorical principles and the orally transmitted ritual speeches of Book 6. Yet in their own Nahuatl incipit to the book the copyists describe the discourses it contains as follows:

> Here begins the sixth book in which are told the various words of prayer ['tlatlatlauhtiliztlatolli'] with which they prayed to those who were their gods; and how they made noble speech ['tecpillatouaia'], through which they displayed rhetoric ['rethorica'] and moral philosophy ['philosophia moral'] as is evident in the discourses.[120]

Despite having to rely on Spanish loan words for 'rhetoric' and 'moral philosophy', the Mexican scholars nonetheless signal the relevance of those categories in this

[117] *HG* 6.22 [1969 vii, 122]. Compare a mother's advice to her daughter in 6.19 [1969 vii, 100]: 'And thy speech is not to come forth hurriedly. As thou art to speak, thou art not to be brutish, not to rush, not to disquiet. Thy speech is to come forth in tranquility and with gentleness. Thou art neither to lift up nor to lower much [thy voice]. As thou art to speak, as thou art to address one, as thou art to greet one, thou art not to squeak. Thou art not to murmur. Straight forward is thy speech to come forth; in medium voice is it to come forth; nor art thou to make it fanciful.'

[118] Quintilian, *Institutio* 11.3.32.

[119] TORQUEMADA, *MI* 15.18 [1977 v, 77–9]; MENDIETA, *Historia* 3.19 [1870, 226].

[120] *HG* 6.1 [1969 vii, 1].

context. As Aristotle pointed out, rhetoric can be displayed without conscious acquisition of it as an art.[121]

But Sahagún's tendentious Spanish title, *De la Rethorica, y philosophia moral, y theologia,* conveys that the book was *about* those arts, and for obvious reasons does not reveal that many of the speeches in Book 6 were a form of idolatrous liturgy.[122] The friar's packaging of those speeches as rhetoric throughout the Spanish translation was a ploy that was sustained by his prologue to the book, by his translations of the short explanatory prefaces in Nahuatl to the individual chapters, and by the last three chapters (reviewed in the next subsection). In the end, Sahagún's prologue, with its focus on persuasion and the importance Mexicans had accorded to 'rhetoricians' as statesmen, had little concrete relevance to the material it introduced.

Short prefaces to each chapter—excerpted in Nahuatl and Spanish in Appendix 1.7 below—commend the value of the content to come, without offering very meaningful insights on it. The critical vocabulary in Nahuatl is limited, making frequent recourse to the same terms: *tlatolli*, 'word', could be rendered into Spanish as *lenguaje* (style or expression), *materia* (subject matter), or *vocablos* (words); *machiotlatolli,* 'sign-word', 'example word', became *maneras de hablar*, 'figures of speech'. The Nahuatl prefaces also employed loan words like *metaphoras* and *sentencias,* which in turn came from Latin—the frequent recurrence of those terms was because the selection of choice metaphors, an aspect of *elocutio,* appealed to Renaissance readers.[123]

The Spanish versions of the Nahuatl prefaces often have a technical air that is lacking in the originals. For example, 'mjec in vncan moteneoa tecpilatlatolli', 'there is spoken a very noble discourse', became 'usa en ella de muchos colores retoricos', 'he makes use of many rhetorical colours.'[124] Again, the Nahuatl preface to a speech given by the commoners' representative to the new *tlatoani,* or ruler, in Chapter 11 remarks simply,

> iece injn tlatolli, amo cenca maviçauhqui, in juh achto omjto.
>
> This speech is not as marvellous as the previous one.

But in the Spanish translation, classical literary terminology is used to amplify that verdict:

[121] Aristotle, *Rhetoric* 1.1, 1354a.

[122] 'Theologia' in this context implies discourse about the gods rather than prayers addressed to them, while 'philosophia moral' meant something like 'the science of behaviour', as *moral* derives from the Latin *mos*, 'custom', just as *historia moral* designates a social or ethnographic history.

[123] Cf. prefaces to *HG* 6.1, 6.4, 6.20, 6.27, excerpted in Appendix 1.7 below. Juan Luis Vives gave primacy to *elocutio* over the other four canons of rhetoric (*De causis corruptarum artium*, in *Opera omnia* vi, 159–62, cited in Mack 2005, 70). Vives' *De ratione dicendi* (1533) was primarily a manual of style.

[124] *HG* 6.13 [1969 vii, 63].

no lleva esta oracion tanta gravedad, ni tanto coturno como la pasada.

This speech does not convey so much gravity, nor so much of the *cothurnus* ['grand style'] as the last.[125]

Overall, the Spanish prefaces attribute to the Nahuatl speeches a degree of rhetorical accomplishment that they do not really possess—but the purpose of Sahagún's Spanish translation of the entire text of Book 6 was to deliver the 'Rethorica' that had been promised in the title. The lists of idioms and expressions in Nahuatl in the three final chapters contributed to this strategy.

(ii) The *Adagios, Çaçaniles,* and *Methaphoras*: Book 6, chapters 41–43

Renaissance Latin rhetorical manuals often close with a list of figures of speech or idioms, in imitation of the Roman *Rhetorica ad Herennium*.[126] That was the model for *Historia general* Book 6, the last three chapters of which are devoted to adages, riddles, and metaphors.[127] Such devices had been a staple of classical rhetorical manuals and Erasmus used them to enable students to acquire *copia*, abundance of expression in Latin.[128] The Dutch humanist's first collection of 818 proverbs, the *Adagiorum collectanea* (1500), proved a great success: after many increasingly extended editions, a final full version, *Adagiorum chiliades* ('Thousands of adages'), containing 4,151 adages was printed in Basel in 1536. These volumes incorporate very brief phrases from Latin literature as well as fuller proverbs, accompanied by an explanatory commentary.

While lists of sayings and metaphors had also been compiled in Spain, Erasmus' *Adagia* is the obvious template for chapter 41 of *Historia general* Book 6, entitled 'Adagios'.[129] This chapter consists of Nahuatl *tlatlatolli*, 'sayings', varying in length from one or two words to a sentence, succeeded by an explanation, also in Nahuatl—all accompanied with a parallel Spanish translation (Figure 8.5). Sometimes an equivalent saying in Spanish was given in lieu of a literal rendering: 'Ixpetz', 'The astute one', was given as 'Merlin'; and 'Tlanj xiqujpilvilax', 'A sack-dragger deep down', became 'A wolf in sheep's clothing' ('lobo en piel de oveja').[130]

[125] *HG* 6.11 [1969 vii, 57]: *cothurnus*, a term of Greek origin, referring to the boot worn by actors in tragedies, probably drawn from Horace, *Ars poetica* 80, 280.

[126] *Ad Herennium* 4.13.19–4.55.69.

[127] Mack 2011, 208–26; Vickers 1988, 295: 'All rhetoric-books offer a classification of verbal devices.'

[128] *Ad Herennium* 4.17.24; Aristotle, *Rhetoric* 2.21, 1394a–1395b; cf. Quintilian, *Institutio* 9.3.98.

[129] Pedro Díaz de Toledo's *Proverbia Senecae* (1495) and the *Refranes que dizen las vieja* (1508) of Íñigo López de Mendoza, the Marquis of Santillana, are Spanish collections cited in Ríos Castaño 2014b, 64.

[130] *HG* 6.41 [1969 vii, 220–1].

Libro, 6, de la Rethorica

muchos resbaladeros y cay das en este mundo.

Es lo mismo que arriba se ya dicho que apenas ay quien se pueda escapar de caer en algun peccado.

Con ninguna cosa sale de quãtas comiença.

¶ Este refran se dize: del que comiença a deprender algun officio o sciencia y luego le dexa y pasa a otro y con ninguno sale: por esto dizen del ayamo quatlatlatztza: como si dixesse en nada asienta.

No ay que confiar en parientes o a muertos y a ydos no ay amigos.

¶ Dizesse este refran: de los que estan en necessitad o los mesmos lo dizen de si mismos porque no ay nadie que entonce los fauorezca y ansi dizen aiac matlacpa teca. quiere dezir todos me an desamparado.

iquac mitoa. Quenvel ximimatia titeocuitlamichin.

Tlaalaui, tlapetzcaui intlalticpa

¶ Çan ieno iuhqui ino mito: aço quinitzquitiapa qualli inemiliz: ça tepan itla ipan vetzi tlatlaculli, in maiuhqui omalauh çoquititlan.

Aiemo quatlatlatztza.

¶ Itechpa mitoa: in amoçan centlamantli quimotequitia, çan amo tle nelti: aço quimomachtia cuicatl, çan avel quichioa: iene quimomachtia latin, anovel quichioa: iene castillantlatolli quimomachtia, amo novel quimati. Inaquin iuhquichioa y, vel itechpa mitoa. Aiemo quatlatlatztza.

Aiac matlacpa teca.

¶ Iquac mitoa: intla aca itla itequiuh, itla ic tlapalevia ymocuicuiltia, mona nenequi: quitoa. Ma nicaoa y notequiuh: in iquac iuhquichioa in, in momati aço cenca ic tlaçotlaloz, mauiztililoz: auh çan ic tlaiolitlacoa: niman ic caoaltilo. Auh

Figure 8.5 Spanish translation accompanying original Nahuatl adages and their explanations, *Florentine Codex*, 1577, Book 6, chapter 41. Biblioteca Laurenziana, Florence, Ms. Med. Palat. 219, f. 195v.

The influence of humanist pedagogy is evident in the explanations given for some of the maxims. The adage 'Aiemo quatlatlatztza', literally, 'He does not yet lay eggs from the head', is translated into Spanish as 'Con ninguna cosa sale de quantas comjença' ('Nothing comes out of all the attempts to begin'). There is then an elucidation in Nahuatl:

> This is said of one who does not accomplish a task, and nothing comes of it. Perhaps he studies a song but cannot master it. A little later he studies Latin; neither can he master it. A little later on he studies the Castilian tongue; neither can he master it.[131]

Here the Mexican writers refer to the kind of training they had themselves received (incidentally confirming that the students at the College of Santa Cruz learned Latin before they studied Spanish).

That Latin education shaped their commentary on another adage: 'Oc cepa iuhcan iez, oc ceppa iuh tlamanjz in jqujn, in canjn', 'Once again it shall be, once again it shall exist, sometime, somewhere.'[132] The interpretation in Nahuatl is as follows:

> What happened long ago and no longer happens, will happen another time. What existed long ago, will exist again. Those who are living now, will live anew, will exist.[133]

This introduces a further suggestion, extraneous to the adage itself, that what happened in the past—as well as the present—will happen and exist again. Irrespective of the conceptions of cyclical time that may have been held by the Aztecs, it was in their study of Latin literature that the native scholars are more likely to have come across the idea that past scenarios would recur again. Among other texts, as indicated earlier, they certainly knew Virgil's fourth *Eclogue*, which predicted the return of the Golden Age of Saturn.[134]

But instead of simply translating the Nahuatl explanation quoted above, Sahagún expressed his opposition to it, and ventured to identify its classical source:

[131] *HG* 6.41 [1969 vii, 228]: 'Itechpa mjtoa: in amo çentlamantli qujmotequjtia, can amo tle nelti: aço qujmomachtia cujcatl, çan avel qujchioa: ie ne qujmomachtia latin, ano vel qujchioa: ie ne castillan tlatolli qujmomachtia, amo no vel qujmati.'

[132] *HG* 6.41 [1969 vii, 235].

[133] 'In tlein mochioaia cenca ie vecauh, in aiocmo mochioa: auh oc ceppa mochioaz, oc ceppa iuh tlamanjz, in juh tlamanca ie vecauh: in iehoantin, in axcan nemj, oc ceppa nemjzque, iezque.' The English translation given above is from Sullivan 1963, 127.

[134] Virgil, *Eclogue* 4.5–6; cf. *Aeneid* 6.745–51; Ovid, *Metamorphoses* 15.165–85. Tedeschi 2012, 495 also reads this *adagio* in terms of cultural transfer, noting the indigenous Mexican scholars' reception of Aesop and Ovid.

> This proposition is Plato's, and the devil taught it here because it is erroneous and very false. It is contrary to faith too, as it means that the things that were will come back into being as they were in past times, and the things that exist now will exist again: in such a way that, according to this error, those who are alive now will come back to live, and the world as it is now will come back into being in the same way, which is very false and very heretical.[135]

The friar's association of that particular view with Plato was actually prompted by a chapter in the *City of God,* in which Saint Augustine censured pagan philosophers for the belief that past ages and events would return.[136] Sahagún was thus rebutting the heretical Greco-Roman doctrine which he believed had coloured the Indian Latinists' interpretation of the Mexican adage, rather than whatever was conveyed by the adage itself. His wording suggests the writers had picked up this notion in the college ('el diablo la enseño aca', 'The devil taught it here'), where texts of Plato as well as the *City of God* were definitely available by the 1570s.[137]

Chapter 42 of *Historia general,* Book 6 contains riddles, 'çaçanilli' or *zazanilli*—a term that also connotes short tales and was used for the fables in the Nahuatl translation of Aesop.[138] There is a brief definition of 'çaçanilli' at the beginning of the Nahuatl text as 'the so-called "what-is-its", with which riddles are made as if they were mysteries'.[139] Sahagún thus introduced the chapter (in Spanish):

> Some of the many *çaçaniles* of which that Mexican race makes use: they are like 'What is a so-and-so?' in our language.[140]

[135] *HG* 6.41 [1969 vii, 235]: 'Esta proposicion es de platon y el diablo la enseño aca porque es erronea es falsissima es contra la fe qual qujere dezir las cosas que fueron tornaron a ser como fueron en los tiempos pasados y las cosas que son agora serã otra uez: de manera que segun este error los que agora viuen tornaran a biujr y como esta agora el mundo tornara a ser de la mjsma manera lo qual es falsissimo y hereticissimo.' Cf. HERNÁNDEZ, *De antiquitatibus Novae Hispaniae* (c. 1575) 3.3.

[136] Augustine, *De civitate Dei* 12.14, entitled 'De revolutione saeculorum' (cf. Tatian, *Oratio ad Graecos* 5; Nemesius, *De natura hominis* 5 for similar Christian polemics).

[137] Appendix 1.3 below: [61], [121].

[138] Cf. Karttunen 1992, 346 on *zazanilli.* In the entry on 'çaçanilli', MOLINA, *Vocabulario* (1571) [2013], 13v, has 'consejuelas para hazer reyr' ('tales to induce laughter'), and gives 'dezir consejuelas para pasar el tiempo' ('tell tales to pass the time') for *çaçanilhuia.* The explanation of 'Ixpetz' in *HG* 6.41 [1969 vii, 220] has 'çaçanilli' in the sense of riddle.

[139] *HG* 6.42 [1969 vii, 237]: 'Vncan mjtoa: cequj çaçanjlli, in mjtoa çaçan tleino, injc moçaçanjlvia, in juhqujma monaoaltotoca'. Cf. Sullivan 1963, 131.

[140] 'De algunos çaçanjles de los muchos que vsa esa gente mexicano [*sic*]: que son como los que cosa y cosa de nuestra lengua.'

The indication that this form was typically Mexican is borne out by nearly all the riddles to come, including the first example given:

> What is a little blue-green jar filled with popcorn? Someone is sure to guess our riddle; it is the sky.

Only two of the forty-six riddles in the chapter involve identification of items introduced by the Spaniards: 'sacapuch', the European sackbut, is the answer to the seventh riddle, and 'tocamisa', 'shirt' (the Spanish *camisa* preceded by the Nahuatl possessive *to-*), is the answer to the twenty-sixth.

Nonetheless, puzzles like these abounded in Europe both in Latin and in vernacular traditions. Although Cicero did not recommend the *aenigma* for rhetorical adornment and Quintilian considered it an obscure form of allegory, Augustine and later Christian authors like Isidore of Seville were inclined by their study of scripture to accept the *aenigma* as a figure of speech that required appropriate interpretation.[141] Some Latin verse riddles collected in Symphosius' *Aenigmata* were popularized in the *Historia Apollonii*, which also had a rich transmission in Spanish and many other languages.[142] In the 1500s, Lilio Gregorio Giraldi listed and explained Greek and Roman *aenigmata*, while Angelo Poliziano, Thomas More, and Joachim Camerarius were among the Renaissance Latin writers who concocted riddles of their own.[143] Most importantly, Erasmus had published his *Apophthegmatum opus* in 1531, a collection of *aenigmata* and witticisms drawn from a digest attributed to Plutarch. Just as Erasmus' *Adagia* were the obvious model for the 'adagios' in chapter 41 of *Historia general*, Book 6, his apothegms—which also supplied students with a repertoire of expressions for their own Latin writing—directly inspired the assembly of 'çaçanilli' in chapter 42. That collection must have been designed in part to offer a comparable resource for learners of Nahuatl.

Aristotle had held that *aenigmata* were a good source of metaphors, because metaphors were a type of riddle.[144] Metaphors themselves, 'methaphoras', are the subject of the final chapter of Book 6. The short Nahuatl heading that prefaced chapter 43 signalled its benefit to the language-learner:

[141] Cicero, *De oratore* 3.167; Quintilian, *Institutio* 8.6.52; cf. Lausberg 1998, 400 [§899]; Augustine, *De Trinitate* 15.9 on the 'Pauline mirror' of I Corinthians 13:12 ('We see now through a glass in a dark manner'); Isidore, *Etymologies* 1.37.24 on Judges 14:14 ('out of the strong came forth sweetness'): Cook 2001. Cf. the *tezcatl* 'mirror' discussed in Chapter 5, p. 180 above.

[142] Laird 2005.

[143] GIRALDI, *Libelli duo* (1551) contains his *Libellus, in quo aenigmata pleraque antiquorum explicantur*, traditionally dated to 1539; REUSNER, *Aenigmatographia* (1599) is an anthology of enigmas by humanist authors.

[144] Aristotle, *Rhetoric* 1.2, 1405b.

> Some figures of speech, called metaphors; difficult phrases accompanied by their explanations and interpretations.[145]

The corresponding Spanish heading provided by Sahagún, on the other hand, promises examples of rhetorical elegance: 'Some refined metaphors, with their explanations' ('de algunas methaphoras delicadas con sus declarationes').[146]

Fray Andrés de Olmos had assembled a similar group of Nahuatl sayings that he had suggested were 'metaphorical', but without actually calling them metaphors or offering any judgement on their quality:

> The following manners of speaking are metaphorical, because the literal text means one thing and the sense another, although some tend towards a gloss of the literal text and others involve a sense other than that of the literal text they come from.[147]

Olmos was cautious about distinguishing too rigidly between the literal and general senses of these expressions. The 'manners of speaking' he listed each comprised a title or theme in Spanish, heading a series of untranslated phrases in Nahuatl, as in this example:

> la doctrina sancta que sale del coraçon ha de ser tenida en mucho y no menospreciada.
>
> *yn toptli, in petlacalli. amo ytech axiuani, amo tzitzquiloni amo analoni, amo tlacaauilli, yehica in teyollotlan in meya, in quiça in qualli ueueyutl atlatlaçaloni.*[148]
>
> Holy doctrine that comes from the heart has to be held at great value and not despised.
>
> *The coffer and the reed chest are not to be grasped, not to be gripped, not to be seized, they are not the idle things of mortals, because from the place of the heart goodness and what is venerable well up and emerge, not to be thrown aside.*[149]

145 Sullivan 1963, 139; *HG* 6.43 [1969 vii, 241]: 'cequi machiotlatolli, in ijtoca methaphoras, in ohouj tlatolli: ioan in imelaoaca, in jcaqujztica.'

146 Anderson 1966 presents another early collection of metaphors; see also Maxwell and Hanson 1992, 19. Hanson 1994 notes features common to the collections.

147 OLMOS, *Arte de la lengua mexicana* (1547) 3.8 [2002, 177] (cf. n. 97 above): 'Las siguientes maneras de dezir son metaphoricas, porque una cosa quiere dezir la letra y otra la sentencia, aunque algunas vayan a letra glosada y otras se puedan aplicar a otro sentido del que van.' Cf. Maxwell and Hanson 1992, 75.

148 OLMOS, *Arte* (1547) 3.8 [2002, 181].

149 The translation here is adapted from Maxwell and Hanson 1992, 104–5.

A version of this very same expression in the *Historia general* shows how such idioms were spotlighted as 'metaphors' in Book 6, chapter 43. The key words from Olmos' phrase above, 'yn toptli, in petlacalli', were presented as a lemma, followed by an explanation, given first in Nahuatl and next in Spanish:

> Nahuatl lemma:
>
> Toptli, Petlacalli ['The Coffer, the Reed Chest']
>
> Nahuatl explanation:
>
> Injn tlatolli itech mjtoaia: in aqujn vel qujpia in jchtacatlatolli, piallatolli: anozo in jtla aqualli ijxpan muchioaia: aiac vel qujnextiliaia, vel toptli, vel petlacalli: mjtoaia. Vel qujpia in tlatolli, anozo tenemjliz. ['This saying was said of one who guarded well the secrets, the entrusted words, or something evil which had occurred in his presence. To no one could he disclose it; he was indeed like a coffer, like a reed chest. It was said he guarded well the words, or one's conduct.']
>
> Spanish explanation:
>
> Esta letra qujere dezir Cofre Arca. Y por methaphora qujere dezir. Persona que guarda bien el secreto que le esta encomendado o persona muy callada.[150] ['The literal meaning is 'Coffer, Ark'. As a metaphor it means: A person who guards well the secret entrusted to him or a person who can keep very quiet.']

As with the 'adagios', the literal meaning of each idiom is distinguished from its broader sense. In the Spanish elucidations the words 'por methaphora' are frequently used (as they are here) to claim a figurative quality for the Nahuatl idiom. Thus Sahagún's Spanish text changed Olmos' flexible conception of 'ways of speaking' into a list of formal metaphors that were more in line with classical canons. That process is illustrative of the general way in which material and testimonies incorporated into the *Historia general* were modified to fit European humanist paradigms.[151]

The Spanish translation sometimes added or changed wording to modify the sense of the Nahuatl. 'Out of the clouds, out of the mists' ('Mixtitlan aiauhtitlan'), which designated people never before seen, is one example. The original explanation of the phrase in Nahuatl that was provided by the scribes of the *Historia general* can be given in English as follows:

> This was said about people very illustrious and very great, who had never been seen, who had never been known, who had never been beheld

[150] *HG* 6.43 [1969 vii, 247].

[151] Hanson 1994, citing Dibble 1982, 20, likens Sahagún's transformation of the idioms listed by Olmos to the way depictions in the *Florentine Codex* deviated from the indigenous style of the Sahagún's earlier *Primeros Memoriales.*

> anywhere before. And so, when the Spaniards came here, throughout all Mexico it was said: 'Out of the clouds, out of the mists.' It was also said about those who were highly esteemed and very rich.[152]

Sahagún's purported translation, however, does not mention the Spaniards:

> As a metaphor it is said of some notable person who came to a place or kingdom which was not expecting him and who brings great advantage to the republic: and so the people say 'mjxtitlan aiauhtitlan oqujçaco' which means: someone unexpected and unknown has come from the sky or from among the clouds.

Conversely the terms 'kingdom' and the 'republic' are introduced, and the verb 'oqujçaco', 'has come', is surreptitiously added to the Nahuatl saying under discussion. The effect is to change the original reference to illustrious and hitherto unknown personages into a response to an unanticipated but fortunate political turn of events brought about by a stranger. That manipulation is of obvious ideological interest with regard to the Spanish incursion in Mexico.

There are many more idioms listed as 'metaphors' in chapter 43 that conjoin two words or two images in order to convey a single idea. These pairings are not poetic or rhetorical in any strong sense, but instances of a common feature of the Nahuatl language known as 'diphrasis'.[153] 'Ocelopetlatl, quappetlatl', 'the jaguar mat, the eagle mat', is an example from early in the chapter. This expression was explained there—in Nahuatl—as meaning 'where the strong and valiant are, whom no one can vanquish'.[154] The ensuing elaboration, though, introduced another diphrasis, in the form of single word, *altepetl*:

> And they also said: 'There stand the jaguar wall and the eagle wall which protect the city ['altepetl']'—*which means: water and mountain* ['quitoznequj: in atl in tepetl'].

The gloss, here italicized, shows that a form of the transference amounting to metaphor in European tradition was actually a standard constituent of many common terms in Nahuatl: the word for city was not at all elevated or rhetorical. But that

[152] Sullivan 1963, 145. Cf. *HG* 6.43 [1969 vii, 244]. The expression was used in the Mexica speaker's address to the Spaniards in SAHAGÚN, *Colloquios* (1564) 1.7 (line 892 in Klor de Alva 1982, 116) and in Montezuma's speech to Cortés in *HG* 12.16 [1955 xiii, 44].

[153] The use of 'bread and butter' for 'sustenance' illustrates this kind of effect in English, and Latin has several such idioms, e.g. *igne et ferro*, 'by iron and fire', for warfare. Garibay 1940, 115 defined *difrasismo* in Nahuatl as 'expressing a single idea by means of two words which have a self-contained meaning, whether by being synonyms or related' (my translation). Cf. Lockhart 1992, 394 on 'double phrasing'.

[154] *HG* 6.43 [1969 vii, 244].

helpful parsing of *altepetl* by the Nahuatl writers was not translated into Spanish—presumably because it risked conveying to readers that other 'metaphors' listed in this chapter were not really the product of deliberate artifice.

That example alone illustrates the different ways in which the Nahuatl text and the Spanish text operate throughout Book 6. The function of the original speeches and the *copia* of idioms in Nahuatl was exemplary, reminiscent of the text books of Latin usage that were favoured by Erasmus and other humanist educators.[155] On the other hand, the function of the Spanish translation, which was not always faithful to its source, was to frame and aestheticize the Nahuatl discourses in the book, giving readers the impression that the Mexicans had possessed a conscious art of rhetoric.

The Spanish title Sahagún gave to Book 6 was designed to make its exotic content appear more recognizable, in accord with the way pre-Hispanic Mexicans were characterized in its prologue—as a people who, like the ancient Greeks or Romans and modern Europeans, set great store by the art of persuasion. That characterization is in line with Sahagún's earlier portrayal of the Mexica leaders in the *Colloquios y Doctrina christiana* as rhetorically accomplished respondents to the Franciscan Twelve.[156] Las Casas, Torquemada, and other missionaries were in any case using the Nahuatl discourses like those collected by Olmos as evidence for the native Mexicans' moral virtue and intellectual sophistication. Sahagún's own persistent characterization of the discourses presented in the *Historia general* as 'rhetoric' had a comparable ideological dimension.

V. Conclusions

The illustrated bilingual text finalized in the *Florentine Codex* remains an unparalleled resource for contemporary researches into pre-Hispanic Mexican society, so that far more is now known about the Aztecs than the Anglo-Saxons. The source text in Nahuatl, based on actual testimonies from native informants about life and customs in pre-Hispanic Mexico, was only later translated into Spanish, and some parts of that text—notably the ritual speeches in Book 6—were of genuine indigenous origin.

Nonetheless, the *Historia general* as a whole was fundamentally European in its conception, structure, and style. While Fray Andrés de Olmos' lost *Tratado de las antigüedades mexicanas* was an obvious precedent in New Spain, several classical, medieval, and Renaissance encyclopaedias have long been recognized as relevant precursors, and Vincent of Beauvais' *Speculum maius* appears to have been the model for the final organization of the *Florentine Codex*. Saint Augustine's *City of God* inspired the confutations of Aztec religion in the Spanish prologues and appendices to

[155] Cf. Chapter 3, I above and Sloane 1991 on the function of ERASMUS, *De copia* (1512).
[156] Cf. Chapter 5, IV (i) above.

individual books of the *Historia general,* in which Augustine's manner of discrediting the pagan Roman beliefs and practices is often invoked or imitated. The recurrent use of Latin and of Latinisms was a humanist tendency, and terminology from classical rhetoric is deployed throughout Book 6 to support Sahagún's claims for the nature of its content. There are also some classical references in the prologues to other books of the *Historia general*—to Rome, Troy, Hercules, and Aeneas—and Roman gods are used to characterize Aztec divinities in the Spanish text of Book 1.

In notable contrast to other sixteenth-century chronicles and tracts about the Indians in New Spain, classical authors are barely ever mentioned: Virgil and Cicero are each referred to on a single occasion in the Spanish text, and the sole Renaissance authority mentioned is Calepino's dictionary. The few fleeting analogies drawn between Mexican and the Greco-Roman antiquity in the prologues are not developed, because they were meant to serve only as elementary illustrations for European readers. Sahagún had no interest in pursuing comparisons between Aztec and Greco-Roman gods for their own sake: extirpation of the idolatry of the Mexicans required an understanding of its specific nature, and deeper comparisons would not have contributed to that understanding.

The Nahuatl text of the *Historia general* does not name any classical personages, peoples, or places at all, but certain passages clearly evoke episodes in Roman and late antique literature. The similarities of the rule of Quetzalcoatl to the reign of Saturn and the convergences between the circumstances of Cihuacoatl's departure and those of the death of Pan are too specific and detailed to be coincidental. It is just conceivable that Sahagún planted such allusions to Virgil, Josephus, and Eusebius in order to bring the original testimonies into line with Franciscan millenarian expectations—after all, the friar did resort to *legerdemain* to present the discourses in Book 6 as examples of rhetoric. That possibility seems remote, though: millenerianist Franciscans tended to express their views in forthright terms.[157] In any case, Sahagún was free to offer his own interpretations of the Nahuatl material in his prologues, as he frequently did.

Those appropriations of classical and early Christian authors are more plausibly attributed to the Nahuatl-speaking Latinists who transcribed and translated the testimonies of the original informants. Martín Jacobita, rector of the College of Santa Cruz, and Antonio Valeriano, whose own Latin writing echoed a range of authors including Virgil, were among those 'experts in three languages, Latin, Spanish and Indian' whom Sahagún named as his assistants.[158] The most likely explanation for the alignments of Mexican and classical myth in the Nahuatl text is that the collegians were seeking to make sense of the legacies they recorded in the light of the European literature and Christian eschatology with which they were familiar.

[157] Cf. Chapter 1, p. 17 above.

[158] These native scholars are listed in Appendix 1.4 below.

A relevant parallel is offered by the way in which illustrators of the *Florentine Codex* frequently made use of images and motifs from Renaissance drawing or painting to represent Mesoamerican subjects.[159]

The preceding survey of the different uses of humanist learning in the *Historia general* has foregrounded the dialogical nature of the work. As well as differentiating the agency of the native Latinists from that of Sahagún himself, it has been important to call attention to the crucial distinction—which is all too often underplayed—between those indigenous Latinists who mediated the primary material in Nahuatl and the indigenous elders of Texcoco, Tlatelolco, and Mexico City, far better versed in their ancestral traditions, who first supplied it.

[159] Baird 1993, 32–7, 122–38; Magaloni Kerpel 2020, 66–74.

9

Universal Histories for Posterity

Native Chroniclers and Their European Sources

'The teaching of Latin to Indians has stopped', wrote Fray Juan de Torquemada in the 1590s, 'because they are so burdened with toils and everyday responsibilities, with no time to think of developing their knowledge or spiritual concerns, and the ministers of the church are demoralised.' The friar explained that as enthusiasm for training native governors had diminished, the College of Santa Cruz went into decline, teaching only reading and writing to large numbers of local children.[1] Although Fray Juan Bautista oversaw the publication of Christian texts in Nahuatl at Tlatelolco into the 1600s, the college was no longer a nucleus for composition and translation in the Mexican language, and the Franciscans' investigation of native history and beliefs had also come to an end.[2]

Indigenous scholarly activity did continue in the seventeenth century, as native and mestizo authors of privileged standing wrote on their own initiative rather than at the behest of a religious order. In Nahuatl or in Spanish they recorded the complex histories of their ancestral territories in the Valley of Mexico, from their mythical origins to the time of the Spanish incursion and beyond.[3] The chronicles they produced were lengthier and more developed than the accounts of local polities that Indian principals had supplied in their Latin petitions or other documents written in the mid-1500s. Some of these later writers relied on European forms of

[1] TORQUEMADA, *Monarchia Indiana* (1615), = *MI*, 15.43 [1977 v, 178]. Other colleges for the Indians were faring no better: Gibson 1964a, 383.

[2] BAUTISTA, *Advertencias para los Confesores* (1600), *Libro de la miseria y brevedad de la vida del hombre* (1604), *Vida y milagros del Bienaventurado Sanct. Antonio de Padua* (1605), *Sermonario* (1606). Bautista also collaborated with the Indian scholar Agustín de la Fuente on the *Comedia de los Reyes* (c. 1610), a drama about the Epiphany. Cf. Hernández de León-Portilla 1988 i, 53–100; Tavárez 2000 and Pascoe 2017 on the printer Cornelius Adrian Caesar. Baudot 1995, 514–24 deals with evidence for Philip's prohibitions and the confiscation of Indian histories, examining the consequences for Franciscan chroniclers.

[3] Studies include Lockhart 1992, 376–92; Velazco 2003; Villella 2016, 112–48; Gruzinski 2018, 265–302 on Pomar; Townsend 2017 on Nahuatl chronicles.

Aztec Latin. Andrew Laird, Oxford University Press. © Oxford University Press 2024.
DOI: 10.1093/oso/9780197586358.003.0010

knowledge to mediate Nahuatl traditions: the following consideration of ways in which they did so serves as a coda to the preceding chapters.

This discussion will review the work of four chroniclers, with particular focus on the use they made of classical and humanist literature. Given that little is known about the intellectual formation of these authors or the environments in which they operated, such a survey can at least throw light on their reading, and on the different ways in which they embellished their accounts of the Mexican past. After showing how Diego Muñoz Camargo and Hernando de Alvarado Tezozomoc employed analogies from Roman literature (Section I), the distinctive practices of two seventeenth-century historians will then be examined in more detail: Chimalpahin, who cited classical sources as authorities to validate his annalistic history in Nahuatl (Section II), and Fernando de Alva Ixtlilxochitl, for whom certain Greco-Roman and Renaissance texts served as literary models (Section III). These chroniclers used evocations of European antiquity far more dynamically than previous indigenous scholars, in order to convey by association the importance of Mexican history (Section IV).

I. Classical illustrations in the works of Diego Muñoz Camargo and Hernando de Alvarado Tezozomoc

In both of his histories of Tlaxcala, Diego Muñoz Camargo (1528–1600) expressed admiration for the polity and its pre-conquest history, while identifying himself with the Spaniards, whom he refers to as 'our own', 'los nuestros'. The author's bifocal perspective can be explained by his mixed parentage as the son of a Spanish conquistador by a Tlaxcalteca woman, as well as by his experience of mediating between cultures: until 1545 he was brought up in Mexico City, where he served as a page at the viceregal court, before he moved to Tlaxcala and forged connections with the local indigenous elite.[4] Muñoz Camargo met many celebrated prelates and friars—Fray Julián Garcés, Fray Juan de Zumárraga, Vasco de Quiroga, and Fray Bartolomé de las Casas—and it is likely that the Franciscans had a part in his education.[5]

The historian's first work, *Descripción de la ciudad y provincia de Tlaxcala,* was commissioned as a 'relación geográfica' of Tlaxcala. Such *relaciones* were supposed to supply systematic responses to the *Instruction y memoria* (1577), an official

[4] Cf. Velazco 2003, 192–5; Villella 2016, 134–40. As a child, he was entrusted with explaining the rudiments of Christianity to a group of Indians whom Cabeza de Vaca had brought back from his expedition to Florida: MUÑOZ CAMARGO, *Descripción* (c. 1585) [1984, 127].

[5] MUÑOZ CAMARGO, *Historia* (1592), 85r–85v [2013, 232–3]. Gibson 1950, 208 notes that the historian was probably buried at the convent of San Francisco in Tlaxcala, suggesting his closeness to the order. TORQUEMADA, *MI* 4.80 [1975 ii, 247] gives a brief notice of Muñoz; León-Portilla 1983, 152–77 examines the friar's use of his work.

questionnaire about all of Spain's new territories in the Indies, but Muñoz Camargo's meandering narrative was an unusual example of the form.[6] The *Descripción* contained 156 ink drawings that correspond to known images in the *Lienzo de Tlaxcala*: the text may have been a historical prose version of the tapestry's visual account of Tlaxcala's alliance with the conquistadors against the Mexica (Plate 3).[7] The author presented the *Descripción* to Philip II in person, on an embassy to Spain between 1583 and 1585. In order to signal the literary quality of his *relación*, Diego Muñoz Camargo adorned the dedication with a succession of classical *sententiae*, all from books that were available in New Spain.[8] The first, correctly ascribed to Plato (although Muñoz Camargo almost certainly found it in a citation by Cicero), emphasizes the obligations imposed on a writer by his country: 'man was not born for himself alone, but also for his sweet homeland and friends'.[9] The second, lifted directly from Vegetius' dedication of his treatise on warfare to the Emperor Valentinian, underlines the importance of a ruler's endorsement of a book: 'only the work to which the office of prince gives authority should be considered perfect and finished'.[10] Finally, a longer *exemplum* about Artaxerxes amplifies an anecdote culled from Plutarch's *Lives*:

> And so I hope that, despite the rudeness of my style, [this book] will be received with the equability which you show on receiving greater things; because if ARTAXERXES, king of the Persians, [whom] the knights and lords of his kingdom were offering jewels and medals of inestimable price, received with joy the water of the River Kura, which a rustic, who had

[6] Anon., *Instructio[n] y memoria, de las relaciones* (1577) [1984]. Cline 1972 catalogues the *relaciones* for New Spain; Gruzinski 1991, 77–103 is an important discussion. Cf. Acuña 1981, 25 on Muñoz Camargo's *Descripción*.

[7] Kranz 2010, 53–68; cf. Chapter 1, p. 39 above.

[8] Yhmoff Cabrera 1996 i, 369–73; ii, 621–8 lists early editions of Cicero's *De officiis* and Plutarch's *Lives* from libraries and convents in Mexico: both works were in the College of Santa Cruz by the 1570s: Appendix 1.3 below.

[9] MUÑOZ CAMARGO, *Descripción* (c. 1585) [1984, 33]: 'Vnas veces me daba esfuerzo aquella celebrada sentencia del divino PLATÓN, que no nació el hombre para sí solo, sino también para su dulce patria y amigos'; cf. Cicero, *De officiis* 1.22 (paraphrasing pseudo-Plato, *Letters* 9, 358a): 'Vt praeclare scriptum est a Platone, non nobis solum nati sumus ortusque nostri partem patria vindicat, partem amici' ('As was famously written by Plato, we are not born for ourselves alone; our country claims one share in our being, and our friends another').

[10] MUÑOZ CAMARGO, *Descripción* (1585) [1984, 33]: 'según el famoso VEGECIO, aquella obra se debe tener por perfecta y acabada, a la cual el oficio de príncipe diere autoridad'; cf. Vegetius, *De re militari*, Book 1, preface: 'Antiquis temporibus mos fuit bonarum artium studia mandare litteris atque in libros redacta offerre principibus, quia neque recte aliquid inchoatur, nisi post Deum fauerit imperator' ('In ancient times it was customary to commit endeavours in the literary arts to writing and to offer them, produced in book form, to princes, because nothing is started off correctly unless, after God, the emperor favours it').

> nothing else to serve him, brought him with great love and reverence in his own hands—if [Artaxerxes], bowing his royal head with great kindness and greatness, drank it, how can one who has greater kindness and prudence not receive this small service, even if it is from the hand of my rustic talent?[11]

The later *Historia de Tlaxcala* (c. 1592) developed from the *Descripción*.[12] Both works contain cursory mentions of Greeks, Romans, Trojans, or Carthaginians, and both present scenarios that resemble specific episodes in Roman history. The heroic death of the general Regulus at the hands of the Carthaginians, for instance, is recalled by an account of Tlahuicole, the Tlaxcalteca warrior who, as a captive of the Mexica, preferred an honourable death to their offer of freedom. Another example is that of Maxixcatzin, the *tlatoani* who secured Tlaxcala's alliance with Spain: his role resembles that of Massinissa, the king of Numidia who had changed sides to fight with Rome against Carthage in the second Punic war.[13] Such implicit parallels, no less than Muñoz Camargo's overt references to ancient Mediterranean peoples, were designed to aggrandize the content of his histories.

The smaller number of illustrations from classical literature employed by the native chronicler Hernando de Alvarado Tezozomoc (1535–1613) operate in a similar way. Tezozomoc, who seems to have worked as a translator of Nahuatl and Spanish, produced two separate chronicles, one in each language.[14] His *Coronica mexicana*, 'Chronicle of Mexico' (1598), began with the migration of the Aztecs from Aztlan to Mexico City, and culminated in the Spanish conquest. This history, though written in Spanish, derived from native records and oral tradition, retaining some conventions of Nahuatl style.[15] At the same time, it adopted a European

[11] MUÑOZ CAMARGO, *Descripción* (1585) [1984, 33]: 'Y ansí espero que, no mirando la rudeza de mi estilo, será recibida con aquella igualdad que acostumbra recibir mayores cosas; por que si ARTAJERJES rey de los persas . . . le ofreciendo los caballeros y señores de su reino joyas y preseas de inestimable precio recibió con alegría el agua del río Ciro que un rústico, no teniendo otra cosa con qué servirle, con gran amor y reverencia en sus propias manos le traía, a las cuales, inclinando su real cabeza con gran benignidad y grandeza, la bebió, ¿cómo no recibirá este pequeño servicio quien posee mayor benignidad y prudencia, aunque sea de mano de mi rústico ingenio?' Cf. Plutarch, *Life of Artaxerxes* 5.

[12] Mignolo 1987 notes generic distinctions between the *Descripción* and the *Historia*, despite their overlapping content.

[13] MUÑOZ CAMARGO, *Descripción* (c. 1585), 66r–67r, and *Historia de Tlaxcala* (1592), 53r–53v [2013, 132–4] on Tlahuicole; *passim* on Maxixcatzin; cf. Livy, *Ab urbe condita*, 'Periocha' 18 on Regulus, and 24.48–9 on Massinissa.

[14] ALVARADO TEZOZOMOC, 'Tlalamatl Huauhquilpan', 1v (1598), a legal document in Nahuatl, has a portrait of the author with the caption 'nahuatlato AlBarado', 'the Nahuatl speaker Alvarado', conveying that he worked as a translator: Cortés 2011. Mariscal 1946 conjectured on the basis of this and other testimonia that he lived until 1613; Peperstraete and Kruell 2014, 318 report his name on a document of 1610.

[15] Lockhart 1992, 390.

perspective, so that classical references provide analogies to explain practices or entities specific to Mexico. The first example occurs in a description of Montezuma II's trusted counsellors:

> They were very secretive, so that no one in the city knew of them, because they kept the Mexican senate very secret, just as the Romans did in the Capitol.[16]

The second is in an account of a prophecy made to Montezuma:

> Some people of old predicted that there would come and populate these lands ones who were to be called *tzoçuilycxique* [= *tzocuilicxique*, 'goldfinch-footed'] or else named *çenteycxiques* [single-footed]: they are those that are found in the deserts of Arabia burned by the high sun and they have just one foot on a very large leg that they use as their shade, they use their ears as coverings, and have heads in their chests.[17]

The *tzocuilicxique* are a conflation of three quite distinct humanoid species described by Pliny and Saint Augustine, all of which featured in a single passage of Isidore of Seville's *Etymologies*:[18]

> People believe that the Blemmyans in Libya are born as trunks without heads, with a mouth and eyes in the chest . . . they tell of the Panotians of Scythia, whose ears are so large that they cover their whole body . . . The race of Sciopods is said to live in Ethiopia; they have only one leg, and are amazingly fast-moving. The Greeks call them *skiopodes* ('shade-footed

[16] ALVARADO TEZOZOMOC, *Coronica mexicana* (1598), cap. 97 [2001, 97]: 'estauan muy secretos, que nenguno de la çiudad sabían dellos, porque el senado mexicano guardauan mucho secreto, como los rromanos [*sic*] lo guardauan en el Capitollio.' Cf. Cicero, *Ad Atticum* 4.17.3; *Historia Augusta* 20.12.3 (on the Gordians): 'senatus consultum tacitum fieret . . . ne quid forte proderetur' ('a decree of the Senate was passed in secret . . . so that nothing could by any chance be disclosed'). *Historia Augusta*, an anonymous Roman collection of imperial biographies, circulated in various editions after Bonus Accursius' *editio princeps* (1475).

[17] ALVARADO TEZOZOMOC, *Coronica mexicana* (1598), cap. 110 [2001, 476]: 'algunos antiguos les dexaron profetizado que los que abían de benir a rreynar y pobrar estas tierras que abían de ser llamados *tzoçuilycxique* y por otro nombre *çenteycxiques*, que son aquellos que están [en] los desiertos de Arabia que el alto sol ençiende, [que] son, que tienen un pie solo, de una pata muy grande, con que se hazen sombra, y las orejas les sirben de fraçadas, [que] tienen la cabeça en el pecho.'

[18] Pliny, *Historia naturalis* 7.2; Augustine, *De civitate Dei* 16.8. There were more than ten different editions of the *Etymologies* between 1470 and 1530, and the work reached New Spain with the missionaries: pp. 18, 35–6, 38, and 150 above.

Monſtra hu-
mana.

ueniens ardor ſolis. Confinxerunt ueteres multa monſtra quæ in hac terra aſſerunt in-
ueniri, præſertim Solinus & Me
gaſtenes ſcribūt, per diuerſos In
diæ montes eſſe nationes capiti-
bus caninis, armatas unguibus,
amictas ueſtitu tergorum, ad ſer
monem humanū nulla uoce ſed
latratibus tantum ſonantes aſpe
ris rictibus. Gangis fontē qui
accolūt, nullius ad eſcam opis in
digent, odore uiuunt pomorum
ſylueſtrium, longiusqꝫ pergētes,
eadem illo in præſidio gerunt, ut
olfactu alantur. Quod ſi tetriorē
fortè ſpiritū traxerint, exanima-
ri eos certum eſt, & illorum ali-
quos in Alexandri caſtris fuiſſe memoriæ traditum eſt. Legimus monoculos quoqꝫ in India eſſe. Quoſdam etiam tam inſigniter auritos, ut aures ad pedes defluant, atqꝫ in alter-
utram earum decubent, quarum duricie arbores conuellant. Quoſdam item ſingulis pedi
bus & adeo latis quidem, ut ubi ſe defendendi à calore uelut reſupinati, his totaliter inum-
brentur. Legitur etiam gentem quandam eſſe, quæ in iuuenta eſt cana, in ſenectute uero ni

Figure 9.1 Human monsters in Sebastian Münster, *Cosmographia universalis,* Basel 1550, 1080. John Carter Brown Library.

> ones') because when it is hot they lie back on the ground and are shaded by the great size of their feet.[19]

Tezozomoc's statement that the *tzocuilicxique* are found in the deserts of Arabia indicates that they were to be identified with the beings in the classical sources. The connection may have been made to render the creatures in the pre-Cortesian prophecy more credible, or at least more recognizable, to readers who may well have been familiar with the common medieval and Renaissance depictions of the Blemmyans, Panotians, and Sciopods (Figure 9.1).[20]

Tezozomoc's second work, the *Chronica Mexicayotl,* 'Chronicle of Aztec Mexico' (1609), which was in Nahuatl, glorified Tenochtitlan and its rulers—for the benefit of those descended from the Mexica Tenochca, and perhaps also for the edification of readers who hailed from different Nahuatl-speaking polities. The text has sometimes been incorrectly attributed to Chimalpahin (cf. Section II below), despite an unequivocal affirmation in the preface:[21]

[19] Isidore, *Etymologies* 11.3.17, 19, 23: 'Blemmyas in Libya credunt truncos sine capite nasci, et os et oculos habere in pectore . . . Panotios apud Scythiam esse ferunt, tam diffusa magnitudine aurium ut omne corpus ex eis contegant . . . Sciopodum gens fertur in Aethiopia singulis cruribus et celeritate mirabili: quos inde σκιόποδας Graeci vocant, eo quod per aestum in terra resupini iacentes pedum suorum magnitudine adumbrentur.'

[20] Equivalences between Aztec and Roman gods in SAHAGÚN, *Historia general* = *HG,* Book 1 may have had a comparable function: Chapter 8, II above.

[21] Chimalpahin, who copied the earliest known manuscript, made several interpolations but only occasionally named himself when he did so. The authorship of parts of the *Chronica Mexicayotl* is thus

> But now it is the year 1609. I, don Hernando de Alvarado Teçocomoc, am also a grandson of the late lord, the great ruler Moteucçomatzin Xocoyotl, who guarded and governed the great *altepetl* here, Mexico Tenochtitlan. I issued from his beloved daughter, the lady, the noblewoman, my mother, named doña Francisca de Moteucçoma. She was the wife of the lord don Diego de Alvarado Huanitzin, my parent, my father.[22]

After thus identifying himself, the author explained that his work was based on ancient records and on the testimonies of noble elders, including his father and his uncle, Pedro de Montezuma.[23] The *Chronica Mexicayotl* begins with a teleological narrative of the Aztecs' foundation of Mexico Tenochtitlan, which is ascribed alternately to two divine agencies: the demonic Huitzilopochtli had 'conversed with the Azteca and lived among them as their friend' during their migration to Mexico, while the Christian God had also inclined them to move southward to their destined home in Mexico for another reason:

> so that the Spaniards would go to them and change their way of life, and so that their spirits and souls would be saved, in the way that in times past the people of Rome brought it about, as well as the people of Spain, *the Spaniards who then expanded over all the world* ['yn españolesme yn huel ixquich yc omocenmanque in ipā cemanahuatl'].[24]

The phrase italicized here echoes the language that had been used only a few lines earlier to describe the divine plan for the Aztecs to 'spread, expand everywhere over various lands' ('omotecaco omoçecenmanaco y nepapan nohuiampa tlallipan'). Alvarado Tezozomoc thus set the early history of his ancestors in parallel to that of the Romans and that of the Spaniards, to highlight the preeminence of the Tenochca among the other native peoples inhabiting the Valley of Mexico.

difficult to determine: BOTURINI BENADUCI, 'Catalogo' (1746), §VIII [2015, 217] first ascribed the work to Chimalpahin, and Schroeder 2011 has made a detailed case for this, but Peperstraete and Kruell 2014 firmly attribute the *Chronica Mexicayotl* to Alvarado Tezozomoc on internal evidence. Another indication of Tezozomoc's authorship is noted in Chapter 6, III (iii) n. 113 above.

[22] ALVARADO TEZOZOMOC, *Chronica Mexicayotl* (1609) [1997, 63]: cf. the genealogy in Appendix 1.5 below.

[23] ALVARADO TEZOZOMOC, *Chronica Mexicayotl* (1609), 19r–19v [1997, 64]. Lockhart 1992, 389–91 notes the Nahuatl chronicle's affinities with the *Coronica mexicana*.

[24] ALVARADO TEZOZOMOC, *Chronica Mexicayotl* (1609), 20v [1997, 66].

II. Classical authorities in Chimalpahin's Nahuatl annals

Domingo Francisco de San Antón Muñón Chimalpahin Cuauhtlehuanitzin, as he called himself, states that he was born on the night of 26–27 May 1579 in Amecameca Chalco, some thirty miles southeast of Mexico City.[25] He was probably first schooled there, at the large Dominican Convent of the Assumption. Like other indigenous chroniclers, Chimalpahin took pride in his place of origin, and his coverage of pre-Hispanic times gave particular attention to Amecameca. But after he began to live in Mexico City, his accounts of the post-conquest era focused more on Tenochtitlan.[26]

Chimalpahin moved to the capital in 1593–1594 to take up an appointment as a residential warden of the church of San Antonio Abad.[27] The position offered access to indigenous records and European books: San Antonio, in the *barrio* of Xoloco, was near the Convent of San Francisco, which had been connected to the college of San José de los Naturales and was renowned for its extensive library.[28] Chimalpahin evidently consulted two volumes printed in Mexico City in 1606, around the time he began writing: his knowledge of astrology and European geography came from Henrico Martínez' popular *Reportorio de los tiempos*; and he reproduced a Nahuatl passage about eclipses from Fray Juan Bautista's *Sermonario en lengua mexicana*.[29]

Chimalpahin wrote almost entirely in the Mexican language but his best known annals, the *Diario* (c. 1624) and the eight cycles of the *Relaciones* (c. 1630), refer to works by Spanish, Latin, and Greek authors.[30] The *Diario* covers events in the Valley

[25] CHIMALPAHIN, *Relaciones* 7 (c. 1630), 218v [1998 ii, 248]. The Nahuatl names came from his ancestors Chimalpahin and the *tlatoani* Cuauhtlehuanitzin: Schroeder 1991, 1–13.

[26] Lockhart 1992, 388.

[27] CHIMALPAHIN, *Relaciones* 8 (c. 1630), 225r, 234v [1998 ii, 270, 294].

[28] 16,417 volumes were brought from the Convent of San Francisco to the National Library of Mexico in 1867: Payno 1869, 13. Segura Martínez *et al.* 1991–2000 catalogue the convent's holdings. Schroeder 1991, 13–20 makes important conjectures about Chimalpahin's intellectual environment and the sources available to him.

[29] CHIMALPAHIN, *Diario* (c. 1624), 142–4 [2006, 178–80] quotes BAUTISTA, *Sermonario* (1606), 196: cf. Schmidt 2021; Tavárez 2010, 19–20. Martínez Baracs 2007b, 291 suggests that the achievements of Mexican scholars described by Bautista inspired Chimalpahin. An unpublished study by Carlos Diego Arenas Pacheco shows how sources named or recalled in the *Relaciones* 1 and 2 were transmitted to Chimalpahin.

[30] Compare the lists compiled in Rafael Tena's edition of CHIMALPAHIN, *Relaciones* [1998 ii, 389–90] and in Messiaen 2003, 224, although the *Martyrologium Romanum* (cf. nn. 38–39 below) is not in Tena's list and Bautista's *Sermonario* is absent from both. The dates of Chimalpahin's manuscripts can only be approximate: cf. the editors' introduction to CHIMALPAHIN, *Diario* (c. 1624) [2006, 10–14].

of Mexico during 1589–1615, some of which the author observed himself. The end of the entry for 1608 counts back to the very creation of the world:

> When the universe was made and created at the very beginning, it was six thousand, three hundred and sixty-one years before now, the end of the year of our lord God 1608.[31]

The dates of the Flood and the foundation of the city of Rome are used to situate the first settlement of Mexico 1,524 years before, in 84 AD: 'it was then that the ancient Chichimeca who had come to Aztlan Teocolhuacan gradually began to come in this direction, to . . . disperse here in the land called New Spain'. For the next entry, which details the election of officials for the Audiencia of New Spain, the year of 1609 is counted down from the Roman Emperor Vespasian's sack of Jerusalem in 70 AD. The destruction of Jerusalem had loomed large in Franciscan religious theatre because of the subject's perceived similarities to the fall of the Aztec capital of Mexico Tenochtitlan.[32]

Chimalpahin's *Relaciones* are his *magnum opus*, covering the periods from the Creation to 1612. In the original manuscript, the year that heads each entry is given in both the Mexican and Christian system of reckoning.[33] Despite some extensive digressions, the annalistic style of the work is viewed as typical of a long-standing Nahuatl tradition. Many autochthonous Mexican records (including those with pictorial components) offer precedents for his use of certain dates as anchors, and for the practice of counting backward and forward in time.[34] Such Nahuatl annals addressed similar concerns to those of the yearbooks of medieval Europe: successions of principals, conflicts, memorable deeds, plagues, droughts, natural events, and occasional supernatural phenomena. Another fundamental feature common to both traditions was the central place given to the community in which the records were produced, whether it was an *altepetl*, a town, a region, a royal court, or a monastery.[35]

Yet the archetype and model for all the post-classical annals in the Christian west—Isidore of Seville's *Chronicon*—had adopted a universal perspective. The short version of the *Chronicon*, which Isidore had incorporated into Book 5 of his

[31] CHIMALPAHIN, *Diario* (c. 1624), 72 [2006, 116]: 'Yn iquac yn itzinpeuhyoc. yn ochihualoc yn yocoyalloc cemanahuatl. ye caxtoltzonxihuitl ypan caxtolpohualxihuitl. ypan yepohualli ypã ce xihuitl. ynic axcan ypan in yn itlamian yxiuhtzĩ tt° Dios. de 1608 años.'

[32] Burkhart 2010; Sell and Burkhart 2009, 243–80; cf. Chapter 8, n. 65 above.

[33] CHIMALPAHIN, *Relaciones* (1630) [1949–1952].

[34] Lockhart 1992, 387 (following a survey of prior records at 345–86); Schroeder 2010b, 102. Boornazian Diel 2018 interprets the pictorial annals of the *Codex Mexicanus* (c. 1583).

[35] Cf. White 1987, 5–11, 14–15. Cf. Woolf 2019, 117: 'Chimalpahin's annals for post-Conquest times follow a pattern familiar to any reader of medieval chronicles.' Woolf also notes that Chimalpahin's 'vision of history embraced the whole world'.

Etymologies, must have been mediated in some form to Chimalpahin, however indirectly.[36] Isidore's year-count began with the Creation of the world 5,210 years before Christ was born and continued into Isidore's own lifetime in the 600s. Similarly, the chronology in the *Relaciones* ran from the Creation until the period Chimalpahin was writing, and set the birth of Christ just eleven years after the date given by Isidore:

> our Lord was born 5,199 years after the creation of the world, according to the count of the *Martyrologium Romanum*, 2,957 after the Flood, and 2,015 from the birth of Abraham; and 1,510 from the departure of the people of Israel from Egypt; and 1,032 after David was anointed king in the sixty-fifth week, according to Daniel's prophecy; and in the 194th Olympiad, 752 years after the foundation of Rome, and 42 years into Octavian's rule.[37]

This preliminary note on the Mexican calendar is given in Spanish at the beginning of the second *Relación*, stating that the reckoning came from the *Martyrologium Romanum* (1583).[38] Chimalpahin's entire list of events from biblical and secular history to situate the nativity appears to be taken verbatim from that source.[39] The Spanish note is followed by a Nahuatl version that is generally accurate, although 'in the 194th Olympiad' ('en la olimpiada cienta y noventa y quatro') is wrongly translated as '194 *years from* the Olympiad', and 'olimpiada' is incorrectly taken to mean 'cleansing':

> in nechipahualiztli yn motenehua la olimpiada ye iuh chiuhcnapohualxihuitl ypan matlactli onnahui xihuitl.
>
> From the cleansing that is called the Olympiad it was one hundred and ninety-four years.

[36] Isidore, *Etymologies* 5.39. The *Chronicon* was based on Saint Jerome's adaptation of Eusebius' chronicle. Cf. n. 18 above on the *Etymologies* in New Spain.

[37] CHIMALPAHIN, *Relaciones* 2, 10v [1998 i, 60].

[38] The *Martyrologium Romanum* (1583) was published after the Gregorian calendar had been adopted in 1582.

[39] The Latin text of the *Martyrologium* translated in Chimalpahin converges with the Proclamation of the Birth of Christ in the Roman Rite: 'Anno a creatione mundi, quando in principio Deus creavit caelum et terram, quinquies millesimo centesimo nonagesimo nono; a diluvio autem, anno bis millesimo nongentesimo quinquagesimo septimo; a nativitate Abrahae, anno bis millesimo quintodecimo; a Moyse et egressu populi Israel de Ægypto, anno millesimo quingentesimo decimo; ab unctione David in Regem, anno millesimo trigesimo secundo; Hebdomada sexagesima quinta, juxta Danielis prophetiam; Olympiade centesima nonagesima quarta; ab urbe Roma condita, anno septingentesimo quinquagesimo secundo; anno Imperii Octaviani Augusti quadragesimo secundo.'

This characterization of the Olympiad seems to be based on a mistaken connection between *olimpiada* and the Spanish word for cleaning, *limpiar*, but it fortuitously tallies with information provided by Isidore of Seville. Isidore had preceded his *Chronicon* with a brief excursus 'on Olympiads, *lustra* and jubilees', which explained that the Roman *lustrum* imitated the Olympiad and that 'it was called a 'lustrum' because the city of Rome was *purified* ['lustrabatur'] every five years'.[40]

There are further occasions on which Chimalpahin seems to be drawing from unspecified European sources. For instance, a remark in Spanish on the fall of the Mexica, stating that 'everything in the world waxes and wanes' ('Todas las cosas deste mundo cresen y menguan'), was a commonplace, found in the Bible and in a number of classical texts.[41] Sahagún had already applied it to the changing fortunes of the Aztecs, and it was the theme of a classically styled oration, reminiscent of a tragic soliloquy, attributed to Montezuma in Francisco Cervantes de Salazar's *Chronica de la Nueva España* (1566).[42]

Whether or not it was ever known to Chimalpahin, the standard Latin translation of Plato by Marsilio Ficino was the ultimate source for the quotations from the *Timaeus* and the *Letters* (both given in Nahuatl) that open Chapter 1 of the first *Relación*.[43] The chapter then evokes prefatory formulae from Diogenes Laertius, Lactantius, Eusebius, and Augustine; from the Renaissance encyclopaedists Caelius Rhodiginus, Battista Egnazio, and Antonius Sabellicus; and from the Book of Genesis. It is held that all those authors had invoked God's authority before embarking upon their work: 'And the ancient writers always began in the name of God, in their treatment of God.'[44] But that was not, despite what Chimalpahin claims, the case with Diogenes Laertius, a Greek author who lived in the 200s AD:

> And the one named Diogenes Laertius in the 'Lives of the Sages' called *philosophers*, at the point of explaining the foundations of knowledge, of *philosophy*, begins by showing how our lord God is the principle of divine

[40] Isidore, *Etymologiae* 5.37. MOTOLÍNIA, *Memoriales* (c. 1541), 123v [1996, 551] had earlier invoked 'olympiades' to try to make sense of the Aztecs' use of four signs—Tochtli, 'Rabbit'; Acatl, 'Reed'; Tecpatl, 'Flint'; and Calli, 'House'—as names for the years. Cf. Chapter 2, IV (iv) above.

[41] CHIMALPAHIN, *Historia o chronica* (c. 1610–1629), 14r–14v [1997 i, 54]; cf. Ecclesiastes 1; Wisdom 5:9; I Corinthians 7:31; Seneca, *Epistles* 107.8; Herodotus, *Histories* 1.86–7; Xenophon, *Cyropaedia* 7.2; Plutarch, *Solon* 8.24; Justinus, *Epitome of Pompeius Trogus* 1.7; Boethius, *Consolatio* 2.2; Sahagún, *HG*, Book 1, Prologue [1982 i, 47].

[42] SAHAGÚN, *HG* Book 1, Prologue [1982 i, 47]; CERVANTES DE SALAZAR, *Chronica* 4.113 [1971 ii, 48–9].

[43] FICINO, *Platonis Opera* (1485). Augustine and other Latin authors referred to Plato's *Timaeus* as '[*De*] *Constitutione Mundi*': cf. CHIMALPAHIN, *Relaciones* 1 (c. 1630), 1v [1998 i, 30].

[44] CHIMALPAHIN, *Relaciones* 1 (c. 1630), 6r [1998 i, 32]: 'Auh i yehuantin yn aquique tlacuilloque yn cenca ye huecauh mochipa pehuaya ytechpatzinco ycatzinco yn Dios ynic yehuatzin Dios.'

science: that is what he left written in the first words of the book he composed. . . .[45]

Diogenes Laertius did not make any such comment about God. The impression that he had done so probably derived from Ambrogio Traversari's dedication of his Latin translation of the *Lives of the Philosophers* to Cosimo de' Medici in which Traversari had stated that Diogenes' doctrines were 'largely in agreement with Christian truth.'[46]

The quotation from Sophocles that ends the first chapter of the *Relaciones*—a very loose translation of the first lines of the *Trachiniae*—is a felicitous comment on annalistic historiography, a form of writing that by its nature can never lay claim to closure:

> It is stated that in the text of the *Sentencias* one named Sophocles the tragic poet said: 'In short, there is nothing that may be deemed good and fortunate until its end is underway.'[47]

Although no collection of *sentencias*, 'sayings', was ever attributed to Sophocles in antiquity, the loan words 'poeta tragico' reveal the true origin of this citation: Bartholomaeus Marlianus' collection, *Sophoclis tragici poetae . . . sententiae*, '*Sententiae* of Sophocles the tragic poet', printed in Rome in 1545.[48] It is important to emphasize, however, that Chimalpahin would not have had direct knowledge of this volume or of any other texts or editions of the classical authors whom he names.[49]

While the use of Greco-Roman *exempla* had come to be an occasional feature of Nahuatl literary discourse ever since Fray Juan de Gaona's *Colloquios de la paz* was first composed in the 1540s, the invocation of classical sources as authorities was

[45] CHIMALPAHIN, *Relaciones* 1 (c. 1630), 6r [1998 i, 32]: 'Auh i yehuatl ytoca Diogenes Laercio yn ipa ynnemilliz yn tlamatinime, yn mitohua motenehua philosophos, i ye quitoz quitenehuaz yn itzinpeuhcapa yn tlamachilliztli philosophia, nimann ic compehualtia yn quiteyttitia quitenextillia yn queni nehuatzin teoyxtlamachilliztzintli yn t[o]t[ecuiy]o Dios, yn quichiuh tlatolpeuhcatenonotzalliztli yn ipan iamauh oncan quihto.' The italics above indicate Spanish loan words in the original Nahuatl.

[46] TRAVERSARI, *Diogenes Laertius, Vitae et sententiae philosophorum* (1472). Traversari's Latin translation, first made in 1433, was translated into Italian. Cf. Kraye 2007, 98; Stinger 1977.

[47] CHIMALPAHIN, *Relaciones* 1 (c. 1630), 6r [1998 i, 32]: 'yn mitohua motenehua ypa yn i*Sentencias* in iyamauh yn itoca Sophocles poeta tragico quitohuaya: "Ca ça niman amo tle oncatqui qualli yectli ytzonquizca y nepepeuhcayotl." '

[48] MARLIANUS, *Sophoclis tragici poetae sententiae* (1545), CIIIIr thus translates Sophocles, *Trachiniae*, verses 1–3 into Latin: 'Est vetus verbum apud homines vulgatum: / mortalium neminem, priusquam moriatur, / percipere posse felix ne sit, an infelix' ('There is an old saying put forth among men that no mortal can tell before he dies whether he is fortunate or unfortunate').

[49] Cf. n. 29 above.

always more typical of writing in formal disciplines, such as philosophy, theology, history, and science. Chimalpahin's oeuvre thus represents a new phase in the development of Nahuatl, canonizing it as a vehicle for scholarship as well as a medium for literature. The annalist evidently sought to ensure that his own language could compete with the Spanish vernacular, and it is also conceivable that he was claiming for Nahuatl a status more comparable to that of Latin.

III. Classical models in Fernando de Alva Ixtlilxochitl's portrayal of Nezahualcoyotl

Fernando de Alva Ixtlilxochitl (c. 1580–1650) was mainly of Spanish parentage, but he could claim descent on his mother's side from the ancient rulers of the Acolhua capital of Texcoco, which had belonged to the Aztec Triple Alliance. He became a judge and governor (successively in Texcoco, Tlalmanalco, and Chalco) and his associates included the viceroy Luis de Velasco, Constantino Huitzimengari, son of the Purépecha scholar don Antonio, and possibly Fray Juan Torquemada.[50] Alva Ixtlilxochitl's histories, based on interviews with native elders and on codices that he had collected himself, fused thorough knowledge of Mexican and Acolhua traditions with humanist learning in some remarkable ways.

The *Relación sucinta,* 'Condensed narrative' (c. 1605); *Compendio histórico del reino de Texcoco,* 'Historical compendium of the kingdom of Texcoco' (1608); and the unfinished *Historia de la nación chichimeca,* 'History of the Chichimec people' (1625–1640), all give prominence to Alva Ixtlilxochitl's ancestor Nezahualcoyotl, a renowned *tlatoani* of Texcoco in the 1400s (Plate 15). The Franciscan chronicler Motolinía had been the first to liken Nezahualcoyotl to the biblical King David; in their subsequent histories, both Fray Gerónimo de Mendieta and Torquemada, apparently inspired by Fray Andrés de Olmos, presented the ruler as an opponent of polytheism and a scrupulous legislator.[51] It was long believed that Nezahualcoyotl had composed some of the Nahuatl lyrics collected in the *Cantares mexicanos* and poems of the *Romances,* which the mestizo chronicler Juan Bautista de Pomar had appended to the *Relación de Texcoco* (1582).[52] Alva Ixtlilxochitl himself characterized

[50] Don Constantino is mentioned in ALVA IXTLILXOCHITL, *Historia de la nación chichimeca* (c. 1625–1640), cap. 91 [1977 ii, 245]. Brian 2016, 57, 29–31, 94–5; Whittaker 2016; and Townsend 2014 consider Alva's scholarly development and his associates.

[51] MOTOLÍNIA, *Memoriales* (1541), 94r–102v [1996, 441–67, at 443 and 466]; MENDIETA, *Historia* (c. 1596) 2.6, 3.2 [1870, 83–4, 181–2]; TORQUEMADA, *MI* 2.45, 2.51–3, 11.26 [1975 i, 214–17, 228–34; 1977 iv, 70–3]. Cf. Baudot 1995, 179, 182 on Olmos as a source. Rovira 2009 views later sixteenth-century accounts of Nezahualcoyotl as a response to the inquisitorial trial and execution of his grandson don Carlos Ometochtzin for idolatry in 1539.

[52] POMAR, *Romances de los señores de la Nueva España* (1582) [2009]; for discussion of Nezahualcoyotl's authorship, cf. Garibay 1993 i, 12–17; Lee 2008, 44.

Nezahualcoyotl as a 'model for good and outstanding princes', maintaining that the histories of his life in painted codices were tantamount to Xenophon's account of the education of the Persian king Cyrus.[53] A passage of Alva's *Relación sucinta*, which laid stress on the wisdom of the *tlatoani* of Texcoco, is worth quoting in full:

> He was a wise man, and in his great knowledge he pronounced the following words to which the divine Plato and other great philosophers added nothing: *Ypan yn chiucnauhtlamanpan meztica yn tloque nahuaque ypalnemohuani teyocoyani ycelteotl oquiyocox ynixquex quexquix mita yn amota*, which means 'Beyond the nine levels [of heaven] is the creator of heaven and earth through whom creatures live, and one sole god who created all things visible and invisible'.[54] Accordingly he called Heaven 'Ilhuicac', a place of endless glory, and Hell he called 'Mictlan', which means place of death without end. He attained and declared all these things, and he spent many years reflecting on the secrets of divinity, and as he did not have the law of the gospel, he kept to idolatry, although, as can be gleaned from the songs the natives sing to this day and from their histories and paintings, he often said that Huitzilopochtli, god of the Mexicans, and their idols were demons who kept them deceived, and that although they sacrificed to them, it was for no other reason than that they should not suffer harm to their persons and worldly goods, since they were always threatened by them.[55]

[53] ALVA IXTLILXOCHITL, *Compendio* (1608), 'Undécima relación' [1975 i, 439]: 'los historiadores antiguous que pintaron la vida de este singular príncipe hacen lo que se cuenta de Xenofonte, que todos dicen de él, que en la vida escribió de Ciro, rey de los persas, no fue tanto su intento escribir vida de un hombre particular, cuanto pintar un buen rey en las partes que conviene que tenga . . . no tenía más de poner delante del rey Nezahualcoyotzin, porque fue un dechado de buenos y excelentes príncipes. . . .' Latin and vernacular translations of Xenophon's *Cyropaedia* from the 1500s show its popularity as a prototype of the *speculum principis*: Marsh 1992. Brian 2016, 96–107 considers the relation of contemporaneous literature on princely education to Alva Ixtlilxochitl's writing. The dates for Alva's works given here follow the reassessment of the traditional chronology in Whittaker 2016, 57–65.

[54] The reconstruction of this Nahuatl sentence from the manuscript is based on Whittaker 2016, 48 and is used here: the wording in O'Gorman's text is in the next note.

[55] ALVA IXTLILXOCHITL, *Relación sucinta* (c. 1605), [sc. 'Relación'] 11 [1975 i, 404–5]: 'Fue hombre sabio, y por su mucho saber declaró estas palabras que siguen que el divino Platón y otros grandes filósofos no declararon más, que fue decir: *Y pan yn Chahconauhtla manpan* [*sic*] *meztica intloque nahuaque ypai nenohuani teyocoyani ic el téotl* [*sic*] *oquiyócox ynixquex quéxquix mita ynamota* [*sic*], que quiere decir: 'después de nueve andanas está el criador del cielo y de la tierra, por quien viven las criaturas, y un solo dios que crió las cosas visibles e invisibles. Asimismo llamó al cielo Ylhuicac, lugar de gloria inacabable, y al infierno Mictlan, que quiere decir lugar de muerte sin fin. Todas estas cosas declaró y alcanzó, y anduvo muchos años especulando divinos secretos, y como le faltó la ley evangélica siguió la idolatría, aunque él, como se ve en los cantos que tienen hoy día los naturales y en las historias y pinturas, muchas veces dijo que Huitzilopuchtli, dios de los mexicanos, y los ídolos eran

Many elements of that description recall Juan Bautista de Pomar's earlier avowal that Nezahualcoyotl believed in one 'Maker of heaven and earth, [who] sustained everything made and created by him, [who] had never been seen in human form or body, or in any other figure'. Pomar had further stated that Nezahualcoyotl supposed his creator to 'inhabit a place after nine levels . . . to which the souls of the virtuous went after death, while those of the wicked went to another place of horrible work'.[56]

The wording of the Nahuatl sentence (given in the quotation above), in which Alva Ixtlilxochitl attributed this doctrine to Nezahualcoyotl, could have come from a traditional source—and it happens to resemble part of a composition in the *Cantares mexicanos* entitled 'Atequilizcuicatl', 'Water-Pouring Song'. The lyric alludes to the Aztecs' war against the Spaniards and their leaders' colourful voyage to another world. The expressions 'chiucnauhtlamanpan', 'the nine levels', and 'ycelteotl', 'one God alone', are also conjoined in the same song, in reference to the Christian heaven:

> For in nine levels dwell thy princes, Angels, and they give Thee pleasure,
> God alone: Archangels, Virtues, Powers, Principates.[57]

The conjunction of Platonic and Christian thinking in both of those Nahuatl quotations originated in the writing of the Florentine Neoplatonist Marsilio Ficino, whose Latin works were well known in New Spain. His *Theologia Platonica*, 'Platonic Theology' (1482), described the nine levels of heaven under the Empyreum (Figure 9.2) and posited a celestial region inhabited by angels, to which souls akin to them were carried up, along with the contrasting nine levels of the false demons, to which other souls sank down.[58] These realms correspond to Nezahualcoyotl's

demonios que les traían engañados, y que aunque ellos les hiciesen sacrificio no era sino porque no los hiciesen daño en sus personas y bienes temporales, porque siempre les amenazaban.'

[56] POMAR, *Relación de Texcoco* (1582) [1986, 69–70]: 'había uno solo y que este era el Hacedor del cielo y de la tierra, y sustentaba todo lo hecho y lo criado por él, y que estaba donde no tenía segundo, y en un lugar después de nueve andanas, y que no se había visto jamás en forma ni cuerpo humano, ni en otra figura, y que al lugar donde estaba iban á parar las almas de los virtuosos después de muertos, y que las de los malos iban á otro lugar de penas y trabajos horribles.' Cf. Brian 2016, 101.

[57] *Cantares mexicanos* (1560s–1580s), 59v [1985, 338]: 'Can chiucnautlamantlini yc onnemio in mopillohuan in Agelosme mitzhuelamachtia on ycelteotl huiya Alcagel, Biltotesme, Potestates, Pilincipatos.'

[58] FICINO, *Theologia Platonica* (1482) 18.8 [2006 vi, 13]. The Latin text summarized above reads, 'His novem felicium gradibus apud Platonicos octo caelorum plagae ac nona super caelum excogitata regio congrue accommodari videntur; apud Orphicos autem octo caeli atque sub luna aethereus ignis; apud Christianos circuli sub empyreo novem. Quilibet enim ad illam potissimum regionem habitu quodam simili, quasi naturali levitate, feruntur, cuius habitatoribus angelis sese in vita praecipue similes reddiderunt. Similiter quoque Christiani reprobos animos in novem reproborum daemonum gradus quibus se vivendo fecere similes ipsa similitudine quasi pondere naturali, putant praecipitari.'

Figure 9.2 The celestial spheres in Peter Apian, *Cosmographia*, Antwerp, 1539, 4r. John Carter Brown Library.

glorious heaven of Ilhuicac, 'place of sky', and the deathly hell of Mictlan.[59] Alva Ixtlilxochitl aligned Huitzilopochtli and the other Aztec idols that Nezahualcoyotl called 'demonios' with Ficino's 'reprobi daemones', or false demons. It is no coincidence that Sahagún and other missionaries who were well versed in early Christian literature had regarded Aztec divinities as deceiving 'demons'.[60]

The account of Nezahualcoyotl's wisdom in the *Relación sucinta* closes with an unusual detail:

> In memory of those nine levels of heaven as he understood it, he ordered a tower of nine storeys to be constructed in Tezcoco, the ruins of which can be seen to this day, which was called Chililitli.[61]

[59] Cf. Schwaller 2006 on the Nahuatl idea of Ilhuicac.

[60] Chapter 8, II above.

[61] ALVA IXTLILXOCHITL, *Relación sucinta* (c. 1605), '[Relación] 11' [1975 i, 405]: 'y en memoria de las nueve andanas que hallaba, según él lo entendía, mandó hacer una torre en Tezcuco de nueve sobrados que hoy día se ve en sus ruinas, que se llamaba Chililitli.'

Ficino's *Theologia Platonica* had referred to comparable man-made representations of heaven in the ancient Mediterranean, describing one in particular:

> Archimedes of Syracuse made a bronze model of heaven in which all the movements of the seven planets were very accurately worked just as they are in the heavens, and the device itself revolved like heaven. I leave aside the pyramids of Egypt, the buildings of the Romans and Greeks, and their work in metal and glass.[62]

Ficino's mention of this model in the context of his discussion of 'diligence in the arts and in governance' ('artium et gubernationis industria') could account for Alva Ixtlilxochitl's own inclusion of an edifice constructed to recall the heavens in a portrayal of his royal ancestor's princely virtues.[63]

Yet the *Relación sucinta* offered no account of why Nezahualcoyotl supposedly called the tower 'Chililitli' or of what the name meant. An explanation comes in the later *Historia de la nación chichimeca,* which gives a fuller description of the king's architectural simulacrum of the nine heavens. It was topped by a spire, honouring the unknown and unseen creator of all things:

> . . . [T]he exterior was adorned with stars against a black background, and the inside was inlaid with gold, gems and precious feathers set out for the god . . . without any statue or attempt to represent his image . . . In the ninth level there was an instrument that they called 'chililitli' from which this temple and tower took its name; and also other musical instruments, such as cornets, flutes, conches, and a metal coffer which they called 'tetzilacatl' that served as a bell . . . and especially what was called the chililitli.[64]

There is at least one attestation of *chililitli* in Nahuatl as a copper cymbal struck by a pine mallet.[65] The curious emphasis on musical instruments in this narrative and

[62] FICINO, *Theologia Platonica* (1482) 13.3 [2004 iv, 170]: 'Archimedes Siracusanus aeneum caelum fecit in quo omnes septem planetarum motus verissime conficiebantur ut in caelo et ipsum volvebatur ut caelum. Mitto Aegyptiorum pyramides, Romanorum Graecorumque aedificia, metallorum officinas et vitri.'

[63] Toussaint 2002.

[64] ALVA IXTLILXOCHITL, *Historia de la nación chichimeca* (1625–1640), cap. 45 [1977 ii, 126]: 'era por la parte de afuera matizado de negro y estrella, y por la parte interior estaba todo engastado en oro, pedrería y plumas preciosas, colocándolo al dios . . . sin ninguna estatua ni formar su figura . . . En el noveno sobrado estaba un instrumento que llamaban chililitli de donde tomó el nombre este templo y torre; y en él asimismo otros musicales, como las cornetas, flautas, caracoles y un artesón de metal que llamaban tetzilacatl que servía de campana . . . y en especial el llamado chililitli.'

[65] SAHAGÚN, *HG* 2.25 [1981 iii, 77]; Stevenson 1968, 39–40.

the special importance of the *chililitli* might at first appear to have originated in an indigenous tradition.

But the cosmos had been presented as a musical harmony of spheres in Plato's *Republic*—the principal source for Ficino's account of the heavenly regions. According to Plato, a Siren was positioned on each of the eight rotating concentric circles of the cosmos: seven of them were planetary and one with fixed stars constituted the outermost revolving orbit: 'Each Siren . . . sounded a single note, and all eight notes together made a single harmonious sound [*harmonia*].' The whole arrangement was explicitly visualized in that closing section of the *Republic*, known as the Myth of Er: 'one is bound to picture it as a hollow wheel with the others fitting snugly inside it like those jars which fit into one another . . . and their circular rims, looked at from above, form a solid surface.'[66] Plato also argued in the *Laws* that music had a direct bearing on statecraft because it could exert a strong influence on the character of individuals and of society as a whole.[67] Ficino himself placed still more emphasis on the utility of music for government because he deemed it to have an important role in a prince's moral education, enabling him to develop his judgement and to instill true laws and virtues.[68]

These associations may well have led Alva Ixtlilxochitl to link musical instruments to Nezahualcoyotl.[69] In addition, the *chililitli* could be endowed with an iconic value: the copper disc, suspended vertically, approximates to Plato's image of the circular rims of the rotating planets, which looked like a solid surface when viewed from above; and it also recalls Archimedes' revolving bronze model of the celestial bodies. In the absence of other hypotheses, one conceivable explanation for the prominence given in this narrative to the *chililitli*, and for the tower being named after it, could be its value as a visual representation of the cosmos.

The presentation of Nezahualcoyotl as a model for princes whose beliefs and practices were already in accord with principles of Renaissance Neoplatonic thought was only thinly disguised: the tactic is comparable to that of the Church Fathers of late antiquity who had sometimes defended certain pagan authors on the basis that their writings foreshadowed Christian teaching. Nonetheless, this attempt to elevate the ancient realm of Texcoco in the eyes of his Spanish readers remains responsible for an enduring view of the historical Nezahualcoyotl as a philosopher-king, poet, and monotheist.[70]

[66] Plato, *Republic* 10, 616c–17c.

[67] Plato, *Laws* 7, 810–22.

[68] Kristeller 1943, 289–323 and Walker 1958, 3–29 explain the place of music in Ficino's thought; cf. Vanhaelen 2017; Rees 2002, 355 on Ficino's view of its role in princely education.

[69] Nezahualcoyotl is depicted with a tubular *tlalpanhuehuetl*, 'field drum', on his back in the *Codex Ixtlilxochitl* (c. 1582): Plate 15.

[70] León-Portilla 1956; 1972.

IV. Conclusions

None of the chroniclers discussed above attended the College of Santa Cruz in Tlatelolco.[71] Their works offer de facto proof that indigenous and mestizo scholars were able to receive a humanist education in Tlaxcala, Texcoco, and Amecameca as well as in Mexico City. While Latin letters by alumni of Santa Cruz had contained references to sources that were largely mediated by Erasmus, the writers of these histories in Nahuatl and Spanish recalled many more classical authors.

There is a discernible shift from the use of illustrative *exempla* from Greco-Roman literature by Diego Muñoz Camargo and Hernando de Alvarado Tezozomoc to the more adventurous and individualistic endeavours of Chimalpahin and Fernando de Alva Ixtlilxochitl in the 1600s. Chimalpahin was not a mere spokesman for the pre-Hispanic past but a modernizer as well: his fusion of European and indigenous styles of record-keeping served to elevate Nahuatl as a potential literary medium for his contemporaries and successors. Alva de Ixtlilxochitl's innovation was not just to cite classical and Renaissance texts but also to emulate them, occasionally using their topics and themes to enrich his narration. In fact he revealed that his knowledge of Mediterranean antiquity had prompted historical curiosity about his Mexican forebears:

> From my youth, I always had a great desire to know about events which took place in this New World which were no less than those of the Romans, Greeks, Medes and other pagan republics of universal renown; though, after the changing of the times and the collapse of my ancestors' dominions and estates, their histories remained in obscurity.[72]

All four of the chroniclers whose work has been adumbrated in this chapter recognized the symbolic value of classical antiquity, which they exploited as part of a strategic design to confer prestige on their region, or *altepetl*, and to affirm the significance of the Indian past in world history. It was not only Spanish scholars and missionaries, but also native and mestizo authors who were responsible for comparing Mexico's former grandeur to that of ancient Greece and Rome.

[71] *Pace* Garibay 1953–1954 [2007]: the supposition that these authors studied at Santa Cruz has persisted.

[72] ALVA IXTLILXOCHITL, *Sumaria relación de la historia general de esta Nueva España* (c. 1625), 'Dedicatoria' [1975 i, 526]: 'Desde mi adolescencia tuve siempre gran deseo de saber las cosas acaecidas en este Nuevo Mundo que no fueron menos que las de los romanos, griegos, medos y otras repúblicas gentílicas que tuvieron fama en el universo; aunque con la mudanza de los tiempos y caída de los señoríos y estados de mis pasados, quedaron sepultadas sus historias.'

10

General Conclusions and *Envoi*

> What makes a subject difficult to understand—if it is significant, important—is not that some special instruction about abstruse things is necessary to understand it. Rather it is the contrast between the understanding of the subject and what most people want to see. Because of this, the very things that are most obvious can become the most difficult to understand. What has to be overcome is not difficulty of the intellect but of the will.
>
> —Ludwig Wittgenstein, *Philosophie/The Big Typescript* (1933)[1]

I.

The spread of humanism in the 1500s was not confined to Europe. Studies of grammar, logic, and rhetoric published in New Spain matched and sometimes superseded those produced in Italy, the Low Countries, and Iberia. Scientific enquiries, histories of the Indies, pioneering investigations of Amerindian society, and a culture of translation opened up new forms of knowledge. All these endeavours came in the wake of the profound social and technological changes effected as a consequence of the Spanish incursion, which had rapidly transformed Mexico City into a colonial capital with its own centres of learning, a printing press, and a thriving market in imported books.

Such developments are commonly identified with the Renaissance, which had never been a uniform phenomenon: the interactions humanists had with ruling groups differed from one country to another, as did their domains of expertise. While scholars in European academies were generally engaged in antiquarian investigations or the philological study of texts in Latin, Greek, or Hebrew, those in the Valley of Mexico belonged to the religious orders and were concerned with the theory and practice of converting the Indians and the mastery of their languages. At the same time, the 'Christian turn' in sixteenth-century humanism was evident on both sides of the Atlantic: sacred literature was studied by ecclesiastics and by

[1] Wittgenstein 1933, §86 [1993, 161].

Aztec Latin. Andrew Laird, Oxford University Press. © Oxford University Press 2024.
DOI: 10.1093/oso/9780197586358.003.0011

members of the laity alike; late antique and medieval authors were widely read; and Desiderius Erasmus' thought on religion and language was especially influential.

Historians continue to underplay the enormous importance of Erasmus of Rotterdam in early colonial Mexico. His radical thinking, inspired by the example of the early Christian fathers, lay behind the strategies of prominent churchmen, who tacitly quoted or alluded to his work in all kinds of contexts. The Dutch humanist's views on princely education were implemented by Franciscan instructors—who also used his textbooks to teach Latin to their Indian students. In addition, Erasmus' advocation of a common medium to propagate the Gospel, in conjunction with his methods of linguistic pedagogy, had inspired the friars' approach to indigenous tongues. Nebrija's works were the principal template for their grammars and dictionaries, but Olmos, Gilberti, and other missionary linguists transferred the humanist strategy of identifying examples of good usage in Latin to Amerindian languages, which were seen to possess their own quality of elegance. The illustrations of Latin expression in Erasmus' *Colloquia*, *Adagia*, and *Apophthegmata* were a particular model for Fray Bernardino de Sahagún's collections of idioms in Nahuatl.

The first alphabetic texts in the Mexican language were accurate translations from Latin of liturgy, biblical lectionaries, and other material required for evangelical purposes. The rendering of Joachim Camerarius' Latin version of Aesop's fables into Nahuatl may have been a by-product of this process. Preparation of Christian literature in the Mexican language was the principal intellectual activity at the Imperial College of Santa Cruz, although awareness of this point is limited, largely owing to the renown of the *Florentine Codex*. In fact, movement from Latin to Nahuatl characterized nearly all the scholarly activity of the friars and their Indian collaborators at Tlatelolco. The scheme of Latin grammar governed *artes* of native languages and even the process of translating from Spanish: the Nahuatl version of Sahagún's *Colloquios y Doctrina christiana*, for instance, required the assistance of translators who were Latinists—and the Spanish source text had been structured on the principles of classical rhetoric.

Many misconceptions about the translations made by the native collegians have arisen from the widespread assumption that they were fluent in Nahuatl with a flawed command of Latin. The students at Santa Cruz de Tlatelolco, however, were in a peculiar diglossic situation. As young children, they had been sequestered from their families and immersed in Latin: the knowledge they had of their Mexican mother tongue would not have been as systematic. The challenge they would have faced in making translations lay not in comprehending the Latin sources, but in finding the correct and appropriate idiom with which to convey the content in the target language of Nahuatl.

The conventions of Latin inevitably provided the matrix for the earliest original formal compositions in the Mexican language. Works like Fray Juan de Gaona's *Colloquios de la paz* were based on medieval preceptive dialogues, incorporating references to classical and Christian authors. Such compositions, authored in collaboration with indigenous scholars, helped to elevate the status of Nahuatl and institute it as a language of letters in its own right. The themes and generic features of Latin writing that had given rise to vernacular literatures in medieval Europe generated Nahuatl literature in a similar way, although this fact has been little recognized. The process of evolution would continue into the 1600s: Hernando de Alvarado Tezozomoc, Domingo Chimalpahin, and other native chroniclers adapted traditional indigenous record-keeping to construct new forms of historiography, and the striking Nahuatl narratives of the Virgin of Guadalupe, presented in Luis Laso de la Vega's *Huei Tlamahuiçoltica* (1649), fused a range of influences.[2]

Several texts authored at Tlatelolco were configured, in whole or in part, as 'mirrors for princes', including Alonso de Molina's Nahuatl translation of Denis the Carthusian's *De regimine politiae,* Fray Juan de Mijangos' *Espejo divino,* Juan Badiano's Latin herbal *Libellus de medicinalibus Indorum herbis,* and even the translations of Aesop. A clinching example from the mid-1500s is an anonymous work in Nahuatl, *Izcatqui yníntezcaamauh, in tlahtoque,* 'Behold a mirror-book for rulers'.[3] *Speculum* literature had enjoyed perennial popularity in Europe and would continue to abound in the Hispanic world, at least until the end of the seventeenth century. Both New Spain's first viceroy and the first bishop of Mexico actually regarded the education of an indigenous governing class as a practical objective. Although historians have long been swayed by Robert Ricard's opinion that the College of Santa Cruz was founded to train a Mexican clergy, Sahagún makes clear that this purpose had never been the case, and a friar at the college was formally censured for proposing that Indians should enter the priesthood. The real reason that students selected from the Indian nobility received an advanced education in Latin was to prepare them for positions of leadership.

The polished Latin petitions to the Spanish crown by native rulers and governors show that they reflected on their status as Indians in colonial society, and they also anticipated the indigenous chroniclers of the next generation who would write more extensive histories of their ancestral polities. Thus many Mexicans who were authors of texts in Latin, Spanish, and Nahuatl were not merely scribes and translators but also humanists in the fullest sense. Even though Renaissance thinkers and writers have not always been called 'intellectuals', the term is a suitable descriptor for these indigenous scholars and governors, just as it would be for *letrados* in Spain, or Italian civic humanists in the fifteenth and sixteenth centuries.[4]

Spaniards frequently used analogies from Greco-Roman history and literature to provide favourable accounts of Mexico and its peoples. Indian writers themselves

[2] Brading 2001, 80–8; Poole 1997, 110–26; Laird 2021, 34–5; cf. Appendix 3 below.

[3] Alcántara Rojas 2022 is a valuable preliminary survey.

[4] Ramos and Yannakakis 2014, 1–17; see further Linz 1972; Celenza 2017.

employed classical *exempla* in their Latin letters—and those who worked on the *Florentine Codex* sometimes instinctively relied on their knowledge of Greco-Roman literature to interpret the Mexican past. Born after the Spanish conquest and educated as Christians, they would have found some beliefs of their forebears difficult to understand or explain.[5] Later indigenous or mestizo chroniclers like Diego Muñoz Camargo and Fernando de Alva Ixtlilxochitl, on the other hand, affirmed—or even contrived—parallels between the kingdoms of pre-Cortesian Mexico and Greece or Rome as a way of aggrandizing the dominions of their ancestors.

The practice of presenting Mexican legacies in terms of European classical paradigms became more varied and elaborate over the course of the colonial period and into the nineteenth century.[6] Carlos de Sigüenza y Góngora, for instance, used each of the Aztec emperors to illustrate a different Roman princely virtue in his *Theatro de virtudes políticas*. The book was published in 1680, which Sigüenza counted as the year 353 (from the foundation of the city of Mexico in 1327 AD) and which he ostentatiously styled in Roman fashion as 'Anno a Mexico Condit. CCC L III'. More serious comparisons between Greco-Roman and Aztec civilization were made by the Jesuit historian Francisco Javier Clavigero in his *Storia antica del Messico*, 'Ancient History of Mexico' (1780).

The classicizing tendency was sustained well into the twentieth century by the two *doyens* of Nahuatl literary studies in Mexico. Ángel María Garibay and Miguel León-Portilla both aestheticized the Nahuatl texts they edited, purging them of Christian references and formatting them in lines of verse so that they resembled classical lyric poems or dramatic choruses.[7] Garibay, himself an accomplished classicist, had discerned analogies between ancient Greek and the Mexican language, and identified Nahuatl genres of 'lyric', 'epic', and 'theogony'. León-Portilla also Hellenized the Aztecs: his seminal book, *La filosofia náhuatl en sus fuentes* (1956), translated into English as *Aztec Thought and Culture* (1963), accorded a form of dualism to the ancient Mexicans. León-Portilla subscribed to some sixteenth-century characterizations of Nahuatl primary sources, and hinted at further analogies with pre-Socratic, Platonic, and Aristotelian philosophy.[8]

[5] Cf. Gruzinski 1988, 6: 'Pre-Hispanic history and archaeology have frequently forgotten that the majority of testimonies we have of the pre-Cortesian epoch were elaborated and redacted in the context of upheaval in a nascent New Spain, and they offer, above all else, a reflection of that period' (my translation).

[6] Keen 1971; see also Earle 2007, Laird 2010a.

[7] Payàs 2004, 545–7.

[8] See Garibay 1932, Garibay 1945, Garibay 1953–1954, Garibay 1965, and León-Portilla 1956. Segala 1989 and Segala 1992 were an early challenge to the status quo instituted by such studies.

II.

Several areas of enquiry related to this study remain to be explored. The uses made of Latin by members of religious and indigenous elites need to be assessed in terms of the broader symbolic value attached to the language in New Spain. Numerous sources call attention to the fact that Latin prayers and formulae were incomprehensible to the larger indigenous population, just as they were to the masses in Europe. Fray Pedro de Gante's *Doctrina christiana en lengua mexicana* thus introduced the Nahuatl translation of the *Ave Maria*:

> Jnin latin tlatolli camo ticcaqui. ma tiquitocan totlatolpan.[9]
>
> These Latin words you do not understand. Let us say it in our language.

Speakers at the Council of Trent had already affirmed that the Latin rite induced a sense of reverence in those who could not understand it.[10] Fray Alonso de Molina included Nahuatl entries for both 'Latin' and 'Latinity' in his Spanish-Nahuatl dictionary, which was expressly compiled for those preaching to natives.[11] By making Indians aware of Latin and conveying a sense of its importance, missionaries were in effect affirming a social division based on knowledge of the language.[12]

The varied interactions between Latin and Nahuatl in writing of the sixteenth and seventeenth centuries have yet to be properly surveyed. A wide range of Christian texts, from catechisms to lives of saints and dramas on religious subjects, were written wholly or partly in Nahuatl by native scholars trained in Latin. The manuscripts of the Nahuatl Gospels and Epistles require more critical study, and examination of them in relation to the Roman Rite could well highlight ideological or doctrinal questions, while enhancing an understanding of fundamental categories of the Mexican language. The trilingual *Dictionarium* described in Chapter 5 has relevant heuristic potential, as it provides direct Nahuatl equivalents—or explanations—of Latin terms. In addition, original compositions in Nahuatl from the 1500s incorporate quotations or passages derived from Latin authorities without always stating

[9] GANTE, *Doctrina christiana* (1553), 79v; cf. 81r, where the Latin *Salve Regina* is followed by the words 'Jnic huel ticcaquizque to tlatolpan monequi tiquitozque', 'So that we can understand it, it is necessary that we say it in our words', quoted in Burkhart 2001, 117.

[10] Coletti 1987, 27, 220–2; Waquet 2001, 41–50; Chapter 5, III above on Cardinal Pacheco.

[11] MOLINA, *Aqui comiença un vocabulario* (1555), 152v gives 'latin tlatolli' for the Spanish 'Latin lengua latina' and supplies two terms for 'Latinidad desta lengua' (i.e. pure Latin style): 'latin tlatollotl', 'Latin word-ness' and 'latin tlatoliztli', 'eloquence in Latin'. The earlier anonymous *Dictionarium* (Chapter 5 above) has 'latin tlatolli ' for 'Latin, lengua latina' and 'latin tlatoliztli' for 'Latinidad desta lengua'.

[12] Bourdieu 1977; Bourdieu 1991, 37–104. Waquet 2001, 230–1 considers the 'relations of authority, inevitably assymetric, that used to exist between those who knew Latin and those who did not'.

their provenance. Identification of those authorities would facilitate interpretation of the works in which they appear—as would consideration of the degree to which humanist rhetorical and dialectical patterning governed their construction.

Some Nahuatl literature from the 1500s is deemed to be of pre-Hispanic origin. That corpus could be reviewed, if not reassessed, in view of the present enquiry. Two distinct sets of texts associated with an autochthonous Mexican tradition of admonitory discourse are commonly referred to as 'huehuetlatolli', although they were produced for different purposes. One was ethnographic: the book of pagan 'tlatlatlauhtiliztlatolli', ritual speeches and prayers, couched as rhetoric and moral philosophy by Sahagún in the *Florentine Codex*. The other was the earlier collection of exemplary texts with which Fray Andrés de Olmos originally supplemented his *arte* of Nahuatl. These texts, which survive in Olmos' hand or in versions separately transmitted by Fray Juan de Torquemada, Alonso de Zorita, and Fray Juan Bautista, are often conceived in terms of a hypothetical Mexican 'ancient word'. Yet they seem to have originated as models of linguistic usage for missionaries, and many of them conveyed an explicitly Christian message: they should be viewed in relation to the preceptive Franciscan Nahuatl texts and dialogues with which they have obvious communities.

The currents of indigenous thought and protocols of performance that have been discerned in the *Cantares mexicanos* ('Songs in the Mexican Language') and the *Romances de los señores de la Nueva España* will probably always elude conclusive interpretation.[13] At the same time, European religious and literary themes evident in these sixteenth-century texts could be further analysed: native nobles like Antonio Valeriano and Francisco Plácido who are named in the *Cantares* were involved in their composition, and the mestizo chronicler Juan Bautista de Pomar may have compiled the *Romances*.[14]

The full extent of the interference of biblical episodes, classical and Christian literature, and even Renaissance demonology in chronicles and histories of Mexico by Indians and Spaniards alike has still not been taken into account.[15] Many very specific examples have gone unnoticed, such as the view Francisco Cervantes de Salazar attributed to Montezuma that his subjects 'were more prone to obey out of fear than out of love', which was really a Roman literary commonplace.[16] As well as making explicit references to European antiquity, Cervantes de Salazar's *Chronica*

[13] *Cantares mexicanos* (1560s–1580s), ed. Bierhorst 1985, 7–130; ed. León-Portilla, Curiel Defossé, and Reyes Equigas 2011 i, 209–95: see further Segala 1989, 137–81. Tomlinson 2007, 9–92 is another adventurous reading of the text.

[14] Gruzinski 2018, 265–302.

[15] Rozat Dupeyron 1993 is a pioneering examination of accounts of the Spanish conquest.

[16] CERVANTES DE SALAZAR, *Dialogi* (1554), 290r: 'metu magis quam amore eos parere dixit saepe Moteççuma'; *Chronica* (c. 1566) 1.16 [1971 i, 129]. Cf. Cicero, *Philippics* 1.33–4; Seneca, *Thyestes* 207–10; pseudo-Seneca, *Octavia* 454–9.

de la Nueva España (c. 1566) and Fray Diego Durán's *Historia de las Indias de Nueva España* (c. 1581) relate episodes that may have been suggested by Greco-Roman myth and history. Fray Juan de Torquemada's *Monarchia Indiana* (1615), a providential narrative in twenty-one books of Mexico's development from its legendary origins to the late 1500s, has itself been likened to Livy's history of Rome. Multiple titles by more than four hundred classical, medieval, and humanist authors are mentioned in the course of Torquemada's history.[17]

Alonso de Zorita, a Latinist educated at Salamanca and a judge in the Audiencia of New Spain, drew from every source at his disposal—Franciscan chronicles, conquistadors' memoirs, indigenous testimonies, and codices—to compile his comprehensive *Relación . . . de la Nueva España* (1585). Zorita's further knowledge of classical and humanist literature surpassed Torquemada's, making the *Relación* a remarkable endeavour in scientific antiquarianism.[18] Two extensive Latin works of ethnohistorical interest were written in the later sixteenth century: Francisco Hernández' *De antiquitatibus Novae Hispaniae* (c. 1575) and José de Acosta's *De procuranda Indorum salute* (1588). Though Hernández's study of ancient Mexico shared much of its content with Sahagún's researches, it contains descriptions of Aztec dance, music, and song that are not attested elsewhere.[19]

The ways in which humanist learning determined European responses to different languages and societies could be explored in many other settings. Vinko Paletin, who joined Francisco de Montejo's campaign in Yucatán in the 1530s, claimed to have found Punic inscriptions in Chichen Itza and held that the Maya were of Carthaginian descent.[20] In sixteenth-century Michoacán, as in the Valley of Mexico, Franciscan friars and their indigenous students worked together, producing Christian texts in Purépecha—that situation accounts for the apparent intrusion of vignettes from Virgil's *Aeneid* into an early account of Tarascan myth.[21] And in the southern region of Oaxaca, Dominican missionaries and their converts also collaborated on the translation of catechisms and sermons into numerous Zapotec languages.[22]

Before Latin was studied in New Spain, it had already been taught to youths from native elites in the reclaimed emirate of Granada in Andalusia and on the Caribbean island of Hispaniola. The same would be done in Peru, where excerpts

[17] Frost 1983.

[18] Vigil 1987.

[19] HERNÁNDEZ, *De antiquitatibus* (c. 1575) 2.6, 58r–60r [1945: 94–6].

[20] PALETIN, *De jure et justitia belli contra indos* (c. 1560), 66r. Cf. Laird and Šoštarić 2019; Lupher 2003, 167–86.

[21] ALCALÁ, *Relación de Michoacán* (c. 1540) 1.4, 67r–68r [2013, 25–8] describes the priests of Xaratanga turning into snakes and entering Lake Pátzcuaro (recalling *Aeneid* 2.199–227, especially 2.208–9) and a council of the gods in 3.9, 36r–37v [233–6].

[22] Farriss 2018.

from Aesop and Ovid along with a large corpus of religious material were translated into Quechua; and mestizo chroniclers presented Andean civilization in terms of Greco-Roman models. The groundwork needs to be done on accounts of Amerindian legacies in Charcas (now Bolivia), in the Viceroyalty of New Granada (corresponding to Colombia, Ecuador, and Venezuela), in the Southern Cone, and in Brazil.[23] There is a further range of writing in Latin from Africa, Asia, and the Pacific—not all of which was produced by authors of European origin.

The obvious fact that Renaissance humanism acquired its global reach as a consequence of imperial expansion, though, calls for careful reflection about how these avenues of enquiry should be explored.[24] Europeans used their systems of learning and education as instruments of control in the process of colonization, and they inscribed their own interests and agenda into their representations of the peoples they had subjected.[25] Although the ideological dimensions of ethnography, as a product of empire, have long been acknowledged, historians of scholarship still tend to regard their field as a domain largely remote from social praxis.[26] Study of Greco-Roman legacies in the form of 'classical reception' is even more problematic, not least in colonial contexts, because it presupposes the centrality of classics, which it also seeks to affirm.[27] Even if interdisciplinary or inclusive approaches are accommodated, such a centripetal methodology serves the ends of classicists above all, and regularly leads to a distortion of historical realities.[28] In that respect, practitioners of classical reception are all too comparable to those early missionaries in the Americas who subordinated whatever knowledge they acquired of indigenous cultures and languages to their own end of promulgating the Christian message.

The circulation of classical and patristic literature in sixteenth-century New Spain followed trends in Europe, but it did have consequences for perceptions and even policies with regard to the Indians. Knowledge of classical texts could also have a more haphazard effect on the way in which Nahuatl legacies were viewed. The first image of Mexico City ever published in Europe (Plate 16) offers an intriguing example: a woodcut map of Tenochtitlan printed in Nuremberg in 1524, along with

[23] Important Latin documents are in the eight volumes of *Monumenta Mexicana* covering 1570–1605, edited by Zubillaga and Rodríguez 1956–1991, and in other series of the *Monumenta Historica Societatis Iesu* initiated in 1894. Many manuscripts brought to Italy by the Jesuits after their expulsion from Spanish and Portuguese territories are listed in Revelli 1926, Burrus 1959, Guzmán 1964, Torre Villar 1980, Hervás y Panduro 2007, and Hervás y Panduro 2009.

[24] Bolaños and Verdesio 2002, 1–50; Bernheimer 1995.

[25] Asad 1973.

[26] Sandys 1908 and Ligota and Quantin 2006 are among many examples, spanning the twentieth century.

[27] Laird 2010b, 359–63; Laird 2019a, 136–8.

[28] Historical realities, in this context, amount to what is deemed history by conventional lights: cf. White 1987, 24, 30 on the 'community of historians'.

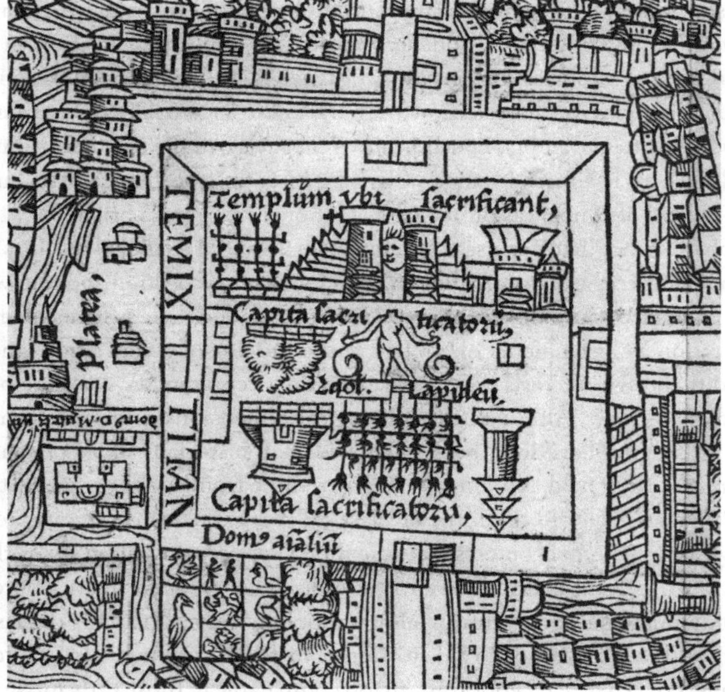

Figure 10.1 Map of Tenochtitlan, detail of central panel, *Praeclara Ferdinandi Cortesii de Noua maris Oceani Hyspania narratio*, Nuremberg, 1524. John Carter Brown Library.

Pietro Savorgnano's Latin translation of Hernán Cortés' letters to Charles V.[29] The labels and captions on the map were also in Latin, but the pictorial design must have been based on an indigenous original.[30] A central panel (Figure 10.1) shows the sacred precinct of Tenochtitlan with the Great Temple of Huitzilopochtli and Tlaloc.[31] The sun, depicted as a human face, appears in a space between the two sections of that double pyramid: the actual edifice had in fact been aligned to channel the sun into that space at the equinox.[32] That detail is connected to the

[29] CORTÉS, *Praeclara . . . de Noua maris Oceani Hyspania narratio* (1524) incorporated the map. The colouring in the copy held at the Newberry Library was a later addition.

[30] Mundy 1998.

[31] This is labelled 'Templum vbi sacrificant', 'Temple where they sacrifice'. The words 'Capita sacrificatorum', 'Heads of those sacrificed', designate the skull racks (*tzompantli*) to the left of the pyramid and above the 'Dom*us* a*n*imali*um*', Montezuma's zoo. 'Idol*um* Lapide*um*', 'Stone Idol', probably refers to a large statue of the decapitated goddess Coatlicue, which stood in the precinct: Matos Moctezuma 2017, 21–3.

[32] MOTOLINÍA, *Memoriales* (c. 1541), 13r [1995, 170]: 'Esta fiesta caía estando el sol en medio del Uchilobos', 'This festival occurred when the sun was in the midst of the [temple of] Huitzilopochtli'. Cf. Šprajc 2000; Galindo Trejo 2015.

map's title, 'TEMIX TITAN', because in ancient Roman poetry the sun was routinely personified as 'Titan'—notably in references to its position, to its course across the sky, or to the passage of days.[33] But the proper toponym, 'Tenochtitlan', is commonly derived from *te-noch-titlan*, 'By the prickly pear on the rock', in line with the legend of the city's foundation.[34] Here it seems that Cortés' approximation of 'Temixtitan', retained in Savorgnano's Latin text, prompted whoever devised the captions for this map to present a classical term for the sun as a component of the Mexican name.[35]

Misunderstandings and false recognitions were a common feature of early modern ethnography, which relied on elements from a familiar repertoire in order to interpret and convey what was unfamiliar. Deeply held Christian beliefs were bound to frame the first European representations of the pre-Hispanic world—a consideration that historians of Mesoamerica have always taken into account. The influence of humanist learning and scholarly practices on writing in early colonial Mexico, though often overlooked, was just as profound. The true sophistication of many sixteenth-century texts in Nahuatl, as well as those in Latin and Spanish, will be better recognized once this influence becomes more widely acknowledged.

[33] Cicero, *Aratea* 585; Virgil, *Aeneid* 4.119, 6.725; Ovid, *Metamorphoses* 1.10, 2.118, 10.79. Cf. Pfundstein 1997, 23 n. 5; Fontenrose 1940, 436, 444.

[34] Cf. Introduction, p. 1 above. The etymology is open to question: Karttunen 1992, 225; Lockhart 2001, 233; Whittaker 2021, 146.

[35] The sun was prominent in indigenous pictorial accounts of the Spanish conquest of Mexico: Chapter 6, II (i) above.

Appendix 1

CATALOGUES AND CONSPECTUSES

Appendix 1.1: Synopses of Renaissance Latin grammars and of the first *artes* of Nahuatl and Purépecha

1.1.1 Niccolò Perotti, *Rudimenta grammatices,* 1473

[Untitled account of the function and parts of grammar]
- De nomine
- De uerbo
- De participio
- De pronomine
- De praepositione
- De aduerbio
- De coniunctione
- De constructione orationis incipit foeliciter
- De uerbis impersonalibus incipit foeliciter
- De comparatiuis
- De figuris
- De componendis epistolis
- Peroratio

1.1.2 Antonio de Nebrija, *Introduciones latinas,* c. 1487

LIBRO PRIMERO, Los nombres por proporcio & semeiança de los quales declinan los otros:
- La declinacion delos pronombres
- La declinacion delos nombres griegos
- La declinacion delos nombres barbaros
- Las cuatro coniugaciones regulares

Las formaciones dellas. Los uerbos irregulares
Reglas para conocer & iuntar las ocho partes de la oracion

LIBRO SEGUNDO, Del genero del nombre:
Dela declinacion del nombre
Delos nombres defectiuos
Delos praeteritos delos uerbos
Delos supinos de los uerbos
Dela composicion de los uerbos

LIBRO TERCERO, Preguntas dela grammatica & de sus quatro partes:
Preguntas dela orthographia & letra
Preguntas dela prosodia & syllaba
Preguntas dela etymologia & dicion
Preguntas del nombre
Preguntas del pronombre
Preguntas del uerbo
Preguntas del participio
Preguntas del aduerbio
Preguntas dela interiecion
Preguntas dela coniuncion
Preguntas que partes dela oracion se ponen vnas por otros
Preguntas dela construction
Preguntas delas figuras de construction

LIBRO QUARTO, Delos cinco generos delos uerbos:
Delos uerbos de diuersos generos o en vn genero diuersas species
Delos uerbos impersonales
Delos infinitivos
Delos gerundios
Delos supinos
Delos participios
Dela construction delos nombres.

1.1.3 Fray Andrés de Olmos, *Arte de la lengua mexicana*, 1547

PRIMERA PARTE (Untitled), 23r–43v:[1]
c. 1 Delas partes dela oracion en general
c. 2 Delas diferencias que ay de pronombres
c. 3 Delos pronombres que se juntan a los verbos y nombres, etcetera
c. 4 Delos pronombres posesiuos
c. 5 Dela combinacion que hacen algunos pronombres entre si

[1] This is the pagination of the BNE manuscript.

c. 6 Delo que pierden los nombres juntandose con los pronombres *no, mo, y*
c. 7 Delos nombres primitiuos sustantiuos y de como forman el plural
c. 8 Delos nombres sustantiuos deriuatiuos
c. 9 Delos deriuatiuos sustantiuos que descienden de verbos
c. 10 Delos nombres adjetiuos primitiuos
c. 11 Delos verbales adjectiuos
c. 12 De ciertas particulas que se juntan a los nombres y con ellas se hacen diminutiuos
c. 13 Delos nombres compuestos comparatiuos y superlatiuos

SEGUNDA PARTE, De los verbos y de la conjugacion y formaçion dellos, 44r–84v:
c. 1 Dela conjugacion de los verbos regulares
c. 2 Dela formacion dellos
c. 3 Dela formacion del preterito
c. 4 Dela formacion de la passiua e impersonal
c. 5 Delos verbos irregulares
c. 6 Delos verbos *eo, is* y *venio, venis*
c. 7 De algunas particulas que se juntan con verbos actiuos
c. 8 De otras que se juntan con todos verbos
c. 9 De como los verbos se juntan con los pronombres
c. 10 Delos verbos neutros
c. 11 Delos verbos deriuativos
c. 12 Delos verbos compuestos
c. 13 Delos verbos reuerenciales

TERCERA PARTE, Partes dela oracion indeclinables, y de la orthographia y tambien dealgunas maneras de hablar, 85r–102v:
c. 1 Delas preposiciones
c. 2 Delos aduerbios en comun
c. 3 Delos aduerbios locales y temporales
c. 4 Delos aduerbios numerales
c. 5 Delas conjunctiones e interjectiones
c. 6 Dela orthographia
c. 7 De unas maneras de hablar comunes
c. 8 Dela manera de hablar que tenian los viejos en sus platicas y despues de pondra una platica de las que solia hacer antiguamente un padre a su hijo: en que se descubre mucho de la propiedad dela lengua y en esto se incluye y concluye la tercera parte.

1.1.4 Fray Maturino Gilberti, *Arte de la lengua de Michuacan*, 1558

PROLOGO [Rules on writing and pronunciation], 7r–11v

PRIMERA PARTE, 12r–41r:
- Declinacion de los nombres substantiuos
- Conjugacion [del verbo] *hurandahpen*
- Conjugacion del *Sum, es*
- Conjugacion [del verbo] *Harani*
- Conjugacion [del verbo] *Arani*

SEGUNDA PARTE, Las ocho partes de la oracion, 41r–109r:
- Delos nombres substantiuos
- Delos pronombres
- Delos verbos
- Delos aduerbios
- Delos participios
- Delas preposiciones
- Delas conjunctiones
- Delas interjecciones
- Delos vocablos del parentesco
- Delos vocablos dela affinidad
- Palabras para preguntar de matrimonio

TERCERA PARTE, Dela orthographia phrasis y ornato, de la composicion delos verbos, del modo de contar, del modus dicendi, 109r–174r:
- De la orthographia
- Del phrasis y ornato desta lengua
- Dela composicion delos verbos
- Delas particulas
- De los modos de contar enesta lengua
- Modos dicendi
- Dela cuenta de los dias
- Delas partes de la noche.[2]

1.1.5. Fray Maturino Gilberti, *Grammatica Maturini*, 1559

PRIMA PARS, 5r–42r:	De Octo partium orationis cursu
SECUNDA PARS, 42r–49v:	De Concordantia partium
TERTIA PARS, 49v–66v:	De Genere

[2] Gilberti, *Arte* (1558), 174v–176v [2004, 337–9] has a more detailed table of contents.

QUARTA PARS, 66v–93r:	De Regimine verbi aliarumque orationis partium
QUINTA PARS, 93v–107v:	De Accento simul et quantitate solius penultimae
SEXTA PARS, 117v–137r:	De Ornatu linguae latinae
SEPTIMA PARS, 137r–168v:	Quaedam pro pueris linguae latiné salutandi, valedicendi, percontandi exercitamenta ac formulae ex Erasmo Roterodamo aliisue doctissimis.

Appendix 1.2: Books purchased in 1559 by Antonio Huitzimengari, native governor of Michoacán

• Source: Mendoza, 'Poder de Francisco de Mendoza librero' (1562). Municipal Archive of Pátzcuaro. Books listed in this document were identified in Jiménez 2002.

10 August 1559

Los libros que don Antonio Uichimingar debe a mí, Francisco de Mendoza son los siguentes:

[1]	*Vn cornù copia*	Niccolò Perotti, *Cornu copiae seu linguae Latinae commentarii.* Venice: Paganinus de Paganinis, 1489.
[2]	*trejo su per evangelia*	Gutierre de Trejo, *In sacrosancta Iesu Christi quattuor Euangelia... commentarij.* Seville: Petrus de Luxan, 1554.
[3]	*lengua de erasmo*	Erasmus, *La lengua de Erasmo roterodamo romançada.* Toledo: Ayala, 1533.
[4]	*divino r[ost]ro per tres liciones*	Unidentified.
[5]	*fuenllana de musica di vihuela*	Miguel de Fuenllana, *Libro de Música para Vihuela, Orphenica lyra.* Seville: Montesdoca, 1554.
[6]	*frey juan bermudez*	Juan Bermudo, *Comiença el libro . . . de instrumentos musicales.* Osuna: Juan Leon, 1554.

25 September 1559

[7]	*Suma Gayetana*	Tomasso de Vio 'Cayetano', *Summa sacrae theologiae . . . divo Thoma Aquinate commentariis illustrata.* Lyon: Hugo a Porta, 1558.

[8]	*P[r]o[b]lemas de Villalobos*	Francisco de Villalobos, *Libro intitulado los problemas de Villalobos que tracta de cuerpos naturales y morales.* Zamora: Juan Picardo, 1543.
[9]	*Vocabulario [en len] g[ua]*	Fray Maturino Gilberti, *Vocabulario en la lengua de Mechuacan.* Mexico City: Joannes Paulus, 1559.
[10]	*El Tholomeo*	Claudius Ptolemy, *Geographia.* Various editions: e.g. Cologne 1540, Lyon 1541, Basel 1545.
[11]	*Vocabulario del Antonio in 4º*	Antonio de Nebrija, *Dictionarium,* c. 1495. Various editions and titles.
[12]	*de un Dialogo Democrates*	Juan Ginés de Sepúlveda, *De convenientia militaris disciplina cum Christiana religione dialogus qui inscribitur Democrates.* Rome: Antonius Blandus 1535; Spanish translation, *Dialogo llamado Democrates.* Seville: Juan Cromberger, 1541.
[13]	*de un Osias Marco*	Ausias March, *Las obras del famosíssimo Philosopho y Poeta mossen Osias Marco cavallero de nación catalán.* Seville: Ioan Canalla, 1553.
[14]	*de unas horas longetas en latin que por la cedula de las espaldas parece*	Unidentified liturgical book of lessons and prayers.

In margin: *Cuenta de lo que debe don Antonio gobernador de Michuacan*

Appendix 1.3: Books at the Imperial College of Santa Cruz in Tlatelolco, 1572–1584

• Source: An anonymous manuscript often known as the 'Codex of Tlatelolco' (c. 1587). A title in eighteenth-century lettering had been added to the original folio volume: 'Imperial Colegio de Indios titulado Santa Cruz, fundado en el Convento de Santiago Tlatelolco de Religiosos Franciscanos'. The document contained records of the college from 1550 to 1587, including inventories of books held there that were compiled in 1572, 1574, and 1582.[3] The original manuscript cannot now be located, but it was edited and published as the 'Códice de Tlatelolco' in García Icazbalceta 1892 ii, 241–71.

[3] Cf. Chapter 4, III above for the significance of these inventories.

The authors and titles of all the books that were given incompletely or incorrectly in the inventories are reconstructed below. An asterisk [*] following details of a specific edition indicates that identification can be confirmed on the basis of a surviving copy, print history, or other evidence. More often, an inclusive date span (e.g. 1472–1592) is given for the period in which there were repeated printings of a title before 1600. Titles followed by a question mark [?] are more tentative conjectures.

Not all the volumes from Tlatelolco in the Sutro Mexicana Collection, now in San Francisco State University Library and catalogued in Mathes 1982 [1985], were in the college in the 1500s. For those volumes which can be connected with the items in these inventories, the words 'College' and/or 'Convent' after the year of publication in the right-hand column indicate whether they originally belonged to the College of Santa Cruz or to the Convent of Santiago.

The books from Santa Cruz recorded in Fray Francisco Antonio de la Rosa Figueroa, *Diccionario bibliográphico* (c. 1758) also included titles acquired after the college's decline as a teaching institution. Listings in that catalogue, however, may help to confirm or refine some of the identifications made here.

31 July 1572

[1]	*Item, un Vocabulario Calepino grande, encuadernado en tablas.* Cf. [6] [84]	Ambrogio Calepino, *Dictionarium.* 1502–1600.
[2]	*Item, otros dos Vocabularios de Antonio de Librija.* Cf. [18] [111]	Antonio de Nebrija, *Dictionarium ex Hispaniensi in Latinum sermonem.* Numerous editions 1492–1600.
[3]	*Item, un Arte de Gramática de comento de Antonio de Librija.* Cf. [19] [22] [53] [112]	*Antonio de Nebrija, *Introductiones in latinam grammaticam*. Granada. 1540. Convent. Numerous editions of *Ars/Introductiones* c. 1485–1595.
[4]	*Item, un libro de las Epístolas de S. Jerónimo, encuadernado en tablas.* Cf. [68]	St. Jerome, *Epistolae.* 1468–1600.
[5]	*Item, otro libro llamado Apiano de beliz*	Appian, *De bellis.* 1472–1592.

[6]	*Item, otro libro Vocabulario de Ambrosio Calepino.* Cf. [1] [84]	Calepino, *Dictionarium.*
[7]	*Item, otro libro Filosofía Natural*	Franz Titelmans, *Philosophiae Naturalis.* Editions printed 1535–1572.
[8]	*Otro libro grande encuadernado en tablas intitulado Gayo Plinus.* Cf. [80]	Pliny, *Natural History.* Various editions 1469–1571.
[9]	*Item, otro libro intitulado de Santo Tomás de Aquino.* Cf. [87] [97]	*St. Thomas Aquinas, *In Evãgelium beati Joannis Evãgeliste aurea expositio.* Paris: Joannes de Porta 1520. Convent. *Aquinas, *Prima pars Summe theologie.* Venice: Antonius de Giunta. 1522. Convent.
[10]	*Item, otro libro de la Historia Imperial, en romance*	Pedro Mexía, *Historia imperial y cesarea.* Printed 1540–1579.
[11]	*Item, otro libro Vocabulario que se dice Catolicón*	Johannes Balbus, *Catholicon seu Vocabularius universalis.* Printed 1460–1514.
[12]	*Item, dos vocabularios en lengua castellana en la mexicana, hechos por el P. Fr. Alonso de Molina*	*Alonso de Molina, *Aqui comiença el vocabulario, en la lengua castellana y mexicana.* Mexico: Juan Pablos, 1555.
[13]	*Otro libro de Quintiliano.* Cf. [67]	*Quintilian, *Institutionum oratoriarum.* Paris: Nicolaus Savetier, 1527. Convent.
[14]	*Otro llamado Plutarco.* Cf. [62] [79]	*Plutarch, *Ethica sive Moralia: Opera.* Basel: Michaelis Isingrinius, 1552. Convent.
[15]	*Otro libro intitulado Repertorio General succinctum . . . super de la Teulugía de Grabiel Biel*	*Gabriel Biel, *Repertorium generale et quatuor libros sententiarum* (Commentary on Peter Lombard's *Sententiae*). Lyon: Jacobus Mit, 1527. College.
[16]	*Otro libro intitulado Despauterio de latinidad.* Cf. [39]	Johannes Despauter, *Commentarii grammatici.* 1536–1582.
[17]	*Otro Vocabulario Eclesiástico*	*Rodrigo Fernández de Santaella, *Vocabulario eclesiastica.* Seville: Johannes Regnitzer, Magnus Herbst, and Thomas Glockner, 1499.
[18]	*Otro Vocabulario de Antonio de Librija.* Cf. [2]	Nebrija, *Dictionarium.*
[19]	*Otro Arte de comento de Librija.* Cf. [3] [22] [53] [112]	Nebrija, *Ars grammatica/Introductiones.*

[20]	*Otro libro de Gramática de Martiniano*. Cf. [69] below	*Martianus Capella, *De arte grammatica*. Editions of this book from *De nuptiis*, all printed in 1500.
[21]	*Otro libro de Lóxica del Maestro Silíceo*	Siliceus (Juan Martínez Guijarro), *Logica brevis*. 1518–1530.
[22]	*Otro Arte de Antonio de Librija de comento*. Cf. [3] [19] [53] [112]	Nebrija, *Ars grammatica/Introductiones Latinae*.
[23]	*Item, una Blibia* [*sic*] *en latín*. Cf. [29] [38] [57] [70]	**Biblia cum summariorum apparatu*. Paris: I. Preul, 1523. Convent. *Nicolaus de Lyra, *Textus Bibliae cum glossa ordinaria*, 6 vols. Basel: Langendorff and Frobenius 1506--1508. Convent, College. **Bibliae cum glossa ordinaria*, 6 vols. Lyon: Ioannes Mareschal, 1529. College. **Biblia; D. Dionysii Carthusiani Enarrationes piae ac eruditae*. Cologne: Iohannes Soter and Melchior Novesanus, 1533. Convent. **Biblia; Catena aurea super Psalmos*. Paris: Jehan Petit, 1534. Convent. **Biblia; Arnobii Afri vetusti pariter ac laudatissimi scriptoris commentarii*. Basel: Hieronymus & Nicolaus Episcopius, 1537. Convent.
[24]	*Otro libro de Catón*. Cf. [98] below	Pseudo-Cato, *Disticha moralia* or *Disticha de moribus*. Many editions: 1450–1572.
[25]	*Otro libro de Epístolas Opus Regali*. Cf. [72] below	*Johannes Ludovicus Vivaldus, *De Contritionis veritate aureum Opus Fratris Joannis Viualdi de Monte Regali*. 1508–1518.
[26]	*Otro libro de Marco Antonio*. Cf. [102]	Marcus Antonius Sabellicus, *Opera*, or *Historiae*. Various works by this author printed 1480–1600.
[27]	*Otro libro Rrechardos de mediav*[a]. Cf. [88] below	Book by Ricardus de Mediavilla (Richard of Middleton).
[28]	*Otro libro Dealética de Filosofía*	*Joannes Caesarius, *Dialectica . . . Quid sit philosophia*. Paris: Gaudoul, 1533. Prior printings 1526–1533.[4]
[29]	*Otro libro Blibia* [*sic*]. Cf. [23] [38] [57] [70]	Bible.

[4] Cf. Chapter 4, n. 125.

[30]	*Otro libro de las Epístolas de S. Pablo*	*Denis the Carthusian, *In omnes Beati Pauli epistolas commentaria.* Cologne: Petrus Quentell, 1538. College.
[31]	*Otro libro que se intitula las Epístolas de Mantuano*	Pico della Mirandola, Battista Mantovano, *Auree epistole Ioannis pici Mirandule . . . cum elegiaca ipsius ad deum de precatoria duabus que epistolis Fratris baptiste Mantuani carmelite.* 1508.
[32]	*Otro libro del Nuevo Testamento.* Cf. [48]	New Testament [Erasmus, *Novum instrumentum* 1516; Erasmus, *Novum Testamentum* 1516–1536].
[33]	*Otro libro que se dice los Oficios de Cicerón.* Cf. [114], also [41]	Cicero, *De officiis.* 1450–1600.
[34]	*Otro libro de Epístolas de Erasmo.* Cf. [109]	Possibly Erasmus, *Epistolae familiares.* Basel: Barphtholomaeus Westhemerus, 1538. Various collections of *Epistolae* printed 1515–1561.
[35]	*Otro libro de Bita Criste cartuxano.* Cf. [40]	*Ludolph of Saxony, *Vita Christi Cartuxano.* Seville: Juan Cromberger, 1537. Convent *Ludolph of Saxony, *Vita Christi Cartuxano.* Seville: Jacome Cromberger, 1543–1551. Convent and College.
[36]	*Otro libro de sante Salustio [sic].* Cf. [42] [49] [56] [101]	*Sallust, *De L. Sergii Catilinae coniuratione, ac Bello Iugurthino historia.* Antwerp: Johannes Loe, 1543. Convent. *Sallust, *In Catilina Iugurthaque Crispi Sallusti,* c. 1550, no place of publication. Convent. *Sallust, *Coniuratio Catilinae et bellum Iugurthinum.* Lyon: Antonius Gryphius, 1578. Convent
[37]	*Otro libro que se dice Aureli de latinidad*	*Aurelius Augustine, *Opuscula plurima.* Venice: Dionysius Bertochus, 1491. Convent. *Aurelius Augustine, *Omnium operum tomus primus.* Lyon: Sebastianus Honoratus, 1563. College.
[38]	*Item, otra Blibia.* Cf. [23] [29] [57] [70]	Bible: see [23] above.

[39]	*Item, otro libro Despauteri de latinidad*	Despauter, *Commentarii grammatici*: see [16] above.
[40]	*Otro libro que se dice bita Cristi.* Cf. also [35]	Ludolf of Saxony, *Vita Christi.* Lyon: Iacobus Huguetan, 1555. College.
[41]	*Item, otro libro de las oraciones de Tulio Cicerón*	Cicero, *Orationes.* Frequently printed 1450–1600.
[42]	*Item, otro libro que se dice Salustii.* Cf. [36] [49] [56] [101]	Sallust, *Catilina* and/or *Iugurtha.*
[43]	*Unas Epístolas de S. Pablo.* Cf. [30] [44]	Epistles of St. Paul.
[44]	*Otras Epîstolas de S. Pablo.* Cf. [30] [43]	
[45]	*Otro libro de Bautista Mantuano.* Cf. [51] [85] [103]	Battista Mantovano, *Bucolica/Parthenice*?
[46]	*Otro libro de Contentus mundi de Jason*	Jean de Gerson, *De contemptu mundi.* 1483–1587.
[47]	*Otro libro Manual Espiritual*	*Martín de la Azpilcueta, *Manual de confesores & penitentes.* Salamanca: Andreas de Portonariis, 1556. College.
[48]	*Otro Testamento Nuevo.* Cf. [32]	New Testament.
[49]	*Otro libro de Salusti de latinidad.* Cf. [36] [42] [56] [101]	Sallust, *Catilina* and/or *Iugurtha.*
[50]	*Otro libro que se dice Proxinasmata de lógica*	*Augustinus Hunnaeus, *Progymnasmata logices puriori sermone.*
[51]	*Otro libro intitulado Bautista Mantuano.* Cf. [45] [85] [103]	Battista Mantovano.
[52]	*Otro libro Despauterio pequeño.*	Johannes Despauter, *Rudimenta.* Editions printed 1515–1600. (Incorporated into the *Commentarii*: [16] [39] above).
[53]	*Otro Arte de Antonio de Librija.* Cf. [3] [19] [22] [112]	Nebrija, *Ars grammatica/Introductiones.*
[54]	*Otro libro de Arte canto llano*	Gonzalo de Martinez Biscargui, *Arte de canto llano.* 1508–1550.

[55]	*Otro libro intitulado Cosmografía Camponi*	*Giovanni Francesco Camocio, *Cosmographia universalis . . . Camotii.* Venice: Ad signum Pyramidis, 1569.
[56]	*Item, otro libro de Saludio.* Cf. [36] [42] [49] [101]	Sallust: see [36].
[57]	*Item, otra Blibia escrita de mano en pergamino.* Cf. [23] [29] [38] [70]	Manuscript copy of the Bible.
[58]	*Item, un libro Silva de varia lección, en romance*	Pedro Méxia, *Silva de varia leccion.* 1540–1570.
[59]	*Item, otro libro de la destruición de Troya*	*Guido della Colonna, *La chronica Troyana: En que se contiene la total y lamentable destruycion dela nombrada Troya.* Toledo: Miguel Ferrer, 1562.

• The 1572 inventory ends with these words: *El juez preguntó bajojuramento á Tomé López, mayordomo, José de Castañeda, lector, y Martín Jacobita, rector, si el colegio tenía otras cosas. Contestaron que no.*

13 December 1574[5]

Inventory of books in the college made in the presence of Fray Alonso de Molina and Fray Bernardino de Sahagún.

[60]	*Un libro Opera Divi Ambrosii*	St Ambrose, *Divi Ambrosii omnia opera.* 1492–1586.
[61]	*Otro, Divi Agustini de Civitate Dei*	St Augustine, *De civitate Dei.* 1475–1596.
[62]	*Otro, de Plutarchus de Viris Illustribus.* Cf. [14]	*Plutarch, *Vitae comparatae illustrium virorum.* Basel: Thomas Guarinus, 1573. Convent.
[63]	*Titus Livius*	Livy, *History*: editions 1469–1600.
[64]	*Historia Imperial en romance*	Pedro Mexía, *Historia imperial y cesarea.*1545–1579.
[65]	*Chronica Santo Antonii Florentini*	St. Antoninus of Florence, *Chronica Antonini: Historiae Domini Antonini Archipraesulis Florentini.*1477–1543.
[66]	*Divi Cipriani Opera*	*St Cyprian, *Opera divi Caecilii Cypriani.* Paris: Bertholt Rembolt, 1512. Convent. *Opera, Antwerp: Joannes Steelsius. 1568. Convent.

5 '1584' in García Icazbalceta 1892 ii, 259 should read '1574'.

[67]	*Quintíliani Inst. Orat.* Cf. [13]	Quintilian, *Institutio oratoria.*
[68]	*Divi Hieronimi Epistolarum Liber*. Cf. [4]	St. Jerome, *Epistles.*
[69]	*Marciani Capele Opus.* Cf. [20] above	*Martianus Capella, *Opus de Nuptiis Philologi[a]e et Mercurii libri duo.* Vicenza: Henricus de Santo Urso, 1499.
[70]	*Tres Blibias* (in margin: *ojo falta una*). Cf. [23] [29] [38] [57]	See [23] above for editions in Tlatelolco.
[71]	*Libri Paralipomenon*	*Libri Regvm IIII. Paralipomenon . . .* [St Jerome, books of Old Testament]. 1526–1570
[72]	*Opus Regali.* Cf. [25] above	*Vivaldus, *De Contritionis veritate . . .*
[73]	*Postille totius anni*	*Postill[a]e maiores totius anni.* Various editions 1500–1580.
[74]	*Boecius de Consolacioni xhic cun comendis*	*Boethius, *De consolatione. De consolatu Philosophiae . . . Nouissime cum Sancti Thomae . . . com[m]entarijs.* Venice: O. Scotus, 1524.[6] Many editions 1470–1600.
[75]	*Logica Aristotiles*	*Aristotle, *Logica Aristotelis: Libri logicorum ad archetypos recogniti.* Paris: Joannes Parvus, 1541. Convent.
[76]	*Catolicon.* Cf. [11]	Johannes Balbus, *Catholicon.*
[77]	*Diogenes de vitis*	*Diogenes Laertius, *Laertii Diogenis De vitis Philosophorum* (ed. Ambrogio Travesari). Rome: Georgius, 1473.[7]
[78]	*Prudenti poeti opera*	*Aurelius Prudentius, *Prudentii poetae opera.* Venice: Aldus Manutius, 1501–1502.
[79]	*Plutarchi Opuscula*	Plutarch, *Opuscula.* 1509–1572.
[80]	*Plini Secundi ystoria naturalis.* Cf. [8]	Pliny, *Natural History.*
[81]	*Logica fratre Alfonsi a uera cruzi*	*Fray Alonso de la Vera Cruz, *Recognitio summularum* ('*Sumulas*' in later 1584 inventory) *cum textu Petri Hispani & Aristotelis.* Salamanca: Jo. Baptista à Terra Nova, 1573. Convent.

[6] The transcribed title follows this particular edition.

[7] Other editions include Henricus Stephanus (Paris, 1570) but Traversari's title was recalled by Cabrera and Chimalpahin (pp. 178 and 306 above).

[82]	*Dialectice titilmani*	Franz Titelmans, *Dialecticae Considerationis Libri Sex.* 1543–1564.
[83]	*Flavi Josephi de antiquitatibus*	Josephus, *De antiquitatibus Iudaicis.* 1499–1564.
[84]	*Tres Calepini.* Cf. [1] [6]	Calepino, *Dictionarium.*
[85]	*Duo liber Parthenices mariani cun.*	Battista Mantovano, *Parthenice mariana.* 1500–1524.
[86]	*Manual Espiritual del P. frai Xpoual Ruiz.* Cf. [47] above	[*Manual de adultos.* Mexico: Juan Cromberger. 1540]?
[87]	*Tercia Pars beati Tome.* Cf. [9] [97]	*St. Thomas Aquinas, *Tertia p[ar]s sum[ma]e in Theologia.* Venice: Philippus Pincius, 1512. Convent. **Summae theologicae tertia pars.* Paris: Claude Chavallon, 1514. Convent.
[88]	*Ricardi super quartum Sent.* Cf. [27]	Ricardus de Mediauilla*(Richard of Middleton), *Perspicacissimi in quartum sententiarum theologicarum Petri Lombard.* 1517.[8]
[89]	*Filosophia naturalis cun paraphrasi*	*Jacques Lefèvre d'Etaples, Franciscus Vata[b]lus, Totius francisi batalii. Philosophiae naturalis Paraphrases.* c. 1512–1539.
[90]	*Seis libros de Luis bibas*	Juan Luis Vives, *Linguae Latinae exercitatio/ Colloquia.* 1531–1597.
[91]	*Un libro de ysopete*	Aesop's Fables: many editions printed 1450–1574.
[92]	*Dos libros hymnorum cun comendariis*	Books of hymns with commentary.
[93]	*Dos Vocabularios del P. Fr. Alonso de Molina*	See [12] above.
[94]	*Un Repertorio de Chaves en romance*	Gerónimo Chaves, *Chronographia, o Repertorio de los tiempos.* 1516–1586.
[95]	*Tractatus de contentus mundi.* Cf. [46]	Thomas à Kempis, *De contemptu mundi,* cf. Gerson [46] Erasmus, *De contemptu mundi* listed in 1574 inventory [109].
[96]	*Logica de Siliceo.* Cf. [21]	Siliceus, *Logica brevis.* 1518–1531.

[8] Compare [27] above. Place of publication not known. The only extant copy of the 1517 imprint is in Madrid.

[97]	*Logica Sancii* Cf. [9] [87]	*St Thomas Aquinas, *Logica Sancti Thomae de Aquino*. Venice: Hieronymus de Hippolyto, 1496.
[98]	*Catonculus muy viejo.* Cf. [24]	A copy of Cato's Distichs, probably made from a manuscript of Aymeric of Angouleme's textbook, *Ars lectoria* (c. 1086 AD), in which Cato was unusually referred to as 'Catonculus'.
[99]	*Contextus seu Epítome. Hay más: Dialéctica Aristóteles.—Doctrina Aristotelis, . . . Accessit breue epitome totius Dialecticae*	*Fray Alonso de la Vera Cruz, *Resolutio dialectica cum textu*. Salamanca: Joannes Baptista à Terranova, 1569.
[100]	*Seduli duo*	Sedulius: Various editions 1501–1573 [cf. *Sedulii mirabilium divinorum libri . . . Iuvenci de Evangelica historia libri quatuor. Aratoris historiae apostolicae libri duo*. Venice: Aldus Manutius, 1502] *Antonio de Nebrija, 1531, *Sedulii paschale cum commento*. Alcala: Michaelis de Eguia. Convent.
[101]	*Tres libros de Salustiani.* Cf. [36] [42] [49] [56]	Sallust, for editions in Tlatelolco, see [36] above.
[102]	*Sabelicus*. Cf. [26]	Sabellicus, *Opera/Historiae*.
[103]	*Baptista Mantuano bucolicorum.* Cf. [45] [51]; also [85]	Battista Mantovano, *Bucolica*. 1498–1598.
[104]	*Petri Criniti de diciplina*	Petrus Crinitus, *Commentarii de honesta disciplina*. Various editions 1504–1598.
[105]	*Tartareti Logica*	Pierre Tartaret, *Expositio super textu logices Aristotelis*. 1493–1514.
[106]	*Jubenal*	*Juvenal, *Satyrae sexdecem ab Antonio Mancinello expositio*. Lyon: Johann Klein, 1515. College.
[107]	*Otro libro de Gerson de oraciones*	*Joannes Gerson, *Opera*. Basel: A. Petrus, 1517. Convent.
[108]	*Virgilio*	Virgil or possibly *St Vigilius, *B[eati] Vigili martyris et episcopi Tridentini opera*. Cologne: Arnold Birkmann, 1555. Convent.

[109]	*Erasmo de Conscribentis*	Erasmus, *Opus de conscribendis epistolis.* 1517–1587.
[110]	*Un arte Despauterio*	Despauter, *Rudimenta* or *Commentarii grammatici.*
[111]	Dos Vocabularios de Ant° de Nibrija	Nebrija, *Dictionarium.*
[112]	Cinco artes de Ant° de Nibrija. Cf. [3] [19] [22] [53]	Nebrija, *Ars grammatica.*
[113]	*Vocabulario Eclesiástico.* Cf. [17]	Fernández de Santaella, *Vocabulario.*
[114]	*Otro libro de los oficios de Cicerón.*	Cicero, *De officiis*: see [33] above.

8 March 1582

This shorter inventory repeats items listed above, but specifies Erasmus as author of a '*Contentus* [*Contemptu*] *mundi*' and names the '*Sumulas*' [*Summulae*] of Fray Alonso de la Vera Cruz. These titles are added:

[115]	*Logia Magistri Sante Carranza*	*Sancho Carranza de Miranda, *Progymnasmata logicalia magistri Santii Carranca de Miranda.* Paris: Johannes Parvus, 1517.
[116]	*Doctrina Christiana*	[Pedro de Gante, *Doctrina christiana en lengua mexicana.* Mexico: Juan Pablos, 1553; Pedro de Córdoba, *Dotrina Chr[ist]iana para instrucción & información delos indios* Mexico: Juan Cromberger, 1544]?
[117]	*Otra Doctrina christiana*	See [116] above
[118]	*Oficio de Nombre de Jesus*	[*Incipit devotissimum officium gloriosissimi nominis Jesu.* Rome: Antonius Bladus Asulanus, 1539]?
[119]	*Opus marciali*	*Martial, *Epigrammatum Opus.* Venice: Joannes de Colonia, 1475.
[120]	*Sedulli paschali*	*Antonio de Nebrija, 1531, *Sedulii paschale cum commento.* Alcala: Michaelis de Eguia. Convent.
[121]	*y un platón*	Plato, *Opera omnia.* 1472–1592.

Appendix 1.4: Named alumni of the College of Santa Cruz

(i) Alumni teaching at the college mentioned in the 'Codex of Tlatelolco' (1587):
Pablo Nazareo, 'rector'
Martín Exidio, 'conciliari'
Antonio Valeriano, 'lector'
Martín Jacobita, 'lector'
Joaquín, 'lector'
Gregorio, 'lector'
Antonio Ramírez, 'lector'
José de Castañeda, 'lector'
Gregorio de Medina, 'lector'
Alonso Lejerano, 'lector'
Mateo Sánchez, 'repetidor'
Bonifacio Maximiliano, 'repetidor'
Gaspar de Torres, 'maestro de primeras letras'

(ii) Collegians described in the Prologue of Bautista, *Sermonario* (1606):
Hernando de Ribas
Don Juan Berardo
Diego Adriano
Don Francisco Bautista de Contreras
Esteban Bravo
Don Antonio Valeriano
Pedro de Gante (Pedro Atecpanecatl)
Agustín de la Fuente

(iii) Collegians named by Sahagún in *Colloquios y Doctrina christiana* (1564), 27v and in *Historia general* (1580), Book 2, Prologue:

Latinists:	Antonio Valeriano
	Alonso Vegerano
	Martín Jacobita
	Andrés Leonardo (*Colloquios* only)
	Pedro de San Buenaventura (*HG* only)
Scribes (*HG*):	Diego de Grado
	Bonifacio Maximiliano
	Mateo Severino

(iv) Juan Badiano, *Libellus de medicinalibus Indorum herbis* (1552) states that he was a *praelector* at the college: Appendix 2.2.2 below.

(v) For Miguel of Cuauhtitlan, cf. Mendieta, *Historia ecclesiastica Indiana* 4.23 and Chapter 4, p. 129 above.

Appendix 1.5: Genealogies for Pedro de Montezuma, Antonio Valeriano, Antonio Cortés Totoquihuatzin, and Hernando de Alvarado Tezozomoc[9]

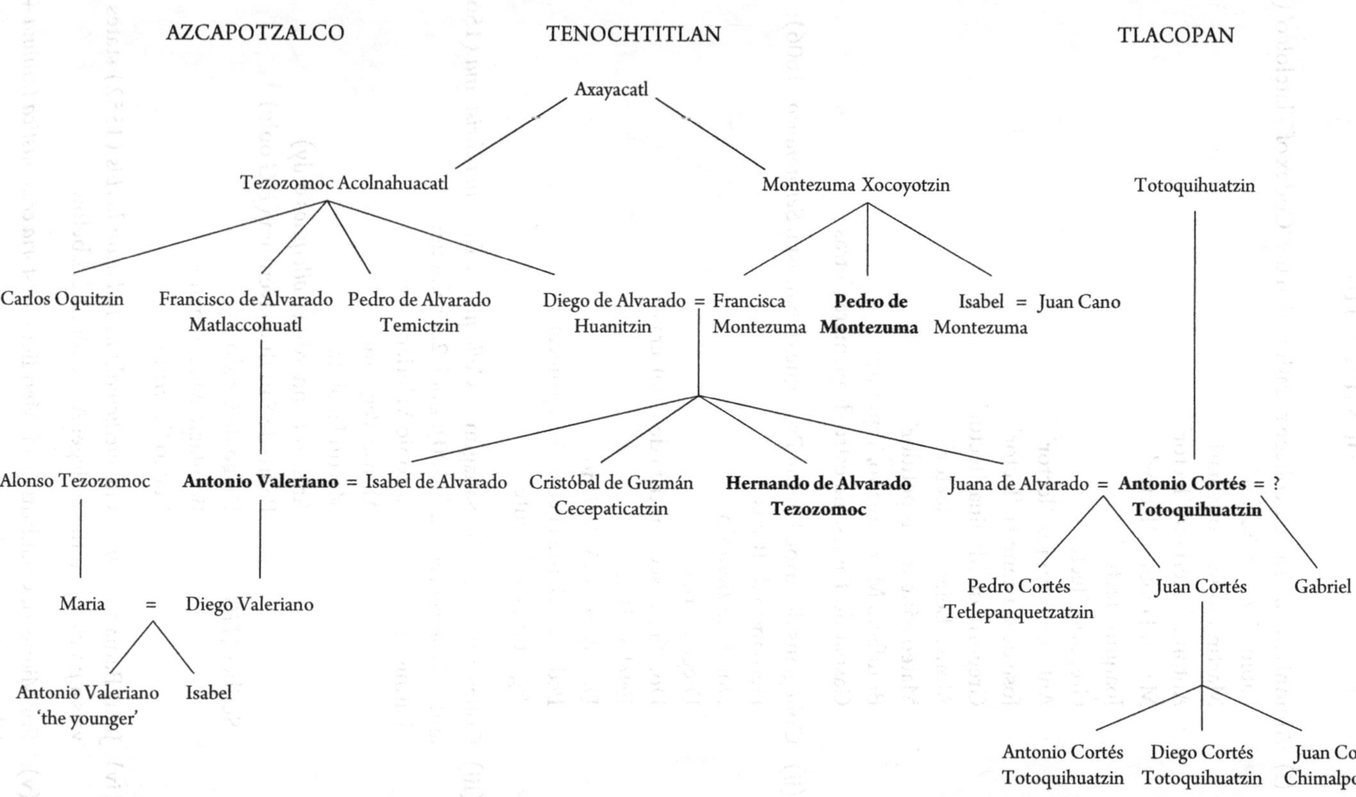

[9] Table adapted from Castañeda de la Paz 2013, 467, *Cuadro* 11: 'Linaje de don Antonio Valeriano'. Cf. ALVARADO TEZOZOMOC, *Chronica Mexicayotl* (1609); CHIMALPAHIN, *Codex Chimalpahin* (c. 1621); CHIMALPAHIN, *Diario* (1624).

Appendix 1.6: Titles and morals of Aesop's Fables in Latin and Nahuatl

1.6.1 Titles of fables in Aldus Manutius, Joachim Camerarius, and *Nican ompehua y çaçanillatolli* (BNM Ms. 1628 bis)

Aldus/Frobenius 1534 [pages]	Camerarius, 1538 folios	BNM Ms., 1550s (?)
1. Aquila & vulpes [103–5]	1. Aquila et vulpes 38v–39r	
2. Aquila & scarabeus [105–7]	2. Aquila et scarabeus 39r–39v	
3. Philomela & accipiter [107]	3. Luscinia et Accipiter 39v–40r	
4. Vulpes & hircus [107–9]	4. Vulpes et Hircus 40r–40v	1. *Quaquauhtentzone yhuan coyotl* (Goat and coyote)
5. Vulpes & leo [109]	5. Vulpes et Leo 40v	2. *Coyotl yhuan tequani miztli* (Coyote and fierce mountain lion)
6. Feles & gallus [109–11]	6. Feles & Gallus 40v	
7. Vulpes (i) [111]	7. Vulpeculae 41r	3. *Cocoyo* (Coyotes)
8. Vulpes & rubus [111–13]	8. Vulpes et Sentes 41v	
9. Vulpes & crocodilus [113]	9. Vulpes et Crocodilus 41v	4. *Acuetzpali yhuan coyotl* (Alligator and coyote)
10. Galli & perdix [113–15]	10. Gallinae et Perdix 41v–42r	5. *Cihuatotolme yhuan centetl tototl ytoca perdiz* (Hens and sparrow bird called 'partridge')
11. Vulpes (ii) [115]	11. Vulpes 42r–42v	6. *Coyotl* (Coyote)
12. Carbonarius & fullo [115]	12. Carbonarius et Fullo 42v	7. *Ce tecollati yhuan tlapacqui* (Charcoal burner and fuller)
13. Piscatores (i) [115–17]	13. Piscatores 42v–43r	
14. Iactator [117]	14. Gloriator 43r	
15. Impossibilia promittens [117]	15. Votum quod solvi non posset 43r–43v	8. *Nehtolle yn ahmo huel moneltilia* (The promise that was not kept)

Aldus/Frobenius 1534 [pages]	Camerarius, 1538 folios	BNM Ms., 1550s (?)
16. Malignus [117–19]	16. De Apollonis tentatore 43v–44r	
17. Piscatores (ii) [119]	17. Piscatores (ii) 44r	9. *Tlahtlamaque* (Fishermen)
18. Deceptor [119–21]	18. Fraudulentus 44r–44v	
19. Ranae [121]	19. Ranae 44v	10. *Cuicuia* (Frogs)
20. Senex et mors [121–3]	20. De Sene et Morte 45r	11. *Huehuento yhuan miquiztli* (Old man and death)
21. Anus et medicus [123]	21. De Anu Laborante ex oculis 45r–45v	12. *Ylamaton yxcocoxqui* (Old woman with bad eyes)
22. Agricola & filii ipsius [123–5]	22. Rusticus et Filii Illius 45v–46r	13. *Milahcatl yhuan ypilhuan* (Farmer and his sons)
23. Herus & canes [125]	23. Herus et Canes 46r	14. *Chichime yhuan intecuio* (Dogs and their master)
24. Mulier et gallina [125–7]	24. Mulier et Gallina 46r	15. *Ycnocihuatl yhuan ycihuatotol* (Widow and her hen)
25. Morsus a cane [127]	25. Vulneratus a Cane 46v	16. *Ce tlacatl chichi quiquêtzo* (Man bitten by a dog)
26. Adulescentuli & coccus [127]	26. Adolescentes et Cocus 46v–47r	17. *Telpopochtotonti yhuan (cozinero) molchichiuhqui* (Youths and the cook)
27. Inimici [127–9]	27. Inimici 47r	18. *Mococoliani* (Enemies)
28. Felis & mures [129]	28. Feles & Mures 47r–47v	19. *Mizton yhuan quimichti* (Cat and mice)
29. Vulpes & simius [131]		
30. Thunnus & delphin [131]	29. Thunnus et Dephinus 47v	
31. Medicus & aegrotus [133]	30. Medicus et Aegrotus 47v–48r	20. *Tticitl yhuan cocoxqui* (Doctor and invalid)
32. Auceps & vipera [133]	31. Auceps et Anguis 48r	21. *Totohanqui yhuan cohuatl* (Birdcatcher and snake)
33. De fibro [133–5]	32. Fiber 48r–48v	

Aldus/Frobenius 1534 [pages]	Camerarius, 1538 folios	BNM Ms., 1550s (?)
34. Canis & coccus [135]	33. Canis et Cocus 48v	22. *Chichi yhuan molchichiuhqui* (Dog and cook)
35. Canis & lupus [135–7]	34. Canis et Lupus 48v–49r	23. *Chichi yhuan cuitlachtli* (Dog and wolf)
36. Canis & gallus [137]	35. Canis et Gallus 49r–49v	24. *Itzcuintli yhuan oquichquanaca* (Dog and hen)
37. Leo & rana [137]	36. Leo et Rana 49v	25. *Tequani miztli yhuan cuiatl* (Fierce mountain lion and frog)
38. Leo & asinus & vulpes [137–9]	37. Leo, Asinus, Vulpes 49v–50r	26. *Miztli tequani yhuan asno yhuan coyotl* (Fierce mountain lion, ass, and coyote)
39. Leo & ursus [139]	38. Leo et Vrsus 50r	27. *Miztli tequani yhuan cuitlachtli* (Fierce mountain lion and wolf)
40. Vates [139–41]	39. Divinator 50v	28. *Tlaachtopayhytohuani* (Soothsayer)
41. Formica & columba [141]	40. Formica et Columba 50v	29. *Azcatl yhuan huilotl* (Ant and dove)
42. Vespertilio & rubus & mergus [141–3]	41. Vespertilio, Rubus, Hirundo 50v–51r	30. *Tzinacatl, quanhuitzli cuicuitzcatl* (Bat, thornbush, swallow)
	42. Lignator et Mercurius 51r–51v	
43. Aegrotus & medicus [143]	43. Aegrotus et Medicus 51v–52r	31. *Cocoxqui yhuan tiiçitl* (Invalid and doctor)
44. Lignator & Mercurius [143–5]		
45. Asinus & hortulanus [145–7]	44. Asinus et Olitor 52r	32. *Asno yhuan quilchiuhqui* (Ass and gardener)
46. Auceps & cassita [147]	45. Auceps et Cassita 52r–52v	33. *Totoanqui yhuan acatzanatl* (Birdcatcher and thrush)
47. Viator [147]	46. Viator 52v	
48. Puer & mater [149]	47. Puer et Mater 52v–53r	34. *Piltontli yhuan ynan* (Boy and his mother)

Aldus/Frobenius 1534 [pages]	Camerarius, 1538 folios	BNM Ms., 1550s (?)
49. Pastor & mare [149–51]	48. Pastor et Mare 53r–53v	35. *Ychcapixqui yhuan hueyatl* (Shepherd and sea)
50. Punica & malus [150]	49. Malus et Pirus 53v	
51. Talpa [151]	50. Talpa 53v	
52. Vespae & perdices [151–3]	51. Vespae et Perdices 54r	
53. Pavo & monedula [153]	52. Pavo et Monedula 54r	36. *Quetzaltototl yhuan toznene* (Quetzal bird and parrot)
54. Singularis animal & vulpes [153]	53. Aper et Vulpes 54r–54v	
55. Cassita [153–5]	54. Cassita 54v	
56. Hinnulus [155]	55. Hinnuleus 54v	
57. Lepores & ranae [155–7]	56. Lepores et Ranae 54v–55r	37. *Cicihti yhuan cuicuia* (Hares and frogs)
58. Asinus & equus [157]	57. Asinus et Equus 55r–v55	38. *Asno yhuan cauallo* (Ass and horse)
59. Avarus [157–9]	58. Avarus 55v–56r	39. *Tlahtlametl* (Miser)
60. Anseres & grues [159]	59. Anseres et Grues 56r	40. *Tlalalacame yhuan cacanauhti* (Wild geese and ducks)
61. Testudo & aquila [159]	60. Testudo et Aquila 56r–56v	41. *Ayotl yhuan quauhtli* (Turtle and eagle)
62. Pulex [159]	61. Pulex 56v	
63. Cerva [161]	62. Cervus 56v–57r	42. *Quauhtlamaçatl* (Wild deer)
64. Cerva & leo [161]	63. Cervus et Leo 57r	
65. Cerva & vitis [161–3]	64. Cerva et Vitis 57r	43. *Quauhtlacihuamaçatl yhuan xocomecatl* (Forest doe and vine)
66. Asinus & leo [163]	65. Asinus et Leo 57v	44. *Asno yhuan leon tequani* (Ass and fierce 'lion')
67. Olitor & canis [163]	66. Olitor et Canis 57v	
68. Sus & canis (i) [163–5]	67. Sus et Canis (i) 57v–58r	
69. Sus & canis (ii) [165]	68. Sus et Canis (ii) 58r	
70. Serpens & cancer [165–7]	69. Anguis et Cancer 58r–58v	

Aldus/Frobenius 1534 [pages]	Camerarius, 1538 folios	BNM Ms., 1550s (?)
71. Pastor & lupus [167]	70. Pastor et Lupus 58v	45. *Ychcapixqui yhuan coyotl* (Shepherd and coyote)
72. Leo & lupus [167–9]	71. Leo et Lupus 59r	46. *Leon tequani yhuan cuitlachtli* (Fierce 'lion' and wolf)
73. Mulier [171]	72. Mulier et Maritus ebriosus 59v	
74. Cycnus [171]	73. Olor 60r	
75. Aethiops [171]	74. Aethiops 60r	47. *Ce cahcatzactli* (Black man)

1.6.2 Society and art of government in the morals of Nahuatl fables 33–47

• Each passage below from the *Nican ompehua y çaçanillatolli* (BNM ms.) is followed by an English translation from the Nahuatl and then by the source text in Camerarius, *Fabellae Aesopicae plures* (1538).

33. *Totoanqui yhuan acatzanatl*, 'Birdcatcher and Thrush' [*Auceps et cassita*]
Yni çaçanilli techmachtia ca niman ahmo huel oncan nemohua yn altepetl yttic yn canin tepachohua çanno yehuantin teca mocahcayahua tetlacuihcuilia yhuan tetolinia.
(The fable teaches us that one cannot live well in a state where those who govern people are the ones who deceive them, steal from them, and harm them.)
[*Fabula monet, male coli atque habitari cum oppida tum domus, in crudelitate & rapinis principum.*]

36. *Quetzaltototl yhuan toznene*, 'Quetzal Bird and Parrot' [*Pavo et Monedula*]
Yni çaçanilli techmachtia. Ca yn iquac pehpenalo tlahtoque in quimocuitlahuizque altepetl hamo yehuatl mottaz yn inchipahualiz yn inqualnexiliz, ça yehuatl mottaz yn inchicahualiz yhuan yn imixtlamatiliz yn innezcaliliz.
(This fable teaches us: when the rulers are chosen to look after the town, beauty and looks should not be considered, but only strength, prudence, and aptitude.)
[*Monet fabula, in principibus legendis non speciem modo, sed etiam virtutem & sapientiam spectari oportere.*]

37. *Cicihti yhuan cuicuia*, 'Hares and Frogs' [*Lepores et Ranae*]
Yni çaçanilli quihttoznequi ca yn aq[uiq]ue motolinitinemi tlalticpac ayc moyollalia yn innetolliniliz yn aquique quitzacuia tlalticpac ynic motolinia.
(This fable means that those who live in misery on earth find comfort in the misery of those who are the lowest on earth, who live the most miserably.)
[*Fabula ostendit, afflictis aliorum miserias solatio.*]

38. Asno yhuan cauallo, 'Ass and Horse' [*Asinus et Equus*]
Yni çaçanilli techmachtia. Ca yn macehualti hamo monequi yn techmoxicozque yn tlattoque yhuan in motlacamati: çan monequi ye toyollo pachihuiz yn tlein cehcenyacâ oquinmomaquili totecuiyo Dios yehica ca yn tlattoque yhuan motlacamati occenca miecpa ohuitiliztli quinamiqui.
(This fable teaches us: common people have no need to envy their rulers and the rich; our hearts should be content with what our God gives to each one of us, for in fact the rulers and the rich very often have to confront danger.)
[*Docet fabula, non esse principatus & opes propter splendorem appetendas, sed in consideratione inuidiae & discriminum, in quibus principes & opulenti versantur, bono consulendam tenuem fortunam, & mediocritatem vitae. Itaque & Plato Vlyssis animam elegisse ait vitam hominis priuati & non negociosi, neglectis omnibus aliis, honoribus & opulentia, potentiaque praeclaris.*]

40. Tlalalacame yhuan cacanauhti. 'Geese and Ducks' [*Anseres et Grues*]
Yni çaçanilli quihtoznequi: ca yniquac centetl altepetl pehualo: yn icnotlaca yciuhca teixpampa yehua: Auh in mocuiltonohuani achi mochipa mamalti mochihua, ypampa in tlatquihuaque yn necuiltonoleque hamo axcan huel teixpampa yehua.
(The fable means that when a town is conquered, the poor people are the first to flee. But the rich are nearly always made prisoners, because they have possessions and riches, and find it difficult to flee so quickly.)
[*Ostendit fabula, vrbe capta cum pauperes plerunque vim hostilem effugiant, diuites in potestatem hostium venire, & in seruitutem abduci.*]

44. *Asno yhuan león, tequani*. 'Ass and Wild Lion' [*Asinus et Leo*]
Yni çaçanilli techmachtia ca miequintin oncate macehualti yçanilihuiz quinmoxictia yn mahuiztililoni, ynca mahuiltiznequi, auh yniquac hamo ynnehmachpa quicuitihuetzi, yn ca motzoncui.
(This fable teaches us: there are many common people who resent without thought those who are honoured, and make fun of them. But when they catch those [common people] without warning, they quickly seize them as captives.)
[*Fabula significat, saepe imbecilles per occasionem adoriri territos inimicos, sed eosdem gerentes se improuide & elate, a confirmatis facile et celeriter opprimi.*]

46. *Leon tequani yhuan cuitlachtli.* 'Wild Lion and Wolf' [*Leo et Lupus*]
Yni çaçanilli techmachtia. Ca miequintin onnemi yn ahqualli yn ahyectli tlahtolli quitechihchihuilia ynic tetlanmihquania, auh çan no yehuantin ynpan mocuepa, çan no yehuantin quinqua yn intlahtol.
(This fable teaches us: there are many whose bad and malignant talk prepares a trap for others in order to get rid of them. But those words turn back on them, and they are eaten.)
Fabula docet, qui alteri struat malum, eum sibi laqueos quibus capiatur nectere.

47. *Ce cahcatzactli.* 'Black Man' [*Aethiops*]
Yni çaçanilli techmachtia, ca yn quenami ceceyaca yyeliz yn ipan tlacat; ayac huel occentlamantli ypan quicuepiliz.
(This fable teaches us that in whatever way each one is born is one's nature; nobody can change it into another.)
Significat fabula nullo pacto mutari ingenia & naturas, sed retinere insitas semper proprietates, & quasi personas attributas sibi. Recte igitur dicitur & hoc apud Aristophanem: Non poteris rectum cancris inducere gressum, Ne leves horrentis echini reddere sentes.

• The Bancroft manuscript adds a second moral to *Ce cahcatzactli*:
Yni çaçanilli techmachtia ca niman ahmo huel oncan nemoa in altepetl itic in cani tepachoa çan no yehuanti teca mocaiahua tetlacuicuilia ihuan tetolinia.
(The fable teaches us that one cannot live well in a state where those who govern people are the ones who deceive them, steal from them, and harm them.)
[*Fabula monet, male coli atque habitari cum oppida tum domus, in crudelitate & rapinis principum.*]

Appendix 1.7: Types and qualities of the speeches in Book 6 of the *Florentine Codex*

Chapter	Type of speech	Addressee(s)	Speaker(s)	Function	Comment on quality of speech in Nahuatl text	Corresponding comment in Spanish text
1	Prayer	Tezcatlipoca	Unspecified group	Seeking relief from plague	cenca maviçauhquj in machiotlatolli in metaphoras	vsan de muy hermosas metaphoras y maneras de hablar
2	Prayer	Tezcatlipoca	Priests	Seeking wealth/relief from poverty		
3	Prayer	Tezcatlipoca	Priests	Seeking help in war	cenca quaqualli in metaphoras, in machiotlatolli injc tlatoaia	que contiene muy delicadas metaphoras y muy elegante lenguaje
4	Prayer	Tezcatlipoca	Priests	To aid new ruler in his office	cenca ohovi in sentencias in vncan moteneoa	que contiene sentencias muy delicadas
5	Prayer	Tezcatlipoca	Principal priest	Death of ruler, need for successor	mjec in vncan moteneoa: in quaqualli tlatolli	muchas delicadezas en sentencia, y en lenguaje
6	Prayer	Tezcatlipoca	Principal priest	Requesting death of bad ruler	cenca qualli in tlatolli, ioan cenca quaqualli in metaphoras	se pone muy estremado lenguaje y muy delicadas metaphoras
7	Prayer Ritual counsel	Tezcatlipoca Wrongdoer	Priest (*sátrapa*) Priest	Response to sinner's confession Consolatory advice to wrongdoer		
8	Prayer	Tlaloc (and Chicomecoatl)	Priests	Plea for rain	cenca maviçauhqui in tlatolli	Contiene muy delicada materia
9	Prayer	Tezcatlipoca	New ruler	Request for aid in ruling	cenca miec in jnecnomachiliztlatol	se humila de muchas maneras
10	Court oration	New ruler (*tlatoani*)	Great priest, noble, or dignitary 'who knew the words well'	Long speech/prayer to ruler after investiture	in vel qujmatia tlatolli cenca maviçauhqui injn tlatolli, ioan cenca ohovi in machiotlatolli: cenca quaqualli in tenonotzaliztlatolli	es platica de alguno persona muy principal uno de los satrapas o de algun pilli o tecutli el que mas apto era para hacerla; tiene maravilloso lenguaje y muy delicadas metaforas y admirabiles avisos

Chapter	Type of speech	Addressee(s)	Speaker(s)	Function	Comment on quality of speech in Nahuatl text	Corresponding comment in Spanish text
11	Court oration	New ruler	Dignitary	Good wishes of common people after previous speech	iece injn tlatolli, amo cenca maviçauhqui, in juh achto omjto	no lleva esta oracion tanta gravedad, ni tanto coturno como la pasada
12	Court oration	Nobles	New ruler	Reply and thanks for good wishes		
13	Court oration	Nobles	Nobleman	Speech on kingship in lieu of above	in vel qujmatia tlatolli, in vel mjmatinj catca: mjec in vncan moteneoa tecpillatlatolli	bien hablado y bien entendido; usa en ella de muchos colores rethoricos
14	Court oration	Citizens	New ruler	Moral instruction		
15	Court oration	Citizens	Nobleman	Praise of ruler, seconding exhortation		
16	Court oration	Ruler, nobles and citizens	Noble elder	Gratitude to ruler, and clarification of instruction		
17	Parental instruction	Ruler' sons	Ruler	Advice on conduct and kingship	vncan motenenoa, centlamātli cenca qualli, tenonotzaliztlatolli, nen emjliztilonj	Del razonamiento lleno de muy buena doctrina en lo moral . . .
18	Parental instruction	Ruler's daughter	Ruler	Advice on life and conduct	cenca qualli in tlatolli, injc qujnnonotzaia	hablanlas con muy tiernas palabras y en cosas muy particulares
19	Parental instruction	Ruler's daughter	Mother	Advice on social conduct	Injn tlatolli oc cenca vel neiollotilotilozquja, intla ic temachtilonj, ca cenca qualli in tlatolli: tel mocuecuepaz, in tlein amo monequj: cenca intech monequi in tel pupuchti, in jchpupuchti	mas aprovecharian estas dos platicas dichas en el pulpito, por el lenguaje y estilo que estan (*mutatis mutandis*) a los moços, y moças
20	Parental instruction	Son	Father, noble, ruler	Humility, pleasing gods and men	miec in maviçauhqui tlatolli ioan in machiotlatolli, ioan in cecencamatl tlatolli	del lenguaje y afectos . . . con maraujllosas maneras de hablar y con delicadas metaphoras y propissimos vocablos

(continued)

Chapter	Type of speech	Addressee(s)	Speaker(s)	Function	Comment on quality of speech in Nahuatl text	Corresponding comment in Spanish text
21	Parental instruction	Son	Father, noble, ruler	Advocation of chastity	mjiec tlaneujujliztlatolli, ioan machiotl moteneoa: cenca qualli in tlatolli, ioan oc cequj mjiec tepapaqujlti	con muchas comparationes y ejemplos muy al proposito con excellente lenguaje; tratando esta materia ofrecese tocar otras muchas cosas gustosas de leer
22	Parental instruction	Son	Father, noble, ruler	Conduct and prudence in public		
23	*Short exhanges of dialogue in account of procedure for having sons marry*					
24	Orations occasioned by pregnancy	Pregnant woman's kin	Husband's elders	Announcement of pregnancy		
		Husband's elders	Pregnant woman's kin	Announcement of pregnancy		
25	Orations occasioned by pregnancy	Pregnant woman	Parents of husband	Exhortations, advice on pregancy		
		Parents and in-laws	Elder kinsman of husband	Exhortations, advice on pregancy		
		Parents of pregnant woman	Elder kinsmen of husband	Gratitude for their words		
		Elders	Pregnant woman	Recognition of advice given		
26	Oration for pregnancy	Family of couple	An elder of either family	Need for a midwife		
27	Oration occasioned by pregnancy	Midwife	Old woman relative	Entreaty for services	mjiec in moteneoa in neiollotilonj, cenca qualli in tlatolli in juh tlatoa cioa, ioan cenca quâqualli in metaphoras	donde se ponen muchas cosas apetitosas de leer y de saber y muy buen lenguaje mugeril y muy delicadas metaphoras
		Family of couple	Midwife	Agreement to deliver the child		
		Midwife	Kinswomen of pregnant woman	Exhortation to proceed		
		Kinswomen	Midwife	Advice on care for pregant woman		
28	Oration for pregnancy	Woman about to give birth	Midwife	Encouragement for delivery	Mjiec in moteneoa in tepapaqujlti	donde hay cosas bien gustosas de leer

Chapter	Type of speech	Addressee(s)	Speaker(s)	Function	Comment on quality of speech in Nahuatl text	Corresponding comment in Spanish text
29	Prayer/Oration for pregnacy	Woman dead in childbirth	Midwife	Valediction and praise to woman deified as one of the *ciuapipiltin*		
30	Oration at birth of a child	Infant (girl)	Midwife	Salutation welcoming newborn, before cutting umbilical cord		
31	Oration on birth of a child	Infant boy and infant girl	Midwife	Speeches consecrating the boy to war and the girl to the household.		
32	Prayers	Chalchiutlicue Infant	Midwife Midwife	Prayers for purification of infant and to wash away evil		
	Admonition	Infant	Midwife	Preparation for sorrows of life		
33	Orations after birth of a child	Mother	Midwife	Praise for valour and admonition	cenca qualli in tlatolli: oc cenca iehoatl injc tlacuepa mjxiuhquj	donde ay muy esmeraldo lenguaje, en especial enla respuesta dela partera
		Midwife	Old woman	Praise and speculation		
	Admonition	Kin of child	Midwife	Humility; child's uncertain future		
34	Orations after birth of a child	Infant	Ruler/noble/merchant	Admonition of future travails		enbiauan a hazer esto a algun viejo honrado sabio y bien hablado, el qual primeramente hablaba al njño con lenguaje muy tierno y amoroso, lleno de mil dixes
		Mother	Ruler/noble/merchant	Salutation		
		Infant's carers	Ruler/noble/merchant	Rejoicing at birth, unknowable future		

(*continued*)

Chapter	Type of speech	Addressee(s)	Speaker(s)	Function	Comment on quality of speech in Nahuatl text	Corresponding comment in Spanish text
35	Orations after birth of a child	Parents Ambassador Infant, mother, old women and men	Ambassador of city Elder kinsman Ambassador	Recognition of child, unknown future Response on behalf of child, parents, elders Succession of greetings to each addressee for birth of child in a common family		
36	Orations after birth of a child	Parents, old men and women	Soothsayer	Prophecies according to date of infant's birth		
37	Prayers for newborn child	Chalchiutlicue & other gods	Midwife	Bathing and naming of infant boy		
38	Prayers for newborn child	Chalchiutlicue & other gods	Midwife	Bathing of infant girl		
39	Prayer	Quetzalcoatl	Priests	Prayer for youth entering *calmecac*		
40	Admonitions	Boy Girl	Elders Old woman	Advice on entering *calmecac* Advice on entering *calmecac*		
41	*Adages*				in cequj tlâtlatolli, itoca adagios, inqujtoaia, ioan in qujtoa	de algunos de los adagios que esta gente mexicana usaua
42	*Riddles*				cequi çaçanilli, in mjtoa çaçan tleino, injc moçaçanjlvia, in juhqujma monaoaltotoca	de algunos çaçaniles delos muchos que vsa esta gente mexicana: que son como los que cosa y cosa de nuestra lengua
43	*Metaphors*				cequj machiotlatolli, injtoca methaphoras, in ohoui tlatolli: ioan inj melaoaca, in jcaqujztica	de algunas methaphoras delicadas con sus declarations

Appendix 2

TEXTS AND TRANSLATIONS

The Latin and Spanish texts below are 'semi-diplomatic' transcriptions that retain the spelling and style of the sources, but expand typographic or scribal abbreviations, with the missing letters italicized. When conjectures or corrections have been made, the original wording is given in footnotes.

Appendix 2.1: Fray Julián Garcés, *De habilitate et capacitate gentium*, 1537, on the conduct and scholarly capability of the Indians of New Spain

• Source: GARCÉS, *De habilitate et capacitate gentium* (1537), 3–5, 7–9
John Carter Brown Library, Providence: BA537.G215d

2.1.1 Accomplishments and conduct of native pupils

[p. 3] SANCTISSIMO DOMINO NOSTRO Paulo III. Pontifici Maximo frater Iulianus Garces ordinis prędicatorum, Episcopus primus Tlaxcalen*sis*. In noua Hispania Indiarum Caesaris Caroli, salutem sempiternam dicit.

QVae circum nouellum gregem ecclesiae sanctae aggregatum, tibi beatissime pater acquisitum nouerim, declarare non pigebit, quatenus exultare valeat spiritus tuus in domino salutari. Et ne prologi lo*n*ga enarratione tibi praecipue, qui tot ac tantis totius orbis negotiis prouidere debes, fastidium generem, rem ipsam in valuis aggredior. Nulla sunt obstinatione orthodoxae fidei infesti, aut peruicaces (vt Iudaei & Mahumetani) Indorum paruuli. Christianorum decreta non hauriunt modo, sed exhauriunt, ac veluti ebibunt: citius hi & alacrius articulorum fidei seriem & consuetas orationes quam Hispanorum infantes ediscunt, & tenent quicquid // [p. 4] a nostris traditur. Aluntur intra monastioru*m* ambitum, per suas classes & contubernia, per scolas &

doctrinam.[1] Ex ditioribus trecenteni: quadringentini: quingenteni. Et *sic* de singulis ordinatim secundum magnitudinem ciuitatum & oppidorum & multitudinem ciuium ceu eorum vicinorum: Non clamosi, non iurgiosi, non litigiosi, non inquieti, non discoli, non tumidi, non iniuriosi, placidi, pauidi, disciplinati, ad magistros obtemperantissimi, obsequiosi ad sodales, non querulosi, non mordaces, non contumeliosi, omni prorsus vitio (quo nostrates pueruli scatent) liberi. Secundum quod illa etas patitur. Ad liberalitatem propēsissimi: vtrum vni vel multis des nihil interest, quia quod vni datum est singulis impartiendum curant: parsimonia mirabili, non bibaculi, non gulosi, ingenita & velut innata modestia ac disciplina. Siquidem videre est eos ordinate seriatimque incedentes, seu sedere seu stare iubeantur, seu flexis poplitibus prosterni ad puluinaria: Praeter suum tla cuali (*sic* enim communem escam appellant) post panem seu tlaxcali, nihil obnixe flagitantes. habent enim & nostrates fructus omnes. id est quorum semina ab Hyspania allata sunt: Tanta est terrae feracitas ac foecu*n*dia, Habe*n*t & suos fructus. Iam vero ingenii docilitas supra modum, seu cantare iubeas, seu legere, scribere, pingere, fingere, caeteraque id genus liberalium artium & aliarum ad rudimenta omnia perspicaces & acutissimi intellectus dexteritate singulari, quod praeter coeli clementiam ac temperiem (vt saepe mihi animo reuoluenti occurrit) prestat mira in cibo simplicitas ac parsimonia. Cum intra monasteria fratru*m* ac disciplinam arceantur, nulla a maioribus querimonia, questioue fit, qu*od* inaequali disparitate tractentur, qu*od* severius castigentur qu*od* a pedagogis tardius ad domos dimittantur, quod ęqualibus inaequalia, aut imparibus paria demandētur offitia. Contradicit nemo, nullus obiurgat, sed parentum cura ac solertia ad id tendit, vt quam eruditissimus in Christianismo suus natus euadat. Iam vero ecclesiasticus cantus, seu organicus seu armoniacus seu rithmicus, absolutissime ab eis perdiscitur, ita vt extrarii[2] musici non magnopere // [p. 5] desyderentur. Qui in campo pugiles exercebantur campestrati vocabantur (teste Augustino) quia femoralibus eorum pudenda uelabantur, quae campestraria dicebantur & perizomata in literis sacris (indi tomastli dicunt[3]) apud quos tanta cura & verecundiae obseruatio vt in publicum etiam tantilli infantuli (de mexico loquor) sine tomaxtli, id est, subligari prodeat nemo.

TRANSLATION

[p. 3] TO OUR MOST HOLY LORD Pope Paul III, Fray Julián Garcés of the Order of Preachers, first Bishop of Tlaxcala in New Spain of the Indies of Emperor Charles, wishes eternal health.

What I have come to know about the new little flock herded to the holy Church and acquired for you, most blessed father, will be no burden to declare, as it will make your spirit rejoice in the Lord our saviour. In order not to cause irritation by the

[1] 1537: coutubernia, per scolas & doctriuia

[2] 1537: exrratii

[3] 1537: ind_ tomastli dicant

delivery of a lengthy prologue to you of all people, as you have to oversee so many great concerns all over the world, I shall get to the point, even as I stand at the door. The little children of the Indians have no obstinate hostility to the orthodox faith, and they are not stubborn (like Jews and Mohammedans). Not only do they imbibe Christian principles, but they also absorb them as if they were drinking them up: more quickly and readily than Spanish children they learn thoroughly the articles of faith in order, and the standard prayers, and they keep hold of whatever// [p. 4] is passed on to them by our people. They are nurtured in the environment of the monasteries in classes and groups, for lectures and instruction. From the wealthier ones, there are 300, 400, or 500 of them. The size of each group is in due proportion to the size of the cities and towns and to the greatness of the number of citizens or those living in the environs. They are not rowdy, quarrelsome, contentious, difficult, haughty, or offensive, but placid, timid, disciplined, highly obedient to their teachers, and accommodating to their colleagues, and they are not complaining, sharp-tongued, or abusive. They are indeed free of all vice (with which our own children are plagued), considering inclinations at that age. They are very much disposed to generosity: it makes no difference whether you give something to one of them or to many of them, because they take pains to share what is given to one with every other. Their frugality is remarkable; they are not given to drinking, nor gluttonous; they have a moderation and restraint instilled and virtually inborn, whether indeed one is to see them walking along in an orderly file, whether they are bidden to sit or stand up, or to kneel down before shrines on bended knee. Other than their *tla cuali* (for so they call the common meal, from the word for bread), or *tlaxcali*, they demand nothing strenuously. They have all our produce, that is to say, those things for which seeds have been imported from Spain—so great is the fecundity and bounty of the earth—and they have their own produce too. In fact their educational ability is above average—whether you bid them sing, read, write, paint, or make something. Where the liberal and other arts are concerned, their understanding of all the basics is perceptive and acute, showing a singular dexterity. Apart from the clemency and temperance of the skies, the astonishing simplicity and frugality of their diet is what explains this (as has often struck me when I turn my mind to the question). Once they settle in the monasteries of our brothers for training, no complaint or questioning is ever made by the older ones that they are being handled unfairly or inequitably, that they are punished too severely, that they are sent home too late by their teachers, or that unequal obligations are placed on those equal to them or equal ones on those unequal to them. No one contradicts, none is reproachful, but the care and preoccupation of the parents are directed to the end that their son should come forth as well versed in Christianity as possible. Accordingly, church music, whether instrumental, plain or contrapuntal, is so thoroughly learned that musicians from abroad are not greatly// [p. 5] missed. The fighters who used to train in the Campus Martius were called *campestrati* on Saint Augustine's testimony, because they covered their private parts with loincloths that used to be called *campestria* or, in sacred writings, *perizomata* (the Indians say *tomaxtli*). Amongst these Indians there is such a high regard for and observance of modesty that no one, not even a little child, would appear in public without *tomaxtli,* that is, without something around their waist.

2.1.2 Indians' intelligence and literacy; comparison of their ancestors to the ancient Spaniards

[p. 7] rationis optime compotes sunt & integri sensus & capitis, sed insuper nostratibus pueri istorum & vigore spiritus & sensuum viuacitate dexteriori in omni agibili & intelligibili praestantiores reperiuntur. De maioribus quod barbara feritate ac crudelitate vltra humanum modum fuerint audiui, vtpote antropofagi, id est, humanarum carnium voratores: truces ac cruenti, sed quanto crudeliores & immaniores fuere tanto acceptius Deo holocaustum offeretur si bene conuertantur: Cuius pars maxima nos sumus, si tales erga eos extiterimus verbo & exemplo, manu, lingua, quales eos nobis si in similem casum incidissemus voluissemus habere, lucri facere animas eorū laboremus, pro quibus Christus fudit sanguinem. Barbariem eis & idolatriam obiicimus quasi meliores habuerimus patres nostros a quibus ductamus originem, quousq*ue* beatus Iacobus apostolus eisdem praedicavit, eosq*ue* ad fidei cultum conuertit, ex pessimis optimos reddens: vnde tot clarissima martirum doctorum, & virginum lumina emicuerunt, quos hic longum esset & non necessarium recēsere. Quis dubitat durante seculo multos ex his sanctissimos futuros, & omni virtute conspicuos: Nunquid Sertorio apud Hispanias res agente, submissa est cerua quae fatidica putaretur: Ecce ceruam, id est, brutum animal Hispani prophetisam, id est// [p. 8] fatidicam ac deam adorabant. Feritas Hispanorum quondam tanta erat, vt Sylius Italicus ex Italica Bethicae ciuitate oriūdus, dicat de maioribus suis eulogium inclytum.

Prodiga gens animi & properare facillima mortem[4]:
Namq*ue* vbi transcendit florentes viribus annos,
Impatiens aeui spernens venisse senectam,
& fati[5] modus in dextra est.

Viriatus ille quem teste Iustino (de gentilitate loquor) Hyspania habuit clarissimum ducem, pastor erat armentarius. At post Christianismum susceptum, cum fide veram nobilitatem haereditate possidemus, tot milites, tot duces praeclarissimos, quibus & Roma imperatoribus vsa mirum in modum creuit, ac in id quod de ea audiuimus prouecta est. Si tam inculta & vepribis errorum obsita Hyspania ante

[4] 1537: morte
[5] 1537: facti

apostolorum praedicatione*m* postea tales fructus siue in seculo siue in ecclesia parturiuit, quales futuros nunquam antea credidissent, quia haec mutatio dexterae excelsi, dent mihi tantis pro eodem omnipotentis Dei ac domini liberatoris cunctorum auxilio, fauore, & patrocinio mirabilem fortasse Indorum populum in hoc nouo mundo reperto futurum? Nunquid (ait Esaias) abbreuiata est manus Domini vt saluare nequeat: Quo tempore Sertorius in Hyspania apud semiferos homines Romanorum dux erat literas Hyspani et graecas & latinas nouera*nt* ab his nationibus subiugati, verum tame*n* est, quod si Hyspania proprias vires agnouisset (ait Trogus) nunquam Romanis colla dedisset, literas ergo Hyspani didicerant, verum tamen est, nec eorum linguam minus callebant, & semibarbari adhuc erant. Quid mirum, si miselli isti in extremo terrarum margine constituti, nullo cultorum hominum commertio, nullas usq*ue* hodie literas assecuti, beluarum instar essent, nullum animal habentes pro vectura ipsi aselli bipedes omnia ruri domiq*ue* vectitarent, nulla exterorum hominum notitia, nullo cultu, aut victu, aut vestitu, aliisq*ue* humanae vitae ornamentis pręditi, nullo literarum commertio, nullo vehiculorum aut nauigiorum usu, inculti essent ac pene barbari & c. Si omnibus his pręditi[6] Hyspani tales prisco tempore extitere: Quid de his desperandum: Cum de nobis a nostris minime// [p. 9] desperatum sit: Cum in ea regione tam illustres viri †evaserint in vtroq*ue* homines†[7]: Ecce *sic* benedicetur omnis homo qui timet d*o*min*u*m ait Psalmista: sequitur & videas filios filiorum tuorum, qui sunt homines noui mundi indiginae, q*ui* fide & virtutibus eos quorum sunt ministerio ad fide*m* conversi, forte superaturi sunt. Et quoniam eos penitus literas non didicisse praedixerim (palinodiam[8] cano) pingebant enim non scribebant, id est non literis sed imagini*b*us vtebantur: Siquidem absentibus seu tempore seu loco memorabile vellent significare: quod & Lucanus insinuat in haec verba.

Phoenices primi, famae si creditur ausi
Mansuram rudibus vocem signare figuris
Nondum flumineas Memphis contexere biblos
Nouerat, & saxis tantum, volucresq*ue* feraeq*ue*,
Sculptaq*ue* seruabant magicas animalia linguas.

Nunc vero tanta est ingenii eorum felicitas (de pueris loquor) vt & latine & Hyspane scribant, nostris pueris elegantius Latine sciant atq*ue* loquantur: non minus quam nostri qui se eius rei studio dedidere.

[6] 1537: hiis prędicti
[7] 1537: homine
[8] 1537: palanodiam

TRANSLATION

[p. 7] They have mastery of excellent reasoning, coherent sense, and thought, but the children of these people, above and beyond those of our own country, turn out to be pre-eminent in every aspect of action and intelligence, in their liveliness of spirit and in the alert dexterity of their responses. Concerning their ancestors I have heard that they were of a barbarous savagery and cruelty beyond any human limit, insofar as they were *anthropophagi*; that is to say they consumed the flesh of humans. They have been violent and bloodthirsty, but the more cruel and dreadful they have been, the more welcome may be the tribute that would be offered to God if they were to be converted. The greatest part of the gain to be made is up to us: if we conduct ourselves by word and example, with our hands and our tongues in the way that, if we had ended up in a similar situation, we would have wanted to have them treat us; we should toil to win their souls, for which Christ shed his blood. We object to their barbarism and idolatry as if the ancestors, from whom we ourselves originate, had been any better, until such time as the blessed apostle James preached to them and converted them to observance of the faith, turning them from the worst into the best. From then on there flashed forth so many luminaries of martyrs, learned men, and virgins whom it would take too long to survey—and it is not necessary. Who doubts that as a century passes there will be many of these Indians who will be very saintly, conspicuous in every virtue? Is it not the case that a deer that was thought to possess the gift of fortune telling was deployed by Sertorius when he was conducting campaigns in Spain? Indeed it was a hind, a dumb animal the Spaniards venerated as a// [p. 8] prophetess or fortune teller and goddess. The ferocity of the Spaniards was once so great that Silius Italicus, who came from the city of Italica in Baetica, pronounces this glorious eulogy of his very own ancestors:

> A people reckless of life, who readily hurry to death.
> When a man, past his years of strength and prime,
> Is impatient of longevity and spurns the advance of old age,
> He uses his own sword-arm to end the span of his life.[9]

On the testimony of Justinus (I am talking of pagan antiquity), Viriatus, whom Spain held as its most eminent ruler, was a cattleherd.[10] But after Christianity was adopted, we now possess through our faith true nobility in our inheritance: so many soldiers, so many glorious generals. By employing them as emperors Rome itself grew in a wondrous way, and was brought forward to become all that we have heard. If Spain was so uncivilized and overgrown with the thorns of error before the preaching of the apostles, but afterwards bore such fruit in the secular world and

[9] Silius Italicus, *Punica* 1.225–8.

[10] Justinus, *Epitome of Trogus*, 44.2.

in the church, such as they never before thought there would be, because a change was made by the hand of Him on high, my opponents should concede that, by the same help, favour, and protection of God and Lord, liberator of all, the people of the Indies in this newly discovered world might become wonderful in ways just as great. Has, as Isaiah says, 'the hand of the Lord become shortened so he cannot redeem'?[11] When Sertorius was in Spain among the half-wild inhabitants as general of the Romans, those ancient Spaniards had come to know of Greek and Latin writing, having been subjugated by those peoples. But it is true that if Spain had known her own strength (says Trogus), she would never have bowed her neck to the Romans.[12] The Spaniards had therefore learned the Romans' alphabet, and they were no less skilled in their language even though they were still semi-barbarians.

What wonder is it if these poor little ones on the farthest border of the world, having no dealings with educated people, having no understanding of letters until this day, should be like wild animals? They have no beasts of burden, but they themselves carry everything to and from the field and the home, like asses on two feet. They have had no word of other human beings, no education or any means of sustaining themselves or clothing, or other adornments of human existence, no dealings with letters, no use of vehicles or boats. What wonder is it that they should be uneducated, virtually barbarians, and so on? If those aforementioned Spaniards with all these advantages were such in a past age, why should we despair of these people? Since we// [p. 9] despaired not a bit about ourselves and since in that region there were such illustrious men, such people should emerge in both places. 'Behold thus shall be blessed the man that fears the Lord', says the Psalmist.[13] And he continues, 'Mayst thou see thy children's children'[14]: these are the human inhabitants of the new world, who are perhaps about to surpass in faith and in their virtues those by whose ministry they have been converted to the faith. Since I pronounced that the Indians have never learned literacy, I now sing a 'palinode': they used to paint instead of write. That is to say they used pictures instead of letters if ever they wanted to signify anything to those not present in the same time and place. Lucan also hints at it in these words:

The Phoenicians first presumed, if tradition is believed,
To seal their utterances for posterity in crude signs.
Not yet had Egypt learned to weave together river reeds,
And only birds and beasts and other animal designs
Conserved the speech of wise men for their needs.[15]

[11] Isaiah 50:2.

[12] Justinus, *Epitome of Trogus*, 44.5.8.

[13] Psalms 127:4.

[14] Psalms 127:6.

[15] Lucan, *Pharsalia* 3.220–4.

Now they are blessed with such great talent (I mean the young men) that they write in both Latin and Spanish. They know and speak Latin more elegantly than our own young men; and no less than our people who have devoted themselves to study of this subject.

Appendix 2.2: Juan Badiano, *Libellus de medicinalibus Indorum herbis*, Dedication and Coda, 1552

• Source: BADIANO, *Libellus* (1552), 1r–1v, 63r–63v
Library of INAH (National Institute of Anthropology and History), Mexico

2.2.1 Title and dedication

[1r] Libellus de medicinalibus Indorum herbis, quem quidam Indus Collegii sanctę Crucis medicus composuit, nullis rationibus doctus, sed solis experimentis edoctus. Anno domini seruatoris 1552: ~

Clarissimo domino Francisco de Mendoza, illustrissimi superioris huius Indię proregis domini Antonij de Mendoza filio optimo Martinus de la Cruz indignus seruus salute*m* precatur plurimam et prosperitatem.

CVm in te omnium uirtutum decora atque ornamenta & bonoru*m* munera, quę a quouis mortali desiderantur reluceant, domine magnificentissime, nescio profecto, quid in te potissimum laudem. Equidem non uideo, quibus laudibus efferam insignem uestrum amorem: quibus uerbis gratias agam uestro beneficio qu*am* maximo. Pater enim tuus, Vir christianissimus simul et piissimus, uerbis consequi nequeam qu*am* maxime omnium mihi benefecerit. Quicquid enim sum, quicquid possideo & quicquid nominis habeo, illi debeo. Nihil par nihilue dignum inuenire// [1v] possum illius beneficientię. Ingentes quidem gratias agere possum męcenati[16] meo: sed referre minime. Quam ob rem me, quantus[17] sum, offero, dedico, consecroque in mancipium. Neque uero ei soli, sed etiam tibi, mi Domine clarissime, obtestantissimum singularis amoris signum et testimonium. Non enim alia de caussa ut ego quidem suspicor hunc libellum herbarium et medicamentarium tantopere efflagitas quam ut Indos apud Sacrum Cęsaream Catholicam regia*m* maiestatem &si immeritos commendes. Vtinam librum regis conspectu dignum Indi faceremus, hic enim prorsus indignissimus est, qui ueniat ante conspectum tantae maiestatis. Sed memineris nos misellos pauperculos Indos omnibus mortalibus inferiores esse: & ideo ueniam nostra a natura nobis insita paruitas, & tenuitas meretur. Nunc igitur hunc libellum, quem tuo nomini, Vir magnificentissime, omni iure debeo

[16] 1552: mercenati

[17] 1552: quantus quantus

nuncupare, precor ut eo animo de manu seruuli tui suscipias quo offertur, aut quod non mirabor eijcias quo meretur. Vale. Tlatilulci. Anno Domini Seruatoris, 1552.

Tuae excellentię seruus addictissimus.

TRANSLATION

Booklet on the Indians' medicinal herbs, which an Indian physician of the College of Santa Cruz has compiled, one taught not by any systems but instructed by experimental results alone. In the year of our Lord and saviour 1552: ~

To the most renowned Don Francisco de Mendoza, excellent son of the most illustrious Proregent of this upper India, Don Antonio de Mendoza, Martín de la Cruz, his unworthy servant, wishes all health and prosperity.

Since the splendor and adornments of every virtue and the gifts of goodness desired by every mortal are reflected in you, most magnificent lord, I really do not know how to praise you of all people. Certainly I do not know what commendations I am to utter in praise of your extraordinary affection or with what words I am to give thanks for your boundless kindness. As for your father, a very religious and pious man, I am unable to put into words how he has benefited me most of all. Whatever I am, whatever I possess, whatever reputation I have, I owe to him. I can find nothing to equal or match// [1v] this benefit. I can declare a huge debt of gratitude to my patron, but I can hardly pay it back. For that reason, I offer, dedicate, and consecrate myself, all that I am, to his service. And not to him alone, but to you too, my most renowned master, I pledge myself as a sign and testimony of affection beyond compare. As I suppose, you are requesting this little herbal and medicinal treatise for no other reason than to commend the Indians, unworthy though they are, to his Sacred Caesarean and Catholic Royal Majesty. If only we Indians were to make a book worthy of the king's glance: this book is obviously very unworthy of coming before the glance of such great majesty. But bear in mind that we poor little wretched little Indians are inferior to all mortals, and our smallness and insignificance ingrained in us by nature therefore merits pardon. So now this little book, which I must by every principle dedicate to you, most eminent sir, I beg you to receive in the spirit in which it is offered from the hand of your little servant or else—and I will not wonder at this—cast it away to whatever place it deserves. Farewell. Tlatelolco, in the year of our Saviour, 1552.

A servant most bound to your excellency.

2.2.2 Juan Badiano, Coda to the reader

[63r] Juannes Badianus, interpres, candido lectori S.

Qvicquid operę in huius libelli herbarij qualicunq*ue* uersione a me collocatum est, Lector *praeter*quam optime, iterum atq*ue* iterum oro, boni consulito. Equidem malebam id laboris mihi perire, quam tuam censuram exactissimam subire. Porro compertum habeas me in hac editione aliquot succisiuas horas locasse non iactandi ergo ingenij, quod propemodum nihil est, sed obedientię tantum quam optimo iure debeo ęis huius Diui Jacobi hispanorum apostoli et patroni electissimi sacerdoti eidemq*ue* Antistiti admodum reuerendo patri franciscano fratri Jacobo de Grado, qui onus hoc meis humeris// [63v] imposuit. Vale in Christo Servatore. Tlatilulci in Sanctae Crucis Collegio Divę Marię Magdalenę sacratis ferijs. Anno ab orbe restituto Milessimo quingentessimo quinquagessimo secundo.

Finis libelli herbarij quem latinitate donauit Joannes Badianus, natione Indus, patria Xuchimilcanus eiusdem Collegij praelector.

Gloria semper ei sit cuius munere uerti,
Quem cernis librum, lector amice bone.

TRANSLATION

Juan Badiano, the translator, offers greetings to the fair reader.
Whatever effort I have put into the translation of this little herbal, such as it is, most eminent reader, again and again I beg you to look kindly on it. Indeed I would prefer that this work of mine came to nothing, than to subject it to your most exacting criticism. What is more, you should be well aware that I spent several spare hours on this publication—not to show off my talent, which is almost non-existent, but out of the obedience I owe rightly and properly to the very priest and Rector of this house of Saint James, apostle and most fitting patron saint of the Spanish, namely to the Reverend Father and Franciscan Brother Jacobo de Grado. It was he who placed this burden// [63v] on my shoulders. Fare well in Christ the Saviour. Tlatelolco, in the College of Santa Cruz, on the sacred Feast of Saint Magdalene. In the year one thousand five hundred and fifty-two from the restitution of the world.

End of the little herbal put into Latin by Juan Badiano, an Indian by race, a native of Xochimilco, and a teacher in the same College.

Glory to Him by whose gift I translated the book you behold, good friend and reader.

Appendix 2.3: Antonio Cortés Totoquihuatzin, Letter to Emperor Charles V, 1552

• Source: CORTÉS TOTOQUIHUATZIN, 'S. C. C. Majestati' (1552) Archive of the Indies, Seville: Patr. 184, 45

[p. 1]

1. *Sacrę Catholicę* Cęsareę Majestati Antonius cortes Rector populi de tlacoban[18] omnesq*ue* alij conciues humile seruitium impendunt.

Tam alta est tua Celsitudo, atque cesarea majestas, Cesar invictissime, vt vbique gentium non tam imperium longe lateque patens, quam illa tui animi *Xp*ianitas per omnium ora sonet in finesque orbis terrę divulgetur; ac non supremi imperij fidissimum custodem solum, sed & *Xp*ianae fidei, defensorem optimum esse, atque acerrimum propugnatorem contra vel gentilium vel hereticorum incursus omnes affirment.[19] Quo fit, vt in te verissimum illa sancti Job comprobemus: Nimirum Militiam hominis vitam esse super terram:[20] quippe tuum studium eo semper tendere videtur, quo gentes barbaras, ethnicos et demonum cultores, dei denique inimicos oppugnes, ac e tenebris in lucem *Xp*ianorum pellucidam in ipsum scilicet justiciae solem, qui *Xp*us omnium seruator est, educas, hosque victos pacifices, illustres, *Xp*o tandem lucrifacias. **2.** Quam Rem in nobis es foelicissime operatus, qui vbi per tuos hispanos, demonum agmen horrendum profligasti, et *Xp*ianismum introduxisti, nostram hanc prouinciam, pace, ac quiete summa collocasti, quae etsi majorum no*st*ror*um* stragem, bonorum temporalium jacturam non minimam doleat, tamen tuum immortale beneficium agnoscit quam humillime. Magna que ex parte sum*m*um et illud sane ineffabile gaudium nobis prouenit quod tibi vt pote imperatori inuictissimo, humanissimo, ac denique *Xp*ianissimo subjectos esse sciamus. Id quod consolationi maximae nobis est, nosq*ue* bono esse animo jubet, nec certe est, cur timeamus, literis cum tua cesarea majestate agere. Nam etsi abjectissimae conditionis homines censeamur, nulliusque precii apud hispanos videamur, tua tamen illa saepe experta lenitas, et animi candor, amorq*ue* vnicus, quem erga indigenas hactenus gessisti et geris, et te gestur*um* speramus, quo nostras causas atque nostri aflictiones, l*ite*ris, jam postq*ua*m non datur veras audire et reddere voces declaremus cogere videtur. **3.** Age ergo, pientissime imperator, nobis tuas patientissimas aures accommodare dignerjs, cum in dies nos gemamus ob ingentia grauamina quę nobis ex immoderatis tributis, et seruitiis multis prouenire constat, quibus nos jndi atterimur omnes, sed maxime nos tlacopanenses, quibuscum agitur pejus, miserius iniquiusque, quam vt excogitari possit. Quam Rem numq*ua*m nobis est datum declarare tuo sacro isti senatui, tum ob loci intercapedinem tum ob nullam nunciorum potestatem. Porro nacti temporis opportunitatem, fidissimumque quorumdam Religiosorum auxilium non omissimus quo minus literis istis explicaremus nostr*arum* miseri*arum* congeriem quam hic plorantes describimus, ea potissimum est de aflictione que e tributis, evenit quam, obsecramus, parumper equo animo accipere ne grauare:

[18] Here 'tlacoban' is uninflected, but 'tlacubam' (**13**) and 'tlacubae' (**15**) also occur; cf. 'tlacubanenses' (**12**), 'tlacopanenses' (**3**), and 'tlacopanensem' (**4**). Nahuatl pronunciation does not distinguish *o* from *u*, or the unvoiced *p* from the voiced *b*: Launey 2011, 3–8.

[19] 'ōēs affirmēt': addendum in left margin of ms.

[20] Job 7:1: militia est vita hominis super terram et sicut dies mercennarii dies eius.

4. ¶Ante omnia asserimus nullum alium populum tributo*rum* multitudine premi vehementer qu*am* nostrum populum tlacopanensem, qui a nostro commendatorio nomine Joanne Cano hactenus est grauatus tributis superfluis quę quotannis tribuimus, ab eo non solum sed etiam a filia moteçoma quam in vxorem habuit, que etsi nostri sanguinis nostraeq*ue* patriae fuit, tamen adeo ab humanitate aliena fuit vt pietatis loco et naturalis amoris quo sese vnius terrae et gentis homines ama*nt*, tyrannidem exercuerit: et nos qui a preclaris et nobilibus patribus sumus orti, loco seruorum tenuerit. **5.** Vtriq*ue*// [p. 2] horum octogessimo quoque die tribuimus sexcenta argenteorum pondo, viginti vestes, quas nauas, totidem vestes quas vipiles nostri voca*nt* hispani, et sindones viriles totidem, ac etiam totidem indica femoralia que hic apud nos vulgo mastiles appellantur. Preterea, quolibet die damus quinq*ue* gallinas indicas, quarum unaqueque stat duobus argenteis, et octo frumentorum onera, quorum vnum quodque duobus valet argenteis, etiam atque etiam nonnulla fructuum g*ene*ra que a nobis sum*mo* sudore queruntur,[21] comparanturque[22] sex argenteis. His addimus quatuor coturnices quas etiam duobus argenteis emimus, Necnon et ducentas placentulas nomine apud nos tortillas, onera lignorum etiam sex damus, et pabulorum decem, carbonum duo grandja onera, vnum fasciculum ted*arum* quas ocote vocant, candelas tres nigras †seu† huius terrae. Hęc quidem omnia singulis diebus tribuimus. Infine autem cuiuslibet anni, mille frument*orum* mensuras que hanegas vocantur, et semper quolibet anno, colimus duos agros pregrandes quibus colendis maxima fit populo aflictio.

6. ¶Dictus Ioannes Cano minime Contentus his duos hispanos locavit sibi custodes, vnum in suis hortis, alterum in suis prediis que sunt estanciae, quorum vnicuique vnoquoque die vnam gallinam damus precio duo*rum* argente*orum*, vnum lignorum onus, pipera multa que axi dicu*n*tur, dimidiam partem vnius orbis salis, et ducentas placentas, deniq*ue* his cum Joanne Cano quasi tribus comendatarijs seruimus:

7. ¶Nec his rebus fit satis illi, verum etiam viginti homines in sua domo seruiunt, qui sunt presto ad ejus jussa capescenda, quindecim etiam seruiunt in suis hortis, totidem occupandis in custodiendis ouibus et capris. Qui quidem homines in tantum labori seu potius seruituti addicuntur vt diebus festis et dominicis nec sacrum nec concionem, nec doctrinam *XP*ianam quam discendam a nobis obnixissime iubes, audire sinantur minime; itaque immemores suae anime salutis veluti pecora in montibus semper agunt atque in hortis. Etsi negotium quod illis est iniunctum non diligenter agunt, suis vestibus spoliantur, et q*ua*m pessime tractantur.

8. ¶Preterea, illis que taxata sunt in moderatione tributorum nobis concessa non est contentus, verum alia multa sua propria autoritate exegit atque eflagitauit a n*ost*ro populo. De qua re nos fuimus conquesti apud hunc senatum quem habent

[21] 1552: querutur [sc. quaeruntur]

[22] 1552: comparatur

Jllustrissimus Prorex d*omin*us lodouicus de velasco ac ceteri tui consiliarii, quibus nostris afflictionem audientibus et volentibus nos tributorum aliqua parte relevare, Dictus Joan[n]es Cano minime acquiescit, neq*ue* justiciam quam nobis faciunt admittit, sed negotium totum et causam ad tuam cesaream majestatem deferre vult, vt isthic terminetur et finiatur per istum senatum. Quod quidem si facit, erit nobis max*im*o incom*m*odo atque grauamine. Nam non poterimus isthuc adesse ob penuriam rerum maximam & loci intercapedinem quam maxime longam. Quamobrem supplicibus verbis petimus, vt, si isthic est finienda Causa nostra, fiat nobis tributorum noua moderatio que conformis sit n*os*trae pauperiej et numero nostri populi qui non attingere potest tria millia hominum etiam pueros numerando, ceterum oramus vt que preter moderationem tribus accepit Joannes tuo jussu restituat.

9. ¶Insuper non tantum excessit tributorum moderationem, sed etiam in tribus locis a nobis accepit, idq*ue* contra nostram voluntatem tres agros pregrandes latitudine sed maxima longitudine, vbi hortos fecit. Jn vno quidem atotoc nomine, parietes altos et domus multas easdemque superbas construximus multo sumptu pecunia*rum* nostra*rum*: pro quibus faciendis ne vnum quidem numisma soluit, et gen*er*a arbor*um* que in eo plantauimus, nos ipsi quesiuimus, et plantauimus et nutriuimus max*im*o labore. Hunc quidem hortum possederat prior maritus d*ominae* ysabel filiae moteçoma supra dictę: quo mortuo successit Joannes Cano et factus ejus maritus mordicus tenuit et tenet, et nobis eum petentibus respondet hunc agrum seu hortum suę mulierj deberi a suo patre moteçoma jure hereditario. Quod quidem q*ua*m falsum// [p. 3] sit plurimi testantur. Atq*ue* eam ob rem amore quem ad Deum †p*at*rem no*st*rum† geris iubeas[23] nobis concedi hunc agrum cum omnibus domibus factis a nobis.[24]

10. ¶In altero vt pote in agro nomine tetlolinca, quem abhinc octodecim annis accepit Joannes Cano, plantauit vites multas: quem quando accepit vtens dolo hęc verba nobis proposuit seu potius dedit. Scitis hispanos esse cupidissimos terrarum, atque ideo ne hunc agrum, vbi genera florum multa habetis, a vobis accipiant in eo plantabo vites causa conservandi eum: et quicquid fructus terra produxerit mihi vobiscum commune erit; et ager ipse semper vestri iuris sicut hactenus erit. hęc quidem dixit, tamen iam permultos annos dictum agrum possidet et non modo non ipsum agrum restituit, sed nec fructus terrę. Petimus ergo summopere vt hic ager malicia quada[m] acceptus nobis reddatur, cum is iuste nostro dominio debeatur.

11. ¶In vltimo loco nomine tepetlapan manet quidam ager minime sterilis, vbi multas arbores plantauimus et parietes altos circumduximus. Hunc quidem agrum iniustissime acceptum Joannes Cano abhinc iam quatuor decim annis volens ire

[23] 1552: ad deum p[ ]um ge[ ]is iubeas. Zimmermann 1970: ad deum patrem nostrum generis iubeas. Pérez-Rocha and Tena 2000: ad deum purum geris iubeas

[24] 1552: domibus deo factis a nobis

in hispaniam vendidit cuidam hispano no*min*e Joanni de Burgos, pro quo millia et ducenta pondo auri recepit. Petimus hunc etiam iussu tuę sacrę maiestatis nobis reddi cum iure ad nos pertineat qu*am* ad Joannem Canum.

12. ¶Audisti clementissime rex, nos tlacubanenses non modo multitudine tributorum grauari, sed et priuari nostris agris et alijs multis possessionibus. Nec locus esse videtur dicendi impresentiarum quot quantosque agros a nostro populo hispani acceperint et accipiant modo vbi vel hortos vel prędia faciant. Beneficiu*m* ergo nobis immortale fuerit idque quam maxime contendimus vt que tributa hactenus dedimus dicto Joanni Cano et suae vxori filiae mutecuçome, posthac sacrę maiestati demus et nos nostraque omnia in numero tuorum seruorum, qui tibi seu officialibus tuis tributa soluunt, habere digneris, et quod a tua pietate obtinere malumus est vt moderata sint omnia tributa et seruitia, que impendimus et vt id rectius fieri possit, oramus tuam clementiam, vt vir certe xrianus et probus nec no*n* et Indorum amans Jacobus Ramirez Visitator tuus mandato tuo ad nos veniat et proprijs oculis et tributa et seruitia videat, vt ipse iuxta nostrum modum post tandem tributa moderetur et populum nostrum seruitijs superfluis releuet, qui et videat an praedia omnia, dico estantia et horti omnes in nostro oppido manentes recte possideantur ab hispanis et a nostro Commendatorio Joanne Cano. Demum vt ipse iusticiam rectissimam nobis faciat. Qua in re vnicum nobis beneficium futurum est.

13. ¶Hic nonnulla adijcere licet quibus nostrum statum pristinum intelligas quibusq*ue* suasus facile nobis concedas que efflagitamus. primo quidem certiorem facimus tuam excelentissimam maiestatem has indias antiquis in temporibus fuisse diuisas in tres partes nimirum mexicum, tlacubam, et tetzcocum atq*ue* ex consequenti tres dominos seu rectores habuisse qui dominabantur aliorum populorum circumiacentium. Jd quidem cum notum sit hispanis impugnatoribus harum Jndiarum et potissimum religiosis, qui nobis sanctam Catholicam fidem declarauerunt, no*n* est quod pluribus exponamus. Quoniam igitur noster populus nunq*uam* seruiuit quin potius illi seruitus magna impensa est ab alijs: maximo nobis grauamini est quod tam inmoderata soluamus quotannis et (quod peius est) priuemur nostris terris et aliis possessionibus. Eam ob causam genibus flexis oramus vt nos tributis maxime releues et si fieri potest, vnum ex populis qui seruiebant nobis, nostro dominio ascribas, vt vel nos iuuet in dandis tributis, vel nostrae pauperiei succurrat. **14.** Hic silentio prętereundum no*n* est dictum Joannem Canum a nobis segregas[s]e tria oppida seu estancias vnam capoloac, aliam ocoyacac, tertiam tepeuexoyocam, que antiquis in temporibus ad nos pertinebant. Eas inquit Joannes Cano a tua inuictissima maiestate obtinuisse vt seorsum// [p. 4] seruirent et nobiscum vna minime soluerent tributa tamen cum hinc versus hispaniam est profectus dixit se illas petiturum a tuo senatu vt simul daremus tributa. Digneris mandare Joanni Cano vt illas seorsum no*n* habeat, sed simul annua tributa soluamus, quo mutuo nos releuemus tributis.

15. ¶Reliquum significo omni subiectione[25] et reuerentia ego tuus cliens humilis Anthonius Cortes meum patrem nomine totoquihuatzin fuisse pręsidem[26] et rectorem huius tlacubę tempore belli hispanorum qui sciens hispanos tuos cum domino Marchione Del valle iam venisse gauisus[27] est impendio et illis no*n* nulla munera misit et accedentes ad hoc nostrum oppidum obuijs[28] manibus, vt dicitur, recepit et res necessarias eis affatim ministrauit. Et sequentia verba Marchioni proposuit. **16.** Prosperrime veneris cum tuo exercitu sciasq*ue* nos tibi et ei cuius nomine venis esse paratos ad serviendum: et quem adoras deum eundem colam cum toto meo populo: Ecce tibi fanum deorum meorum destrue et ingredere illud et quicquid in eo inuentum tibi placuerit accipe et vtere. Pręterea hic sunt filie meę quas in vxores ducere possunt tui qui tecum veniunt vt e vobis nepotes et neptes nos*t*ras habeamus. Cęterum scias me nol[l]e gerere bellum contra te et tuum exercitum, ne meus populus male pereat, sed quod magis volo est quoniam sunt multę gentes mihi inimice nunq*uam* a me expugnatae maximum mihi juuamen fuerit si omnes nos debellemus. Hęc sunt quidem verba, inuictissime imperator que meus pater proposuit Marchioni, nec credas hec omnia a veritate abhorrere cum hec cum[29] hispani tum Jndi testentur. **17.** his addo dictum meum patrem sepe prohibuisse Muntecuhçomam mexici rectorem quo minus bellum gereret contra hispanos, tamen ipse mei patris admonitionem co*n*temnens parauit bellum. Porro hispani fugientes mexicum transiuerunt per hunc populum meum quibus quoniam cum illis inierat amicitiam rursum res necessarias victui largitus est et eos liberauit fame ingenti qua co*n*sumebantur vlteriusque progressi sunt post quorum recessum meus pater fuit mortuus no*n* quidem bello sed infirmitate quadam. Transeunte vno anno hispani redierunt mexicum contra quos ne bellum inirent mexicani eos obnixe alij filij patris mei qui mihi erant fratres, monuerunt, qui pro bono malum recipientes occissi sunt a mexicanis, quorum vnus vocabatur tepanecatzintli, alter tlacatecatzintli. **18.** Ex quibus omnibus colliges meos fratres mortem obijsse propter tuos hispanos et meum p*at*rem te recepisse vt pote dominum nec tibi in aliquo contra dixisse, quinpotius tuis semper seruisse ac perinde tibi. His omnibus fretus audeo implorare tuum auxilium ne ergo patere nos grauari tributis sed iube vt ad tuum imperium pertineat hic noster populus et minime ad Joan*n*em Cano et filiam Muntehcuçcome et horum filios a quibus sit satis nos perpessos fuisse ea que mala nobis intulerunt. Quo mentio facta de hispanis habeatur vera hic subijcio testium nomina que sunt Melchior Vasquez, Joannes Çacancatl, Gaspar tlacateuhtli, Balthasar, Benedictus, Thoribius, et alii multi homines hi omnes sunt Jndi, hispani vero sunt qui sequuntur Bernardinus De tapia.

[25] 1 Timothy 2:11: in omni subjectione

[26] 1552: pręsentem

[27] 1552: gauissum

[28] 1552: obijs

[29] 1552: tum

19. Et vt quae petimus in summa sint dicta, paucis Repitimus. primum et precipuum est, vt que tributa damus Joanni Cano, demus tuae sacrę majestati. 2^{m}. vt Visitator Jacobus Ramirez nostrum visitet populum, et taxet omnia tributa 3^{m}. vt Agros a Joanne et alijs hispanis acceptos jubeas nobis reddi: & qui in nostro oppido manent predia que nobis relinquant. Vltimum vt que extra tributorum moderationem accepit Joannes nobis restituat et premium laboris nostri quem habuimus in edificandis domibus quas non tenebamur construere, soluat nobis. Dat. Mexici & tlacoban, Kalendis decembris. 1552 a*nnos asi*

	antonius cortes	
melchior vasquez		geronymo de suero
//[p. 5]		
joannes çacancatl	benedictus	thoribius
Petrus de santamaria	Jacobus	Gaspar tlacateuctli
martinus	balthasar xolotecatl	michael

TRANSLATION

[p. 1] To his Holy, Catholic, and Caesarean Majesty, Antonio Cortés, Ruler of the people of Tlacoban, and all other fellow citizens render humble service.

1. So lofty is your eminence and Caesarean majesty, most invincible Caesar, that among peoples everywhere the Christian quality of your soul, as well as your empire stretching far and wide, sounds on the lips of all and is proclaimed to the ends of the earth; and all men affirm that you are not only the most faithful guardian of the highest empire, but also the best defender of the Christian religion and the most vigorous champion against the incursions of either pagans or heretics; this has led us to commend those words of the holy prophet Job [7:1] as very true in your case, without any doubt: 'The life of man upon earth is warfare', since your exertions seem always to be directed towards fighting against barbarous peoples, pagans and worshippers of devils, in a word, against God's enemies, then leading them from darkness to the clear light possessed of Christians, indeed to that very Sun of Righteousness [Malachi 4:2] which is Christ, saviour of all, and towards pacifying them once conquered, enlightening them, and at last winning them for Christ.

2. To this end you have laboured very happily among us: here by the agency of your own Spaniards you have overthrown the dreadful army of devils and introduced Christianity, in utmost peace and tranquility you have established our province, which has the humblest recognition of your immortal kindness, even though it may grieve at the slaughter of our elders and at the very great loss of our worldly wealth. To a large degree, our knowledge that we are subject to the most invincible, the most humane, and in fact most Christian of emperors, is the source of a great and clearly inexpressible joy to us. This is of very great reassurance to us; it bids us be in good spirits as we certainly have no reason to be afraid of engaging in correspondence with your Caesarean majesty. For though we may be judged to be humans of the lowest condition and may be seen to be of no worth in the eyes of Spaniards, your oft-proven gentleness and goodwill and the singular affection which you have so far shown and still show to native people, and which we hope you will show again, seems to compel us to declare our pleas and afflictions in writing, now that we are no longer granted the opportunity to hear and respond to your actual words in person.

3. So then, most pious of Emperors, deign to lend us your most patient ears, since from one day to another we are groaning because of the huge and weighty burdens that, it is recognized, come upon us from excessive tribute and much servitude by which all of us Indians are worn down, but especially we Tlacopaneca, for whom conditions are worse, more wretched, and unfair than could be imagined. This was a matter which it was not granted to us to declare to your sacred Council, because of the remoteness of its location and because we had no power to send delegates. Wherefore benefiting from the opportunity of the moment and from the very loyal support of certain friars, we have not failed to set out in this letter the mass of misfortunes that we lament as we describe them here, the most pressing of which is the hardship that has resulted from the tribute. We beg you to hear us briefly on this subject and not be annoyed:

4. Before all else, we affirm that no other people is so severely oppressed by such a multitude of tributes as our people of Tlacopan, which up to now has been burdened with excessive annual payments by our *encomendero*, Juan Cano by name—and not only by him but also by Montezuma's daughter whom he took for a wife. Even though she was of our own blood and native land, she was herself so remote from fellow feeling that instead of the duty and natural love that men of the same race and country usually show to one another, she exercised tyranny and kept us in the position of slaves, when we were born of renowned and noble parents. **5.** To each of these two,// [p. 2] every eighty days, we pay six hundred silver pesos, twenty garments, which the Spaniards call *naguas*, the same number of what our people call *huipiles*, the same number of finely woven male garments, and the same number again of Indian loincloths, which among us here are commonly named *mastiles*. In addition, on any day, we give five Indian hens, each one of which costs two silver pesos, and eight weights of grain each worth two silver pesos, and over and above that, very many types of produce that are sought with the greatest of effort and bought for six silver pesos. To those things we have to add four partridges, which we actually buy for two silver pesos, and furthermore two hundred of the little pancakes we name *tortillas*; we also give six loads of wood, ten of fodder, two large loads of charcoal, a bundle of the pitchpine torches that are called *ocote*, three black candles, which are of this land. So we pay all these things as tribute each day. And at the end of every year we give a thousand measures of grain, which are called *hanegas*, and always in any given year we cultivate two huge fields, the cultivation of which is a very great hardship imposed on the people.

6. The aforementioned Juan Cano, not happy with this, positioned one of his two Spanish guards in his gardens, and the other on the farms that are his estates. To each of them on each day we give one hen worth two silver pesos, one load of wood, many peppers that are called *axi*, half of a wheel of salt, and two hundred tortillas, so that we provide service to these men along with Juan Cano, as if we had three *encomenderos*.

7. Not even those provisions are enough for him, as twenty men serve in his house ready to take his orders, another fifteen provide service in his gardens, and the same number are employed in guarding his sheep and goats. Those men are bound to so much work—or rather servitude—that on holy days and Sundays they are hardly ever allowed to hear the sacred rites, sermons, or the Christian doctrine that you very strenuously bid us learn, and so they are unmindful of the salvation of their souls; rather like cattle they always live in mountains and gardens. And if they do not diligently go about this work which is imposed upon them, they are robbed of their clothes and treated in the worst way possible.

8. Furthermore, he is not happy about what has been calculated in the assessment of the tributes granted to us—he has actually used his own authority to exact and demand forcefully many other things from our people. We had complained about that matter before the council held by the most illustrious Viceroy Don Luis de Velasco and your other councillors who heard of our hardship and wanted to relieve us of our tribute to some degree. But the said Juan Cano does not at all assent, nor does he accept the judgements they are making on our behalf, but wants to refer the whole business and the plea to your Caesarean majesty, to be concluded there and settled by your Council. It will cause us great hardship and trouble if he indeed does this, as we will be unable to go there and attend, owing to the great scarcity of our resources and to the distance of the location, which is as far away as it could possibly be. For that reason with our humble words we ask, if our case is to be settled there, that the new rate of our tribute may be made in line with our poverty and the number of our community, which cannot come near three thousand men, even counting the boys. We also plead that Juan may, at your bidding, return what he has received in three [places] that is above the rate.

9. What is more, not only has he gone beyond the rate for our tributes, but he has also received from us in three locations—and this against our will—three fields colossal in breadth and also great in length, which he has made into gardens. In fact, in one of them named Atotoc we built high walls and many houses, magnificent ones, spending a lot of our own money: he did not spend a single coin for these things to be done, and the varieties of trees we planted on the site, we ourselves sought out, planted, and nurtured with a great deal of work. The previous husband of the aforementioned doña Isabel, the daughter of Montezuma had owned this garden, and on his death, Juan Cano, becoming her husband and his successor, held and holds fast to this property, and when we ask him for it he replies that this field or "garden" was legally due to his wife as an inheritance from her father Montezuma.// [p. 3] Very many attest to how untrue this is. So on that account with the love you bear to God, first may you order the field with all the homes we made to be granted to us.

10. Another case is that of the territory named Tetlolinca, which Juan Cano received eighteen years ago and planted with many vines.[30] When he took it using his trickery, he put to us, or rather left us with, these deceitful words: 'You know the Spaniards are very covetous of land, and because of this, so that they do not take from you this field where you grow many kinds of flowers, I will plant vines in it in order to keep it. Whatever produce the land brings forth will be common to me and to all of you; and the territory will always be yours by rights as it has been up to now.' That is what he said, but for many years he has been in possession of the said area and not only has he not given back the territory itself, but he has not given us any of the produce from the land either. We therefore earnestly beg that this territory, taken by a cunning kind of malice, be returned to us, since it is rightly due to come under our ownership.

11. In the last place called Tepetlapan there is still a very fertile field, where we planted many trees, and we built high walls around it. Juan Cano most unjustly took this field fourteen years ago now, and as he wanted to go to Spain, sold it to a certain Spaniard by the name of Juan of Burgos: he received one thousand two hundred gold pesos for it. We ask that this too be returned to us by the order of your sacred majesty, since by rights it belongs to us rather than to Juan Cano.

12. You have heard, most merciful king, that we Tlacopaneca are not only being weighed down with a multitude of tributes, but also being deprived of our fields and many other possessions. It does not seem to be the place to speak at the present time of how many and how large are the lands the Spaniards have taken, and still take, where they make either gardens or farms. It would therefore be an immortal kindness to us, and one that we are striving for to the utmost, from now on to give to your sacred majesty the tributes, which, up to now, we have given to the said Juan Cano and his wife the daughter of Montezuma, and that you may deem us and all our own worthy of being in the number of your servants, who pay tribute to you and your officials, and what we choose to obtain from your piety is that all the tributes and services we provide may be kept within due limits; and so that it may be possible for this to be done more rightly, we beg your mercy, that a man undoubtedly Christian and upright as well as very much a lover of the Indians, Jacobo

[30] Tetlolinca (now San Lorenzo Totolinga, Naucalpan) was subject to Tlacopan: *Memorial de los pueblos* (1550s), 1 [1970, 5].

Ramírez, may come to us by your decree as your Visitor, to see with his own eyes the tributes and services we provide; so that in accordance with our own measure, he may henceforth assess our tribute and relieve our people from excessive service; and so that he should see whether all the farms (I mean the estates and all the gardens left in our town) are rightly held by the Spaniards, and by our *encomendero* Juan Cano: finally that he should render us the justice that is most correct. In this matter the benefit to us is something that would be unparalleled.

13. Here we may add some things through which you may understand our former state and by which you may be easily persuaded to grant us what we ask. In the first place, then, we inform your most excellent majesty that in former times these Indies were divided into three parts, namely Mexico, Tlacuba, and Texcoco, and as a consequence they had three lords or rulers who ruled the other surrounding peoples. Now since that is known to the Spanish invaders of these Indies and especially to the religious men who declared the Catholic faith to us, there is no need to relate the matter in more words. Since therefore our own people was never in servitude, but, rather, great service was paid to it from others, it is the greatest of burdens to us that we should pay such excessive tribute every year and (what is worse) be deprived of our lands and other possessions. For that reason, on bended knee we pray that you relieve us from our tribute to the greatest degree, and, if it can be arranged, that you allocate to our dominion one of the peoples who used to be in our service, either to help us in paying tributes or ease our poverty. **14.** At this point the fact should not be passed over in silence that the aforementioned Juan Cano took three towns or estates away from us: one was Capoloac, another Ocoyacac, and the third Tepeuexoyocan, which in former times used to belong to us. Juan Cano said that he had obtained these from your most invincible majesty// [p. 4] to render service separately, and not at all to pay tribute jointly with ourselves. But when he went from here and set off for Spain, he said he would seek those estates from your Senate, so that we should pay our tribute jointly. May you deign to command Juan Cano not to possess those estates separately, but ensure that we provide our annual tribute together, so that we might mutually have some relief from making payments.

15. One remaining thing that I, your humble subject Antonio Cortés, should point out in all submissiveness and reverence is that my father, Totoquihuatzin by name, had been chief and ruler of Tlacopan at the time of the war with the Spaniards. Knowing that your Spaniards had already come with their commander the Marquis del Valle, he greatly rejoiced, sent several gifts to them and, as they approached this town of ours, he welcomed them, as the saying goes, 'with open arms' and provided all that they needed in abundance. He then proposed the following to the Marquis: **16.** 'May your arrival with your army be most auspicious, and may you know that we are prepared to serve you, and him in whose name you come. Along with my people I will worship the same god you revere. Here you have the shrine of my gods: destroy it; go in and take and make use of anything you find there that you like. Furthermore, here are my daughters—the men who have come with you can take them as wives, so that we may share grandsons and granddaughters. In any case, you should know that I have no wish to wage war against you and your army, lest my people come to a bad end. Rather there is something I want far more: since there are many nations hostile to me that I have never managed to defeat, it would be a very great help to me if we could subdue them together.' Those are the very words, invincible emperor, which my father put to the Marquis and you should not think that any of these things that both Spaniards and Indians attest are inconsistent with the truth. **17.** To that I add that my aforementioned father often tried to prevent Montezuma, the ruler of Mexico, from campaigning against the Spaniards, but in defiance of my father's warning he nonetheless prepared for war. What is more, the Spaniards fleeing Mexico passed through this community of mine, which, as it had already entered into an alliance with them, again supplied them with all the things they needed to survive, and freed them from the severe hunger that was devastating them, and they made further advances. After their departure, my father died, not actually in combat, but of an illness. One year went by and the Spaniards returned to Mexico, and the Mexicans were strenuously warned not to enter into a war against them by my father's other sons, who were my brothers. Receiving an evil return for their good deed my brothers were killed by the Mexicans: one was called Tepanecatzintli, and the other Tlacatecatzintli. **18.** From all this, you will gather that my brothers met their end for the sake of your own Spaniards and that my father welcomed you indeed as his lord, and did not contradict you in any respect, but rather always served your own people in the same way as he served you. Counting on all this, I presume to beg your help, so that you do not suffer us to be weighed down by tributes, but bid this district of ours belong to your empire and not at all to Juan Cano and the daughter of Montezuma and their sons from whom we have suffered enough with the ills they have inflicted on us. In order that the mention made of the Spaniards be deemed true, I append here the names of witnesses: Melchior Vasquez, Juan Xacancatl, Gaspar Tlacateuhtli, Balthasar, Benedicto, Toríbio, and many other men. These are all Indians, but there are Spaniards too, whose names follow: Bernardino de Tapia.

19. And so that what we ask for may be summed up, we ask for it again in a few words. First and foremost is that we may give to your sacred majesty the tributes we give to Juan Cano. Second, that the Visitor Jacobo Ramírez may come to our people and reckon the value of all our tributes. Third, that you order the lands taken by Juan and the other Spaniards to be given back to us and that those who reside in our town give up the estates which are ours. The last is that Juan restore to us whatever he has received in excess of his tributes, and pay us the price of the work we put into building houses we were not obliged to construct. Signed in Mexico and Tlacoban, on the Kalends of December 1552, as follows:

Antonio Cortes

Melchior Vasquez Geronimo de Suero

//[p. 5]

Juan Xacancatl Benedicto Toribio

Petrus de Santamaria Jacobo Gaspar Tlacateuctli

Martín Balthasar Xolotecatl Michael

Appendix 2.4: Rulers of Azcapotzalco, Letter to Philip II of Spain, 1561

• Source: VALERIANO, 'Inuictissimo Hispaniarum Regi' (1561)
Archive of the Indies, Seville: Legajo Mexico, 1842

[p. 1]

Inuictissimo Hispaniarum Regi ac V. Caroli
Imperatoris heredi felicissimo Philippo Azcaputzalcani
omnium infimi famuli su*m*mam
felicitatem comprecant*ur*.

Superbum ac pene improbum cuiq*ue* videbitur, Felicissime Rex, nos o*mn*ium infimos ad te inter homines supremum regem l*itt*eras destinare, ad quem non sat firmo animo scribere solent qui vel regia dignitate vel eruditione varia sunt insigniti. At cum nos mancipia et quidem humillima simus, & l*itt*eras siue diuinas siue humanas necdum a limine salutauerimus, annon temerarium omnino fuerit nos scribere non ad principem quemq*uam* sed ad te talem ac tantum Regem? Vt etiam si tuos seruos vltro nos offeramus vix digni iudicemur; Qui enim aut quales sumus? Nempe pauperes, miseri, barbari, tales deniq*ue* quorum predecessores suę tempore gentilitatis fuere admodum rustici, abiecti, nudi et corporis et animę dotibus, inter quas primas habent virtutes ac l*itt*erę, quas profecto ne per somnium quidem nouere. Cum hęc omnia veritate sint fulta, quid faciundum censes? Nunq*uam* ne indis audendum cum Principe, Rege ve, aut Imperatore? Imo vero, audendum q*uam* maxime, ne extremę pusillanimitatis esse credamur, et siqua est animis insita timiditas, est procul abigenda, audaces enim fortuna iuuat, timidosque repellit. Adhęc ausum non minimum prestat id quod l*itt*eris est proditum, nimir*um* principes non christianos solum, verum et ethnicos in suos subditos fuisse mites, benignos, clementes: eosdemque in suis querellis aut quibusuis petitionibus lubentissime audisse. Cui rei argumento est Adrianus Imperator, et is pro multis vn*us* sufficiet, qui transiens in itinere a muliere quadam rogatus vt eam audiret, cum respondisset sibi ocium non esse, audiuit ab ipsa muliere: Noli ergo imperare: tum conuersus ęquissimo animo eam audiuit. A quo te absimilem credere nefas esse ducimus, quippe qui sis adeo benignus, humanus, pius cum erga cęteros cuiusuis status et ordinis homines tum erga nos indigenas: in quibus tua pietas non tam verbis qu*am* factis est declarata. Qua re tua pietate freti modeste magis q*uam* audacter tuę Cęsareę Maiestati, quę animum ad scribendum impellere[31] breuitate qu*am* maxima fieri// [p. 2] potuerit proponemus, quę omnia in ordinem redigentur quo clarius distinctiusque cognosci queant quę a tua clementia consequi conamur.

[**1**] Primum. Si quid est quod nostrum satis male animum habeat, est, qu*od* nostrum oppidum, cuius fines terrar*um* quondam longe lateq*ue* protendebantur modo intra angustos et arctos contineatur. Quod mirum alicui videri non debet, cum hispani non solum, sed et nostrę nationis homines nobis confines maximam agrorum partem, ex his qui ceu res hęreditarię ab auis atauisque nostris sunt relicti, per nefas vsurparint. Neque vero nobis multum reclamantibus vnquam bene successit, partim quia pecuniis destitueremur partim qu*ia* comendatarius esset semper absens, qui erat Franciscus de montero, prouincię Yucatanę preses. Sed quorsum hec? Certe vt intelligas tlacubanenses impresenti*arum* multos ex n*ost*ris agris habere iniuste: De quibus etsi abhinc duodeuiginti annis aut eo plus inter nos et illos est mota lis apud senatores non fuit tamen decisa: quod sane incurię non est ascribendum sed morborum variis generibus quę illis annis in Indos crassabantur simul et comendatarij absentię. Porro eos iure hereditario ad nos pertinere clare indicat caussę liber, quę tunc temporis est acta. Eiusdem rei est luculentissimus testis Licen*tia*tus Ceynos qui nuper ab hispania in hanc regionem se rursum recepit. Necnon et noster qui est hoc tempore comendatarius Licen*tia*tus Maledonatus, qui preses Insulę sancti Dominici fuit, qui tuam Cęsaream Maiestatem certiorem efficiet non modo per ea quę de hoc negotio a fide dignissimis didicit sed etiam per quasdam terrarum descriptiones. Ac proinde vbi caussam optime noris, per eum quem in Deum Opt. Max. geris purum amorem, mandare digneris vt nobis restituantur. Atq*ue* hęc satis de primo.

[**2**] Secundum. In picturis quibusdam quas isthuc transmittimus invenire licet, hispanos multos sibi, iure an inuria ipsi viderint, predia multa accepisse intra ipsos quos tam arctos limites modo habemus, nec sine nostrorum damno et incommodo, quippe aut ab eis aut ab eorum famulis sepenumero maletractentur, pręcipue dum vel n*ost*ros terminos obseruare laboramus aut ab eis quas habent pecudes tempore sementis abigimus. Quare ne quispiam alius hispanus posthac predium aliquod rursum accipere audeat, a tua Clementia summopere contendimus vt quępiam regia cedula tuę Cęsareę Maiestatis chyrographo munita ad nos transmittatur in defensionem simul et conservationem terminor*um*, quibus nostri oppidi agri concluduntur.

[31] 1561: impullere

[3] 3.ᵐ Quoniam seruitia publica quę mexici impenduntur aut templis struendis aut excolendis hispanorum agris magnę vexationi nobis extant et eo vsq*ue* vt nulla transeat hebdomada quin in ea multi ex nobis (cum tamen perpauci simus) adhęc seruitia impendenda distribuantur, triginta quidem ad structionem ecclesię Diui Dominici, viginti vero ad hispanorum predia, decem autem ad Ędem sacratissimę Virginis archiepiscopalem, quinque etiam ad templum (quod vulgo guadalope dicitur) virginis Marię; inde fit vt ecclesiam quam iam a multis annis inceptam habemus, ad finem vsq*ue* protrahere minime valeamus, sed nec impresentiar*um* incipere monachorum// [p. 3] monasterium, qui in quibusdam domibus satis humilibus commorantur apud nos. Quare a tua Clementia suppliciter petimus vt spacio annorum aliquot ab omnibus seruitiis publicis immunes relinquamur, donec et ecclesiam et monasterium perstruamus. Adhęc quoniam in animo est nostram gentem dispersam in vnum coadunare, ędiculasque nostras callibus ornare quo humanus cultus qui Xp*isti*anitatis basis magna videtur in nobis regnet et barbaries ipsa iamiam exulet, suplicamus terq*ue* quaterq*ue* non nobis denegetur petitum.

[4] 4.ᵐ Etsi n*ost*rum oppidum est modo exiguum, verumtamen olim non fuit minima prouincia inter alias quas sane excellebat antiquitate & nobilitate. Antiquitate quidem, Nam antiquorum annales edocent conditum fuisse abhinc millessimo quingentessimo vigessimo quinto anno. Nobilitate vero, quia qui vbiq*ue* populorum sunt nobiles seu ingenui suam traxisse originem ex Azcaputzalco vniuersi vno ore fatentur. Atq*ue* eam ob rem, quos terrarum terminos habebat trium dier*um* itinere ex omni parte comprehendebantur. Pręterea quicquid in montibus continetur, qui circumiacent oppido n*ost*ro, totum erat in vtilitatem nostram nemine obstante, nam trabes, tabulas, ligna acapna et lapides cedere,[32] etiam precio nullo soluto cuicumq*ue* licebat. Post vero, non incuria nostra, sed tyrannide potius tlacubanenses cum reliquis oppidulis, quę circumiacent et syluas cedreas & lapidicinas ita sibi ascripserunt vt iam nulli nostrorum liceat quicquam ex eis cedere: quamqu*am* persoluamus precium simul et ad id faciendum regii senatus Mexici schędulas habeamus. Quocirca a tua Clementia submisse postulamus vt quemadmodum abhinc viginti annis communes nobis erant una cum aliis ita sint in posterum; nec quisquam ad cedendum aut trabes aut lapides inhibeat, qua in re authoritatem tue Cesaree Maiestatis exoptamus.

[5] 5.ᵐ Nostrum oppidum fuisse quondam prouinciam et quidem magnam in testimonium complurima adduci possunt: inter quę hęc duo pręcipua existimamus. Vnum quidem, quod constet liquido satis populos multos vectigales habuisse quorum oppida hęc ferme fuere: Quauhnahuac, Tetelpa, Xilotepec, Matlatzinco, Cohuatepec, Cempohualla, Nanacapa, quę quidem omnia annua tributa pendere tenebantur, idque antequam a Marchione Cortesio prouincia Mexicana expugnaretur. Alterum, quod ex eo tanqu*am* ex fonte vberrimo deriuata sint non pauca oppida quę prius

[32] Sc. cędere (caedere)

non erant nisi colonię ductę a domino n*ost*ri oppidi qui Dicebatur, Teçoçomoctli, dominus profecto generosissimus, ditissimus & (quod maius est) vita longissimus qui secundum antiquorum memoriam vixisse fertur centum et sexaginta sex annis: nec plures esse annos pręterqu*am* centum et triginta tres ex quo e uiuis concessit. Hic itaq*ue* coloniis a se factis in dominos pręfecit suos filios quos perplures habuit; nam maiorem filium moriens hic suo loco substituit dominum et hęredem nomine, Ylhuicamina. Atq*ue* vt rem paucis aperiamus. Mexicani cum oppugnati fuere ab azcaputzalcanis iuxta montem no*min*e, Chapoltepec, in quem prius applicuere ex longa ac diutina peregrinatione, postea errabundi hinc inde pellebantur ignorantes omnino quem locum ad habitandum eligerent: eos miseratus dictus, Teçoçomoctli, ea in parte loci vbi nunc est, Tenuchtitla, collocandos// [p. 4] mandauit. Qui quidem mexicani octoginta annis seruiere oppido n*ost*ro ei pro tributo persoluendo quę ex lacu capere poterant pisces, ranas, anseres, aliaq*ue* id genus aquatilia. Inter quos tandem orta nescio qua dissensione qui a communi consortio desciuere vocati sunt, tlatilolcani, a quodam terre aggere in medio lacus posito in quem transiere amissa iam amicitia. Quibus iam segregatis a mexicanis dominus Teçoçomoctli dedit in primatem et rectorem filium appellatum Quaquapitzahuac. 2.a colonia est vocata, Tlacuba, cuius colonis idem dominus Teçoçomoctli duos filios constituit, vnum no*min*e Aculnahuacatl, alterum vero, Tzaqualcatl: quibus mortuis reliqui coloni in nostrum oppidum proditores extitere vtpote qui dolo et fraude dominium azcaputzalcanor*um* sibi vindicarint. Vnde est factum vt nunc videatur prouincia Tlacuba, cum prius tamen fuerit colonia facta a Teçoçomoctli. 3.a est dicta, Coyohuaca, vbi fuit dominus Maxtlato. 4.a est, atlacuihuaya, vbi fuit dominus Yepcohuatl. 5.a Huitzilopochco, cuius dominus fuit Yztachecatl. 6.a cohuatlayauhca nunc Mexico subiecta, eius dominus fuit, Tecocohua. 7.a est Tultitla, cuius dominus fuit Tepanonoc. 8.a est Tepechpa, cuius primas fuit Quahquauhtzi. 9.a est Aculma, vbi dominus est factus Teyolcocohua. 10.a est Tulquauhyoca, cuius dominus fuit Teuhtlehuac. 11.a est Cuitlachtepec, vbi fuit domina filia nomine Xocotzi, 12.a est Chiappa, vbi fuit domina filia nomine, tomiyauh. 13.a est Ayotochco, cuius dominus fuit Yohuallatohua. 14.a est Oztoticpac, dominus cuius fuit Tlacacuitlahua. 15.a est quecholac, vbi fuit domina alia filia. Quę omnia clariora euadent ex pictura quadam, vbi hę colonię describuntur simul et nomina filiorum Teçoçomoctli qui dominati sunt singulis coloniis. Caussa vero, quare hęc in medium adducamus est vt nostrum hoc oppidum quod iam monstrauimus prouinciam fuisse quondam nomine Ciuitatis donetur a tua Clementia.

[**6**] 6.[m] Penes nos sunt iam a multis annis quędam n*ost*ri oppidi insignia, quę quominus ab aliquo irrita credantur confirmanda tua Cęsarea authoritate maxime volumus, quippe optime n*ost*rę Reipub. statum declarant. Inprimis depingitur formica, nec abs re, quia a formica suum sortitur nomen nostrum oppidum: Paries vero qui turris pinnas videtur habere muros quorumdam mercatorum signat, fortissimos sane, quos tamen ob suam egregiam fortitudinem maiores nostri solo equauere. Deinde subsequitur cor, quod quidem quemadmodum est vitę fons et origo, ita

nostrum oppidum fuit origo totius nobilitatis quę in populis huius nouę hispanię est dispersa. Huic connectitur ornamentum quod simile Episcoporum thiarę videtur, tali namque insigniebantur priscis temporibus Indorum domini. Super hęc omnia est crux, significans crucem Domini, quam asiaticis prędicauit philippus Dei Apostolus, cui quidem in honorem ecclesia huius oppidi est dicata.

[7] 7.^{m} Haud nobis est obscurum diuinum illud oraculum: Sapientia cor stabilit, ventis pondus ponit. Ex quo clarissimum omnibus redditur l*itt*era*rum* cognitione Xp*ist*ianorum corda in fide maxime corroborari, atque hos qui aliquando gentilitatis ventis agitati fuere, pondus in sua christianitate habere. Porro cum in nobis recens sit plantata vitę arbor verę vitalis, ipsa videlicet fides catholica, quę vt altius radices mittat, nostro oppido conuenientissimum iudicamus nos etiam mus*arum* domo donari debere, quam vt in hoc n*ost*ro oppido fundare valeamus, copiam a tua Cęsarea Maiestate expetimus, vbi etsi// [p. 5] scientiarum o*mn*ium genera edoceri non debeat, at certe Grammatica cum lingua hispana quę commodius pręlegi possunt a quibusdam nostris qui sermonem latinum perinde ac hispani sępe sunt professi.

[8] 8^{m}. Ante hispanorum aduentum mercatum quem, *tianquizco*, vocamus alibi q*uam* in n*ost*ro oppido fuisse semper habitum, qui ambigat est nemo, qui ab omnibus ita frequentabatur, vt non tam certis quam continuis diebus in eo venderentur varie merces, ac pene infiniti serui atque captiui, qui hoc in loco solum venui exponebantur. Postea vero, ita est factum, vt oppidum quodque vel minimum sua propria authoritate mercatum iam habeat, atque apud nos mercatus iam non fiat, nisi dumtaxat die vno qualibet hebdomada, *scilicet* die sabbati, quod est in omnium detrimentum. Ideoque tuam Cęsaream Maiestatem testamur atque obsecramus, vt mercatus qui hoc in loco celebrabatur quotidie, adminus duobus diebus habeatur, die Martis et die iam pręfixo.

Habes iam, Xp*ist*ianissime Rex, quę a tua summa clementia obtinere desideramus, quę etiam quia iusta, quia honesta, quia vtilia, eadem vt concedantur nobis hortari possunt. Neque vero quicq*uam* dehortetur nostra omnium vilitas & paupertas, qui licet Iro pauperiores atq*ue* alga viliores simus: sumus tamen *Sacrę Catholicę Cęsareę Magestatis* serui fideles atq*ue* iam in christianorum albo relati per fidem Catholicam atq*ue* sacri baptismatis alio*rum*q*ue* sacramentorum susceptionem. Quę res sola caussa sufficiens esse potest quominus in nostris petitionibus nobis deesse possis, quia Christianissimus, quia maxime potens, quia natura liberalissimus. Ne vero modum seu septa vt dicitur epistola transiliat, iam hic finem capiet, si tamen subiecero fuisse in votis ad hispaniam duos ex nobis mittere qui negotia declarare possent, sed per Proregem non licuit nec super ea re plus molesti esse voluimus, quod sciremus te etiam idem nolle. Qua de caussa visum est has l*itt*eras destinare quibus sane vltra iam humiliter petita, etiam a Deo Opt. Max. tuę Cęsareę Maiestati precamur vitam longeuam, regna ampla in terris & gloriam semper duraturam in celis. Datę Azcaputzalci, quarto Idus Februarii, Anno vero a Xp*ist*o nato Quingentessimo sexagessimo primo supra Millessimum.

Tuę S. C. C. Magestatis

Infimi seruj

// [p. 6]

don hernando de molina governador		Don baltasar hernandez governador	
Po. zacharias alcalde		Pedro dionisio alcalde	
Antonio Valerjano		Fran.co Placido	Fran. delos angeles
Diego de s. filipe Regidor	pedro garçia Regidor	Fran. chalcocalqui Regidor	Martin gano Regidor
Don Martin de. s. matheo	Martin de.s.to domingo	Martin de sa. miguel	

// [p. 7]

*A la S. C. C. M. del inuictissimo rey nro señor don Filipe, en los reynos de Esp. Es del pu*º *de azcapoçalco para su Magestad.*

TRANSLATION

[p. 1]

To the invincible King of both Spains, Emperor Charles V's
most fortunate heir, Philip,
the Azcapotzalca, servants most lowly of all
wish the utmost happiness.

It will seem to anyone proud, if not ill judged, that we, the most lowly of all, are sending a letter to you as the supreme king among men, to whom even those endowed with royal rank or a range of erudition do not write in too confident a spirit. But as we are vassals and indeed of the most insignificant sort, and as we have not yet greeted the realm of letters, whether divine or human, even from the threshold, is it not altogether rash for us to write to any prince, let alone to a king such as yourself, so great, that even if we offer ourselves as your slaves of our own accord we may scarcely be judged worthy? Who, then, or what are we? Nothing but paupers, wretches, barbarians, such as whose forebears in the time of their paganism were altogether rustics, abject, bare of endowments for body and soul, amongst which the virtues and letters hold first place: things they did not even know in their dreams. Since this is all grounded on truth, what do you judge we should do? Should the Indians never dare to speak with a prince, king, or emperor? On the contrary, we must so dare to the utmost, in order not to be believed cowardly in the extreme—and if there is any timidity ingrained in our mind we should drive it far away, since Fortune helps the bold and drives back the fearful. Daring this is very well supported by what is shown in literature: there is no doubt that not only Christian princes but pagan ones, too, have been lenient, kind, and merciful to their own subjects and they have been very willing to hear their complaints or suits of every kind. The emperor Hadrian is proof of this principle and this one figure will serve for many. On a journey he was making he was asked by a certain woman to hear her: when he replied that he did not have time, he heard that very woman say 'In that case, do not be an emperor.' At that he was moved to hear her very readily. We deem it very wrong to believe you are different from him, in so far as you are so kind, humane, and dutiful to other men, of whatever station and rank, as you are to us natives, amongst whom your piety has been shown, not so much by your words as by your deeds. So then, relying on that piety of yours, more modestly than boldly, we shall set out for your Caesarean Majesty, in the greatest brevity// [p. 2] possible, what incited our desire to write, all of which will be assembled in order so that the things we are trying to obtain from your clemency can be clearly and distinctly discerned.

[**1**] First. If there is anything that weighs very heavily on us, it is the fact that our town, the boundaries of which once used to stretch far and wide, is now held within narrow and reduced limits. This need not appear surprising to anyone, since not only the Spaniards but also men of our own people, neighbours on our borders, have wickedly usurped the greatest part of the fields that were left to us as an inheritance by our grandfathers and ancestors. And indeed our frequent protests have not had a good outcome, partly because we are destitute of money and partly because our *encomendero*, who was Francisco de Montejo, is always away, as he is governor of the province of Yucatán. But what is the purpose of all this? It is so you may understand that the people of Tlacopan have in the present circumstances unjustly taken possession of many of our fields. Although a legal case about them was lodged before the *Oidores* some eighteen years ago or more, it has not been resolved. That is plainly not attributable to neglect but to the various kinds of diseases that were heavily afflicting the Indians as well as to the absence of the *encomendero*. What is more, the register of the case which was conducted at the time clearly shows that the fields belong to us by right of inheritance. A very trustworthy witness of the same matter is the *Licenciado* Ceynos who recently returned to this area from Spain.[33] And there is also the man who is our *encomendero* at the present time, the *Licenciado*

[33] Francisco Ceynos was *oidor* in the Second Audiencia of New Spain (1531–1536) over which Sebastián Ramírez de Fuenleal presided.

Maldonado, who was in charge of the island of Santo Domingo, and who will inform your Caesarean Majesty—not only of what he has learnt about this business from very reliable witnesses, but also from certain maps of these lands. And accordingly when you have become very well acquainted with the case, by the pure love which you hold for God, the Best and Greatest, may you think it right to command that our fields be returned to us. And that is enough about the first point.

[**2**] Second. In some pictures which we are sending over, it may be discerned that many Spaniards—whether justly or unjustly, they themselves will see—have taken many estates for themselves, even from within those very constrained borders we now have, causing considerable losses and disadvantages to our people, the more so because our people are again and again mistreated by the Spaniards and their servants, especially when we are striving to guard our borders, or when we drive their cattle from them in the sowing season. So, in order that no other Spaniard may henceforth presume to take possession of any estate, we earnestly entreat from your clemency that some royal seal of your Caesarean Majesty, fortified by your handwriting, may be sent to us for both the protection and preservation of our borders, by which the fields of our town are enclosed.

[**3**] 3rd. As the forms of public servitude which are imposed in Mexico City for the construction of temples or for the cultivation of the Spaniards' fields are a source of great vexation for us, to the point that no week passes in which many of us, few though we are, are not allocated to these imposed labours: thirty men for building the church of St Dominic, twenty for the farms of the Spaniards, ten for the archiepiscopal shrine of the most sacred Virgin, and five again for the temple of the Virgin Mary (which is commonly known as Guadalupe). It has thus come about that we are in no way able to carry through to the end the church we have which was begun several years ago, nor even at the present time to begin the monastery // [p. 3] for the monks who are lodging among us in some very modest dwellings. So we humbly beseech of your clemency that for the interval of some years we may be left exempt from all public works, until we complete building both our church and our monastery. In addition it is our desire to unite our scattered people into one, and provide our houses with pathways: so that human order, which appears to be a crucial basis for Christianity, may prevail and barbarism be banished abroad, we beg once and again not to be denied this request.

[**4**] 4th. Even though our town is now small, at one time it was not at all the smallest province among others which it definitely surpassed in antiquity and nobility: in antiquity, as annals of the ancients tell us that it was founded one thousand, five hundred and twenty-five years ago; and in nobility because everywhere peoples of noble or pure stock all declare with one accord that they have derived their origins from Azcapotzalco. And in line with that, the town's boundaries used to be recognized as being three days' journey away in every direction. Moreover, whatever is contained in the mountains surrounding our town was all for our own use, and no one stood in our way, so that any one of us was permitted to cut timber, planks, dry

wood for smokeless fuel, and even stones, free of charge. But later on, not through our own carelessness but rather as a result of arbitrary rule, the Tlacubans along with further little towns in the vicinity appropriated for themselves both the cedar groves and the quarries of stone so that none among us is allowed to cut anything from them, although we would pay the price and have written permission of the Royal Audiencia [*Senatus*] of Mexico to do so. Wherefore we humbly beg of your clemency that the things we held in common, along with others twenty years ago may be so for the future, and that no one may prohibit us from either cutting timber or quarrying stone: in this matter we greatly desire the authority of your Caesarean Majesty.

[**5**] 5th. Several points can be adduced to our testimony that our town was once a province, and indeed a great one. Among them we consider these two to be pre-eminent. One is that it may be clearly agreed that the province had a good number of peoples as *terrazgueros*: their towns altogether were: Quauhnahuac, Tetelpa, Xilotepec, Matlatzinco, Cohuatepec, Cempohualla, and Nanacapa, all of which had to pay an annual tribute, before the province of Mexico was taken in battle by the Marquis Cortés. The other pre-eminent point is that Azcapotzalco was the richest source for the origin of very many towns, which were earlier nothing but settlements founded by the lord of our own town who was called Tezozomoc, indeed a very honourable lord, very wealthy and what is more, very long-lived as, according to the record of our elders he is said to have lived one hundred and sixty-six years, and that there have been not more than a hundred and thirty-three years since he departed from the living. He put his sons, of whom he had several, as lords over the settlements he had himself made; and on his death he appointed, as lord and heir in his place, his elder son named Ylhuicamina. So that we might reveal the matter in a few words, when the Mexica had been attacked by the Azcapotzalca near the mountain called Chapultepec, on which the former had earlier settled after a long period of wandering, and were now again driven to wander about from one place to another, having no idea where they should choose to live, the said Tezozomoc, taking pity on them, decreed// [p. 4] that they should be settled in a part of the region where Tenochtitlan is now. And so the Mexicans served our town for eighty years, by paying as tribute the things they were able to gather from the lake: fish, frogs, ducks, and other kinds of aquatic animals. In the end, after some kind of conflict arose among them, those who seceded from the community were called 'Tlatilolcani' after a certain mound of earth that is positioned in the middle of the lake. This was where they migrated when good relations could not be recovered. To these people, once they had separated from the Mexica, the lord Tezozomoc gave as chief and ruler his son, who was named Quaquapitzahuac. Their second settlement was called Tlacuba: the same lord Tezozomoc put in charge of its settlers his two sons, one named Aculnahuacatl, the other Tzaqualcatl. Once they died the settlers showed themselves as traitors to our town, in so far as they used guile and deceit to lay claim to what was the dominion of the Aztcapotzalca for themselves. So it came

about that Tlacuba now seems to be a province, when before it had been a settlement founded by Tezozomoc. The third is called Coyoacán, where Maxtlato was lord. The fourth is Atlacuihuaya, where Yepcohuatl was lord; fifth, Huitzilopochco, whose lord was Yztachecatl. The sixth, Cohuatlayauhca, is now subject to Mexico; its lord was Tecocohua. The seventh is Tultitla, whose lord was Tepanonoc. The eighth is Tepechpa, whose principal was Quahquauhtzi. The ninth is Aculma, where Teyolcocohua became lord. The tenth is Tulquauhyoca, whose lord was Teuhtlehuac. The eleventh is Cuitlachtepec, where there was a lady who ruled, a daughter named Xocotzi. The twelfth is Chiappa, where the mistress was a daughter named Tomiyauh. The thirteenth is Ayotochco, whose lord was Yohuallatohua. The fourteenth is Oztoticpac, whose lord was Tlacacuitlahua. The fifteenth is Quecholac, where the mistress was another daughter named Azcalxoch. The sixteenth is Totomihuaca, whose mistress was a daughter named Tlacochcue. All this will emerge more clearly from a picture where these settlements are drawn along with the names of the children of Tezozomoc who ruled each of these settlements. The reason that we are making all these things known, is so that this town of ours which we have already shown was once a province might, through your clemency, be endowed with the title of city state.

[**6**] 6th. For many years now we have had insignia for our town, which, so that they may not be thought worthless by anyone, we very much want to be endorsed by your Caesarean authority, since they very clearly signal the status of our republic. Foremost in them an ant is depicted, and not without significance, because our town happens to take its name from the ant; then a wall which seems to have the pinnacles of a tower symbolizes the walls of a market, very strong ones indeed, which, however, because of their outstanding strength our ancestors razed to the ground. Then follows a heart, because just as that is the source and origin of life, so our town has been the origin of all the nobility that has been scattered among the peoples of New Spain. Adjoined to it is a form of adornment that looks similar to the mitre worn by bishops, for it was with such a thing that the lords of the Indians were decorated in former times. Above all of these is a cross, symbolizing the cross of the Lord which was proclaimed to the people of Asia by Philip, God's apostle, in whose honour this town's church is dedicated.

[**7**] 7th. The following divine oracle is not at all obscure to us: 'Wisdom steadies the heart, giving it weight against the winds.' From this it is rendered very clear to all that the hearts of Christians are very greatly strengthened in the faith through knowledge of letters, and that those who were at one time buffeted by the winds of paganism now have constancy in their Christianity. Furthermore, since the living tree of true life has only been recently planted among us, namely that of the Catholic faith, and so that it may extend its roots all the more deeply, we ourselves consider it very advantageous for our town to be endowed with a home for the Muses, and we seek from your Caesarean Majesty// [p. 5] the resources to enable us to found it in our own town. Although there may be no need for all the sciences to be taught there,

instruction in Latin and the Spanish language can certainly be provided by some of us who have frequently taught it as well as the Spaniards have.

[**8**] 8th. No one may debate the fact that a market which we call the *tianquizco* was always held in our town and elsewhere before the arrival of the Spaniards. It was frequented by everyone so that, not just on certain days but on every day, a variety of merchandise was to be sold and a virtually endless number of slaves and captives who in this place alone were put up for sale. Subsequently it has come about that any town, even a very small one, may now have a market by its own authority, but in our case a market may no longer be held, unless it may be on one given weekday, in fact on Saturday. This is to the detriment of us all. So we call upon and entreat your Caesarean Majesty to allow the market, which used to be held daily in this place, to be accommodated on at least two days, Tuesdays and on the day already arranged.

You now have before you, most Christian of kings, all that we yearn to obtain from your utmost clemency, things that even as they are just, as they are honourable, and as they are practical, can incline you to grant them to us. And may the poverty and worthlessness common to us all not in any way dissuade you—for though we are poorer than Irus and more worthless than seaweed, we are nonetheless loyal servants of your holy Catholic Caesarean Majesty, and we are already counted in the register of Christians on the strength of our Catholic faith and our adoption of holy baptism and the other sacraments. That alone can be sufficient cause for you not to fail us in our petitions, as you are very Christian, as you are greatly powerful, and as you are by nature most generous. And so that this letter may not exceed the appropriate limit or 'go beyond the pale', as the expression goes, may it come to an end here, once I have added however that there had been a desire to send two of us to Spain so that they might represent these concerns, but permission was not granted by the Viceroy and we did not want to cause any further trouble with that matter, because we knew you did not want that either. With regard to our plea, it seemed best to send this letter, with which in addition to the requests we have humbly made, we beseech from God, the Best and Greatest, a long life for your Caesarean Majesty, extensive kingdoms on earth, and everlasting glory in heaven. Written in Azcapotzalco, on the fourth day before the Ides of February [10th] in the true year, the one thousand, five hundred and sixty first, from Christ's birth [1561].

Your Holy Catholic Caesarean Majesty's lowly servants,//[p. 6]

Don Hernando de Molina
Governor

Don Baltasar Hernández
Governor

Pedro Zacharias
Mayor

Pedro Dionisio
Mayor

Antonio Valeriano

Francisco Plácido

Francisco de los Ángeles

Diego de San Filipe	Pedro Garçia	Francisco Chalcocalqui	Martín Cano
Ruler	Ruler	Ruler	Ruler

Don Martín de San Matheo Martín de Santo Domingo Martín de San Miguel

// [p. 7]
To the Holy Catholic and Caesarean Majesty of our most invincible king and lord, Don Felipe in the realms of Spain. From the people of Azcapotzalco to his Majesty.

Appendix 2.5: Antonio Valeriano, Letter to Fray Juan Bautista, c. 1600

• Source: BAUTISTA, *Sermonario* (1606), Prologue, unnumbered page
John Carter Brown Library, Providence: BA606.J91a

Hic litterarum gerulus, ad vestram Paternitatem portat, id quod mihi traducendum iussisti. Nescio profecto, an in traductione eius sim fęlix. Multa quippe in eo sunt pręgnantia; vt nesciam in quem sensum meliorem verti debeant. Si quid est erratum, parcas obsecro. Et tuam grauem censuram adhibeas: & his litteris tam male formatis simul & ignoscas: illiturę enim videntur potius, quam litterę. Nec mirum vestrę Paternitati videatur: manus n*amque* iam vacillant: oculi caligant, & aures occlusę. Iterum atq*ue* iterum parcas. Deus Optimus Maximus longęvam tuę paternitati vitam concedat. De Mexico. Tui amantissimus, &si indignus. Antonius Valerianus. Hęc ille.

TRANSLATION

The bearer of this letter is delivering to Your Paternity the thing that you bade me translate. I know not for sure whether I am successful in my translation of it. Indeed there are many things in it weighty with implication, so that I do not know what is the better sense into which they should be rendered. I beg you to pardon anything done in error, and to apply to it your authoritative censorship; and at the same time to overlook these badly formed letters: for they appear to be litterings rather than letters. And that should seem no wonder to Your Paternity: as my hands now quiver, my eyes grow dim and my ears are blocked. Again and again pardon. May God Best and Greatest grant a long life to Your Paternity. From Mexico City. Most devoted to you, though unworthy. Antonio Valeriano.

Appendix 2.6: Fray Bernardino de Sahagún, Reply of the Mexica lords to the Franciscan Twelve, 1564

• Source: SAHAGÚN, *Colloquios y Doctrina christiana* (1564), 35r, 37r
Vatican: Archivum Secretum Vaticanum, Armario I, vol. 91

The division of the text into sections marked A–G follows that of the manuscript.

[35r] luego vno de los doze (con el interprete) los repito todo lo q*ue* el dia antes abian d*ic*ho a los señores. desque lo ouiero*n* oydo leuantose vno de los satrapas y capta*n*do la benevolencia a los doze, començo ahablar y hizo vna larga platica segun que se sigue.

¶Cap°. siete, en que se pone la respuesta que los satrapas dieron alos doze sobre la arriba d*ic*ho.

Señores nu*est*ros, personas principales y de mucha estima, seais muy bie*n* venidos, y llegados a n*uest*ras tierras y pueblos: no somos dignos nosotros tan baxos y soezes de ver las caras de tan valerosas personas: aos traydo dios nu*est*ro señor paraque nos rigais: ignoramos donde y quetal sea el lugar do*n*de abeis venido y donde mora*n* n*uest*ros señores y dioses: por que abéis venido por la mar entre las nubes y nieblas (camino que nunca supimos). embia os dios entrenosotros por ojos oydos y boca suya: el q*ue* es inuisible y esp*irit*ual, en vosotros senos muestra visible://[34]
//[36r] y oymos con n*uest*ras orejas sus palabras cuyos vicarios soys: emos oydo las palabras de aquel por cuya virtud biujmos y somos, las quales no*s* abéis traydo y co*n* admjracion emos oydo las palabras del señor del mundo que por n*uest*ro amor os a acá embiado y ansí mjsmo nos abeis traydo el libro de las celestiales y diuinas palabras. **A.** Pues qué podremos dezir en v*uest*ra p*re*sencia, que palabras podremos endereçar a v*uest*ras orejas que sean dignas de ser oydas de tales personas: nosotros que somos como nada, personas soezes y de muy baxa condicio*n*, y que por hierro nos a*p*uesto n*uest*ro señor en las esqujnas de su estrado y silla: pero no obsta*n*te esto con dos o tres razo*n*es responderemos y contra diremos las palabras de aquel que nos dio[35] su ser nu*est*ro señor por qujen somos y biujmos: por ventura provocaremos su yra co*n*tra nosotros y nos despeñaremos, y sera lo que diremos causa de n*uest*ra perdicion, por ventura ya nos desecha: pues q*ue* emos de hazer los que somos hombres baxos y mortales? si muriéremos muramos, si perecieramos, perezcamos, que a la verdad los dioses tambie*n* murieron (no recibais pena señores n*uest*ros) por que co*n* delicadez y curiosidad queremos examjnar los diujnos secretos (bien ansí como si con temeridad a hurto quisiesemos entre abrir el cofre de las riquezas

[34] Folio 35v contains a Nahuatl translation of the Spanish text on fol. 35r.

[35] 1564: de

para ver lo que esta enel). **B.** Aueis nos d*ic*ho que no conocemos a aq*ue*l por qujen tenemos ser y vida y que es señor del cielo y dela t*ie*rra: ansi mjsmo dezis q*ue* los q*ue* adoramos no son dioses: esta manera de hablar haze se nos muy nueua y es nos muy escandalosa, espantamonos de tal dezir como este: porque los padres y ante pasados q*ue* nos enge*n*draro*n* y regiero*n*, no nos dixero*n* tal cosa: mas antes ellos nos dexaro*n* esta costumbre que tenemos de adorar n*uest*ros dioses: y ellos los creyero*n* y adoraro*n* todo el tie*m*po q*ue* biuieron sobre la t*ie*rra: ellos nos e*n*senaro*n* de la manera q*ue* los abiamos de honrar y todas las cerimonjas y sacrificios q*ue* hazemos ellos nos los enseñaro*n*: dexaron nos d*ic*ho q*ue* mediante estos biuimos y somos y que estos nos merecierо*n* par*a* q*ue* fuesemos suyos y los seruiesemos en innumerables siglos. antes q*ue* el sol come*n*çase a resplandecer nj a aver dia: ellos dixero*n* q*ue* estos dioses que adoramos nos da*n* todas las cosas necesarias a n*uest*ra vida corporal el mayz, los frisoles, la chía etc. aestos demandamos la pluuja para q*ue* se crí*en* las cosas de la tierra. **C.** estos n*uest*ros dioses poseen[36] deleytes y riq*ue*zas grandes. todos los deleytes y riquezas son suyas: habitan e*n* lugares muy deleytosos do siemp*re* ay flores y v*er*duras y grandes frescur*as* (lugar no conocido, ni sabido de los mortales que se llama tlalocan) donde jamas ay hambre pobreza nj enfermedad: ellos so*n* los q*ue* dan las honrras, cauallerias, dignidades y reynos el oro y la plata, plumajes, piedras p*re*ciosas. **D.** No hay memoria del t*iem*po e*n* q*ue* come*n*çaron a s*er* honrrados, adorados y estmados: por ventura aun siglo odos de q*ue* esto se haze at*iem*po sin cue*n*ta: q*ui*en tiene memoria de q*uando* ni como començaro*n* aquellos celebres y sagrados lugares donde se hazian milagros y se dauan respuestas q*ue* se llaman tula*n*, vapalcalco, xuchatlapa*n*, tamoancham, youalliycha*n*, teutiuaca*n*. Los habitadores destos lugares ya d*ic*hos se enseñorearo*n* y *reynaron* en todo el mundo; estos dan honrra, fama nombrada, reynos y gl*or*ia y señorios. **E.** Cosa de gra*n* desatino y liuiandad seria destruir nosotros las antiq*ui*ssimas leyes y costu*m*bres q*ue* dexaro*n* los p*ri*meros pobladores desta t*ie*rra q*ue* fuero*n* los chichimecas, los tulanos, los de colhua, los tepanecas: enla adoracio*n*, fe, y seru*ic*jº de los sobre d*ic*hos, en*que* emos nacido y nos emos criado y a esto estamos habituados, y los tenemos imp*res*os e*n* n*uest*ros coraçones. **F.** O *señores* n*uest*ros y p*rin*cipales gra*n*de aduertencia deueis tener enq*ue* no hagais algo por do*n*de alboroteys y hagais hazer algu*n* mal hecho a v*uest*ros vasallos. como podra*n* dexar los pobres viejos y viejas aquello en*que* toda su vida se a*n* criado: mjrad q*ue* no in curramos enla yra de n*uest*ros dioses: mjrad q*ue* no se leua*n*te co*n*tra nosotros la ge*n*te popular, silos dixeramos q*ue* no so*n* dioses los que hasta *aquí* siem*pre* an tenido por tales. **G.** Co*n*ujene co*n* mucho acuerdo y muy despacio mjrar este negocio señores n*uest*ros: nosotros no nos satisfacemos ni nos *per*suadimos de lo q*ue* nos a*n* d*ic*ho ni ente*n*demos, nj damos credito a lo que de nue*st*ros dioses se nos a d*ic*ho: pena os damos, señores y padres e*n* hablar desta manera: presentes estan los *señores* q*ue* tiene*n* el cargo de regir el reyno y republicas

[36] 1564: pose en

deste mu*n*do; de vna manera sentimos todos: que basta auer p*er*dido, basta q*ue* nos *an* tomado la pote*n*cia y iuridicio*n* real; e*n*lo q*ue* toca a n*uest*ros dioses: antes moriremos q*ue* dexar su *seruicj*º. y adoracio*n*, estaes nuestra determinacio*n*. haced lo que//[37] [37r] qujsiéredes: lo d*ic*ho basta en respuesta y contra dicion de lo que nos abeis dicho no tenemos mas que dezir, señores n*uest*ros.

TRANSLATION

Then one of the Twelve (with the translator) repeated to the satraps and priests everything they had said before to their lords. After they heard it, one of the satraps got up and, seeking the goodwill of the Twelve, began to speak and he gave a long speech as follows:

Chapter seven, which contains the reply given by the satraps to the Twelve on what was said above.

Our lords, leaders of great esteem, may you be very welcome, having come to our lands and towns. We are not worthy ourselves, so low and dirty, to see the faces of such valorous people. Our Lord sent you here to rule us. We do not know where or from what place you have come, or where our lords and gods abide, because you have come by sea, among clouds and mists (a way we have never known). God sent you among us as eyes and hearers, and as his mouth. He who is invisible and spiritual shows himself as visible to us in you; and with our ears we hear his words, of which you are representatives. We have heard the words of him, through whom we live and exist, which you have brought, and in wonder we have heard the words of the Lord of the world, who for love of us has sent you here; and so indeed you have brought us the book of heavenly and divine words.

A. What can we say in your presence? What words can we direct to your ears that would be worth being heard from persons such as ourselves? We who are as nothing, dirty people of a very low condition, whom in error our Lord placed on the corner of his platform and his seat. Even so we offer a response, and with two or three arguments we shall counter the words about him who gave us his being, our Lord through whom we exist and live. Perhaps we will provoke his wrath against us and cast ourselves down, and what we say will be the cause of our ruin; perhaps he is already casting us aside, so what is there for us to do, as we are lowly humans and mortals? If we are to die, let us die; if we are to perish, let us perish; as in truth the gods died too. (May you not be aggrieved, our lords).

B. You have told us that we do not know him, the one through whom we have existence and life, and who is Lord of heaven and earth. Likewise, you say those whom we worship are not gods. This way of speaking is very new and very shocking to us: we are horrified at such speech, because our fathers and forefathers, who engendered and

[37] Fol. 36v contains a Nahuatl translation of the Spanish text on fol. 37r.

ruled us, did not tell us such a thing. They left us this custom of having to worship our gods; they believed in them and worshipped them all the time they lived upon the earth; they taught us the ways we had to do [the gods] honour; they taught us all the ceremonies and sacrifices we perform: they told us that through them [the gods] we live and exist and that these gods had a claim on us so that we belonged to them and served them for countless centuries before the sun began to shine and before there was day; they said that those gods we worship give us all the things necessary for bodily life: maize, beans, *chia*, etc.; we ask them for rain, for the things of the earth to grow.

C. These gods of ours possess delights and great riches; all delights and riches are theirs; they live in very delightful places where all is always flowers, greenery, freshness (a place neither known nor familiar to mortals, which is called Tlalocan), where there is never hunger, poverty, or sickness; they are those who grant honours, chivalry, dignity and kingdoms, gold and silver, feathers, precious stones.

D. There is no memory of the time when they began to be honoured, worshipped, and esteemed; perhaps it was a century or two after the time without reckoning, [but] no one has a memory of when or how those famous sacred places began, where miracles were wrought and a response was given, and which are called Tula, Huapalcalco, Xuchatlapan, Tamoanchan, Yohualichan, Teotihuacan. The inhabitants of those places named were lords and rulers of all the world; they give honour, renowned fame, kingdoms, glory, and lordship.

E. It would be a matter of grave error and crassness to destroy the very ancient laws and customs that the first settlers of this earth left us—those who were the Chichimeca, those of Tula, the Tepaneca—the worship, faith, and service of the above-mentioned [gods] in which we are born and brought up, and we are habituated to this and we hold them impressed on our hearts.

F. O our lords and leaders. You must receive a grave warning not to do anything that might cause agitation or something very bad to be done to your vassals. How will poor old men and woman who have been raised this way all their lives be able to accept this? See that we do not incur the anger of our gods; see that the ordinary people do not rise up against us, if we were to tell them that those gods, which they have always held as such until now, are not gods.

G. Our lords, it is advisable to proceed slowly and calmly in this matter: we are not satisfied and we are not persuaded by what you have told us, nor do we understand or give credence to what has been said to us about our gods. We cause you pain, lords and fathers, to speak in this way: here present are lords who have the charge of ruling this kingdom and the republics of this world; we are all of one accord: that it is enough to have lost, that it is enough that they have taken power and royal jurisdiction from us; where our gods are concerned we would die before leaving their service and worship. That is our determination: do what you wish. Enough has been said in response and in contradiction of what you have told us. We have no more to say, our lords.

Appendix 3

EXCURSUS ON ANTONIO VALERIANO AND THE VIRGIN OF GUADALUPE

The celebrated apparitions of the Virgin of Guadalupe, which reputedly occurred in Tepeyac in 1531, are described in a Nahuatl narrative, *Nican mopohua*, 'Here it is related.' The authorship of that text has often been credited to the native Latinist Antonio Valeriano (c. 1521–1605), although there is no attestation of the *Nican mopohua* before it was published as part of the *Huei tlamahuiçoltica*, 'Great Miracle' (1649) by Luis Laso de la Vega.[1]

The first association of Valeriano's name with the Guadalupan tradition was made in 1675 by the priest and scholar Luis Becerra Tanco, who claimed that 'Juan Valeriano' had recounted the apparitions to his own uncle, Gaspar de Praves, who died in 1628.[2] Ascription of the *Nican mopohua* to Antonio Valeriano arose from Carlos de Sigüenza y Góngora's testimony that the Mexican scholar had written about the miracles in a Nahuatl manuscript that Fernando de Alva Ixtlilxochitl acquired and translated into Spanish.[3] The historian Lorenzo Boturini Benaduci argued that this Nahuatl text was the same as the one that Laso de la Vega had published.[4] Boturini's supposition was enthusiastically endorsed by the Jesuit Juan José de Eguiara y Eguren in the *Bibliotheca Mexicana* (1755):

> Let us wholeheartedly place a golden crown on the writings of our Valeriano, attributing to him alone the one published in the Mexican language in Mexico City in 1649 . . . We do then attribute this golden work to our Valeriano, by

[1] LASO DE LA VEGA, *Huei Tlamahuiçoltica* (1649) appeared after the first publication on the subject in Spanish: SÁNCHEZ, *Imagen de la Virgen María, Madre de Dios de Guadalupe* (1648). Sousa, Poole, and Lockhart 1998, 5–18 consider the relation between these texts.

[2] BECERRA TANCO, *Felicidad de México* (1675), 17r [1982, 329]: Brading 2001, 92.

[3] SIGÜENZA Y GÓNGORA, *Piedad heroyca* (c. 1690) [1960, 65]; cf. Poole 1997, 165–70 on the transmission of Sigüenza's claim.

[4] BOTURINI BENADUCI, *Idea de una nueva historia* (1746), 'Catálogo', XXXIV [2015, 263, 267].

> following the footsteps of our own most learned Arbiter and Historian, Don Carlos de Sigüenza.[5]

That position has been defended by several influential modern historians.[6] Yet there is no actual evidence to support it: none of the numerous sixteenth-century sources for Valeriano offers anything that could link him to the *Nican mopohua*.

Miguel León-Portilla sought to reconcile Edmundo O'Gorman's hypothesis that Valeriano wrote the *Nican mopohua* in 1556 with the lack of any contemporaneous reference to the events it relates. León-Portilla suggested that Valeriano was sufficiently impressed by the *neixcuitilli*, the Franciscans' Nahuatl dramas, to develop a confabulation of his own: a *relación* that combined the traditional style and content of *cuicatl*, indigenous song, with the conventions of European miracle narrative. The purpose of the *relación* would have been to celebrate and explain—in poetic rather than in historically veridical terms—the popular cult of Mary-Tonantzin, established at Tepeyac by the 1550s, and the veneration of her image.[7] Valeriano was indeed involved with religious drama: Chimalpahin records that 'gobernador don Antonio Valeriano' and Fray Juan de Torquemada were among the nine founding members of the *Cofradía de la Soledad* instituted in the chapel of San José at the Convent of San Francisco in Mexico City on 12 April, Good Friday, of 1591.[8] The *Cofradía* staged dramatic productions of an exemplary nature, and Torquemada himself composed 'comedias o representaciones' in Nahuatl, probably drawing from Valeriano's linguistic knowledge.[9]

León-Portilla's suggestion recalled a hypothesis proposed two centuries earlier by the priest and politician Fray Servando Teresa de Mier:

> Or else the history of Guadalupe is a comedy of the Indian Valeriano, forged on Aztec mythology concerning Tonantzin, to be represented in Santiago [Tlatelolco], where he was a professor, by the young Indian college students, who in that time were accustomed to represent in their language the farces that they called sacramental *autos*, which were in vogue in the sixteenth century.[10]

[5] EGUIARA Y EGUREN, *Bibliotheca Mexicana* (1755), 290–1: 'Auream plenè coronidem Scriptis Valeriani Nostri imponamus, vindicantes ipsi edita Mexico anno 1649 idiomate Mexicano ... Vindicamus autem aureum Valeriano nostro Opusculum istud, vestigia legentes Critici Historiographi eruditissimi nostri D. Caroli de Siguenza.'

[6] Cuevas 1931; Burrus 1979; O'Gorman 1986; León-Portilla 2000b; Martínez Baracs 2015.

[7] León-Portilla 2000b, 43–7.

[8] CHIMALPAHIN, *Relaciones* 7 (c. 1630), 224r [1998 ii, 268–9].

[9] TORQUEMADA, *Monarchia Indiana* 20.79 [1975–1983 vi, 395]; Horcasitas 2004 i, 100–1.

[10] MIER Y NORIEGA, 'Carta VI' (1797) [1982, 852]: 'ó la historia de Guadalupe es una comedia del indio Valeriano, forjado sobre la mitología azteca, tocante á la *Tonantzin*, para que la representasen

Teresa de Mier's theory was later elaborated by Joaquin García Icazbalceta, who noted that the *Nican mopohua* contained positive references to Tlatelolco and could have been divided into acts for a dramatic performance.[11]

But such a scenario—whether at the Convent of Santiago or the College of Santa Cruz—can hardly have been less likely: the Franciscans were expressly opposed to the veneration of the Virgin of Guadalupe because they believed it was encouraging the Indians to practice idolatry. A prominent teacher at the college, Fray Francisco de Bustamante, preached a public sermon on 6th September 1556 criticizing the new archbishop of Mexico, the Dominican Alonso de Montúfar, for promoting devotion to the Virgin of Guadalupe.[12] Bustamante's view was widely shared by witnesses: another friar at Tlatelolco, Fray Luis, described such devotion as 'drunkenness . . . a veneration which we all deplore'.[13] Fray Bernardino de Sahagún later explained that Tepeyac had been the site where Mexicans had formerly worshipped their goddess Tonantzin, whose name means 'Our mother', and he lamented that preachers there were now giving the same name to the Virgin, an association he called a 'Satanic invention'.[14] There would have thus been little reason for Valeriano to become involved with the Guadalupan cult, as he had a lifelong association with the Franciscans at Tlatelolco and had worked so closely with Sahagún, as well as with Fray Juan Bautista and Fray Juan de Torquemada.[15]

Antonio Valeriano did make an oblique reference to the Virgin of Guadalupe in the Latin letter to Philip II he signed with the other rulers of Azcapotzalco in 1561. The third request in the letter was for people from the town to be exempted from works required by the Spaniards—including construction of the archbishop's palace consecrated to the Virgin Mary and of a temple to the Virgin of Guadalupe, which would have been at Archbishop Montúfar's behest:

> no week passes in which many of us, few though we are, are not allocated to imposed labours: thirty men for building of the *church* ['ecclesiae'] of St Dominic, twenty for the farms of the Spaniards, ten for the archepiscopal

en Santiago, donde era catedrático, los inditos colegiales, que en su tiempo acostumbraban representar en su lengua las farsas que llamaban autos sacramentales muy de boga en el siglo diez y seis.'

[11] García Icazbalceta 1896, 67–9, in Poole 1997, 222.

[12] The sermon's content and witnesses' sympathetic reactions can be gleaned from the report Montúfar commissioned the following day: anon., *Información que el arzobispo* (1556) [1891]: Torre Villar and Navarro de Anda 1982, 36–141.

[13] Anon., *Información que el arzobispo* (1556) [1982, 69]: 'esa borrachera, porque ésa es un devoción que nosotros todo estamos mal con ella'. The witness was probably Fray Luis Cal, the Franciscan guardian of Tlatelolco: Velázquez Rodríguez 1931, 6–9, 41; Ricard 1933 [1966], 188–9; Poole 1997, 59–64.

[14] SAHAGÚN, *Historia general* (1580) 11.12 [1982 i: 90], Spanish text; cf. Chapter 8, III above.

[15] Karttunen 1995, 118.

palace of the most sacred Virgin, and five again for *a temple* ['templum'] *of the Virgin Mary (which is commonly called Guadalupe)*. It has thus come about that we are in no way able to carry through to the end the *church* ['ecclesiam'] we have, which was begun several years ago, nor even at the present time to begin the monastery for the monks who are lodging among us in some very modest dwellings.[16]

A forthright expression of opinion about the veneration of the Virgin of Guadalupe fostered by the secular clergy would not have been relevant or politic, but there are a couple of important innuendos conveyed by the words and phrases italicized above. First, the parenthesis in the manuscript, 'which is commonly called Guadalupe', 'quod vulgo Guadalope [*sic*] dicitur', here qualifies the edifice of the temple. Yet it was far more conventional to apply the title of 'Guadalupe' to the Virgin herself, and it is notable that the writer refrains from doing so. Secondly, while 'templum' carries connotations of pagan religion, the church that Valeriano hoped would be completed in Azcapotzalco is, in contrast, repeatedly called an 'ecclesia'—the Greek term adopted as the customary Latin word for church.[17] In this context the distinction between *templum* and *ecclesia* appears to be pointed, given that Sahagún remarked that in Tepeyac, the site of the shrine of the Virgin of Guadalupe, 'the Mexicans used to have a *temple* ['templo'], dedicated to the mother of the gods.'[18]

Valeriano thus signalled his lack of enthusiasm for the emergent Guadalupan cult, but his choice of words primarily served to highlight the pressing need for the church of San Felipe and the adjacent Dominican monastery to be built in Azcapotzalco. That objective was achieved: both were completed by 1565.[19]

[16] Cf. Appendix 2.4, item [3] above.

[17] Palmer 1954, 186: 'Even where it would have been possible to find a Latin equivalent [for a Greek Christian technical term], undesirable pagan associations often ruled it out of court. *vates* or *fatidicus* could not do service for *propheta* nor *templum* or *fanum* for *ecclesia*.'

[18] SAHAGÚN, *HG* 11.12 [1982 i, 90].

[19] Ricard 1966, 70, 334 n. 65.

BIBLIOGRAPHY

Abbreviations

Archives and libraries

AGI	Archivo General de Indias, Seville, Spain
AGN	Archivo General de la Nación, Mexico
AGS	Archivo General de Simancas, Spain
AHN	Archivo Histórico Nacional, Spain
BANC	Bancroft Library, Berkeley
BLAC/JGI	Benson Latin American Collection/Joaquín García Icazbalceta Collection, University of Texas Library, Austin
BNE	Biblioteca Nacional de España, Madrid
BNF	Bibliothèque nationale de France, Paris
BNM	Biblioteca Nacional de México
Bodleian	Bodleian Library, Oxford
JCB	John Carter Brown Library, Providence, Rhode Island
MARI	Middle American Research Institute, Tulane University, New Orleans
MNA	Museo Nacional de Antropología, Mexico
Newberry	The Newberry Library, Chicago
NLC	National Library of Congress, Washington, DC
Vat. Lat.	Biblioteca Apostolica Vaticana

Journals, book series, publishers, and institutions

ACMRS	Arizona Center for Medieval and Renaissance Studies, Phoenix
AHR	*American Historical Review*
AJP	*American Journal of Philology*
ASD	*Opera Omnia Desiderii Erasmi Roterodami*, Amsterdam Edition
BAE	Biblioteca de autores españoles, Madrid
BAR	British Archaeological Reports
CLAR	*Colonial Latin American Review*

CONACULTA	Consejo Nacional para la Cultura y las Artes, Mexico
CSIC	Consejo Superior de Investigaciones Científicas, Spain
CUP	Cambridge University Press
CWE	*Collected Works of Erasmus*, Toronto: University of Toronto Press
ECN	*Estudios de Cultura Náhuatl*
EHN	*Estudios de Historia Novohispana*
ESL	*Edizione di Storia e Letteratura*
FCE	Fondo de Cultura Económica
HAHR	*Hispanic American Historical Review*
HEL	*Histoire Épistémologie Langage*
IIFL	Instituto de Investigaciones Filológicas, Mexico
IIH	Instituto de Investigaciones Históricas, Mexico
IJCT	*International Journal of the Classical Tradition*
INAH	Instituto Nacional de Antropología e Historia, Mexico
JHI	*Journal of the History of Ideas*
JOLCEL	*Journal of Latin Cosmopolitanism and European Literature*
JWCI	*Journal of the Warburg and Courtauld Institutes*
JWI	*Journal of the Warburg Institute*
OCD	*Oxford Classical Dictionary* (fourth edition)
OLD	*Oxford Latin Dictionary*
OUP	Oxford University Press
RAE	Real Academia Española, Madrid
RAH	Real Academia de la Historia, Madrid
REAA	*Revista Española de Antropología Americana*
SUP	*Studi Umanistici Piceni*, Sassoferrato, Italy
UMSNH	Universidad Michoacana de San Nicolás Hidalgo
UNAM	Universidad Autónoma de México
UP	University Press

• As place of publication, 'Mexico' designates Mexico City.

Other abbreviations

ed(s).	editor(s)
edn(s).	edition(s)
Eng.	English
et al.	*et alii*, and others
Fr.	Frater, Fray, or Frère
facs.	facsimile
ms(s).	manuscript(s)
n.s.	new series
OFM	*Ordo Fratrorum Minorum*, Order of Friars Minor
orig.	original(ly)
repr.	reprint(ed)
SJ	*Societas Jesu*, Society of Jesus
s.n.	*sine nomine*, no name given
Sp.	Spanish
s.v.	*sub verbo*, under the heading of
tr.	translation, translated
transcr.	transcription

PRIMARY SOURCES

(I) ANONYMOUS TEXTS AND CODICES, BY TITLE

Annals of Juan Bautista = *Anales/Códice de Juan Bautista,* c. 1569 [ms. copy in Lorenzo Boturini Library, transc. Reyes García, Luis, 2001, *¿Cómo te confundes? ¿Acaso no somos conquistados? Anales de Juan Bautista,* Mexico: Biblioteca Lorenzo Boturini].

Annals of Tlatelolco = *Anales de Tlatelolco,* c. 1550, *BNF Ms Mexicain 22-23* [edited by Berlín, Heinrich 1980, Mexico: Porrúa; edited by Tena, Rafael 2004, Mexico: Cien de México; Eng. translation by Lockhart 1993, 256–73].

Auctores octo morales, 1400s [edited by Raenerius, Johannes, *Autores octo morales* 1538, Lyon: Theobaldus Paganus; translated by Pepin, Ronald E. 1999, *An English Translation of Auctores Octo, a Medieval Reader,* Lewiston NY: Edwin Mellen Press]. *See also* ERASMUS, DESIDERIUS, 1539.

Cantares mexicanos, 1560s–1580s, BNM, Ms. 1628 bis, 1–85 [facs. León-Portilla 1994; edn., Eng. translation by Bierhorst, John 1985, Stanford: Stanford UP; edited, Sp. translation by León-Portilla, León-Portilla, Curiel Defossé, and Reyes Equigas 2011 i–ii.2].

Codex Aubin, c. 1576–1608, British Museum, Am2006, Drg.31219 [1902 *Códice Aubin: Manuscrito Azteca,* edited by Peñafiel, Antonio 1902, Mexico: Secretaría de Fomento; facs. edn. edited by Dibble 1963; online edn. forthcoming: https://codexaubin.ace.fordham.edu].

Codex Borgia, 1400s–1500s, Vatican Apostolic Library, Borg.mess. [edited by Seler, Eduard 1904–1909, 3 vols., Berlin: Druck von Gebr. Unger].

Codex Huixquilucan (*Hemenway Codex*), c. 1660–1750, Tozzer Library, Harvard University [facs. edited by Harvey, Herbert R. 1993, *Códice Techialoyan Huixquilican Estado de México,* Mexico: Goberno del Estado de México].

Codex Ixtlilxochitl, c. 1582, BNF, Ms. Mexicain 55-71 [edited by Durand-Forest, Jacqueline de 1976, Graz: Akademische Druck- und Verlagsanstalt].

Codex Magliabechiano, mid-1500s, Biblioteca nazionale centrale di Firenze, Cod. Magl. XIII, 11, 3 [facs., edited, translated by Nuttall, Zelia 1983, *The Codex Magliabechiano and the Book of the Life of the Ancient Mexicans,* 2 vols., Berkeley: University of California Press].

Codex Mendoza, c. 1542, Bodleian, MS.Arch.Selden.A. [facs. edited by Berdan, Frances F. and Rieff Anawalt, Patricia 1992, 4 vols. Berkeley: University of California Press].

Codex Mexicanus, c. 1583, BNF, Ms. Mexicain 23-24 [online https://gallica.bnf.fr/ark:/12148/btv1b55005834g].

Codex Osuna, 1565, BNE [1947 facs. edited by Chávez Orozco, Luis 1947, Mexico: Instituto Indigenista Interamericano].

Codex Ramírez, see TOVAR, JUAN DE.

Codex Techialoyan García Granados, 1600s, MNA [facs. edited by Noguez, Xavier 1992, Toluca: El Colegio Mexiquense].

Codex Telleriano-Remensis, c. 1563, Mexico, BNF, Ms. Mexicain 385 [facs. edited by Quiñones Keber, Eloise 1995, Austin: University of Texas Press].

'Codex of Tlatelolco' = 'Imperial Colegio de Indios titulado Santa Cruz', c. 1587, lost ms. [edited by García Icazbalceta 1892 ii; 241–70; excerpted in Appendix 1.3].

Codex Tlatelolco, c. 1562, pictorial codex, INAH [edn. Noguez, Xavier and Valle, Perla 1989, *Códice de Tlatelolco,* Mexico: Secretaría de Relaciones Exteriores].

Codex Tudela, c. 1540; Spanish text and glosses c. 1554, Museo de América, Madrid 70.400 [facs. edited by Jiménez Moreno and Robertson 1980].

Codex Xolotl, c. 1542 [edited by Dibble, Charles E. 1980, 2 vols., Mexico: IIH].

'*Códice franciscano*' = *Relación particular y descripción de toda la Provincia del Santo Evangelio que es de la Orden de San Francisco . . . al Visitador Lic. Juan de Ovando,* c. 1570 [edited by García Icazbalceta, Joaquín 1889 *Códice franciscano: Siglo XVI* (*Nueva colección de documentos* ii), Mexico: Francisco Díaz de León].

Dictionarium ex Hispaniensi in Latinum sermonem (Vocabulario trilingüe), c. 1545, Newberry, Ayer Ms. 1478. *See also* NEBRIJA, ANTONIO DE, 1516.

Incipiunt Epistolae et Evangelia, quae in diebus dominicis per anni totius circulum leguntur. Traducta in linguam Mexicanam, c. 1550, Newberry, Ayer Ms. 1467.

Incipiunt epistolae et evangelia, quae in diebus dominicis per totius anni circulum leguntur. Traducta in linguam mexicanam c. 1560, Biblioteca Capitular de Toledo, Ms. 35-22, 7r–215v.

Información que el arzobispo de México D. Fray Alonso de Montúfar mandó practicar con motivo de un sermón . . . [de] Fray Francisco de Bustamante, acerca de la devoción y culto de Nuestra Señora de Guadalupe, 1556, ms., Archive of Basilica of Guadalupe [edn. 1891, Mexico: Irineo Paz; partial edn. Torre Villar and Navarro de Anda 1982, 36–141].

Instructio[n] y memoria, de las relaciones que se han de hazer para la descripción de las Indias, 1577, Madrid: s.n. [edn. Acuña 1984, Mignolo 1987, 479–84].

Izcatqui ynintezcaamauh, in tlahtoque, c. 1550, in *Miscelánea sagrada*, 1550s–1570s, fols. 101–124.

Martyrologium Romanum: Ad novam kalendarii rationem et ecclesiasticae historiae veritatem restitutum, 1583, Rome: Domenicus Basa.

Memorial de los pueblos sugetos al señorio de Tlacupan y de los que tributauan a Mexico, Tezcuco y Tlacupan, 1550s, Mexico, AGI, Aud. Mex. 256 [edited by Zimmermann 1970, 5–8].

Miscelánea sagrada, 1550s–1570s, BNM, Ms. 1477 (275 fols.) [edn., Sp. translation and study by Alcántara Rojas, Berenice and Sánchez Aguilera, Mario Alberto, 3 vols., in progress].

Nican ompehua y çaçanillatolli, 1550s?, BNM, Ms. 1628 bis, 179r–191v [facs. edited by León-Portilla 1994; edn., Sp. translation by Tena, Rafael, in León-Portilla, Curiel Defossé, and Reyes Equigas 2019 iii, 569–630; edn., Sp. translation in Torres López 2019, 258–351].

Nican vmpeua y çaçanillatolli, 1550s?, BANC, MSS. M-M 464 [edn., German translation, Eng. translation by Kutscher, Brotherston, and Vollmer 1995].

Romances de los señores de la Nueva España, see POMAR, JUAN BAUTISTA DE.

Sequuntur communes epistolae de apostolis, c. 1552, Biblioteca nazionale Braidense, Milan, Manoscritti, AH_X.9 [edn., Latin translation by Biondelli 1858].

Tam de Tristibus quam de Ponticis, 1577, Mexico: Antonius Ricardus.

'*Vocabulario trilingüe*', see *Dictionarium* above.

(II) MANUSCRIPT AND PRINT SOURCES BEFORE 1800 (BY AUTHOR)

ACCURSIUS, BONUS, ed. c. 1478, *Aesopi Fabulae Graece et Latine*, Milan: Bonus Accursius; repr. 1480.

ACOSTA, JOSÉ DE, 1588, *De procuranda Indorum salute = De natura noui orbis libri duo, et De promulgatione euangelii, apud barbaros, siue De procuranda Indorum salute libri sex*, Salamanca: Guillelmus Foquel [edn., Sp. translation by Pereña, Luciano 1984, 1987, *De procuranda Indorum salute*, 2 vols., Madrid: CSIC].

ACOSTA, JOSÉ DE, 1590, *Historia natural y moral de las Indias*, Seville: Juan de León [edn. Alcina Franch, José 2003, Madrid: Dastin; Eng. translation by López-Morillas, Frances 2002, *Natural and Moral History of the Indians*, Durham, NC and London: Duke UP].

AGRICOLA, RUDOLPH (RODOLPHUS), 1515, *De inventione dialectica Libri Tres*, Leuven: Theodoricus Martinus (orig. c. 1476–1479) [edn. Mundt, Lothar 1992, Tübingen: Niemeyer; Eng. translation by McNally, J.R. 1967, 'Rudolph Agricola's *De inventione Libri Tres*: A Translation of Selected Chapters', *Speech Monographs* 34.4: 393–422].

ALBERTI, LEON BATTISTA, c. 1462, *De componendis cyfris* (15 extant mss.) [edited by Buonafalce, Augusto, with Eng. translation by Mendelsohn, Charles J. and Kahn, David 1997, *A Treatise on Ciphers*, Turin: Galimberti].

ALBERTI, LEON BATTISTA, 1568, 'La cifra', in *Opuscoli morali* of Alberti, Venice: Francesco Franceschi, 200–23.

ALBORNOZ, RODRIGO DE, 1525, 'Carta al emperador Carlos V', Mexico City, 15 December, AGI Patronato 184, ramo 2 [edn. García Icazbalceta 1858 i, 484–511; transcr. Company Company 2008, 23–47].

ALCALÁ, Fr. JERÓNIMO DE, c. 1540, *Relación de Michoácan* [edited by Le Clézio, Jean-Marie Gustave, 2016, Zamora: Colegio de Michoacán; Eng. translation by Craine, Eugene R. and Reindorp, Reginald C. 1970, *The Chronicles of Michoacán*, Norman: University of Oklahoma Press].

ALEGRE, FRANCISCO JAVIER, c. 1767, *Historia de la Compañía de Jesus en Nueva-España que estaba escribiendo en el tiempo de su expulsión*, edited by María de Bustamante, Carlos, 1841, 3 vols., Mexico City: J.M. Lara.

ALVA IXTLILXOCHITL, FERNANDO DE, c. 1603, *Sumaria relación de todas las cosas que han sucedido en la Nueva España y de muchas cosas que los tultecas alcanzaron . . .* [edn. s.v. ALVA IXTLILXOCHITL 1975 i, 261–395].

ALVA IXTLILXOCHITL, FERNANDO DE, c. 1605, *Relación sucinta en forma de memorial de la historia de la Nueva España* [edn. s.v. ALVA IXTLILXOCHITL 1975 i, 395–413].

ALVA IXTLILXOCHITL, FERNANDO DE, 1608, *Compendio histórico del reino de Texcoco* [edn. s.v. ALVA IXTLILXOCHITL 1975 i, 415–521]

ALVA IXTLILXOCHITL, FERNANDO DE, c. 1625, *Sumaria relación de la Historia general de esta Nueva España* [edn. s.v. ALVA IXTLILXOCHITL 1975 i, 523–49].

ALVA IXTLILXOCHITL, FERNANDO DE, c. 1625–1640, *Historia de la nación chichimeca* [edn. s.v. ALVA IXTLILXOCHITL 1977 ii, 7–263].

ALVA IXTLILXOCHITL, FERNANDO DE, 1975, 1977, *Obras históricas*, edited by O'Gorman, Edmundo, 2 vols., Mexico: UNAM-IIH.

ALVARADO TEZOZOMOC, HERNANDO DE, 1598, *Coronica mexicana* [2001 edited by Díaz Migoyo, Gonzalo and Vázquez Chamorro, Germán, 2001, *Crónica mexicana*, Madrid: Dastin].

ALVARADO TEZOZOMOC, HERNANDO DE, 1598, 'Tlalamatl Huauhquilpan', INAH Library.

ALVARADO TEZOZOMOC, HERNANDO DE, 1609, *Chronica Mexicayotl*, MS. 354 vol. III, 18r–63r, MNA [edited, Eng. translation by Anderson, Arthur J.O. and Schroeder, Susan 1997, *Codex Chimalpahin Volume 1*, Norman: University of Oklahoma i, 61–177]; BNF, Ms. 311 [edited, Sp. translation by León, Adrián 1998, *Crónica mexicayotl*, Mexico: IIH; orig. 1949].

ÁLVAREZ, MANUEL, 1572, *Emmanuelis Alvari e Societate Iesu de institutione grammatica libri tres*, Olyssipone (Lisbon): Ioannes Barrerius [repr. 1594, Mexico: Vidua Pedri Ocharte].

ANCHIETA, JOSÉ DE, 1563, *De gestis Mendi de Saa*, Lisbon: João Álvares.

ANGLICUS, BARTHOLOMAEUS, c. 1240, *De proprietatibus rerum*, various mss. [Sp. translation, s.v. BURGOS, VICENTE DE]

ANTONIO, NICOLÁS, 1672, *Bibliotheca Hispana nova sive Hispanorum scriptorum qui ab anno MD. ad MDCLXXXIV. floruere notitia*, Rome: N.A. Tinassius; repr. Madrid: Ibarra, 1788 [facs. 1996 of 1788 edn., 2 vols., Madrid: Visor].

ANUNCIACIÓN, Fr. JUAN DE LA, 1577, *Sermonario en lengua mexicana*, Mexico: Antonio Ricardo.

AQUINAS, SAINT THOMAS, 1474, *Expositio super Job ad litteram*, Esslingen: Conrad Fyner [translated by Damico, Anthony 1989, *The Literal Exposition on Job*, Oxford: OUP].

ARA, Fr. DOMINGO DE (DEHARA), 1560, *Ars tzeldaica facta a r[everend]o fr. Domenico de Ara, in Bocabulario de lengua tzeldal según el orden de Copanabastla*, BANC, MSS. M-M 479, fols. 129r–132r [edited by Acuña 1983, 217–22; 1986 *Vocabulario de lengua tzeldal según el orden de Copanabastla*, edited by Mario Humberto Ruz, Mexico: UNAM].

ARA, Fr. DOMINGO DE, c. 1560, *Egregium opus fratris Dominici Dehara*, ms., Newberry, VAULT Ayer Ms. 1688.

ARIAS MONTANO, BENITO, 1569, *Rhetoricorum Libri IV. . . cum annotationibus Antonij Moralij Episcopi Meschuacanensis*, Antwerp: Christophorus Plantinus.

ARNAULD, ANTOINE and LANCELOT, CLAUDE, 1660, 'Port Royal Grammar' = *Grammaire générale et raisonnée contenant les fondemens* [sic] *de l'art de parler*, Paris: P. Le Petit [edn. Brekle, Herbert E. 1966, Stuttgart-Bad Cannstatt: Frommann; Eng. translation by Rieux, Jacques and Rollin, Bernard E. 1975, *General and Rational Grammar: The Port-Royal Grammar*, The Hague: Mouton].

ÁVALOS, *Licenciado* and BONILLA, *Licenciado*, 1576, 'Carta del Santo Oficio de México al Consejo de la General Inquisición', AGN, Mexico (ramo Inquisición): 22 March 1576 [edited by Fernández del Castillo 1982, 35–7].

BADIANO, JUAN, 1552, *Libellus de medicinalibus Indorum herbis*, Tlatelolco, ms., INAH [facs., edn., Sp. translation, introduction by Garibay, Ángel María (with essay studies by various authors) 1991, *Martín de la Cruz, Libellus de medicinalibus Indorum herbis: Manuscrito azteca de 1552*, 2 vols., Mexico: FCE, Insituto Mexicano del Seguro Social; orig. Mexico: Instituto Mexicano del Seguro Social, 1964; Eng. translation by Gates, William 2000, *An Aztec Herbal*, Mineola NY: Dover].

BALBUS, JOHANNES, 1460, *Catholicon, seu Vocabularius universalis et prosodia vel grammatica*, Mainz: Johannes Gutenberg.

BAUTISTA (BAUTISTA VISEO), Fr. JUAN, 1600, *Advertencias para los Confesores de los naturales*, 2 vols., Mexico: Convento de Santiago Tlatelolco, por M. Ocharte [edited by Murillo Gallegas, Verónica 2014, Mexico: Porrúa].

BAUTISTA VISEO, Fr. JUAN, c. 1601, *Huehuetlahtolli*, Mexico: s.n. (printed at Convent of Tlatelolco), JCB: B601.J91h [facs. edited by León-Portilla, Miguel, Sp. translation by Silva Galeana, Librado 2011, *Huehuetlahtolli: Testimonios de la antigua palabra*, Mexico: FCE].

BAUTISTA VISEO, Fr. JUAN, 1604, *Libro de la miseria y brevedad de la vida del hombre . . . en lengua mexicana*, Mexico: Diego López Dávalos.

BAUTISTA VISEO, Fr. JUAN, 1605, *Vida y milagros del bienaventurado Sanct. Antonio de Padua*, Mexico: Diego López Dávalos.

BAUTISTA VISEO, Fr. JUAN, 1606, *Sermonario = A Jesucristo N.S. ofrece este Sermonario en lengua mexicana*, Mexico: Diego López Dávalos, JCB: BA606.J91a [Prologue, edited by García Icazbalceta 1954, 474–8].

BAUTISTA VISEO, Fr. JUAN and Fuente, Agustín de la, c. 1610, *Comedia de los Reyes* [edited, Sp. translation by Paso y Troncoso, Francisco del 1902, Florence: Salvador Landi].

BEAUVAIS, VINCENT DE, c. 1259, *Speculum maius*, various mss. [edited 1473, Strasbourg: Johann Mentelin].

BECERRA TANCO, LUIS, 1675, *La felicidad de México en el principio y milagroso origen que tuvo el santuario de la Virgen María Nuestra Señora de Guadalupe . . .*, Mexico: Viuda de Bernardo de Calderón [edited by Torre Villar and Navarro de Anda 1982, 309–33].

BENAVENTE, Fr. TORIBIO DE, see MOTOLINÍA

BIBLIANDER (BUCHMANN), THEODOR, 1548, *De ratione communi omnium linguarum et literarum commentarius*, Zurich: Christoph Froschauer [edited by Amirav, Hagit and Kirn, Hans-Martin 2011, Geneva: Droz].

BOCCACCIO, GIOVANNI, 1472 *Genealogię deorum gentilium libri* [edn. Romano, Vincenzo, 1951, 2 vols., Bari: Laterza; Eng. translation of books 1–4, Solomon 2011].

BOTURINI (BOTTURINI) BENADUCI, LORENZO, 1746, *Idea de una nueva historia general de la América septentrional*, Madrid: Juan de Zuñiga, incorporating 'Catálogo del museo histórico indiano . . .' [Eng. translation by Poole, Stafford 2015, *Idea of a General History of North America*, Norman: University of Oklahoma Press].

BREYDENBACH, BERNARD VON, 1486, *Peregrinatio in Terram Sanctam*. Mainz: Erhard Reuwich.

BRUNO, GIORDANO, 1582, *De umbris idearum*, Paris: Aegidius Gorbinus [edited by Sturlese, Rita 1991, Florence: Olschki].

BURGOS, VICENTE DE, 1494, *Propriedad de las cosas*, Toulouse: Henricus Mayer.

CABRERA, Fr. CRISTÓBAL 1540, *Argumenta in epistolas Pauli*, ms., Vat. Lat. 1164 [listed in Kristeller 1963–1996, 2: 311 and in Burrus 1960].

CABRERA, Fr. CRISTÓBAL, 1540, 'Dicolon Icastichon', *Manual de adultos*, last two leaves, Mexico: En casa de Juan Cromberger, JCB: BA544.Z94d [facs., Sp. translation by García Icazbalceta 1954; edited, Eng. translation by Laird 2019b, 84–5].

CABRERA, Fr. CRISTÓBAL, c. 1540, 'Epigrams' = *In philosophorum, oratorum, historicorumque classicorum opera extemporalia epigrammata*, ms., Vat. Lat. 1165, fols. 105–9. [edn. Laird 2013].

CABRERA, Fr. CRISTÓBAL, c. 1540, 'Ad Emmanuelem Florez sanctae Mexicanensis Ecclesiae Decanum extemporalis epistola', ms., Vat. Lat. 1165 [edn., Eng. translation by Laird 2017b]

CABRERA, Fr. CRISTÓBAL, 1548, *Meditatiunculae ad... principem Philippum*, Valladolid: Franciscus Ferdinandez Cordubensis.

CABRERA, Fr. CRISTÓBAL, 1549, *Flores de consolación, Dirigidas ala muy yllustre y muy generosa Señora, la señora Doña Iuana de Zuñiga Marquesa del Valle*, Valladolid: Francisco Fernandez de Cordova.

CABRERA, Fr. CRISTÓBAL, 1567, *Escuela de la disciplina y doctrina christiana*, Medina del Rioseco, Spain, ms., Vat. Lat. 5033, fol. 196.

CABRERA, Fr. CRISTÓBAL, 1582, *De solicitanda infidelium conversione*, Rome, 25 January, ms.,Vat. Lat. 5026, 29r–50v [edn. Martín Ortiz 1974, 413–61; edn./Sp. translation of 41v–50v, Campos 1965, 129–42; Eng. summary, Burrus 1961].

CAESARIUS, JOHANN (JOANNES), 1526, *Dialectica . . . in decem tractatus digesta . . . Appendix, in qua ex Alcinoo philosopho platonico declarat quid sit philosophia, . . . tum ex Marsi[lio] Fici[no] quot sint apud ph[il]os[ophorum] disserendi genera*, Cologne: Eucharius Cervicornus.

CALEPINO, AMBROGIO, 1502, *Dictionarium*, Reggio Emilia: Dionysius Bertoch.

CAMERARIUS, JOACHIM, 1538, *Aesopi Phrygis fabvlarvm celeberrimi avtoris vita: Fabellae Aesopicae plvres quadringentis, quædam prius etiam, multæ nunc primum editæ*, Tübingen: Ulrichus Morhardus.

CARDANO, GEROLAMO, 1550, *De subtilitate libri XXI ad Illustriss. Principem Ferrandum Gonzagam*, Nuremberg: Johannes Petreius [edited by Spon, Charles 1663, *Hieronymi Cardani Opera omnia*, vol. 3, Lyon: J.A. Huguetan and M.A. Ravaud; repr. 1966, Stuttgart-Bad Canstatt, 352–672; 2013 translation by Forrester, John, 2 vols., Tempe: ACMRS].

CAROCHI, HORACIO 1645, *Arte de la lengua mexicana, con la declaración de los adverbios de ella*, Mexico: Por Iuan Ruyz [edited, Eng. translation by Lockhart, James 2001, *Grammar of the Mexican Language with an Explanation of Its Adverbs*, Stanford: Stanford UP].

CARTHUSIANUS, DIONYSIUS (DENIS THE CARTHUSIAN), 1532, *Opera minora*, 2 vols., Cologne: Johannes Soter.

CASTAÑEGA, Fr. MARTÍN DE 1529, *Tratado de las supersticiones y hechicerías*, Logroño: Miguel de Eguia [edited by Alejandro Campagne, Fabián 1997, Buenos Aires: Publicaciones de la Universidad].

CERVANTES DE SALAZAR, FRANCISCO, 1554, *Dialogi = Ad Ludovici Vivis Valentini exercitationem, aliquot Dialogi*, Mexico: Ioannes Paulus [edn., Sp. translation by García Icazbalceta, Joaquín 1875; Sp. translation by O'Gorman 1963; facs. ed León-Portilla, Miguel 2001, *México en 1554: Tres diálogos latinos*, Mexico: UNAM; Eng. translation by Sheperd, Barrett and Lee, Minnie; edited by Castañeda, Carlos E. 1953, *Life in the Imperial and Loyal City of Mexico in New Spain*, Austin: University of Texas Press].

CERVANTES DE SALAZAR, FRANCISCO, c. 1566, *Chronica de la Nueva España*, ms., BNE Mss. 2011 [edited by Magallon, Manuel 1971, *Crónica de la Nueva España*, 2 vols., Madrid: Atlas].

CHACÓN, ALFONSO (ALPHONSUS CIACCONUS), 1744, *Bibliotheca libros et scriptores ferme cunctos ab initio mundi ad annum MDLXXXIII, Ordine alphabetico complectens*, Amsterdam: J.C. Arksteeum & H. Merkum.

CHIMALPAHIN, DOMINGO, c. 1610–1629, *Historia o Chronica y con su Calendario*, MNA, Ms. 354 vol. III,, 1r–16v [edn., Eng. translation by Schroeder, Susan and Anderson, Arthur J.O. 1997 i, 26–59, s.v. CHIMALPAHIN, 1621].

CHIMALPAHIN, DOMINGO, 1621, *Codex Chimalpahin* (MNA, Ms. 354 vol. III), edn., Eng. translation by Schroeder, Susan and Anderson, Arthur J.O. 1997, 2 vols., Norman: University of Oklahoma Press.

CHIMALPAHIN, DOMINGO, c. 1624, *Diario*, BNF, Ms. Mexicain 220 [edn., Sp. translation by Tena, Rafael 2001, Mexico: CONACULTA; edn., Eng. translation by Lockhart, James, Schroeder, Susan, and Namala, Doris 2006, *Annals of His Time*, Stanford: Stanford UP].

CHIMALPAHIN, DOMINGO, c. 1630, *Relaciones*, BNF, Ms. Mexicain 74 [facs. edited by Mengin, Ernst 1949–1952, *Eight Relations*, Copenhagen: Corpus Codicum Americanorum Medii

Aevi; edn., Sp. translation by Tena, Rafael 1998, *Las ocho relaciones y el Memorial de Colhuacan*, 2 vols., Mexico: CONACULTA; *Septima relación de las Différentes histoires originales*, edited by García Quintana, Josefina 2003, Mexico: IIH].

CHIMALPAHIN, DOMINGO, 1631, *Memorial breve acerca de la fundaçión de la ciudad de Culhuacan*, BNF, Ms. Mexicain 74, 15r–67v [edn., Sp. translation by Tena, Rafael 1998 i, 72–175, s.v. CHIMALPAHIN, c. 1630].

CHIMALPOPOCA, FAUSTINO, 1876, *Lógica en el idioma mexicano por Chimalpopoca/Elementa logica[e] Jo. Gott.l. Hein. versa in idiomate Nahuatl ad usum Indorum (vulgo dicto) de Tenochtitlan*, BANC, MSS. M-M-474.

CHRYSOSTOM = CHRYSOSTOMUS, DIVUS JOANNES, 1530, *Opera*, 5 vols., Basel: Officina Frobeniana.

CIUDAD REAL, Fr. ANTONIO DE, c. 1586. *Relación breve y verdadera de algunas cosas de las muchas que sucedieron al padre fray Alonso Ponce* [edn. 1872, 2 vols., Madrid: Viuda de Calero].

CLAVIGERO, FRANCESCO SAVERIO (FRANCISCO JAVIER CLAVIJERO), 1780, *Storia antica del Messico cavata da' migliori storici spagnuoli, e da' manoscritti, e dalle pitture antiche degl' indiani*, 4 vols., Cesena: G. Biasini. [Sp. translated by by Clavigero, edited by Cuevas, Mariano 2003, *Historia antigua de México*, Mexico: Porrúa].

CLEYNAERTS, NICOLAS (CLENARDUS, CLENARD), 1557, *Institutiones ac meditationes in Graecam linguam*, Lyon: Macé Bonhomme (originally two works: *Institutiones in linguam Graecam*, Paris: Lodovicus Cyanius, 1530; *Meditationes Graecanicae*, Leuven: Bartholomaeus Gravius, 1531).

CLEYNAERTS, NICOLAS, 1559, *Tabula in grammaticen Hebraeam*, Paris: Martinus Iuvenis; orig. Leuven: Thierry Martens, 1529.

COLUMBUS, CHRISTOPHERUS, c. 1504, *Libro de las profecías* [edn. Rusconi, Roberto and translated by Sullivan, Blair 1997, *The Book of Prophecies Edited by Christopher Columbus*, Berkeley: University of California Press].

CORONEL, Fr. JUAN DE, 1620, *Arte en lengua maya*, Mexico: Emprenta de Diego Garrigo, por Adrián César [edn. Acuña, René 1998, Mexico: UNAM].

CORTÉS, HERNÁN, 1520, 'Segunda carta-relación al Emperador: Fecha en Segura de la Sierra á 30 de octubre de 1520' [edn. CORTÉS, 1866, 51–157; Eng. tr. s.v. CORTÉS, 1986, 47–159].

CORTÉS, HERNÁN, 1522, 'Tercera carta-relación al Emperador: Cuyoacan á 15 de mayo de 1522' [edn. CORTÉS 1866, 161–272; Eng. tr. s.v. CORTÉS 1986, 160–281].

CORTÉS, HERNÁN, 1524, *Praeclara Ferdina[n]di Cortesii de Noua maris Oceani Hyspania narratio sacratissimo. ac Inuictissimo Carolo Romanoru[m] Imperatori semper Augusto, Hyspaniaru[m]*, Nuremberg: Fredericus Peypus.

CORTÉS, HERNÁN, 1526, 'Quinta carta de relación' = 'Carta al Emperador. Méjico 3 de setiembre de 1526' [edn. CORTÉS 1866, 395–492; tr. s.v. CORTÉS 1986, 338–447].

CORTÉS, HERNÁN, 1866, *Cartas y relaciones de Hernán Cortés al Emperador Carlos V*, edited by Pascual de Gayangos, Paris: A. Chaix.

CORTÉS, HERNÁN, 1986, *Letters from Mexico*, translated by Pagden, Anthony, New Haven: Yale UP.

CORTÉS TOTOQUIHUATZIN, ANTONIO, 1552, 'Don Antonio Cortés y otros yndios piden a S.M.', Tlacopan, 6 January, AGI Patronato 184, 45 [facs. edited by Zimmermann 1970, 1, Ia; edn. Pérez-Rocha and Tena 2000, 161–2].

CORTÉS TOTOQUIHUATZIN, ANTONIO, 1552, 'Sacra Cathólica, Cesarea Magestad, Don Antonio Cortés, tlatouani o caçique del pueblo llamado Tlacopan . . . y los alcades y regidores', Tlacopan, 6 January, AGI, Audiencia de México, 91, ramo 1 [edn. Pérez-Rocha and Tena 2000, 163–5].

CORTÉS TOTOQUIHUATZIN, ANTONIO, 1552, 'S. C. C. Majestati Antonius cortes Rector populi de Tlacoban' (Latin letter to Charles V), Tlacopan, 1 December, ms. AGI, Patr. 184, 45 [facs., edited by Zimmermann 1970, 2–5; edn., Eng. translation Appendix 2.3].

CORTÉS TOTOQUIHUATZIN, ANTONIO, 1561, 'Carta de don Antonio Cortés y de los alcaldes y regidores de Tlacopan al rey Felipe II', Tlacopan, 20 February, AGI, Audiencia de México, 168 [edited by Pérez-Rocha and Tena 2000, 245–7].

CORTÉS TOTOQUIHUATZIN, ANTONIO, 1566, 'Don Antonio Cortés caçique y los demas principales del pueblo de Tacuba, sobre que se ponga en la corona real', Mexico, 15 March), AGI, Justicia 1029 [edited by Pérez-Rocha and Tena 2000, 333–68].

CORTÉS TOTOQUIHUATZIN, ANTONIO, 1574, 'Jueves ic XXIX ilhuitl metztli . . . ,' Tlacopan, 29 April, BNF, Ms. Mexicain 115 [Nahuatl facs. edn., German translation by Zimmermann 1970, 12–13; Sp. translation by Pérez-Rocha and Tena 2000, 373–8].

CRUZ, MARTÍN DE LA, 1552, *Libellus*, *see* BADIANO.

CRUZ, Fr. RODRIGO DE LA, 1550, 'Carta al Emperador Carlos V', Ahuacatlan, 4 May, edited by Solano 1991, 45.

DANTE ALIGHIERI, c. 1305, *De vulgari eloquentia* (*editio princeps*), Paris: Joannes Corbon [edited, translated by Botterill, Steven 1996, Cambridge: CUP].

DÁVILA PADILLA, AGUSTÍN, 1596, *Historia de la fundación y discurso de la prouincia de Santiago de Mexico, de la Orden de Predicadores*, Madrid: Pedro Madrigal [repr. 1625, 1955 Brussels: Ivan de Meerbeque, in facs., edited by Millares Carlo, Agustín 1955, Mexico: Academia Literaria].

DESPAUTER, JOHANN (JOHANNES DESPAUTERIUS), 1536, *Commentarii grammatici*, Lyon: Thibaud Payen; repr. 1537, Paris: ex officina Roberti Stephani.

DÍAZ DE LUCO, JUAN BERNAL, 1545, *Aviso de curas muy provechoso para los que exercitan el oficio de curar animas*, Alcalá de Henares: Joan de Brocar.

DÍAZ DEL CASTILLO, BERNAL, 1568–1575, *Historia verdadera de la conquista de la Nueva España* [2011 edited by Serés, Guillermo, Madrid-Barcelona: RAE-Galaxia Gutenberg].

DOLCE, LODOVICO, 1562, *Dialogo di M. Lodovico Dolce nel quale si ragiona del modo di accrescere e conservare l'arte di memoria*, Venice: Giovanni Battista & Melchiorre Sessa.

DURÁN, Fr. DIEGO, 1579, *El calendario antiguo*, BNE, Vitr/26/11, fols. 316–44 [edited by Camelo Arredondo, Rosa de Lourdes and Romero, José Rubén 2002, *Fray Diego Durán: Historia de las Indias*, Mexico: CONACULTA, vol. 2, 221–93; translated by Horcasitas, Fernando and Heyden, Doris 1975, *Book of the Gods and Rites of the Ancient Calendar*, Norman: University of Oklahoma, 383–470].

DURÁN, Fr. DIEGO, c. 1581, *Historia de las Indias de Nueva España e Islas de Tierra Firme* (*Codex Durán*), BNE, Vitr/26/11, fols. 1–226. [edited by Camelo Arredondo, Rosa de Lourdes and Rubén Romero, José 2002, 2 vols., Mexico: CONACULTA; Eng. translation by Heyden, Doris 2010, *History of the Indies of New Spain*, Norman: U. of Oklahoma Press].

EGUIARA Y EGUREN, JUAN JOSÉ DE, 1755, *Bibliotheca Mexicana, sive eruditorum historia virorum*, Mexico: in aedibus authoris [facs. edited by Torre Villar, Ernesto de la 1986 vol. 1, Mexico: UNAM].

ERASMUS, DESIDERIUS, c. 1489, *Conflictus Thaliae et Barbariei* [edn. Hoven, René 2013, ASD I-8, 343–67].

ERASMUS, DESIDERIUS, 1500, *Adagia =Adagiorum collectanea*, Paris: Johann Philippi; expanded repr. 1508, *Adagiorum chiliades tres*, Venice: Aldus Manutius. *See* ERASMUS 1536 for the final complete edition.

ERASMUS, DESIDERIUS, 1503, *Encheiridion militis Christi*, in *Lucubratiunculae aliquot Erasmi*, Antwerp: Theodoricus Martinus [edited by Domański, Juliusz and Marcel, Raymond 2016, ASD V-8; translated by Fantazzi, Charles 1988, CWE 66, 1–128].

ERASMUS, DESIDERIUS, 1511, *De ratione studii ac legendi interpretandique auctores*, Paris: Joris Biermans [edn. Margolin, Jean-Claude 1971, ASD I-2, 79–151; translated by McGregor, Brian 1978, CWE 24, 661–92].

ERASMUS, DESIDERIUS, 1511, *Praise of Folly = Moriae encomium id est Stultitiae Laus*, Paris: Gilles de Gourmon [edn. Miller, Clarence H. 1979 ASD IV-3; translated by Radice, Betty 1986, CWE 27, 77–154].

ERASMUS, DESIDERIUS, 1512, *De copia = De duplici copia verborum ac rerum commentarii duo*, Paris: In aedibus Ascensianis [edn. Knott, Betty I. 1988, ASD I-6; translated by Knott, Betty I. 1978 CWE 24, 279–659].

ERASMUS, DESIDERIUS, 1515, *Libellus de constructione octo partium orationis*, Basel: in officina Frobeniana [edn. Cytowska, M. 1973, ASD I-4:105–43].

ERASMUS, DESIDERIUS, 1516, *Epistolae = Erasmi Roterodami Epistole*, Leipzig: Valentinus Schumann.

ERASMUS, DESIDERIUS, 1516, *Institutio principis Christiani*, Basel: Johannes Frobenius [edn. Herding, O. 1974, ASD IV-1, 95–219; translated by Cheshire, Neil M. and Heath, Michael J. 1986, CWE 27, 199–288].

ERASMUS, DESIDERIUS, 1516, New Testament = *Novum Instrumentum omne*, Basel: Johannes Frobenius [repr. 1516, 1519, 1522, 1527, 1536 as *Novum Testamentum omne*, edited by Brown, Andrew J., 2000–2013, ASD VI-1–VI.4].

ERASMUS, DESIDERIUS, 1516, *Paraclesis ad lectorem pium* (published with *Novum Instrumentum*), Basel: Johannes Frobenius [edn. Béné, Ch. 2013, ASD V-7, 279–98; translated by Dalzell, Ann 2019, 'The Paraclesis of Erasmus of Rotterdam to the Pious Reader', in *The New Testament Scholarship of Erasmus*, edited by Sider, Robert D., Toronto: University of Toronto Press, 393–422].

ERASMUS, DESIDERIUS, 1517, *De querela pacis vndique gentium eiectae profligataeque*, Basel: Johannes Frobenius (first Frobenius edn. in *Polydori Vergilii proverbiorum liber*, Basel, 1516) [edn. Herding, Otto 1977 ASD IV-2, 60–100; translated by Radice, Betty 1986, CWE 27, 293–322].

ERASMUS, DESIDERIUS, 1518, *Colloquia familiaria = Familiarium colloquiorum formulae*, Basel: Johannes Frobenius [edn. Halkin, L.-E., Bierlaire, F., and Hoven, R., 1972, ASD I-3, 31–103; translated by Thompson, Craig R. 1997, CWE 39-40]

ERASMUS, DESIDERIUS, 1520, *Antibarbari = Antibarbarorum liber unus*, Basel: Johannes Frobenius [edn. Kumaniecki, Kazimierz 1969, ASD I.1: 7–138; translated by Mann Phillips, Margaret 1978, CWE 23, 1–122].

ERASMUS, DESIDERIUS, 1520, *Apologia de In principio erat sermo*, Basel: Johannes Frobenius [1703–1706 ed. *Opera Omnia*, IX, 111–22, Leiden; translated by Drysdall, Denis D. 2015, CWE 73, 13–40].

ERASMUS, DESIDERIUS, 1520, *Conficiendarum epistolarum formula* [edn. s.v. 1522, *Opus de conscribendis epistolis*; translated by Fantazzi, Charles, 1985, CWE 25: 258-67].

ERASMUS, DESIDERIUS, 1521, *De contemptu mundi epistola*, Leuven: Theodoricus Martinus [edn. Dresden, Sem, ASD V-1, 1–87; translated by Rummel, Erika CWE 66, 131–75].

ERASMUS, DESIDERIUS, 1522, *Epistula nuncupatoria ad Carolem Caesarem: Exhortatio ad studium euangelicae lectionis* [2005 *Exhortation à la lecture de l'évangile: Le texte Latin*, edited by Bedouelle, Guy, Turnhout: Brepols].

ERASMUS, DESIDERIUS, 1522, *Opus de conscribendis epistolis . . . recognitum ab autore*, Basel: Johannes Frobenius [edn. Margolin, Jean-Claude 1971, ASD I-2, 205–579; translated by Fantazzi, Charles, 1985, CWE 25: 1–254].

ERASMUS, DESIDERIUS, 1523, *In Evangelium Lucae Paraphrasis*, Basel: Johannes Frobenius [edn. Bloemendal, Jan 2018, ASD VII-2, translated by Phillips, Jane E., 2003, CWE 47–48].

ERASMUS, DESIDERIUS, 1525, *Lingua*, Basel: Johannes Frobenius [revised edn. Waszink, J. H. 1989 ASD IV-1; translated by Fantham, Elaine and Rummel, Erika 1989, CWE 29, 249–412]. *See also* PÉREZ DE CHINCHON.

ERASMUS, DESIDERIUS, 1528, *De recta Latini Graecique sermonis pronuntiatione*, Basel: in officina Frobeniana [edn. Cytowska, M. 1973, ASD I-4: 1–103; translated by Pope, Maurice, 1985, CWE 26, 347–476].

ERASMUS, DESIDERIUS, 1529, *Paraphrasis seu potius Epitome in Elegantiarum libros Laurentii Vallae*, Cologne: Joannes Gymnicus [edn. Heesakkers, C.L. and Waszink, J.H. 1973, ASD I-4, 187–351].

ERASMUS, DESIDERIUS, 1529, *Opus Epistolarum . . . per autorem, diligenter recognitum (Lib. 1–24)*. Basel: Ex officina Frobeniana [edited by Allen, P.S. 1906–1958, *Opus epistolarum*,

12 vols., Oxford: Clarendon Press; tr. 1975–2013, *Correspondence of Erasmus,* 15 vols. Toronto: University of Toronto Press].

ERASMUS, DESIDERIUS, 1531, *Apophthegmata = Apophthegmatum opus* [edn. Meer, Tineke ter 2010, ASD IV-4; translated by Fantham, Elaine 2014, CWE 37-38].

ERASMUS, DESIDERIUS, 1535, *Ecclesiastes = Ecclesiastae sive De ratione concionandi libri quatuor,* Antwerp: Michaelis Hillenius [edn. Chomarat, Jacques, 1991–1994, ASD, V-4, V-5; translated by Butrica, James L.P. 2015, CWE 67-68].

ERASMUS, DESIDERIUS, 1536, *Adagia = Adagiorum chiliades,* Basel: Ex officina Frobeniana [edn. Heinimann, Felix and Kienzle, Emanuel 1981 ASD II-1–II-8; various translators, 1981–2006, CWE 30-36].

ERASMUS, DESIDERIUS, 1538, *Epistolae familiares,* Basel: Barphtholomaeus Westhemerus.

ERASMUS, DESIDERIUS, 1539, *Autores cum suis commentis scilicet Catonis Romani sententiae morales Distichis descriptae . . .,* Lyon: Matthias Bonhome.

ERASMUS, DESIDERIUS, 1567, *Catonis Disticha moralia, cum scholiis,* Seville: *apud* Alonso Escribano, *apud* Andrea Pescioni.

ERASMUS, DESIDERIUS, and EGNATIUS, JOANNES BAPTISTA, ed., 1546, *Vitae Caesarum quarum scriptores hi C. Svetonius Tranquillus, Dion Cassius, Aelius Spartianus . . . ,* Basel: Hieronymus Frobenius.

ESCALONA, Fr. ALONSO DE [?], 1500s, 'Dominica in albis', BNM, Ms. 1482, 237r–240r.

FERNÁNDEZ DE OVIEDO, Gonzalo, 1535–1557, *La historia general y natural de las Indias* [edited by Tudela Bueso, Juan Pérez de 1959, 5 vols., BAE 117–21, Madrid: Ediciones Atlas].

FERRER, SAINT VINCENT, 1300s, *Sermones de peccatis capitalibus prout septem petitionibus orationis Dominicae opponuntur* [edited 1729 *Opera, seu sermones de tempore et sanctis,* Augsburg: Joannes Strotter, 29–57].

FICINO, MARSILIO, 1482, *Theologia Platonica de immortalitate animarum,* Florence: Antonio Miscomini [edited, Eng. translation by Hankins, James 2001–2006, *Platonic Theology,* 6 vols., Cambridge, MA: Harvard I Tatti Library].

FICINO, MARSILIO, 1485, *Platonis Opera latine, interprete Marsilio Ficino, cum Vita Platonis ab eodem Ficino,* Florence: Laurentius Venetus (*see also* CAESARIUS).

FLORENCIA, FRANCISCO DE, 1694, *Historia de la provincia de la Compañía de Jesús de Nueva España,* Mexico: J.J. Guillena Carrascoso.

FOCHER, Fr. JUAN DE (Fr. JOHANNES), 1574, *Itinerarium Catholicum proficiscentium ad infideles convertendos,* Hispali [Seville]: Alfonsus Scribanus [edited by Eguiluz, P. Antonio 1960, *Itinerario del misionero en América,* Madrid: Librería General Victoriano Suárez].

GALLANDE, PIERRE (PETRUS GALLANDIUS), ed., 1543, *M. Fabii Quintiliani eloquentissimi de Institutione oratoria libri XII . . . ,* Paris: Michaëlis Paruus.

GANTE, Fr. PEDRO DE (Pieter de Muer), 1529, 'Dilectissimi patres fratres et sorores', Mexico, 27 June, in ZIERIXEENSES, *Chronica,* 124v–127r [edited by García Icazbalceta 1954, 100–2].

GANTE, Fr. PEDRO DE (Pieter de Muer), 1532, 'Carta al emperador', Mexico, 31 October, AHN, Diversos Colecciones, 22, N.13 [edn. 1877, *Cartas de Indias,* Madrid: Ministerio de Fomento, 51–3].

GANTE, Fr. PEDRO DE (Pieter de Muer), 1553, *Doctrina christiana en lengua mexicana,* Mexico: Juan Pablos [facs. edited by Torre Villar, Ernesto de la 1981, Mexico: Centro de Estudios Históricos Fray Bernardino de Sahagún].

GANTE, Fr. PEDRO DE (Pieter de Muer), 1558, 'Carta de Fr. Pedro de Gante al Rey D. Felipe', Mexico [edited by García Icazbalceta 1941, 220–7].

GAONA, Fr. JUAN DE, c. 1540, *Colloquios de la paz, y tranquilidad christiana, en lengua mexicana,* Ms. 35–22, Chapter Library, Toledo, Spain, 265r–326v; another ms. version with variants, *El siguiente tratado hizo El padre frai Juan de gaona con sus discipulos,* in *Miscelánea sagrada* (s.v)., fols. 75r–100v; edn. Fr. Agustín de Zárate, 1582, Mexico: Pedro Ocharte.

GAONA, Fr. JUAN DE, c. 1600, *Colloquios de la paz, y tranquilidad christiana: Interlocutores; Un Religioso y un collegial,* anonymous translation into Otomí, Newberry, Ayer Ms. 1648.

GARCÉS, HENRIQUE, tr. 1591, *Francisco Patricio, De Reyno, y de la institución del que ha de Reynar.* Madrid: Luis Sanchez.

GARCÉS, Fr. JULIÁN, 1537, *De habilitate et capacitate gentium sive Indorum novi mundi nuncupati ad fidem Christi capessendam, & quam libenter suscipiant.* Rome s.n., JCB, BA537.G215d [facs. Hanke 1976, 376–89, Lobato Casado 1988; edn., Eng. translation by Laird 2014; fols. 2v–3v, 4v–5v excerpted in Appendix 2.1].

GARCÉS, Fr. JULIÁN and ZUMÁRRAGA, Fr. JUAN DE, 1529, 'Carta de los Ilmos. Sres. Dn. Fr. Julián Garcés, Obispo de Tlaxcala y Dn. Fr. Juan de Zumárraga, Electo Obispo de México, a un noble señor de la Corte, Consejero de los Reyes', AGI-J 1018, Mexico, 7 August [edited by Cuevas 1946 i, 455–6; García Icazbalceta 1947 iv, 99–102].

GARCILASO DE LA VEGA, INCA, 1609, *Primera parte de los Commentarios reales,* Lisbon: Pedro Crasbeeck [edited by Arañíbar, Carlos 1991, *Comentarios reales,* Mexico: FCE; Eng. translation by Livermore, Harold V. 1965, *Royal Commentaries of the Incas and General History of Peru,* Austin, University of Texas Press].

GERVASE OF TILBURY, c. 1211, *Otia imperialia* [edn., Eng. translation by Banks, S.E. and Binns, J.W. 2002, Oxford: OUP].

GIL, 'MAESTRE', 1527, *Libro de medicina llamado Macer,* Valladolid: Miguel de Eguía.

GILBERTI, Fr. MATURINO, 1558, *Arte de la lengua de Michuacan,* Mexico: en casa de Iuan Pablos [1987 facs. edited by Warren, J. Benedict, Morelia, Michoacán: Fimax Publicistas; 2004 edited by Monzón, Cristina, Zamora: El Colegio de Michoacán].

GILBERTI, Fr. MATURINO,1559, *Dialogo de Doctrina Christiana en la lengua d[e] Mechuaca[n]. Hecho y copilado de muchos libros de sana doctrina,* Mexico: Iuan Pablos Bressano.

GILBERTI, Fr. MATURINO, 1559, *Grammatica Maturini tractatus omnium fere que Grammatices studiosis tradi solent,* Mexico: En la oficina de Antonio Espinosa [2003 edited by Lucas González, Rosa, 2 vols, Zamora: El Colegio de Michoacán].

GILBERTI, Fr. MATURINO, 1559, *Vocabulario en lengua de Mechuacan,* Mexico City: Casa de Iuan Pablos Bressano [1989 facsimile, edited by Warren, J. Benedict, Morelia, Michoacán: Fimax Publicistas; 1997 edited by Zavala, Agustín Jacinto, Martínez, Clotilde, and Warren, J. Benedict, Zamora: El Colegio de Michoacán].

GINÉS DE SEPULVEDA, see SEPÚLVEDA, JUAN GINÉS DE.

GIRALDI (GYRALDUS), LILIO GREGORIO, 1551, *Libelli duo, in quorum altero Aenigmata, plerique antiquorum, in altero Pythagorae Symbola sunt explicata,* Basel: Joannes Oporinus.

GRANADA, Fr. LUIS DE, 1576, *Ecclesiastica rhetorica sive de ratione concionandi libri sex,* Lisbon: Antonius Riberius.

GRANADA, Fr. LUIS DE, 1585, *Breve tratado en que se declara de la manera que se podrá proponer la doctrina de nuestra santa fe y religión cristiana á los infieles* [1848 reprint, *Biblioteca de autores españoles,* edited by Bonaventura, Carles Aribau, vol. 8: *Obras de Fray Luis de Granada* 2: 596–611, Madrid: Ribadeneyra].

GUEVARA, Fr. ANTONIO DE, 1528, *Libro áureo de Marco Aurelio, emperador y eloquentissimo orador,* Seville: Jacobo Cromberger [edited by Blanco, Emilio 1994, *Obras Completas de Fray Antonio de Guevara* vol. 1, Madrid: Biblioteca Castro-Turner].

GUEVARA, Fr. ANTONIO DE, 1539, *Epistolas familiares del illustre señor don Antonio de Gueuara.* Valladolid: Juan de Villaquiran [edited by Cossio, José María de 1950, *Epístolas familiares* vol. 1, Madrid: Aldus].

GUEVARA, Fr. ANTONIO DE, 1539, *Una decada de Cesares, las vidas de X Emperadores Romanos, a Trajano ad Alexandrum.* Valladolid: Juan de Villaqueran.

HEGIUS [VON HEEK], ALEXANDER, 1480s, *Invectiva in modos significandi,* editio princeps in Hegius, *Dialogi,* 1503, Deventer: Richard Paffraet [edn. IJsewijn, Jozef 1971, Forum for Modern Language Studies 7: 299–318]

HEINECKE, JOHANN GOTTLIEB, 1740, *Elementa philosophiae rationalis et moralis,* Venice: Typographia Balleoniana.

HERNÁNDEZ, FRANCISCO, c. 1575, *De antiquitatibus Novae Hispaniae libri tres,* RAH, Ms. 9-2101 [facs. 1926, Mexico: Museo Nacional de Arqueología, Historia y Etnografía; Sp.

translation by García Pimentel, Joaquín 1945, *Antigüedades de la Nueva España*, Mexico: Pedro Robredo].

HUITZIMENGARI, DON ANTONIO, 1553–1554, 'Información de méritos y servicios de don Antonio Huitzimengari, hijo del último cazonci de Michoacán', AGI, PatronatoReal, ficha 13, legajo 60, ramo 3, número 2 [edn. Aguilar González, J. Ricardo and Afanador Pujol, Angélica J. 2019, *Don Antonio Huitzimengari: Información y vida de un noble indígena en la Nueva España del siglo XVI*, Morélia: UMSNH/UNAM, 107–212.

INNOCENT III (INNOCENTIUS TERTIUS), POPE, c. 1196, *De contemptu mundi et miseria conditionis humanae* [1855 *Patrologia Latina*, edited by Migne, J.-P. *et al.*, Paris: J.-P. Migne, cols. 701–46; repr., *Innocentii III Romani pontificis opera omnia*, vol. 217, Turnhout: Brepols].

INNOCENT III (INNOCENTIUS TERTIUS), POPE, 1540, *De sacro altaris mysterio*, Antwerp: Joannes Steelsius.

LANDA, Fr. DIEGO DE, 1568, *Relación de las cosas de Yucatán* [edited by León Cazares, María del Carmen 2003, Mexico: CONACULTA].

LAS CASAS, Fr. BARTOLOMÉ DE, 1535, *Carta a un personaje de la corte*, Granada de Nicaragua, 15 October [edited by Pérez de Tudelea y Bueso, Juan 1958, *Obras escogidas*, vol. 5, Madrid: Atlas, 65].

LAS CASAS, Fr. BARTOLOMÉ DE, 1539, *De unico vocationis modo omnium gentium ad veram religionem* [edn./Sp. translation by Millares Carlo, Agustín 1942, *Del único modo de atraer a todos los pueblos a la verdadera religión*, Mexico: FCE; edn. Castañeda Delgado, Paulino and García del Moral, Antonio 1992, *Obras completas*, vol. 2, Madrid: Alianza; Eng. translation by Sullivan, Francis Patrick, in Parish 1992, 63–182].

LAS CASAS, Fr. BARTOLOMÉ DE, c. 1552, *Apologia = Argumentum Apologiae Rmi. Dni. Fratris Bartholomei a Casaus, Episcopi quondam chiapensis adversus Genesium Sepulvedam, theologum cordubensem* [edited by Losada, Ángel 1975, *Apología*, Madrid: Editora nacional; edited by Abril Castelló, Vidal 2000, Salamanca: Junta de Castilla y León; Eng. translation by Poole, Stafford 1992, *In Defense of the Indians*, De Kalb: Northern Illinois UP.]

LAS CASAS, Fr. BARTOLOMÉ DE, c. 1558, *Apologética historia sumaria* [edited by O'Gorman, Edmundo 1967, 2 vols., Mexico: UNAM].

LAS CASAS, Fr. BARTOLOMÉ DE, c. 1560, *Historia de las Indias* [edited by Pérez de Tudela Bueso, Juan and López Oto, Emilio 1961, *Obras escogidas* vol. 2, Madrid: Atlas; edited by Millares Carlo, Agustín and Hanke, Lewis 1965, 3 vols., Mexico: FCE; edited by Ángel Medina, Miguel, Pérez Fernández, Isacio, and Ángel Barreda, Jesús, 1994, *Obras completas*, vols. 3–5, Madrid: Alianza].

LAS CASAS, Fr. BARTOLOMÉ DE, 1571 *'De regia potestate' = Explicatio quaestionis utrum reges vel principes iure aliquo vel titulo, et salva conscientia, cives ac subditos a regia corona alienare, et alterius domini particularis ditioni subiicere possint?* Frankfurt: Wolfgang Griesstetter [edited by Pereño, Luciano, Pérez Prendes, J.M., Abril, Vidal, and Azcarraga, Joaquín 1984, *De regia potestate*, Madrid: CSIC].

LAS CASAS, Fr. BARTOLOMÉ DE, and SANTO TOMÁS, Fr. DOMINGO DE, 1560, 'Memorial del obispo fray Bartolomé y fray Domingo de Santo Tomás', ms. [edited by Pérez de Tudela Bueso, Juan 1958, *Obras escogidas de Fray Bartolomé de las Casas*, Madrid: Atlas, 465–9].

LASO (LASSO) DE LA VEGA, LUIS, 1649, *Huei Tlamahuiçoltica*, Mexico: Juan Ruyz [edited, Eng. translation by Sousa, Poole, and Lockhart 1998].

LEÓN PINELO, ANTONIO, 1629, *Epitome de la Bibliotheca Oriental i Occidental, Nautica i Geografica*, 4 vols., Madrid: Iuan Gonzalez.

LIPSIUS, JUSTUS, 1584, *De constantia*, Antwerp: Plantijn.

LÓPEZ, JERÓNIMO, 1541, 'Carta de Jerónimo López al Emperador', Mexico City, 20 October [edn. García Icazbalceta 1866 ii, 141–54].

LÓPEZ, JERÓNIMO, 1545, 'Carta de Jerónimo López al Emperador', 25 February [edn. Paso y Troncoso 1939 iv, 150–79].

LÓPEZ DE COGULLUDO, DIEGO, 1688, *Historia de Yucathan, Sacada a luz por Francisco de Ayeta*, Madrid: Juan Garcia Infanzon [facs. edited by Rubio Mañé, Jorge Ignacio 1957, Mexico: Editorial Academia literaria].

LÓPEZ DE GÓMARA, FRANCISCO, 1554, *La historia general de las Indias, y todo lo acaescido enellas dende que se ganaron hasta agora y la conquista de Mexico y dela Nueua España*, Antwerp: Martin Nutius [1941 edn. *Historia general de las Indias*, Madrid: Espasa Calpe].

LORENZANA Y BUITRÓN, FRANCISCO ANTONIO, 1769, *Concilios provinciales, primero y segundo, celebrados en la muy noble y muy leal ciudad de Mégico en los años 1555 y 1565*. Mexico: Imprenta de Joseph Antonio Hogal.

LYRA, NICHOLAS OF, 1502, *Biblia Latina cum Glossa ordinaria: Et literali moralique expositione*, Basel: Jo. de Amerbach, Jo. Petri de Langendorf, Jo. Froeben [facs. of Strasbourg 1481 *editio princeps*, edited by Froehlich, Karlfried K. and Gibson, Margaret T. 1992, 4 vols., Turnhout: Brepols].

MACER FLORIDUS, [AEMILIUS], 1511, *Carmen de herbarum virtutibus*, Paris: Jehan Petit (1200s orig.); see also GIL, 1527.

MAGNUS, OLAUS, 1555, *Historia de gentibus septentrionalibus*, Rome: Joannes Maria de Viottis.

MANUTIUS, ALDUS, ed., 1505, *Vita, & Fabellæ Aesopi*, Venice: Aldus.

MANUTIUS, ALDUS, ed., 1534, *Aesopi Phrygis uita et fabellae*, Basel: Johannes Frobenius.

MARBAIS, MICHEL DE (MICHAEL DE MARBASIO), c. 1270, *Summa de modis significandi*, Paris [edited by Kelly, Louis Gerard 1995, Stuttgart-Bad Cannstatt: Frommann-Holzboog].

MARCHESINUS, JOHANNES, 1470, *Mammotrectus super Bibliam*, Mainz (Civitas Maguntina): Petrus Schoiffer.

MARIANA, JUAN DE, 1599, *De rege et regis institutione libri III*, Toledo: Petrus Rodericus.

MARLIANUS, BARTHOLOMAEUS, 1545, *Hoc libello haec continentur Sophoclis tragici poetae vita . . . Eiusdem poetae sententiae pulcherrimae*. Rome: Antonius Bladus Asulanus.

MARTÍNEZ, HENRICO, 1606, *Reportorio de los tiempos, Historia natural desta Nueva España*. Mexico: Emprenta del mesmo autor.

MARTYR D'ANGHIERA, PETER (PETRUS MARTYR ANGLERIUS), 1530, *De orbe novo decades*, Complutum (Alcalá de Henares): Michaelis d'Egina [edited by Mazzacana, Rosanna and Magioncalda, Elisa 2005, *Pietro Martire d'Anghiera, De orbe Novo Decades*, 2 vols., Genoa: Università di Genova].

MELANCHTHON, PHILIPP, 1550, *Fabellae Aesopicae qvaedam notiores, et in scolis vsitatae*, Leipzig: Valentinus Papa.

MENDIETA, Fr. GERÓNIMO DE, c. 1596, *Historia = Hystoria ecclesiastica yndiana compuesta par el P[adr]e Fray Geronimo de Mendieta*, BLAC, Ms., JGI 1120 [edn. García Icazbalceta, Joaquín 1870, *Historia eclesiástica indiana*, Mexico: Antigua Librería, Portal de Agustinos, facs. 1993, Mexico: Porrúa].

MENDOZA, FRANCISCO DE (bookseller), 1559, 'Poder de Francisco de Mendoza, librero de México al regidor de Pátzcuaro, Juan Fernández, para cobranza', Archivo Municipal de Pátzcuaro, Michoacán, Serie Pátzcuaro, expediente 35' [edited by Jiménez 2002; cf. Appendix 1.2].

MERULA, GIORGIO, ed., 1503, *Censorini de die natali liber aureus*, Milan: Joannes Angelus Scinzenzeler.

MERULA, GIORGIO, 1519, 1521, *Scriptores historiae Augustae: Neruae & Traiani atq[ue] Adriani Caesarum vitae ex Dione*, Venice: Aldus.

MEXÍA FERNANGIL, DIEGO, 1617, *La segunda parte del Parnaso antartico de divinos poemas*, BNF, Ms. Espagnol 389, fols. 182–196.

MEXÍA (MEJÍA), PEDRO, 1540, *Silva de varia lección*, Seville: Dominico de Robertis [edn. Castro Díaz, Antonio 1989, Madrid: Cátedra].

MIER Y NORIEGA, Fr. SERVANDO DE TERESA DE, 1797, 'Carta VI', *Cartas al Dr Muñoz sobre la aparición de Nuestra Señora de Guadalupe*, Burgos [edited by Torre Villar and Navarro de Anda 1982, 838–61].

MIJANGOS, Fr. JUAN DE, 1607, *Espejo divino, en que pueden verse los padres y tomar documento para acertar a doctrinar bien a sus hijos y aficionallos a las virtudes*, Mexico: Diego Lopez Davalos.

MIJANGOS, Fr. JUAN DE, 1624, *Primera parte del Sermonario, dominical, y sanctoral, en lengua mexicana*, Mexico: Ioan de Alcaçar.

MINAYA, Fr. BERNARDINO DE, c. 1559, *Memorial* 'Muy Católica Majestad' (Letter to Philip II), ms., AGS, Sección de Estado, Legajo 892, fols. 197ff. [edited by Hanke 1937: 99–101].

MOLINA, Fr. ALONSO DE, 1546, *Doctrina christiana breve traduzida en lengua mexicana*, Mexico: Juan Pablos? [partially surviving work described in Hernández de León-Portilla 1988 ii, 276].

MOLINA, Fr. ALONSO DE, c. 1550, *Izcatqui yn innemiliz yn tepachoa* (translation of CARTHUSIANUS, 1532 ii, 319–34), BNF, Ms. Mexicain 367, fols. 294–343; and in *Miscelánea sagrada*, 1550s–1570s, 156v–66v (entitled *Innemiliz yn tepachoani*).

MOLINA, Fr. ALONSO DE, 1555, *Aqui comiença vn vocabulario enla lengua castellana y mexicana*, Mexico: Iuan Pablos [facs. edited by Galeote, Manuel 2001, Málaga: Universidad de Málaga].

MOLINA, Fr. ALONSO DE, 1571, *Vocabulario en lengua castellana y mexicana y mexicana y castellana*, Mexico: Antonio de Spinosa [repr. retaining 1571 pagination, edited by Platzmann, Julio 1880, 2013 facs. edn., Mexico: Porrúa].

MOLINA, Fr. ALONSO DE, 1571, *Arte de la lengua mexicana y castellana*, Mexico: En casa de Pedro Ocharte [facs., edn. Hernández de León-Portilla, Ascensión 2014, Mexico: UNAM].

MONTAIGNE, MICHEL DE, 1580–1595, *Essais* [edited by Thibaudet, Albert and Rat, Maurice 1962, *Montaigne: Oeuvres complètes*, Paris: Gallimard].

MONTESINO, Fr. AMBROSIO, 1512, *Epistolas y Euangelios delos domingos y festiuidades principales*, Toledo: s.n.

MONTÚFAR, Fr. ALONSO DE, 1556, Información que el arzobispo de México D. Fray Alonso de Montúfar mandó practicar con motivo de un sermón: Que en la fiesta de la Natividad de Nuestra Señora (8 de setiembre de 1556) predicó . . .' [edited by Bustamente, Francisco 1888, Madrid: La Guirnalda].

MORE, THOMAS, 1518, *Utopia = De optimo reipublicae statu, deque nova insula, Vtopia, libellus uere aureus . . .* , Basel: Johannes Frobenius; orig. Basel 1516 [edited by Logan, George M., Adams, Robert M., and Miller, Clarence H. 1995, *Utopia: Latin Text and English Translation*, Cambridge: CUP].

MORE, THOMAS, with ERASMUS, 1521, *Luciani Samosatensis Saturnalia, Cronosolon, id est, Saturnalium legum lator, Epistolae Saturnales . . .* Basel: Johannes Froben[ius].

MORENO, JUAN JOSEPH, 1766, *Fragmentos de la vida, y virtudes del V. Illmo. y Rmo. Sr. Dr. D. Vasco de Quiroga . . .* , Mexico, Imprenta del Real y más Antiguo Colegio de S. Idelfonso [edited by León Alanis, Ricardo 1998, Morelia: UMSNH].

MOTOLINÍA, Fr. TORIBIO DE BENAVENTE, c. 1541, *Memoriales*, Ms. JGI 31 [edn. Dyer, Nancy Joe 1996, *Memoriales: Libro de oro*, Mexico: Colegio de México].

MOTOLINÍA, Fr. TORIBIO DE BENAVENTE, c. 1543, *Historia de los indios de la Nueva España* [edn. O'Gorman, Edmundo 2001, Mexico: Porrúa, orig. 1969; Eng. translation by Steck, Francis Borgia 1951, *Motolinía's History of the Indians of New Spain*, Washington, DC: Academy of American Franciscan History].

MOTOLINÍA, Fr. TORIBIO DE BENAVENTE, 1555, 'Carta al Emperador Carlos V', Tlaxcala, 2 January [edn. in MOTOLINÍA, *Historia de los indios*, edited by O'Gorman 2001, 295–316].

MOTOLINÍA, Fr. TORIBIO DE BENAVENTE, undated, three sixteenth-century manuscripts: (i) *Origen de los Mexicanos*; (ii) *Historia de los Mexicanos por sus pinturas*; (iii) *Relación de la genealogía y linaje de los Señores que han señoreado esta tierra de la Nueva España*, BANC, MSS M-M 448, MSS M-M 438–49 [edn. García Icazbalceta 1941 iii, 240–56].

MUÑOZ CAMARGO, DIEGO, c. 1580–1585, *Descripción de la ciudad y provincia de Tlaxcala de las Indias y del Mar Oceano para el buen gobierno y ennoblemiciento dellas*, Glasgow University Library, Sp Coll MS Hunter 242 (U.3.15) [facs. edited by Acuña, René 1981, Mexico: UNAM; edn. Acuña 1984, Relaciones geográficas del siglo XVI: Tlaxcala, Mexico: UNAM].

MUÑOZ CAMARGO, DIEGO, 1592, *Historia de Tlaxcala*, BNF, Ms. Mexicain 210 [edited by Reyes García, Luis 2013, Tlaxcala: Universidad Autónoma de Tlaxcala].

NAZAREO DE XALTOCAN, PABLO, 1556, Letter to Philip II, 'Invictissimo Hispaniarum omniumque Indiarum . . . Domino Philippo', Mexico, 11 February; 1556, Letter to Isabel of Valois, 'Serenissimae Hispaniarum . . . Reginae', Mexico, 12 February; 1566, Letter to Philip, 'Sacrae Catholicae Magestati', Mexico, 17 March, AGI, ms., Audiencia de México, 168 [facs., edited, Sp. translation by Zimmermann 1970, 18–31, Tafeln 13–29; edited, Sp. translation by Osorio Romero 1990, 1–34, cf. Pérez Rocha and Tena 2000, 333–67].

NEBRIJA, ANTONIO DE (LEBRIJA, NEBRISSENSIS), c. 1487, *Introductiones Latinae = Introduciones latinas contrapuesto el romance al latín*, Salamanca: Anton de Centenera [edited by Esparza, Miguel Ángel and Calvo, Vicente 1996, Münster: Nodus Publikationen].

NEBRIJA, ANTONIO DE, 1492, *Comiença la gramatica que nuevamente hizo el maestro Antonio de Lebrixa sobre la lengua castellana.* Salamanca s.n. [edited by Lozano, Carmen 2011, *Antonio de Nebrija: Gramática sobre la lengua castellana*, Barcelona: Galaxia Gutenberg, 2011].

NEBRIJA, ANTONIO DE, c. 1495, *Dictionarium ex Hispaniensi in Latinum sermonem.* Salamanca: s.n. [1989 facsimile, *Vocabulario español-latino*, Madrid: RAE].

NEBRIJA, ANTONIO DE, c. 1495, *Introductiones Latinae*, Salamanca: s.n.

NEBRIJA, ANTONIO DE, 1516 (1520), *Dictionarium ex Hispaniensi in Latinum sermonem*, Seville [repr. of shorter 1513 edn.; orig. Salamanca 1495].

NIGER, FRANCISCUS, 1480, *Brevis grammatica*, Venice: Theodorus Herbipolensis.

OLMOS, Fr. ANDRÉS DE, 1547, *Arte de la lengua mexicana*, Ms., BNE, RES/165/1 [facs., transcribed and edited by Hernández de León-Portilla, Ascensción and León-Portilla, Miguel 2002, Mexico: UNAM]. BANC, HHB-MM-454; BNF, Ms. Espagnol 259; BNF, Ms. Mexicain 364; NLC, S-III-48-C, 4ac. 8; MARI, 497-2017-051 [critical edition, Téllez Nieto 2022].

OLMOS, Fr. ANDRÉS DE, 1551–1552, *Tratado sobre los siete pecados mortales*, in *Sermones de fiesta*, BNM, Ms. 1488, 312v–387v [edited by Baudot, Georges 1996, Mexico: UNAM].

OLMOS, Fr. ANDRÉS DE, 1553, *Tratado de hechicerías y sortilegios*, BNM, Ms. 1488, 390v–407r [edited by Baudot, Georges 1990, Mexico: UNAM].

OROZ, Fr. PEDRO, 1586, *Relación de la descripción de la Provincia del Santo Evangelio: Que es en las Indias Occidentales que llaman la Nueva España* [edited by Chauvet, Fidel de Jesús 1947, Mexico: Impresora Mexicana de J. Aguilar Reyes; Eng. translation by Chavez, Angélico 1972, *The Oroz Codex*, Washington, DC: Academy of American Franciscan History].

PALETIN, VINKO (VINCENTIUS PALETINUS), c. 1560, *De jure et justitia belli contra Indos ad Philip. Hisp. Regem*, Ms., Lilly Library, Indiana University Bloomington, LMC 1962, fols. 1–80 [Sp. orig. *Tratado del derecho y justicia dela guerra que tienen los reyes de España contra las naciones dela Yndia Ocidental*, 1559, Ms., RAH, Colección Salazar y Castro, *N 75*, fl. 68 112, edited by Šanjek, Franjo; Sp. transcription and Croatian translation by Polić-Bobić, Mirjana 1994, *Rasprava o pravu i opravdanosti rata što ga španjolski vladari vode protiv naroda Zapadne Indije (1559)*, Zagreb: Nakladni zavod Globus].

PALSGRAVE, JOHN, 1530, *Lesclarcissement de la langue françoyse*, London: Richard Pynson.

PANÉ, Fr. RAMÓN, 1498, *Relación acerca de las antigüedades de los indios* [edited by Arrom, Juan José 1974, Mexico: Siglo XXI; Eng. translation by Griswold, Susan C., Durham, NC and London: Duke UP].

PASTRANA, JUAN, 1497, *Grammatica Pastranae sive Speculum puerorum*, Lisbon: Valentim Fernandes.

PATRIZI, FRANCESCO (FRANCISCUS PATRICIUS SENENSIS), 1531, *De regno et regis institutione libri IX*, Paris: Galeotus a Prato, *See also* GARCÉS, HENRIQUE, 1591.

PAUL III, POPE (ALESSANDRO FARNESE), 1537, 'Sublimis Deus', Rome, 2 June [facs. Cuevas 1914, 88; Eng. translation by Hanke 1937, 71–2].

PÉREZ DE CHINCHÓN, BERNARDO, 1533, *La lengua de Erasmo nuevamente romançada por muy elegante estilo*, Toledo: Ayala [edited by Severin, Dorothy S. 1975, Madrid: Aguirre Torre].

PÉREZ DE RIBAS, ANDRÉS, 1645, *Historia de los triunfos de nuestra santa fe entre gentes las más bárbaras y fieras del nuevo orbe*, Madrid: Alonso de Paredes.

PEROTTI, NICCOLÒ, 1473, *Rudimenta grammatices*, Rome: Conrad Sweynheym and Arnold Pannartz, Ms. Vat. Lat. 6737 [edn. Percival, W. Keith 2010, Kansas: University of Kansas Libraries, http://hdl.handle.net/1808/6453].

PEROTTI, NICCOLÒ, 1489, *Cornu copiae seu linguae Latinae commentarii*, edited by Odaxius, Ludovicus, Venice: Paganinus de Paganinis [edn. Charlet, Jean-Louis, Furno, Martine, Pade, Marianne, Ramminger, Johann, Harsting, Pernill, Stok, Fabio, and Abbamonte, Giancarlo 1989–2001, 8 vols., Sassoferrato: Istituto di Studi Piceni].

PICHARDO, JOSÉ ANTONIO, c. 1800, *Traduccion* [sic] *de Algunas Fabulas de Esopo en lengua mexicana*, BNF, Ms. Mexicain 287.

POMAR, JUAN BAUTISTA DE, 1582, *Relación de la ciudad y provincia de Texcoco* (17th-c. copy of orig.), BLAC, Genaro García Collection G58-G57 [edited by Acuña, René 1986, *Relaciones geográficas del siglo XVI*, vol 3, Mexico: UNAM].

POMAR, JUAN BAUTISTA DE, 1582, *Romances de los señores de la Nueva España*, ms., BLAC, MS CDG-980 (G-59) [edited, Eng. translation by Bierhorst, John 2009, *Ballads of the Lords of New Spain*, Austin: University of Texas Press].

POSTEL, GUILLAUME, 1538, *De originibus, seu de Hebraicae linguae et gentis antiquitate*, Paris: Dionysius Iescuier.

PUBLICIUS, JACOBUS, 1482, *Oratoriae artis epitoma*, Venice: Erhard Ratdolt; repr. 1485, 1490.

QUIRINI, ANGELO MARIA, ed., 1744–1757, *Epistolarum Reginaldi Poli S.R.E. cardinalis et aliorum ad ipsum par[te]s I–V*, 5 vols., Brixiae (Brescia): Joannes Maria Rizzardi.

QUIROGA, VASCO DE, 1531, 'Carta del licenciado quiroga, oidor de la audiencia de Santo Domingo, al Consejo de Indias, sobre la venida de aquel Obispo a la presidencia de dicho Tribunal, y sobre otros asuntos', 14 August [edited by anon. 1870 *Colección de documentos inéditos relativos al descubrimiento conquista y organización de las antiguas posesiones españoles de América y Oceania, sacados de los archivos del reino y muy especialmente del de Indias*, Madrid: José María Pérez, 1870, vol. 13, 420–9].

QUIROGA, VASCO DE, 1535, 'Información en derecho', BNE, Ms. 7369, fol. 4–fol. 159 [1868 *Colección de documentos inéditos relativos al descubrimiento, conquista y organización de las antiguas posesiones españoles de América y Oceania, sacados de los archivos del reino y muy especialmente del de Indias* [edited by Torres de Mendoza, Luis, Madrid: J.M. Pérez, 1868, vol. 10, 333–513].

QUIROGA, VASCO DE, 1559, 'Petición', 3 December, *Inquisición*, vol. 43, No. 6 [edited by Warren 1987, facsimile of GILBERTI, *Arte de la lengua de Michuacan*, li–lii].

QUIROGA, VASCO DE, 1561, 'El Obispo de Michoacan al Consejo de Indias', 17 February, AGI, Audiencia de México, leg. 374, fols. 9–10 [edited by Campos, Leopoldo 1965, *Vasco de Quiroga y el Arzobispado de Morelia*, Mexico: Jus, 155–8].

RABELAIS, FRANÇOIS, 1532, *Pantagruel*. Lyon: Claude Nourry [edn. Saulnier, Verdun L. 1965, Geneva: Droz].

RAMÍREZ DE FUENLEAL, SEBASTIÁN, 1533, 'Carta a la emperatriz, del obispo de Santo Domingo', Mexico, 8 de agosto [edited by Paso y Troncoso, Francisco del 1939, *Epistolario de Nueva España 1505–1818*, Mexico: Antigua Librería Robredo, vol. 3, 116–18].

REMESAL, ANTONIO DE, 1620, *Historia de las Indias Occidentales y Particular de la Gouernación de Chiapa, y Guatemala*. Madrid: Por Francisco de Abarca y Angelo [edited by Sáenz de Santa María, Carmelo 1988, 2 vols., Mexico: Porrúa].

REUCHLIN, JOHANNES, 1506, *De rudimentis Hebraicis libri III*, Phorce (Pforzheim): Thomas Anshelm [repr. 1974, Hildesheim: Georg Olms].

REUSNER, NICOLAUS, 1599, *Aenigmatographia, sive Sylloge aenigmatum . . .*, Frankfurt.

RINCÓN, ANTONIO DEL, 1595, *Arte mexicana compuesta por el Padre Antonio del Rincón de la compañia de Iesus.* Mexico: Casa de Pedro Balli [repr., edited by Peñafiel, Antonio 1885, Mexico: Secretaría de Fomento].

RIOFRÍO, BERNARDO DE, 1688, 'Por el Venerable Dean, Y Cavildo de la Santa Iglesia de Mechoacan, como Patron de los dos Hospitales . . .', Mexico, 4 February, JCB, BA688-R585p.

ROMBERCH, JOHANNES, 1520, *Congestorium artificiose memorie,* Venice: Giorgio Rusconi.

ROSA FIGUEROA, Fr. FRANCISCO ANTONIO DE LA, c. 1758, *Diccionario bibliográphico, alphabético e índice sylabo repertorial de quantos libros sencillos existen en esta librería de este convento de NPS Francisco de México,* BNM, Ms. 10266.

ROSATE, ALBERICUS DE (ALBERICO DA ROSCIATE), 1481, *Dictionarium juris,* Bologna: Heinricus de Colonia.

RUEUS, FRANCISCUS, 1547, *De gemmis iis praesertim quarum divus Joannes Apostolus in sua Apocalypsi meminit: De aliis quoque quarum usus hoc aeui apud omnes percrebuit, libri duo,* Paris: Christian Wechel.

RUIZ, Fr. FRANCISCO, 1540, *Index locupletissimus duobus tomis digestus in Aristotelis Stagiritae opera quae extant . . . ,* Sahagún, Léon: Sanctorum martyrum Facundi & Primitivi Coenobius.

RULERS OF AZCAPOTZALCO, 1561, 'Inuictissimo Hispaniarum Regi', Azcapotzalco, 1561, ms., AGI: Legajo Mexico, 1842 [transcr., Eng. tr. Appendix 2.4].

SAHAGÚN, Fr. BERNARDINO DE, 1540s, *Postillas sobre las Epístolas y Evangelios de los Domingos de todo el año* (1540s) [edited by Anderson, Arthur J.O. 1993, *Adiciones, Apéndice a la postilla y Ejercicio cotidiano,* Mexico: UNAM].

SAHAGÚN, Fr. BERNARDINO DE, 1558–1561, *Primeros memoriales* [transcr. Sullivan, Thelma D. 1997, *Palaeography of Nahuatl Text with English Translation,* Norman: University of Oklahoma Press].

SAHAGÚN, Fr. BERNARDINO DE, 1563, *Sermonario = Siguense unos sermones de dominicas y de sanctos en lengua mexicana.* Newberry, Ayer Ms. 1485 [edn., Sp. translated by Sánchez Aguilera, Mario Alberto, Mexico: UNAM, IIH, 2022].

SAHAGÚN, Fr. BERNARDINO DE, 1564, *Colloquios y Doctrina christiana con que los doze frayles de San Francisco, enbiados por el Papa Adriano sesto y por el Emperador Carlos qujnto, convirtieron alos indios de la Nueva España enlengua mexicana y española,* ms., Archivum Secretum Vaticanum, Armario I, vol. 91 [facs., edn. León-Portilla, Miguel 1986, *Coloquios y doctrina cristiana,* Mexico: Fundación de Investigaciones Sociales; transcr., Eng. tr. of fols. 35r and 37r in Appendix 2.7].

SAHAGÚN, Fr. BERNARDINO DE, 1570, *Breve compendio de los ritos idolátricos que los indios de la Nueva España . . . Pio V dicatum* [edited by Oliger, Livario 1942, Rome: Schola Typographica Pius X].

SAHAGÚN, Fr. BERNARDINO DE, c. 1580, *HG = Historia general de las cosas de Nueva España,* ms., Biblioteca Medicea Laurenziana, Florence, Ms. Med. Palat. 218-220, [Nahuatl edn. and Eng. translation by Dibble and Anderson 1950–1982, *Florentine Codex,* 12 vols, Salt Lake City and Santa Fe: School of American Research; Sp. edn. Garibay, Ángel María 2016, Mexico: Porrúa (orig. 1969); Sp. edn., García Quintana, Josefina and López Austin, Alfredo 1989, 2 vols., Mexico: CONACULTA].

SAHAGÚN, Fr. BERNARDINO DE, 1583, *Psalmodia Christiana,* Mexico: Pedro Ocharte [edited, Eng. translation by Anderson, Arthur J. O. 1993, Salt Lake City: University of Utah Press].

SAHAGÚN, Fr. BERNARDINO DE, c. 1585, *Kalendario mexicano, latino y castellano,* BNM, Ms. 1628 bis, fols. 86–100 [facs. León-Portilla, Miguel 1994; edited by Iguíniz, Juan B., 1918 'Calendario atribuido a fray Bernardino de Sahagún', *Boletín de la Biblioteca Nacional* 12, 189–232].

SAHAGÚN, Fr. BERNARDINO DE, 1586, *Arte divinatoria que usaban los mexicanos,* BNM, Ms. 1628 bis, fols. 101–25 [facs. León-Portilla, Miguel 1994; transc. of 'Prólogo', 'Al lector', 'Capítulo 1', García Icazbalceta 1954, 382–7].

SALINAS, MIGUEL DE, 1540, *Rhetorica en lengua castellana,* Alcalá de Henares: Joan de Brocar.

SÁNCHEZ, MIGUEL, 1648, *Imagen de la Virgen María, Madre de Dios de Guadalupe,* Mexico: Bernardo Calderón [edited by Torre Villar and Navarro de Anda 1982, 152–281].

SÁNCHEZ BAQUERO, PEDRO, 1573, 'Patri Everardo Mercuriano, Gen', Mexico, 8 March [edited by Zubillaga SJ, Félix 1956, *Monumenta Mexicana* i, 52–74].

SÁNCHEZ BAQUERO, PEDRO, c. 1580, *Fundación de la Compañía de Jesús en Nueva España* [edited by Ayuso SJ, Félix 1945, Mexico: Patria].

SANCTIUS, FRANCISCUS (SÁNCHEZ DE LAS BROZAS, FRANCISCO, 'el Brocense'), 1562, *Verae breuesque grammatices Latinae institutiones,* Lyon: Haeredes Seb. Gryphij.

SANCTIUS, FRANCISCUS (SÁNCHEZ DE LAS BROZAS, FRANCISCO, 'El Brocense'), 1587, *Minerva seu de causis linguae Latinae,* Salamanca: Ioannes [et] Andreas Renaut, fratres [edited by Sánchez Salor, Eustaquio and Chaparro Gómez, César 1995, Cáceres: Instituto Cultural El Brocense].

SANDOVAL, ALONSO DE, 1627, *De instauranda Aethiopum salute, natvraleza, policia sagrada i profana, costvmbres i ritos, disciplina i catechismo evangelico de todos etiopes,* Seville: Por Francisco de Lyra [edn. 1956, Bogotá: Empresa Nacional de Publicaciones].

SANTA MARÍA, Fr. DOMINGO DE, TORAL, Fr. FRANCISCUS DE, and VERA CRUZ, Fr. ALONSO DE LA, 1559, 'Sacra Catholica y Real Magestad', Tlaxcala, 1 May [edited 1877, *Cartas de Indias,* Ministerio de Fomento, Madrid: Manuel G. Hernández, 141–3].

SANTO TOMÁS, Fr. DOMINGO DE, 1560, *Grammatica o Arte de la lengua general de los Indios de los reynos del Peru,* Valladolid: Francisco Fernandez de Córdova [edited by Cerrón-Palomino, Rodolfo 1995, Cuzco: Centro Bartolomé de las Casas].

SAVETIER, NICOLAUS, 1527, ed., *M. Fabii Quintiliani Oratoriarum institutionum libri,* Paris.

SCALIGER, JOSEPH JUSTUS (the younger), 1583, *Opus novum de emendatione temporum in octo libros tributum,* Paris: Sebastien Nivelle, Mamert Patisson.

SCALIGER, JOSEPH JUSTUS (the younger), 1599, *Diatriba de Europaeorum linguis; editio princeps* 1610, in *Opuscula varia,* Paris: H. Beys.

SCALIGER, JULIUS CAESAR (the elder), 1540, *De causis linguae Latinae libri XIII,* Lugdunum [Lyon]: Gryphius.

SCALIGER, JULIUS CAESAR (the elder), 1557, *Exotericarum exercitationum liber quintus decimus: De subtilitate ad Hieronymum Cardanum,* Lutetiae [Paris]: Michaelis Vascosanus.

SEPÚLVEDA, JUAN GINÉS DE, 1535, *Democrates = De convenientia militaris disciplina cum Democrates Christiana religione dialogus qui inscribitur Democrates,* Rome: Antonius Blandus [Sp. tr. 1541, *Dialogo llamado Democrates,* Seville: Juan Cromberger].

SEPÚLVEDA, JUAN GINÉS DE, c. 1545, *Democrates secundus sive de iustis belli causis* [edn., Sp. translation by Losada, Ángel 1951, Madrid: CSIC, Instituto Francisco de Vitoria].

SIGÜENZA Y GÓNGORA, CARLOS DE, 1680, *Theatro de virtudes políticas, que constituyen á un Príncipe,* Mexico: Viuda de Bernardo de Calderón [edited by Moreno de los Arcos, Roberto, *Teatro de virtues políticas,* Mexico: UNAM, 1986].

SIGÜENZA Y GÓNGORA, CARLOS DE, c. 1690, *Piedad heroyca de Don Fernando Cortés, Marqués del Valle,* Mexico, incomplete mss. at BLAC and Biblioteca Pública del Estado de Jalisco, Guadalajara [edited by Delgado, Jaime 1960, Madrid: J. Porrúa Turanzas].

SOLÓRZANO PEREIRA, JUAN DE, 1629–1639, *De Indiarvm ivre disputationes sive De iusta Indiarum Occidentalium inquisitione, acquisitione, et retentione tribvs libris,* 2 vols., Madrid: Francisci Martinez [edn. Baciera, Carlos 1994–2001, 4 vols., Madrid: CSIC; Spanish tr. 1647, *Politica indiana: Sacado en lengua castellana de los dos tomos del derecho; Govierno municipal de las Indias Occidentales,* Madrid: Diego Diaz de la Camera].

STEPHANUS, ROBERTUS (ROBERT ESTIENNE), 1551, *Dionis Nicaei, rerum Romanarum a Pompeio Magno, ad Alexandrum Mamaeae filium epitome, Ioanne Xiphilino authore, & Guilielmo Blanco Albiensi interprete,* Paris: Robertus Stephanus.

SUÁREZ DE ESCOBAR, PEDRO (Fr. PEDRO DE MEDELLÍN), 1591, *Primera parte del libro intitulado Espejo divino de vida christiana,* Madrid: La biuda de Alonso Gomez.

THEVET, Fr. ANDRÉ DE, 1553, *Histoyre du Mechique*, BNF, Ms. Français 19031, 79r–88v [edited by Jonghe, Edouard de 1905, '*Histoyre du Mechique*, manuscrit français inédit du XVIe siècle', *Journal de la Société des Américanistes*, n.s., 2: 1–41].

TLAXCALA, JUAN DE, 1541, 'Verba sociorum domini petri tlacauepantzi', Tula, 6 September, AGN, Vínculos y mayorazgos, vol. 256, fols. 9r–12r. [edn., Sp. translation by Rosas Herrera, Gregorio 1946, *Tlalocan* 2: 150–62; edn., Sp. translation by Pérez-Rocha and Tena 2000, 141–9].

TOLEDO, FRANCISCO DE, 1578. *Introductio in dialecticam Aristotelis*, Mexico: Antonius Ricardus, in Collegio Sanctorum Petri & Pauli.

TORO, Fr. GABRIEL DE, c. 1536, *Thesoro de misericordia divina y humana, sobre el cuidado que tuvieron los antiguos, gentiles, hebreos y christianos, de los necesitados*, Salamanca: s.n. [repr. 1548, Salamanca: Juan de Junta; edn. Rodríguez Cacho, Lina and Quirós García, Mariano, 1999, *Tesoro de misericordia*, Madrid: RAE].

TORQUEMADA, Fr. JUAN DE, 1615, *Monarchia Indiana = Los veinte iun Rituales i Monarchia indiana, con el origen y guerras de los indios ocidentales, de sus Poblaçones, Descubrimiento, Conquista, Conversion y otras cosas maravillosas de la mesma tierra discribuydos en tres tomos*. Seville: Mathias Clavijo [edited by León-Portilla, Miguel, 1975–1983, *Monarquía indiana*, 7 vols., Mexico: IIH].

TOURNAI, Fr. GUIBERT DE, 1200s, *Tractatus de pace* [edited by Longpré, Ephrem 1925, Florence: Collegium S. Bonaventurae, Quaracchi].

TOVAR, JUAN DE, c. 1582–1587, *Codex Ramírez* = (1) *Relación del origen de los indios que habitan en la Nueva España según sus historias*, INAH Library [facs. edited by Orozco y Berra, Manuel 1944, *Codex Ramírez*, Mexico: Leyenda] = (2) *Historia de la benida de los yndios apoblar Mexico*, JCB Codex/Ind/2: 30289 [edited by Kubler, George and Gibson, Charles 1951, *The Tovar Calendar: An Illustrated Mexican Manuscript*, New Haven: Yale UP].

TRAVERSARI, AMBROGIO (AMBROSIUS TRAVERSARIUS), tr. 1472 *Diogenes Laertius: Vitae et sententiae philosophorum*, Rome: Georg Lauer (ms. orig. 1433).

TREBIZOND, GEORGE OF (TRAPEZUNTIUS, GEORGIUS), tr. 1470, *Eusebius Caesariensis: De euangelica praeparatione*, Venice: Nicolaus Jenson.

TREBIZOND, GEORGE OF (TRAPEZUNTIUS, GEORGIUS), 1522, *Rhetoricorum libri*, Basel: Valentinus Curio; repr. 1538, Paris: Christianus Wechelus, 1538 [facs. of 1538 edn., edited by Deitz, Luc 2006, Hildesheim and New York: Georg Olms].

VALADÉS, Fr. DIEGO, 1579, *Rhetorica Christiana: Ad concionandi et orandi usum . . .* , Perusia (Perugia): Petrumiacobus Petrutius; repr. 1582 [facs., Sp. translation by Herrera Zapién, Tarsicio, Pimentel Álvarez, Julio, Castro Pallares, Alfonso, and Palomares Chávez, Esteban 1989, *Retórica cristiana*, Mexico: FCE].

VALADÉS, Fr. DIEGO, 1581, *Catholicae assertiones contra praecipuos aliquot hereticorum errores*, ms., Vaticanus Ottobonensis 582, 43r–97v [edited by Löfstedt, Bengt and Talkovic, Scott 1998. Lund: Lund University].

VALDÉS Y SALAS, FERDINAND DE, 1559, *Cathalogus librorum qui prohibentur . . .* , Valladolid [Pinciae]: Sebastianus Martinez.

VALENCE, PIERRE, 1528, *Introductions in Frensshe for Henry the Yonge Erle of Lyncoln*, London: Wynkyn De Worde.

VALERIANO, ANTONIO (and rulers of Azcapotzalco), 1561, 'Inuictissimo Hispaniarum Regi', AGI: Legajo Mexico, 1842 [transcr., Eng. tr. Appendix 2.4].

VALERIANO, ANTONIO, c. 1600, 'Hic litterarum gerulus', Letter to Fr. Juan Bautista), in BAUTISTA c. 1606, *Sermonario*, 'Prologo', s.p. [transcr., Eng. tr. Appendix 2.5].

VELASCO, LUIS DE (Viceroy), 1551, 'Mandato en relación con la autorización que se da a Martín de la Cruz para ejercer como curandero 27 de mayo de 1551', AGN, 148v–149r [edited by Zavala 1982, 231].

VERA CRUZ, Fr. ALONSO DE LA, 1554, *Dialectica resolutio cum textu Aristotelis*, Mexico: Joannes Paulus Brixensis.

VERA CRUZ, Fr. ALONSO DE LA, 1554, *Recognitio summularum cum textu Petri Hispani, & Aristotelis*, Mexico: Joannes Paulus Brixensis.

VERGARA, FRANCISCO DE, 1537, *De Graecae linguae grammatica*, Alcalá: Michaelis de Eguía.

VETANCURT (BETANCOURT), AUGUSTÍN DE, 1697, *Menologio franciscano*, Mexico: Maria de Benavides.

VIEIRA, PADRE ANTÓNIO, 1662, *Sermão da Epifania* [edited by Cidade, Hernane 1940, *Padre António Vieira. Vol. 3: Sermões prègados no Brasil II*, Lisbon: Agência Geral das Colónias].

VILLANUEVA, DOCTOR, 1572, 'Información sobre fray Maturino Gilberti', Mexico, AGI, Indif. Gral., leg 1227 [transcr. Escobar Olmedo, Armando 1989, in GILBERTI, 1559 *Vocabulario*, edited by Warren 1989, 19].

VITERBO, ANNIUS OF (JOHANNES ANNIUS VITERBENSIS), 1498, *Antiquitates = Commentaria . . . super opera diversorum auctorum de antiquitatibus loquentium*, Rome: Eucharius Silber.

VIVES, JUAN LUIS, 1522, *Commentarii ad libros de Civitate Dei D. Aurelii Augustini*, Leuven: s.n. [edited by Pérez Dura, Jorge and Estéllez González, José María 1992, *Opera Omnia* II, Valencia: Universitat de València—Instituto de Cultura Juan Gil Albert].

VIVES, JUAN LUIS, 1531, *De disciplinis libri XX* (*De corruptis artibus* in 7 books, *De tradendis disciplinis* in 5 books, *De artibus* in 8 books) Antwerp: Michael Hillenius [translated by Watson, Foster 1913, *Vives, on Education*, Cambridge: CUP].

VIVES, JUAN LUIS, 1533, *Ioannis Lodovico Viuis Valentini De ratione dicendi libri tres: De consultatione*, Leuven: Bartholomeus Gravius [edited, translated by Walker, David J. 2017, Leiden and Boston: Brill].

VIVES, JUAN LUIS, 1534, *De conscribendis epistolis*, Antwerp: Hillen [edited, translated by Fantazzi, Charles 1989, Leiden and New York: Brill].

VIVES, JUAN LUIS, 1538, *Linguae Latinae exercitatio Ioannis Lodo. Vivis*, Cologne: s.n.

VIVES, JUAN LUIS, 1555, *Opera in duos distincta tomos: Quibus omnes ipsius lucubrationes*, Basel: Jacobus Parcus [contents listed in Yhmoff Cabrera 1996 iii, 464–6].

ZIERIXEENSES (DE ZIERIKZÉE), Fr. AMANDUS, 1534, *Chronica compendiosissima ab exordio mundi vsq[ue] ad annum Domini millesimum quingentesimu[m] trigesimu[m] quartum*, Antwerp: Simonis Cocus.

ZORITA (ZURITA), ALONSO DE, 1576, *Breve y sumaria relación de los señores de la Nueva España*, Mexico [edited by García Icazbalceta, Joaquín and Ramírez Cabañas, Joaquín 1942, Mexico: UNAM; translation by Keen, Benjamin 1963, *The Lords of New Spain*, London: Phoenix House].

ZORITA (ZURITA), ALONSO DE, 1585, *Relación de la Nueva España: Relación de algunas de las muchas cosas notables que hay en la Nueva España y de su conquista y pacificación y de la conversión de los naturales de ella* [edn. Ruiz Medrano, Ethelia, Wiebke, Ahrndt, and Mariano Leyva, José 1999, 2 vols., Mexico: Cien de México].

ZUMÁRRAGA, Fr. JUAN DE, 1529, 'Carta a su Majestad, del Electo Obispo de México', Tenuxtitan-Mexico, 27 August, Letter to Emperor Charles V [edited by García Icazbalceta 1947 ii, 169–249].

ZUMÁRRAGA, Fr. JUAN DE,1533, 'Insigne memorial . . . ante el Real Consejo de Indias' [edited by Garcia Icazbalceta 1947 iv, 114–16.

ZUMÁRRAGA, Fr. JUAN DE, 1537, 'La instrucción que yo el Obispo de México doy a mis procuradores', Mexico, February 1537 [edited by García Icazbalceta 1947 iv, 130–41].

ZUMÁRRAGA, Fr. JUAN DE, 1544, *Dotrina breue muy prouechosa de las cosas que pertinecen ala fe catholica*, Mexico: Juan Cromberger.

SECONDARY LITERATURE

Abellán Giral, Concepción 1991. *Studies in the Humanism of Antonius Nebrissensis: His Biography and His Grammatical Theory*. Doctoral dissertation, Royal Holloway and Bedford New College, University of London.

Abbott, Don Paul 1996. *Rhetoric in the New World: Rhetorical Theory and Practice in Colonial Spanish America*. Columbia: University of South Carolina Press.

Acker, Geertrui van 1992. 'El humanismo cristiano en México: Los tres flamencos', in *Historia de la evangelización de América: Simposio Internacional, Ciudad del Vaticano, 11–14 de mayo de 1992*, edited by Jose Escudero Imbert. Vatican City: Libreria Editrice Vaticana, 795–819.

Acuña, René 1981. 'Estudio preliminario', in MUÑOZ CAMARGO, 1585 [1981], 9–47.

Acuña, René 1983. 'Arte gramatical para una lengua iletrada: La *Ars Tzeldaica* de fray Domingo de Ara', *Nova Tellus* 1: 207–27.

Acuña, René, ed. 1984. *Relaciones geográficas del siglo XVI: Tlaxcala*. Mexico: UNAM.

Acuña, René, ed. 1988. *Vasco de Quiroga, De debellandis indis: Un tratado desconocido*. Mexico: UNAM.

Acuña, René, ed. 1995. *Fray Julián Garcés: Su alegato en pro de los naturales de Nueva España*. Mexico: UNAM.

Adams, J.N. 2013. *Social Variation and the Latin Language*. Cambridge: CUP.

Adler, William 1994. '*Ad verbum* or *ad sensum*: The Christianization of a Latin Translation Formula in the Fourth Century', in *Pursuing the Text: Studies in Honor of Ben Zion Wacholder on His Seventieth Birthday*, edited by John Reeves and John Kampen. Sheffield: Sheffield UP, 321–48.

Afanador-Pujol, Angélica Jimena 2015. *The Relación de Michoacán (1539–1541) and the Politics of Representation in Colonial Mexico*. Austin: University of Texas Press.

Alcántara Rojas, Berenice 2008. 'Cantos para bailar un cristianismo reinventado: La nahuatlización del discurso de evangelización en la *Psalmodia Christiana* de Fray Bernardino de Sahagún'. Doctoral dissertation, IIF-UNAM.

Alcántara Rojas, Berenice 2022. 'Un espejo de príncipes en lengua náhuatl y otros opúsculos para la educación del buen gobernante', in *Vestigios manuscritos de una nueva cristiandad*, edited by Berenice Alcántara Rojas, Mario Alberto Sánchez Aguilera, and Tesiu Rosas Xelhuantzi. Mexico: UNAM, 253–80.

Alejos-Grau, Carmen José 1994. *Diego Valadés, educador de la Nueva España: Ideas pedagógicas de la Rethorica Christiana*. Pamplona: Eunate.

Allen, Michael J.B. and Rees, Valery, with Davies, Martin, ed. 2002. *Marsilio Ficino: His Theology, His Philosophy, His Legacy*. Leiden, Boston, Cologne: Brill.

Álvarez Morán, María Consuelo, and Iglesias Montiel, Rosa María 2001. 'La traducción de la *Genealogia deorum* y su papel de difusora de la mitología clásica', *Cuadernos de filología italiana: Extra* 8: 215–40.

Amador de los Ríos, José 1861–1865. *Historia crítica de la literatura española*. 7 vols. Madrid: Joaquín Muñoz.

Anderson, Arthur J.O. 1966. 'Refranes en un Santoral en Mexicano', *ECN* 6: 55–61.

Anderson, Arthur J.O. 1983. 'Sahagún's Doctrinal Encyclopedia', *ECN* 16: 109–22.

Andrés Martín, Melquiades 1976. *La teología española en el siglo XVI*. 2 vols. Madrid: Biblioteca de Autores Cristianos.

Andrews, J. Richard 1974. *An Introduction to Classical Nahuatl*. Norman: University of Oklahoma Press.

Angelelli, Ignacio 1970. 'The Techniques of Disputation in the History of Logic', *Journal of Philosophy* 67: 800–15.

Asad, Talal, ed. 1973. *Anthropology and the Colonial Encounter*. Atlantic Highlands, NJ: Humanities Press.

Asensio, Eugenio 1960. 'La lengua compañera del imperio', *Revista de Filología Española* 43: 399–413.

Ashworth, E. Jennifer 1982. 'Eclipse of Medieval Logic', in *The Cambridge History of Later Medieval Philosophy*, eds. Norman Kretzmann, Anthony Kenney, Jan Pinborg, and Eleonore Stump. Cambridge: CUP, 785–96.

Ashworth, E. Jennifer 2008. 'Developments in the Fifteenth and Sixteenth Centuries', in Gabbay and Woods 2008, 609–43.

Austin, J.L. 1971. 'Performative-Constative', in *Philosophy of Language*, edited by J.R. Searle. Oxford: OUP, 13–22.

Aveni, Anthony 2012. *Circling the Square: How the Conquest Altered the Shape of Time in Mesoamerica*. Philadelphia: American Philosophical Society.

'Ayac' 2014. 'Aesop's Fables: General Notes', *Nahuatlahtolli* (web log post), September 19, https://nahuatlahtolli.wordpress.com/2014/09/19/aesops-fables-general-notes. Accessed November 2022.

Báez Rubí, Linda, 2005. *Mnemosine novohispánica: Retórica e imágenes en el siglo XVI*. Mexico: UNAM.

Baird, Ellen T. 1993. *The Drawings of Sahagún's Memoriales: Structure and Style*. Norman: University of Oklahoma Press.

Baldwin, T.W. 1944. *William Shakespeare's Small Latine and Lesse Greeke*. 2 vols. Urbana: University of Illinois.

Barker, Nicolos and Kaplan, Sue Abbe, eds. 2001. *The Aldine Press: Catalogue of the Ahmanson-Murphy Collection*. Berkeley: University of California Press.

Barlow, Robert H. 1945a. 'Some Remarks on the Term "Aztec Empire"', *The Americas* 1.3: 345–9.

Barlow, Robert H. 1945b. 'La Crónica X: versiones coloniales de la historia de los mexica tenochca', *Revista Mexicana de Estudios Antropológos* 7: 70–6.

Baron, Hans 1966. *The Crisis of the Early Italian Renaissance*. Princeton: Princeton UP.

Bartosik-Vélez, Elise 2014. *The Legacy of Christopher Columbus in the Americas*. Nashville: Vanderbilt UP.

Bataillon, Marcel 1932. *Érasme au Mexique*. Algiers: Société historique algérienne.

Bataillon, Marcel 1937. *Erasme et l'Espagne: Recherches sur l'histoire spirituelle du XVIe siècle*. Paris: E. Droz; reprinted Geneva: Droz, 1998. [Sp. tr. 2007. *Erasmo y España: Estudios sobre la historia espiritual del siglo XVI*, tr. Antonio Alatorre. Mexico: FCE; first published 1950].

Baudot, Georges 1968. 'La biblioteca de de los evangelizadores de México: Un documento sobre Fray Juan de Gaona', *Historia mexicana* 17.4: 610–17.

Baudot, Georges 1976. 'La Belle et la Bête dans le folklore náhuatl du Mexique central', *Cahiers du monde hispanique et luso-brésilien* 27: 53–61.

Baudot, Georges 1987. Review of Sahagún, *Coloquios*, edited by León-Portilla 1986, *Vuelta* 13.1: 48–9.

Baudot, Georges 1991. 'Fray Toribio Motolinía denunciado antes de la Inquisición por fray Bernadino de Sahagún', *ECN* 21: 127–32.

Baudot, Georges 1993. 'Dieu et le Diable en langue nahuatl dans le Mexique du XVIème siècle avant et après la conquête', in *Langues et cultures en Amérique Espagnole coloniale*, ed. Marie Cécile Bénassy-Berling, Jean-Pierre Clément, and Alain Milhou, Paris: Presses de la Sorbonne Nouvelle, 145–57.

Baudot, Georges 1995. *Utopia and History in Mexico: The First Chronicles of Mexican Civilization 1520–1569*. Niwot: UP of Colorado; French orig. Toulouse: Privat, 1976.

Bauer, Ralph 2019. *The Alchemy of Conquest: Science, Religion, and the Secrets of the New World*. Charlottesville and London: University of Virginia Press.

Bayard, Jean-Pierre 1978. *Le symbolisme du Caducée*. Paris: Guy Trédaniel.

Bayardi, Citlalli 2016. 'Figuras retóricos en el *Coloquio de los Doce*', in Hernández and Máynez 2016, 123–48.

Beckjord, Sarah H. 2007. *Territories of History: Humanism, Rhetoric and the Historical Imagination in Colonial Spanish America*. University Park: Pennsylvania State UP.

Benjamin, Walter 1969. 'Theses on the Philosophy of History', in *Illuminations*, edited by Hannah Arendt; tr. H. Zorn. New York: Schocken, 253–64.

Bentley, Jerry H. 1983. *Humanists and the Holy Writ: New Testament Scholarship in the Renaissance*. Princeton: Princeton UP.

Beristáin de Souza, José Mariano 1883. *Biblioteca Hispano Americana septentrional*. 2 vols. Mexico: Fuente Cultural; 5 vol. orig. Mexico: Alejandro Valdés, 1816–1821.

Bernheimer, Charles, ed. 1995. *Comparative Literature in the Age of Multiculturalism*. Baltimore: Johns Hopkins UP.

Berrens, Stefan 2004. *Sonnenkult und Kaisertum von den Severern bis zu Constantin I (193–337 n. Chr.)*. Stuttgart: Franz Steiner.

Beuchot, Mauricio 1997. 'Presencia de Nebrija en la Nueva España: Julián Garcés y Bartolomé de las Casas', in *Memoria del coloquio La Obra de Antonio y su Recepción en la Nueva España,* edited by Ignacio Guzmán Betancourt and Eréndira Nansen Díaz. Mexico: INAH, 145–51.

Beuchot, Mauricio 1998. *History of Philosophy in Colonial Mexico,* tr. Elizabeth Mill. Washington, DC: Catholic University of America Press, 1998; Sp. orig. 1997, *Historia de la filosofía en el México colonial,* Barcelona: Herder.

Bierhorst, John 1992. *History and Mythology of the Aztecs: The Codex Chimalpopoca.* Tucson: University of Arizona Press.

Biondelli, Bernardino 1858. *Evangeliarium, epistolarium et lectionarium Aztecum sive Mexicanum, ex antiquo codice depromptum.* Milan: Typis Jos. Bernardoni Qm. Johannis.

Black, Robert 2001. *Humanism and Education in Medieval and Renaissance Italy: Tradition and Innovation in Latin Schools from the Twelfth to the Fifteenth Century.* Cambridge: CUP.

Black, Robert 2015. 'First Steps in Latin: The Teaching of Reading and Writing in Renaissance Italy', in *Learning Latin and Greek from Antiquity to the Present,* ed. Elizabeth Archibald, William Brockliss, and Jonathan Gnoza. Cambridge: CUP, 99–117.

Bleichmar, Daniela 2019. 'Painting the Aztec Past in Early Colonial Mexico: Translation and Knowledge Production in the *Codex Mendoza*', *Renaissance Quarterly,* 72.4: 1362–415.

Bloch, Marc 1961. *Feudal Society,* tr. I.A. Manyon. 2 vols. Chicago: University of Chicago Press.

Bolaños, Alvaro Félix and Verdesio, Gustavo, eds. 2002. *Colonialism Past and Present: Reading and Writing about Colonial Latin America Today.* Albany: State University of New York Press.

Bolgar, R.R. 1954. *The Classical Heritage and Its Beneficiaries.* Cambridge: CUP.

Bolzoni, Lina 2001. *The Gallery of Memory: Literary and Iconographic Models in the Age of the Printing Press,* tr. Jeremy Parzen. Toronto: University of Toronto Press.

Boni, Giacomo 1906. 'Leggende', *Nuova Antologia: Rivista di Lettere, Scienze ed Arti* 41 (fasc. 837): 3–39.

Boone, Elizabeth Hill 1983. *The Codex Magliabechiano and the Lost Prototype of the Magliabechiano Group.* Berkeley: University of California Press.

Boone, Elizabeth Hill 1998. 'Pictorial Documents and Visual Thinking in Postconquest Mexico', in *Native Traditions in the Postconquest World,* edited by Elizabeth Hill Boone and Tom Cummins. Washington, DC: Dumbarton Oaks, 149–99.

Boone, Elizabeth Hill 2019. 'Fashioning Conceptual Categories in the Florentine Codex: Old-World and Indigenous Foundations for the Rulers and the Gods', in Peterson and Terraciano 2019, 95–109.

Boone, Elizabeth Hill, Burkhart, Louise, and Tavárez, David 2017. *Painted Words: Nahua Catholicism, Politics and Memory in the Atzaqualco Pictorial Catechism.* Washington, DC: Dumbarton Oaks Research Library and Collection.

Boornazian Diel, Lori 2018. *The Codex Mexicanus: A Guide to Life in Late Sixteenth-Century New Spain.* Austin: University of Texas Press.

Borgeaud, Philippe 1988. *The Cult of Pan in Ancient Greece.* Chicago: University of Chicago Press.

Boruchoff, David A. 2003. 'Sahagún and the Theology of Missionary Work', in Schwaller 2003, 59–102.

Botley, Paul 2004. *Latin Translation in the Renaissance: The Theory and Practice of Leonardo Bruni, Giannozzo Manetti and Desiderius Erasmus.* Cambridge: CUP.

Boucher, Philip P. 1992. *Cannibal Encounter: Europeans and Island Caribs, 1492–1763.* Baltimore: Johns Hopkins UP.

Bourdieu, Pierre 1977. 'The Economics of Linguistic Exchange', *Social Science Information* 16.6: 645–68.

Bourdieu, Pierre 1991. *Language and Symbolic Power,* tr. Gino Raymond and Matthew Adamson, edited, introduced by John B. Thompson. Cambridge: Polity.

Brading, David A. 1991. *The First America: The Spanish Monarchy, Creole Patriots and the Liberal State 1492–1867*. Cambridge: CUP.

Brading, David A. 2001. *Mexican Phoenix: Our Lady of Guadalupe; Image and Tradition across Five Centuries*. Cambridge: CUP.

Branham, R. Bracht 1985. 'Utopian Laughter: Lucian and Thomas More', *Moreana* 86: 23–43.

Breva Claramonte, Manuel 2008. 'Grammatization of Indigenous Languages in Spanish America: The Mental Language, Language Origin and Cultural Factors', *HEL* 30.2: 11–24.

Brian, Amber 2016. *Alva Ixtlilxochitl's Native Archive and the Circulation of Knowledge in Colonial Mexico*. Nashville: Vanderbilt UP.

Briggs, Charles 1999. *Giles of Rome's De regimine principum: Reading and Writing Politics at Court and University, c.1275–c.1525*. New York: CUP.

Brind'Amour, Pierre 1983. *Le Calendrier romain*. Ottawa: Éditions de l'Université d'Ottawa.

Brotherston, Gordon 1987. 'Aesop in Aztec', in Kutscher, Brotherston, and Vollmer, 1987, 11–49.

Brotherston, Gordon 1993. *Book of the Fourth World: Reading the Native Americas through Their Literature*. Cambridge: CUP.

Browne, Walden 2000. *Sahagún and the Transition to Modernity*. Norman: University of Oklahoma Press.

Bruno, Daniel and Míguez, Néstor 2016. 'Conquest and Evangelization: The Bible in Colonial America', in Cameron 2016, 828–42.

Bull, Malcolm 2005. *The Mirror of the Gods: Classical Mythology in Renaissance Art*. Oxford: OUP.

Burke, Peter 1989. 'The Renaissance Dialogue', *Renaissance Studies* 3: 1–12.

Burke, Peter 1995. 'America and the Rewriting of World History', in *America in European Consciousness*, edited by Karen Ordahl Kupperman. Chapel Hill: Omohundro Institute of Early American History and Culture, 33–51.

Burkhart, Louise M. 1986. 'Sahagún's 'Tlauculcuicatl', a Nahuatl Lament', *ECN* 18: 181–218.

Burkhart, Louise M.1988. 'The Solar Christ in Nahuatl Doctrinal Texts of Early Colonial Mexico', *Ethnohistory* 35.3: 234–56.

Burkhart, Louise M. 1989. *The Slippery Earth: Nahua-Christian Moral Dialogue in Sixteenth-Century Mexico*. Tucson: University of Arizona Press.

Burkhart, Louise M. 1996. *Holy Wednesday: A Nahua Drama from Early Colonial Mexico*. Philadelphia: University of Pennsylvania Press.

Burkhart, Louise M. 2001. *Before Guadalupe: The Virgin Mary in Early Colonial Nahuatl Literature*. Austin: University of Texas Press.

Burkhart, Louise M. 2003. 'On the Margins of Legitimacy: Sahagún's *Psalmodia* and the Latin Liturgy', in Schwaller 2003, 103–16.

Burkhart, Louise M. 2010. 'The Destruction of Jerusalem as Colonial Nahuatl Historical Drama', in Schroeder 2010a, 74–100.

Burrus, Edward J. 1959. 'Hispanic Americana in the Manuscripts of Bologna, Italy', *Manuscripta* 3: 131–47.

Burrus, Edward J. 1960. 'Cristóbal Cabrera (c. 1515–98), First American Author: A Checklist of His Writings in the Vatican Library', *Manuscripta* 4: 67–89.

Burrus, Edward J. 1961. 'Cristóbal Cabrera on the Missionary Methods of Vasco de Quiroga', *Manuscripta* 5.1: 17–27.

Burrus, Edward J. 1968–1976. *The Writings of Alonso de la Vera Cruz: The Original Texts with English Translation*. 5 vols. Rome: Jesuit Historical Institute.

Burrus, Edward J. 1979. *A Major Guadalupan Question Resolved: Did General Scott Seize the Valeriano Account of the Guadalupan Apparitions?* Washington, DC: Center for Applied Research in the Apostolate.

Bursill Hall, G.L. 1971. *Speculative Grammars of the Middle Ages: The Doctrine of Partes Orationes of the Modistae*. The Hague: Mouton.

Burton, Gideon 2007. 'From *Ars dictaminis* to *Ars conscribendi epistolis*' [sic], in Poster and Mitchell 2007, 88–101.

Bustamante García, Jesús 1989. *La obra etnográfica y lingüística de Fray Bernardino de Sahagún*. Madrid: Universidad Complutense.

Bustamante García, Jesús 1990. *Fray Bernardino de Sahagún: Una revisión crítica de los manuscritos y su proceso de composición*. Mexico: UNAM.

Calnek, Edward 1988. 'The Calmecac and Telpochcalli in Pre-Conquest Tenochtitlan', in Klor de Alva, Nicolson, and Quiñones Keber 1988, 169–77.

Cameron, Euan, ed. 2016. *The New Cambridge History of the Bible. Volume 3: From 1450 to 1750*. Cambridge: CUP.

Campana, Augusto 1946. 'The Origin of the Word "Humanist"', *JWCI* 9: 60–73.

Campbell, D.J. 1936. 'The Birthplace of Silius Italicus', *Classical Review* 50: 55–58.

Campos, Leonardo 1965. 'Métodos misionales y rasgos biográficos de don Vasco de Quiroga según Cristóbal Cabrera, Pbro.', in *Don Vasco de Quiroga y Arzobispado de Morelia*, edited by Manuel Ponce. Mexico: Jus, 107–55.

Canellis, Aline 2016. 'Jerome's Hermeneutics: How to Exegete the Bible?', in *Patristic Theories of Biblical Interpretation*, edited by Tarmo Toom. Cambridge: CUP, 49–76.

Cañizares-Esguerra, Jorge 1999. 'New World, New Stars: Patriotic Astrology and the Invention of Indian and Creole Bodies in Colonial Spanish America, 1600–1650', *AHR* 104.1: 33–68.

Cañizares-Esguerra, Jorge 2001. *How to Write the History of the New World: Histories, Epistemologies, and Identities in the Eighteenth-Century Atlantic World*. Stanford: Stanford UP.

Carrasco, Pedro 1984. 'The Extent of the Tepanec Empire', in *The Native Sources and the History of the Valley of Mexico: Proceedings of the 44th International Congress of Americanists Manchester 1982*, edited by Jacqueline de Durand-Forest. Oxford: BAR, 73–92.

Carrasco, Pedro 1999. *The Tenochca Empire of Ancient Mexico: The Triple Alliance of Tenochtitlan, Tetzcoco, and Tlacopan*. Norman: University of Oklahoma Press.

Carreño, Alberto María 1949. 'The Books of Fray Juan de Zumárraga', *The Americas* 5.3: 311–30.

Carreño, Alberto María 1961. *La Real y Pontificia Universidad de México, 1536–1865*. Mexico: UNAM.

Carrera de la Red, Avelina 1998. 'Las cartas de Pablo Nazareo y el latín en el México del s. xvi', *Nova Tellus* 16: 129–48.

Carrera Stampa, Manuel 1960. *El escudo nacional*. Mexico: s.n. 1960 [repr. Mexico: Secretaría de Gubernación, 1994].

Carruthers, Mary 1993. 'The Poet as Master Builder: Composition and Locational Memory in the Middle Ages', *New Literary History* 24.4: 881–904.

Carruthers, Mary 2008. *The Book of Memory: A Study of Memory in Medieval Culture*. Cambridge: CUP.

Carver, Robert 2001. '"True Histories" and "Old Wives' Tales": Renaissance Humanism and the "Rise of the Novel"', *Ancient Narrative* 1: 322–49.

Caso, Alfonso 1927. *El Teocalli de la Guerra Sagrada*. Mexico: Talleres Gráficos de la Nación.

Castañeda, Carlos E. 1952. 'Pichardo, Jose Antonio', *Handbook of Texas*, edited by Webb, Walter Prescott, Caroll, H. Bailey, Friend, Llerena B.,Caroll, Mary Joe, and Nolen, Louise. Austin: Texas State Historical Association, 2: 374.

Castañeda de la Paz, María 2009. 'Central Mexican Coats of Arms', *Ethnohistory* 56.1: 125–61.

Castañeda de la Paz, María 2013. *Conflictos y alianzas en tiempos de cambio: Azcapotzalco, Tenochtitlan y Tlatelolco (siglos XII–XVI)*. Mexico: UNAM, Insituto de Investigaciones Antropológicas.

Castillo Farreras, Victor Manuel 1971. 'El bisiesto náhuatl', *ECN* 9: 75–104.

Cave, Terence 2008. *Thomas More's Utopia in Early Modern Europe: Paratexts and Contexts*. Manchester: Manchester UP.

Celenza, Christopher S. 2017. *The Intellectual World of the Italian Renaissance: Language, Philosophy and the Search for Meaning*. Cambridge: CUP.

Cervantes, Fernando 1991. *The Idea of the Devil and the Problem of the Indian: The Case of Mexico in the Sixteenth Century*. London: Institute of Latin American Studies.

Cervantes, Fernando 1994. *The Devil in the New World: The Impact of Diabolism in New Spain*. New Haven and London: Yale UP.

Cervantes, Fernando 2016. 'The Bible in European Colonial Thought', in Cameron 2016, 805–27.

Chaparro Gómez, César 2003. 'Retórica, historia y política en Diego Valadés', *Norba: Revista de historia* 16.2 [1996/2003]: 403–19.

Chavero, Alfredo 1948. *Sahagún*. Mexico: Vargas Rea.

Chavez [sic] OFM, Angélico, 1972. *The Oroz Codex*, Washington, DC: Academy of American Franciscan History.

Chiapelli, Fredi, ed. 1976. *First Images of America: The Impact of the New World on the Old*. 2 vols. Berkeley: University of California Press.

Chipman, Donald E. 2005. *Moctezuma's Children: Aztec Royalty under Spanish Rule, 1520–1700*. Austin: University of Texas Press.

Christensen, Mark Z. 2013. *Nahua and Maya Catholicisms: Texts and Religion in Colonial Central Mexico and Yucatan*. Stanford: Stanford UP.

Christensen, Mark Z. 2014. *Translated Christianities: Nahuatl and Maya Religious Texts*. University Park: Pennsylvania State UP.

Chuchiak IV, John F. 2007. 'Forgotten Allies: The Origins and Roles of Native Mesoamerican Auxiliaries and *Indios Conquistadores* in the Conquest and Colonization of Yucatan, 1526–1697', in *Indian Conquistadors*, edited by Laura E. Matthew and Michel R. Oudijk. Norman: University of Oklahoma Press, 175–226.

Clarke, M.L. 1996. *Rhetoric at Rome: A Historical Survey*. London: Routledge (orig. London: Cohen and West, 1953).

Clay, Diskin 1992. 'Columbus's Senecan Prophecy', *AJP* 113.4: 617–20.

Clayton, Mary L. 1989. 'A Trilingual Spanish-Latin-Nahuatl Manuscript Dictionary Sometimes Attributed to Fray Bernardino de Sahagún', *International Journal of American Linguistics* 55.4: 391–416.

Clayton, Mary L. 2003. 'Evidence for a Native-Speaking Nahuatl Author in the Ayer *Vocabulario Trilingüe*', *International Journal of Lexicography* 16: 99–119.

Cline, Howard F. 1972. 'The *Relaciones Geográficas* of the Spanish Indies, 1577–1648', in *Handbook of Middle American Indians. Volume 12: Guide to Ethnohistorical Sources, Part One*, edited by Robert Wauchope, Howard F. Cline, and John B. Glass. Austin: University of Texas Press, 183–242.

Cline, Howard F. and Glass, John B., eds. 1973 *Handbook of Middle American Indians. Volume 13: Guide to Ethnohistorical Sources, Part Two*. Austin: University of Texas Press.

Cobo Betancourt, Juan Fernando 2014. 'Colonialism in the Periphery: Spanish Linguistic Policy in New Granada, c. 1574–1625', *CLAR*, 23.2: 118–42.

Codoñer, Carmen and González Iglesias, Juan Antonio, eds. 1994. *Antonio de Nebrija: Edad Media y Renacimiento*. Salamanca: Ediciones Universidad de Salamanca.

Coleman, David 2003. *Creating Christian Granada: Society and Religious Culture in an Old-World Frontier City, 1492–1600*. Ithaca and London: Cornell UP.

Coletti, Vittorio 1987. *L'éloquence de la chaire: Victoires et défaites du latin entre Moyen Âge et Renaissance*. Paris: Éditions du Cerf; Italian orig. Casale Monferrato: Marietti, 1983.

Company Company, Concepción, ed. 2008. *Documentos lingüísticos de la Nueva España: Altiplano central*. Mexico: UNAM.

Connell, William F. 2011. *After Moctezuma: Indigenous Politics and Self-Government in Mexico City, 1524–1730*. Norman: University of Oklahoma Press.

Conte, Gian Biagio 1986. *The Rhetoric of Imitation*, tr. Charles Segal. Ithaca: Cornell UP.

Cook, Eleanor 2001. 'The Figure of Enigma: Rhetoric, History, Poetry', *Rhetorica* 19.4: 349–78.

Cook, Sherburne F. and Borah, Woodrow 1979. *Essays in Population History: Mexico and California, Volume Three*. Berkeley: University of California.

Copeland, Rita 2007. 'The History of Rhetoric and the *Longue Durée*: Ciceronian Myth and Its Medieval Afterlives', *The Journal of English and Germanic Philology* 106.2: 176–202.

Coroleu, Alejandro 1998. 'Humanismo en España', in *Introducción al Humanismo del Renacimiento*, edited by Jill Kraye. Madrid: CUP, 295–330.

Coroleu, Alejandro 2004. 'On the Awareness of the Renaissance', in *Il latino nell'età dell'Umanesimo: Atti del convegno di Mantova, 26–27 ottobre 2001*. Florence: Leo Olschki, 3–15.

Coroleu, Alejandro 2008. 'Anti-Erasmianism in Spain', in Rummel 2008, 73–92.

Corona Núñez, José 1982. 'Antonio Uitziméngari, Primer Humanista Tarasco', in *Humanistas Novohispanos de Michoacán*, edited by Silvio Zavala. Morelia: UMSNH, 49–61.

Cortés, Rocío 2011. *'El "nahuatlato Alvarado" y el "Tlalamatl Huauhquilpan": Mecanismos de la memoria colectiva de una comunidad indígena*. New York: Hispanic Seminary of Medieval Studies.

Cortés Castellanos, Justino 1987. *El catecismo en pictogramas de Fr. Pedro de Gante*. Madrid: Fundación Universitaria Española.

Courcelle, Pierre 1957. 'Les exégèses chrétiennes de la quatrième Églogue', *Revue des Études Anciennes* 59: 294–319.

Cram, David 2013. 'Linguistic Eschatology: Babel and Pentecost in Seventeenth-Century Linguistic Thought', *Language & History* 56: 44–56.

Crossgrove, William C. 2010. 'Macer Floridus', *Oxford Dictionary of the Middle Ages*, . Oxford: OUP, vol. 3, 1063.

Cuevas SJ, Mariano, ed. 1914. *Documentos inéditos del siglo XVI para la historia de México*. Mexico: Taller del Museo Nacional de Arqueología, Historia y Etnología [repr. Mexico: Porrúa, 1975].

Cuevas SJ, Mariano 1931. 'Documentos escritos en pro de las Apariciones Guadalupanas: Su autenticidad. Su valor', en *Memoria del Congreso Nacional Guadalupano: Discursos, conclusiones, poesías*. Mexico: Escuela Typográfica Salesiana, 97–108.

Cuevas SJ, Mariano 1946–1947. *Historia de la iglesia en México*. 5 vols. Mexico: Patria.

Cummings, Brian 2009. 'Erasmus and the End of Grammar: Humanism, Scholasticism, and Literary Language', *New Medieval Literatures* 11: 249–70.

Cummins, Thomas B.F. 1995. 'From Lies to Truth: Colonial Ekphrasis and the Act of Crosscultural Translation', in *Reframing the Renaissance*, edited by Claire Farago. New Haven: Yale UP, 152–74.

Curtius, Ernst Robert 1953. *European Literature and the Latin Middle Ages*. Princeton and Oxford: Princeton UP; German orig. Bern: Francke 1947.

Dannenfeldt, Karl H. 1955. 'The Renaissance Humanists and the Knowledge of Arabic', *Studies in the Renaissance* 2: 96–117.

Dealy, Ross 1975. *Vasco de Quiroga's Thought on War: Its Erasmian and Utopian Roots*. Bloomington: Indiana UP.

Dealy, Ross 1976. *The Politics of an Erasmian Lawyer*. Malibu: Undena.

Dehouve, Danièle 2000. 'Un dialogue de sourds: Les Colloques de Sahagún', in *Les rituels du dialogue*, edited by Aurore Monod Becquelin and Philippe Erikson. Nanterre: Société d'ethnologie, 199–234.

Dehouve, Danièle 2014. 'La parole des anciens ou huehuetlahtolli, une trouvaille franciscaine', in *Nouveaux chrétiens, nouvelles chrétientés dans les Amériques, XVI*[e]*–XIX*[e] *siècles*, edited by Pierre Ragon. Paris: Presses Universitaires de Paris Ouest, 47–60.

Dekkers, Eligius and Fraipont, Jean, eds. 1956. *Sancti Aurelii Augustini Enarrationes in Psalmos*. Turnhout: Brepols.

Delany, Carol 2006. 'Columbus' Ultimate Goal: Jerusalem', *Comparative Studies in Society and History* 48.2: 260–92.

den Haan, Annet 2016. *Giannozzo Manetti's New Testament: Translation Theory and Practice in Fifteenth-Century Italy*. Leiden and Boston: Brill,

Díaz Cíntora, Salvador, ed. 1996. *Fábulas de Esopo en náhuatl*. Mexico: UNAM.

Dibble, Charles E. 1963. *Historia de la nación mexicana*. Madrid: José Porrúa Turanzas.

Dibble, Charles E. 1982. 'Sahagún's *Historia*', in Dibble and Anderson 1982, vol. 1, 9–23.

Dibble, Charles E. and Anderson, Arthur J.O., eds and tr. 1950–1982. *Florentine Codex: General History of the Things of New Spain*. 13 vols. Santa Fe, NM and Salt Lake City, UT: School of American Research and University of Utah Press.

Ditchfield, Simon 2017. 'Translating Christianity in an Age of Reformations', *Studies in Church History* 53: 164–95.

Ditchfield, Simon, Methuen, Charlotte, and Spicer, Andrew, eds. 2017. *Translating Christianity*, Studies in Church History 53. Cambridge: CUP on behalf of the Ecclesiastical History Society.

Domínguez Torres, Mónica 2011. 'Claiming Ancestry and Lordship: Heraldic Language and Indigenous Identity in Post-Conquest Mexico', in *Negotiating Difference in the Hispanic World from Conquest to Globalisation*, edited by Eleni Kefala. Chichester: Wiley-Blackwell, 70–86.

Domínguez Torres, Mónica 2013. *Military Ethos and Visual Culture in Post-Conquest Mexico*. Farnham: Ashgate.

Dorez, Léon 1932. *La Cour du Pape Paul III*. 2 vols. Paris: Ernest Leroux.

Dubois, Claude-Gilbert 1970. *Mythe et langage au seizième siècle*. Paris: Ducros.

Dubois, Claude-Gilbert 1985. *L'imaginaire de la Renaissance*. Paris: PUF.

Dubrow, Heather 1994. 'The Term Early Modern', *Proceedings of the Modern Language Association* 109.5: 1025–6.

Duffin, Christopher John 2007. 'Alectorius: The Cock's Stone', *Folklore* 18.3: 325–41.

Dumont, Raphaèle 2016. 'Teatro en Tlatelolco: Los indígenas salen a escena', in Hernández and Máynez 2016, 93–106.

Duverger, Christian 1987. *La conversión de los indios de Nueva España*. Mexico: FCE.

Earle, Rebecca 2007. *The Return of the Native: Indians and Myth-Making in Spanish America, 1810–1930*. Durham, NC: Duke UP.

Eco, Umberto 1997. *The Search for the Perfect Language*, tr. James Fentress. Malden: Blackwell; Italian orig. Rome and Bari: Laterza, 1993.

Eden, Kathy 2000. '*Koinonia* and Friendship between Rhetoric and Religion', in *Rhetorical Invention and Religious Enquiry: New Perspectives*, ed. Walter Just and Wendy Olmstead. New Haven: Yale UP, 305–22.

Eden, Kathy 2001. *Friends Hold All Things in Common: Tradition, Intellectual Property, and the Adages of Erasmus*. New Haven: Yale UP.

Edmonson, Munro S. ed. 1974. *Sixteenth-Century Mexico: The Work of Sahagún*. Albuquerque: University of New Mexico Press.

Egido, Aurora 1998. 'Erasmo y la Torre de Babel', in *España y América en una perspectiva humanista: Homenaje a Marcel Bataillon*, edited by Joseph Pérez. Madrid: Casa de Velázquez, 11–34.

Elliott, J.H. 1970. *The Old World and the New, 1492–1650*. Cambridge CUP.

Elliott, J.H. 1989. 'The Court of the Spanish Habsburgs: A Peculiar Institution', in *Spain and Its World, 1500–1700: Selected Essays*, by Elliott. New Haven: Yale UP, 142–61.

Elliott, J.K., ed., tr., 1999. *Apocryphal New Testament*. Oxford: OUP.

Elschenbroiche, Adalbert 1990. *Die deutsche und lateinische Fabel in der frühen Neuzeit*. 2 vols. Tübingen: Niemeyer.

Errington, Joseph 2008. *Linguistics in a Colonial World*. Malden: Blackwell.

Escalante Gonzalbo, Pedro 2019. 'The Art of War, the Working Class, and Snowfall', in Peterson and Terraciano 2019, 63–74.

Escobar Chico, Ángel 1997. 'La pervivencia del corpus teológico ciceroniano en España', *Revista Española de Filosofía Medieval* 4: 189–202.

Esperabé de Artega, Enrique 1914. *Historia pragmática e interna de la Universidad de Salamanca*. 2 vols. Salamanca: Fr. Núñez Izquierdo.

Estarellas, Juan 1962. 'The College of Tlatelolco and the Problem of Higher Education for Indians in 16th Century Mexico', *History of Education Quarterly* 2.4: 234–43.

Estrada Torres, María Isabel 2000. 'San Juan Tenochtitlan y Santiago Tlatelolco: Las dos comunidades indígenas de la Ciudad de México; 1521–1700'. Dissertation, Universidad Autónoma Metropolitana, Unidad Iztapalapa, Mexico.

Fabregat Barrios, Santiago 2003. 'Presencia y función de los mitos clásicos en la *Historia general y natural de las Indias* de Gonzalo Fernández de Oviedo y Valdés'. *Epos* 19: 67–88.

Farriss, Nancy 2018. *Tongues of Fire: Language and Evangelization in Colonial Mexico*. New York: OUP.

Fernández, Justino 1991. 'Las miniaturas que ilustran el códice', in BADIANO, *Libellus de medicinalibus Indorum herbis* (1552) [1991], vol. 2, 101–6.

Fernández del Castillo, Francisco 1982. *Libros y libreros en el siglo XVI*. Mexico: FCE; orig. Mexico: AGN, 1914.

Fernández Gallardo, Luis 2016. 'Los studia humanitatis según Alonso de Cartagena', *Atalaya: Revue des études romanes* 16 (2016), http://journals.openedition.org/atalaya/1907. Accessed January 2023.

Fernández López, Jorge 2002. 'Rhetorical Theory in Sixteenth-Century Spain: A Critical Survey', *Rhetorica* 20: 133–48.

Fernández-Armesto, Felipe 1992. 'Aztec Auguries and Memories of the Conquest of Mexico', *Renaissance Studies* 6: 287–305.

Fernández-Santamaria [sic], J.A. 1977. *The State, War and Peace: Spanish Political Thought in the Renaissance 1516–1559*. Cambridge: CUP.

Foley, John Miles 1991. *Immanent Art: From Structure to Meaning in Traditional Oral Epic*. Bloomington: Indiana UP.

Foley, John Miles 1995. *The Singer of Tales in Performance*. Bloomington: Indiana UP.

Foley, John Miles 2002. *How to Read an Oral Poem*. Urbana and Chicago: University of Illinois Press.

Fontán Pérez, Antonio 1986. 'El humanismo español de Antonio de Nebrija', in *Homenaje a Pedro Sáinz Rodríguez. Vol. 2: Estudios de lengua y literatura*. Madrid: Fundación Universitaria Española, 209–28.

Fontenrose, James E. 1940. 'Apollo and the Sun-God in Ovid', *AJP* 61.4: 429–44.

Forbes, Thomas R. 1973. 'The Capon Stone', *Bulletin of the New York Academy of Medicine* 49.1: 48–51.

Fragnito, Gigliola 2014. 'Paolo III', in *Dizionario biografico degli Italiani*, edited by Alberto Maria Ghisalberti, vol. 81. Rome: Istituto della Enciclopedia italiana, 98–107.

Frost, Elsa Cecilia 1983. 'Fuentes bíblicas, clásicas y contemporáneas de *Los veintiún libros rituales y Monarquía Indiana*', in TORQUEMADA, *Monarquía indiana*, vol. 7. Mexico: UNAM, 267–74 [cf. TORQUEMADA, Fr. JUAN DE, 1615, above].

Frugoni, Arsenio, ed., 1950. *Carteggio Umanistico di Alessandro Farnese*. Florence: Leo Olschki.

Fuchs, Barbara 2001. *Mimesis and Empire: The New World, Islam, and European Identities*. Cambridge: CUP.

Fuller, Amy 2015. 'The Evolving Legend of La Llorona'. *History Today* 65.11: 39–44.

Fumaroli, Marc 1994. *L'âge de l'eloquence: Rhétorique et 'res litteraria' de la Renaissance au seuil de l'époque classique*. Paris: Albin Michel.

Gabbay, Dov M. and Woods, John, eds. 2008. *Handbook of the History of Logic. Volume 2: Medieval and Renaissance Logic*. Amsterdam: Elsevier.

Gaillemin, Béatrice 2014. 'Les catéchismes testériens: Un corpus homogène?', in *Nouveaux chrétiens, nouvelles Chrétientés dan les Amériques, xvie–xixe siècles*, edited by Pierre Ragon. Paris: Universitaires de Paris Ouest, 83–104.

Galindo Trejo, Jesús 2015. 'Templo Mayor, Tenochtitlan—Calendar and Astronomy', in *Handbook of Archaeoastronomy and Ethnoastronomy*, edited by Clive L.N. Ruggles. New York: Springer, 743–7.

García Cubas, Antonio 1896. *Diccionario geográfico, histórico y biográfico de los Estados Unidos Mexicanos*. 5 vols. Mexico: Las Escalerillas.

García de Cortázar y Ruiz de Aguirre, José Ángel, ed. 1999. *Cristianismo marginado: Rebeldes, excluidos, perseguidos; Actas del XI Seminario sobre Historia del Monacato*. Aguilar de Campoo [sic]: Fundación Santa María la Real.

García Icazbalceta, Joaquín, ed. 1858, 1866. *Colección de documentos para la historia de México*. 2 vols. Mexico: J.M. Andrade (repr. 2 vols. Mexico: Porrúa 1971).

García Icazbalceta, Joaquín, ed. 1875. *México en 1554: Tres diálogos latinos*. Mexico: Antigua Librería Andrade.

García Icazbalceta, Joaquín, ed. 1892. *Códice Mendieta: Documentos franciscanos, siglos XVI y XVII*. 2 vols. Mexico: Francisco Díaz de León.

García Icazbalceta, Joaquín, ed. 1896. *Carta acerca del origen de la imagen de Nuestra Señora de Guadalupe*. Mexico: Verdad.

García Icazbalceta, Joaquín, ed. 1941. *Nueva colección de documentos para la historia de México*. 3 vols. Mexico: Salvador Chávez Hayhoe; orig. Mexico: Antigua Librería Andrade y Morales, 1889.

García Icazbalceta, Joaquín 1947. *Don Fray Juan de Zumárraga: Primer obispo y arzobispo de México*, edited by Rafael Aguayo Spencer and Antonio Castro Leal. 4 vols. Mexico: Porrúa.

García Icazbalceta, Joaquín 1954. *Bibliografía mexicana del siglo XVI: Catálogo razonado de libros impresos en México de 1539 a 1600*, edited by Agustín Millares Carlo. Mexico: FCE; orig. Mexico: Antigua Librería de Andrade y Morales, 1886.

Garibay (Garibay Kintana), Ángel María 1932. *La poesía lírica azteca: Esbozo de síntesis crítica*. Mexico: Ábside.

Garibay, Ángel María 1940. *Llave del Náhuatl*. Mexico: Porrúa.

Garibay, Ángel María 1945. *Épica náhuatl: Divulgación literaria*. Mexico: UNAM.

Garibay, Ángel María 1953–1954. *Historia de la literatura náhuatl*. 2 vols. Mexico: Porrúa [repr. 2007, 3rd edn].

Garibay, Ángel María 1965. *Teogonía e historia de los mexicanos*. Mexico: Porrúa.

Garibay, Ángel María, ed. 1969. *Fr. Bernardino de Sahagún, Historia general de las cosas de Nueva España*. 4 vols. Mexico: Porrúa [repr. 2016].

Garibay, Ángel María 1993. *Poesía náhuatl*. 3 vols. Mexico: UNAM.

George, Edward V. 2009. 'Humanist Traces in Early Colonial Mexico: Texts from the Colegio de Santa Cruz de Tlatelolco', in *Litterae Humaniores: Del Renacimiento a la Ilustración*, edited by Ferrán Grau Codina, José María Maestre Maestre, and Jordí Pérez Durá. Valencia: Universitat de València, 279–91.

Gerbi, Antonello 2010. *The Dispute of the New World: The History of a Polemic, 1750–1900*, tr. Jeremy Moyle. Pittsburgh: University of Pittsburgh Press, 2010; Italian orig. Milan and Naples: Riccardo Ricciardi, 1955.

Giard, Luce 1984. 'Du latin médiéval pluriel des langues, le tournant de la Renaissance', *HEL* 6.1: 35–55.

Gibson, Charles 1950. 'The Identity of Diego Muñoz Camargo', *HAHR* 30.2: 195–208.

Gibson, Charles 1952. *Tlaxcala in the Sixteenth Century*. New Haven: Yale UP.

Gibson, Charles 1964a. *The Aztecs under Spanish Rule: A History of the Indians of the Valley of Mexico*. Stanford: Stanford UP.

Gibson, Charles 1964b. 'The Pre-Conquest Tepanec Zone and the Labor Drafts of the Sixteenth Century', *Revista de Historia de América* 57/58: 136–45.

Gil, Juan 1990. 'El latín en América: Lengua general y lengua de élite', in *Acta de I Simposio de Filología Iberoamericana (Sevilla, 26 al 30 de marzo de 1990)*. Zaragoza: Libros Pórtico, 97–135.

Gil Fernández, Luis 1967. 'El humanismo español del siglo XVI', *Estudios Clásicos* 51: 211–97.

Gil Fernández, Luis 1981. *Panorama social del humanismo español*. Madrid: Alhambra.

Gilbert, Claire M. 2020. *In Good Faith: Arabic Translation and Translators in Early Modern Spain*. Philadelphia: University of Pennsylvania Press.

Gingerich, Willard 1988. '*Chipahuacanemiliztli*: The Purified Life in the Discourses of Book VI, *Florentine Codex*', in Josserand and Dakin 1988, vol. 2, 517–43.

Glass, John B. 1964. *Catálogo de la Colección de Códices*. Mexico: INAH.

Glass, John B. 1975. 'A Census of Middle American Testerian Manuscripts', in *A Handbook of Middle American Indians. Volumes 14 and 15: Guide to Ethnohistorical Sources, Parts Three and Four*, edited by Robert Wauchope and Howard F. Cline. Austin: University of Texas Press, 281–96.

Gómez de Orozco, Federico 1945. 'Costumbres, fiestas, enterramientos y diversas formas de proceder de los indios de la Nueva España', *Tlalocan* 2.1: 37–63.

Gómez Moreno, Ángel 1994. *España y la Italia de los humanistas: Primeros ecos*. Madrid: Gredos.

Gonzalbo Aizpuru, Pilar 1990. *Historia de la educación en la época colonial: El mundo indígena*. Mexico: El Colegio de México.

González Casanova, Pablo 1924. 'Un cuento griego en el folklore azteca', *Ethnos* 3: 16–24.

González Gómez, José Antonio 2004. *Antropología e historia en Azcapotzalco: Estudio histórico sobre la dinámica cultural, económica y política de una población del noroeste de la Cuenca de México (siglos XVI y XVII)*. Escuela Nacional de Antropología e Historia, INAH, dissertation.

González González, Enrique 1987. *Joan Lluis Vives: Del escolaticismo al humanismo*. Valencia: Generalitat Valenciana.

González Rodríguez, Jaime 1981. *La idea de Roma en la historiografía indiana (1492–1550)*. Madrid: CSIC.

González Vega, Felipe 2010. '*Ex grammatico rhetor:* The Biblical Adventures and Rhetorical Maturity of Antonio de Nebrija between the *Apologia* and the *Tertia quinquagena*', in *Humanism and Christian Letters in Early Modern Iberia (1480–1630)*, ed. Barry Taylor and Alejandro Coroleu. Newcastle upon Tyne: Cambridge Scholars Publishing, 9–36.

González Vera, Francisco 1868. 'De los primeros misioneros en Nueva España y Carta de Pedro de Gante', *Revista de España* 3.11: 384–402.

Grafton, Anthony T. 1991. *Defenders of the Text: The Traditions of Scholarship in an Age of Science, 1450–1800*. Cambridge, MA: Harvard UP.

Grafton, Anthony T. 1993. *Joseph Scaliger: A Study in the History of Classical Scholarship. Volume II: Historical Chronology*. Oxford: Clarendon Press.

Grafton, Anthony T., Shelford, April and Siraisi, Nancy 1992. *New Worlds, Ancient Texts: The Power of Tradition and the Shock of Discovery*. Cambridge, MA: Harvard UP.

Gravelle, Sarah Stever 1988. 'The Latin-Vernacular Question and Humanist Theory of Language and Culture', *JHI* 49: 367–87.

Green, Lawrence D. and Murphy, James J. 2006. *Renaissance Rhetoric: Short Title Catalogue*. Aldershot, Ashgate, and Burlington: Ashgate.

Green, R.P.H., ed. 1995. *Augustine, De Doctrina Christiana*. Oxford: Clarendon Press.

Green, R.P.H., tr. 2008. *Saint Augustine, On Christian Teaching*. Oxford: OUP.

Greenblatt, Stephen 1991. *Marvelous Possessions: The Wonder of the New World*. Chicago: University of Chicago Press.

Greenblatt, Stephen, ed. 1993. *New World Encounters*. Berkeley: University of California Press.

Greenleaf, Richard E. 1961. *Zumárraga and the Mexican Inquisition 1536–1543*. Washington, DC: Academy of American Franciscan History.

Griffin, Clive 1991. *Los Cromberger: La historia de una emprenta del siglo XVI en Sevilla y Méjico*. Madrid: Ediciones de Cultura Hispánica.

Gruzinski, Serge 1988. *La colonisation de l'imaginaire: Sociétés indigènes et occidentalisation dans le Mexique espagnol, XVIe–XVIIIe siècle*. Paris: Gallimard.

Gruzinski, Serge 1991. *La colonización de lo imaginario: Sociedades indígenas et occidentalización en el México español; Siglos XVI–XVIII*, translation by Jorge Ferreiro. Mexico: FCE.

Gruzinski, Serge 2002. *The Mestizo Mind: The Intellectual Dynamics of Colonization and Globalization*, translated by Deke Dusinberre. London: Routledge.

Gruzinski, Serge 2018. *La machine à remonter le temps*. Paris: Fayard.

Gruzinski, Serge and Mermet, Gérard 1994. *L'aigle et la sibylle: Fresques indiennes du Mexique*. Paris: Imprimerie nationale.

Guilliem Arroyo, Salvador 2013. 'The Discovery of the Caja de Agua of Tlatelolco: Mural Painting from the Dawn of New Spain', *CLAR* 22.1: 19–38.

Gutiérrez, Gustavo 2003. *Las Casas: In Search of the Poor of Jesus Christ*, translated by Robert R. Barr. Eugene: Wipf and Stock; Sp. orig. 1992, *En busca de los pobres de Jesucristo*, Lima: Instituto Bartolomé de las Casas.

Guzmán, Eulalia 1964. *Manuscritos sobre México en archivos de Italia*. Mexico City: Sociedad Mexicana de Geografía y Estadística.

Guzmán Betancourt, Ignacio 2002. 'Antonio del Rincón (1556–1601): Primer gramático mexicano', *ECN* 33: 253–65.

Guzmán Betancourt, Ignacio, and Nansen Díaz, Eréndira, eds. 1997. *Memoria del coloquio La Obra de Antonio y su Recepción en la Nueva España*. Mexico: INAH.

Hamann, Byron Ellsworth 2013. 'Object, Image, Cleverness: The *Lienzo de Tlaxcala*', *Art History* 36.3: 518–45.

Hamann, Byron Ellsworth 2015. *The Translations of Nebrija: Language, Culture, and Circulation in the Early Modern World*. Amherst: University of Massachusetts Press.

Hamann, Byron Ellsworth 2018. 'Comparison and Seeing in the Mediterratlantic', in Laird and Miller 2018, 57–73.

Hamilton, Alastair 1996. 'Humanists and the Bible', in Kraye 1996, 100–17.

Hampe Martínez, Teodoro 1999. 'Sobre la Escolástica virreinal peruana: El P. Leonardo de Peñafiel, comentarista de Aristóteles', in *La tradición clásica en el Perú virreinal*, edited by Hampe Martínez. Lima: Fondo Editorial Universidad Nacional Mayor de San Marcos, 69–100.

Hanke, Lewis 1937. 'Pope Paul III and the American Indians', *Harvard Theological Review* 30.2: 65–102.

Hanke, Lewis 1949. *The Spanish Struggle for Justice in the Conquest of America*. Philadelphia: University of Pennsylvania Press.

Hanke, Lewis 1976. 'The Theological Significance of the Discovery of America', in Chiapelli 1976 i, 363–89.

Hankins, James 1995. 'The "Baron Thesis" after Forty Years and Some Recent Studies of Leonardo Bruni', *JHI*, 56.2: 309–38.

Hankins, James, ed. 2000. *Renaissance Civic Humanism: Reappraisals and Reflections*. Cambridge: CUP.

Hankins, James, ed. 2007. *The Cambridge Companion to Renaissance Philosophy*. Cambridge: CUP.

Hanks, William F. 2010. *Converting Words. Maya in the Age of the Cross*. Berkeley, Los Angeles, and London: University of California.

Hanson, Craig A. 1994. 'Olmos and Sahagún', in *Chipping Away on Earth: Prehispanic and Colonial Nahua Studies in Honor of Arthur J.O. Anderson and Charles E. Dibble*, edited by Eloise Quiñones Keber. Culver City: Labyrinthos Press, 29–35.

Hassig, Debra 1989. 'Transplanted Medicine: Colonial Herbals of the Sixteenth Century', *Res: Anthropology and Aesthetics* 17/18: 30–53.

Hausrath, August 1957–1959. *Corpus fabularum Aesopicarum*. 2 vols. Stuttgart: Teubner.

Heath, Shirley 1986. *La política del lenguaje en México: De la colonia a la nación*. Mexico: Secretaría de Educación Pública.

Heikel, Ivar A. 1902. *Über das Leben Constantins: Constantins Rede an die heilige Versammlung; Tricennatsrede an Constantin; Die griechischen christlichen Schriftsteller der ersten drei Jahrhunderte* 7.1. Leipzig: Hinrichs, 149–92.

Helmer, Ángela 2009. 'La semántica cultural del ají [axí]', in *Visiones del encuentro de dos mundos en América*, ed. Mercedes Montes de Oca and Claudia Parodi. Mexico: UNAM, 61–78.

Hellquist, Elof 1922. *Svensk etymologisk ordbok*. Lund: C.W.K. Gleerups.

Henderson, John 2007. *The Medieval World of Isidore of Seville*. Cambridge: CUP.

Henderson, Judith Rice 2007. 'Humanism and the Humanities: Erasmus' *Opus de Conscribendis Epistolis* in Sixteenth-Century Schools', in Poster and Mitchell 2007, 141–77.

Hernández, Esther and Máynez, Pilar, eds. 2016. *El Colegio de Tlatelolco: Síntesis de historias, lenguas, y culturas*. Mexico: Destiempos.

Hernández de León-Portilla, Ascensión 1986. 'Un primerísimo ensayo de análisis etimológico de toponimias y otros vocablos nahuas', *ECN* 18: 219–29.

Hernández de León-Portilla, Ascensión 1988. *Tepuztlahcuilolli: Impresos en náhuatl*. 2 vols. Mexico: UNAM.

Hernández de León-Portilla, Ascensión 2007. 'Fray Alonso de Molina y el proyecto indigenista de la Orden seráfica', *EHN* 36: 63–81.

Hernández de León-Portilla, Ascensión and León-Portilla, Miguel 2009. *Las primeras gramáticas del Nuevo Mundo*. Mexico: FCE.

Hernando Cuadrado, Luis Alberto 2008. 'Nebrija y la Etimología', *Analecta Malacitana*, 31: 79–105.

Herrejón Peredo, Carlos 1989. *El Colegio de San Miguel de Guayangareo*. Morelia: UMSNH.

Herrera Meza, María del Carmen, López Austin, Alfredo, and Martínez Baracs, Rodrigo 2013. 'El nombre náhuatl de la Triple Alianza', *ECN* 46: 7–35.

Hervás y Panduro, Lorenzo 2007. *Biblioteca Jesuítico-Española (1759–1799)*, edited by Antonio Astorgano Abajo. Madrid: Libris.

Hervás y Panduro, Lorenzo 2009. *Biblioteca Jesuítico-Española II: Manuscritos hispano-portugueses en siete bibliotecas de Roma*, edited by Antonio Astorgano Abajo. Madrid: Libris.

Hinojo Andrés, Gregorio 2015. 'Influencias clásicas en el *Libellus de medicinalibus Indorum herbis*', in *Humanismo y pervivencia del mundo clásico. Vol. V: Homenaje al profesor Juan Gil*, edited by José María Maestre Maestre, Sandra Inés Ramos Maldonado, Manuel Antonio Díaz Gito, María Violeta Pérez Custodio, Bartolomé Pozuelo Calero, and Antonio Serrano Cueto. Alcañiz and Madrid: CSIC and Insituto de Estudios Humanísticos, 709–37.

Hofmann, J.B.–Szantyr, Anton 1965. *Lateinische Syntax und Stylistik*. Munich: C.H. Beck.

Holzapfel OFM, Herbert 1948. *The History of the Franciscan Order*, translated by Antonine Tibesar OFM and Gervase Brinkman OFM. Teutopolis IL: St Joseph Seminary.

Homza, Lu Ann 2004. *Religious Authority in the Spanish Renaissance*. Baltimore: Johns Hopkins UP.

Horcasitas, Fernando 2004. *Teatro náhuatl*. 2 vols. Mexico: UNAM; orig. 1974.

Houghton, Luke 2019. *Virgil's Fourth Eclogue in the Italian Renaissance*. Cambridge: CUP.

Humboldt, Alexander von 1810. *Vues des Cordillères et monuments des peuples indigènes de l'Amérique*. Paris: Schoell. [Eng. translation by Helen Maria Williams, *Researches, Concerning the Institutions and Monuments of the Ancient Inhabitants of America, with Descriptions and Views of Some of the Most Striking Scenes in the Cordilleras!* 2 vols. London: Longman and Company, 1814].

Hyma, Albert 1965. *The Christian Renaissance: A History of the 'Devotio Moderna'*. Hamden CT: Archon Books; orig. Grand Rapids, The Reformed Press, 1924.

Hyman, Malcolm D. 2005. 'Terms for 'Word' in Roman Grammar', in *Antike Fachtexte/Ancient Technical Texts*, edited by Thorsten Fögen. Berlin: De Gruyter, 155–70.

Iguíniz, Juan B. 1918. 'Calendario atribuido a fray Bernardino de Sahagún', *Boletín de la Biblioteca Nacional* 12: 189–232.

Janka, Markus 1997. *Ovid, Ars Amatoria, Buch 2: Kommentar*. Heidelberg: Carl Winter.

Jardine, Lisa 1982. 'Humanism and the Teaching of Logic', in *The Cambridge History of Later Medieval Philosophy*, ed. Norman Kretzmann, Anthony Kenney, Jan Pinborg, and Eleonore Stump. Cambridge: CUP, 797–807.

Jardine, Lisa 1988. 'Humanistic Logic', in Schmitt and Skinner 1988, 173–98.

Jeanne, Boris 2011. 'Mexico-Madrid-Rome: Sur les pas de Diego Valadés; Une étude des milieux romaines tournés vers le Nouveau Monde à l'époque de la Contre-Réforme (1568–1594)'. 2 vols. Doctoral dissertation, EHESS Paris.

Jensen, Kristian 1996. 'The Humanist Reform of Latin and Latin Teaching', in Kraye 1996, 63–81.

Jiménez Abollado, Francisco Luis and Ramírez Calva, Verenice Cipatli 2011. *Pretensiones señoriales de Don Pedro Moctezuma Tlacahuepantzin Yohualicahuacatzin*. Hidalgo: Universidad Autónoma del Estado de Hidalgo.

Jiménez, Nora 2002. '"Príncipe" indígena y latino: Una compra de libros de Antonio Huitziméngari (1559)'. *Relaciones* (Zamora, Michoacán) 23.91: 133–60.

Jiménez Moreno, Wigberto and Robertson, Donald, eds. 1980. *José Tudela de la Orden: Códice Tudela*. Madrid: Cultura Hispánica, 207–9.

Johansson K., Patrick 2002. 'Los Coloquios de los Doce: Explotación y transfuncionalización de la palabra indígena', in *La otra Nueva España: La palabra marginada en la Colonia*, edited by Mariana Masera. Mexico: UNAM, 211–34.

Johnson, Paul 2000. *The Renaissance: A Short History*. New York: Random House.

Josserand, J. Kathryn and Dakin, Karen, eds. 1988. *Smoke and Mist: Mesoamerican Studies in Memoriam of Thelma D. Sullivan*. 2 vols. Oxford: BAR.

Justeson, John S. 1986. 'The Origin of Writing Systems: Pre-classic Mesoamerica', *World Archaeology* 17.3: 437–58.

Kagan, Richard 1974. *Students and Society in Early Modern Spain*. Baltimore: Johns Hopkins UP.

Kalyuta, Anastasya 2008. 'La casa y hacienda de un señor mexica: Un estudio analítico de la "Información de doña Isabel de Moctezuma"'. *Anuario de Estudios Americanos* 65.2: 13–37.

Kalyuta, Anastasya 2011. 'El arte de acomodarse a dos mundos: La vida de don Pedro de Moctezuma Tlacahuepantli según los documentos del Archivo General de la Nación (México D.F.) y el Archivo General de Indias (Sevilla, España)', *Revista Española de Antropología Americana*, 41.2: 471–500.

Karttunen, Frances 1988. 'The Roots of Sixteenth-Century Mesoamerican Lexicography', in Josserand and Dakin 1988, vol. 2, 545–59.

Karttunen, Frances 1992. *An Analytical Dictionary of Nahuatl*, Norman: University of Oklahoma Press; orig. Austin: University of Texas, 1983.

Karttunen, Frances 1995. 'From Court Yard to the Seat of Government: The Career of Antonio Valeriano, Nahua Colleague of Bernardino de Sahagún', *Amerindia*, 19/20: 113–20.

Karttunen, Frances 2000, 'Interpreters Snatched from the Shore: The Successful and the Others', in *The Language Encounter in the Americas*, edited by Edward G. Gray and Norman Fiering. New York and Oxford: Berghahn Books, 215–30.

Karttunen, Frances and Lockhart, James 1987. *The Art of Nahuatl Speech: The Bancroft Dialogues*. Los Angeles: UCLA Latin American Center Publications.

Keen, Benjamin 1971. *The Aztec Image in Western Thought*. New Brunswick: Rutgers UP.

Keil, Heinrich, ed. 1855. *Grammatici Latini*. 2 vols. Leipzig: Teubner.

Kennedy, George A. 1990. '"Truth" and "Rhetoric" in the Pauline Epistles', in *The Bible as Rhetoric: Studies in Biblical Persuasion and Credibility*, edited by Martin Warner. London: Routledge, 195–221.

Kennedy, George A. 1999. *Classical Rhetoric and Its Christian and Secular Tradition from Ancient to Modern Times*. Chapel Hill: Univerity of North Carolina Press, 137–82.

Kenney, E.J., ed. 1971. Lucretius, *De rerum natura Book III*. Cambridge: CUP.

Kerson, Arnold L. 2001. 'Fray Juan de Zumárraga, primer obispo y arzobispo de México: Humanista y evangelizador', in *Memoria, XIII Encuentro Nacional de Investigadores del pensamiento novohispano*, edited by Enrique Luzán Salazar. Mexico: Universidad Autónoma de Aguascalientes, 15–37.

Kline, Sarah L. 2008. 'The Native Peoples of Central Mexico', in *The Cambridge History of the Native Peoples of the Americas. Volume 2: Mesoamerica, Part 2*, ed. Richard E.W. Adams and Murdo J. Macleod. Cambridge: CUP 187–222.

Klor de Alva, J. Jorge 1982. 'La historicidad de los *Coloquios* de Sahagún', *ECN* 15: 142–84.

Klor de Alva, J. Jorge, Nicholson, H.B., and Quiñones Keber, Eloise, eds. 1988. *The Work of Bernardino de Sahagún: Pioneer Ethnographer of Sixteenth-Century Aztec Mexico*. Albany: Institute for Mesoamerican Studies, 169–77.

Knight, Alan 2002. *Mexico: From the Beginning to the Spanish Conquest*. Cambridge: CUP.

Kobayashi, José María 1985. *La educación como conquista: Empresa franciscana en México*. Mexico: Colegio de México; orig. 1974.

Kohl, Benjamin G. 1992. 'The Changing Concept of the "studia humanitatis" in the Early Renaissance', *Renaissance Studies* 6.2: 185–209.

Konetske, Richard, ed. 1953–1958. *Colección de documentos para la historia de la formación social de Hispanoamérica, 1493–1810*. 3 vols. Madrid: CSIC.

Krailsheimer, A.J. 1948. 'Rabelais and the Pan Legend', *French Studies* 2.2: 158–61.

Kranz, Travis Barton 2007. 'Sixteenth-Century Tlaxcalan Pictorial Documents on the Conquest of Mexico', in *Sources and Methods for the Study of Post-Conquest Mesoamerican Ethnohistory, Provisional Version*, eds. James Lockhart, Lisa Sousa, and Stephanie Wood. Eugene: University of Oregon Wired Humanities Project, http://whp.uoregon.edu/Lockhart/index.html.

Kranz, Travis Barton 2010. Visual Persuasion: Sixteenth-Century Tlaxcalan Pictorials in Response to the Conquest of Mexico', in Schroeder 2010a, 41–73.

Kraye, Jill 1988. 'Moral Philosophy', in Schmitt and Skinner 1988, 303–86.

Kraye, Jill, ed. 1996. *Cambridge Companion to Renaissance Humanism*. Cambridge: CUP.

Kraye, Jill 2007. 'The Revival of Hellenistic Philosophies', in Hankins 2007, 97–112.

Krebs, Christopher B. 2005. *Negotiatio Germaniae: Tacitus' Germania und Enea Silvio Piccolomini, Giannantonio Campano, Conrad Celtis und Heinrich Bebel*. Göttingen: Vandenhoeck and Ruprecht.

Krippner-Martínez, James 2001. *Rereading the Conquest: Power, Politics and the History of Early Colonial Michoacán, 1521–1565*. University Park: Pennsylvania State UP.

Kristeller, Paul Oskar 1943. *The Philosophy of Marsilio Ficino*. New York: University of Columbia Press.

Kristeller, Paul Oskar 1963–1996. *Iter italicum: A Finding List of Uncatalogued or Incompletely Catalogued Humanistic Manuscripts of the Renaissance in Italian and Other Libraries*. 6 vols. 4 vols. of supplements. London: Warburg Institute.

Kristeller, Paul Oskar 1965. 'The Moral Thought of Renaissance Humanism', in Kristeller, *Renaissance Thought II: Papers on Humanism and the Arts*. New York: Harper and Row, 1965, 20–68.

Kristeller, Paul Oskar 1974. *Humanismus und Renaissance I: Die antiken und mittelalterlichen Quellen*. Munich: W. Fink.

Kristeller, Paul Oskar 1988. 'Humanism', in Schmitt and Skinner 1988, 113–37.

Kristeller, Paul Oskar, Kranz, F. Edward, *et al.* 1960–2020. *Catalogus translationum et commentariorum: Mediaeval and Renaissance Latin Translations and Commentaries; Annoted Lists and Guides*. 13 vols. Washington, DC: Catholic University of America Press.

Kubler, George 1948. *Mexican Architecture of the Sixteenth Century*. 2 vols. New Haven: Yale UP.

Kupperman, Karen Ordahl, ed. 1995. *America in European Consciousness*. Chapel Hill: Omohundro Institute of Early American History and Culture.

Kutscher, Gerdt, Brotherston, Gordon, and Vollmer, Günter, eds. 1987. *Aesop in Mexico: Die Fabeln des Aesop in aztekischer Sprache; Text mit deutscher und englischer Übersetzung/A 16th Century Aztec Version of Aesop's Fables*. Berlin: Mann.

Labarre, Albert, 1975. *Bibliographie du Dictionarium d'Ambrogio Calepino*. Baden-Baden: Koerner.

Lacadena, Alfonso and Wichmann, Søren 2008. 'Longitud vocálica y glotalización en la escritura jeroglífica náhuatl', *REAA*, 38: 121–50.

Laird, Andrew 1999. *Powers of Expression, Expressions of Power: Speech Presentation and Latin Literature*. Oxford: OUP.

Laird, Andrew 2005. 'Metaphor and the Riddle of Representation in the *Historia Apollonii Regis Tyri*', *Ancient Narrative—Supplement* 4: 225–44.

Laird, Andrew 2007. 'Latin America', in *A Companion to the Classical Tradition*, edited by Craig W. Kallendorf. Malden, MA: Blackwell, 222–36.

Laird, Andrew 2009. 'Bartolo da Sassoferrato and the Dominion of Native Americans: The *De debellandis Indis* and Las Casas' *Apologia*', *SUP* 29: 365–73.

Laird, Andrew 2010a. 'The Cosmic Race and a Heap of Broken Images: Mexico's Classical Past and the Modern Creole Imagination', in *Classics and National Cultures*, edited by Susan Stephens and Phiroze Vasunia. Oxford: OUP, 163–81.

Laird, Andrew 2010b 'Reception', in *The Oxford Handbook of Roman Studies*, edited by Alessandro Barchiesi and Walter Scheidel. Oxford: OUP, 349–68.

Laird, Andrew 2012. 'Niccolò Perotti nel Nuovo Mundo: I *Rudimenta grammatices* e le *Cornu copiae* nel Michoacán (Messico) del XVI secolo', *SUP* 32: 51–69.

Laird, Andrew 2013. 'Franciscan Humanism in Post-Conquest Mexico: Fray Cristóbal Cabrera's Epigrams on Classical and Renaissance Authors', *SUP* 33: 195–215.

Laird, Andrew 2014a. 'Humanism and the Humanity of the Peoples of the New World: Fray Julián Garcés, *De habilitate et capacitate gentium*, Rome 1537', *SUP* 24: 183–225.

Laird, Andrew 2014b. 'Nahuas and Caesars: Classical Learning and Bilingualism in Post-Conquest Mexico; An Inventory of Latin Writings by Authors of the Native Nobility, *Classical Philology*, 109.2: 150–69.

Laird, Andrew 2016a. 'Orator, Sage and Patriot: Cicero in Colonial Latin America', in *The Afterlife of Cicero*, edited by Gesine Manuwalt. London: Institute of Classical Studies, University of London, 121–43.

Laird, Andrew 2016b. 'Aztec and Roman Gods in Sixteenth-Century Mexico: Strategic Uses of Classical Learning in Sahagún's *Historia general*', in Pohl and Lyons 2016, 147–67.

Laird, Andrew 2017a. 'Classical Letters and Millenarian Madness in Post-Conquest Mexico: The *Ecstasis* of Fray Cristóbal Cabrera (1548)', *IJCT* 24.1: 78–108.

Laird, Andrew 2017b. '*Hispani hic peccant*: Fray Cristóbal Cabrera's Verse Epistles from New Spain (Vat. Lat. 1165)', *SUP* 37: 81–110.

Laird, Andrew 2018a. 'Colonial Grammatology: The Versatility and Transformation of European Letters in Sixteenth-Century Spanish America', *Language & History* 61: 52–9.

Laird, Andrew 2018b 'Responding to the *Requerimiento*: Imagined First Encounters between Natives and Spaniards in Sixteenth-Century Mexico', *Republics of Letters* 5.3: 1–19.

Laird, Andrew 2019a. 'American Philological Associations: Latin and Amerindian Languages', *Transactions of the American Philological Association* 149.2: 117–40.

Laird, Andrew 2019b. 'Humanism and Experience in the Poetry of Fray Cristóbal Cabrera (1513–1598), in *The Rise of Spanish American Poetry 1500–1700: Literary and Cultural Transmission in the New World*, ed. Rodrigo Cacho Casal and Imogen Choi. Cambridge: Legenda, 81–100.

Laird, Andrew 2019c. 'From the *Epistolae et Evangelia* (c. 1540) to the *Espejo divino* (1607): Indian Latinists and Nahuatl Religious Literature at the College of Tlatelolco', *JOLCEL* 2: 2–28.

Laird, Andrew 2020. 'Metamorphosis and *Mestizaje*: Ovid in Latin Writing from Europe to New Spain (1516–1577), in *Latin and Vernacular in Renaissance Iberia, III: Ovid from the Middle Ages to the Baroque*, ed. Barry Taylor and Alejandro Coroleu. Manchester: SPLASH Editions, 131–41.

Laird, Andrew 2021. 'The White Goddess in Mexico: Apuleius' Latin, Spanish and Nahuatl Legacy in New Spain', in *The Afterlife of Apuleius*, ed. Florence Bistagne, Carole Boidin, and Raphaele Mouren. London: Institute of Classical Studies, 27–46.

Laird, Andrew 2024. 'The Earliest Known Text in Latin by a Nahuatl Speaker: Juan de Tlaxcala, "Verba sociorum domini petri tlacauepantzi" (1541)', *Ethnohistory* 71.2.

Laird, Andrew and Miller, Nicola, ed. 2018. *Antiquities and Classical Traditions in Latin America*. Malden, MA, Chichester, and Oxford: Wiley.

Laird, Andrew and Šoštarić, Petra 2019. 'A Croatian Conquistador in Mayan Yucatán: Vinko Paletin's *De jure et justitia belli contra Indos*', *Colloquia Maruliana* 28: 191–200.

Lampe, G.W.H. 1961. *A Patristic Greek Lexicon*. Oxford: Clarendon Press.

Lane Fox, Robin 1986. *Pagans and Christians: In the Mediterranean World from the Second Century AD to the Conversion of Constantine*. London: Viking/New York: Knopf.

Lara, Jaime 2006. 'Roman Catholics in Hispanic America', in The *Oxford History of Christian Worship*, edited by Geoffrey Wainwright and Karen B. Westerfield Tucker. New York: OUP, 633–50.

Lara, Jaime 2008. *Christian Texts for Aztecs: Art and Liturgy in Colonial Mexico*. Notre Dame: University of Notre Dame Press.

Larracoechea Bengoa, José María 1987. *Notas históricas de la Villa de Durango*. Bilbao: Mensajero.

Laugesen, Anker Teilgard 1962. 'La roue de Virgile: Une page de la théorie littéraire du Moyen-Âge', *Classica et Medievalia* 23: 248–73.

Launey, Michel 2011. *An Introduction to Classical Nahuatl*, tr. Christopher Mackay, Cambridge: CUP.

Lausberg, Heinrich 1998. *Handbook of Literary Rhetoric*, translated by M. Bliss, A. Jansen, and D. Orton. Leiden: Brill; German orig. Munich: Max Hueber, 1960.

Lawn, Brian 1993. *The Rise and Decline of the Scholastic 'Quaestio Disputata': With a Special Emphasis on Its Use in the Teaching of Medicine and Science*. Leiden: Brill.

Lee, Jongsoo 2008. *The Allure of Nezahualcoyotl: Pre-Hispanic History, Religion and Nahua Poetics*. Albuquerque: University of New Mexico Press.

Lejarza, Fidel de 1948. 'Franciscanismo de Cortés y Cortesianismo de los Franciscanos', *Missionalia Hispanica* 5: 43–136.

León, Nicolás 1886. *Noticia y descripción de un códice del Ilmo. D. Fr. Bartolomé de las Casas*. Morelia: Escuela de Artes a Cargo de J.R. Bravo.

León, Nicolás 1888. 'Reyes Tarascos y sus desciendentes hasta la presente epoca', *Anales del Museo Michoacano 1*: 115–78.

León-Portilla, Ascensión, see Hernández de León-Portilla, Ascensión.

León-Portilla, Miguel 1956. *La filosofía náhuatl estudiada en sus fuentes*. Mexico: UNAM [repr. 2006; Eng. translation by Jack Emory Davies 1963, *Aztec Thought and Culture*, Norman: University of Oklahoma].

León-Portilla, Miguel 1962. *Broken Spears: The Aztec Account of the Conquest of Mexico*. Boston: Beacon Press.

León-Portilla, Miguel 1969. 'Ramírez de Fuenleal y las antigüedades mexicanas', *ECN* 8: 9–49.

León-Portilla, Miguel 1972. *Nezahualcoyotl: Su vida y pensamiento*. Texcoco: Gobierno del Estado de México.

León-Portilla, Miguel 1980. 'Un testimonio de Sahagún aprovechado por Chimalpahin—los olmecas en Chalco-Amaquemecan', *ECN* 14: 95–129.

León-Portilla, Miguel 1983. 'Fuentes de la *Monarquía indiana'*, in Torquemada, *Monarquía indiana*. Mexico: UNAM, vol. 7, 93–266 [cf. TORQUEMADA, Fr. JUAN DE, 1615, above].

León-Portilla, Miguel, ed. 1994. *Cantares mexicanos (facsimilar)*. Mexico: Instituto de Investigaciones Bibliográficas.

León-Portilla, Miguel 1999. 'De la oralidad de los códices a la *Historia general:* Transvase y estructuración de los textos allegados por fray Bernardino de Sahagún', *ECN* 29: 65–141.

León-Portilla, Miguel 2000a. 'Aztecas, disquisiciones sobre un gentilicio', *ECN* 31: 307–13.

León-Portilla, Miguel 2000b. *Tonantzin-Guadalupe: Pensamiento náhuatl y mensaje cristiano en el 'Nican mopohua'*. Mexico: FCE.

León-Portilla, Miguel 2002. *Bernardino de Sahagún, First Anthropologist*, translated by Mauricio J. Mixco. Norman: University of Oklahoma Press; Sp. orig., Mexico: UNAM, 1999.

León-Portilla, Miguel 2015. 'Una carta inédita de don Antonio Valeriano, 1578, *ECN* 49: 199–207.

León-Portilla, Miguel, Curiel Defossé, Guadalupe, and Reyes Equigas, Salvador. 2011–2019, *Cantares mexicanos*. 3 vols. Mexico: UNAM-IIH.

Leonard, Irving 1992. *Books of the Brave: Being an Account of Books and of Men in the Spanish Conquest and Settlement of the Sixteenth-Century New World*. Berkeley, Los Angeles, and Oxford: University of California Press; orig. Cambridge: Harvard University Press, 1949.

Ligota, Christopher and Quantin, Jean-Louis, eds. 2006. *History of Scholarship: A Selection of Papers from the Seminar on the History of Scholarship Held Annually at the Warburg Institute*. Oxford: OUP.

Lillo Castañ, Victor and Camino Plaza, Laura 2021. 'Dos epístolas latinas de fray Juan de Zumárraga y Juan Bernal Díaz de Luco sobre la evangelización del Nuevo Mundo', *Translat Library* 3.1: 1–35.

Linz, Juan J. 1972. 'Intellectual Roles in Sixteenth- and Seventeenth Century Spain', *Daedalus*, 101.3: 59–108.

Lobato Casado, Abelardo 1988. 'El obispo Garcés y la Bulla *Sublimis Deus*', in *Actas del I Congreso Internacional sobre los Dominicos y el Nuevo Mundo: Sevilla: 21–25 de abril de 1987*. Madrid: Deimos, 739–96.

Lockhart, James 1992. *The Nahuas after the Conquest: A Social and Cultural History of the Indians of Central Mexico, Sixteenth through Eighteenth Centuries*. Stanford: Stanford UP.

Lockhart, James, ed., tr. 1993. *We People Here: Nahuatl Accounts of the Conquest of Mexico*. Berkeley and Los Angeles: University of California Press.

Lockhart, James 2001. *Nahuatl as Written*. Stanford: Stanford UP.

Loera de la Llave, M.A. 1994. '*Historia sive litterae*: Una biografía carolingia de Notker Balbulus, la historiografía desde la antigüedad y Fray Bernardino de Sahagún', *Literatura Mexicana* 5.2: 301–33.

López Luján, Leonardo 2015. 'Under the Sign of the Sun: Eagle Feathers, Skins, and Insignia in the Mexica World', in *Images Take Flight: Feather Art in Mexico and Europe 1400–1700*, ed. Alessandra Russo, Gerhard Wolf, and Diana Fane. Munich: Hirmer, 132–43.

López Piñero, J.M. 1979. *Ciencia y técnica en la sociedad española de los siglos XVI y XVII*. Barcelona: Labor Universitaria.

López Rodríguez, Miguel 1979. *El Colegio Real de Santa Cruz de la Fe de Granada*. Salamanca: Ediciones Universidad de Salamanca.

López Sarrelangue, Delfina Esmeralda 1965. *La nobleza indígena de Pátzcuaro en la época virreinal*. Mexico: UNAM-IIH.

Losada, Ángel 1971. 'Controversy between Sepúlveda and Las Casas', in: *Bartolomé de las Casas in History*, ed. Juan Friede and Benjamin Keen. DeKalb: Northern Illinois UP, 279–309.

Lozano Guillén, Carmen 2008. 'Elementos de poética en la gramática latina: El género lírico', *Cuadernos de filología clásica: Estudios latinos* 28.1: 95–113.

Lupher, David A. 2003. *Romans in a New World: Classical Models in Sixteenth-Century Spanish America*. Ann Arbor: University of Michigan Press.

Lupton, J.H. 1909. *A Life of John Colet D. D.* London: G. Bell and Sons.

Lyons, Claire L. and Pohl, John M.D. 2010. *The Aztec Pantheon and the Art of Empire*. Los Angeles: The J. Paul Getty Museum.

MacCormack, Sabine 1991. *Religion in the Andes: Vision and Imagination in Early Colonial Peru*. Princeton: Princeton UP.

MacCormack, Sabine 1998. 'The Incas and Rome', in *Garcilaso de la Vega: An American Humanist, A Tribute to José Durand*, edited by José Anadón. Notre Dame: University of Notre Dame Press, 8–31.

MacCormack, Sabine 2007. *On the Wings of Time: Rome, the Incas, Spain and Peru*. Princeton: Princeton UP.

Mack, Peter 1993. *Renaissance Argument: Valla and Agricola in the Traditions of Rhetoric and Dialectic*. Leiden: Brill.

Mack, Peter 1996. 'Humanist Rhetoric and Dialectic', in Kraye 1996, 82–99.

Mack, Peter 2005. 'Vives's *De ratione dicendi*: Structure, Innovations, Problems', *Rhetorica* 23.1: 65–92.

Mack, Peter 2011. *A History of Renaissance Rhetoric 1380–1620*. Oxford: OUP.

Maclean, Ian 1984. 'The Interpretation of Natural Signs: Cardano's *De subtilitate* versus Scaliger's *Exercitationes*', in *Occult and Scientific Mentalities*, edited by Brian Vickers. Cambridge: CUP, 231–52.

Magaloni Kerpel, Diana 2020. *El Códice Florentino y la creación del Nuevo Mundo*. Mexico: Editorial Raíces-INAH.

Mahlmann-Bauer, Barbara 2008. 'Catholic and Protestant Textbooks in Elementary Latin Conversation', in *Scholarly Knowledge: Textbooks in Early Modern Europe*, edited by Emidio Campi, Simone de Angelis, Anja-Silvia Goening, and Anthony T. Grafton. Geneva: Librairie Droz, 341–90.

Maillard Álvarez, Natalia 2018. 'Early Circulation of Classical Books in New Spain and Peru', in Laird and Miller 2018, 26–40.

Mann, Nicholas 1996. 'The Origins of Humanism', in Kraye 1996, 1–19.

Mannheim, Bruce 1989. 'La memoria y el olvido en la política lingüística colonial', *Lexis* (Lima) 13: 13–46.

Marcocci, Giuseppe 2020. *The Globe on Paper: Writing Histories of the World in Renaissance Europe and the Americas*, translated by Richard Bates. Oxford: OUP.

Marcus, Leah S. 1992. 'Renaissance/Early Modern Studies', in *Redrawing the Boundaries: The Transformation of English and American Literary Studies*, edited by Stephen Greenblatt and Giles B. Gunn. New York: Modern Language Association of America, 41–63.

Mariscal, Mario 1946. 'Un retrato y una firma ilustres en papeles del siglo XVI', *Filosofía y Letras* (Mexico) 12.24: 315–20.

Marrone, Daniela 2000. *L'apologeticon di Battista Spagnoli*. Mantua: Accademia Nazionale Virgiliana di Scienze Lettere e Arti.

Marrou, Henri-Irénée. 1976. *Patristique et humanisme: Mélanges*. Paris: Le Seuil.

Marsh, David 1992. 'Xenophon', in Kristeller and Kranz 1960–2020, vol. 7, 75–196.

Marshall, Peter K. 1983, 'Scriptores Historiae Augustae', in Reynolds 1983, 354–6.

Martín Baños, Pedro 2019. *La pasión de saber: Vida de Antonio de Nebrija*. Huelva: Universidad de Huelva.

Martín Ortiz, Eduardo 1974. *La coacción de infieles a la fé según Cristóbal Cabrera*. Seville: Pontificia Universitas Gregoriana.

Martínez, José Luis, ed. 1986. *Entrevista de Gonzalo Fernández de Oviedo a Juan Cano en septiembre de 1544*. Mexico: Ambos Mundos.

Martínez Baracs, Rodrigo 2005. *Convivencia y utopía: El gobierno indio y español de la 'ciudad de Mechuacan', 1521–1580*. Mexico: FCE.

Martínez Baracs, Rodrigo 2006. *La perdida Relación de la Nueva España y su conquista de Juan Cano*. Mexico: INAH.

Martínez Baracs, Rodrigo 2007. 'El triunfo de la Virgen y gozo mexicano', *Literatura Mexicana* 18.2: 5–37.

Martínez Baracs, Rodrigo 2007b. 'El Diario de Chimalpáhin' *ECN* 38: 283–312.

Martínez Baracs, Rodrigo 2015. 'Notas sobre la elaboración del *Nican Mopohua*', in *De la historia económica a la historia social y cultural: Homenaje a Gisela von Wobeser*, edited by María del Pilar Martínez López-Cano. Mexico: UNAM-IIH, 315–32.

Martínez Baracs, Rodrigo and Espinosa Morales, Lydia 1999. *La vida michoacana en el siglo XVI: Catálogo de los documentos del siglo XVI del Archivo Histórico de la Ciudad de Pátzcuaro*. Mexico: INAH.

Martínez López-Cano and María del Pilar, eds. 2006. *La Universidad novohispana en el siglo de oro*. Mexico: UNAM.

Massing, Jean Michel 1995. 'From Greek Proverb to Soap Advert: Washing the Ethiopian', *JWCI* 58: 180–201.

Mathes, Miguel 1982. *Santa Cruz de Tlatelolco: La primera biblioteca académica de las Américas*. Mexico: Secretaría de Relaciones Exteriores.

Mathes, Miguel 1985. *The America's* [sic] *First Academic Library, Santa Cruz de Tlatelolco*. Sacramento: California State Library.

Mathes, Miguel 1995. 'La imprenta en Tlatelolco', *Boletín del Instituto de Investicaciones Bibliográficas* 7: 121–42.

Matos Moctezuma, Eduardo 2017. 'Ancient Stone Sculpture: In Search of the Mexican Past', in *The Oxford Handbook of the Aztecs*, edited by Enrico Rodríguez-Alegría and Deborah L. Nichols. Oxford: OUP, 21–8.

Matthews Sanford, Eva 1949. 'Famous Latin Encyclopedias', *Classical Journal* 44: 462–7.

Maxwell, Judith M. and Hanson, Craig A. 1992. *Of the Manners of Speaking That the Old Ones Had: The Metaphors of Andrés de Olmos in the TULAL Manuscript*. Salt Lake City: University of Utah Press.

May, James M. and Wisse, Jakob, eds. 2001. *Cicero: On the Ideal Orator*. Oxford: OUP.

Mayer, Alicia 2008. *Lutero en el Paraíso: La Nueva España en el espejo del reformador alemán*. Mexico: UNAM.

Máynez, Pilar 2008. 'Sobre el origen del lenguaje y la diversidad lingüística: La Babel de México', *ECN* 39: 207–23.

Maza, Francisco de la 1945. 'Diego Valadés, escritor y grabador franciscano', *Anales del Instituto de Investigaciones Estéticas* 4.13: 15–44.

Maza, Francisco de la 1968. *La mitología clásica en el arte colonial de México*. Mexico: Instituto de Investigaciones Estéticas.

Mazzocco, Angelo 1993. *Linguistic Theories in Dante and the Humanists: Studies of Language and Intellectual History in Late Medieval and Early Renaissance Italy*. Leiden: Brill.

McLaughlin, Martin L. 1995. *Literary Imitation in the Italian Renaissance: The Theory and Practice of Literary Imitation in Italy from Dante to Bembo*. Oxford: Clarendon Press.

McNally, Robert E. 1966. 'The Council of Trent and Vernacular Bibles', *Theological Studies* 27: 204–27.

McRae, Duncan 2016. *Legible Religion: Books, Gods and Rituals in Roman Culture*. Cambridge, MA: Harvard UP.

Megged, Amos 2010. *Social Memory in Ancient and Colonial Mesoamerica*. Cambridge: CUP.

Méndez Arceo, Sergio 1952. *La Real y Pontifícia Universidad de México: Antecedentes, tramitación y despacho de las reales cédulas de erección*. Mexico: Consejo de Humanidades.

Méndez Plancarte, Gabriel 1946. *Humanistas mexicanos del siglo XVI*. Mexico: UNAM.

Merino Jerez, Luis 2007. *Retórica y artes de memoria en el humanismo renacentista*. Cáceres: Universidad de Extremadura.

Merino Jerez, Luis 2020. 'Iacobus Publicius' *Ars memorativa*: An Approach to the History of the (Printed) Text'. *Acta Universitatis Carolinae Philologica* 2: 85–105.

Messiaen, S.A.D. 2003. 'Some Interesting Observations on Chimalpahin by Use of His *Diferentes historias originales*', *ECN* 34: 219–56.

Mignolo, Walter D. 1987. 'El mandato y la ofrenda: *La descripción de la ciudad y provincia de Tlaxcala* de Diego Muñoz Camargo, y las *Relaciones de Indias*', *Nueva Revista de Filología Hispánica* 35.5: 451–84.

Mignolo, Walter D. 1992. 'On the Colonization of Amerindian Languages', *Comparative Studies in Society & History* 34.2: 301–30.

Mignolo, Walter D. 1995. *The Darker Side of the Renaissance: Literacy, Territoriality, and Colonization*. Ann Arbor: University of Michigan Press.

Mijáres, Ivonne 2014. *Catálogo de Protocolos del Archivo General de Notarías de la Ciudad de México, Fondo Siglo XVI*. Mexico: IIH, http://cpagncmxvi.historicas.unam.mx/catalogo.jsp.

Minns, Denis and Parvis, Paul, eds. 2009. *Justin, Philosopher and Martyr: Apologies*. Oxford: OUP.

Miranda, Francisco 1982. *América espera*, edited by José Luis Salcedo-Bastardo. Caracas: Biblioteca Ayacucho.

Miranda Godínez, Francisco 1972. *Don Vasco de Quiroga y su Colegio de San Nicolás*. Morelia: Fimax.

Moffitt Watts, Pauline 1991. 'Hieroglyphs of Conversion: Alien Discourses in Diego Valadés' *Rhetorica Christiana*', *Memorie Domenicane* 22: 405–33.

Moisan, Jean-Claude 1997. 'Les rhétoriques de Francisco Sánchez de las Brozas et le système Ramiste', in *Autour de Ramus: Texte, théorie, commentaire*, eds. Kees Meerhoff and Jean-Claude Moisan. Québec: Nuit Blanche, 195–216.

Momigliano, Arnaldo 1950. 'Ancient History and the Antiquarian', *JWCI* 13: 285–315.

Monfasani, John 1976. *George of Trebizond: A Biography and a Study of His Rhetoric and Logic*. Leiden: Brill.

Monzón, Cristina 1997. 'La influencia de Nebrija en la gramática p'urhépecha de Gilberti', in *Memoria del Coloquio: La obra de Antonio Nebrija*, in Guzmán Betancourt and Nansen Díaz 1997, 107–19.

Monzón, Cristina 1999. 'Innovations in a Vernacular Grammar. A Comparison of Fray Maturino Gilberti's Latin and Tarascan Grammars', in *History of Linguistics 1996. Volume 1: Traditions in Linguistics Worldwide*, edited by David Cram, Andrew R. Linn, and Elke Nowak. Amsterdam and Philadephia: John Benjamins, 147–54.

Monzón, Cristina 2009. 'The Tarascan Lexicographic Tradition in the 16th Century', in *Missionary Linguistics IV/Lingüística misionera IV: Lexicography*, edited by Otto Zwartjes, Ramón Arzápalo Marín, and Thomas C. Smith. Amsterdam and Philadelphia: John Benjamins, 165–95.

Monzón, Cristina 2012a. 'Intertextual Unity in the Franciscan Friar Juan Baptista de Lagunas's Opus of 1574', *Historiographia Linguistica* 39: 243–58.

Monzón, Cristina 2012b. 'Remodelling the Tarascan Religious World: 16th-Century Translations and Its Survival into the 21st Century', in Zwartjes, Zimmermann, and Schrader-Kniffki 2012, 113–30.

Moore, John C. 1981. 'Innocent III's *De miseria humanae conditionis*: A *Speculum Curiae*?', *Catholic Historical Review*, 67.4: 553–64.

Morales OFM, Francisco 1993. 'Los Franciscanos y el primer arte para la lengua náhuatl: Un nuevo testimonio', *ECN* 23: 53–81.

Moreno de Alba, José G. 1996. 'Indigenismos en las *Décadas del Nuevo Mundo* de Pedro Mártir de Anglería', *Nueva Revista de Filología Hispánica* 44.1: 1–26.

Moss, Ann, 2003. *Renaissance Truth and the Latin Language Turn*. Oxford: OUP.

Moyer, Anne E. 2020. 'Who Were the Florentines? Etruscan Roots', in *The Intellectual World of Sixteenth-Century Florence: Humanists and Culture in the Age of Cosimo I*, by Moyer. Cambridge: CUP, 29–70.

Much, Rudolf 1967. *Die Germania des Tacitus*. Heidelberg: Carl Winter.

Müller, Paola 2010. 'L'*imago* come *medium* conoscitivo del *De arte rhetorica* (1569) di Cipriano Soarez', *SUP* 30: 307–16.

Mundy, Barbara E. 1996. *The Mapping of New Spain: Indigenous Cartography and the Maps of the Relaciones geográficas*. Chicago: University of Chicago Press.

Mundy, Barbara E. 1998. 'Mapping the Aztec Capital: The 1524 Nuremberg Map of Tenochtitlan: Its Sources and Meanings', *Imago Mundi* 50: 11–33.

Mundy, Barbara E. 2015. *The Death of Aztec Tenochtitlan, the Life of Mexico City*. Austin, University of Texas Press.

Murillo Gallegos, Verónica 2010. 'En náhuatl y en castellano: El dios cristiano en los discursos franciscanos de evangelización', *ECN* 41: 297–316.

Murillo Gallegos, Verónica 2016. 'Filiaciones escotistas ante el Concilio de Trento: Fray Juan Bautista de Viseo, *Advertencias para los Confesores* (1600)', *Anuario de Filosofía Argentina y Americana* 27: 93–155.

Myers, Kathleen Ann 2008. *Fernández de Oviedo's Chronicle of America: A New History for a New World*. Austin: University of Texas Press.

Nader, Helen 1972. *The Mendoza Family in the Spanish Renaissance, 1350 to 1550*. Berkeley: University of California Press.

Nelson, William 1973. *Fact and Fiction: The Dilemma of the Renaissance Storyteller*. Cambridge, MA: Harvard UP.

Nesvig, Martin Austin 2006, 'The "Indian Question" and the Case of Tlatelolco', in *Local Religion in Colonial Mexico*, edited by Nesvig. Albuquerque: University of New Mexico Press, 63–89.

Nesvig, Martin Austin 2009. *Ideology and Inquisition: The World of the Censors in Early Mexico*. New Haven: Yale UP.

Nettel, Patricia 1993. 'Cosmovisión y cultura material franciscana en los pueblos de indios de Nueva España según Fray Diego Valadés (una perspectiva etnográfica)', in *Franciscanos y el mundo religioso en el México virreinal*, edited by Francisco Morales and Cecilia Frost. Mexico: UNAM, 39–53.

Nicolau D'Olwer, Luis, ed. 1956. *Fray Toríbio de Benavente: Relaciones de la Nueva España*, Mexico: UNAM.

Nicolau D'Olwer, Luis 1987. *Fray Bernardino de Sahagún 1499–1590*, translated by Mauricio J. Mixco. Salt Lake City: University of Utah; Sp. orig., Mexico: Instituto Panamericano de Geografía e Historia, 1952.

Nicolau D'Olwer, Luis and Cline, Howard F. 1973. 'Sahagún and His Works', in Cline and Glass 1973, 186–203.

Niederehe, Hans-J. 2004. 'La *Gramática de la lengua castellana* (1492) de Antonio de Nebrija', *Boletín de la Sociedad Española de Historiografía Lingüística* 4: 41–52.

Noreña, Carlos G. 1970. *Juan Luis Vives*. The Hague: Nijhoff.

Nouilhon, Michèle 1989. 'Les lectisternes républicains', in *Entre hommes et dieux: Le convive, le héros, le prophète*, edited by Annie-France Laurens. Besançon: Annales littéraires de l'Université de Besançon, 27–42.

Nowak, Elke, ed. 1999. *Languages Different in All Their Sounds: Descriptive Approaches to Indigenous Languages of the Americas, 1500 to 1850*. Münster: Nodus.

Ødemark, John 2017. 'Preaching with Pictures, Transforming Memories: Catechisms and Images as Contact Zones in Sixteenth Century New Spain', in *Translating Catechisms, Translating Cultures: The Expansion of Catholicism in the Early Modern World*, edited by Antje Flüchter and Rouven Wirbser. Leiden and Boston: Brill, 331–67.

O'Gorman, Edmundo, ed., tr. 1963. *Cervantes de Salazar: México en 1554 y Túmulo imperial*. Mexico: Porrúa.

O'Gorman, Edmundo, ed. 1975–1977. *Fernando de Alva Ixtlilxóchitl: Obras históricas*. 2 vols. Mexico: UNAM.

O'Gorman, Edmundo 1986. *Destierro de sombras: Luz en el origen y culto de Nuestra Señora de Guadalupe del Tepeyac*. Mexico: IIH.

Olaechea Labayen, Juan Bautista 1958. 'Opiniones de los teólogos españoles sobre dar estudios mayores a los indios', *Anuario de Estudios Americanos* 15: 113–97.

Olivier, Guilhem 2016. 'The Mexica Pantheon in Light of Graeco-Roman Polytheism: Uses, Abuses, and Proposals', in Pohl and Lyons 2016, 189–214.

O'Malley, John 2013. *Trent: What Happened at the Council*. Cambridge, MA: Belknap.

Ong, Walter J. 2002. *Orality and Literacy: The Technologizing of the Word*. London and New York: Routledge.

O'Rourke Boyle, Marjorie 2004. 'A Conversational Opener: The Rhetorical Paradigm of John 1:1', in *A Companion to Rhetoric and Rhetorical Criticism*, edited by Walter Jost and Wendy Olmsted. Malden and Oxford: Blackwell, 60–79.

Orozco y Berra, Manuel 1830. *Noticia histórica de la conjuración del Marqués del Valle: Años de 1565–1568*. Mexico: Tipografía de R. Rafael.

Ortega Sánchez, Delfín 2011. *Diego Valadés: Conquistador extremeño de Nueva España*. Seville: Punto Rojo.

Ortiz de Montellano, Bernardo 1993. *Medicina, salud, y nutrición aztecas*. Mexico: Siglo XXI.

Osorio Romero, Ignacio 1976. *Tópicos sobre Cicerón en México*. Mexico: UNAM.

Osorio Romero, Ignacio 1979. *Colegios y profesores jesuitas que enseñaron latín en Nueva España (1572–1767)*. Mexico: UNAM.

Osorio Romero, Ignacio 1980. *Floresta de gramática, poética y retórica en Nueva España (1521–1767)*. Mexico: UNAM.

Osorio Romero, Ignacio 1984. 'Tres joyas bibliográficas para la enseñanza del latín en el siglo XVI novohispano', *Nova Tellus* 2: 192–200.

Osorio Romero, Ignacio 1990. *La enseñanza de latín a los indios*. Mexico: UNAM.

Pade, Marianne 2005. 'Niccolò Perotti's *Cornu Copiae*: Commentary on Martial and Encyclopedia', in *On Renaissance Commentaries*, edited by Marianne Pade. Hildesheim: Georg Olms, 49–63.

Padley, G.A. 1976. *Grammatical Theory in Western Europe, 1500–1700: The Latin Tradition*. Cambridge: CUP.

Padley, G.A. 1985 and 1988. *Grammatical Theory in Western Europe, 1500–1700: Trends in Vernacular Grammar*. 2 vols. Cambridge: CUP.

Pagden, Anthony 1982. *The Fall of Natural Man: The American Indian and the Origins of Comparative Ethnology*. Cambridge: CUP.

Palencia-Roth, Michael 1985. 'Cannibalism and the New Man of Latin America in the 15th and 16th-Century European Imagination', *Comparative Civilizations Review* 12: 1–27.

Palmer, L.R. 1954. *The Latin Language*. London: Faber.

Palomera SJ, Esteban J. 1962. *Fray Diego Valadés, OFM: Evangelizador humanista de la Nueva España; Su obra*. Mexico: Jus.

Palomera SJ, Esteban J. 1963. *Fray Diego Valadés, OFM: Evangelizador humanista de la Nueva España; El hombre y su epoca*. Mexico: Jus.

Pardo, Osvaldo 2004. *The Origins of Mexican Catholicism: Nahua Rituals and Christian Sacraments in Sixteenth-Century Mexico*. Ann Arbor: University of Michigan Press.

Paris, Gaston 1878. *La légende de Trajan*. Paris: Imprimerie nationale.

Parish, Helen Rand, ed., tr. 1992. *Bartolomé de las Casas, The Only Way*. New York and Mahwah: Paulist Press.

Pascoe, Juan 2017. *Cornelio Adrián César: Impresor flamenco en México 1597–1633*. Tacambaro, Mexico: El Taller Martìn [sic] Pescador, en colaboración con la Biblioteca Francisco de Burgoa de Oaxaca y The John Carter Brown Library.

Paso y Troncoso, Francisco del, ed. 1939–1942. *Epistolario de la Nueva España*. 16 vols. Mexico: Antigua Librería Robredo.

Patterson, Annabel M. 1970. *Hermogenes and the Renaissance: Seven Ideas of Style*. Princeton: Princeton UP.

Payàs, Gertrudis 2004. 'Translation in Historiography: The Garibay/León-Portilla Complex and the Making of a Pre-Hispanic Past'. *Meta: Journal des traducteurs/ Meta: Translators' Journal* 49.3: 544–61.

Payno, Manuel 1869. *Las bibliotecas de México*. Mexico: La Imprenta del Gobierno en Palacio.

Paz y Meliá, Antonio 1892. *Nobiliario de conquistadores de Indias*. Madrid: M. Tello.

Pelling, C.B.R. ed. 1988. *Plutarch, Life of Antony*. Cambridge: CUP.

Peñafiel, Antonio 1900. *Fábulas de Esopo en idioma mexicano*. Mexico: Secretaría de Fomento.

Peperstraete, Sylvie 2007. *La "Chronique X": Reconstitution et analyse d'une source perdue fondementale sur la civilisation aztèque*. Oxford: Archaeopress.

Peperstraete, Sylvie and Kruell, Gabriel Kenrick 2014. 'Determining the Authorship of the *Crónica mexicayotl*: Two Hypotheses', *The Americas* 71.2: 315–38.

Percival, W. Keith 1975. 'The Grammatical Traditions and the Rise of the Vernaculars', *Current Trends in Linguistics* 13: 231–75 [Percival 2004: Study I].

Percival, W. Keith 1981. 'The Place of the *Rudimenta Grammatices* in the History of Latin Grammar', *Res Publica Litterarum* 4: 233–64 [Percival 2004: Study VIII].

Percival, W. Keith 1989. 'The Influence of Perotti's *Rudimenta* in the *Cinquecento*', in *Protrepticon: Studi di letteratura classica e umanistica in onore di Giovannangiola Secchi-Tarugi*, edited by Sesto Prete. Milan: Centro Internazionale di Studi Umanistici, 91–100 [Percival 2004: Study X].

Percival, W. Keith 1996. 'Italian Affiliations of Nebrija's Latin Grammar', in *Italia ed Europa nella linguistica del Rinascimento*. Vol. 1, edited by Mirko Tavoni. Ferrara: Franco Cosimo Panini, 99–112 [Percival 2004: Study XII].

Percival, W. Keith 1999. 'Nebrija's Linguistic Oeuvre as a Model for Missionary Linguistics', in Nowak 1999, 15–29 [Percival 2004: Study XIV].

Percival, W. Keith 2004. *Studies in Renaissance Grammar*. Aldershot: Ashgate.

Pérez-Rocha, Emma 1982. *La tierra y el hombre en la Villa de Tacuba durante la época colonial*. Mexico: INAH.

Pérez-Rocha, Emma 1998. *Privilegios en lucha: La información de doña Isabel Moctezuma*. Mexico: INAH.

Pérez-Rocha, Emma and Tena, Rafael 2000. *La nobleza indígena del centro de México después de la conquista*, Mexico: INAH.

Peterson, Jeanette Favrot 2019. 'Images in Translation', in Peterson and Terraciano 2019, 21–36.

Peterson, Jeanette Favrot and Terraciano, Kevin, eds. 2019. *The Florentine Codex: An Encyclopedia of the Nahua World of Sixteenth-Century Mexico*. Austin: University of Texas Press.

Perry, Ben E. 1952. *Aesopica*. Urbana: University of Illinois Press.

Pfundstein, James M. 1997. 'Per astra ad aspera: Aeneid 6.725', *Vergilius* 43: 22–30.

Phelan, John Leddy 1956. *The Millennial Kingdom of the Franciscans in the New World: A Study of the Writings of Gerónimo de Mendieta*. Berkeley and Los Angeles: University of California Press.

Phillips Jr, Henry, ed., tr. 1883. 'History of the Mexicans as Told by Their Paintings', *Proceedings of the American Philosophical Society* 21: 616–51.

Piho, Virve 1972. 'Tlacatecutli, tlacochtecutli, tlacatéccatl y tlacochcálcatl', *ECN* 10: 315–28.

Pohl, John M.D. and Lyons, Claire 2016. *Altera Roma: Art and Empire from Mérida to Mexico*. Los Angeles, Cotsen Institute of Archaeology Press, UCLA.

Pollnitz, Aysha. 2017. 'Old Words and the New World: Liberal Education and the Franciscans in New Spain (1536–1601)', *Transactions of the Royal Historical Society* 27: 123–52.

Poole, Stafford 1963. 'The Church and the Repartimientos in the Light of the Third Mexican Council, 1585', *The Americas* 20: 3–36.

Poole, Stafford 1965. 'War by Fire and Blood—the Church and the Chichimecas, 1585', *The Americas* 22: 115–37.

Poole, Stafford 1981. 'Church Law on the Ordination of Indians and *Castas* in New Spain', *HAHR* 61.4: 637–50.

Poole, Stafford 1997. *Our Lady of Guadalupe: The Origins and Sources of a Mexican National Symbol, 1531–1797*. Tucson: University of Arizona Press.

Poster, Carol and Mitchell, Linda C. eds. 2007. *Letter-Writing Manuals and Instruction from Antiquity to the Present*. Columbia: University of South Carolina Press.

Prem, Hanns J. 1992. 'Aztec Writing', in *Supplement to the Handbook of Middle American Indians Vol. 5*, edited by V.R. Bricker. Austin: University of Texas Press, 53–69.

Prem, Hanns J. 1997. *The Ancient Americas: A Brief History and Guide to Research*, tr. K. Kurbjuhn. Salt Lake City: University of Utah Press.

Prescott, William Hickling 1843. *History of the Conquest of Mexico*. New York: Harper and Brothers [1915: 2 vols. Oxford, London, Edinburgh, and Glasgow: Humphrey Milford and OUP].

Pym, Antony 2000. *Negotiating the Frontier: Translators and Intercultures in Hispanic History*. Manchester: St Jerome.

Ramírez, José Fernando 1898. *Adiciones á la biblioteca de Beristáin: Opúsculos históricos*. 2 vols. Mexico City: V. Agüeros.

Ramírez Calva, Verenice Cipatli 2010. *Caciques y caciquazgos indígenas en la región de Tollan, siglos XIV–XVII*. Zamora: El Colegio de Michoacán.

Ramírez Vidal, Gerardo 2005. 'Fray Diego y los indios', in *Acerca de Diego Valadés. Su Retórica christiana*, edited by Bulmaro Reyes Correa, Gerardo Ramírez Vidal, and Salvador Díaz Cíntora. Mexico: UNAM, 9–32.

Ramminger, Johann 2020. 'Language and Cultural Memory in the *Antiquitates* of Annius of Viterbo', *Nordic Journal of Renaissance Studies* 17: 35–66.

Ramos, Gabriela and Yannakakis, Yanna, eds. 2014. *Indigenous Intellectuals: Knowledge, Power, and Colonial Culture in Mexico and the Andes*. Durham, NC: Duke UP.

Raven, James 2011. 'Classical Transports: Latin and Greek Texts in North and Central America before 1800', in *Books between Europe and the Americas: Connections and Communities, 1620–1860*, edited by Leslie Howsam and James Raven. Basingstoke: Palgrave Macmillan, 157–86.

Read, Malcolm K. 1980. '*Exempla* versus *ratio*: A Re-appraisal of a Crisis in Renaissance Linguistics', *Transactions of the Philological Society*, 78: 141–52.

Redmond, Walter B. 1972. *Bibliography of the Philosophy in the Iberian Colonies of America*. The Hague: Nijhoff.

Rees, Valery 2002. 'Ficino's Advice to Princes', in Allen, Rees, and Davies 2002, 339–58.

Reeves, Marjorie. 1999. *Joachim of Fiore and the Prophetic Future: A Medieval Study in Historical Thinking*. Stroud: Sutton.

Reff, Daniel T. 2005. *Plagues, Priests and Demons: Sacred Narratives and the Rise of Christianity in the Old World and the New*. Cambridge: CUP.

Regier, Willis Goth 2019. 'Erasmus and Aesop', *Erasmus Studies* 39.1: 51–74.

Reinhardt, Klaus 1987. 'Das Werk des Nikolaus von Lyra im mittelalterlichen Spanien', *Traditio* 43: 321–58.

Rekers, Ben 1972. *Benito Arias Montano (1527–1598)*. London: Warburg Institute, Leiden: Brill.

Restall, Matthew 2003. *Seven Myths of the Spanish Conquest*. Oxford: OUP.

Restall, Matthew, Sousa, Lisa, and Terraciano, Kevin, eds. 2005. *Mesoamerican Voices: Native Language Writings from Colonial Mexico, Yucatan, and Guatemala*, Cambridge: CUP.

Retief, Francois Pieter and Cilliers, Louise 2006. 'Snake and Staff Symbolism in Healing', *Acta Theologica* 26.2: 189–99.

Revelli, Paolo 1926. *Terre d'America e Archivi d'Italia*. Milan: Fratelli Treves.

Rex, Richard 2016. 'Humanist Bible Controversies', in *The New Cambridge History of the Bible. Vol. 3: 1450–1750*, edited by Euan Cameron. Cambridge: CUP, 61–81.

Reyes, Alfonso 1960. 'Apéndice sobre Virgilio y América', in *Obras completas*, by Reyes, vol. 11. Mexico City: Fondo de Cultura Económica, 178–81.

Reyes Equiguas, Salvador 2016. 'El *scriptorium* del Colegio de la Santa Cruz de Tlatelolco a través de los Códices *Florentino* y *De la Cruz-Badiano*', in Hernández and Máynez 2016, 26–38.

Reynolds, Leighton D. ed. 1983. *Texts and Transmission: A Survey of the Latin Classics*. Oxford: Clarendon Press.

Ricard, Robert 1933. *La 'conquête spirituelle' du Mexique: Essai sur l'apostolat et les méthodes missionaires des ordres mendiants en Nouvelle-Espagne de 1523–24 à 1572*. Paris: Institut d'Ethnologie [translated by Lesley Byrd Simpson, 1966, *The Spiritual Conquest of Mexico*. Berkeley and Los Angeles: University of California].

Rico, Francisco 1981. 'Un prólogo al Renacimiento español: La dedicatoria de Nebrija a las *Introducciones latinas* (1488)', in *Homenaje al profesor Marcel Bataillon: Seis lecciones sobre la España de los Siglos de oro (Literatura y historia)*, edited by Pedro Manuel Piñero Ramírez and Rogelio Reyes Cano. Seville: Universidad de Sevilla, 59–94.

Richter, Annegret 2015. *Geschichte und Translation im kolonialen Mexiko: Eine Untersuchung ausgewählter historischer Schriften von Fernando de Alva Ixtlilxochitl, Diego Muñoz Camargo und Hernando Alvarado Tezozomoc*. Hildesheim, Zurich, and New York: Georg Olms.

Riddle, John M. 1984. 'Dioscorides', in Kristeller *et al.* 1984, vol. 4, 1–143.

Ríos Castaño, Victoria 2014a. *Translation as Conquest: Sahagún and Universal History of the Things of New Spain*. Frankfurt am Main and Madrid: Vervuert/Iberoamericana.

Ríos Castaño, Victoria 2014b. 'Translating Purposes and Target Audiences in Sahagún's *Libro de la Rethorica* (c. 1577), in *Missionary Linguistics V/Lingüística Misionera V: Translation Theories and Practice*, edited by Otto Zwartjes, Klaus Zimmermann, and Martina Schrader-Kniffki. Amsterdam and Philadelphia: John Benjamins, 53–83.

Ríos Castaño, Victoria 2015. 'The Translation of Aesop's Fables in Colonial Mexico', *Trans* 19.2: 243–62.

Rives, J.B. 1999. *Tacitus: Germania; Translated with Introduction and Commentary*. Clarendon Press.

Rizzo, Silvia 2002. *Ricerche sul latino umanistico*. Rome: ESL.

Robertson, Donald 1959. *Mexican Manuscript Painting of the Early Colonial Period: The Metropolitan Schools*. New Haven: Yale UP.

Robertson, Donald 1966. 'The Sixteenth-Century Mexican Encyclopedia of Fray Bernardino de Sahagún', *Cahiers d'Histoire Mondiale* 9.3: 617–27.

Robins, R.H. 1997. *A Short History of Linguistics*. London: Longman.

Rodríguez Cruz, Agueda María 1977. *Salmantica docet: La proyección de la Universidad de Salamanca en Hispanoamérica*. Salamanca: Universidad de Salamanca.

Rodríguez Garrido, José A. 2005. 'La Égloga *El Dios Pan* de Diego Mexía Fernangil y la Evangelización en los Andes a inicios del siglo XVII', in *Manierismo y transición al Barroco: Memoria del III Encuentro Internacional sobre Barroco*, edited by Norma Campos Vera. Navarra: Universidad de Navarra, 307–19.

Roest, Bert 2004. *Franciscan Literature of Religious Instruction before the Council of Trent*. Leiden and Boston: Brill.

Rojas Silva, Alejandra 2018. '*Gardens of Origin and the Golden Age in the Mexican Libellus de medicinalibus Indorum herbis (1552)*', in Laird and Miller 2018, 41–56.

Rojas Silva, Felipe 2022. 'Babylonians in Sixteenth Century Mexico: Comparative Antiquarianism in the Work of Sahagún', in *The Allure of the Ancient: Receptions of the Ancient Middle East, ca. 1600–1800*, edited by Margaret Geoga and John Steele. Leiden and Boston: Brill, 284–309.

Romeo, Rosario 1954. *Le scoperte americane nella coscienza italiana del Cinquecento*. Milan: Riccardo Ricciardi.

Romero Galván, José Rubén 2006. 'Tezozomoc, Fernando de Alvarado', in *The Oxford Encyclopedia of Mesoamerican Cultures*, vol. 3, edited by Davíd Carrasco. New York: OUP, 2001, 219–20.

Romm, James 1993. 'New World and "novos orbes": Seneca and the Debate over Ancient Knowledge of the Americas', in *The Classical Tradition and the Americas: European Images of the Americas and the Classical Tradition*, ed. Wolfgang Haase and Meyer Reinhold. Berlin and New York: De Gruyter, 77–116.

Rovira, Jose Carlos 2009. 'Nezahualcoyótl en la crónica hispánica y mestiza', in *Los límites del Océano: Estudios filológicos de crónica y épica en el nuevo mundo*, edited by Guillermo Serés and Mercedes Serna Arnáiz. Barcelona: Universitat Autónoma de Barcelona, 191–206.

Rowe, John Howland 1965. 'The Renaissance Foundations of Anthropology', *American Anthropologist* 67: 1–20.

Rozat Dupeyron, Guy 1993. *Indios imaginarios e indios reales en los relatos de la conquista de México*. Mexico: Tava Editorial (repr. Xalapa: Universidad Veracruzana, 2002).

Rubial-García, Antonio 2011. 'Los escudos urbanos de las patrias novohispanas', *EHN* 45: 17–46.

Ruiz Bañuls, Mónica 2009. *El huehuetlatolli como discurso sincrético en el proceso evangelizador novohispano del siglo XVI*. Rome: Bulzoni.

Ruiz Medrano, Ethelia 2010. *Mexico's Indigenous Communities: Their Lands and Histories*. Boulder: UP of Colorado.

Rummel, Erika, ed. 2008. *Biblical Humanism and Scholasticism in the Age of Erasmus*. Leiden and Boston: Brill.

Russell, D.A. 2001. *Quintilian: The Orator's Education*. 4 vols. Cambridge, MA: Harvard UP.

Sagaón Infante, Raquel 1998. 'Testamento de Isabel Moctezuma', *Anuario Mexicano de Historia del Derecho* 10: 753–60.

Said, Edward W. 1978. *Orientalism*. New York: Random House.

Sakamoto, Kuni 2016. *Julius Caesar Scaliger, Renaissance Reformer of Aristotelianism: A Study of His Exotericae Exercitationes*. Brill: Leiden.

Salmon, Vivian 1960. 'A Pioneer of the "direct method" in the Erasmus Circle', *Latomus*, 19.3: 567–77.

Sánchez Aguilera, Mario Alberto 2019. 'La doctrina desde el púlpito: Los sermones del ciclo de Navidad de Fray Bernardino de Sahagún'. Doctoral dissertation, IIF-UNAM.

Sánchez Aguilera, Mario Alberto 2022. 'Hacia una nueva caracterización del *Manual del cristiano* de fray Bernardino de Sahagún: La obra y sus tratados', *ECN* 63: 15–66.

Sandoval Aguilar, Zazil and Rojas Rabiela, Teresa, eds. 1991. *Lenguas indígenas de México: Catálogo de manuscritos e impresos en lenguas indígenas de México, de la Biblioteca Nacional Antropología e Historia*. Mexico: Biblioteca Gonzalo Aguirre Beltrán.

Sandstrom, Alan R. 2017. 'The Aztecs and Their Descendants in the Contemporary World', in: *The Oxford Handbook of the Aztecs*, ed. Deborah L. Nichols and Enrique Rodríguez-Alegría. New York: OUP, 707–20.

Sandys, J.E. 1908. *A History of Classical Scholarship*. 2 vols. Cambridge: CUP.

Santamarina Novillo, Carlos 2007. 'Los *azteca-tepaneca*: En torno a su origen y gentilicio', *REAA* 36: 61–81.

Saunders, Nicholas 2001. 'A Dark Light: Reflections on Obsidian in Mesoamerica', *World Archaeology* 33.2: 220–36.

Sayers, Dorothy L. 1948. *The Lost Tools of Learning*. London: Methuen.

Schellhase, Kenneth C. 1976. *Tacitus in Renaissance Political Thought*. Chicago: University of Chicago Press.

Schilling, Robert 1992. 'Roman Gods', in *Roman and European Mythologies*, edited by Yves Bonnefoy, Chicago: University of Chicago Press, 68–75.

Schmidt, Stephanie 2021. 'Conceiving of the End of the World: Christian Doctrine and Nahua Perspectives in the Sermonary of Juan Bautista Viseo', *Ethnohistory* 68.1: 125–45.

Schmitt, Charles B. and Skinner, Quentin, eds. 1988. *The Cambridge History of Renaissance Philosophy*. Cambridge: CUP.

Schroeder, Susan 1991. *Chimalpahin and the Kingdoms of Chalco*. Tucson: University of Arizona Press.

Schroeder, Susan, ed. 2010a. *The Conquest All Over Again: Nahuas and Zapotecs Thinking, Writing and Painting Spanish Colonialism*. Brighton, Portland, and Toronto: Sussex Academic Press: 101–23.

Schroeder, Susan 2010b. 'Chimalpahin Rewrites the Conquest', in Schroeder 2010a, 101–23.

Schroeder, Susan 2011. 'The Truth about the *Crónica mexicayotl*', *CLAR* 20.2: 233–47.

Schroeder, Susan and Anderson, Arthur J.O., eds. 1997. *Codex Chimalpahin*. 2 vols. Norman: University of Oklahoma Press.

Schroeder, Susan, Cruz, Anne J., Roa de la Carrera, Cristián, and Tavárez, David E., eds. 2010. *Chimalpahin's Conquest: A Nahua Historian's Rewriting of Francisco López de Gómara's La conquista de México*. Stanford: Stanford UP.

Schwaller, John Frederick 2001. *A Guide to Nahuatl Manuscripts Held in United States Repositories*. Berkeley: American Academy of Franciscan History.

Schwaller, John Frederick, ed. 2003. *Sahagún at 500: Essays on the Quincentenary of the Birth of Fr. Bernardino de Sahagún, OFM*. Berkeley: Academy of American Franciscan History.

Schwaller, John Frederick 2006. 'The *Ilhuica* of the Nahua: Is Heaven Just a Place?' *The Americas* 62:3: 391–412.

Segala, Amos 1989. *Histoire de la littérature nahuatl (sources, identités, représentations)*. Rome: Bulzoni Editore.

Segala, Amos 1992. 'La literatura náhuatl: ¿Un coto privado? (Respuesta del Dr. Amos Segala al Dr. Miguel León-Portilla)', *Caravelle* 52: 209–19.

Segura Martínez, Salvia Carmen, Pérez Luna, Julio Alfonso, and Carreño Velázquez, Elvia, eds. 1991–2000. *Catálogo de la Biblioteca del Convento Grande de San Francisco de Ciudad de México*. 5 vols. Mexico: UNAM.

Sell, Barry D. 2010. 'Perhaps Our Lord, God, Has Forgotten Me: Intruding into the Colonial Nahua (Aztec) Confessional', in Schroeder 2010a, 181–205.

Sell, Barry D. and Burkhart, Louise M., eds. 2009. *Nahuatl Theater. Volume 4: Nahua Christianity in Performance*. Norman: University of Oklahoma Press.

Serafino, Gregorio 2015. 'Las plegarias en náhuatl de La Montaña de Guerrero: Testimonios y recopilaciones', *ECN* 50: 329–53.

Seznec, Jean 1972. *Survival of the Pagan Gods: The Mythological Tradition and Its Place in Renaissance Humanism and Art*, tr. Barbara F. Sessions. Princeton: Princeton UP.

SilverMoon 2007. 'The Imperial College of Tlatelolco and the Emergence of a New Nahua Intellectual Elite in New Spain (1500–1760)'. Doctoral dissertation, Duke University.

Simón, Pedro 1942. *Historial de la expedición de Pedro de Ursúa al Maranón y de las aventuras de Lope de Aguirre*. Lima: Sanmartí.

Simpson, William 1890. *Bibliotheca Mexicana, or, A Catalogue of the Library of . . . José Fernando Ramírez*. London: Norman and Son.

Singer, Peter N. ed. 1997. *Galen: Selected Works*. Oxford: OUP.

Singleton, Charles S. 1973. *Dante Alighieri, The Divine Comedy, Purgatorio 2: Commentary*. Princeton: Princeton UP.

Sirinelli, Jean 1961. *Les vues historiques d'Eusèbe de Césarée durant la période prénicéenne*. Dakar: Université de Dakar.

Skinner, Quentin 1978. *The Foundations of Modern Political Thought. Volume 1: The Renaissance*. Cambridge: CUP.

Skinner, Quentin 1988. 'Political Philosophy', in Schmitt and Skinner 1988, 387–452.

Skutsch, Otto 1968. *Studia Enniana*. London: Athlone Press.

Skutsch, Otto 1985. *The Annals of Q. Ennius Edited with Introduction and Commentary*. Oxford: Clarendon Press.

Sloane, Thomas O. 1991. Schoolbooks and Rhetoric: Erasmus' *Copia*', *Rhetorica* 9.2: 113–29.

Small, Jocelyn Penny 1993. *Wax Tablets of the Mind: Cognitive Studies of Memory and Literacy in Classical Antiquity*. London: Routledge.

Smith-Stark, Thomas C. 2004. 'Phonological Description in New Spain', in *Missionary Linguistics II: Orthography and Phonology*, edited by Otto Zwartjes and Cristina Altman. Amsterdam: John Benjamins, 3–64.

Snyder, Jon R. 1989. *Writing the Scene of Speaking: Theories of Dialogue in the Late Italian Renaissance*. Stanford: Stanford UP.

Solano, Francisco de, ed. 1991. *Documentos sobre política lingüística en Hispanoamérica (1492–1800)*. Madrid: CSIC.

Solomon, Jon, ed. 2011. *Giovanni Boccaccio, Genealogy of the Pagan Gods, Volume 1*, Cambridge, MA and London: I Tatti.

Solmsen, Friedrich 1932. 'Drei Rekonstruktionen zur antiken Rhetorik und Poetik', *Hermes* 67: 133–54.

Somolinos D'Ardois, Germán 1991. 'Estudio histórico', in BADIANO, *Libellus de medicinalibus Indorum herbis* (1552) [1991], 165–91.

Sousa, Lisa, Poole, Stafford, and Lockhart, James 1998. *The Story of Guadalupe: Luis Laso de la Vega's Huei Tlamahuiçoltica of 1649*. Stanford: Stanford UP.

Spitler, Susan 2005. 'Colonial Mexican Calendar Wheels: Cultural Translation and the Problem of "Authenticity" ', in *Painted Books and Indigenous Knowledge in Mesoamerica*, edited by Elizabeth Hill Boone. New Orleans: Middle American Research Institute, 271–88.

Šprajc, Ivan 2000. 'Astronomical Alignments at the Templo Mayor of Tenochtitlan, Mexico', *Journal for the History of Astronomy* 31: S10–S40.

Springer, Carl P.E. 2011. *Luther's Aesop*. Kirksville, Montana: Truman State UP.

Steck OFM, Francis Borgia 1944. *El Primer Colegio de América*. Mexico: Centro de Estudios Históricos Franciscanos.

Stevenson, Robert M. 1968. *Music in Aztec and Inca Territory*. Berkeley and Los Angeles: University of California Press.

Stinger, Charles L. 1977. *Humanism and the Church Fathers: Ambrogio Traversari (1386–1439) and Christian Antiquity in the Italian Renaissance*. Albany: State of New York UP.

Stols, Alexandre A.M. 1992. 'Descripción del códice', in BADIANO, Libellus de medicinalibus Indorum herbis (1552) [1991], 93–100.

Stroh, Wilfried 2008. 'De origine vocum "humanitatis" et "humanismi"', *Gymnasium* 115: 535–71.

Suárez Roca, José Luis 1992. *Lingüística misionera española*. Oviedo: Pentalfa.

Sullivan, Thelma D. 1963. 'Nahuatl Proverbs, Conundrums, and Metaphors, Collected by Sahagún', *ECN* 4: 93–177.

Sullivan, Thelma D. 1974. 'The Rhetorical Orations or *Huehuetlatolli* collected by Sahagún', in Edmonson 1974, 79–111.

Tanner, Marie, 1993. *The Last Descendant of Aeneas: The Hapsburgs and the Mythic Image of the Emperor*. New Haven: Yale UP.

Tavárez, David E. 2000. 'Naming the Trinity: From Ideologies of Translation to Dialectics of Reception in Colonial Nahua Texts, 1547–1771', *CLAR* 9.1: 21–4.

Tavárez, David E. 2010. 'Reclaiming the Conquest: An Assessment of Chimalpahín's Modifications to *La conquista de México*'. In Schroeder, Cruz, Roa de la Carrera, and Tavárez 2010, 17–34.

Tavárez, David E. 2011. *The Invisible War: Indigenous Devotions, Discipline, and Dissent in Colonial Mexico*. Stanford: Stanford UP.

Tavárez, David E. 2013a. 'A Banned Sixteenth-Century Biblical Text in Nahuatl: The Proverbs of Solomon', *Ethnohistory*, 60.4: 759–62.

Tavárez, David E. 2013b. 'Nahua Intellectuals, Franciscan Scholars and the *Devotio Moderna* in Colonial Mexico', *The Americas*, 70.2: 203–35.

Tavárez, David E. 2019. 'Aristotelian Politics among the Aztecs: A Nahuatl Adaptation of a Treatise by Denys the Carthusian', in *Transnational Perspectives on the Conquest and Colonization of Latin America*, edited by Jenny Mander, David Midgley, and Christine Beaule. London: Routledge, 141–55.

Tedeschi, Stefano 2012. 'Un refranero mestizo?', *Bulletin of Hispanic Studies* 89.5: 483–96.

Téllez Nieto, Heréndira 2010. *Vocabulario trilingüe en español-latín-náhuatl atribuido a fray Bernardino de Sahagún*. Mexico: INAH.

Téllez Nieto, Heréndira 2015a. 'La tradición gramatical clásica en la Nueva España: Estudio y edición crítica del *Arte de la lengua mexicana* de Fray Andrés de Olmos'. Doctoral dissertation, Universidad Complutense de Madrid.

Téllez Nieto, Heréndira 2015b 'La tradición textual latina de las Fábulas de Esopo en lengua náhuatl', *Latomus*, 74.3: 715–34.

Téllez Nieto, Heréndira 2019a. Latinidad, tradición clásica y *nova ratio* en el Imperial Colegio de la Santa Cruz de Santiago Tlatelolco', *JOLCEL* 2: 30–55.

Téllez Nieto, Heréndira 2019b. 'Los Colloquios de la paz y tranquilidad christiana de Fray Juan de Gaona: El primer tratado teológico-filosófico del siglo XVI en náhuatl (y otomí)', *Aevum* 93.3: 723–48.

Téllez Nieto, Heréndira 2022. *Andrés de Olmos, Arte de le lengua mexicana*. Frankfurt: Vervuert Verlagsgesellschaft.

Téllez Nieto, Heréndira and Baños Baños, José Miguel 2018. 'Traducciones bíblicas en lenguas indoamericanas: El Evangeliario náhuatl de la Biblioteca Capitular de Toledo (Mss 35-22)', *Revue d'histoire ecclésiastique* 113.3–4: 656–89.

Téllez Nieto, Heréndira and Baños Baños, José Miguel 2019. 'Los *Uehuetlahtolli* de Fray Andrés de Olmos: *Linguae Mexicanae exercitatio*', *Revista de Letras* (São Paulo) 59.1: 83–95.

Tena, Rafael 1992. *El calendario mexicana y la cronografía*. Mexico: INAH.

Tena, Rafael 2019. 'Fábulas de Esopo: Etudio introductorio', in León-Portilla, Curiel Defossé, and Reyes Equigas 2019 iii, 569–74.

Thompson, Craig R. 1940. *Translations of Lucian by Erasmus and St. Thomas More*. Ithaca: Cornell UP.

Thompson, D'Arcy Wentworth 1895. *A Glossary of Greek Birds*. Oxford: Clarendon Press.

Tibesar, Antonine 1988. Review of *The America's* [sic] *First Academic Library, Santa Cruz de Tlatelolco* [Mathes 1985], *The Americas* 44.5: 509–10.

Todorov, Tzvetan 1984. *The Conquest of America: The Question of the Other*. New York: Harper and Row.

Tomlinson, Gary 2007. *The Singing of the New World: Indigenous Voice in the Era of European Contact*. Cambridge: CUP.

Torre Villar, Ernesto de la 1980. *Testimonios históricos mexicanos en los repositorios europeos: Guía para estudio*. Mexico: Instituto de Estudios y Documentos Históricos.

Torre Villar, Ernesto de la and Navarro de Anda, Ramiro, eds. 1982. *Testimonios históricos guadalupanos*. Mexico: FCE.

Torres López, Juan Carlos 2019. 'De la zorra al coyote: Aspectos de la tradición semiótica y cultural de las fábulas de Esopo al náhuatl en los siglos XVI–XVII'. Doctoral dissertation, UNAM.

Toussaint, Stéphane 2002. 'Ficino, Archimedes and the Celestial Arts', in Allen, Rees, and Davies 2002, 307–26.

Townsend, Camilla 2003. 'Burying the White Gods: New Perspectives on the Conquest of Mexico', *AHR* 108.3: 659–87.

Townsend, Camilla 2014. 'Introduction: The Evolution of Alva Ixtlilxochitl's Scholarly Life', *CLAR* 23.1: 1–17.

Townsend, Camilla 2017. *Annals of Native America: How the Nahuas of Colonial Mexico Kept Their History Alive*. New York: OUP.

Trexler, Richard C. 1987. 'From the Mouths of Babes: Christianization by Children in New Spain', in *Church and Community 1200–1600: Studies in the History of Florence and New Spain*. Rome: ESL, 549–74.

Tudeau-Clayton, Margaret and Berry, Philippa, eds. 2003. *Textures of Renaissance Knowledge*. Manchester: Manchester UP.

Turovsky, Barak 2016. 'Found in Translation: More Accurate, Fluent Sentences in Google Translate', *The Keyword Google Blog*, November 15, www.googblogs.com/author/barak-turovsky/page/2/. Accessed November 2022.

Umberger, Emily 1998. 'New Blood from an Old Stone', *ECN* 28: 241–56.

Utrera, Fr. Cipriano de 1932. *Universidades de Santiago de la Paz y de Santo Tomás de Aquino y Seminario Conciliar de la ciudad de Santo Domingo de la Isla Española*. Santo Domingo: Padres Franciscanos Capuchinos.

Van Engen, John 2008. *Sisters and Brothers of the Common Life: The Devotio Moderna and the World of the Later Middle Ages*. Philadelphia: University of Pennsylvania Press.

Van Zantwijk, Rudolph 1990. 'El concepto del 'Imperio Azteca en las fuentes históricas indígenas', *ECN* 20: 201–11.

Vanhaelen, Maude 2017. 'Cosmic Harmony, Demons, and the Mnemonic Power of Music in Renaissance Florence: The Case of Marsilio Ficino', in '*Sing Aloud Harmonious Spheres': Renaissance Conceptions of the Pythagorean Music of the Spheres*, edited by Jacomien Prins and Maude Vanhaelen. Abingdon: Routledge, 101–22.

Velazco, Salvador 2003. *Visiones de Anáhuac: Reconstrucciones historiográficas y etnicidades en el México colonial*. Guadalajara: Universidad de Guadalajara.

Velázquez Rodríguez, Primo Feliciano 1931. *La aparición de Santa María de Guadalupe*. Mexico: Patricio Sanz.

Verástique, Bernardino 2000. *Michoacán and Eden: Vasco de Quiroga and the Evangelization of Western Mexico*. Austin: University of Texas Press.

Vergara Ciordia, Francisco and Comella Gutiérrez, Beatriz 2014. 'La recepción de la obra de Vicente de Beauvais en España', *Cauriensia* 9: 375–405.

Vicente Castro, Florencia and Rodríguez Molinero, José Luis. 1986. *Bernardino de Sahagún: El primer antropólogo en Nueva España (siglo XVI)*. Salamanca: Ediciones Universidad.

Vickers, Brian 1988. *In Defence of Rhetoric*. Oxford: OUP.

Vidal Díez, Mònica 2007. *El Vocabulario hispano-latino (1513) de AE. A. de Nebrija: Estudio y edición crítica*. PhD dissertion: Departmento de Humanidades, Universidad Carlos III de Madrid.

Viesca Treviño, Carlos 1995a. 'Y Martín de la Cruz, autor del Códice de la Cruz Badiano, era un médico tlatelolca de carne y hueso', *ECN* 25: 479–98.

Viesca Treviño, Carlos 1995b. 'El códice de la Cruz-Badiano, primer ejemplo de una medicina mestiza', in *El mestizaje cultural y la medicina novohispana del siglo XVI*, edited by José Luis Fresquet Febrer and José María López Piñero. Valencia: Universitat de València, 71–89.

Viesca Treviño, Carlos 1996. 'Las alteraciones del sueño en el *Libellus de medicinalibus Indorum herbis*', *ECN* 26: 147–61.

Vigil, Ralph H. 1987. *Alonso de Zorita: Royal Judge and Christian Humanist 1512–1585*. Norman: University of Oklahoma Press.

Villar Villamil, Ignacio de 1933. *Cedulario heráldico de conquistadores de Nueva España*, Mexico: Talleres gráficos del Museo nacional de arqueología, historia y etnografía.

Villaseñor, Raul 1953. 'Luciano, Moro, y el utopismo de Vasco de Quiroga', *Cuadernos Americanos* 68: 155–75.

Villella, Peter B. 2016. *Indigenous Elites and Creole Identity in Colonial Mexico, 1500–1800*. New York: CUP.

Vollmer, Günter 1987. 'Handschriften und Edition der aztekischen Aesop-Texte'/'Manuscripts and Editions of the Nahuatl Text', in Kutscher, Brotherston, and Vollmer 1987, 206–41.

Vollmer, Günter 1989. 'Esopo para mexicanos o el intento de enseñar a indígenas una vida prudente', in *América: Encuentro y asimiliación; Actas segundas jornadas de historiadores americanistas Santa Fe, Granada; 7 a 12 octubre de 1988*. Granada: Diputación Provincial, 97–108.

Wagner, Henry Raup 1944. *The Rise of Fernando Cortés*, Berkeley: The Cortes [sic] Society.

Walker, D.P. 1958. *Spiritual and Demonic Magic, from Ficino to Campanella*. London: The Warburg Institute.

Waquet, Françoise 2001. *Latin: Or the Empire of a Sign*, translated by John Howe. London: Verso.

Warren, J. Benedict 1994. 'El siglo XVI de Maturino Gilberti', *Relaciones, Estudios de Historia y Sociedad*, 60: 277–90.

Warren, J. Benedict 1998. *Vasco de Quiroga en África*. Morelia: Fimax Publicistas.

Waterworth, James, ed., tr. 1848. *The Canons and Decrees of the Sacred and Oecumenical Council of Trent*. London: Dolman.

Wear, Andrew 1995. 'Early Modern Europe 1500–1700', in *The Western Medical Tradition: 800 BC to AD 1800*, edited by Lawrence I. Conrad, Michael Neve, Vivian Nutton, Roy Porter, and Andrew Wear. Cambridge: CUP, 215–370.

Weckmann, Luis 1992. *The Medieval Heritage of Mexico*. New York: Fordham Univerity Press; Sp. orig. *La herencia medieval de México*, Mexico: FCE.

Weiss, Roberto 1964. *The Spread of Italian Humanism*. London: Hutchinson.

Wernicke, Konrad 1903. 'Pan', in *Ausführliches Lexikon der griechischen und römischen Mythologie* vol. 3, Abteilung 1, edited by Wilhelm Roscher. Leipzig: Teubner 1347–481.

White, Hayden 1987. *The Content of the Form: Narrative Discourse and Historical Representation*. Baltimore: Johns Hopkins UP.

Whittaker, Gordon 2009. 'The Principles of Nahuatl Writing', *Göttinger Beiträge zur Sprachwissenschaft* 16: 47–81.

Whittaker, Gordon 2016. 'The Identities of Fernando de Alva Ixtlilxochitl', in *Fernando de Alva Ixtlilxochitl and His Legacy*, edited by Galen Brokaw and Jongsoo Lee. Tucson: University of Arizona Press, 29–76.

Whittaker, Gordon 2021. *Deciphering Aztec Hieroglyphs*. Oakland: University of California Press.

Wilkerson, S. Jeffrey K. 1974. 'The Ethnographic Works of Andrés de Olmos, Precursor and Contemporary of Sahagún', in Edmonson 1974, 27–77.

Williams, Franklin B. 1981. 'Utopia's Chickens Come Home to Roost', *Moreana* 18.69: 77–8.

Williams, Robert A. 1992, *The American Indian in Western Legal Thought*. Oxford: OUP.

Wilson, N.G. 1992. 'The Name Hythlodaeus', *Moreana* 29.110: 33–4.

Wittgenstein, Ludwig 1993. *Philosophical Occasions 1912–1951*, edited, translated by James Carl Klagge and Alfred Normann. Indianopolis: Hackett.

Wittkower, Rudolph 1938. '"Grammatica": From Martianus Capella to Hogarth', *JWI* 2.1: 82–4.

Wittkower, Rudolph 1939. 'Eagle and Serpent: A Study in the Migration of Symbols', *JWI* 2.4: 293–325.

Wittkower, Rudolph 1949. *Architectual Principles in the Age of Humanism*. London: Warburg Institute.

Wölfflin, Eduard 1933. *Ausgewählte Schriften*, edited by Gustav Meyer. Leipzig: Dieterich'sche Verlagsbuchhandlung.

Woolf, Daniel 2019. *A Concise History of History: Global Historiography from Antiquity to the Present*. Cambridge: CUP.

Wright Carr, David Charles 2012. '*Teoatl tlachinolli:* Una metáfora marcial del centro de México', *Dimensión Antropológica* (*año* 19) 55: 11–37.

Xelhuantzi, Tesiu R. 2017. 'El *Verba sociorum* y la apropriación colonial por la nobleza náhuatl', *Intercambios: Estudios de Historia* y *Etnohistoria* 2: 11–15.

Xelhuantzi, Tesiu R. 2018. 'La palabra náhuatl', https://www.scribd.com/document/413329773/Tesiu-r-Xelhuantzi-La-Palabra-Nahuatl.

Yates, Frances A. 1966. *The Art of Memory*. London: Routledge and Kegan Paul.

Yates, Frances A. 1975. *Astraea: The Imperial Theme in the Sixteenth Century*. London and Boston: Routledge and Kegan Paul.

Yhmoff Cabrera, Jesús 1975. *Catálogo de obras manuscritas en latín de la Biblioteca Nacional de México*. Mexico: UNAM.

Yhmoff Cabrera, Jesús 1996. *Catálogo de los impresos europeos del siglo XVI que custodia la Biblioteca Nacional de México*. 3 vols. Mexico: UNAM.

Zavala, Silvio 1937. *La 'Utopía' de Tomás Moro en la Nueva España y otros estudios*. Mexico: Antigua Librería Robredo.

Zavala, Silvio 1955. *Sir Thomas More in New Spain*. London: Hispanic and Luso-Brazilian Councils (reprinted in Zavala 1998, *Recuerdo de Vasco de Quiroga*, Mexico: Porrúa, 81–93).

Zavala, Silvio 1982. *Libros de asientos de la gobernación de la Nueva España: Período del virrey don Luis de Velasco, 1550–1552*. Mexico: AGN.

Zavala, Silvio 1995. *Ideario de Vasco de Quiroga*. Mexico: Colegio de México; orig. 1941.

Zimmermann, Günter 1970. *Briefe der indianischen Nobilität aus Neuspanien an Karl V und Philipp II um die Mitte des 16. Jahrhunderts*. Munich: Klaus Renner.

Ziolkowski, Jan M. 2006. 'Mastering Authors and Authorizing Masters in the Long Twelfth Century', in *Latinitas Perennis. Volume 1: The Continuity of Latin Literature*, edited by Wim Verbaal, Yanick Maes, and Jan Papy. Leiden and Boston: Brill, 93–118.

Ziolkowski, Jan M. and Putnam, Michael C.J., eds. 2008. *The Virgilian Tradition: The First Fifteen Hundred Years*. New Haven: Yale UP.

Zubillaga SJ, Félix and Rodríguez SJ, Miguel Ángel, eds. 1956–1991. *Monumenta Mexicana*, 8 vols. Rome: Monumenta Historica Societatis Iesu.

Zulaica Gárate, Román 1939. *Los franciscanos y la imprenta en México en el siglo XVI*. Mexico: Pedro Robredo.

Zwartjes, Otto 2000. Review of *Languages Different in All Their Sounds* [Nowak 1999], *Romansk Forum* 12: 120–36.

Zwartjes, Otto 2014. 'Algunas observaciones sobre el *Vocabulista arauigo en letra castellana* (1505) de Pedro de Alcalá y el *Vocabulario español-latino* (c. 1495) de Antonio de Nebrija', in *Métodos y resultados actuales en Historiografía de la Linguística*, edited by María Luisa Calero Vaquera, Alfonso Zamorano Aguilar, María del Carmen García Manga, María Martínez Atienza, and Francisco Javier Perea Siller. Münster: Nodus Publikationen, 753–62.

Zwartjes, Otto 2016. 'Métodos de enseñanza y aprendizaje de lenguas en la Nueva España: El Colegio de Tlatelolco', in Hernández and Máynez 2016, 174–203.

Zwartjes, Otto, Zimmermann, Klaus, and Schrader-Kniffki, Martina, eds. 2012. *Missionary Linguistics V/ Lingüística Misionera V*, Amsterdam and Philadelphia: John Benjamins.

INDEX

Tables and figures are indicated respectively by *t* and *f* following the number of the page on which they appear. Entries for monarchs, popes and viceroys give the dates of their reigns or periods in office.

The manufacturer's authorised representative in the EU for product safety is Oxford University Press España S.A. of El Parque Empresarial San Fernando de Henares, Avenida de Castilla, 2 – 28830 Madrid (www.oup.es/en or product.safety@oup.com). OUP España S.A. also acts as importer into Spain of products made by the manufacturer.

Printed in the USA/Agawam, MA
August 8, 2025

891738.006